D0221139

WOMEN IN EARLY MODERN ENGLAND

WOMEN IN EARLY MODERN ENGLAND

1550–1720

SARA MENDELSON

and

PATRICIA CRAWFORD

CLARENDON PRESS · OXFORD

1998

Oxford University Press, Great Clarendon Street, Oxford OX2 6DP

Oxford New York
Athens Auckland Bangkok Bogota Bombay
Buenos Aires Calcutta Cape Town Dar es Salaam
Delhi Florence Hong Kong Istanbul Karachi
Kuala Lumpur Madras Madrid Melbourne
Mexico City Nairobi Paris Singapore
Taipei Tokyo Toronto Warsaw
and associated companies in
Berlin Ibadan

Oxford is a trade mark of Oxford University Press

Published in the United States
by Oxford University Press Inc., New York

British Library Cataloguing in Publication Data
Data available

Library of Congress Cataloging in Publication Data
Mendelson, Sara Heller, 1947–
Women in early modern England, 1550–1720/Sara Mendelson and Patricia Crawford.
p. cm.
Includes bibliographical references (p.).
1. Women—England—History—Modern period, 1600– 2. Women—England—History—Renaissance, 1450–1600. I. Crawford, Patricia (Patricia M.) II. Title.
HQ1599.E5M46 1998
305.4'0942–dc21 97–33337

ISBN 0–19–820124–9

1 3 5 7 9 10 8 6 4 2

Typeset by J&L Composition Ltd, Filey, North Yorkshire
Printed in Great Britain by
Bookcraft Ltd., Midsomer-Norton
Nr. Bath, Somerset.

Preface

Many people have asked us how we came to collaborate on a book, and how we have managed our joint labours. The answer to the first of these questions is that we decided (one afternoon in Oxford in 1982) that it would be a good idea to write a book together. One of us immediately produced a rough outline. We then began to work, and soon found that we had embarked on a larger project than we initially envisaged because there was so little secondary source material to draw upon. We realized that we would be engaged in archival research on many subjects which interested us. Fifteen years later, we have come to what we feel is a reasonable stopping-place.

As to how we have managed our collaboration, we have shared ALL the work that went into the making of the book. We drew up lists of archival sources, apportioned research tasks between the two of us, and exchanged notes and transcriptions. In similar fashion we divided the book into sections and were each allotted our share of the writing. We have exchanged ideas and drafts and revisions by every means of communication known to woman. We have carried on daily conversations by email, and at intervals we were able to meet on the same continent—whether in Australia, England, or North America—where we have enjoyed the hospitality of each other's family and friends.

Looking at our final script, we can no longer determine which of us was first to have a particular idea or to write a particular phrase, nor do we wish to parcel out credit or blame between the two of us. It has truly been a shared project, and as a symbolic expression of our indistinguishable roles—since we cannot superimpose our names on precisely the same spot—we have subverted the hierarchy of the alphabet on the title-page.

For others who might plan on collaboration, we offer useful advice which we received as messages in fortune-cookies (consumed at some of our innumerable shared meals): 'Friendship will be the secret of your success'; 'Retain your sense of humour'; and finally, 'Nothing is impossible for your willing heart'.

P. C. and S. M.

Perth, Western Australia, and
Hamilton, Ontario, Canada
March 1997

Preface

Acknowledgements

Were we to express the full sense of our indebtedness to all the archivists, colleagues, and friends who have helped make this book possible, then the preface would attain the length of a monograph in itself. We offer these brief acknowledgements as a token of our deep gratitude to all.

We begin with warm thanks to the librarians and archivists who have assisted our research, especially the staff of the following: the Bodleian Library (with particular thanks to the staff of the Duke Humfrey), the British Library (with special thanks to Michael Crump and Frances Harris), Dr Williams's Library, the Folger Shakespeare Library, the Guildhall Library, the Greater London Record Office, the London Friends' Library, Mills Library at McMaster University, and the Library of the University of Western Australia. We are grateful to the staff at county record offices and local archives, particularly the following: the Borthwick Institute, the Cumbria Record Office, the Devon Record Office, the Essex Record Office, the Hereford and Worcester County Record Office, the Hertfordshire County Record Office, the Norfolk Record Office, Oxford Archives, and the Somerset Record Office. We acknowledge the kindness of the Worshipful Company of Fishmongers, who allowed xerox copying from the typed calendar of their records, and the History of Parliament Trust, who permitted us to consult their records. It is a pleasure to acknowledge the generosity of colleagues who have shared references and archival material, including Ian Archer, Gerald Aylmer, Judith Bennett, Sylvia Bowerbank, Helen Brash, David Cressy, Julian Davies, Ian Gentles, Frances Harris, Felicity Heal, Cynthia Herrup, Sarah Jones, Anne Kugler, Anne Laurence, Mary O'Connor, Margaret Pelling, Patricia Phillips, Mary Prior, Keith Thomas, Tim Wales, Richard Wall, Joe Ward, Helen Weinstein, Amanda Whiting, and Sonya Wynne. Hassell Smith has kindly allowed access to his Bacon database at the Centre for East Anglian Studies.

Many colleagues and friends have generously shared their unpublished or forthcoming work, or have allowed us to consult their unpublished theses, including Richard Adair, Ian Archer, Judith Bennett, Maxine Berg, Sylvia Bowerbank, Vivien Brodsky, Linda Campbell, Miranda Chaytor, Maria Cioni, David Cressy, Julian Davies, T. A. Davies, Kevin Dillow, Frances Dolan, Amy Erickson, Doreen Evenden-Nagy, Judy Everard, Mary Fissell, Amy Froide, Ian Gentles, L. M. Glanz, Joan Goldsmith, Laura Gowing,

Paul Griffiths, Isobel Grundy, Loreen Guisé, Frances Harris, Ann Hughes, Martin Ingram, Sarah Jones, Frances Kelly, D. Kirby, Anne Kugler, Anne Laurence, Peter Lawson, Beverly Lemire, David Lemmings, Carole Levin, Stephen MacFarlane, Phyllis Mack, Nancy Klein Maguire, J. L. McIntosh, Charlotte Merton, Jodi Mikalachki, Craig Muldrew, Mary O'Connor, Katherine Park, Margaret Pelling, Christine Peters, Wilfrid Prest, Mary Prior, Judith Richards, Michael Roberts, R. C. Sawyer, Winfried Schliener, Pamela Sharpe, Hilda Smith, Jennifer Stine, the late Valerie Drake Taylor, Joan Thirsk, Barbara Todd, Tim Stretton, Tim Wales, Claire Walker, Garthine Walker, Amanda Whiting, Daniel Woolf, and Melinda Zook.

Our manuscript has greatly benefited from comments and criticism by those who have read portions of the text, including Judith Bennett, Sylvia Bowerbank, Victoria Burrows, Frances Harris, Peter Lawson, David Lemmings, Jane Long, Phyllis Mack, Katharine Massam, Mary O'Connor, Margaret Pelling, Maureen Perkins, and Lisa Schnell. We are grateful to Alan Dodds for help with conversions. For generous assistance with illustrations, we are greatly indebted to Jean Miller at the Folger Shakespeare Library, and especially to Helen Weinstein. We should also like to thank Michael Belson, Anna Illingworth, and Tony Morris at Oxford University Press for their patience and hard work, and Pat Lawrence for her meticulous copy-editing.

Patricia Crawford acknowledges with thanks the financial support of the Australian Research Council, the Folger Shakespeare Library, The University of Western Australia (for a 75th Anniversary Award), and the History Department of the University of Western Australia. She offers especially warm thanks to the many friends who have offered interest, support, and encouragement in Australia, Canada, England, and the United States, especially Sylvia Bowerbank, Victoria Burrows, Leonore Davidoff, the late Geoffrey Elton, Laura Gowing, Val Hasler, Gail Jones, Jane Long, Phyllis Mack, Philippa Maddern, Katharine Massam, Mary O'Connor, Lyndal Roper, and Keith Thomas; for generous hospitality, Ursula and Gerald Aylmer, Mary and Kenneth Green, Anne Laurence, Phyllis Mack, the Mendelson family, Mary Prior, Gareth Roberts, Lois Rutherford, and Bob Scribner; and most significantly of all, thanks to Sara, co-author and dear friend, and to husband, Ian.

Sara Mendelson acknowledges with gratitude the assistance of the Social Sciences and Humanities Council of Canada, for its generous financial support for this and other related projects for more than a decade; the University of Toronto, for administering a Canada Research Fellowship and a series of Canada Council research grants; and the Arts Faculty at the University of Western Australia, for a visiting fellowship. She offers especially warm thanks to friends in Oxford and elsewhere for hospitality and other acts of kindness, including Ian and Patricia Crawford, Penny Gouk, Anne Laurence, Carole Levin, Adina and Sander Mendelson, Joseph Mendelson, Avner and Leah Offer, Patricia Phillips, Mary Prior, Gareth Roberts, and Ruth Widmann; to former teachers Mike Zuckerman and Charles Gray; to Keith Thomas, for his inspiring example and sustaining presence over the years; to Sylvia Bowerbank and Mary O'Connor, without whose critical acumen and unflagging support this author's share of the book would never have been finished; to her mother Miriam Heller and sister Elizabeth Heller, for their encouragement; to co-author Trish, to whom her debt of gratitude is far greater than can be expressed, let alone repaid; to Alan, David, and Daniel Mendelson for their help and support and humour and long-suffering forbearance, and chiefly for their very existence.

Contents

List of Illustrations

Abbreviations

BDBR	*Biographical Dictionary of British Radicals*
BL	British Library, London
Bodl.	Bodleian Library, Oxford
CSPD	*Calendar of State Papers Domestic*
DNB	*Dictionary of National Biography*
DWL	Dr Williams's Library, London
EHR	*English Historical Review*
fo.	folio of manuscript
Folger	Folger Shakespeare Library, Washington, DC
GLRO	Greater London Record Office
Guildhall	Guildhall Library
HMC	*Historical Manuscripts Commission Reports*
HWJ	*History Workshop Journal*
JBS	*Journal of British Studies*
LF	London, Friends' Library
LPS	*Local Population Studies*
OA	Oxfordshire Archives
OED	*Oxford English Dictionary*
PRO	Public Record Office
RO	Record Office
sig.	signature, or gathering of pages in an early printed book
STC	A. W. Pollard and G. R. Redgrave, *A Short-Title Catalogue of Books . . . 1475–1640*, 2nd edn., 2 vols. (1976–86)
TRHS	*Transactions of the Royal Historical Society*
TT	Thomason Tract, reference number, British Library
Wing	D. Wing, *Short-Title Catalogue of Books printed in England . . . and of English Books . . . 1641–1700*, 2nd edn., 3 vols. (New York, 1972–88)

Note concerning Dates and Spellings

The year has been taken to begin on 1 January, not 25 March as in the Old Style calendar.

In quotations from manuscript sources, spellings and punctuation have been modernized for ease of reading by non-specialists. Quotations from primary printed sources have been cited verbatim, with silent corrections of typos and using modern typography.

Glossary of Terms

churching	church ceremony following childbirth, before which a woman should not appear in public
Civil War	the years 1642–9, a period of military conflict between the forces of king and Parliament, ending in the king's execution and the abolition of monarchy in 1649
Interregnum	the years 1649–60, when the country was ruled without a king
Restoration	Charles II returned to England in 1660
Reformation	Religious changes of the sixteenth century by which England became a Protestant country
feme covert	married woman, under coverture
feme sole	legal status of being a single woman; or being permitted to act legally as such
lying-in	childbirth
nuncupative	oral will
Puritan	term used here broadly to refer to movement in the Church for reform, but with specific (and debated) meanings over the period covered here
Quakers	members of the Society of Friends, a religious movement which began in the 1650s. A key tenet was the equality of all souls before God
recusant	term used technically for those who refused to attend the Established Church, but frequently used of Catholics

INTRODUCTION

> If one could bequeath ones experience to those one leaves behind one, it would be the best legacy one could give, and was that, I remember, I wished my grandmother could have left me when she died though she had not given me a farthing besides . . .
>
> Mary Clarke to Edward Clarke, 29 October 1697

Mary Clarke, recounting to her husband the occurrences of everyday life, was conscious of the inestimable value of female experience.[1] But unlike lands and goods, which can be traced directly by historians, the legacy of women's lived experiences in past ages is not easily recovered. While a few educated women (like the author of our epigraph) had both the desire and the ability to reflect on their existence in their own words, the vast majority can be glimpsed only fleetingly, through an entry in a parish register, a few lines recorded by the clerk of a court, or a passing mention by fathers, husbands, or sons.

This book originated as a series of questions, all of which could be summed up in one overarching question: what was women's experience of life and the world in early modern England? As historians, we believed we knew a great deal about men's lives. But our knowledge of ordinary women, of the majority of the female populace, was relatively limited.

Our shared search for the legacy of women's lives was inaugurated early in the 1980s. Although we were determined to write a collaborative, feminist history of women in early modern England, we felt isolated at the time, for there was no 'field' to speak of. While the 1970s had seen great strides in studies of medieval and nineteenth-century English women, research into the intervening centuries seemed to lag behind, leaving the sixteenth and seventeenth centuries as the neglected Dark Ages of women's history. The bibliography of secondary sources about ordinary women consisted of Alice Clark's *Working Life of Women in the Seventeenth Century* (1919), which had

[1] Som. RO, Clarke Letters, DD/SF 4515/124, Mary Clarke to Edward Clarke, 29 Oct. 1697.

been published more than sixty years earlier, and little else.[2] Over the intervening years, an entire interdisciplinary field has matured along with our book.[3] The excitement we have felt at witnessing the growth of scholarly interest in the lives of early modern women has immeasurably enriched our own work.

From our very first efforts to draft a list of topics for our study, we sought to survey the plural 'women' in a diversity of situations, rather than construct a monolith labelled 'woman'. It seemed essential to try to comprehend 'women's experiences' not as a simple linear description of female behaviour, but as an intricate process of interactions.[4] There was the interplay between the dominant male discourse and women's own perceptions. Even more complicated was the interaction of the entire spectrum of male and female perceptions, and of social and economic institutions, with women's biology and physiology as it changed over a lifetime. There were all the myriad circumstances in which individual women might find themselves, variables of age, social rank, matrimonial and familial and sexual status, and geographical locale. To this long list of parameters we found it necessary to add personal and contingent factors, such as the doctrinal convictions which united or separated women along religious and political lines.

But it is impossible to comprehend everything at once, to recapture the boundless complexity of existence in plain historical prose. Gradually, the original question—what were women's experiences of life in early modern England—became divided and subdivided into a sequence of related questions. Our approach was to group the parameters that influenced women's lives into separate categories, to find out as much as we could about each category, and to explore resonances and common themes, the ways in which patterns of gender linked disparate categories.

We set out with what seemed to us obvious and elementary questions. What was the typical female biography, the sequence of life-stages from birth to death for the majority of the female populace; how did it differ from the typical male biography? In similar fashion, we explored the possible existence of a popular culture rooted in women's experience. Social histor-

[2] Aside from Keith Thomas's ground-breaking essay, 'Women and the Civil War Sects' (1958), in 1980 there was little to add to older works listed in G. Davies, *Bibliography of British History: Stuart Period, 1603–1714* (2nd edn., 1970), 331. (Thomas's essay was not even included in the 1970 edition.)

[3] The field now has an interdisciplinary association devoted to it, the Society for the Study of Early Modern Women, under whose auspices early modern scholars have held a series of conferences and launched several publications.

[4] For more recent thoughts on this topic, see J. Scott, '"Experience"', in J. Butler and J. Scott (eds.), *Feminists Theorize the Political* (1992), 22–40.

ians had identified the elements of 'popular culture' for the male half of the populace. Did ordinary women have a culture of their own, or were they mere onlookers or passive sharers in male popular culture?[5]

Much was known about men's occupations at different social levels and in diverse geographical locales; what work did ordinary women do? What was their economic role, in what ways did it relate to (or differ from) that of men? How did its parameters evolve over the course of centuries? Although historians of women all owe an incalculable debt to the pioneering labours of Alice Clark, her theoretical interpretation of women's working lives had begun to be challenged on several grounds during the 1980s. Yet there was (and still is) no consensus among historians as to what kind of paradigm should be substituted for Clark's model.

Conventional political narratives of early modern England were written on the assumption that men were the only citizens, and consequently the only true political actors, aside from four female monarchs. Was this scenario a true representation of political reality? Or did women other than queens regnant claim a share of civil rights and privileges during this period? Could a narrative be constructed showing ways in which ordinary women exercised some form of political agency?[6]

Our project entailed an extensive search of the archives, locating and analysing thousands of documents, most of which appeared to have been deliberately framed to withhold from us the answers to our questions about women's lives. Sharing our concerns with other feminist historians, we devised ways and means of getting around the intractability of the sources, developing techniques of reading against the grain, using conventional sources in innovative ways, and finding new sources on which we could deploy the traditional methods we had learned as students.

Eventually we assembled a collection of answers to our questions. But in the process of interrogating the sources, we observed aspects of women's experiences in early modern England that were puzzling and unexpected, calling out for explanation. Our research had unearthed a new series of questions, far more intriguing than the list with which we had started. Some of the anomalies we observed confirmed our original suspicion that the structure of women's history differed from men's history, what historians term the 'conventional narrative'. If men's history was taken to be the standard linear model, whether in the form of a whiggish ascent to liberal democratic individualism, or a socialist descent to wage-slavery and indus-

[5] See Ch. 4. For the absence of gender in modern social history, see the review by G. Eley in *HWJ*, 35 (1993), 206–20, of the three volumes edited by F. M. L. Thompson, *The Cambridge Social History of Britain, 1750–1950* (Cambridge, 1990).

[6] See Ch. 7.

trial degradation, then women's history evidently followed a non-linear or non-intuitive path. Why, for example, did certain women manage to assert formal civil and political rights at the beginning of our period, and why did these rights deteriorate or disappear over the course of the seventeenth century, at the very moment when non-élite men were making larger claims for their inclusion in the political nation?[7]

Other questions concerned ways in which historians had not fully understood the lives of ordinary people of both sexes, of men as well as women. Not only did the working lives of plebeian women fail to conform to the mono-occupational professional labels with which early modern officials tried to classify everyone. Many plebeian men did not appear to fit into the mono-occupational model either. At the lowest economic level, both women and men were apparently described more accurately by a paradigm that assumed a multiple occupational subsistence identity, not a single professional work identity.[8] We were beginning to glimpse a new perspective on the lives of both sexes, although we had begun asking our questions about women.

Still other puzzles arose from common themes that emerged from the evidence we had amassed. Why was women's experience of marriage so similar across the class spectrum, when we had predicted that structural factors related to social and economic rank would play more of a role in creating disparate patterns?[9] An obsession with the control of female sexuality, with women's dependent and submissive self-presentation as the outward sign of sexual subjection, also seemed to crop up in what we regarded as alien contexts. Why did the paternalistic structure of female employment assess women according to their sexual reputation, rather than their fitness for the task at hand? What assumptions about gender led the judiciary to trust the testimony only of those female witnesses who presented a chaste and modest demeanour? Conversely, why did the wrong religious or political convictions bar a woman from being certified as a midwife, an occupation we had assumed was a private medical skill, not a public political office?

In discovering new sources and new questions, we rejoiced in the rich diversity, the sheer fascination offered by a 'thick' description of women's lives in the early modern period. Yet our ultimate aim has been to go beyond a mere delineation of women's beliefs and behaviour, however rich and detailed. Our book is the record of a struggle to understand the whole of

[7] See Ch. 1 for women's rights as citizens, and Ch. 7 for their political activities.

[8] See Ch. 5. [9] See Ch. 3.

early modern English history in a new way, initially from ordinary women's viewpoint, but in the end from everyone's viewpoint, from the monarch down to the illegitimate child placed by hostile parish officials in the household of strangers.

Both of us were trained as conventional historians, yet our thinking has been profoundly altered by feminist theory and the debates of recent years. As historians, we had learned a source-based model of historical inquiry, with a paradigm of the scholar as competitive individualist. But when we asked new questions about the past, we found a simple source-based approach too limited for our purposes. In the early 1980s, the archival work which we needed in order to provide answers to our questions still remained to be done. The magnitude of the task we set for ourselves, of rewriting the history of early modern England from women's perspective, was too daunting for one person. Rather than work as solitary scholars, we developed techniques of collaboration. At the same time, we have gained assistance from many other scholars, and have benefited from being part of an international network of historians engaged in similar enterprises. Writing feminist history has been a kind of extended conversation with many generous people. While the authorial 'we' represents our shared thoughts, we have retained our individual perspectives, leaving echoes of two different voices to convey to the reader our sense of an ongoing discussion.

DEFINING TERMS AND CONCEPTS

Early modern England was a hierarchical society with gradations of social degree or rank. The term 'élite' is used as shorthand for the wealthiest and most educated members of society, from the nobility to the minor gentry. 'Middling' characterizes the group of men and women whose relative prosperity distinguished them from about one-third of the population who lived in poverty. The terms 'ordinary' or 'plebeian' refer to the mass of the female population. All terms used to designate the non-élite sector of society have their difficulties; although we refer to the majority as 'labouring' women, the word conveys the false impression that women of the middling and upper ranks did no work. The nomenclature for social and economic distinctions is likewise contentious: 'class' has been used as a synonym for socio-economic levels, rather than in a Marxist sense, although we also refer to 'social levels' and to 'rank'.

The term 'patriarchy' originally referred to the classical notion that fathers should rule. Although the understanding of patriarchy in the political sphere shifted during the seventeenth century, the authority of fathers in the domestic sphere remained unchallenged. By the end of the seventeenth century, monarchs might hold their crowns at the invitation of Parliament; but society still recognized the God-given right of husbands and fathers to govern wives, children, and servants. We shall use the term 'patriarchy' in two ways: first, in the seventeenth-century sense, to characterize a political system based on the dominion of a husband and father over his household; and secondly, as a modern analytical concept to refer to a social system which favours men over women.[10]

As used in this book, the term 'feminism' also has both an early modern and a late twentieth-century meaning. Feminism can be understood as a critique of women's position in society and as a desire to improve it. Rather than a well-defined set of goals or a specific programme, feminism takes diverse forms in different historical contexts. In early modern England, women expressed feminist views in a number of ways. Some voiced their criticisms of injustices suffered by the female sex; others adopted forms of resistance which we can read as subversive.[11] We use the term 'gender order' to refer to the rules which society endorsed about relationships between the two sexes, and about the respective roles assigned to each sex. While all societies have a gender order, each culture has its own distinctive set of rules at a particular point in time.[12]

READING THE SOURCES

Mary Beale, whose self-portrait is reproduced opposite (Fig. 1), portrayed herself in warm, glowing colours. Dressed in her working clothes, she holds the tools of her trade, absorbed in the skilled profession which has earned her financial success and social renown. She gazes directly at the viewer (or is it at her own image?), her features animated with an intelligent, searching expression. In the intimate seclusion of her studio, she displays the disarray of her uncovered hair, the sensuous flesh-tones of her neck and bust.

[10] See S. Walby, *Theorizing Patriarchy* (Oxford, 1990).

[11] For further discussion and relevant footnotes, see Ch. 4.

[12] J. J. Matthews, *Good and Mad Women: The Historical Construction of Femininity in Twentieth-Century Australia* (Sydney, 1984), 14–16.

FIG. 1. Self-Portrait *c.*1675. Mary Beale (1633–99), who depicted herself in several self-portraits, chose to present herself here as a working artist

FIG. 2. Young woman in a cart. Ordinary women depicted in contemporary sources did not choose how they would be portrayed

In contrast, the young woman shown arriving in London in a cart (Fig. 2) had no say in the way she was represented. With her head covered and her body muffled to the neck, she is nevertheless presented as an object, exposed to the stares of crowds of male bystanders. The black-and-white woodcut does not even reveal the duller hues of the homespun in which she was probably clothed. Her picture exemplifies the situation of most early modern women. So far as we know, there are no surviving pictorial works by plebeian women who portrayed themselves. While a few well-educated women enjoyed the luxury of projecting their own image on to paper or canvas, the vast majority were represented by others, if they were represented at all.

What is true of pictorial representations is to a large extent true of written documents. Women are everywhere and nowhere in the archives. Few were able to express their own views directly; we must reconstruct the evidence for a female narrative from a wide range of indirect source materials. Because documents were shaped by the purposes of the institutions and individuals who created them, every text has its own perspective. Each text offers a different kind of challenge.

The traditional methods of scholarship, which entail discovering as much as possible about the circumstances in which documents were created and preserved, are indispensable for women's history. Early editing was notoriously bowdlerizing of references to women. For example, male nineteenth-century editors deleted all references to menstruation in texts.[13] Wherever possible, we have used the original archival sources. Secondly, we have developed techniques of reading against the grain, of asking where women are absent as well as present in the documents. While there is no single or definitive reading of any text, the careful use of many different kinds of sources in conjunction with each other can provide a more balanced and nuanced account of social realities.

One of our aims is to open up the range of source materials about women and to demonstrate their possibilities through case-studies. Every piece of evidence provides a partial access to women's lives; frequently one document is illuminated by another type of source. For example, in elucidating a 1680 court case about the marriage of two women, we have referred to contemporary ballads about same-sex unions, to literature about cross-dressing, and to medical treatises about hermaphroditism.[14] Each chapter is based on as wide an array of sources as we have been able to find.

Contemporary hierarchies of sex and social class magnify the difficulties of unravelling the evidence, masking or distorting our view of women's lives. There are problems of male bias and misogyny, both in the original creation of documents, and subsequently in scholars' selection and interpretation. Many sources relating to women have been relegated to the historical scrap heap. In the late nineteenth century, the parliamentary papers of Sir

[13] See R. Houlbrooke (ed.), *English Family Life, 1576–1716: An Anthology from Diaries* (Oxford, 1988), 105–8.

[14] See Ch. 4; for a fuller account, see P. Crawford and S. Mendelson, 'Sexual Identities in Early Modern England: The Marriage of Two Women in 1680', *Gender & History*, 7 (1995), 362–77.

Simonds D'Ewes were rightly found to be significant, but his rich archival collections of personal correspondence were dismissed as 'family matters of no historical significance'.[15]

Husbands and heirs were more likely to preserve female memoirs when these depicted marriage and family members in a positive light. The earl of Bridgewater had his beloved wife's private meditations, including an essay on marriage, copied into a handsome memorial volume after her death.[16] Some husbands edited their wives' diaries and memoirs as a labour of love.[17] In contrast, women's critical voices were suppressed. Fearing that others might read it, Samuel Pepys ordered his wife to destroy a memoir she had composed about the unpleasantness of her life, because it was 'so piquant, and wrote in English and most of it true'. When she refused, he forced the papers from her, 'and tore them all before her face'.[18]

The vast majority of the female population were of middling or plebeian status; yet the bulk of surviving evidence relates to the upper ranks. In the past, scholars have been apt to focus on élite women, partly because evidence about their lives is more plentiful. Like all social historians interested in the lives of ordinary people, we have been forced to extract much of our information from records generated by the literate minority. Wherever the sources permit us to do so, we have featured the lives of plebeian women, drawing attention to the dissimilar experiences of women of different social ranks.

As an antidote against the gender bias inherent in the sources, we have tried to privilege women's own words, rather than rely on masculine accounts of female attitudes and experiences. Writings by women are more numerous than many historians have acknowledged; these include diaries, autobiographies, letters, manuscript treatises, and printed works.[19] A few letters by ordinary women have survived, although far more rarely than those of the peerage and the gentry. We have, for example, a wet-nurse's letter about arrangements for undertaking a charge.[20] Women kept books of recipes for medicines and cookery, and collected tips about house-

[15] See *DNB*, D'Ewes.

[16] BL, MS Egerton 607, E. Egerton, countess of Bridgewater, 'Meditations'.

[17] e.g. A. Walker, *The Holy Life of Mrs Elizabeth Walker* (1690); S. Bury, *An Account of the Life and Death of Mrs. Elizabeth Bury* (Bristol, 1720).

[18] *The Diary of Samuel Pepys*, ed. R. Latham and W. Matthews, 11 vols. (1970–83), iv. 9–10; S.H. Mendelson, 'Stuart Women's Diaries and Occasional Memoirs', in M. Prior (ed.), *Women in English Society, 1500–1800* (1985), 184.

[19] See P. Crawford, 'Women's Published Writings, 1600–1700', and Mendelson, 'Stuart Women's Diaries', in Prior (ed.), *Women in English Society, 1500–1800*.

[20] BL, MS Harleian 382, fo. 182, 10 May 1639.

wifery. Material objects, such as embroidered gifts, can offer clues about women's perceptions of the world.[21]

In our exploration of the lives of ordinary women, we have made extensive use of the records of the church and secular courts. Here a caveat is necessary: while female testimony appears to offer direct access to women's own voices, the historian must be constantly aware that every word spoken by a woman was recorded and edited by male officials.[22] Texts reflect the demands of the court situation: the recording practices of clerks, the attempt to shape the words of litigants and witnesses into answers which conformed to the legal framework within which each court functioned. Women's words were also filtered through the barrier of men's expectations, for contemporary authorities constructed the criminality of women differently from that of men.

BOUNDARIES AND TOPICS, THEMES AND ARGUMENTS

Our time-frame encompasses what may be loosely termed the 'early modern' era, extending from about 1500 to 1750. While the issues relate broadly to this longer period, our detailed archival work has focused on the years from 1550 to 1720, a time-span which might be described as the 'long' seventeenth century. Within this broad chronological framework, each topic—discourses about woman, life-stages, culture, work, and politics—follows its own chronology. Because our primary focus is on the lives of ordinary women, we have devoted less space to the experiences of the élite, for whom both the sources and the secondary literature are well known. Some topics for which there is now an extensive literature (such as women's role in witchcraft, or their prominence in radical religion especially in the early Quaker movement) have also been treated with more brevity than their importance warrants. On the other hand, some subjects are absent from our account because the sources have proved intractable despite all our efforts. Only a tiny handful of seventeenth-century women left evidence of their views on female heterosexual desire. Between Aphra Behn's poetic assertion that female modesty was merely a 'necessary bait . . . to gain the dull repute

[21] See Ch. 4.

[22] For discussions of these issues with respect to women, see L. Gowing, *Domestic Dangers: Women, Words and Sex in Early Modern London* (1996); S. Mendelson, '"To Shift For a Cloak": Disorderly Women in the Church Courts', in V. Frith (ed.), *Women and History: Voices of Early Modern England* (Toronto, 1995), 3–18.

of being wise' and Dame Sarah Cowper's proud claim in her diary that she had conceived four children 'without knowing what it is to have an unchaste thought or sensual pleasure', there is little basis for constructing generalizations about women's attitude as a group.[23]

In Chapter 1, we examine the intellectual and cultural 'givens' of early modern society, the world of discourses about gender into which every woman was born. Much recent work has focused on the dominant discourses which constructed woman.[24] These discourses were not self-contained, but mutually supporting; yet in practice their implications were frequently contradictory. Furthermore, even the discourses sometimes abandoned the concept of woman as monolith, recognizing that her condition might vary according to her sexual status—maid, wife, or widow—as well as her age and social position. No one nowadays mistakes prescriptive ideals for experience. Yet we need to acknowledge that experience was expressed through language; thus the multiple layers of competing discourses offer us one mode of access to women's experiences.[25] Discourse provided certain narrative scripts by which women could live their lives and interpret the meaning of events. In some cases women internalized the discourses; in others, they reversed, combined, modified, or ignored them.[26]

While our narrative is prefaced with an examination of the dominant discourses that constructed woman, our main concern is with women's perceptions of their lives from their own point of view. Chapters 2 and 3 describe the sequence of female life-stages from birth to death. Life-stages of women differed from those of men: the patterns of women's lives were shaped by their physiology through a succession of bodily changes, by their sexual and reproductive experiences, and by their relationships to men, as daughters, wives, or widows. In these two chapters we explore the interplay of gender, class, and age, showing how women's lives varied across the social spectrum at different ages.

[23] S. Mendelson, *The Mental World of Stuart Women: Three Studies* (Brighton, 1987), 167; Herts. RO, Panshanger MSS, D/EP/F29, Dame Sarah Cowper, Diary, i. 61.

[24] For examples see I. Maclean, *The Renaissance Notion of Woman: A Study in the Fortunes of Scholasticism and Medical Science in European Intellectual Life* (Cambridge, 1980); L. Woodbridge, *Women and the English Renaissance: Literature and the Nature of Womankind, 1540–1620* (Urbana, Ill., 1984); M. R. Sommerville, *Sex and Subjection: Attitudes to Women in Early-Modern Society* (1995); A Fletcher, *Gender, Sex and Subordination in England, 1500–1800* (New Haven, 1995).

[25] For other modes of gaining access to women's experiences in past ages, see Ch. 4 (material culture); see also R. Porter, 'Review Article: Seeing the Past', *Past and Present*, 118 (1988), 186–205.

[26] For a general discussion of these issues as related to post-structuralist theory, see the special issue *Feminist Studies*, 14 (1988), *passim.*; T. de Lauretis, *Alice Doesn't: Feminism, Semiotics, Cinema* (Bloomington, 1984), 159.

Women's culture, the subject of Chapter 4, was largely ignored by male contemporaries. While some scholars have objected to the idea of a separate female culture, dismissing it as a celebratory phase of older-style women's history, we argue that it was an important part of women's lives. In the early modern setting, female culture was one of the primary modes of women's agency, both in their own lives and as a means of influencing the larger society. Although much of female culture tended to be conservative, supporting the *status quo* by helping women to survive the double oppression of gender and class, certain features of women's traditional culture had a subversive potential. Supported by a sense of shared values, women invaded intellectual and physical spaces which men had claimed as their own.

Chapters 5 and 6 explore the world of women's work. Women's working lives and material circumstances were affected both by gender and by social rank. A large proportion of the population were born poor, living most of their lives at or near the subsistence level. Plebeian women's economy of makeshift differed in significant ways from the lifestyles of the wealthy; yet even so, women's work shared certain characteristics across the social spectrum. While those of the middling ranks were more likely to have a professional occupational designation, women at all levels assumed responsibility for child-care and housewifery. In these chapters we have tried to make visible the work women actually did, and to assess their opportunities for economic survival at different social levels.

Contemporaries claimed the political world, the public sphere, as a man's world; conventional historians have continued the tradition. Political narrative, which remains the dominant mode of historical writing for the early modern period, has been resistant to the inclusion of gender as an analytical category.[27] Yet in certain circumstances, women could be active political agents who subverted the boundaries between the public and the private. In Chapter 7 we seek to show how politics mattered to women, and women to politics. Our narrative begins with the four queens regnant of early modern England, and continues with a survey of women's participation in the political realm in a diversity of social contexts. A case study of the years 1640–60 explores the range of women's activities during the Civil War period. At the end of the 'long' seventeenth century, despite the exclusion of the female sex from liberal theories of social contract, women continued to be active in both mass and élite politics.

In a brief epilogue, we consider the 'shape' of women's history in relation

[27] J. Scott, 'Gender: A Useful Category of Historical Analysis', in her *Gender and the Politics of History* (New York, 1988). For a discussion of this theme at the end of the 18th and early 19th cents., see L. Colley, *Britons: Forging the Nation, 1707–1837* (New Haven, 1992), 248–81.

to the larger society over the course of the early modern era. What were the most significant forces for change in women's lives; where can we identify continuities or stasis? The answer, as we have come to see it, is not a simple linear appraisal of progress or decline. Not only did the givens of the dominant discourse about gender interact in unpredictable ways with women's own perceptions and physiology. Women's agency—and its limitations—is revealed in the mutually evolving relationships between gender and other parameters, between culture and biology, established institutions, and women's acquiescence or resistance against all the constraints that hedged their lives. The implications of this process of interaction affect not only our understanding of early modern history, but our own existence as gendered beings in a world where gender continues to be one of the key parameters that structures our lives.

1

CONTEXTS

The category 'woman' was the subject of endless discourse in early modern England. Through the lenses of medical, scientific, legal, and political frameworks, woman was categorized and known. Because discursive boundaries were not static but were always shifting, contemporary understandings of woman changed throughout the period and in different contexts. Furthermore, there were contradictions and ambiguities as well as similarities and reinforcements between one discourse and another, and even within the same discourse.

In this chapter we shall examine some of the ways in which ideas about gender differences were expressed and perpetuated in early modern England. These ideas will be surveyed under a number of headings: medical understandings of woman's body, religious teachings, the gender bias in legal structures, popular notions, stereotypes, and links between different contexts. But while the social construction of gender difference will be separated into component parts for the sake of clarity, all such distinctions are ultimately artificial. It is necessary at the outset to stress the complex nature of the interactions between different sources of ideas about gender, and between ideology and other structures such as the organization of family life.

To contemporaries, the difference between the two sexes was a fundamental principle upon which society was constructed. Writers assumed that woman was inferior to man. Unresolved was the problem of social levels, the contradictions between class and gender. Contemporaries knew that Queen Anne was not inferior to her lowest footman,[1] but they still insisted that all women ought to be subordinate in some sense.

Although some theorists have attempted to discover the origins of gender hierarchy in a single factor such as the patriarchal family or the division of labour, we make no such claim. Individual elements were interrelated. Axioms about women's inferiority were transported from one discourse to another. In a way, women's disadvantaged status was 'overdetermined' in early modern society. The initial constraints of biology, the symbolism of

[1] M. Astell, *Reflections upon Marriage* (3rd edn., 1706), sig. A.

gender, inherited intellectual notions, social and economic and political institutions, and miscellaneous factors such as technological development all reinforced each other's effect. Axioms about female inferiority proved remarkably resistant to change.

Given the interdependence of mental and material causes, why start with *mentalité*? The priority of the mental realm lies in the importance of context. While all societies engage in the social construction of gender, each epoch represents a different combination of historical parameters which have moulded a unique version of femininity and masculinity. In order to decode the meanings which early modern contemporaries attached to their thoughts and behaviour, we need to offer a brief account of the assumptions about woman which everyone took for granted.

Notions about woman were discussed in medical, scientific, religious, legal, and political texts. In addition to the formal élite discourses which were circulated across Europe in Latin and vernacular texts designed for educated men, there were various popular discourses.[2] Axiomatic to both élite and popular wisdom were notions of female inferiority, the need for subordination, and 'otherness' from man. Much of the discussion of women in early modern society has to date concentrated on these treatises, sermons, manuals, poems, plays, and popular sayings in which the nature of woman was described, so this is one of the better known areas of early modern women's history.[3]

Although this chapter is primarily intended as an introduction to early modern thought for those unfamiliar with the period, we hope that the synthesis we provide may be useful in several ways. First, we have sought to read the discourses, both élite and popular, in a new way, seeking to demonstrate their interrelatedness. We include popular notions from proverbs, jokes, ballads, and chap-books as well as the ideas of the élite. Given the range of traditions, it should not surprise us to find that there were inconsistencies, contradictions, and ambiguities which, as we shall discuss in later chapters, created spaces which women were able to occupy. Because there were contradictions inherent in maintaining an intellectual position which was in many respects contrary to empirical reality, the attempt to define 'woman' was an endlessly fascinating intellectual pursuit. For example, although both God and nature taught that woman was inferior, and

[2] I. Maclean, *The Renaissance Notion of Woman* (Cambridge, 1980); M. R. Sommerville, *Sex and Subjection: Attitudes to Women in Early-Modern Society* (1995).

[3] See, for some examples, L. B. Wright, *Middle-Class Culture in Elizabethan England* (Chapel Hill, NC 1935); L. Woodbridge, *Women and the English Renaissance: Literature and the Nature of Womankind, 1540–1620* (Urbana, Ill., 1984).

therefore she should be under governance, in certain circumstances men recognized that obedience was not the highest good. Duty to God, to her own conscience, might be heroic, as it was in the lauded example of the martyred Ann Askew, a Protestant wife of a Catholic husband who died for her faith. Patriarchy's very resilience created contradictions which made resistances and subversions more possible. Contradictions inherent in the 'system' (more a ramshackle assembly of prejudices) were exploited by subordinate groups.

Secondly, the chapter highlights some areas where further research could be fruitfully undertaken. Currently, the study of literature and literary texts is rich and flourishing, but only recently have historians turned their attention to the law.[4] Furthermore, the practice of law, as well as of medicine, cannot be separated from legal and medical theory. Both ideas and practices are an important part of early modern *mentalité*.

Finally, we argue that we need to understand discourses and stereotypes, in order to explain one of the contexts in which women lived their lives. Women had a limited range of scripts, or stories, by which they could understand their experiences. The stereotypical choices were sharply polarized. Women could be good, proceeding from virginity to marriage and maternity, and die after a virtuously spent widowhood. Or they could be wicked: scolds, whores, or witches. What they could not be, in theory, was independent, autonomous, and female-focused. Thus we need to be sensitive to the silences in discourses as well as the stated words. What was it impossible for women to talk about, at least in men's hearing, because of the way in which the dominant discourse had constructed the female sex?

Women lived their lives within the frameworks of meaning constructed by these discourses. The extent to which their sense of self and identity were shaped by them is one of the larger questions underlying our book. While we have begun with a discussion of contemporary understandings of woman, this does not mean that we believe women were totally defined by discourse. Women's bodies and their material circumstances also played a part in shaping their lives. While we argue that women's experiences were shaped, framed, and interpreted by the discourses which we will refer to as 'dominant', nevertheless women had opportunities for agency and for subversion. They constructed their own meanings and stories. Other chapters in our

[4] S. Staves, *Married Women's Separate Property in England, 1660–1833* (Cambridge, Mass., 1990); A. Erickson, *Women and Property in Early Modern England* (1993); E. Spring, *Law, Land, and Family: Aristocratic Inheritance in England, 1300 to 1800* (Chapel Hill, NC, 1993); J. Kermode and G. Walker (eds.), *Women, Crime and the Courts in Early Modern England* (1994).

book present the dynamic relationship between the discourses of patriarchal dominance and women's daily lives. Here our chief concern is to show how early modern society constructed the idea of woman, so that we can understand the basic parameters of the gender order at this particular historical period.

MEDICAL UNDERSTANDINGS OF WOMAN'S BODY

Sex and gender

The female body was one of the most significant sites where contemporary medical theorists wrote the text of woman's otherness, weakness, inferiority, and passivity. The basic documents in which these biological and medical theories were expounded comprised an international literature published in Latin about the body, health, and sickness. From the sixteenth century onwards, with the advent of printing, texts were translated for a wider lay audience. By the end of the seventeenth century, the gap between medical 'knowledge' and popular ideas about bodies had widened. University-educated physicians promulgated their ideas through their practice as well as through texts. Ultimately, medical theories influenced unlicensed medical practitioners, both male and female, and their patients in turn.

Contemporary theological and legal discourse was informed by medical knowledge. Yet medical axioms were themselves influenced by religious ideology: thus, because woman was created second, because she tempted Adam to the Fall, she was condemned by God to bring forth children in sorrow. There was no point in a physician seeking to prevent painful childbirth. Women themselves accepted many of the physicians' theories, but had alternative sources of knowledge about their bodies based on observation and experience.[5] Even the courts of law were forced, on occasion, to go outside the practice of physicians and turn to women to resolve certain points about conception and pregnancy. In this section we shall explain the main medical assumptions about women's bodies, and discuss how medical theorists explained the distinctively female functions.

Man was the measure of all things, and the female was a deviation from the norm, the 'other'. The very questions physicians debated made woman seem an aberration from human perfection. What was to be said about the differences between women and men? Some followed Aristotle in thinking

[5] P. Crawford, 'Sexual Knowledge in England, 1500–1750', in R. Porter and M. Teich (eds.), *Sexual Knowledge, Sexual Science: The History of Attitudes to Sexuality* (Cambridge, 1994), 91–8.

that a woman was an error in creation, or an imperfect version of the male. But by the sixteenth century, most educated men acknowledged that females had a purpose, even if men continued to share in the joke that all women were a mistake. Some seventeenth-century medical writers explicitly repudiated earlier views: Crooke, in 1615, dismissed the barbarity of calling a woman 'A Creature by the way, or made by mischance' and denying her a soul 'as man hath'.[6] Nature had appointed two sexes for generation, wrote Ross in 1651, never intending, as some thought, to make all creation male.[7] Repeated denials show that the purpose of female existence remained a popular topic of debate, and kept alive the belief that woman was, in herself, problematic.

Bodies were fundamental to early modern conceptions of sexual difference. Because people believed that everyone was either male or female, they were troubled by the possibility of hermaphrodites, and debated the question of what hermaphrodites were. As Laqueur has argued, the question which preoccupied physicians and jurists was the relationship of bodily parts to gender identity. In the case of an hermaphrodite, to which gender did an individual belong?[8] According to Aristotelian tradition, the issue was comparatively straightforward: an hermaphrodite was a female who was possessed of extra matter which could be removed. Such cases were comparatively rare. More worrying was the model from Hippocrates and Galen, which depicted hermaphrodites as beings of an intermediate or indeterminate sex. By masturbation, a woman might so enlarge her clitoris that she became a person truly of a double gender.[9] The possibility of androgyny destabilized the early modern classificatory system upon which the gender order rested.

The female body, like the male, was explained in terms of humoral theory. From the time of Hippocrates and Galen, physicians had believed that the four humours, of which bodies were composed, were governed by the different temperaments of the two sexes; the man was hot and dry, the woman cold and moist.[10] Male and female qualities and virtues derived from their basic make-up. Thus man was active, woman passive; man was

[6] H. Crooke, *Microcosmographia: A Description of the Body of Man* [1615], 258.

[7] A. Ross, *Arcana Microcosmi* (1651), 86.

[8] T. Laqueur, *Making Sex: Body and Gender from the Greeks to Freud* (Cambridge, Mass., 1990), 134–42.

[9] L. Daston and K. Park, 'The Hermaphrodite and the Orders of Nature: Sexual Ambiguity in Early Modern France', *GLQ: A Journal of Gay & Lesbian Studies*, 1 (1995), 419–38; K. Park, 'The Rediscovery of the Clitoris: French Medicine and the Tribade, 1570–1620', in C. Mazzio and D. Hillman (eds.), *The Body in Parts: Discourses and Anatomies in Early Modern Europe* (New York, 1995). We are most grateful to Dr Park for allowing us to read both these papers before publication.

[10] Maclean, *Renaissance Notion of Woman*, 30, 42, 61.

energetic, brave, and strong, while woman was gentle, tender, kind, and timorous. Anatomically, women were less healthful because their passivity subjected them to diseases: 'The passive condition of women is subject unto more diseases and of other sortes and natures then men are.'[11]

The female body was understood as that of the male, modified.[12] Thus the ovaries were referred to as the 'testicles of woman'. Woman's seed was deemed of inferior quality to the man's; man's seed had gone through greater heat, 'becomes more spiritualiz'd, & subtile' while the woman's was 'cruder and lesse digested, from a cruder matter, by lesse perfect Organs'.[13] However, after Harvey's work, *On Generation*, was published, most medical writers agreed that women lacked seed,[14] and by the end of the seventeenth century, theorists were debating whether the child was preformed in either the ova or the male seed.[15]

Physicians believed that heterosexual activity was necessary for the health of women as well as men: 'Moderate Venerie is very expedient for preservation of health.'[16] Yet excessive sexual activity was thought to be weakening and could lead to sterility.[17] As the Bible explained, some adulterous women were so consumed with lust 'that their monethely diseases, procured by inordinate lust eate up and consume their bodies'.[18] Lust could be subdued by Bible reading, meditation, fasting, labour, hard fare, and hard lodging.[19]

Sexuality between women was less discussed than that between men, but was not ignored. Unlike sodomy, it was not a legal offence, so there were no criminal court records.[20] Medical writers distinguished two kinds of lesbian sexuality: rubbing and penetration. While they censured the over-stimulation of the female genital areas, and condemned the practices of

[11] E. Jorden, *A Briefe Discourse of a Disease called the Suffocation of the Mother* (1603), 1.

[12] Laqueur, *Making Sex*, 25–8.

[13] N. Highmore, *The History of Generation* ([28 Oct.] 1651), 89–90.

[14] [T. Gibson], *The Anatomy of Humane Bodies* (1682), 136.

[15] A. McLaren, *Reproductive Rituals: The Perception of Fertility in England from the Sixteenth Century to the Nineteenth Century* (1984), 22–5.

[16] W. Vaughan, *Naturall and Artificial Directions for Health* (1600), 46.

[17] L. Lemnius, *The Touchstone of Complexions* (1576), fo. 105; L. Lessius, *Hygiasticon: Or the Right Course of Preserving Life and Health unto Extream old Age* (Cambridge, 1634), 130.

[18] H. Finch, *The Worlds Great Restauration or the Calling of the Jewes* (1621), 201. Thanks to Wilfrid Prest for this reference.

[19] T. Cogan, *The Haven of Health* (1584), 250–3; Vaughan, *Directions for Health*, 47.

[20] L. Compton, 'The Myth of Lesbian Impunity: Capital Laws from 1270 to 1791', *Journal of Homosexuality*, 6 (1980–1), 11–25; B. Eriksson, 'A Lesbian Execution in Germany, 1721: The Trial Records', *Journal of Homosexuality*, 6 (1980–1), 27–40; T. Van Der Meer, 'Tribades on Trial: Female Same-Sex Offenders in Late Eighteenth-Century Amsterdam', *Journal of the History of Sexuality*, 1 (1991), 424–45.

those they termed 'fricatrices' or 'tribades',[21] their greatest horror was for women who attempted to penetrate each other. Any sexuality between women questioned a fundamental tenet of patriarchal culture, namely the axiom that only men should have sexual access to women, and that heterosexuality, usually with reproductive goals, was the only natural form of sexual behaviour.[22]

Moreover, the blurring of the boundaries between women and men was profoundly disturbing. Women who loved other women sexually were thought to have usurped the roles of men. Androgyny was attacked in stereotypes of the cross-dressed woman, and the hermaphrodite.[23] The possibility of women becoming men destabilized the categories upon which social order depended.

The ways in which the physicians constructed the three physiological functions which distinguished the female from the male—menstruation, parturition, and lactation—show how medical 'knowledge' helped to define woman as inferior to man.

Menstruation

From the time of Hippocrates, woman's womb was understood as the source of 500 miseries to the woman.[24] Medical theories gave substance to the Old Testament view that a menstruating woman was polluted and polluting.[25] Menstruation itself was God-given: as Andrew Borde explained, in *The Breuiary of Helthe*, published in several editions from 1547, 'the cause of this matter is that god hath ordered it to all women from 15 yeres of there age or there about to 50'.[26] One group of physicians explained that women menstruated because their bodies were inefficient, accumulating superfluous blood; menstruation was the means by which they shed the excess. Another theory posited that because women could not purify their blood, as men could, by exercise and heat, they accumulated the impure blood which they shed monthly.[27] There was a class component in both theories. Physicians

[21] Stephen Orgel has earlier references than those cited by the *OED* for these terms; Orgel, conference paper, Hobart, 1994.

[22] Feminist theorists have shown that the 'naturalness' of heterosexuality should be recognized for the social construct it is; R. Braidotti, 'The Politics of Ontological Difference', in T. Brennan (ed.), *Between Feminism and Psychoanalysis* (1989), 96.

[23] *Hic Mulier; or, The Man-Woman* (1620); R. M. Dekker and L. C. van de Pol, *The Tradition of Female Transvestism in Early Modern Europe* (1989).

[24] N. Fontanus, *The Womans Doctour* ([8 Nov.] 1652), 2.

[25] P. Crawford, 'Attitudes to Menstruation in Seventeenth-Century England', *Past and Present*, 91 (1981), 57–65.

[26] A. Borde, *The Breuiary of Helthe* (1547), fo. 90^{v}.

[27] Crawford, 'Menstruation', 50–1.

FIG. 3. Mary Frith, alias Mall Cutpurse. The masculine iconography displayed in this portrait of Mary Frith, who habitually dressed as a man, includes not only her strong heavy features, short hairstyle, man's hat, and sword, but also the male symbolism of the eagle, lion, and ape

believed that women who led active lives and ate poor quality food would have healthier bodies.[28] Idle wealthy women who were richly fed menstruated more than others, and were more liable to ill health since they accumulated more blood.[29]

[28] Cogan, *Haven of Health*, 1–2.

[29] A. Paré, *The Workes of that famous Chirurgion* (1634), 945.

Contemporary medical theorists defined certain patterns of menstruation as disorders or diseases. Amenorrhoea was a disease caused by the unexplained absence of menstruation. Since menstruation was necessary for health, amenorrhoea in turn caused further ills: 'Sometimes Hysterical fits invade', wrote William Drage.[30] Culpeper in the mid-seventeenth century recounted the case of 'a young Virgin in Service in London' who broke out in sores as if with French pox because she had never menstruated.[31] In these cases, physicians usually let blood for amenorrhoea. However, blood-letting was unwise if a woman of child-bearing years had never menstruated, because she might have consumed her blood by her bodily heat, becoming like a man, and a virago: 'such Viragoes, participating so much of the nature of Man, that they seldom or never have any evacuation at all.'[32] Older women who ceased to menstruate became more masculine.[33]

Greensickness and 'mother-fits' were similar disorders which contemporaries believed were caused by the suppression of menstruation or by the corruption of a woman's seed. Younger women were especially prone to greensickness. Medical writers offered a range of remedies including regimes of exercise and spare diet to reduce the amount of blood produced, blood-letting, and marriage. Physicians were not seriously concerned about it: 'It is easily cured by Marriage in young Virgins.'[34]

'Mother-fits', 'strangulation', or 'suffocation of the mother' were also caused by the suppression of menstruation, or corruption of a woman's seed.[35] Too much blood produced seed, which could corrupt the menstrual blood, if not expelled: 'When Seed and Menstrual Blood are retained in Women besides [beyond?] the intent of Nature, they putrefie and are corrupted, and attain a malignant and venomous quality.'[36] A woman's brain was filled with a 'black and dark Smoke' and she was believed to grow melancholy from the stoppage of her terms.[37] Her spirits, suffocated with too much moisture, offended 'the Chamber of Reason'.[38] In its most extreme form, this 'frenzy of the womb' could lead to melancholy, unsteadiness of

[30] W. Drage, *A Physical Nosonomy* (1665), 323.

[31] *Culpeper's School of Physick* ([Oct.] 1659), 246.

[32] R. B[unworth], *The Doctresse: A Plain and Easie Method, of Curing those Diseases which are Peculiar to Women* ([30 May] 1656), 4.

[33] Paré, *Workes*, 947.

[34] J. Pechey, *The Store-house of Physical Practice* (1695), 315.

[35] In 1662 John Graunt referred to a new disease, 'stoppage of the stomach', which he believed similar to greensickness and mother-fits and was likewise cured by marriage; J. Graunt, *Natural and Political Observations* (1662), in *The Earliest Classics*, ed. P. Laslett (1973), 27.

[36] L. Riverius, *The Practice of Physick*, trans. N. Culpeper, A. Cole, and W. Roland (1655), 420.

[37] L. Lemnius, *A Discourse touching Generation* (1667), 268.

[38] S. Purchas, *Purchas his Pilgrim: Microcosmus, or the Historie of Man* (1619), 481–3.

mind, or even madness.[39] Suicidal fancies were also caused by vapours from the womb rising to the brain.[40]

Disturbances in love affairs could also precipitate mother-fits: 'young blossom'd Girls seem to be troubled with another evil . . . and that's their Mother, which must ever and anon be fuming up their throats upon the least disturbance of their Amours.' Robert Burton, the anatomist of melancholy, concluded gloomily that it was almost impossible for young people of a similar age to be together and *not* fall in love. A later writer warned parents not to thwart their daughters, he having seen several young women 'that fell into most terrible fits of the Mother, five or six in a day, upon a rupture of a Marriage'.[41] Young women who had rich diets and idle lives were most at risk.

Mother-fits could also come from a plethora of blood and seed leading to the desire for venery. Excessive blood would be distilled into seed, which would cause an itching sensation. Lemnius linked women's sexual appetites to their bodily forms: fat, ruddy women were full of moisture, and therefore the wetness of their seed sedated their lust. Lean, slender women of declining years were always itching.[42] Some writers recommended a spare diet and hard exercise: 'A sober Diet mitigates the Violence of Passions and Affections', advised *Medicaments For the Poor*.[43] Young women who lived in the country suffered less from mother-fits because their hard labour used up their excessive blood.[44] Physicians therefore let blood from women who did not menstruate or who suffered mother-fits.[45] In one case, a physician purged a woman suspected of being possessed by an ill spirit, 'and restored her matrix [womb] to its former estate'.[46]

If the mother-fits were from retention of seed, then sexual activity (within marriage) was the preferred treatment, as it was for greensickness: 'a good Husband will administer the Cure!'[47] 'Marry your daughters betimes lest they marry themselves' was a popular saw. Fathers should ensure that their daughters married in good time, because 'that Sex is frail,

[39] Lemnius, *Of Complexions*, fo. 105^{v}; D. Sennert, *The Institutions or Fundamentals of the Whole Art . . . of Physick* (1656), 269.

[40] P. de Loyer, *A Treatise of Specters* (1605), fos. 110–110^{v}.

[41] R. Burton, *The Anatomy of Melancholy* (Oxford, 1621), 576; G. Harvey, *Morbus Anglicus: Or the Anatomy of Consumption* (1672), 23–4.

[42] L. Lemnius, *The Secret Miracles of Nature in Four Books* (1658), 152.

[43] J. Prévost *Medicaments For the Poor*, trans. N. Culpeper (2nd edn., Edinburgh, 1664), 30.

[44] Paré, *Workes*, 948.

[45] *Diaries and Letters of Philip Henry of Broad Oak, Flintshire, A. D. 1631–1696*, ed. M. H. Lee (1882), 9, 41–3, 65.

[46] K. Digby, *A Late Discourse* (3rd edn., 1660), 93–4.

[47] *Aristotles Masterpiece* (1710), 104.

and subject to ruine'.[48] Sexual activity was a needful evacuation;[49] a wife was thought to be in a more healthful state than a virgin or a widow.[50] Since a woman's seed untimely retained 'causeth heavinesse, and dulnesse of the body' and corruption,[51] it was proper for afflicted women to use coition to expel the venomous matter.[52] For many of women's menstrual disorders, physicians recommended marriage for virgins and 'often and wanton copulation' for wives.[53] Widows and maids were often 'thorowly cured' of their mother-fits by marriage, wrote Bunworth in 1656.[54]

In extreme cases, with some regard for ethical considerations, medical writers advised each other—usually in Latin—how to masturbate the woman so that her seed would be released. Paré, for example, thought that strangulation of the womb could cause death, so he advised the midwife to tickle the mouth of the woman's womb with her finger.[55]

Mother-fits could be mistaken for witchcraft or demonic possession. Edward Jorden, in his treatise, *The Suffocation of the Mother*, warned people to be circumspect in diagnosing witchcraft since 'the effects of naturall disease be strange to such as haue not looked thoroughly into them'.[56]

By the end of the seventeenth century, physicians were exploring the causes of what they called female hysteria. In 1692, Pechey explained that women were more liable than men to hysteric diseases. Previously, hysteric symptoms were attributed to 'a vitious Womb', but Pechey claimed that 'this whole Disease is occasion'd by the animal Spirits being not rightly dispos'd, and not by Seed and menstruous Blood corrupted'.[57] Theorists had begun to define the symptoms of hysteria as a form of female madness, a categorization which would be of significance for the negative construction of women in the future.

The 'menopause', a term not used until the nineteenth century, was variously referred to as 'the time the Courses are about to leave them', or 'the cessation of the flowers', and thought to occur at about 45 or 50 years of age.[58] In general, early modern medical writers viewed the menopause positively, not as a particularly unfortunate stage in a woman's life. Lemnius

[48] Lemnius, *Generation*, 352. [49] Cogan, *Haven of Health*, 247.
[50] Fontanus, *Womans Doctour*, 4–6. [51] Sennert, *The Institutions of Physick*, 269.
[52] Albertus Magnus, *De Secretis Mulierum* (trans. 1725), 91–2.
[53] Paré, *Workes*, 948. [54] B[unworth], *The Doctresse*, 31.
[55] Paré, *Workes*, 942. Thanks to Winfried Schleiner for allowing us to consult his unpublished paper on the medical ethics involved.
[56] Jorden, *A Briefe Discourse*, epistle dedicatory.
[57] J. Pechey, *A Collection of Chronical Diseases* (1692), 32–3, 49.
[58] Ibid. 82; Lemnius, *Generation*, 356; G. Mauquest de La Motte, *A Treatise of Midwifery* (trans., 1746), 15; Sennert, *Institutions*, 21. For further discussion of estimates of the age of the menopause, see Crawford, 'Attitudes to Menstruation', 66 n. 114.

thought that old women past child-bearing were more quiet 'because their terms are ended'.[59] Into the eighteenth century, however, some physicians continued to believe that disorders increased in older women when they ceased to menstruate.[60]

Some thought that menstrual blood caused bad odours: 'But a woman abounding with excrements, and sending out ill smells by reason of her terms; makes all things worse, and spoils their natural forces and inbred qualities.' If a woman carried nutmegs around to counter her offensive odour, even they would be contaminated and spoiled.[61] Menstrual blood was not only filthy and unpleasant to men, but also dangerous as it could excoriate the penis on contact.[62] Furthermore, menstrual blood was believed to play a powerful role in love magic. Men feared it especially because they could unknowingly consume it in food which had been prepared by women. Even those who discounted the danger in menstrual blood gave more publicity to this belief, as did Crooke in 1615 when he argued against the view that 'Wanton women are wont to bewitch their Lovers with this bloud'.[63] Ross, too, denied that there was power in menstrual blood 'to procure love', suggesting 'this may be an illusion of Satan, who delights in blood'.[64]

Positive writing about menstruation was rare. Even Helkiah Crooke, who sought to explain that menstruation was for health and reproduction, still believed that men found it disgusting. Crooke explained that women menstruated monthly rather than daily, because otherwise no man could 'haue due and comfortable use of a woman. . . . Beside what pleasure or contentment could any man finde in a wife so lothsomely defiled, and that perpetually.'[65]

Parturition

Physicians interpreted pregnancy and childbirth in terms of general medical theories and axioms about the superiority of the male. Because women were constructed for breeding, it followed that they were by nature insatiable for sex and children. Men warned each other to be careful, not 'to be milked by them'.[66]

[59] Lemnius, *Secret Miracles*, 274.

[60] Magnus, *De Secretis Mulierum*, 90.

[61] Lemnius, *Secret Miracles*, 124.

[62] J. Drake, *Anthropologia Nova; Or a New System of Anatomy*, 2 vols. (1707), i. 321. Drake rejected this view as superstitious.

[63] Crooke, *Microcosmographia*, 289.

[64] Ross, *Arcana Microcosmi*, 137.

[65] Crooke, *Microcosmographia*, 293.

[66] Lemnius, *Secret Miracles*, 185.

It was believed that social status mediated a woman's experience of childbearing. Since the childbirth of the well-fed and idle rich woman was likely to be more difficult than that of the poor woman, the two should be treated differently: in 'governing' women in childbed, to treat a country woman like a person of quality would kill her, and vice versa.[67] Class as well as gender was defined in terms of medical discourse.

Various theories of conception were discussed during the early modern period. The most favoured medical view during the sixteenth and first half of the seventeenth centuries stated that the child was formed from both male and female seed: 'the Woman spends her Seed aswel as the Man', and a child was formed from the mixture.[68] Paré's work, translated in 1634, advised a couple how to achieve a simultaneous orgasm.[69] Others thought that woman was merely passive in the process of generation, while the man's seed was active.[70] If it were left to seed to decide the sex of the child, all would be born male, 'since the mans seed is alwaies stronger and hotter than the womans'. Physicians debated what women contributed to the foetus.[71]

Medical theories about conception altered during the seventeenth century. Physicians agreed that women did not spend seed during copulation, and debated whether the foetus was pre-formed in either the sperm or the ovum. Either way, female sexual pleasure became irrelevant. Writers realized that their theories affected women's attitudes to their pregnancies: 'there are some Bawds in our Country that would perswade women that Mothers afford very little to the generation of the child, but only are at the trouble to carry it, . . . as if the womb were hired by Men . . . women grow luke-warm, and lose all humane affections towards their children'.[72]

Although historians have debated whether early modern people had any desire to limit their family size or any knowledge of contraceptive practices before the eighteenth century, evidence suggests that parents did seek to determine the number and sex of their children.[73] Commonplace books and medical treatises contained remedies for barrenness. Medical writers assumed that their readers sought male children: 'Those who seek the

[67] T. Chamberlayne, *The Compleat Midwifes Practice* (1656), 93.

[68] N. Culpeper, *A Directory for Midwives* (1651), 56; *Aristotles Masterpiece* (1690), 6: 'the *Vasa deferentia* in Women, spring from the lowere part of the Testicles'; R. Barret, *A Companion for Midwives, Child-Bearing Women and Nurses* (1699), 47.

[69] Paré, *Workes*, 889. [70] H. Crooke, *Microcosmographia* [1631], 283.

[71] Lemnius, *Secret Miracles*, 9–18; (seed hotter) 20–1.

[72] Lemnius, *Secret Miracles*, 9–10.

[73] L. Stone, *The Family, Sex and Marriage in England, 1500–1800* (1977), 415–24; A. McLaren, *A History of Contraception from Antiquity to the Present Day* (Oxford, 1990), 141–69.

comfort of having wise children, must indeavour that they be born Male; for the Female, through the cold and moist of their Sex, cannot be indowed with so profound a judgment.' Chamberlayne offered six instructions for begetting sons, including how the seed could fall into the right side of the womb, and how the couple should exercise, to consume excessive moisture of seed. (The idle rich would produce daughters.)[74] Presumably, people deduced that the opposite practices or timing of sexual intercourse would either prevent conception or produce a daughter.[75] How to prevent conception was of interest, although some thought such knowledge would lead to sin. People puzzled over why prostitutes, who had frequent intercourse, were barren, and suggested that too much sex had made their wombs too slippery for conception.[76]

Physicians believed that after conception the mother nourished the child with her blood and shaped the child by her imagination.[77] They followed Hippocrates in his belief that males were formed sooner than females.[78] Malformed foetuses and monstrous births were usually blamed on mothers and their sins. Women could produce 'false conceptions', usually termed 'moles'. 'Some say' that true moles were formed when a man's seed was weak and choked with menstrual blood, and that false or windy moles were formed from want of heat in the womb.[79] Other theorists argued that a woman could conceive 'a false mole' without a man, by a mixture of her own seed and menstrual blood.[80] Monsters were the punishment for a couple who had had sexual relations at forbidden times, or who copulated with the 'immoderate desire of lust'.[81] Maternal imagination, which shaped the features of the child, could also deform it. Any sudden fright could damage the foetus. By the end of the seventeenth century, physicians censured the over-indulgence of women's longings during pregnancy; those who continued to work hard and had a spare diet rarely infected their children with disease.[82] Pain in childbirth was generally regarded as an unavoidable punishment from God.

Conception, pregnancy, and childbirth were thus constructed as dangerous times for the mother and child: too much sex, too little seed, the imagination of women, the influence of the stars, all could cause disaster.[83]

[74] T. Chamberlayne, *The Complete Midwifes Practice Enlarg'd* (1659), 288–90.
[75] W. Sermon, *The Ladies Companion, or the English Midwife* (1671), 29.
[76] B[unworth], *The Doctresse*, 50.
[77] Lemnius, *Secret Miracles*, 11–14.
[78] Crooke, *Microcosmographia*, 308.
[79] Sermon, *Ladies Companion*, 31–3.
[80] J. Wolveridge, *Speculum Matricis: Or, the Expert Midwives Handmaid* (1671), 79.
[81] [J. Rueff], *The Expert Midwife* (trans. 1637), 153.
[82] W. Harris, *An Exact Enquiry into . . . the Acute Diseases of Infants* (1693), 11.
[83] Lemnius, *Generation*, 242–3.

Lactation

The third distinctively female function, lactation, was understood as the transformation of blood into milk by the female breasts. Menstrual blood used to nourish the foetus became milk after the child was born: milk 'is nothing else, but the bloud whitened'.[84] Thus the nurse's character, and whatever food she ate or activity she engaged in had the potential to affect the child she fed: 'the propertie and nature of the milke is of power to chaunge and alter the disposition of the Infant.'[85] Widespread through the society was the assumption that the nurse's qualities were transmitted to her child by her milk: 'Do you think the Vulgar have no grounds for this Saying, He sucked in his Malice and Wickedness with his Nurses Milk.'[86] In practice, physicians would advise that a child should be weaned if a nurse was thought to be ill.

Throughout the seventeenth century, medical writers insisted that a mother or nurse could enfeeble her nursling if she engaged in sexual activity. Paré ruled that 'Shee must abstaine from copulation' because sexual activity troubled the blood, diminished the quantity of milk, provoked menstruation, and caused the milk to have a strong quality.[87] Harris repeated similar advice in 1693: 'if she more wantonly entertain the untimely embraces of her Husband, her monthly Visits are renewed by their copulating and so her Milk Corrupteth and groweth soure and the matter for the Milk being otherwise diverted.'[88] Wet-nurses were widely blamed for the ills which befell their charges.

Changes and continuities

There were changes in the medical understanding of a woman's body by the eighteenth century. At the beginning of the early modern period, sexual activity was considered necessary for the bodily health of both men and women. By the end of the seventeenth century, copulation continued to be viewed as necessary for men's health, but no longer for women's. The theoretical links between women and hysteria were stronger at the end of the early modern period. Earlier, a woman was more likely to be labelled as a

[84] J. Guillimeau, *Child-birth or the Happie Deliverie of Women* (1612), 1; J. Hart, *Klinikh, or the Diet of the Diseased* (1633), 330; [Rueff], *Expert Midwife*, 53.

[85] J. Jones, *The Arte and Science of preserving Bodie and Soule in al Healthe* (1579), 8.

[86] *A Dialogue between a Gentleman and a Lady, Relating Chiefly to the Nursing and Bringing up of Children* (1698), 39.

[87] Paré, *Workes*, 909.

[88] Harris, *Exact Enquiry*, 17.

witch than as insane. Madness as a label for 'deviance' filled the place of witchcraft in the eighteenth century.

Yet there were powerful continuities in the axioms of medical theorists. Writers continued to give substance to the view of woman as weak, unstable, and unreliable. The more charitable physicians argued that women could not help their erratic behaviour—'woman-kind are naturally frail'[89]—since they were at the mercy of their imperfect bodies.

Medical discourse and practice constructed woman's body as in a constant state of flux. Her blood assumed so many different forms, as milk, foetal nourishment, and menstrual discharges, all of which seemed, by their very nature, mysterious. Popular writers alleged that woman was unstable because she was influenced by the moon: 'the Moon hath great influence upon all Elementary Bodies; but more upon Women than Men, because they are of her own Sex.'[90] Lemnius cautioned men to be careful of sexual activity at 'the fourth Moon', the time of menstruation, since they could harm their posterity.[91]

Medical and popular theories of the body thus constructed women's bodies as possessing dangerously unstable qualities. The misogynists found in these ideas further justification for not trusting women. All assumed that women, unlike men, were created not as something in themselves, but rather for gestation and man's bodily convenience. Yet female physiological power was very great, and to some degree men were in awe of women. Fearing the female body, they sought to contain and control it.

Medical theories made their greatest impact higher up in the social scale. Elite men read the international literature in Latin as well as English treatises, and supplemented their knowledge with readings from the erotic literature of classical times. At the bottom of the social scale, men and women were more influenced by oral traditions. Discourse about physiological sexual difference played 'a critical role in shaping individuality'.[92] How men thought of women, and how women thought of themselves, were influenced by the medical theorists.

[89] Lemnius, *Secret Miracles*, 14. [90] Culpeper, *Directory for Midwives*, 96.

[91] Lemnius, *Secret Miracles*, 23–4.

[92] S. Greenblatt, 'Fiction and Friction', in T. C. Heller, M. Sosna, and D. E. Wellbery (eds.), *Reconstructing Individualism: Autonomy, Individuality, and the Self in Western Thought* (Stanford, Calif., 1986), 34.

RELIGIOUS TEACHINGS

During the sixteenth and seventeenth centuries, the religious establishment was perhaps the most powerful medium through which theories about human nature and society were disseminated to the general population. Although doctrine was formulated by an élite group of men who constituted the Church hierarchy, the need to promote religious conformity ensured that the Established Church exerted an enormous influence on every sector of the population, either directly or indirectly. Church attendance was compulsory for women as well as men of all ranks, although penalties for recusancy (absence from parish church services) were at certain periods slightly less severe for women.

Aside from expositions of theology and morality, Church teachings dealt with more personal matters such as the sexual relationship between husbands and wives. Clerics also offered information and opinions on public affairs, including local and national political issues. Sermons and 'mass-produced' homilies thus helped to set the terms of reference for popular debates about everything from marital relations to revolutionary politics.

The theology of gender in early modern Europe began with a paradox. On the one hand, Protestant clerics assured women of their equal spiritual status, the doctrine that 'souls have no sex'. Paul had laid the textual basis for this axiom, stating that 'in Christ there is neither Greek nor Jew, slave nor free, man nor woman' [Galations 3:28]. Whether women were fully human, and as such were possessors of souls and capable of salvation, was resolved as a theological issue in women's favour in 585 CE, at the Council of Macon.[93] The decree remained unaltered by the sixteenth-century Reformation; indeed Europeans of every denomination prided themselves on what they regarded as Christianity's superiority to Islam in granting women full spiritual rights. English girls, like boys, attained religious adulthood with their first communion at age 16.

But the doctrine of equal souls did not entitle women to equal participation in the Church's temporal hierarchy. As one cleric explained: 'many women might thinke that by reason of religion, all were equall . . . but . . . Christ hath freed men and women from the bondage of sinne and death, and not from outward subjection.'[94] Women might hope to benefit from the doctrine of 'equal souls' in the next world, but not in the present one.

In practice, men monopolized the institutional expression of religion,

[93] C. L. Powell, *English Domestic Relations* (New York, 1917), 150.

[94] F. Dillingham, *Christian Oeconomy, or Household Government* (1609), 3.

formulating and disseminating religious 'information' about gender issues as well as other matters. They decided points of theology, carried out sacred rituals, and performed all public preaching. The trappings of Protestant symbolism also reinforced a general sense of male spiritual hegemony. Lacking the feminizing aura of the Virgin Mary, Protestant writers laid great stress on the fatherhood of the godhead, as well as the masculine traits and appearance of Christ as bridegroom. The spatial symbolism of church seating, in which the two sexes sat apart in separate areas, also promoted a sense of women's 'otherness' in moral and religious as well as social terms. In church, the dichotomy of sex appeared far less flexible than gradations of social and economic rank. This is not to say that women were barred from any connection with church affairs. But with the exception of the queen regnant, women could claim no formal magisterial role in the religious establishment.

The rationale for women's subordinate status in the Protestant Church was based on contemporary interpretations of passages from the Old and New Testaments, the most important texts being Genesis 2: 18–23 and 3: 16, and Paul's paraphrase of these verses in 1 Corinthians 11: 7–10, 1 Timothy 2: 14, and 1 Peter 3: 1–7. Two fundamental postulates defining women's role in the Christian commonwealth had been deduced from these texts, to be endlessly repeated and elaborated by early modern theologians. The first, an interpretation of Eve's secondary creation from Adam's rib, was the premiss that the woman was made for the man. This was applied specifically to wives' duties to husbands as obedient 'meet helps', and more generally in the assumption that the female sex was subject and subordinate to the male sex.

The second key notion affirmed Eve's moral and intellectual weakness as the primary cause of the Fall and its disastrous sequel for mankind. Again, both specific and general consequences for succeeding generations of women were thought to follow from Eve's behaviour. First, the punishments meted out to Eve entailed special disabilities for wives and mothers. Wifely obedience was not only a duty but a particular scruple for pious women: 'he that wil have a wife in subjection, let him match with a religious woman, for religion teacheth her subjection.'[95]

Women's restriction to a maternal role was taken to be another consequence of the Fall. Eve's punishment of pain in childbirth was generalized to include feminine responsibility for the troubles of rearing as well as bearing offspring. Meanwhile, women's actual sufferings in childbirth served as a

[95] Dillingham, *Christian Oeconomy*, 8–8^{v}.

frequent reminder of Eve's transgression and its consequences for the female sex, while contemporaries of both sexes cited female labour pains as 'proof' of the logic of female inferiority.

Theology defined the good daughter, wife, mother, and widow in terms of her conformity to her role, and laid special stress on the importance of 'relative duties' in women's striving for salvation. It is true that Anglican exegesis tended to be moderate in its intepretation of wifely subjection. The Elizabethan Homily on Marriage, for example, condemned wife-beating without reservation. But such strictures were set in the framework of woman as 'weaker vessel'. Because man was created mentally and physically superior to woman, his reason should enable him to control his wife *without* resorting to force.

In terms of the wider world, theologians' habit of deducing general conclusions from particular incidents in the biblical narrative offered a model for extending the implications of Eve's actions to include all of womankind. In this way the punishment of subjection to Adam was used to justify women's dependent status in every sphere, not just the hierarchical relationship between husband and wife. Writers on legal topics, for example, borrowed from theology to justify female exclusion from the political realm.[96]

The Genesis narrative was understood not only as a symbolic representation of gender roles in marriage and the family, but as a concrete event in the past which accounted for women's loss of power and independence in the secular world. In accord with this historical treatment of the Fall, some theologians conjectured that Eve had been politically equal to Adam before the Fall (dated by Archbishop Ussher at 4004 BCE). Although the question of Eve's pre-lapsarian condition may appear irrelevant to the realities of seventeenth-century life, it became a practical issue for the early Quakers, who believed that they had been reborn to the innocence of the first creation of mankind. This notion involved the corollary that Quaker women need no longer suffer from the social and political consequences entailed by Genesis 3: 16. Some Quakers even collected evidence that the divine penalties had been revoked, as in a letter from Thomas Salthouse to Margaret Fell reporting a woman's painless birth of a daughter: 'before she travailed she brought forth . . . to the praise and honour of him that hath taken away the curse.'[97]

One of the great strengths of religious doctrine was its virtual immunity

[96] T.E., *The Lawes Resolutions of Womens Rights* (1632), 6.
[97] LF, Swarthmore MSS, iii, fo. 158.

from empirical contradiction; theological truths were not considered susceptible to disproof in the same way that scientific theories might be overturned. Women themselves voiced their conviction that certain gender inequalities could never be challenged because scriptural authority was not open to rational debate. The countess of Bridgewater, in a private meditation about marriage, wrote that some women think marriage is an unhappy life because they owe obedience to their husbands. She then added: 'Tis great reason it *should* be so [i.e. that wives should obey their husbands] since we are commanded, by those that are above our capacity of reason, by God himself.'[98]

Some contemporaries believed that there was more room for debate about general issues such as the implications of theology for women's political role (or lack of it). But women were immersed in an intellectual atmosphere in which the politics of the family was intertwined with every other gender issue. As soon as wives were declared subject to husbands, women as a sex were seen as dependent beings who had lost all freedom of action. Only with the changing intellectual climate of the late seventeenth century did a few writers begin to take a fresh look at the scriptural grounds for women's subordination, distinguishing the status of wives from that of widows and spinsters, who had no matrimonial masters. Locke, for example, pointed out that the punishment laid upon Eve entailed no more than wives' obedience to their husbands: 'there is here no . . . Law to oblige a woman to such a Subjection, if the Circumstances either of her Condition or Contract with her Husband should exempt her from it.'[99] But while there were many complexities and ambiguities in the theology of gender, orthodox religious doctrine tended to have a conservative effect on social *mores* and gender relations well into the eighteenth and nineteenth centuries, long after the secular intellectual establishment had begun to debate some gender issues as open questions.

THE LAW AND ITS ADMINISTRATION

The English law and its administration were premissed upon assumptions about the different natures of the two sexes and the law in turn was a

[98] BL, MS Egerton 607, fo. 78^{v}. For similar sentiments about the definitive role of religious authority see M. Astell, *A Serious Proposal to the Ladies*, pt. 2 (1697), 51–4.

[99] J. Locke, *Two Treatises of Government*, ed. P. Laslett (Cambridge, 1960), 191. See also Mary Astell's reinterpretation of Scripture in *Marriage* (1706), 'Second Preface', sigs. a–a4.

powerful influence upon women's lives. The law was one of the fundamental constraints on the personal, civic, and property rights of women.

Contemporaries were aware that the law viewed women and men differently. 'The English laws are composed so far in favor of wives', complained Francis Osborne in the mid-seventeenth century, 'as if our ancestors had sent women to their Parliaments whilst their heads were a woolgathering at home.'[100] Blackstone's dictum in the eighteenth century made the strongest statement of how the laws of England were intended for the protection and benefit of wives: 'So great a favourite is the female sex of the laws of England.'[101] However there were critical voices. Around the end of the sixteenth century, the author of *The Lawes Resolutions of Womens Rights* pointed out that the law treated the sexual transgressions of husband and wife differently, and one mid-eighteenth-century commentator declared that of all the king's subjects, women's condition was 'the most deplorable'.[102]

Historians have rightly pointed out that the legal position of early modern women was not all negative.[103] Amy Erickson's recent study of women and property argues that ordinary women both understood and could use the provisions of the law for their own purposes.[104] Prest has argued cautiously for some 'real improvements' in the early modern period, citing the Statute of Uses (1536), permitting married men to devise land in trust to their wives, the removal of benefit of clergy from convicted rapists in 1576, the raising of the age of consent to marriage for women to 14 years in 1653, and the extension of benefit of clergy to female felons in 1691.[105] None of these historians, however, disputes that the law did treat women and men differently.

Here we are concerned with several issues: how did the law both reflect and reinforce the contemporary gender order? Were women regarded in theory and treated in practice differently from men because of their sex, or because they fell into some situation, such as pregnancy, that was physiologically impossible for men? We suggest that generalization about

[100] F. Osborne, *Advice to a Son* (Oxford, 1656), in L. B. Wright (ed.), *Advice to a Son* (Ithaca, NY, 1962), 65.

[101] W. Blackstone, *Commentaries on the Laws of England* (4th edn., Dublin, 1771), 445.

[102] T.E., *The Lawes Resolutions*, 145: 'as soone as the good wife is gone, the badman will haue her Land, not the third, but euery foote of it.' For the authorship and dating of the work to the late 16th cent., see W. R. Prest, 'Law and Women's Rights in Early Modern England', *The Seventeenth Century*, 6 (1991), 172–5; [H. Chapone], *The Hardship of the English Laws in Relation to Wifes* (1735). Anna Hopkins refers to the secret of Chapone's authorship in correspondence; Bodl., Ballard MS 43, fo. 106 (14 Dec. 1743).

[103] Maclean, *Renaissance Notion of Woman*, 80.

[104] Erickson, *Women and Property*.

[105] Prest, 'Law and Women's Rights', 187 n. 63.

improvement in the legal position of women during the early modern period is too simple.

The law in early modern England was not a system in the sense of being clear, ordered, and widely known. Rather, the law was a series of rules which had evolved over time, and was still fluid. Moreover, the modern distinction between the theory and practice of law is best forgotten at this date.[106] Although several lawyers wrote legal treatises and handbooks, there was no real distinction between theory and practice. The ideas of judges and the lawyers could constitute the law as much as could the decision of MPs expressed as a statute. Thus the administration of the law as well as legal treatises should be considered as legal discourse.

Ideally, all human law aspired to enforce the law of God. In early modern England, there were various kinds of law. Natural law was widely interpreted as that which God had put into the hearts of 'men' to incline them to good behaviour. For example, the love of parents for children was deemed a part of natural law, and therefore axiomatic to the English legal system. Statute law was made in Parliament, and administered by the courts. Common law, based on custom and precedent, was administered in the system of royal courts with the central courts generally supreme. Law based on the king's conscience or equity was administered in the prerogative court of Star Chamber and in Exchequer. Canon law was administered by the church courts. Finally, manorial courts based on custom administered the law of the manor.[107] Each tradition of law required trained and learned men for its interpretation and administration.

Civil, criminal, and ecclesiastical law all began with the axiom that the two sexes were different in their essential nature, and unequal in moral as well as intellectual capacity. As the author of *The Lawes Resolutions of Womens Rights* (1632) explained to his female readers, the world had been divided into two sexes before it was seven days old. Women had nothing to do with either the making or the administration of law: they 'have nothing to do in constituting Lawes, or consenting to them, in interpreting of Lawes, or in hearing them interpreted'. Nevertheless, women were bound by the law: 'they stand strictly tyed to mens establishments, little or nothing excused by ignorance.'[108] Yet although women were much like children—inferior, subordinate, dependent, and therefore excluded from all

[106] J. H. Baker, *An Introduction to English Legal History* (2nd edn., 1979), 1–10, 49.

[107] As Amy Erickson points out, little work has been done on manorial law; A. Erickson, 'Common Law Versus Common Practice: The Use of Marriage Settlements in Early Modern England', *Economic History Review*, 2nd ser., 43 (1990), 24 n. 10.

[108] T.E., *The Lawes Resolutions*, 2.

magisterial roles—there was some small margin of equitable feeling that they were less responsible than males. The law in its framing and administration contained some elements of chivalry towards women as dependants.

Marital status

Neither the Divine Law nor the Law of nature, nay nor yet the civil Law, put any woman under the Subjection of men, but only such as have Husbands; and no shew of reason can be given, for excluding Women from the Inheritance of their Ancestors, or from the administration of it.[109]

Both theory and practice assigned different legal status to single and married women in early modern England. In theory the legal status of the *feme sole* was the same as that of a man. The patriarchal theorist Sir Robert Filmer asserted that all female virgins were born free, and a famous late seventeenth-century judge and legal commentator, Sir Matthew Hale, claimed that although the Roman lawyers made a difference between males and females, he thought 'the measure is the same for both'.[110]

Common law, however, made a sharp distinction between single and married women, treating marriage as the norm: all women were either 'married or to bee married'.[111] Man and wife were one person, and that person was the husband. The only married woman who was not automatically deemed a *feme covert* was a queen.[112] Queens consort could receive gifts of property from their husbands and be sued apart from them.[113]

The implications of the doctrine of coverture—the view that husband and wife were one person at law—affected married women in various ways. The law's protection of wives was limited. For crimes known as *male in se*—treason, keeping a brothel, murder—married women were to answer for themselves. As a husband was legally responsible for his wife, coverture placed her in the same category as children, wards, lunatics, idiots, and outlaws.

A wife had few legal rights over her body in relation to her husband. He had the legal power to administer what was termed 'lawful and reasonable correction', although increasingly domestic advisers denied that he might

[109] T. Craig, *Concerning the Right of Succession to the Kingdom of England* (1703), 83.

[110] R. Filmer, 'The Anarchy of a Limited or Mixed Monarchy', in *Patriarcha and other Political Works* (Oxford, 1949); M. Hale, *Historia Placitorum Coronae*, 2 vols. (1736), i. 17–18.

[111] T.E., *The Lawes Resolutions*, 6.

[112] G. Meriton, *The Touchstone of Wills* (1668), 50.

[113] L. M. Glanz, 'The Legal Position of English Women under the Early Stuart Kings and the Interregnum', Ph.D. diss., Loyola University of Chicago (1973), 254.

beat his wife. A wife could apply to the courts to restrain a husband if she believed that her life was at risk, but she could not sue for bodily harm. (Jurists disagreed about whether a husband whose wife threatened him with what was referred to as 'bodily harm' could seek legal redress.)[114] Cases of marital rape could not be legally sustained. Since neither husband nor wife could testify against each other in court, a wife could not complain against certain actions of her husband.

The doctrine of coverture affected the position of the married woman in relation to property ownership and trading. A wife could make no legal contract, except concerning her clothing and food. Her husband could sell her clothes. Her earnings were not her own, and she could neither sue nor be sued. Any inheritances of personal property she was due were her husband's, unless some specific protection had been made. (One widow ingeniously secured some of her property for the benefit of her married daughter, Alice Thornton, rather than see her bequest swallowed up in her son-in-law's debts.)[115]

Although in theory every person had the right to make a will, from the thirteenth century, common lawyers had argued that since a wife did not own anything, she could not make a will. This position was somewhat modified in the reign of Henry VIII. According to 34 & 35 Hen. VIII, c. 5, a married woman was permitted to make a will with her husband's consent. Mary Prior's study of wives' wills from 1558 to 1700 suggests that a growing number of married women made wills, a trend which Prior attributes to their greater independence and assertiveness.[116]

Some of the special disabilities of married women applied at common law only. Other courts did not make these distinctions, or had as one of their purposes the mitigation of this disadvantage. The court of chancery acted to protect the property interests of wealthy married women who were disadvantaged at common law.[117] Furthermore, although the common law seemed inflexible, various factors affected its administration. The very complexity of a multiplicity of precedents militated against consistency of

[114] W. Gouge, *Of Domesticall Duties* (1622), 390–1; T.E., *The Lawes Resolutions*, 128–9; Stone, *Family*, 325–6; Glanz, 'Legal Position of Women', 45.

[115] *The Autobiography of Mrs. Alice Thornton*, ed. C. Jackson, Surtees Society, 62 (1875), 246–9.

[116] Meriton, *The Touchstone of Wills*, 44–50; M. Prior, 'Wives and Wills, 1558–1700', in J. Chartres and D. Hey (eds.), *English Rural Society, 1500–1800: Essays in Honour of Joan Thirsk* (Cambridge, 1990), 201–25.

[117] M. Cioni, 'The Elizabethan Chancery and Women's Rights', in D. J. Guth and J. W. McKenna (eds.), *Tudor Rule and Revolution: Essays for G. R. Elton from his American Friends* (Cambridge, 1982), 159–82.

judgments. Legal practitioners outside London were sometimes confused about what the law actually was.

In practice some married women could be accepted as *femes sole* by specific local customs, such as the custom of London which permitted a married woman to trade as a *feme sole* merchant,[118] or by a specific warrant. Queen Anne authorized Abigail Masham to receive moneys on the queen's behalf as if she were a *feme sole*.[119] Not all single women possessed sufficient economic resources to enjoy the benefit of trading as a *feme sole*. Furthermore, the increasing importance of the common law during the seventeenth century may have eroded customs which favoured married women's economic rights, as Alice Clark argued.[120]

At the end of the seventeenth century, Locke's theories of contract allowed men to view their position *vis-à-vis* their sovereign as citizens not subjects, but the theory of contract was not extended to the relationship between husband and wife. Yet women saw the illogicality of denying them rights, and increasingly challenged the notion of marriage as slavery from the end of the seventeenth century. As *The Ladies Dictionary* of 1694 observed, 'no Woman ever gave her plight in Marriage with an intent to be a Slave'.[121]

Although it was claimed that the law treated single women the same as men, and that it was only their married status which disadvantaged women, in fact this was not so. A girl was deemed legally of age earlier than a boy. She could consent to marriage at 12, while a boy could not consent until 14. She could make a testament of goods at 12, a boy not until 14.[122] By statute law, the majority of ordinary women between the ages of 14 and 40 could be required to go into service and be under the governance of the head of a household. Although in theory adult males were also liable to compulsory service, in practice the administration of the statute was applied almost exclusively to women.[123]

[118] P. Earle, *The Making of the English Middle Class* (Berkeley, 1989), 160.

[119] F. Harris, 'Women at Court, 1660–1760', unpublished paper, citing BL, Add. MS 63,093, fo. 45. We are grateful to Dr Harris for allowing us to cite her paper.

[120] A. Clark, *Working Life of Women in the Seventeenth Century* (1919), 236–7.

[121] C. Pateman, *The Sexual Contract* (Stanford, Calif. 1988); N.H., *The Ladies Dictionary* (1694).

[122] H. Swinburne, *A Treatise of Spousals* (1686), 50; H. Swinburne, *A Briefe Treatise of Testaments and Last Willes* (1590), 35–6.

[123] 5 Eliz., c. 4. Statute of Artificers (1563). See also Ch. 2 below. In 1777, *The Laws respecting Women*, 103, still stated that all unmarried women aged 12–40 could be compelled to go to service.

Women and property[124]

In most English counties the rule of inheritance among the peers and gentry was primogeniture, by which inheritance followed the male line. A wife's role was to bear heirs so that landed property could be transmitted from one male to another.[125] Nevertheless landed property—'real' property—was not the only kind. Goods and chattels were also property. Everyone had some property, even if they had no land.[126] The most complex body of law related to those women with the greatest property, and the daughters of peers and gentry were frequently involved in legal cases in order to secure their rights.

Under common law, the married woman had a right of maintenance from her husband during his lifetime, and to a proportion of his property on his death; a third if she had children, to half if none. However, a husband whose wife died was entitled, by the 'courtesy of England', to a life interest in her estates.[127] Furthermore, a wife's rights depended on her behaviour, in ways that men's did not: 'if she make an Elopement (which is a mad tricke) Dower is forfeited.'[128]

Wealthy families sought to protect daughters' rights by marriage settlements and trusts. Lands could be kept separate for a woman's own use, or conveyed to trustees who would adminster the land for her separate use. Her rights, which included the right to make bequests, would be upheld by the court of Chancery. During the Elizabethan period, Chancery developed procedures to protect and enforce the property rights of wealthy married women.[129] The court could intervene in ways which undermined a husband's power to bequeath goods by his will. In 1590 Chancery deemed that a husband who left his widow to administer for their children, but left nothing for her, did 'greatly forget the greate love and kyndnes due to such a wief which had most duetyfully behave her selfe towards him and borne him soe many children'.[130]

The property rights of widows of men of higher social status were affected by the rise of the strict settlement and the use of trusts. In theory, strict settlements secured the patrimony of the eldest son of the marriage,

[124] For the best and most comprehensive discussion of this topic, see Erickson, *Women and Property.*

[125] Staves, *Married Women's Separate Property*, 4.

[126] Erickson, 'Marriage Settlements', 23.

[127] K. V. Thomas, 'The Double Standard', *Journal of the History of Ideas*, 20 (1959), 202.

[128] T.E., *The Lawes Resolutions*, 145.

[129] This paragraph is based on M. L. Cioni, 'Women and Law in Elizabethan England with particular reference to the Court of Chancery', Ph.D. diss., University of Cambridge (1974), 219.

[130] Ibid. 188.

and the bride's portion or jointure if she became a widow.[131] But we need to be very careful not to mistake the intention for the effect, as Staves argues in her study of married women's property. In practice, trusts could provide a means by which families were able to undermine the rights of widows.[132] Furthermore, Spring argues very persuasively that the inheritance rights of women in large landowning families declined, as the right of a widow to one-third of her husband's property was transformed into a provision determined before marriage.[133]

Early modern courts were concerned to protect some married women's property rights. If there were a dispute to a title of land, for example, the courts attempted to ascertain whether a wife had consented freely to the sale or had acted under duress, by examining her separately from her husband.[134] At common law, the courts maintained that a husband could not dispose of a wife's property or her dower as he wished.[135]

At lower social levels, the economic situation of widows was affected by changes in the law relating to wills. Complete freedom of testation could reduce the inheritance of widows and children, although the church courts sought to protect their rights.[136] The law allowed for marriage settlements to safeguard the rights of widows, which were especially important should they choose to remarry. The protection of the wife's property dates at least to the sixteenth century. Erickson argues that the wife's interest, not entailment in the main line, was the chief purpose of these settlements, since frequently women entered marriages as widows with the inheritances of their children from a former marriage to be protected from another husband. Further, women's rights to inherit goods were enforced by the ecclesiastical courts.[137]

In practice, when women sought to defend their property rights, they were less successful than men in the courts. Unlike men, whose cases were tried by their peers, women were tried solely by the opposite sex. When women were plaintiffs in cases of grand larceny (the theft of goods valued at a shilling or more), for example, the conviction rate was 44%, whereas the rate for plebeian male plaintiffs (agricultural labourers) was 100%. In cases of petty larceny, women secured convictions in only 50% of

[131] L. and J. C. F. Stone, *An Open Elite? England, 1540–1880* (Oxford, 1984), 73.

[132] Staves, *Married Women's Separate Property*, 204–8.

[133] Spring, *Law, Land, & Family*, 39–65.

[134] Cioni, 'Elizabethan Chancery', 173–4.

[135] Erickson, *Women and Property*, 25.

[136] Baker, *English Legal History*, 321–2; Erickson, *Women and Property*, 25–8.

[137] Erickson, *Women and Property*, 25–7. While Erickson argues that the settlements were more to protect the women rather than the children, we would argue that both motives were present.

cases, compared with 86% of the cases brought by non-agricultural male victims.[138] Women, particularly those of low social status, were less credible than men as plaintiffs.

Common law litigation expanded in the years 1560–1640, but women seem to have played only a minor part as suitors. They had a greater role in Chancery and other conciliar jurisdictions, being a sixth of the 'principal plaintiffs' of all Chancery suits during the second half of the sixteenth century. The proportion of women suitors increased to a quarter of all such cases in the period 1613–1714.[139] However, only in one case in twelve were women the lone plaintiffs in the court of Requests in the Elizabethan period.[140] Some lawyers and judges took a misogynistic attitude to women in the courts, whether as litigants or simply as onlookers. In 1597 the Lord Keeper Egerton ordered that 'base fellows and women and other suitors' should be excluded from the court of Star Chamber, and in 1603 he moved 'that no woman should be a suitor in any court in her own person'.[141] Stretton argues that women may have been discouraged from litigation by their lack of resources and ignorance. Furthermore, women's concern about their reputation may have acted as a barrier. The stereotyped images of women that lawyers employed in pleadings meant that women who pursued their cases at law risked damaging their reputations; they would be labelled as clamorous.[142]

Marriage, separation, child custody

A wife's person was effectively at the mercy of her husband, as the law allowed him to 'correct' her. However, the law courts upheld women's rights to be free from life-threatening violence from her husband, and, in practice, friends and neighbours might intervene if her husband seemed too cruel. The church courts would grant a separation *a mensa et thoro* (from bed and from board) with maintenance for the wife, in such cases.[143]

[138] C. Herrup, *The Common Peace: Participation and the Criminal Law in Seventeenth-Century England* (Cambridge, 1987), 153–5.

[139] Prest, 'Law and Women's Rights', 181–2; Erickson, *Women and Property*, 114–15.

[140] T. Stretton, 'Women and Litigation in the Court of Requests', Ph.D. diss., University of Cambridge (1993), 256.

[141] Prest, 'Law and Women's Rights', 182.

[142] Stretton, 'Women and Litigation', 257–8. For a valuable discussion of the representations of domestic crime, see F. Dolan, *Dangerous Familiars: Representations of Domestic Crime in England, 1550–1700* (Ithaca, NY, 1994).

[143] For a discussion of women's experiences, see Ch. 3 below.

Yet the protection was limited. The law frowned upon the popular custom of wife sale, but sales of wives occurred.[144]

After the Reformation, there was no legal way to end a marriage apart from a separation *a mensa et thoro*, which did not allow either party to remarry. Private acts of separation allowed a wife financial independence in return for indemnifying her husband against her debts. Although in theory this could be beneficial to a wife, in practice the courts were confused. The courts would still allow an estranged husband to seize his wife's goods and earnings. A husband could stop the maintenance if his separated wife committed any sexual misdemeanour.[145]

Wealthy men resented not being able to remarry. Although in the Elizabethan period there was a widespread view that a husband who separated from his wife for her adultery could legally remarry, the Church disapproved, and enforced the laws against remarriage in such cases early in the seventeenth century. During the 1640s and 1650s, individuals such as John Milton challenged the divorce laws, but to no effect. Ultimately more significant was the fact that wealthy, titled men considered an adulterous wife to be a serious problem: her children by another man might become his heirs while he could beget no lawful heirs of his own. After the Restoration, some men sought a remedy through private acts of Parliament for divorce. By the 1690s the House of Lords was of the view that a man, irrespective of his own adultery, was entitled to divorce his adulterous wife and to remarry, and from 1699 onwards there were attempts to turn female adultery into a statutory offence.[146] No wife could obtain an act of Parliament to divorce an adulterous husband.

Custody of children through most of the early modern period was governed chiefly by the view that a child was the property of a father. The husband might legally deny his separated wife not only custody but also access to her own children.

Crimes by and against women

Since it was axiomatic to the legal system that women were passive, not active, the courts assumed that women were accessories rather than

[144] S. P. Menefee, *Wives for Sale: An Ethnographic Study of British Popular Divorce* (Oxford, 1981). Reports of sales were rare, but increased during the 18th century.

[145] L. Stone, *Road to Divorce: England, 1530–1987* (Oxford, 1990), 150–61.

[146] Ibid. 305–17, 320. Cf. earlier attempt to make adultery punishable by death; K. Thomas, 'The Puritans and Adultery: The Act of 1650 Reconsidered', in D. Pennington and K. Thomas (eds.), *Puritans and Revolutionaries: Essays in Seventeenth-Century History presented to Christopher Hill* (Oxford, 1978), 257–82.

instigators of crime. Informally, women were protected when they came before the courts by the belief that they were less likely to be violent and dangerous criminals. This assumption was probably correct, for women's socialization had encouraged them to be more docile and dependent. There was less need to deter by exemplary punishment, because women generally were less a threat to the social order than men. Furthermore, women were less likely than men to be forced to criminal activity, for if they were destitute they might receive poor relief or help from their neighbours.[147]

The law's view of women's offences varied. In some cases, the judges were prepared to privilege women. In 1631 the Attorney-General recommended the pardon of a mother who sheltered her sons who were convicted of the theft of two mares and three cows: one should 'favour a mother in such a case'.[148] But in other instances, the law's view of women made their legal position worse. The law interpreted a husband's violence against his wife in terms of 'due correction'. Female insubordination, and wives' disobedience to husbands was more severely dealt with than excesses of patriarchal authority. If a man killed his wife, he was indicted for murder, but if a wife killed her husband, she was tried for petit treason.[149] Female rioters would be more leniently dealt with if no men had been involved. If women and children came together 'for their own cause', such as to seize grain at a time of famine, and could show that no man had incited them, they were not punishable under the statutes governing unlawful assembly.[150] The law assumed that women's motivation was not to disturb the public order but rather to act together on particular grievances which affected them. Female rioters were not, as males were, a real danger to society, so the law could be more lenient. But a group of women who pulled down enclosures dressed in men's attire were punished in Star Chamber because of 'putting off that shamefastnesse which beseemeth their sexe'.[151]

The law took a selective view of offences. Infanticide was defined as a crime committed by women, and was more severely punished after the statute of 1624 'to Prevent the Murthering of Bastard Children'. Aimed against unmarried mothers, the statute decreed that if a woman concealed a birth and her baby died, she was judged guilty of killing it, unless she could

[147] C. Z. Wiener, 'Sex Roles and Crime in Late Elizabethan Hertfordshire', *The Journal of Social History*, 8 (1975), 41.

[148] *CSPD Charles I, 1629–31*, iv. 346, 382, 476, 489.

[149] M. Dalton, *The Country Justice* (1655), 293.

[150] W. Lambarde, *Eirenarcha, or of the Office of the Justices of Peace* (1614), 180; M. Dalton, *The Countrey Justice* (1618), 196.

[151] Lambarde, *Eirenarcha*, 180; Dalton, *Countrey Justice*, 196, refers to the case.

prove that her child had been born dead.[152] This assumption, of guilt unless innocence could be proved, was contrary to the usual legal principle of presumption of innocence.[153] Furthermore, the law seems to have been rigorously administered. In the period before the Civil War, few of the women convicted of infanticide escaped execution, although only 20 per cent of women convicted of theft without benefit of clergy were executed.[154] In a particularly unhappy case of infanticide in the reign of Charles II, Anne Penny appealed against her sentence to the king, claiming that she had been delivered of a stillborn child, but had neglected to call witnesses. Although testimony from the midwife's and coroner's medical opinion supported her appeal, Charles insisted that Penny had committed a foul crime, and she was duly executed in 1675.[155] By the early eighteenth century, the law was more liberally interpreted, and at the end of the century, the courts usually required the crown to prosecute for murder rather than concealment. The standard defence, that the woman had prepared for the birth of her child by making baby clothes, usually sufficed to secure her acquittal.[156] If a married woman's child died, the burden of proving that she had killed it rested with the crown.

Witchcraft in England, as in early modern Europe, was largely understood as a woman's crime, although this has not featured in all recent historical discussion of the subject.[157] The crime itself was defined by a series of statutes in early modern England.[158] Of those indicted, 93 per cent were women. Macfarlane estimated that of about 2,000 people prosecuted between 1560 and 1706, only about 300 were executed.[159] In New England, Karlsen calculated that of those sent for trial between 1620 and 1725, fifteen

[152] 21 Jac. I, c. 7.

[153] L. Radzinowicz, *A History of English Criminal Law and its Administration from 1750* (1948), i. 431.

[154] Herrup, *Common Peace*, 173–5.

[155] Bodl. Rawlinson MS D. 371, Petitions *temp.* Charles II, fos. 35, 36^{v}; P. C. Hoffer and N. E. H. Hull, *Murdering Mothers: Infanticide in England and New England, 1558–1903* (New York, 1981), 23–6

[156] R. W. Malcolmson, 'Infanticide in the Eighteenth Century', in J. S. Cockburn (ed.), *Crime in England, 1550–1800* (1977), 187–209; K. Wrightson, 'Infanticide in Earlier Seventeenth-Century England', *Local Population Studies*, 15 (1975), 10–22; J. Beattie, *Crime and the Courts in England, 1660–1800* (Oxford, 1986), 113–24.

[157] C. Larner, *Enemies of God: The Witch-hunt in Scotland* (Oxford, 1981), 91; A. L. Barstow, 'On Studying Witchcraft and Women's History: A Historiography of the European Witch Persecutions', *Journal of Feminist Studies in Religion*, 4 (1988), 7–19; cp. J. Sharpe, 'Women, Witchcraft and the Legal Process', in Kermode and Walker, *Women, Crime and the Courts*, 118–20.

[158] For the crime and its history, see K. V. Thomas, *Religion and the Decline of Magic: Studies in Popular Beliefs in Sixteenth and Seventeenth Century England* (1971), 435–68.

[159] A. Macfarlane, *Witchcraft in Tudor and Stuart England* (1970), 62, 160.

of the sixteen convicted witches were women.[160] Some historians have rightly stressed that women were active in the prosecutions of witchcraft, but this should not distract attention from the fact that women rather than men were the main victims.[161] So far as women were concerned, the witchcraft laws were a special hazard which could make some of their traditional practices capital offences.

Male offenders convicted of specified crimes enjoyed benefit of clergy, by which, for certain crimes, they were not punished with death on the first offence. In 1624 the benefit was extended to women in cases of small felonies.[162] There was no literacy test, as there was in the case of men, for the courts assumed that women could not read. Women did not receive the full benefits until 1691.[163] In 1631 at the trial of the earl of Castlehaven, the judges resolved that a man could have benefit of clergy if he stood mute when accused of rape but not of buggery.[164] Although historians have found this a 'curious anomaly', it again reflects the general assumption, which the law shared, that men were of greater value than women: an offence against men was more serious than one against women. Contemporaries were influenced by their concept that buggery was 'unnatural'. Moreover, of course, in cases of rape the testimony offered by a woman was of dubious quality compared with the word of a man in cases of buggery.[165]

Yet there were ways in which women were treated favourably. One privilege the law allowed a woman was to plead her pregnancy as a reason to delay her execution. It is important to note that while this could mean that the sentence was not enforced, in legal terms it postponed but did not cancel the sentence.[166] In practice, juries might ameliorate the law's harshness. Because conviction for the crime of grand larceny carried the death penalty with benefit of clergy, when women's entitlement to the benefit was restricted, juries usually convicted women of the lesser offence of petty larceny for which the penalty was only a whipping.[167] Juries regularly

[160] C. F. Karlsen, *The Devil in the Shape of a Woman: Witchcraft in Colonial New England* (New York, 1989), 47–8. Karlson also argues that the treatment of female suspects was more vindictive; ibid. 50.

[161] J. Sharpe, 'Witchcraft and Women in Seventeenth-Century England: Some Northern Evidence', *Continuity and Change*, 6 (1991), 179–99.

[162] 21 Jac. I, c. 6.

[163] Herrup, *The Common Peace*, 143 and n. 16. In 1691 the continuation of a male literacy test disadvantaged men.

[164] J. Rushworth, *Historical Collections*, 8 vols. (1659), ii. 94–5.

[165] C. Hill, *Society and Puritanism in Pre-Revolutionary England* (1964), 300.

[166] Herrup, *Common Peace*, 143 n. 16.

[167] P. Lawson, 'Patriarchy, Crime and the Courts: The Criminality of Women in Late Tudor and Early Stuart England', unpublished paper, 28–9. We are extremely grateful to Dr Lawson for allowing us to cite his paper, and also for his help with criminal law.

undervalued goods stolen by women. Before 1694, jurors sometimes ensured that female felons would not be hanged for small theft, and later, that women would be whipped instead of merely branded.[168] Juries had enormous flexibility in manipulating punishments, so they could try women on their character, intention, conformity to proper roles, neighbourly repute, and so on. With all-male judge and juries, this flexibility placed even more pressure on women to represent themselves as dependent, subordinate, and not responsible. Jurors' attitudes to women help explain why infanticide was treated so harshly. The women accused were thought to have denied their proper nurturant roles and so were punished with great severity.

Basically, the criminal law saw women as petty criminals or subsistence thieves and judged that they should be punished, but not too severely, unless they started acting like men. If they should, like men, embark on crimes of greater magnitude, such as stealing large amounts of grain or leading riots, then they were treated very rigorously.

Crimes were committed against as well as by women, of which one of the most serious was rape. The basic difficulty for women was that men were strongly persuaded that rape was an accusation 'easily to be made, and hard to be proved'.[169] Legal commentators and judges worried more about how the charge could be sustained than they did about the violation the woman had suffered. Moreover, the law viewed a woman to some extent as male property, so the crime had been committed against her father or husband. A married woman could not prosecute for rape without her husband's consent.[170]

Until late in the seventeenth century, justices were influenced by the theory that women's sexual pleasure was necessary for conception. Thus, as Dalton explained in his handbook for justices, 'If a woman at the time of the supposed Rape do conceive with child by the Ravisher, this is no Rape, for a woman cannot conceive with child, except she doe consent.'[171] When medical theories about conception changed, this caused some doubt about the law. *The Ladies Law* of 1737 explained that 'In ancient Times, it was held not to be a Rape to force a woman, who conceived at the Time; because if she had not consented she could not have conceived; this Opinion hath

[168] Beattie, *Crime and the Courts*, 419–25.

[169] Hale, *Historia Placitorum Coronae*, ii. 635–6; R. Burn, *The Justice of the Peace and the Parish Officer*, 2 vols. (1755), i. 316.

[170] Thomas, 'The Double Standard', 211–13.

[171] Dalton, *Country Justice* (1655), 351 (cap 107); (1666 edn.), 328–9; see also Bodl. MS Eng. Misc. e. 479, MS notes by H. Townshend on *The Compleat Justice* (1661), 238.

been since Questioned.'[172] Very few women attempted to prosecute for rape, and conviction was unlikely unless the girl was under 18.[173]

Female sexuality was central to the law's concern with women. Contemporaries justified a double standard of morality in terms of men's rights to ensure that their biological heirs inherited their property.[174] A wife's infidelity was construed as a kind of theft, taking a husband's property from his rightful heirs. Men's anxieties about achieving some form of immortality may also have played a part in their concern to control the sexuality of women.

Although claims have been made for some improvement in the legal position of women in the early modern period, this improvement relates mainly to the rights of specific groups of women in limited areas. Certainly, the extension of benefit of clergy to women did appear to make the law less discriminatory. The law also increased the protection afforded to some married women as property holders. But, as Staves has argued, there was always a gap between the intention and the effect, and changes in the laws relating to marriage settlements did not, in many cases, help wives, because husbands persuaded them to surrender their jointures. Further work on the practice of law is clearly needed.[175]

We conclude that the legal situation of the majority of women underwent serious erosion in early modern England. After 1624, women were deemed guilty in cases of infanticide unless they could prove their innocence. They were more harshly punished for bastardy. And their traditional involvement in healing and conjuring was more likely to bring them an accusation of witchcraft than it had in the medieval period. Even the protection which the law was said to afford women had the effect of rendering them subordinate, because it treated them as incapable of looking after themselves. Very often women were legally constructed as property and possessions. In so far as women were referred to in terms of animal analogies, such as a cow—'for whose the cow is (as it is commonly said) his is the calf also'[176]—the notion of male ownership was accepted. Young women's opportunities for independence were more restricted by the Statute of Artificers than were young

[172] *The Ladies Law* (1737), 48; Burn, *Justice of the Peace*, i. 315; W. Hawkins, *A Treatise of the Pleas of the Crown*, 2 vols. (1716), i. 108 questions Dalton; Hale, *Historia Placitorum Coronae*, ii. 630.

[173] N. Bashar, 'Rape in England between 1550 and 1700', in London Feminist History Group, *The Sexual Dynamics of History: Men's Power, Women's Resistance* (1983), 37–8, 40.

[174] Thomas, 'The Double Standard', 195–216.

[175] Staves, *Married Women's Separate Property*, 197–208.

[176] MS note in BL copy of E. Coke, *First Part of the Institutes of the Lawes of England* (1628), 373. Thanks to Barbara Todd for this reference.

men's, and, as wives, women were denied all economic independence. Law and custom restricted their employment opportunities, as we shall show in later chapters.

The extent to which women understood their legal position varied according to their social level, education, and experience. A few educated women knew some law and consulted lawyers about their rights. But women needed more than knowledge of their rights: they needed enough self-confidence to demand them.[177] An heiress such as Anne, countess of Pembroke, both knew and secured her rights. She was a wily legal antagonist who triumphed in the face of the opposition of two of her husbands and even of King James himself. Yet all her legal problems stemmed from her position as a female heir. Lower down the social scale, married women were less confident of their legal knowledge: it was common for a woman in the church courts to declare that 'she is [a] married woman & therefore hath no goods of her own, as she taketh it, and hath heard'.[178]

CITIZENSHIP

> . . . we are not tied, nor bound to State or Crown; we are free, not sworn to Allegiance, nor do we take the Oath of Supremacy; we are not made Citizens of the Commonwealth, we hold no Offices, nor bear we any Authority therein; . . . and if we be not Citizens in the Commonwealth, I know no reason we should be Subjects to the Commonwealth. And the truth is, we are no Subjects, unless it be to our Husbands . . .[179]

If we ask to what extent women could participate as citizens in the early modern English polity, we are being deliberately anachronistic. The stark dichotomy we take for granted nowadays, which assumes that men before the twentieth century had the potential to be citizens and women did not, is only a crude approximation to early modern ideas about civic status. It was not clear to contemporaries (nor is it yet clear to historians) precisely what citizenship meant for *men*. Women's civil rights and privileges were even more ambiguously defined, when they were defined at all.[180]

In the earlier part of our period, civil rights represented a continuum or

[177] J. Greenberg, 'The Legal Status of the English Woman in Early Eighteenth-Century Common Law and Equity', *Studies in Eighteenth-Century Culture* (1975).

[178] OA, MS, Oxf. Dioc. papers, c. 96, fo. 8^{v} (1627).

[179] M. Cavendish, duchess of Newcastle, *CCXI Sociable Letters* (1664), 27.

[180] For suffrage as an instance of this principle, see D. Hirst, *The Representative of the People?* (Cambridge, 1975), 18–19.

rather a patchwork of inherited privileges and 'liberties'. Social rank entailed significant legal distinctions between persons. Most male subjects of the crown were not citizens in our present-day sense of the word. Nevertheless, native-born men were thought to possess certain privileges by 'birthright': 'Men may justly have . . . by their very being born in England, that we should not seclude them out of England, that we should not refuse to give them air and place and ground, and the freedom of the highways and other things, to live amongst us.'[181] Appealing to Magna Carta, English men also claimed fundamental rights to life and property, freedom from arbitrary imprisonment, and the defence of these rights by law.

Although the rights to life and property were framed differently for the two sexes, and the concept of trial by one's peers did not take account of gender, English women were presumed to enjoy analogous protection under the law, and 'natural' rights similar to those held by men. Such entitlements associated with birth and locality helped justify women's claims to subsistence and survival, whether as recipients of poor relief or as participants in food and enclosure riots. Natural rights also formed the basis for both married and single women's suits to the Court of Chancery, one of whose functions was the safeguarding of female equitable rights jeopardized by gender distinctions inherent in the common law.[182] It was by birthright, too, that women could claim the privilege of petitioning Parliament, a customary right which women were to transform into a mass political tactic during the Civil War.[183]

Citizenship could be religious, moral, and communal, as well as secular and individual. Society acknowledged (for the most part) that women were human beings, fellow Christians, with souls to be saved. Being born and baptized into the Anglican Church conferred a kind of citizenship, providing grounds for women's election to minor parochial offices, as well as a rationale for political participation by the disenfranchised of both sexes during the 1640s and 1650s. A few female churchwardens were appointed during the sixteenth and seventeenth centuries, and numerous women served as sextons well into the eighteenth century. The parish of St Peter le Poor, for example, noted on 24 April 1690 'that Mrs Margaret Ren Widow have the place of sexton of this parish'.[184]

Women could hold certain offices by inheritance or by royal grant.[185] In 1515 the courts upheld the right of two sisters to inherit the office of High

[181] H. Ireton [in Putney Debates], *Puritanism and Liberty*, ed. A. S. P. Woodhouse (1938), 54.

[182] See Cioni, 'Elizabethan Chancery', 159–82.

[183] See Ch. 7 below.

[184] Guildhall, MS 2423/1, St Peter le Poor, Vestry Minute Book, 1687–1755, fo. 9.

[185] *Commons Journal*, viii. 651, 19 Nov. 1666.

Constable.[186] Both married and single women could be justices of the peace, according to a reading at the Inner Temple in 1503.[187] Early seventeenth-century lawyers knew that Henry VII's mother, Lady Margaret, countess of Richmond, had served in the reign of Henry VII.[188] Anne Clifford, countess of Dorset, Pembroke, and Montgomery, was Sheriff of Westmorland from 1650 until 1675, although it is not clear whether she served in her own person.[189] But the courts denied Lady Russell the right to hold the office of castellan, which she had obtained by reversion, objecting that 'a woman cannot have this office of the custody of a castle, because it appertains to the war, and is to be executed by men only'.[190]

Some women obtained sinecures and places at court. The widowed Lady Jermyn petitioned for the office of Chief Registrar in Chancery, and served by deputy.[191] Dame Lucy Apsley held the office of Custos Brevium for the benefit of her children.[192] Service in the monarch's household was originally seen as a private duty, but by the sixteenth century some places had become salaried offices. In Queen Elizabeth's Privy Chamber, women officers played a significant role in transacting certain suits and other business.[193] There were also female officers in the households of kings, queens consort, and royal children.[194] All who held office, even laundresses, were sworn to their duties and received a salary.[195]

During the sixteenth and early seventeenth centuries, many women were

[186] Duke of Buckingham's case, *The English Reports*, 179 vols. (Edinburgh, 1900–32), lxxiii. 640, decided 1515. After marriage, 'the husband of the eldest may [exercise the office] alone'. Thanks to Judy Everard for this and some other references to office-holders.

[187] B. J. Harris, 'Women and Politics in Early Tudor England', *Historical Journal*, 33 (1990), 269.

[188] C. C. Stopes, *British Freewomen* (1894), 51; B. Putnam, *Early Treatises on the Practice of the Justices of the Peace in the Fifteenth and Sixteenth Centuries* (Oxford, 1924), 194–6. Another woman, Lady Berkeley, apparently served in the reign of Mary Tudor; ibid.

[189] R. Graham, 'The Civic Position of Women at Common Law before 1800', in *English Ecclesiastical Studies* (1929), 363–4. According to Graham, there is no evidence of Anne Clifford's sitting in person.

[190] The Lady Russell's case, *The English Reports*, lxxix. 15.

[191] Glanz, 'Legal Position of English Women', 111.

[192] *CSPD Charles I, 1639–40*, xv. 256–7.

[193] P. Wright, 'A Change in Direction: The Ramifications of a Female Household, 1558–1603', in D. Starkey (ed.), *The English Court from the Wars of the Roses to the Civil War* (1987), 147–72.

[194] See, for example, C. Hibbard, 'The Role of a Queen Consort: The Household and Court of Henrietta Maria, 1625–1642', in R. Asch and A. Birke (eds.), *Princes, Patronage and the Nobility* (1991), 393–414.

[195] G. E. Aylmer, *The King's Servants: The Civil Service of Charles I, 1625–1642* (1961), 474–5, lists female officers in the households of the queen and royal children. For an example of the range of female officers at the court, see Book of Warrants (Charles II), PRO LS 13/252. Thanks to Gerald Aylmer for this reference.

admitted to the privileges of cities and companies. Of twenty poor people who were free of the city of Chester in 1597, at least five were women.[196] Freedom of a city or company did not qualify women to hold office, such as mayor or alderman, nor to participate in making rules and regulations for governing cities, towns, or markets. But those who worked actively for the good of the community might earn the honorary status of 'citizen' even if they held no formal qualifications. It was in this moral and social sense that the pious and charitable Mrs Jane Ratcliffe, the widow of a former mayor, was distinguished in a funeral elegy as a 'Citizen of Chester'.[197]

Female adults were held accountable for a wide range of civic responsibilities. It was assumed that women were subjects in so far as they owed allegiance to Crown and Parliament (although contemporaries were uncertain as to whether women's loyalty should be sworn directly or be represented vicariously by men); women were also bound to obey secular and ecclesiastical laws which pertained to them. Widows and single women paid taxes and parish rates. They also performed civic obligations as householders, including the maintenance of their own property and of communal amenities, and contributions for municipal functions such as the watch. In seventeenth-century Coventry, for example, widows were presented by the constables for their failure to repair streets, scour ditches, remove muckhills, or pay constables' levies.[198]

The duty of constable was one for which women were liable when it fell to their turn by rotation, but they were expected to provide a surrogate.[199] Women's right to serve in person was dismissed by the court of King's Bench in 1635, when the custom of rotation was opposed on the grounds that it might allow a woman to become constable, 'which the law will not permit'.[200] Female tithingmen and parish clerks were appointed very rarely, and appointed substitutes. Elizabeth Attwill, widow, was ordered 'to execute the office of a tithingman by her deputy' in the year 1625.[201] In London, the widow of a former parish clerk was annually elected to the same office from 1694 until 1699 on condition that her son deputize for her.[202]

[196] Stopes, *British Freewomen*, 89; see also 84.

[197] J. Ley, *A Patterne of Pietie or the Religious Life and Death of . . . Mrs Jane Ratcliffe, Widow and Citizen of Chester* (1640). See also P. Lake, 'Feminine Piety and Personal Potency: The "Emancipation" of Mrs. Jane Ratcliffe', *The Seventeenth Century*, 2 (1987), 143–65.

[198] *Coventry Constables' Presentments, 1629–1742*, ed. L. Fox, Dugdale Society (Oxford, 1986), 5, 15, 20.

[199] The Lady Russell's case, *English Reports*, lxxix. 15.

[200] Prouse's case, *English Reports*, lxxix. 940. See J. Kent, *The English Village Constable, 1580–1642* (1986), 58–9.

[201] Devon RO, Quarter Sessions Order Book, 1, 1625–1633, fo. 6.

[202] Guildhall, MS 1196/1, St Katherine Creechurch Vestry Minute Book, 1639–1718, fos. 221, 227, 232^{v}, 233^{v}, 240^{v}.

Although women were called as witnesses in secular and ecclesiastical courts, some judges were troubled at seeing women in this role. In the late sixteenth century, Swinburne debated whether women could be witnesses because of 'the inconstancie and frailty of the feminin Sex'.[203] When Sir Edmund Coke listed categories of people who were incapacitated from being witnesses, he did not include sex among them.[204] Yet there was a body of thought which surfaced intermittently during this period about women's incapacity as witnesses. Rape cases were dominated by the courts' unease at taking the life of a man on the word of a mere woman. In the same way, one historian has suggested that women were punished more severely than men in bastardy cases because juries were reluctant to convict men on the sworn word of women.[205] While considering a testamentary cause in 1666, the House of Commons debated whether the mother of one of the litigants could be admitted as a witness.[206] In a 1682 case, one justice persuaded the others 'that it would not be proper to tender ye oath of a woman'.[207] Common law doubts about the worth of female testimony meant that women could not be compurgators at common law. Borough law did, however, allow female compurgators.[208]

Husbands frequently appointed wives as executrices to their wills in sixteenth- and seventeenth-century England, with the result that widows were responsible for the legal settlement of debts.[209] During the Interregnum, one widow presented her husband's public accounts amounting to over a million pounds.[210] Yet some testators were reluctant to appoint female executors or even call upon female witnesses, believing that women were less capable than men. When Jane Kitchen dictated her will in 1633, there was some difficulty in locating another male witness aside from the scrivener. Kitchen then asked the scrivener whether two women's hands—Alice Powell and Joan Gotobed—'were not as good as one man's hand'; the scrivener replied that the 'two women . . . and he were witness enough'.[211] Mark Brownell's will for 1729 noted that in case of law-suits he appointed his

[203] Swinburne, *Treatise of Testaments*, 188; see Maclean, *Renaissance Notion*, 78, for a similar view among European jurists.

[204] W. Holdsworth, *A History of English Law* (1926), ix. 187–8.

[205] R. A. Marchant, *The Church Under the Law: Justice, Administration and Discipline in the Diocese of York, 1560–1640* (Cambridge, 1969), 224.

[206] *Commons Journal*, viii. 651, 19 Nov. 1666.

[207] C. Horle, 'A Listing of Original Records of Sufferings', typescript, Friends' Library London, i. 27.

[208] M. Bateson, *Borough Customs*, Selden Society, 2 vols. (1904, 1906), ii, p. xxx.

[209] Erickson, *Women and Property*, 156–173.

[210] PRO, E351/440.

[211] Guildhall, MS 9057/1, London Archdeaconry Deposition Books, 1632–38, fos. 34–6.

sons rather than his daughters executors, 'women not being fit for law-suits'.[212]

Nevertheless, women were formally employed by the courts in one area of female expertise, childbirth and other matters related to female sexuality. Courts could empanel and swear a so-called jury of matrons to determine issues which depended on the examination of women's bodies.[213] Since virginity, pregnancy, and childbirth were all part of the female domain, the courts usually accepted female witnesses as authoritative. But the social status of litigants and witnesses could be critical: a jury of matrons was inadequate in the divorce of the Lady Frances Howard from the earl of Essex.[214] In 1688, female witnesses were unable to authenticate the birth of a son to James II.[215] Although juries of matrons were still called in cases such as infanticide during the eighteenth century, the rise of the 'expert' witness increasingly limited women's role.[216]

Regardless of their economic, social, matrimonial, or civic status, ownership of land, or liability for taxes and other civic duties, women were barred by law or custom from many important rights and privileges. Nearly all of these restrictions concerned the exercise of political power or civil authority, whether through office-holding, the franchise, or other formal responsibilities which conferred status on males. Although the rationale employed to exclude women from civic prerogatives varied from one context to another, all such explanations treated the female sex as a separate case. The grounds for women's exclusion were of three types: feminine defect, whether intellectual, moral, or physical; legal dependency created by marriage; and finally, the sexual 'dishonour' which would result if women were permitted to exercise magisterial powers which might subvert the traditional gender hierarchy.[217]

The conventions which barred women from civil rights held by men of the same rank resulted in both theoretical contradictions and practical problems. Women's liability to the 'negative' duties of citizenship appeared inconsistent with their exclusion from civic privileges. Why should women pay taxes, fulfil municipal obligations as householders, display loyalty to king

[212] M. Brownell, *Diary* (1688), in *North Country Diaries*, second series, ed. J. C. Hodgson, Surtees Society, 124 (1914), 178.

[213] J. Oldham, 'On Pleading the Belly: A History of the Jury of Matrons', *Criminal Justice History*, 6 (1985), 1–64.

[214] The court required three ladies to authenticate the midwives' findings. Folger, MS V. b. 21, fo. 51.

[215] R. Weil, 'The Politics of Legitimacy: Women and the Warming-Pan Scandal', in L. G. Schwoerer (ed.), *The Revolution of 1688–1689: Changing Perspectives* (Cambridge, 1992), 65–82.

[216] Oldham, 'Pleading the Belly', 24–9; see also Beattie, *Crime and the Courts*, 362–76.

[217] See Sommerville, *Sex and Subjection*.

and Parliament, and obey the laws of the land if they had no recognized civic identity? Such inconsistencies help explain the widespread confusion about women's proper role in the polity during the early 1640s, when Parliament ordered all adult inhabitants to swear their allegiance in 1641 and 1643. While most localities omitted women from their lists of oathtakers, some noted only the names of women who *refused* to pledge their loyalty. A number of communities listed oaths of widows and single women, and a few parishes took the oaths of all adult inhabitants regardless of sex or matrimonial status.[218]

Some seventeenth-century women exploited the law's ambiguity to plead that the female sex was free of the bonds of civil society. As a group of women declared in an enclosure riot, 'women were lawless, and not subject to the lawes of the realme as men are but might . . . offend without drede or punishment of law'.[219] This was of course an opinion which the courts generally repudiated; nevertheless it offered a logical foundation for female claims to political rights. Margaret Cavendish used a similar argument (quoted above) to define women's status as beyond the control of the laws. Although mistaken in her belief that women never took oaths or held office, the duchess ingeniously argued that unmarried women who were not citizens were not subject to government.[220] Indeed, theologians used analogous reasoning to buttress the claim that women were fully human. The notion that women had no souls was liable to 'let in a Flood of atheism', since women would not care how they lived in this life, if they had no afterlife to fear.[221] Ironically, the assumption that women lacked a civic identity could be transformed to undermine the entire basis of the gender hierarchy.

Contemporaries were well aware that the gender order did not always parallel the hierarchy of rank and wealth, but often cut across it. Women's property and inheritance rights frequently entitled them to prerogatives, sinecures, and appointments from which they might be excluded because of their sex. In a case of conflicting claims, authorities had to decide whether to safeguard property rights at the expense of the gender order, or sacrifice

[218] See below, Ch. 7.

[219] PRO, Star Chamber 8/223/7, quoted in J. Walter, 'Grain Riots and Popular Attitudes to the Law: Maldon and the Crisis of 1629', in J. Brewer and J. Styles (eds.), *An Ungovernable People* (1980), 63.

[220] For similar reasons, some men thought Mary I should be given the same powers as a male monarch: if her power remained undefined, it might be taken to be unlimited, as 'lawless' as that of a conqueror. J. Alsop, 'The Act for the Queen's Regal Power, 1554', *Parliamentary History*, 13 (1994), 267.

[221] 'Timothy Constant' [pseud.?], *An Essay to Prove Women have no Souls* (*c*.1712), 33.

women's proprietary interests so as to maintain female subordination, or contrive a compromise between the two.

A climate of opinion in which female proprietorial claims were gradually eroded, yielding to more sharply defined gender distinctions, can be traced in changing attitudes towards women's eligibility for the franchise and for local office. In Elizabeth's reign, the Privy Council was troubled because a woman had, by her jointure, 'the nomination of the two burgesses for the town of Gatton' to the 1586 Parliament. The objection was not that Mistress Copley was a woman, but that 'she is known to be evil affected'.[222] During the first half of the seventeenth century, there were instances of widows and single women voting in Parliamentary elections under burgess or freehold qualifications.[223] At Worcester in 1640, women shouted their choice by acclamation along with men; in Suffolk, women's votes were at first accepted by the clerks but later struck out by the High Sheriff.

Some women held manorial rights which gave them powers of appointment in elections: in Malton, Yorkshire, the widow and daughters of Colonel Eure claimed the right to appoint the returning officer, and took an interest in the 1660 returns.[224] At Richmond in 1678, women were prevented from casting their votes directly, but were permitted to assign their rights to males.[225] But by 1690, George Petyt's *Lex Parliamentaria* explicitly denied women's right to vote in Parliamentary elections, although previous treatises on Parliament had not mentioned such exclusions from the freehold franchise on the basis of gender.[226]

A similar pattern can be charted in rulings about women's eligibility for parochial and civic office. We have records of women executing the office of churchwarden in their own persons during the sixteenth and early seventeenth centuries: Lucy Seele was churchwarden at Morebath in 1547–8, and Jone Morsse, widow, at Tynemouth in 1554.[227] In 1645, two widows presented accounts for the Somerset parish of St Applegrove.[228] After 1660, however, women held the office only by deputy. Thomasine Coombe was elected churchwarden of Rowe, Devon, in 1676 because of a

[222] A. J. Kempe, *The Loseley Manuscripts and Other Rare Documents* (1836), 242–3.

[223] Hirst, *Representative of the People?*, 18–19; W. Atkinson, 'A Parliamentary Election in Knaresborough in 1628', *Yorks. Archaeological and Topographical Journal*, 34 (1938–9), 213–17.

[224] B. D. Henning (ed.), *History of Parliament: The House of Commons, 1660–1690*, 3 vols. (1983), ii. 479.

[225] R. Fieldhouse, 'Parliamentary Representation in the Borough of Richmond', *Yorks. Archaeological and Topographical Journal*, 44 (1972), 208.

[226] G. Petyt, *Lex Parliamentaria* (1690), 114.

[227] Graham, 'Civic Position of Women', 372.

[228] Ibid. 373.

tenement she enjoyed, but 'being a woman', she gave the office to her son as deputy.[229]

In 1684, when Mary Jacques appealed to the Derby quarter sessions against her appointment as churchwarden, she pleaded her sex as a disqualification, 'that she as a woman was not capable of the office nor by law compellable to serve it'. The court ordered her discharged and a new election held.[230] At elections for churchwarden in the London parish of St Katherine Creechurch during the 1690s, Jewish men were elected and then fined because they could not serve, but no woman was elected churchwarden.[231]

Women were permitted to serve as overseers of the poor or commissioners of the sewers, although one Gray's Inn lecturer argued in 1622 that the 'weakness of their sex' made them unfit to travel, and that their incapacity 'for the most part' to learn the law rendered them incapable of exercising discretion.[232] Nevertheless, women were chosen as overseers of the poor until 1795.[233] The office was an onerous one, which many householders sought to avoid. In Ribchester, Lancashire, where the office was held by rotation, women were appointed at least six times between 1660 and 1800, serving by deputies.[234] By the late eighteenth century, it was resolved that women were liable to serve in case of necessity, but 'where there are a sufficient number of men qualified to serve the office, they are certainly more proper'.[235]

Early in the eighteenth century, the appointment of a female governor of a workhouse at Chelmsford in Essex was questioned as 'not suitable to her sex', but the court upheld her appointment, saying she could act by a deputy.[236] The courts noted that although women were freeholders and contributed to public charges, yet as women could not vote for members of Parliament or coroners, they should not hold public office.[237]

A 1739 dispute which challenged a woman's eligibility to serve as sexton was the exception that proved the rule. The King's Bench upheld the right of the woman to retain her position, remarking upon the 'many women sextons now in London'.[238] Yet a later decision undermined rather than

[229] Devon RO, Chanter 877, Consistory Court Depositions 1676–8, fo. 144.

[230] Graham, 'Civic Position of Women', 374.

[231] Guildhall, MS 1196/1, St Katherine Creechurch Vestry Minute Book, 1639–1718, fos. 202–309^{v}.

[232] Glanz, 'Legal Position of English Women', 112.

[233] Graham, 'Civic Position of Women', 372.

[234] S. and B. Webb, *English Local Government*, 9 vols. (repr. 1963), i. *The Parish and County*, 17 n. 4.

[235] Stubbs case (1788), *English Reports*, cxiii. 219.

[236] *English Reports*, xcii. 174.

[237] *Olive* v. *Ingram*, *English Reports*, xciii. 1068.

[238] Ibid.

strengthened the basis for women's participation in local office. In 1788 the court argued that the office of sexton was 'only a private office of trust, to take care of the church, etc. and therefore a woman may serve it'.[239] By defining the office as private and menial, the court designated it as suitable for women. Conversely, by virtue of their sex women were presumably barred from any local office defined as public and magisterial. A woman could be a sexton in the eighteenth century because the courts deemed this office, by a strange logic, not to 'concern the publick',[240] but for a woman to perform some of the duties of an overseer of the poor was 'inconsistent with the decency of the sex'.[241]

If we examine the range of contexts in which women's civil and political rights were either upheld or rejected over the course of the sixteenth and seventeenth centuries, certain patterns begin to emerge. During the earlier part of our period, a patchwork of arrangements based on custom or local contingencies appears to have predominated. Sixteenth-century cases in some localities showed more concern for inheritance rights than for the sex of the officer.

As time passed, the courts increasingly heard arguments questioning the right of women *as women* to hold office or perform civic duties. By the late seventeenth century, a consensus had emerged which declared women unfit for civic office, and which rated the preservation of the gender order as a higher priority than women's proprietary rights. Women were barred from any office or political privilege that entailed the exercise of magisterial powers over men, unless a male candidate was lacking, as in the case of a female heir to the throne. An alternative arrangement allowed women to hold office on condition they appointed a deputy. But by the eighteenth century, the weight of legal opinion had shifted to the view that women should be excluded entirely from civic duties, which were now deemed 'inappropriate' to their sex.

POPULAR NOTIONS

Notions about gender differences were not the sole province of the educated élite. The labouring classes (and women as well as men) contributed to a common fund of ideas about the sexes. For these groups, culture was transmitted predominantly through speech. Mass illiteracy fostered diverse

[239] Stubbs case (1788), *English Reports*, cxiii. 216.
[240] *Olive* v. *Ingram*, *English Reports*, xciii. 1068.
[241] Stubbs case (1788), *English Reports*, cxiii. 216.

oral traditions, including proverbs and folklore, charms and rhymes, ballads and songs, jokes and anecdotes, 'old wives tales', and nursery and fairy tales.

Information was also communicated and preserved through seasonal customs and festivities, popular and heretical religion, the lore of crafts and skills, magical beliefs and superstitions, lay medical practice and herbal remedies, and local historical traditions. All these genres circulated not only among the mass of the population but also among the wealthy, who enjoyed collecting proverbs, anecdotes, ballads, and medical remedies from their social inferiors. Even sermons were assimilated into the storehouse of oral culture.

A survey of popular notions about gender difference should also include visual and dramatic expressions of common culture. In local communities, jocular or defamatory drawings were sometimes circulated along with rhymes and ballads.[242] Emblem books, woodcuts for ballads and broadsheets, engravings and frontispiece illustrations all helped define beliefs about gender attributes.[243] The symbolic connotations of dress were also highly significant in reinforcing notions of sexual difference, as we can infer from sermons, tracts, and contemporary jokes and anecdotes on this topic.[244]

Although printed pictorial representations were circulated mainly among a literate audience, their symbolism parallels the information which has been recorded from plebeian speech. Such representations entered material culture, as women copied illustrations from printed works for their embroideries.[245] Popular notions about gender were also defined through shame sanctions. Assumptions about gender relations were dramatically enacted through village rites of charivari or rough music, and a well-known vocabulary of visual insult was employed to chastise individual women who had transgressed their proper role.[246]

[242] See for example Bodl., MS Rawlinson B. 382, fos. 397–409, in which the female plaintiff allegedly was the recipient of a 'bawdy, filthy and obscene' drawing and 'Mrs. Fletcher's aid de carrot'. For an example of feminine 'rough music', see GLRO, DL/C/630, Consistory Court Depositions 1632–4, fo. 41^{v}.

[243] For examples of images from emblem books relating to gender stereotypes see H. Diehl, *An Index of Icons in English Emblem Books, 1500–1700* (1986), 20, 23, 43, 46, 54, 58, 63, 65, 79, 80, 85, 101, 115, 123, 148, 149, 163, 173, 175, 186, 212, 214, 219, 220, 222.

[244] See, for example, *Hic Mulier; Or, The Man-Woman* (1620); Folger, MS V. a. 180, fo. 115^{v}; N. Le Strange, *'Merry Passages and Jeasts': A Manuscript Jestbook*, ed. H. Lippincott (1974), 89 (no. 301), 102 (no. 354).

[245] See, for example, Victoria and Albert Museum, T. 117–1936, a silk embroidered portrait of Charles I copied from the frontispiece of *Eikon Basilike*; at least one other embroidered version is known.

[246] For contemporary literary descriptions of 'ridings', complete with social commentary, see R. Greene, *Pinder of Wakefield* (English Reprints, ser. 12 Liverpool, 1956); S. Butler, *Hudibras*, pt. 2, canto 2, lines 585–752. For visual symbolism relating to marital and sex roles, see J. Brand, *Observations on Popular Antiquities*, 2 vols. (1813), ii. 101–21.

Along with oral and visual traditions, a huge volume of printed works circulated among the plebeian classes. Ballads, broadsheets, and pamphlets catered to a mass market. The true size of the audience for popular literature is impossible to calculate, since some of those classified as 'illiterate' were able to read printed works. Those who were not taught to read—particularly women—could listen to ballads and other oral forms of printed genres. Thus there was a great deal of overlap between popular and élite *mentalité* at the border between literate and oral culture.

Like theology and science, popular culture had its own 'origin myths' to account for gender attributes. For example, Sir Nicholas Le Strange included a jocular explanation of sexual difference in his family's collection of anecdotes:

> When man and woman were first made, they had each of them a lace given to lace their Bodyes together, the man had just enough to lace himselfe home, so he left his Tagge hanging downe; the womans prooved somewhat too short, and seeing she must leave some of her body open, in a rage she broake of her Tagge, and threw it away.[247]

Although the tale is irrelevant to Galenic medicine or Anglican theology, it embodies similar assumptions about gender. Women are depicted as the inferior sex, defective from the moment of their creation. Their inferiority is mental and moral as well as physical. The woman's lace is too short, yet she tears it off 'in a rage', exacerbating her defective condition. Thus she brings on herself a further train of evils, and bears some blame for her sex's subordination. Moreover, the man's extra 'tag' and the woman's partially 'open' body suggest, in much the same way as Genesis 3: 16, that phallic sexuality is at once the consequence and the primary symbol of the gender order.

Contemporary proverbs, jokes, anecdotes, and tales give the impression that the axiom of female inferiority was as common among ordinary people as it was among the educated élite. Proverbs echoed the Aristotelian terms for female defect: 'women are at best but necessary evils';[248] they are 'made perfect by men';[249] 'Nature miscarries when she brings forth Women.'[250]

Other common sayings harped on women's flawed physiology: 'A

[247] Le Strange, '*Merry Passages and Jeasts*', 101 (no. 347).

[248] M. P. Tilley, *A Dictionary of the Proverbs in England in the Sixteenth and Seventeenth Centuries* (Ann Arbor, 1950), 747 (W703); see also G. Herbert, *Witts Recreations* (1640), 162, 248, for women as 'necessary harmes' or 'needful evils'.

[249] Tilley, *Proverbs*, 748 (W718).

[250] Herts. RO, Panshanger MSS, D/EP/F36, S. Cowper, Commonplace Book, fo. 374.

Woman, like a German clock, never goes true';[251] 'a ship and a woman are ever repairing'.[252] Proverbs commonly asserted that women were morally frail or inherently wicked. 'A woman is the weaker vessel';[253] 'a man of straw is worth a woman of gold';[254] 'woman is the woe of man';[255] 'women have but two faults: they can neither do well nor say well';[256] 'if a woman were little as shee is good, A peascod would make her a gown & a hood';[257] 'There's no mischief in the world done, But a woman is always one';[258] 'If there be not Hell in Women there's the bottomless pit I am sure.'[259]

That women held a lower status than men in the Great Chain of Being was also implied by their proverbial affinities with the animal world. Women's subhuman nature was insinuated by association: 'He is mad that quarrels with Women or beasts';[260] 'To love a womans soul whilst there are men, is as bad as bestiality whilst there are women.'[261] More often, proverbs matched women with those animals that supposedly exemplified their negative traits. Domestic fowl, particularly geese, suggested women's noisy, timorous, and silly behaviour. Cats, considered sly, deceitful, and sexually promiscuous, were identified with the female sex, as were other animals symbolizing crude sexuality, like the 'salted bitch'.[262] Sexual imagery commonly depicted the man as the rider, the woman as the horse.[263]

Eels, like women, were slippery, impossible to catch or control.[264] Comparing women to monkeys suggested the inanity of female chatter, women's mischievous and destructive behaviour.[265] 'Gossips are frogs', Herbert recorded in his collection of proverbs, 'they drink and talk.'[266] It is noteworthy that women were never compared to the noble 'masculine' animals. A woman was as angry as a wasp, not a lion. Bees had bestial rather than

[251] Tilley, *Proverbs*, 744 (W658). [252] J. Ray, *A Collection of English Proverbs* (1678), 59.
[253] Tilley, *Proverbs*, 743 (W655). [254] Ray, *Proverbs*, 58.
[255] Tilley, *Proverbs*, 744 (W656). [256] Ibid. 748 (W708). [257] Ray, *Proverbs*, 64.
[258] Ibid. 60. [259] Herts. RO, D/EP/F36, Cowper, Commonplace Book, fo. 375.
[260] Tilley, *Proverbs*, 746 (W685).
[261] Herts RO, D/EP/F36, Cowper, Commonplace Book, fo. 374.
[262] 'Cat' was early modern slang for a prostitute; cats were given the female pronoun in 17th-cent. proverbs and tales. See Ray, *Proverbs*, 90; Tilley, *Proverbs*, 743 (W652). For the term 'salted bitch', i.e. a bitch in heat, see, for example, OA, MSS Archd. papers Oxon c. 118, fos. 50–50^v, 57–57^v.
[263] For example a popular joke warned against marrying a widow, because she has 'cast her rider'; Ray, *Proverbs* (1678), 58. For other sexual metaphors see H. Weinstein, '"Hammer and Anvil"; Metaphors of Sex in the Seventeenth-Century English Ballad', unpublished paper, Ninth Berkshire Conference on the History of Women, Vassar, 1993. We are grateful to Dr Weinstein for allowing us to cite her work. [264] Diehl, *English Emblem Books*, 85.
[265] Ibid. 148. [266] G. Herbert, *Outlandish Proverbs* (1640), 275.

magisterial associations for women: 'Swine, women, and bees cannot be turned.'[267]

The idea that women were less than fully human found its most extreme expression in the assertion that they had no souls. This hypothesis, which circulated among the élite as an academic joke,[268] appears frequently in plebeian settings as a proverb or 'common saying.'[269] When George Fox went on a preaching tour in 1647, he came to 'a sort of people that held women have no souls, adding, in a light manner, no more than a goose'.[270] Butler quoted the common rhyme: 'The Souls of Women are so small, That some believe th'have none at all.'[271]

A constellation of major and minor faults was associated with women as a sex. At first sight, these archetypal defects appear to represent the vices or inverse qualities opposed to the ideal female virtues. Instead of being obedient, pious, chaste, and silent as they ought, women were said to be insubordinate, hypocritical, lustful, and garrulous by nature. But the assortment of female defects were also understood by contemporaries as manifestations of a single fundamental defect: female disobedience to male authority, interpreted broadly (and in a multiple sense) as political, psychological, and sexual insubordination. 'A woman does that which is forbidden her';[272] 'Women must have their wills while they live, because they make none when they die';[273] 'Women are always desirous of sovereignty'; 'All women are ambitious naturally.'[274]

Feminine insubordination ranked as an egregious crime not only in its own right, but because it raised the spectre of an inversion of the sexual as well as the political gender hierarchy. A well-known emblem, the picture of a woman's body lacking the head, brings out these multiply linked associations.[275] The caption, 'a headless maid is the worst of all monsters', was read as a triple visual and verbal pun. The maid's 'headless' condition signified that she lacked a male master or 'head', but also implied she had lost her maidenhead, that is, her virginity.

What of the female virtues, whose existence was occasionally conceded in

[267] *Oxford Dictionary of Proverbs*, ed. W. Smith (2nd edn., Oxford, 1952), 637.

[268] See, for example, J. Donne, Probleme vi, 'Why hath the common opinion afforded women soules?', in J. Donne, *Poetry and Prose*, ed. F. Warnke (New York, 1947), 302; Bodl., MS Rawlinson Misc. D. fo. 421; [H. Neville], *The Ladies, A Second Time, assembled in Parliament* (1647), 9; Folger, MS V. a. 180, fo. 126^{v}.

[269] Tilley, *Proverbs*, 748 (W709).

[270] G. Fox, *The Journal of George Fox*, ed. J. Nickalls (Cambridge, 1952), 8–9.

[271] S. Butler, *Genuine Remains*, 2 vols. (1759), 'Miscellaneous Thoughts', i. 246.

[272] Tilley, *Proverbs*, 743 (W650).

[273] Ray, *Proverbs*, 63.

[274] Tilley, *Proverbs*, 747 (W697).

[275] T. Combe, *The Theater of Fine Devices* (1614), no. 16; the proverb is quoted in M. Cavendish, duchess of Newcastle, *Playes* (1662), 269.

FIG. 4. 'My Wife will be my Master; Or, the Married-Mans Complaint against his Unruly Wife' *c.*1640. This ballad woodcut shows the wife brandishing a large skimming-ladle as a weapon; the husband's subjection is underlined by his bare head and kneeling posture. The horns sprouting from his head imply that he has been cuckolded as well as beaten by his wife; the fruit-tree recalls Genesis 3: 16, Eve's punishment of subjection to Adam

the case of a few individual women? Although most popular sources portray women in derogatory guise, a handful of sayings appear at first sight to represent women's qualities in a more positive light. Feminine usefulness or native intelligence was acknowledged in certain contexts. Women's dangerous ordeal in child-bearing was frequently mentioned in their favour, and the 'woman-hater' was told to 'remember, that you had a mother'.[276]

That women worked longer, if not harder, than men was avowed in the common saying that 'A woman's work is never at an end'. Several proverbs paid tribute to female wit. 'A womans advice is best at a dead lift';[277]

[276] Tilley, *Proverbs*, 742 (W637).
[277] Ibid. 745 (W669).

'Womens counsels are sometimes good';[278] 'The Man is the Womans head, but the Woman is sometimes the mans brains';[279] 'A woman [or an 'old woman'] can do more than the devil.'[280] Contemporary ballads and anecdotes devoted an entire genre to the exploits of the 'crafty maid' or the 'cunning wife' who outwitted various stock villains of plebeian life, such as the miller, the tailor, the exciseman, or the priest.[281] Finally, some sayings confessed the superior worth of a few unusual women, if not of the majority. 'A wise woman is the ornament of her house'; 'a good wife's a goodly prize.'[282]

Seen in the larger context, however, the few 'pro-female' sayings were framed in a way which validated a negative view of the sex as a whole. Women's maternal role in sexual reproduction, the crux of their usefulness to men, was subsumed into the image of women as necessary evils. 'Nature chose to make such an ill thing as womankind, rather than lose such a good thing as mankind'; 'none but fools were fit to bear children.'[283] The acknowledgement that women's work was 'never done' implied the corollary that any woman found *not* working was guilty of idle insubordination. This assumption formed the basis of an oft-repeated joke in which a wife asked her husband why he beat her: 'I do nothing.' 'You lazy whore, that's the reason I do beat you', he replied.[284]

Likewise, feminine intelligence was depicted not as true wisdom but as an intuitive leap or a manifestation of low cunning. It was a talent which enabled women to match wits with the devil, or apply their craft to evil aims, but not to compete with men's noble sagacity, the product of rational reflection. 'Women in mischief (in things ill) are wiser than men'; 'Take a woman's first counsel, not her second.'[285] These backhanded compliments increased what was perceived as a 'rationality gap' between the two sexes: whatever their advantages on an intuitive level, women were unfit for rational deliberation, which remained men's prerogative.

Because popular discourses constructed the 'good woman' as exceptional, proverbial expressions which lauded the few women who matched contemporary standards of feminine virtue also tended to reinforce negative stereo-

[278] Tilley, *Proverbs*, 745 (W671). [279] Herts, RO, S. Cowper, Commonplace Book, fo. 375.

[280] Tilley, *Proverbs*, 742–3 (W634, W648).

[281] For examples of the 'crafty maid' and 'crafty wife' genres, see Bodl., Douce Ballads i, fos. 23ᵛ, 127ᵛ; Douce Ballads ii, fos. 167, 175ᵛ, 180ᵛ, 202ᵛ, 220, 255; Bodl., Don. b. 13, pp. 11, 18; *The Roxburghe Ballads*, ed. W. Chappell and J. Ebsworth, 9 vols. in 8 (London and Hertford, 1866–99), ix. 553. [282] Tilley, *Proverbs*, 742 (W642); Ray, *Proverbs*, 58.

[283] Herts. RO, S. Cowper, Commonplace Book, fo. 374.

[284] *A Banquet of Jests* (1634), 232 (no. 260); *Oxford Jests* (1684), 29 (no. 85).

[285] Tilley, *Proverbs*, 744 (W668), 748 (W711).

types of the sex as a whole. Sayings which singled out exceptional women for praise bolstered the impression that the majority were worthless. Moreover, even the best of the sex merely represented a lesser evil: 'I like a thing that's excellent though in an ill kind, as I like a good Woman.'[286] In a popular joke, a man was asked why he had married such a tiny woman? 'Because of evils, the least was to be chosen.'

An interpretation of good women as exceptional instances also helped reconcile the prevailing ideology of misogyny with an empirical reality which constantly contradicted it. 'There's one good wife in the county, and every man thinks he has her', as Roger Whitby quoted in his collection of epigrams.[287] Evidence which pointed to women's equality or superiority could be automatically discounted, either as the exception which proved the rule, or as a defective distortion of virtues which pertained only to males: 'a wise woman is twice a fool.'[288]

Thus popular discourse offered several strategies for admitting the empirical fact that some women did not fit the negative stereotype to which all were assigned. If a few women were wiser and more virtuous than others, their exceptional quality served to throw doubt on the general worth of the female populace as a whole. The ability to reconcile general misogyny with empirical observation which appeared to contradict it was shown not only by men, but by women. Those who won masculine approval could see themselves as honourable anomalies. Thus they could live almost comfortably in a sea of misogyny, so long as they were praised for being 'above their sex'.

STEREOTYPES

A culture offers an individual a range of possibilities: as Phyllis Mack has argued, individual women lived their lives in 'a cage of symbols and stereotypes'.[289] In this section, we shall discuss briefly the main positive and negative stereotypes: the maid, wife, and widow, which apparently constructed all female life-stages; and those of the scold, whore, and witch which encompassed the main deviant categories, in ascending order of seriousness. There are many more stereotypes than we discuss here: for

[286] Herts. RO, S. Cowper, Commonplace Book, fos. 373–5.

[287] Bodl., MS Eng. Hist. 312 (R. Whitby MS notes), fo. 22. See also Ray, *Proverbs*, 58.

[288] Tilley, *Proverbs*, 742 (W643).

[289] P. Mack, *Visionary Women: Ecstatic Prophecy in Seventeenth-Century England* (Berkeley, 1992), 18.

example, the Irish woman, closer to nature, wild and fierce;[290] the country-woman, a synonym for the simple-minded; the town gossip, and fishwife, and so on. Positive stereotypes were presented in eulogies for dead wives and mothers. Individual women were praised as examples of piety. Celebratory images of Elizabeth I multiplied: the virgin queen, Gloriana, and Astrea.[291] One of the questions for the remainder of this book is to understand how much significance these stereotypes had in the lives of early modern women.[292]

Stereotypes were omnipresent in early modern society, deployed both by the élite and the populace at large. They masked the diversity between women, and the operation of power which divided them.[293] Gentlewomen were at little risk from punishment as scolds, whores, and witches, though their behaviour might be stigmatized as garrulous, promiscuous, or dangerous. While in general stereotypes functioned to control and to confine women, the contradictions and ambiguities offered some women opportunities to define themselves differently.

Maid, wife, and widow

Three stereotypes apparently encompassed all female life: maid, wife, and widow.[294] A woman was to be defined by her relationships with a man. Jokes about 'neither maid, wife, nor widow but truly all three' were unravelled as referring to the 'deviant woman' who had never married but was not celibate.

In post-Reformation England, virginity conferred special status only upon extraordinary women, as the example of Queen Elizabeth shows. The Protestant Reformers generally condemned the Catholic ideal of celibacy as against God's ordinance and unnatural. Given the nature of women's bodies, how could nuns possibly contain their sexual desires? Better to marry than to burn.

[290] J. Murphy Lawless, 'Images of "Poor" Women in the Writing of Irish Men Midwives', in M. MacCurtain and M. O'Dowd (eds.), *Women in Early Modern Ireland* (Edinburgh, 1991), 291–4.

[291] F. A. Yates, *Astrea: The Imperial Theme in the Sixteenth Century* (1975); H. Hackett, *Virgin Mother, Maiden Queen: Elizabeth I and the Cult of the Virgin Mary* (1994); C. Levin, *'The Heart and Stomach of a King': Elizabeth I and the Politics of Sex and Power* (Philadelphia, 1994).

[292] L. Code, 'Experience, Knowledge, and Responsibility', in A. Garry and M. Pearsall (eds.), *Women, Knowledge and Reality: Explorations in Feminist Philosophy* (1992), 157–262.

[293] For some of the ideas on which this paragraph depends, see M. Poovey, 'Feminism and Deconstruction', *Feminist Studies*, 14 (1988), 51–65.

[294] [N. Tate], *A Present for the Ladies* (1692); J. Shirley, *The Illustrious History of Women* (1686), 149.

Virginity was prized in young women, but after a woman passed the usual age of marriage, she was an object of suspicion. The term 'old maid' came into wider use in a pejorative sense after the Restoration.[295] By the early eighteenth century, this negative stereotype of the single woman was frequently used, and the term 'spinster', which was earlier used as an occupational designation, took on negative implications. Urban rulers were particularly uneasy about single adult women, viewing them as potential 'bastard bearers'.[296]

The second stereotype, wife, was the archetype of the good woman in post-Reformation Protestant England. Preachers explained that the biblical texts defined the ideal state for a woman as marriage and motherhood, under the governance of a husband. Contemporary moralists elaborated her virtues endlessly: she kept at home, her hands were never idle, she 'never goeth forth but her house was on her back', and reared her children in piety and obedience. Heterosexual activity, as we have seen, was necessary for her health. Her body was designed for domesticity: she was 'a House builded for Generation and Gestation', wrote Purchas in 1619.[297] Kind nature had given her a delicate body 'and designed her only for an easie Life, and to perform the tender Offices of Love'.[298]

The negative stereotype of the wife, depicted largely in popular literature, was the idle city dame, ever gadding, ever about gossiping and tattling. Her morals were loose. She deceived her husband. Especially deplored were the merry gossips who gathered together to waste their husbands' substance and plot their own sexual misdemeanours.[299]

Contemporaries both idealized and criticized wives as mothers. The good mother would be tender and loving, transmitting her own good qualities to her offspring by her breeding of the child in her womb, and by her nursing it at her own breasts. Maternal love was recognized as one of the strongest human emotions which could excuse certain female behaviour outside the stereotype. Faced with a threat to her child, a good mother could become as fierce as a tiger. As one mother herself said, to save her children's souls, a mother will 'venture to offend the world'.[300] Scripture declared that to be a barren wife was one of the greatest misfortunes which could befall a woman.

[295] *OED*.

[296] See, for examples, J. P. Earwaker (ed.), *The Court Leet Records of the Manor of Manchester*, 12 vols. (Manchester, 1884–90), i. 197, 227, 241; ii. 51, 178.

[297] Purchas, *Microcosmus*, 474.

[298] J. Pechey, *A General Treatise on the Diseases of Maids, Big-bellied Women . . . and Widows* (1696), preface, sig. A2.

[299] *A Whole Crew of Kind Gossips, All Met to be Merry* (1609).

[300] D. Leigh, *The Mothers Blessing* (1618), sig. A6.

Want of issue and widowhood were the two greatest curses of woman's life.[301]

Ideally, maternal care was exercised under patriarchal authority, but critics ignored this when they berated mothers for their irresponsibility, and for 'spoiling' children by their over fondness.[302] By the end of the seventeenth century, women's 'natural' capacity for maternity was regularly deployed as an emblem of their unfitness for 'higher' things. Educated men separated reason and feeling, claiming that as women were deficient in reason, they were suited only for domestic duties as wives and mothers.[303]

The third main stereotype, the widow, again featured through both a positive and a negative face. Like other stereotypes, that of the widow worked powerfully because its duality reflected her ambiguous and ambivalent social position.[304] On the one hand, Christianity depicted her as an object of pity, in need of charity and protection. Widowhood was said to be 'accounted by God himself a Condition most deplorable and desolate'.[305] On the other hand, popular culture characterized her as rampantly sexual, calculating, disorderly, and knowing: 'The rich Widow weeps with one eye and casts glances with the other.'[306] Medical theorists constructed the widow's sexuality as voracious: unlike the maid, she knew what sexual pleasure was, and sought it: a young widow will 'bee lesse able to containe and bee chast then when shee was a Virgin'. Sexuality in old widows (and in old men) was termed 'lust' and thought disgusting.[307]

A man's attitude to widows varied depending on whether he identified as a husband or as a suitor. A husband feared that his widow would remarry and prefer another in her affections, that she would waste his painfully gotten estate, and that another man would deplete his children's inheritance.[308] Suitors feared the widow's sexual experience, and resented her

[301] [W. Cragg], *The Widowes Ioy* (1622), 19.

[302] For examples, see P. Crawford, '"The Sucking Child": Adult Attitudes to Child Care in the First Year of Life in Seventeenth-Century England', *Continuity and Change*, 1 (1986), 42–3.

[303] G. Lloyd, *The Man of Reason: 'Male' and 'Female' in Western Philosophy* (1984), 38–56; Pateman, *Sexual Contract*.

[304] M. Rosaldo, 'Women, Culture and Society: A Theoretical Overview', in L. Lamphere and M. Z. Rosaldo (eds.), *Women, Culture and Society* (Stanford, Calif., 1974), 33, suggests that the widow is more anomalous in societies in which a woman is defined exclusively in and through her male relations. Early modern England would fit this model. See also L. Mirrer (ed.), *Upon My Husband's Death: Widows in the Literature and Histories of Medieval Europe* (Ann Arbor, 1992). C. Carlton, 'The Widow's Tale: Male Myths and Female Reality in 16th and 17th Century England', *Albion*, 10 (1978), 118–29.

[305] N. H., *The Ladies Dictionary*, 330.

[306] Tilley, *Proverbs*, 722.

[307] R. Capel, *Tentations: Their Nature, Danger, Cure* (1633), 379, 400–1.

[308] *Sir Walter Raleigh's Instructions to His Son* (1632), in L. B. Wright (ed.), *Advice to a Son: Precepts of Lord Burghley, Sir Walter Raleigh, and Francis Osborne* (Ithaca, NY, 1962), 22.

independence. Negative proverbs reflected their anxieties: 'He who marries a widow will often have a dead man's head in his dish.'[309]

Attitudes to the remarriage of widows were increasingly negative during the early modern period. They thought that the age of the woman should determine whether she remarried. In 1552 Thomas Becon advised the 'true auncient Widdows' to look to their households, serve the Lord, and perform charitable works; 'But as touching the yonger widowes, least they should waxe wanton agaynst Christ, . . . it is conueniente that they marrye againe.'[310] In 1628 a preacher explained that 60 was the age after which it was unseemly to remarry: we dislike the marriage of those over 60 'and speake against it' because there could be no children; there was no need to avoid fornication, because the aged should feel no lust: 'the lecherous old person is hated of God'; and there could be no mutual comfort between two old people.[311]

Widows were frequently equated with old women in contemporary parlance. Stereotypes of the old woman were generally negative. 'Old age had made her Loathsom to man' was a comment made about Elizabeth Cellier in 1679.[312] In old women, scatology replaced sex as a male fear. There were many proverbs and jokes in jest books about women defecating in bed as a revenge for being treated as a drudge, a servant.[313]

The scold, the whore, and the witch

Stereotypes of the disorderly woman abounded in early modern society. Here we will focus on three, the scold, the whore, and the witch, which were, in ascending order of seriousness, those most dangerous to women. All challenged patriarchal control. Each built on specific fears: the scold, of the power of women's tongues; the whore, of unbridled sexuality; the witch, a mirror reversal of all that the patriarchy deemed good in a woman.

Historians have suggested that the period from around the mid-sixteenth century to the Civil War was one which was particularly dangerous to women. Society was obsessed with disorder, and women who challenged the accepted gender order were perceived as a more serious threat.[314]

[309] Tilley, *Proverbs*, 722.

[310] T. Becon, *The Principles of Christian Religion* [1552?], (English Experience, Amsterdam, 1976), sig. J4^{v}

[311] R. Bernard, *Ruths Recompence* (1628), 65.

[312] *Misomastropus: The Bawd's Trial and Execution* (1679).

[313] See, for example, *A Choice Banquet of Witty Jests* (1665), 40, 128–9.

[314] D. E. Underdown, 'The Taming of the Scold: The Enforcement of Patriarchal Authority in Early Modern England', in A. Fletcher and J. Stevenson (eds.), *Order and Disorder in Early Modern England* (Cambridge, 1985), 116–36.

FIG. 5. Anne Bidlestone punished with the scold's bridle. Contemporaries were obsessed with the dangerous power of women's speech. The legal punishment for scolding was the cucking stool, but in Newcastle in 1655, the town ordered that a scold be paraded in an iron cage known as the branks or scold's bridle

Certainly there were more savage punishments and executions of women than at other periods, but it may be premature to talk of a crisis in gender relations before we have a clearer map of the terrain of misogyny at other dates.

The stereotype of the scold developed from the notion that women could not keep quiet. Popular sayings about women's tongues abounded.[315] Scolds were 'disturbers of their neighboures', and local communities were increasingly preoccupied by them from 1560 to 1640.[316] Sometimes scolds were fined, but the legal punishment was one of public shaming. Scolds were to be ducked in a pond or river on a device known as a cucking stool.[317] Even nastier, but illegal, was the public parading of a woman through a town wearing an iron device, the scold's bridle, over her head and tongue. Ralph Gardiner described seeing a woman so led in Newcastle in the 1650s, with a 'tongue of Iron forced into her mouth, which forced the blood out'.[318]

The whore represented unbridled sexuality. Prostitution was thus con-

[315] See Ch. 4 below.

[316] Earwaker (ed.), *Court Leet Records*, iii. 31, 268; Underdown, 'The Taming of the Scold', 117–19; M. Ingram, '"Scolding Women Cucked or Washed": A Crisis in Gender Relations in Early Modern England?', in Kermode and Walker (eds.), *Women, Crime and the Courts*, 48–80.

[317] Ingram, 'Scolding Women Cucked or Washed', in Kermode and Walker (eds.), *Women, Crime and the Courts*, 59–64.

[318] R. Gardiner, *Englands Grievance Discovered* (1655), 110–11. See also Ingram, 'Scolding Women Cucked or Washed', in Kermode and Walker (eds.), *Women, Crime and the Courts*, 48–80.

structed as sexual disorder, a form of deviance, rather than as work. While women of higher social status were usually spared the apellation 'whore', brave satirists occasionally attacked even the kings' mistresses.[319] A whore had lost all womanly qualities, such as modesty, fidelity, and love, and was capable of all kinds of villainy.

Witches were archetypally female. Because women were weak, unstable, lustful, and desirous of power, the devil turned first to them in order to destroy what contemporaries referred to as 'mankind'. Furthermore, the stereotype of the witch focused on women who were old, or widowed, although the patterns of accusation and conviction suggest that this was inaccurate.

The effects on women of discourses about the witch were serious. First, no woman could be unaware of the dangers of witchcraft. While high social status might largely protect a woman from an accusation, even she was not immune; a peer's daughter, Lady Eleanor Davies, who foretold the deaths both of her first husband and of the duke of Buckingham, was later imprisoned for her prophetic writings.[320] Secondly, women were not passive victims of the construction of the witch. They themselves participated in the process both by accusations against other women,[321] and sometimes against men, and a few by themselves seeking to harm others.[322]

CONCLUSIONS

The preceding survey of the dominant notions about woman reveals many intellectual and structural similarities between discourses. Academic theories and popular beliefs both constructed woman as secondary or 'other' in relation to man, confirming the necessity for female dependence and subjection. Just as the axiom of female inferiority defined the misogynistic character of the discourses about woman, the axiom of female dependency shaped the patriarchal character of institutions, their hierarchical rules and organization.

[319] For example, see 'Satire on Old Rowley', *Poems on Affairs of State: Augustan Satirical Verse, 1660–1714*, ed. G. de F. Lord, 7 vols. (New Haven, 1963–75), ii. 184–8.

[320] *BDBR*; E. S. Cope, *Handmaid of the Holy Spirit: Dame Eleanor Davies, Never Soe Mad a Ladie* (Ann Arbor, 1992).

[321] C. Holmes, 'Women: Witnesses and Witches', *Past and Present*, 140 (1993), 45–78; see also, Sharpe, 'Witchcraft and Women', 179–99; J. Sharpe, 'Women, Witchcraft and the Legal Process' in Kermode and Walker (eds.), *Women, Crime and the Courts*, 106–24; and M. Gaskill, 'Witchcraft and Power in Early Modern England: The Case of Margaret Moore', ibid. 124–45.

[322] Larner, *Enemies of God*, 9; Underdown, 'Taming of the Scold', 120–1, assumes that old women accused of witchcraft were actually trying to redress their powerlessness.

Moreover, correspondences between discourses led to symbolic as well as discursive links between different planes of meaning. Nests of interlocking images were perceived partly on a subconscious level, where they were even less susceptible to critical examination. For example, the sun and moon as symbols of the male and female domains were taken to embody a whole range of beliefs about female defect: male and female roles were correlated respectively with light and darkness, good and evil, reason and ignorance, the 'public' domain of politics and the 'private' domain of the household.

Lunar imagery also corroborated female inferiority by stressing women's supposed humoral characteristics. The moon, associated with the menses, marked women as wandering, changing, mentally and morally unstable. During her menstrual periods, Queen Anne was considered 'a little mad' by her male advisers, and consequently unfit for state affairs. It should be noted that women as well as men were taught to think in terms of these symbolic confirmations of gender difference. In her preface to *The Worlds Olio*, the duchess of Newcastle elaborated upon the entire gamut of cosmological metaphors as an explanation for women's 'natural' inferiority:

> God made two great Lights, the one to Rule the Day, the other the Night: So Man is made to Govern Commonwealths, and Women their private Families. . . . and if it be as Philosophers hold, that the Moon hath no Light but what it borrows from the Sun, so women have no strength nor light of Understanding, but what is given them from Men.[323]

Thus the aggregate effect of the whole system of discourses was more than the sum of its parts. Rather than an amorphous collection of discrete disciplines and popular prejudices, the patriarchal paradigm was an organically connected system of thought which was self-referential and self-validating. As a consequence, it tended to shut out resistant or competing discourses. Within a patriarchal world, women found it difficult to articulate their own perceptions and concerns. In specific terms, it was not easy for women to find a framework in which they could voice criticisms of the excesses and abuses of patriarchy, such as domestic violence, incest, and rape. Although much of the political discourse of seventeenth-century England was concerned with challenges to kingly power and to a hierarchical social order, the dominant discourse was much less troubled about the limits of patriarchalism in the domestic context. Indeed, one of the problems with which feminist theorists wrestle is how it might have been possible for

[323] M. Cavendish, duchess of Newcastle, *The Worlds Olio* (1655), 'the Preface to the Reader'.

FIG. 6. The Whore of Babylon. The stereotype of the whore was transported to other negative contexts such as the 'Whore of Babylon', used widely by Protestants to represent the Papacy; the image here illustrates a popular ballad

contemporaries to think in different ways within a culture and a language imbued with patriarchalism.

Of course, there were resistances within the patriarchal construction of gender, as the remainder of this book will show. Patriarchy's own internal ambiguities and contradictions could be exploited by subordinate groups, making a space for subversive ideas and dissident behaviour. During the Civil War years, religious discourse was especially important to those women who challenged many of the central doctrines of patriarchalism, including wives' unquestioning obedience to their husbands, and women's exclusion from the public political world. Occasionally we hear the still, small voice of intellectual dissent, as in the question Mary Astell posed to Lockian liberals at the end of the century: if all men are born free, then why are all women slaves? 'How much soever Arbitrary Power may be dislik'd on a Throne, not Milton himself wou'd cry up Liberty to poor Female Slaves, or plead for the

Lawfulness of Resisting a Private Tyranny.'[324] Nevertheless, patriarchal thought was so deeply bedded into early modern thought that it proved resilient in the face of social change. Individual elements may have shifted, but the paradigm as a whole was not transformed.

This book focuses upon women as the subjects of their own histories, rather than the passive objects of men's discourses. In the following chapters, we shall attempt to deconstruct the category which suggests that to be a woman had a single, unified meaning. All women occupied a position in early modern society as 'woman', but they did not all occupy it in the same way. The evidence about women in past centuries can be explored to show that their experiences were diverse, and their relationships to the dominant powers and to each other were varied. At different times in their lives, the category 'woman' had greater or lesser meaning for women as individuals.

[324] Astell, *Reflections Upon Marriage*, 27.

2

CHILDHOOD AND ADOLESCENCE

In Chapters 2 and 3, we discuss how women experienced the social construction of life-stages in early modern England, focusing on the historical circumstances in which their sense of personal identity was formed. As we have argued in Chapter 1, the 'category' woman interacted with other social and conceptual categories which likewise changed over time. Female experience is not a simple category: it is never, as Diana Fuss points out, 'as unified, as knowable, as universal, and as stable as we presume it to be'.[1] Experiences differed not only from one woman to another, but varied for a single individual over her lifetime. The archetypal female event, childbirth, was not the same for every woman; class, and her previous history, affected her maternity. A woman's understanding of herself as a mother changed over her lifetime.

In these two chapters, we discuss how material circumstances affected women's life-stages. As Crosby argues, gender can recede in the face of other attributes, such as class. While women were seen in the dominant discourse as one category, 'woman', they could at the same time be divided from each other by economic and social status.[2] The more comfortable lifestyles of some women depended on the exploitation of others. There were tensions between women of the same rank, as they competed with each other for sexual partners and social ascendancy.

Central to female life were women's own bodies as well as the discourses about them. Although much modern theory insists upon the primacy of discourse, the importance of physiology placed limits on women's potentiality for 'self-fashioning'.[3] Physiological changes had a cultural meaning, but they were also physically experienced by the woman herself, and played a large part in structuring female existence. Childbirth altered women's bodies, but fatherhood had no corresponding effect on men's physiology.[4]

[1] D. Fuss, *Essentially Speaking* (1989), 114.

[2] C. Crosby, *The Ends of History: Victorians and 'The Woman Question'* (1991), 153–8.

[3] S. J. Greenblatt, *Renaissance Self-Fashioning: From More to Shakespeare* (Chicago, 1980), 166–9.

[4] D. Zohar, *The Quantum Self* (1990), 89–106.

A Man is
firſt an Infant, 1.
then a Boy, 2.
then a Youth, 3.
then a Young-man, 4.
then a Man, 5.
after that, an Elderly-
and at laſt, (man, 6.
a decrepid old Man, 7.
So alſo
in the other ſex,
there are, a Girle, 8.
A Damoſel, 9.
A Maid, 10.
A Woman, 11.
an Elderly Woman, 12.
and a decrepid old
Woman. 13.

FIG. 7. 'The Seven Ages of Man', divided into seven-year periods, were a trope of contemporary thought. Women's lives may be conceptualized differently

As Lyndal Roper reminds us, the inseparability of the body and the psyche implies that not all of an individual's sense of self is created by language and culture: sexual difference is not just a matter of discourse but 'has a bodily dimension' which must be considered in its historical context.[5] To discuss how women experienced their bodies and how their subjectivities were formed, we need a range of source material, preferably from women themselves.

Most people were accustomed to view female life in terms of three stages: maid, wife, and widow. While this tripartite division is sometimes a useful way of discussing early modern women,[6] the plot of the story of the 'maid, wife, and widow' imposes a restricted narrative of normative heterosexual life which excludes a significant proportion of the female populace. Some women were sexually active, although they never married. Moreover, for all practical purposes, many wives were 'without men' just as were single women and widows.

We have depicted women's lives as falling into two broad phases, the first

[5] L. Roper, *Oedipus and the Devil: Witchcraft, Sexuality and Religion in Early Modern Europe* (1994), 16–27.

[6] Amy Erickson demonstrates the utility of these concepts in her excellent study of women's property; A. L. Erickson, *Women and Property in Early Modern England* (1993).

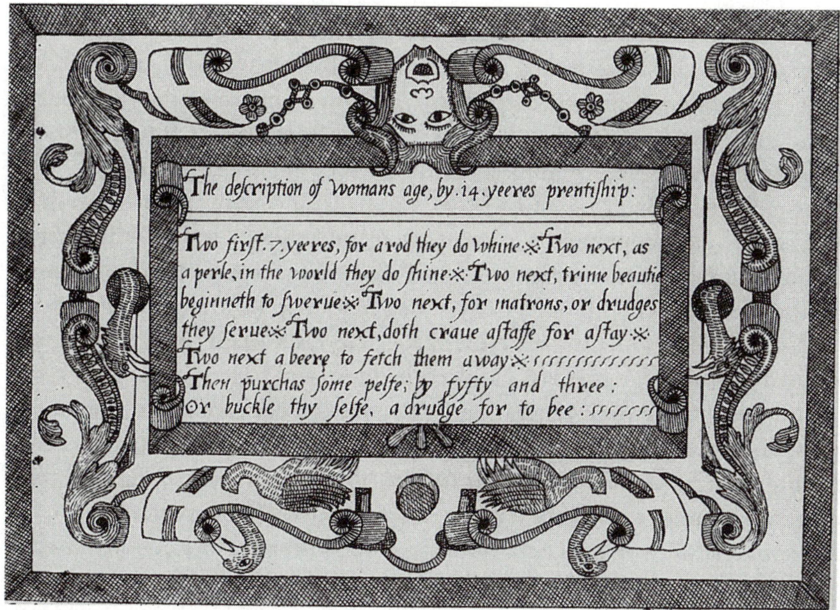

The deſcription of womans age, by .14. yeeres prentiſhip:
Two firſt .7. yeeres, for a rod they do whine ✕ Two next, as
a perle, in the world they do ſhine ✕ Two next, trime beautie
beginneth to ſwerue ✕ Two next, for matrons, or drudges
they ſerue ✕ Two next, doth craue a ſtaffe for a ſtay ✕
Two next a beere to fetch them away ✕
Then purchas ſome pelfe; by fyfty and three:
Or buckle thy ſelfe, a drudge for to bee:

FIG. 8. 'The Description of Womans Age'. Thomas Tusser's verse from *Five Hundred Points of Good Husbandry*, here transcribed by Thomas Trevelyan into his pictorial commonplace book, conceptualized female life-stages as 14-year intervals rather than the 7-year stages applied to males

from birth to the mid-twenties, and the second, adulthood. In discussing life-stages, we have selected points of transition which women themselves perceived as significant. The physical *rites de passage*—menarche, pregnancy, and menopause—have not been used as markers of stages, because we found no women who conceptualized their lives in those terms.

Little direct evidence has survived, even from the educated élite, for the earliest stages of female life. Among ordinary women, the demographic record is easier to reconstruct for those who stayed in one parish for their births, marriages, and deaths. We know comparatively little about the life-stages of vagrant women who moved from place to place, or those who never married. Our most plentiful evidence is about the lives of literate adult women.

EARLY YEARS

Although, across the life-cycle, gender mattered to women more at some stages than at others, women's subjectivity was always gendered. From the moment of birth, the divergence between female and male experience increased at all social levels. By the time children reached adolescence, girls' lives differed markedly from boys'. Some common elements between girls and boys remained, according to their material circumstances and developmental stages. Within a matrix of age and social level, girls' lives were influenced by a range of other variables, including their position in the family and geographical location in countryside or town. While childhood, as a period when a girl received care, may have lasted until around 14 for the élite, childhood was over much sooner for the poorest girls.

During childhood, girls at different social levels learned to be women, the majority of whom mothered children in their turn. The gender order was transmitted to the next generation by the explicit education and training of girls, and by the implicit attitudes and assumptions of the adults who cared for them. Here we discuss how girls learned their roles, depending on their stages of cognitive development, by interaction with their care-givers.[7] We argue that adult women's behaviour developed from an interaction between their developing bodies, their families, especially their mothers who were the primary care-givers, and their class positions in the wider society.

Contemporaries distinguished developmental stages in the years from birth to 14: 'the sucking child', 'the child that can both run and go', the stage of talking, and the child who was potentially useful. Rather than attempt a rigid definition of early modern developmental stages, we shall adopt a roughly chronological approach. Within the years from birth to 14, 7 was significant in dividing childhood into phases. At 7, parish officials could place the poorest children in the households of others. As a servant or apprentice in another family, a girl was expected to contribute to her own maintenance. For the majority of young people, childhood ceased when they went out into service, at whatever age. As a minister wrote to a girl in service, 'You are now come out of the age of childhood'.[8] Although 7 was significant for élite males, who moved away from the nursery and consequently from the company of women, for wealthier girls age 7 was not especially significant; their own protected lives continued.

Contemporaries believed that childhood ceased at around 14. Although writers did not use the term 'adolescence',[9] they recognized that there was a

[7] I. H. Frieze *et al.*, *Women and Sex Roles: A Social Psychological Perspective* (New York, 1978), 114–34.

[8] J. B. Williams (ed.), *The Lives of Philip and Matthew Henry* (1828; 1974), 209.

[9] J. and V. Demos, 'Adolescence in Historical Perspective', *Journal of Marriage and the Family*, 31 (1969), 632–8; I. K. Ben-Amos, *Adolescence and Youth in Early Modern England* (New Haven, 1994), 1–9.

stage of life between the dependence of childhood and the autonomy of adulthood. Criteria for distinguishing the end of childhood varied. Legally, girls could consent to marriage at 12, although, even at the gentry level, few did so. Some writers hint that the onset of menstruation signalled physical maturity; Bacon referred to the onset of 'the flowers' as marking a life-stage.[10] Consummation of a marriage may have been deferred until a young wife began to menstruate; Anne Clopton lived in a state of continence for the first eight months of her marriage with Simonds D'Ewes, presumably until she was deemed physically mature.[11] We do not know precisely the age at which the physical changes associated with menarche occurred. Probably the timing of menarche varied according to a girl's general diet and health; the poorer the diet, the later the onset of menstruation.[12]

Mothers may have seen age 14 or 15 as ending their daughters' childhood; Ann Harrison's mother, who nearly died in childbirth, longed like Hezekiah 'that I may live 15 years to see my daughter a woman'.[13] If a girl married young, adolescence was a brief life-stage, but, in the majority of cases, it was extended because most women married in their mid- to late twenties.

The problems in finding evidence are most serious for the earliest years of a girl's life and for the lives of the poorest girls. Advice literature was increasingly plentiful, but it has little to tell about actual child-rearing practices.[14] Early modern people were less interested in documenting the minutiae of early childhood than we are nowadays. Apart from the childhoods of monarchs, which do not offer a good basis for generalizing about the masses, we have very few accounts of early childhood. Men did not know much about small children; child-care was women's work. Nor did men consider that the earliest years of life were worth talking about, compared with other matters. What 'every woman knows' was not knowledge men valued. Perhaps, too, recollections of their state of dependency as children was disturbing to men.

The voices of young girls and memories of early childhood are hard to discern. Women's own autobiographical memories of the earliest years of

[10] F. Bacon, *The Historie of Life and Death* (1638), 369, 275.

[11] *The Autobiography and Correspondence of Sir Simonds D'Ewes*, ed. J. O. Halliwell, 2 vols. (1845), i. 318–20, 417.

[12] P. Crawford, 'Attitudes to Menstruation in Seventeenth-Century England', *Past and Present*, 91 (1981), 66–7.

[13] *The Memoirs of Anne, Lady Halkett and Ann, Lady Fanshawe*, ed. J. Loftis (Oxford, 1979), 109.

[14] J. E. Meckling, 'Advice to Historians on Advice to Mothers', *Journal of Social History*, 9 (1975), 44–63.

life are complicated and uncertain, for while adult women did tell anecdotes of their childhood, these may have been distilled from family memories and stories. Surviving female autobiographies frequently have a religious bias. The richest source of information about child-rearing is found in the letters of literate women who wrote about the health, behaviour, and well-being of their young. While we have used these sources here, we are conscious that the experiences documented are those relating to wealthier and more privileged childhoods. Nevertheless, even this restricted evidence has not always been used by historians.[15] Although research on various aspects of the childhood of the mass of female children is beginning,[16] there are many things we do not know. Further work on local records may help to fill out the picture, but many silences will remain in the evidence.

How were girls received into the world, compared with boys? Theologically, female and male infants born in post-Reformation England began life on an equal footing. Unlike its Roman Catholic predecessor, the Protestant Church of England specified a single baptismal ceremony for all infants, using the same prayer for girls as for boys and thus affirming its doctrine that souls had no sex.[17] Yet the ritual of churching, carried out a month after birth, already hinted at a higher destiny for male offspring of propertied families. On this occasion the mother was enjoined to think upon 'the Blessing the Family hath received, and especially when an Heir is born'.[18]

In practice, a good deal of contemporary evidence supports the view that even before the birth of a child, élite parents felt differently about the prospect of a son or a daughter. As one preacher observed, 'it is a greater blessing to have a sonne, then a daughter'. More bluntly, the Italian Ochino remarked, 'commonly we rejoyce at the birth of Boyes, and grieve at the birth of Girles'.[19] The existence of gender preferences is most fully docu-

[15] L. Stone, *The Family, Sex, and Marriage in England, 1500–1800* (Oxford, 1977); L. Pollock, *Forgotten Children: Parent–Child Relations from 1500 to 1900* (Cambridge, 1983); L. Pollock, '"Teach Her to Live Under Obedience": The Making of Women in the Upper Ranks of Early Modern England', *Continuity and Change*, 4 (1989), 231–58.

[16] For example, by A. L. Erickson, 'Maternal Management and the Cost of Raising Children in Early Modern England', in R. Wall and O. Saito (eds.), *Social and Economic Aspects of the Family Life Cycle* (Cambridge, forthcoming). We are grateful to Amy Erickson for allowing us to consult her paper before publication.

[17] C. Peters, 'Women and the English Reformation', unpublished paper, 'Women, Text and History' seminar, Oxford, 15 May 1990.

[18] [D. Comber], *A Companion to the Temple* (1684), 214.

[19] R. Bernard, *Ruths Recompence* (1628), 463; [B. Ochino], *A Dialogue of Polygamy* (1657), 62.

mented for the nobility and gentry.[20] In their diaries and letters, many mothers of the upper ranks expressed a wish for a son and were disappointed if the child proved to be a girl. 'My dear love', wrote Anne D'Ewes to her husband in 1641,

It hath pleased God now again the ninth time to restore me from the peril of childbirth: and though we have failed in part of our hope by the birth of a daughter yet we are likewise freed from much care and fear a son would have brought.[21]

Relatives might comfort the parents of daughters by pointing out that the birth of a girl at least demonstrated the couple's fertility. As Thomas Chichely wrote to his daughter, 'Although it be a girl that God hath sent . . . I remember a saying of your Grandfather Russell who said in time it would [turn?] to a boy.'[22] Likewise, when Hannah Brograve bore a child, 'though a daughter, was very welcome . . . because it gave them hope of further issue'.[23] The need to offer such consolation merely underlines the urgency of aristocratic desires for a male heir. Yet even among the élite, women might debate the pros and cons of having male or female offspring. Moreover, the reasons given for a particular gender preference did not always posit the axiom that males were the superior sex. As Dame Sarah Cowper reported in her diary,

I heard some argue, which was most desirable to have Sons or daughters, Specious Reasons were given both ways. A worthy Lady Said She least desired girls, for fear of the disgrace which attends their misbehaviour and ill Conduct, whereas Boys Could Scarce do any thing the world esteemed a fault.[24]

Lower down the social scale, explicit expressions of preference for males are less common.[25] Philip Henry, an ejected Nonconformist minister, favoured male children in general, preaching that the family was strengthened by the birth of sons: 'The more children there are—and the more of them are males, the more likely the family is to bee built up by them.'[26] But in the diary of the Reverend Ralph Josselin, there is no obvious trace of disappointment at the birth of female offspring.[27] At the middling level,

[20] P. Crawford, 'The Construction and Experience of Maternity', in V. Fildes (ed.), *Women as Mothers in Pre-Industrial England* (1990), 19–20.

[21] BL, Harleian MS 379, fo. 112^{v}.

[22] John Rylands Library, Manchester Uni. Lib., Legh of Lyme correspondence, 28 Oct. 1671. For another example of a daughter welcome 'because it gave the hope of further issue', D'Ewes, *Autobiography*, i. 416.

[23] D'Ewes, *Autobiography*, i. 416.

[24] Herts. RO, Panshanger MSS D/EP/F29, Dame Sarah Cowper, Diary, i. 76 (28 Mar. 1701).

[25] Erickson, *Women and Property*, 18, 49, 68–72.

[26] P. Crawford, 'Katharine and Philip Henry and their Children: A Case Study in Family Ideology', *Transactions of the Historic Society of Lancashire and Cheshire*, 134 (1984), 45.

[27] R. Josselin, *The Diary of Ralph Josselin, 1616–1683*, ed. A. Macfarlane (1976), 659 and *passim*.

some families showed a desire for 'equal numbers' in contrast to the aristocratic wish for 'as many boys as possible'.[28] Indeed, in Josselin's musings about the mortality of his children we can glimpse a different aspiration, that of producing matching numbers of each sex.[29] Mary Clarke jokingly referred to the same ideal when informing her husband that since she was not pregnant as she had feared, we 'keep our numbers even'.[30] Some middling rank parents even wanted to have girls.[31] As in all such evidence about emotional attitudes, it would be mistaken to generalize from a handful of examples. Still, literate sources do suggest that parents of the middling ranks were less likely to desire male offspring, a view supported by Amy Erickson in her study of women and property. She found few examples of preference for sons below the gentry level.[32]

The attitudes of the majority of parents remain unclear. Although early modern popular literature displays a good deal of misogyny directed against adult women, there is very little sign of negative feelings about female infants. Ballads and other popular genres usually depict a warm and welcoming attitude to children in general; on rare occasions when a specific prejudice against girls was portrayed, it was unambiguously associated with the squirearchy and represented in very pejorative terms.[33]

Children of every social rank were assigned initially to the care of their mothers. In the nursery, Halifax observed, 'you reign without competition'.[34] Aristocratic women were apt to reserve a supervisory role for themselves while delegating the drudgery to nurses and maidservants, but it is clear from their memoirs and correspondence that they took their educative functions seriously.[35] Women's responsibility for the daily care of children had some important implications for their socialization to gender roles. The dominant influence of mothers during the initial years ensured that boys as well as girls assimilated both a feminine and a universal

[28] See Som. RO, DD/SF 4515, no. 24, Mary Clarke to Edward Clarke, 7 Sept. 1694. For the aristocratic desire for as 'many sons' as possible, see M. Cavendish, duchess of Newcastle, *The Life of William, duke of Newcastle* (1667), 55.

[29] Josselin, *Diary*, 415 (14 Jan. 1658): 'god hath evened my number' on the birth of his daughter Mary.

[30] Som. RO, DD/SF 4515, no. 24.

[31] For example, the parents of London alderman Sir Patience Ward so wanted a girl that they gave him a girl's name. See *DNB*, 'Sir Patience Ward'.

[32] Erickson, *Women and Property*, 49, 68–72.

[33] See, for example, K. Briggs, *A Dictionary of British Folk-tales*, 2 vols. (1970), i. 177, for the tale 'Catskin', which circulated widely in ballad form in the 17th cent.

[34] *Advice to a Daughter* (1688), *Halifax: Complete Works*, ed. J. P. Kenyon (Harmondsworth, 1969), 278.

[35] See, for example, R. Russell, *Letters of Rachel Lady Russell*, 2 vols. (1853), i. 75, 82, 88, etc.; S. Mendelson, 'Stuart Women's Diaries and Occasional Memoirs', in M. Prior (ed.), *Women in English Society 1500–1800* (1985), 198.

component to their education. While élite boys made their escape from the maternal orbit at about age 7, girls remained under their mothers' tutelage to complete an education that was increasingly focused on their prescribed gender role as housekeepers, child-bearers, and child-rearers. Older girls in élite families had little contact with boys of their own age.

In the first year of life, the differences between the lives of girls and boys, rich and poor, was less marked than at other stages. Nutrition was provided by the maternal breast or that of a wet-nurse; daughters of middling families may have fared best here, since they were most likely to be nursed by their mothers at home. Infant and child mortality rates varied during the early modern period; the highest rates were in the first half of the eighteenth century.[36] In London rates were generally higher than in rural areas and varied between richer and poorer parishes, as well as between riverside and inland locations.[37] Although there is insufficient evidence to generalize about female to male survival rates, Richard Wall has suggested that neglect of female children may be inferred from the demographic evidence of skewed sex ratios among children between 1 and 2.[38]

Girls may have been weaned earlier than boys. Yet if weaning was tied to a perceived developmental stage, then parents would have weaned girls earlier than boys because contemporaries thought that girls did most things earlier.[39] Moreover, since male infants were usually weaker and sicklier than their female siblings, then the mother might 'compensate' with a longer nursing period, as she would with any sick, weak child. The evidence of differential neglect at infancy is at this stage ambiguous; certainly more boys than girls died, but more boys were born. Until more demographic work is done that codes for gender, it is difficult to know whether the female mortality rate was affected by adult attitudes. We need to know more about other factors as well, such as the distribution of food resources in a household.

Many variables affected the mortality rates of girls. The majority of

[36] E. A. Wrigley and R. S. Schofield, *The Population History of England, 1541–1871: A Reconstruction* (Cambridge, 1981; 1989), 249.

[37] J. Boulton, *Neighbourhood and Society: A London Suburb in the Seventeenth Century* (Cambridge, 1987), 125; R. Finlay, *Population and Metropolis: The Demography of London, 1580–1650* (Cambridge, 1981), 103–8.

[38] R. Wall, 'Inferring Differential Neglect of Females from Mortality Data', *Annales de démographie historique* (1981), 119–40; G. Reynolds, 'Infant Mortality and Sex Ratios at Baptism as shown by Reconstruction of Willingham, a Parish at the Edge of the Fens in Cambridgeshire', *Local Population Studies*, 22 (1979), 31–6.

[39] Pollock, 'Teach Her to Live Under Obedience', 239–40.

illegitimate children of both sexes were probably at greater risk of death from infanticide than other children,[40] except among the élite, where a father may have been willing to marry his mistress should her child prove to be a boy. The story circulated that when George Monck heard that his mistress, a seamstress, had borne a boy, '"Why then," said he, "she is my wife".'[41] Figures for infanticide do not provide evidence that more girls were killed than boys.[42] Illegitimate children were less likely to be breast-fed than other children, and so may have succumbed to other disorders.[43] Unwanted children born in wedlock may have been neglected and allowed to die, but this would be impossible to prove or quantify.

Literary sources suggest that some noble families took more care of sons than of daughters. When Lady Fanshawe's children fell ill of smallpox, she abandoned her daughters in order to devote all her energies to 'tending my dear son'. She lamented the fact that he had died while his sisters survived.[44] Yet when a granddaughter died, the countess of Denbigh sadly observed 'if she had been the daughter of a King she could not have had no more care taken of her'.[45] Girls were as exposed to physical danger in childhood as boys. They suffered as many accidents through unsupervised play, wandering away and getting lost, getting burned in the fire, falling downstairs or out of windows.[46]

Another way in which historians have attempted to assess adult attitudes to girls compared with boys is to compare the expenditure on their maintenance, education, and training at different social levels. Training by formal apprenticeships involved premiums which can be quantified. Some current research suggests that adults spent similar or even larger sums on the care and education of girls than of boys.[47] From probate accounts, Amy Erickson has calculated that the amount spent on the maintenance of both girls and boys was the same: a median cost per annum of £5. She argues that this is

[40] There is no satisfactory term for children born out of wedlock. The term 'illegitimate' seems preferable to the contemporary 'bastard'.

[41] J. Aubrey, *Brief Lives*, ed. R. Barber (1975), 212.

[42] K. Wrightson, 'Infanticide in Earlier Seventeenth-Century England', *Local Population Studies*, 15 (1975), 12. However, in the case of the single mother, the existence of the child rather than its sex was the main problem.

[43] Justices debated whether infants should be sent to the house of correction to be fed by their mothers. While Fildes has argued that 'finger-fed' babies did survive, there may have been no one to care for illegitimate children.

[44] *Memoirs of Ann, Lady Fanshawe*, ed. Loftis, 139.

[45] Warwickshire CRO, CR 2017/C1, fo. 6, Susan Denbigh to her husband, n.d. (*c*.1642).

[46] Nehemiah Wallington records his 4-year-old daughter's narrow escape from harm when she fell flat into a fire; Guildhall, MS 204, N. Wallington, His Booke, 1630, fo. 435; *The True Protestant Mercury*, 133 (12–15 Apr. 1682) (lost girl).

[47] Pollock, 'Teach Her to Live Under Obedience', 238–9.

reliable evidence of expenditure, because the accounts were usually submitted by or on behalf of women, who had a better sense than male recorders of the value of female household production, and thus a more accurate sense of the cost of keeping a child. The expenditure on the maintenance of poor children from overseers' accounts was only 10 per cent less, suggesting that these figures represent the true cost of maintaining a child. The accounts do show that people from the rank of labourer to yeoman were in the habit of bestowing the same material substance on girls as on boys, at least up to the age of 10.[48] Nevertheless, evidence of similar expenditure may not indicate the attribution of equal value for girls and boys. One reason why equal or larger sums had to be given with girls was that their labour was considered less valuable. Employers demanded a larger premium for females because they were less able to recoup the cost of their keep. But the figures do need to be treated with caution. The regularity of the sum of £5 suggests that accountants may have chosen a standard level of expenditure. While similar payments may have been made for apprenticeships of girls and boys, the unusually large payments made were invariably for boys, not girls. Macfarlane has argued that after age 10, boys required the same maintenance as did adult males, namely £10 per annum. Girls, he argued, cost only £6 per annum, because they earned part of their keep by their labour.[49]

Church court records provide further information about the cost of rearing children. Mary Parrat was an illegitimate child whose supposed father had died when she was 2 years old, leaving her a legacy of £5. The parish refused to take her because her legacy was inadequate; the overseers argued that the *annual* cost of her keep would be £5.[50]

Illegitimate children under 7 might be kept with their mothers.[51] The practice was favoured by officials because it was cheaper than paying someone else for the children's upkeep, not because contemporaries believed that such children had a right to be with their mothers.[52] A poor child of less than 7 years found wandering with both her parents was not herself deemed to be a vagrant; she had a right of settlement with her parents. At the poorest levels of society, even children under 7 were expected to contribute to their

[48] Erickson, 'Maternal Management and the Cost of Raising Children'.

[49] A. Macfarlane, *The Family Life of Ralph Josselin, a Seventeenth-Century Clergyman: An Essay in Historical Anthropology* (Cambridge, 1970), 44.

[50] OA, MS Archdiaconal papers Oxon. c. 118, fos. 41–2.

[51] One justices' handbook asserted that the condition of being 'a Nurse child' extended to seven years; *A Brief Declaration for what Manner of Speciall Nusance* (1636), STC 6453, 35.

[52] M. Dalton, *Countrey Justice* (1618), 32; G. Meriton, *A Guide for Constables, Churchwardens, Overseers of the Poor* (1669), 185; J. Keble, *An Assistance to Justices of the Peace* (1683), 197.

own livelihood. Parents sent daughters as well as sons out to beg, and the parish authorities accepted this practice.[53]

Childhood might end early for the most disadvantaged girls when they were bound as servants or parish apprentices, typically at 7 or 8 years old. Families whose income was below subsistence could rarely afford to support female children. Women who headed households found it even more difficult to keep girls at home; a mother's wages were barely adequate for her own subsistence, and the cash-earning power of dependent female children was insufficient to pay their way. The daughters of vagrants could be separated from their families and settled in the parish where they were born.[54] There are many examples of parents resisting the attempts of the overseers to remove their children.[55]

If the parish was responsible for a girl, parochial officials sought to put her into either an apprenticeship or service. It was assumed that children should maintain themselves by their labour as soon as possible.[56] The parish's object was to compound for a fixed sum for the responsibility for the child; the younger the child, the larger the premium required. Pauper children were the only ones apprenticed before the ages of 13 or 14.[57] Girls could be very young: in 1716 a 3-year-old parish foundling, Levina Dionis, was put out to James Garden for £10, he 'to Qualify her for a servant or otherwise to earn her own living'.[58]

By law, girls were bound until they were 18 years of age or until marriage; boys until 24.[59] In practice, however, local authorities exercised wide discretion.[60] In the agreements signed between parish officials and the master or mistress, the latter took on specified contractual obligations. Typically these included the responsibility for the child's upkeep and welfare for a term of years, at which point the young woman could be placed in the more ordinary forms of service or apprenticeship. In return, the employer was paid a small premium, often with additional money for a set of clothes. Premiums

[53] T. Wales, 'Work, Learning and the Fear of God: The English Poor Laws and the Young, c. 1570–c. 1700'. We are grateful to Tim Wales for allowing us to cite his unpublished paper.

[54] Meriton, *A Guide for Constables* (1669), 94–5, 183–4.

[55] *Minutes of the Norwich Court of Mayoralty, 1630–1631*, ed. W. L. Sachse, Norfolk Record Society, 15 (1942), 103, 235; *Poverty in Early-Stuart Salisbury*, ed. P. Slack, Wilts. Record Society, 31 (1975), 17, 19, 21, 22, 26, etc.

[56] Keble, *An Assistance to Justices of the Peace*, 479; for a discussion of the legislation, see I. Pinchbeck and M. Hewitt, *Children in English Society* (1969), i. 96–8; P. Slack, *Poverty and Policy in Tudor and Stuart England* (1988), 122–31.

[57] Meriton, *Guide for Constables*, 167–8, stated that children must be over 7; P. Sharpe, 'Poor Children as Apprentices in Colyton, 1598–1830', *Continuity and Change*, 6 (1991), 255; Ben-Amos, *Adolescence and Youth*, 58–9.

[58] Guildhall, MS 11,280A/3, Indentures, no. 28.

[59] 39 Eliz., c. 3, quoted in Pinchbeck and Hewitt, *Children in English Society*, i. 98.

[60] Girls bound until 21 according to Meriton, *Guide for Constables*, 168.

for parish apprentices sometimes differed according to gender, but the more significant causes of difference seem to be the age of the child and the region. In early seventeenth-century Bristol, premiums paid by parish authorities averaged about 30*s*.–40*s*., whereas in late seventeenth-century Bristol or London they were as much as five to eight pounds. Rural parishes reveal a similar variation: in Colyton, Devon, amounts ranged from 6*s*. 8*d*. for a 15-year-old boy in 1609 to £9 for a 5-year-old girl in 1621.[61] Girls were normally apprenticed to housewifery, boys to husbandry. The differences in training and pay for these skills had implications for girls' future ability to support themselves.

A glimpse of the life of a young female parish apprentice is found in the autobiography of Mary Hurll, the orphaned daughter of a Marlborough glover. Upon her father's death in 1671 (her mother had died the previous year), 8-year-old Mary was apprenticed to a butcher, to be instructed in the 'Art or Science of Bonelace maker, and alsoe in husewifry or domestrine imployment'. On the same day, her sister Joan was apprenticed to a husbandman, but like Mary she was to be taught lacemaking and domestic employment. Although both sisters were bound to the master, each girl was intended to learn housewifery and the low-paid craft of bone-lacemaking from his wife. The girls' 6-year-old sister was also apprenticed, but for a premium of £5. 10*s*., compared with £2 for the two older girls: presumably the youngest girl required more care and her work would be of less value. Mary recorded that she was neither ill-treated nor overworked, having had the freedom to roam the city with her friends on the Sabbath. Indeed, her sole complaint about the butcher's family was that it was a 'carnal' household in every sense: she deplored the family's indifference to religious matters, especially after her spiritual conversion at the age of 12. Once she had served out her eight-year term, she immediately contracted herself to another service: 'I had then attained the Age of Sixteen, and I was very fearful of being left to myself for fear of Liberty. . . . So I went to serve in another Place Apprentice five Years.' After completing a second apprenticeship, she went to live as her aunt's servant for two years. She was still single when she dictated her memoir.[62]

The complaints of female apprentices or their relatives to the quarter sessions about their treatment offer further glimpses of their lives. In 1659

[61] Sharpe, 'Poor Children as Apprentices', 256.

[62] *An Account of the Remarkable Conversion and Experience of Mary Hurll* (1708); C. Wordsworth, 'The Conversion of Mary Hurll, Lace-Maker's Apprentice at Marlborough, 1675: With her Indentures, 21 June 1671', *Wilts. Archaeological and Natural History Magazine*, 35 (1907–8), 103–13.

John Soper testified to the Devon quarter sessions on behalf of his step-daughter, bound as an apprentice: 'her dame is very cruell and unmercifull unto her, gave her immoderate Corrrection, and by her meanes the poor Girle is become a broke Creature.'[63] Sometimes the courts intervened in cases of physical abuse. Around 1630 in Wiltshire, a female apprenticed to learn bone-lacemaking and sewing had run away eighteen times. Her master and his wife alleged that although she was well fed, she never came home 'but full of vermin'.[64] In 1631 the Norwich mayor's court ordered that Elizabeth Porter was to return to her master, but that he was not to 'correct' (i.e. beat) her. Instead, he was to complain to the mayor or ward alderman if she were to offend again.[65]

If relatives were not there to intervene, cruelty towards young apprentices might not come to public attention unless it was so extreme as to result in death. The Old Bailey sessions for 1681 included two cases of mistresses who had been indicted for killing their female apprentices. Elizabeth Wigenton, a coat-maker by trade, was tried for beating her 13-year-old apprentice to death: 'having set the Girl upon a Piece of Work, she had not done it so well as she required, whereupon she beat her grievously.' At her trial, Elizabeth Wigenton pleaded little in her own defence, merely claiming that she had not meant to kill the girl: 'So that it being proved that she had been a cruel Woman by all her Neighbours, she was found guilty of wilful Murther.'[66] In another case at the same sessions, Sarah Bell was arraigned and tried for fatally wounding her 12-year-old apprentice. Bell had thrown a knife at the girl after she had 'crossed her, in not performing a message she had sent her of'.[67] If a servant or apprentice should die while running away, her master or mistress was not held responsible. In the case of a 9-year-old runaway who died of exposure, the verdict was suicide.[68]

Such cruelty represented one extreme of ill usage towards apprentices. It was considered normal for masters and mistresses to beat their servants so long as they did not use 'immoderate' force. Indeed, the courts themselves could impose a whipping on refractory apprentices. Robert Doughty remarked in his notes on the 1665 Norwich quarter sessions, 'I sent Bridgett Potts a girl of 16 year, an assigned apprentice, to Bridewell for a moderate

[63] Devon RO, QSB Box 64, Easter 1659, loose. [64] *HMC Various*, i. 99.

[65] *Minutes of the Norwich Court of Mayoralty, 1630–31*, 90.

[66] *A True Relation of the Tryals . . . particularly of Elizabeth Wigenton* (1681), 1.

[67] Ibid. 2.

[68] M. Macdonald and T. Murphy, *Sleepless Souls: Suicide in Early Modern England* (Oxford, 1990), 254–5.

whipping, because she had run away from her master six times since last Christmas, for no reason but her roguish disposition.'[69] In both the courts and private households, the biblical admonition against sparing the rod was taken seriously, and girls were subject to physical punishment. Children of both sexes were more liable to public physical punishment if their parents were too poor to pay the fines for their offences. 'Prophane swearing' was punishable with a fine of 12*d*., according to Meriton's *Guide for Constables*, but if the offender was under 12 years and unable to pay, 'then he or she is to be whipped by the constable, or by the Parent, or Master, in the Constable's presence'.[70]

Although children of both sexes were at risk of neglect or cruelty, girls were far more vulnerable to the additional hazard of sexual abuse. A great deal of evidence shows that sexual exploitation of female servants in general was widespread, and it is unlikely that parish apprentices escaped. However, it would be wrong to assume that all poor girls who were apprentices or servants in the households of others were treated with indifference or cruelty. Sometimes families grew very fond of their charges, as did that of the rector of Myddle, who 'adopted' the daughter of a poor weaver burdened with eleven children:

> baptizing the tenth or eleventh, Mr Kinaston said (merrily,) 'Now one child is due to the Parson', to which Parks agreed, and Mr Kinaston choase a girle . . . and brought her up at his own house, and she became his servant . . . [After] several years he gave her in marriage with thirty, some say sixty pounds portion.[71]

Most girls remained with their families, where they were educated by their mothers. They were taught to behave differently from boys. They were to be more restrained, and to preserve their chastity. Bodily comportment for the two sexes was different. While a girl was cautioned about modesty before she was 3, a boy of the same age was urged to 'take up his Coats, and piss like a Man'.[72] Although the dress of girls and boys was the same until the children were 7, boys in wealthier families would be clad in breeches at age 7 and separated from the girls.[73]

The formal content in the education of girls differed from that of boys.

[69] Norfolk RO, AYL 829, notes of quarter session proceedings by Robert Doughty, 1662–5.

[70] Meriton, *Guide for Constables*, 97–8. The explicit 'he or she' is unusual in the handbooks, which normally refer to 'he' only.

[71] R. Gough, *The History of Myddle*, ed. D. Hey (Harmondsworth, 1981), 41.

[72] B. Mandeville, *The Fable of the Bees: Or, Private Vices, Publick Benefits*, ed. F. B. Kaye, 2 vols. (Oxford, 1924), i. 71–2.

[73] A charming letter from Anne, Lady North, of her grandson's breeching ceremony in 1679 is found in *The Autobiography of . . . Roger North*, ed. A Jessopp (1887), 215–16.

Literacy was a basic skill, but the nature and extent of female literate education is controversial, mainly because children acquired literacy skills in a series of discrete stages. Girls were customarily taught to read printed works but not to write. Consequently, the usual indices of literacy based on writing ability bear no relation to the actual extent of women's ability to read. Evidence about female book ownership in probate inventories has also been used to argue that girls learned to read in similar numbers to boys. These figures may be misleading, however, because widows may have inherited books which they were unable to read.[74]

From some literary evidence, we can infer that girls may have learned to read at a very early age, around 4 years or even younger.[75] In many families, the acquisition of literacy was closely linked to religious education. Godly mothers found it convenient to teach piety and reading simultaneously so as to reinforce each other. Once girls had learned their letters, they were launched on the church catechism or the Bible as a practice text for reading.[76] There are several examples of girls able to read the Bible at 4 to 6 years of age.[77] In poorer families, girls were expected to start manual work as soon as they were old enough, so reading had to be fitted in early. Helen Weinstein's work on horn books suggests that more children may have been able to read than we had previously thought. The large body of reading texts which were printed at the end of the seventeenth century met a demand for educational reading.[78]

Girls' formal education in schools is too large a subject to be embarked on here.[79] Yet there are some salient points to be noted. Girls had fewer opportunities for schooling than boys, and their subjects were gender specific. The curriculum for girls of gentry status included a large amount of needlework. Charity schools emphasized sewing, knitting, and spinning rather than reading as a means by which girls might gain a liveli-

[74] Lorna Weatherill's evidence from nearly 3,000 probate inventories showed that the same proportion of women's inventories (19%) revealed books among possessions as did men's inventories. However, women's inventories were only 430 of the total sample, and, of those, the laws about women and property meant that the sample was biased towards widows. L. Weatherill, 'A Possession of One's Own: Women and Consumer Behaviour in England, 1660–1740', *JBS*, 25 (1986), 142.

[75] See, for example, D. Leigh, *The Mothers Blessing* (1616), 4; *Memoirs of the Life of Colonel Hutchinson*, ed. J. Sutherland (Oxford, 1973), 288.

[76] Leigh, *Mothers Blessing*, 47–8; A. Walker, *The Holy Life of Mrs Elizabeth Walker* (1690), 35–40.

[77] Pinchbeck and Hewitt, *Children in English Society*, i. 264–73.

[78] Thanks for this point to Helen Weinstein whose Cambridge Ph.D. dissertation on the subject of the fundamentals of reading is forthcoming.

[79] D. Gardiner, *English Girlhood at School: A Study of Women's Education through Twelve Centuries* (1929); J. Kamm, *Hope Deferred: Girls' Education in English History* (1965); M. Reynolds, *The Learned Lady in England, 1650–1760* (New York, 1920).

hood.[80] From these skills, girls were expected to be able to provide for themselves.

While female as well as male social reformers accepted the premiss that the education of the two sexes should be different, some women tried to improve girls' education. Bathsua Makin pleaded for more intellectual and religious content in girls' schooling, and, towards the end of the century, many wealthier women were involved in charity school educational schemes.[81]

From informal education by their mothers, daughters learned that they in turn would be wives and mothers one day. At the highest social levels, girls were thoroughly indoctrinated in the virtues of modesty, obedience, and subordination to a future husband.[82] In plebeian families, the ideals are less clear. Sometimes girls had a second chance to learn as servants. More rarely, they learned as apprentices. They were trained to be occupied in housewifery, learning cleaning, sweeping, and washing. If the household was more prosperous, then daughters learned brewing, baking, preserving, medical skills, the care of small livestock, and gardening. The significant unspoken content of the curricula for both girls and boys was that the two sexes were different. Since this assumption was so much taken for granted, contemporaries had no need to spell it out.

Few comments from girls about their education survive. Some women recollected as adults that they had been unwilling to learn female skills. A common complaint was needlework. Lucy Hutchinson declared that she hated her needle, and Anne D'Ewes observed that her niece did not want to return to school because she so disliked embroidery 'that she cries almost every day when she goes to it'.[83]

Daughters in the upper ranks were often their parents' favourites. While girls were seen as a drain on the family resources because they required dowries, and were capable of ruining the family honour should they not preserve their reputation for chastity,[84] in practice aristocratic parents may

[80] M. G. Jones, *The Charity School Movement: A Study of Eighteenth-Century Puritanism* (1964), 98–9.

[81] [B. Makin], *An Essay to Revive the Antient Education of Gentlewomen* (1673). Even the anonymous author of a radical scheme for more equality between the sexes in legal matters thought that the ideal training for girls was 'in spinning, carding, sowing [sewing], weaving lace, ribband, tape and other things; in setting of Cushions, Carpets, Hangings, and other things fit for the work of women'; *Chaos: or a discourse* ([18 July] 1659), 47–8. Child thought that girls could be employed 'in mending the Clothes of the Aged, in Spinning, Carding and other linnen Manufactures, and many in Sowing Linnen'; boys, 'in picking Okam, making Pins' and other manufacture; J. Child, *A New Discourse of Trade* (1693), 75; Jones, *Charity School Movement.*

[82] Pollock, 'Teach Her to Live Under Obedience', 244–52.

[83] *Life of Colonel Hutchinson,* 288; BL, Harleian MS 384, fo. 82.

[84] S. Mendelson, *The Mental World of Stuart Women: Three Studies* (Brighton, 1987), 25–6, 64.

actually have found daughters more congenial than sons. Girls had been taught from a very early age to fit harmoniously into any family setting, partly because they would be expected to live with one or more sets of in-laws.[85] Daughters had less difficulty than their brothers in exhibiting the kind of respectful subservience that parents demanded. Paradoxically, the same family might proclaim a theoretical preference for sons but demonstrate greater affection for daughters. To some extent, then, affectionate relations within the family might develop independently of the values of the outside world, and could even operate in contradiction to the hierarchy of gender preference which was such a characteristic feature of early modern society. Ann, Lady Fanshawe, told a story of her mother, who had had three sons, and was sick with a fever after her daughter's birth. Deep in a trance, she struggled to live for Ann's sake: 'the sence of leaving my girle, which is dearer to me than all my children, remained a trouble upon my spirit.'[86]

Little evidence survives about what girls thought of their situations, *vis-à-vis* those of their brothers. If girls were socialized successfully, they accepted their situation as God-given. There are hints of some girls' resentment of their brothers. In her conversion narrative, one woman confessed that as a 10-year-old girl, she had had an impulse to hurt her sleeping baby brother, 'a Brother who was as dear to me as mine own life . . . out of no reason, but an inclination to do harm'. Her adult self attributed this vile temptation to Satan.[87]

If childhood is characterized as a period of limited responsibility, when care is given, then in early modern times, the poorer a girl was, the sooner her childhood ended. All the evidence suggests that daughters of families of higher status were more likely to remain at home under the direct supervision of their mothers. In this sense, the childhood of wealthier girls as a privileged and protected status was prolonged, while independence was forced upon the poorest girls at a very early age.

SERVICE

In early modern times, service was the archetypal 'growing-up' experience for young women.[88] No one was too poor to be a servant or apprentice, and

[85] Mendelson, *Mental World*, 77–8. [86] *Memoirs of Ann, Lady Fanshawe*, 109.

[87] Hurll, *Conversion Exemplified*, 7.

[88] For evidence that service was the 'characteristic' experience of young people at this period, see Ben-Amos, *Adolescence and Youth*. See also R. Wall, 'The Age at Leaving Home', *Journal of Family History*, 3 (1978), 181–202; id., 'Leaving Home and the Process of Household Formation in Pre-Industrial England', *Continuity and Change*, 2 (1987), 77–101; P. Griffiths, *Youth and Authority: Formative Experiences in England, 1560–1640* (Oxford, 1996).

FIG. 9. 'Long Threed Laces Long & Strong'. Laroon's depiction of London street scenes shows poor young children of both sexes selling small wares. The slightly romanticized image does not disguise the fact that the girl is only about 7 years old. For her, childhood had ended early

few were too wealthy. In towns like Bristol, yeomen's and gentlemen's daughters formed a significant proportion of registered female apprentices.[89] Even the nobility had an equivalent of service: aristocratic daughters acquired skills in housewifery and deportment while living in the homes of well-connected kinswomen.[90]

A wide range of households included one or two maidservants. Even poor families might hire a live-in servant to perform heavy drudgery and help with cottage industry.[91] Middling and wealthy households increasingly employed women rather than men for domestic service.[92] Female servants in husbandry worked in general agriculture and in specialized tasks like dairying.[93] Apprenticeships to 'housewifery' or textile trades were common well into the eighteenth century.[94] Thus a significant proportion of the adolescent female population were servants of one kind or another.

Because service was the common experience for young women from a broad spectrum of society, there was no fixed pattern defining its parameters. All the concomitants of service were subject to variation: the age of entry into service; the mixture of domestic with agrarian and industrial tasks included in a maidservant's duties; the length of service and degree of mobility from one household to another; the wages, food, clothes, gifts, and perquisites that made up her salary. These factors were affected by local custom, the social class of mistress and servant, parental occupation and mortality, and even by sibling order.

While financial pressures forced some families to send daughters out to service, many parents tried to prevent girls from leaving home. Elizabeth Walker educated her daughters at home, 'not to save Charges, but avoid Inconveniences' chiefly the 'Vanity or Pride' acquired at girls' boarding schools.[95] Even middling and poorer families kept daughters at home longer

[89] I. K. Ben-Amos, 'Women Apprentices in the Trades and Crafts of Early Modern Bristol', *Continuity and Change*, 6 (1991), 230–3.

[90] Service at court as maid of honour was the most sought-after form for daughters of the nobility, but it was still a form of service. See F. Harris, *A Passion for Government* (Oxford, 1991), 14–17.

[91] See, for example, *The Norwich Census of the Poor, 1570*, ed. J. Pound, Norfolk Record Society, 40 (1971), 25–6, 40, 44, 46, 49, etc. See also *Poverty in Early-Stuart Salisbury*, ed. P. Slack, 'Survey of the Poor, 1625', 65–83, for numerous examples of poor women who kept a young female servant or apprentice.

[92] D. Marshall, *The English Domestic Servant in History* (1949), 4–8.

[93] A. Kussmaul, *Servants in Husbandry in Early Modern England* (Cambridge, 1981), 4, 15, 19, 34, 37–8 ; H. Best, *The Farming and Memorandum Books of Henry Best of Elmswell, 1642*, ed. D. Woodward (Oxford, 1984), 138–42, 150; K. Snell, *Annals of the Labouring Poor* (Cambridge, 1985), 270–319; R. Allen, *Enclosure and the Yeoman* (Oxford, 1992), 57, 159, 215–19, 235.

[94] Gardiner, *English Girlhood at School*, 281–99; Snell, *Annals of the Labouring Poor*, 270–319; B. Hill, *Women, Work and Sexual Politics in Eighteenth-Century England* (Oxford, 1989), 85–102; Ben-Amos, 'Women Apprentices'.

[95] Walker, *Life of Mrs Elizabeth Walker*, 68.

FIG. 10. Susan Gill, maidservant of the Beale family. Charles Beale, husband of artist Mary Beale, sketched their young servant holding her broom, the maidservant's badge of office

than sons. Girls were less likely to go away to school, and were older than male counterparts when they began service.[96] Jane Martindale's parents could not understand her desire to go to London as a lady's maid: 'She

[96] For examples, see *Norwich Census of the Poor*, 33, 40, 45, 46, 49, etc; Boulton, *Neighbourhood and Society*, 126; Wall, 'Age at Leaving Home'.

wanted nothing at home, nor was likely to lacke anything; and if she had a mind to be married, [her] father was then in a good ordinary capacity to preferre her.'[97]

There were two clusters of ages at which girls might enter service. The younger group, made up of orphans and indigent or illegitimate children, were placed in other households to ensure their subsistence.[98] The largest category, however, were those who entered service as a life-stage between puberty and marriage. Ideally, service was meant to offer these young women a safe haven to delay their entrée into adulthood until their mid-twenties, the proper age for marriage, child-bearing, and the independent supervision of a household.

Moral and physical restraint were integral functions of service as an institution. In the eyes of society, all masterless women were disorderly by nature, and were moreover the stimulus for misconduct in others. If an unmarried female lacked paternal supervision, it was deemed essential to place her with a master or mistress who could control her behaviour *in loco parentis*:

> If the mother . . . be a good Huswife, and Religiously disposed, let her have the bringing up of [her daughter]. Place the other . . . in the house of some good Merchant . . . [where] she may learne what belongs to her improvement, for *Sempstrie*, for Confectionary, and all requisits of Huswifery. She shall be sure to be restrained of all ranke company, and unfitting libertie, which are the overthrow of too many of their Sexe.[99]

While in service, young women were to be kept under familial discipline. If employers failed in their duty, they might be rebuked by local officials. The Norwich mayor's court delivered runaway Margaret Harvey, a servant of Matthew Taylor, to Taylor's wife, telling her that she was required to keep Margaret, and 'not suffer her to wander'.[100]

This supervisory role was buttressed by the 1563 Statute of Artificers, which empowered local officials to order unmarried woman between the ages of 12 and 40 into service 'for such wages and in such reasonable sort and manner as they shall think meet'. Any woman who refused could be committed to prison 'until she shall be bounden to serve'.[101] The patriarchal assumptions behind the statute are underlined by the fact that daughters

[97] A. Martindale, *The Life of Adam Martindale*, ed. R. Parkinson, Chetham Society, 4 (1845), 6.

[98] See Sharpe, 'Poor Children as Apprentices in Colyton, 1598–1830', 253–70.

[99] T. Powell, *Tom of All Trades* (1631), 47–8, quoted in Ben-Amos, 'Women Apprentices', 2, 227.

[100] *Minutes of the Norwich Court of Mayoralty, 1630–1631*, 90.

[101] 'Statute of Artificers' (1563), 5 Eliz., c. 4. While in theory men too could be ordered into harvest work, we have found no instances of the Act being applied to adult men in the same way as to women.

living with mothers were often ordered into service, but those with fathers were not.[102]

Women above a certain social level were exempt from the constraints of the Statute of Artificers. Although the author of *The Lawes Resolutions of Womens Rights* cited the statute's provisions for women, he denied its relevance to his propertied female readership, explaining that the statute applied only to 'day laborers'.[103] But at the lower end of the social spectrum, much of the female populace was vulnerable to prosecution under this and subsequent statutes. The Norwich mayor's court frequently ordered young women to be sent to Bridewell if they had not found a service within a specified time limit. Elizabeth Barber, 'liveing at her owne hand', was to be committed to Bridewell until she was retained in service.[104] At Salisbury in 1598, Margery Lane was whipped as a vagrant, then ordered to her native parish, 'there to be employed in work or otherwise as in the . . . statute is provided'.[105]

Indirect evidence confirms the use of the statute against young labouring women. A witness in a Devon defamation suit, 22-year-old Mary Smith, was impugned as 'a poor woman . . . of little credit'. The local constable reported that Mary had been

> questioned and convented before Sir Nicholas Marten a Justice of Peace for not living wth a master . . . Sir Nicholas did enjoin her to procure a master within one month following which she did . . . but did not long tarry with him, by reason whereof she was again brought before a justice, and was threatened to be punished if she did not live with a master. And since that time she hath lived in service.[106]

Women's sense of personal autonomy must have been affected by their awareness that only females, not males, could be forced into service while living on their own as adults. And since local officials were empowered to arrange maidservants' salaries as they thought fit, there was an additional downward pressure on women's wages, exacerbating the large differential that already existed between female and male earnings. Finally, it is significant that the inclusive ages of 12 to 40 corresponded to those years when a woman was susceptible to pregnancy. Service was thus intended as a sexual as well as a physical and economic constraint on young women's liberty. Yet, ironically, the typical unmarried mother who was brought before the secular

[102] *Minutes of the Norwich Court of Mayoralty, 1630–1631*, 82, 103; Walker, *Life of Elizabeth Walker*, 193–4.

[103] T.E., *The Lawes Resolutions of Womens Rights* (1632), 8.

[104] *Minutes of the Norwich Court of Mayoralty, 1630–1631*, 70.

[105] *Poverty in Early-Stuart Salisbury*, ed. P. Slack, 17.

[106] Devon RO, Chanter 866, Consistory Court Depositions 1634–40 (not foliated or paginated), *Flood* v. *Tucker*, 7 Mar. 1635/6, testimony of Edward Panie.

courts was the maidservant who had been impregnated by her master or fellow servant.

Entry into 'life-stage' service ranged from the early to late teens, roughly correlated to the family's wealth yet varying with their demographic circumstances. Parents might keep one daughter at home to help with housewifery and child-care so that the wife could earn supplementary cash in field labour or proto-industry.[107] Other daughters might enter service as situations were found for them, or be contracted to an apprenticeship when parents had saved sufficient cash for a premium.

The flexible and contingent nature of female service is shown by the experiences of the daughters of Leonard and Elizabeth Wheatcroft, a Derbyshire artisan family. By 1679, Elizabeth had borne eleven children, of whom four daughters survived to adulthood.[108] Anna and Esther had already been away from home as children, living with 'friends' while their father was in debtors' prison.[109] In 1675, 11-year-old Esther was sent to Derby with her brother 'to learne sum better work and breeding'.[110] By 1679, 17-year-old Anna was in service in Nottinghamshire, and Leonard had brought Esther 'to sarvis to a place called Routhorne' for two years.[111] Afterwards, Anna went to 'Mr. Horns of Butterly' for one year's service, then stayed home for a year, subsequently going to 'Mr Wollhouse of Glapwell'.[112]

At Chesterfield fair in 1681, Leonard bargained with a bone-lace weaver to take 11-year-old Elizabeth as an apprentice: 'So for 3 pounds 10 shillings we agreed, and bound she was, Sep. 14, being Chesterfeild faire day, for four years.'[113] After Elizabeth's mistress died, Leonard went back to Chesterfield fair and found another, 'one Mary Jennings', to whom Elizabeth was bound for two years. But Mrs Jennings died as well, and Elizabeth lived at home until 1685, when she began two years' service with one 'Catrin Balme'.[114] Meanwhile Anna served in various locations until she married a Yorkshire farmer in 1689.[115]

At age 24, Esther emigrated to London, eventually marrying at the

[107] W. Stout, *The Autobiography of William Stout of Lancaster, 1665–1752*, ed. J. Marshall, Chetham Society (Manchester, 1967), 76, cited in Ben-Amos, 'Women Apprentices', 249 n. 7; L. Wheatcroft, 'The Autobiography of Leonard Wheatcroft', *Journal of Derbyshire Archaeological and Natural History Society*, 18 (1896) and 21 (1899).

[108] Wheatcroft, 'Autobiography' (1899), 41–2.

[109] Wheatcroft, 'Autobiography' (1896), 29.

[110] Wheatcroft, 'Autobiography'(1899), 41.

[111] Ibid. 43. The oldest daughter, Anna, may have been kept at home to help with housekeeping and child-care, since her mother had been working full-time brewing and selling ale since 1668.

[112] Ibid. 44.

[113] Ibid.

[114] Ibid. 46.

[115] Ibid. 49.

advanced age of 44. The youngest daughter, Sarah, alternated between managing her father's household and going out to service while her brother Titus took over the housekeeping. Both father and son welcomed Sarah's return after two years' service with her uncle William: 'after Sarah came hom, I had more liberty, and Titus too, to walke abroad to se our friends and Relations.'[116]

The pattern of ages at which the Wheatcroft daughters went out to service or apprenticeship would appear random, did we not know that their careers were linked to the vagaries of the Wheatcroft family economy. This pattern was in contrast to that of their brothers, who were taught the tailoring trade by their father and then sent to London apprenticeships.[117] Although all the daughters spent time working in other households, they alternated between service and periods at home, depending on the needs of other family members and the opportunities that happened to be available.

The casual and intermittent character of women's training, in which agreements were apt to be private or informal, alerts us to the problems confronting historians who try to make quantitative generalizations about female service. The contract arranged at Chesterfield fair whereby Elizabeth Wheatcroft was apprenticed to learn bone-lace weaving was not likely to have been entered in a central apprenticeship register, nor was there much chance that Anna's and Esther's intermittent terms in rural service or Sarah's stint at her uncle's house would have been caught in the documentary net. Although all the Wheatcroft daughters went out to service in some form, we know of their experiences only because their father recorded his childrens' activities in his journal.[118]

Traditionally, historians have distinguished between three types of female service or training: craft apprenticeship, service in husbandry, and domestic service. To apprentice a child, parents paid a premium to a master or mistress, signing a contract which stipulated that their daughter would be taught a specific trade or skill for a stated term, usually seven to ten years. In service in husbandry, a young woman was hired for a one-year term to perform farming tasks or a mixture of agrarian and domestic labour. In return she was given a

[116] Ibid. 51. [117] Ibid. 45, 47.

[118] As a prolific poet and diarist as well as the town clerk of Ashover, Leonard Wheatcroft was unusually literate for an artisan-labourer; he may have penned his daughter's apprenticeship contract himself. But oral contracts continued to be widely used in business and financial matters by all classes, and certainly by the illiterate majority. See C. Muldrew, 'Credit, Market Relations, and Debt Litigation in Late Seventeenth-Century England', Ph.D. diss., University of Cambridge (1990), 39–88.

small annual wage, usually paid quarterly.[119] Female domestic servants were generally retained for a yearly term and paid their wages in quarterly instalments, although some maidservants were hired by the week or day. Their duties were centred in the household: making fires, cleaning and sweeping, cooking, fetching water, washing dishes and clothes, helping with childcare, running errands, spinning and sewing.

The historical model which attempts to divide female servants into three distinct categories is a problematic one. In the seventeenth century, the borderlines between these forms of female training were blurred, with the greatest overlap in women's domestic duties. From the perspective of a female 'job description', there was a continuum from one type to the others rather than three separate kinds of service.

Although female apprenticeship contracts followed similar forms of wording to that of their male counterparts,[120] documents related to women's training reveal an increasing stress on housewifery and domestic service. In seventeenth-century Bristol, nearly all female apprentices were contracted either as 'servant maids' or else to a combination of craft and household service.[121] As Ilana Ben-Amos has concluded, at this period household service was 'not simply an additional duty which some . . . [female] apprentices were required to perform, but a formal and major obligation of their apprenticeship'.[122] In this respect women's apprenticeship was becoming sharply differentiated from that of men, compared with a greater range of vocational options which had apparently been available to women in earlier centuries.

Similarly, contracts for service in husbandry assumed that whereas men were hired chiefly for outdoor farming tasks, women would perform a combination of domestic and outdoor chores. Job designations for parish apprentices in early seventeenth-century Colyton were routinely distinguished by gender, with boys assigned to service in husbandry and girls to 'housewifery'.[123] In his 1642 memorandum book, Henry Best joked about farmers' assumption that all female servants in husbandry were ready and willing to perform household tasks: 'They will say to a mayde when they hire her that if shee have beene used to washinge, milkinge, brewinge, and

[119] Kussmaul, *Servants in Husbandry*, 37–8.

[120] See, for example, Guildhall, MS 7603/1, the apprenticeship indenture of Rebekah Smith for housewifery (1698), in which the wording is the same as that for male apprentices, including the usual provisos against adolescent male vices: playing cards and dice or haunting taverns and playhouses.

[121] Ben-Amos, 'Women Apprentices', 233.

[122] Ibid. 234.

[123] Sharpe, 'Poor Children as Apprentices', 256.

bakinge, they make noe question but shee can wash the howse and sweepe the dishes.'[124]

Henry Best's derisive transposition of the elements of daily housewifery implies that these domestic chores were undervalued as well as being taken for granted. Women's expertise at 'effeminate' tasks was presumed to be universal and therefore unskilled. In general, the superficially neutral job description of the female craft apprentice or agricultural servant concealed a large domestic component, leading historians to underestimate the degree of sexual differentiation that contemporaries assumed was inherent in young people's training.

Conversely, female household servants were often called upon to perform agrarian or industrial tasks which society defined as 'masculine'. Church court records offer glimpses of young women styled 'famula domestica' (domestic servant) who helped gather or thresh the harvest or perform other field tasks. In a tithe dispute, 20-year-old Margaret Bennett described how she had transported the tithe fruit as part of her duties as Jane Deely's household servant. She had also lent a hand with the barley harvest: 'she went sometimes when her leisure would serve her into the field and did help to rake after . . . Jane Deely's carts when they were laden with barley.'[125] Joan Fowler, 23-year-old 'famula domestica', reported that she and her fellow servants Elizabeth Marshall and John Turner had been 'winnowing of corn together' when some defamatory words were spoken: Joan and Elizabeth winnowed the corn, and John 'put up the corn as it was winnowed and carried it away and brought them more corn to winnow'.[126]

These snapshots of female servants' rural work routine confirm that maidservants' duties in the countryside were not limited to domestic tasks, in spite of traditional prejudices about women's appropriate work roles. Even while nominal job descriptions and wage scales were sharply differentiated by gender, female household servants' informal duties might encroach on masculine occupational prerogatives. It was cheaper for Simon Busby to use his female servants to winnow his grain rather than pay a male thresher day wages to do the job. No doubt Jane Deely's maidservant saved her some harvest wages as well.[127]

The tendency to train maidservants or female relatives informally, thus

[124] Best, *Farming and Memorandum Books*, 141–2.

[125] OA, MS Oxf. Dioc. papers c. 26, 1629–34, fos. 53–53^{v}.

[126] OA, MS Oxf. Dioc. papers c. 26, 1629–34, fos. 90^{v}–1.

[127] In the early 1640s, Henry Best paid threshers and rakers 6*d*. per day. Best, *Farming and Memorandum Books*, 146.

saving the higher costs of male labour, is also evident in artisan families. Women hired as domestic servants in urban or proto-industrial households were employed in preparatory and skilled work in family cottage industry. Indeed, these skills were more often learned in the course of women's domestic service than as part of a formal craft apprenticeship.[128] Beyond basic housewifery, both rural and urban maidservants and apprentices might acquire skills which were considered appropriate to either sex. Nevertheless, neither the mention nor omission of a 'masculine' occupation in female apprenticeship or service contracts can be taken at face value. A girl might be nominally apprenticed to a master, yet learn nothing but housewifery and other feminine skills from his wife. Conversely, some maidservants were contracted to a mistress for domestic service, yet were trained to provide supplementary labour for 'male' chores in husbandry or proto-industry.

An important factor which determined a maidservant's work routine was the size and wealth of the household. At one extreme, large noble households included a host of live-in female personnel allotted to precise vocational niches: house cleaning, laundry, cooking, child-care, and different types of personal service.[129] Lower down the social scale, there were more connections between female and male sectors, with a blurring of gender divisions and a female work routine which took on an increasingly multi-occupational character. At the lowest level, the artisan or labouring family employed a single maid-of-all-work for the full range of household tasks.

In terms of the number of maidservants, most families were closer to the lower end of the spectrum. The yeoman Henry Best, who farmed a substantial Yorkshire manor, kept only two maidservants; so did Elizabeth Walker, the wife of a prosperous clergyman.[130] While managing a large Somerset farm, Mary Clarke had two maidservants in 1694, but decided there was only enough work for one.[131] Many substantial yeoman or 'middling' households included two maidservants at most; artisans' or husbandmen's families could afford only a single one. Thus the typical female servant was the Jill-of-all-trades and mistress of none.

One characteristic of female life-stage service was its high degree of mobility: young women moved from one household to another about as frequently as their male counterparts.[132] Maidservants had several reasons for

[128] Ben-Amos, 'Women Apprentices', 241.

[129] H. Wolley, *The Gentlewomans Companion; Or, a Guide to the Female Sex* (1675), 204–17.

[130] Henry Best's farm, the Elmswell estate, contained 1,293 acres and 28 perches, with additional acreage for pasture. See Best, *Farming and Memorandum Books*, pp. xxiii, 139.

[131] Som. RO, DD/SF 4515, no. 24, Mary Clarke to Edward Clarke, 7 Sept. 1694.

[132] D. Souden, 'Migrants and the Population Structure in English Towns', in P. Clark (ed.), *The Transformation of English Provincial Towns, 1600–1800* (1984), 142–51.

seeking a new household at the end of their term. First, the freedom to leave exerted a slight upward pressure on female wages. Employers disliked training new maidservants each year, and consequently used increased wages as bait to persuade servants to stay. Henry Best, who kept 'two good lusty mayde-servants', noted that Priscilla Browne was first hired (in November 1638) at 18*s.* a year plus a shilling for a godspenny. The second year she received 24*s.*, and the third year, 28*s.* plus 2*s.* for a godspenny. Had she stayed another year, Best would have paid her 38*s.*, and a shilling for a godspenny.[133]

Servants' freedom to migrate encouraged employers to provide adequate food and accommodation, since good living conditions offered a strong inducement to young people to renew their annual contracts.[134] Geographical mobility also presented unmarried women with a wider pool of eligible men, an important consideration since many met their future husbands in or around the households where they served. Some women apparently valued their independence for its own sake. A Devon maidservant, hired to spin by the week, told the courts that although she had been spinning for Joan Bennet and her husband for six weeks, she could 'go from them at every week's end if she pleases'.[135]

Although young women in life-stage service moved frequently from one household to another, their mobility did not enable them to command the same wages as their male counterparts.[136] It is not a coincidence that gender differentials in servants' income were similar to those prevailing for other waged occupations at the time, for it was an economic axiom that female workers should be paid no more than one-half to two-thirds as much as males for comparable work.[137] Maidservants' 'job descriptions' also ensured that they would be undervalued economically as a group. Since housewifery was a large component of every type of female service, maidservants' work took on the negative connotations of female domestic labour, including the assumption that housework was unpaid because it was not really 'work' at all. Moreover, the fact that young women living away from home had few options aside from service was reinforced by statutory law. These factors

[133] Best, *Farming and Memorandum Books*, 139. A godspenny was a cash payment whose acceptance signified that the servant accepted the service contract.

[134] Kussmaul, *Servants in Husbandry*, 40.

[135] Devon RO, Chanter 866, Consistory Court Depositions 1634–40, *Bennet* v. *Deymont*, 28 Nov. 1634 (not foliated or paginated).

[136] For comparison of female and male servants' wages from different geographical regions see M. Roberts, 'Wages and Wage-earners in England, 1563–1725', D.Phil. diss., University of Oxford (1981), 188. See further Ch. 5 below.

[137] Roberts, 'Wages and Wage-Earners', 184–8.

combined to create a bottomless pool of adolescent servile labour which depressed female wages in normal times. Only in exceptional circumstances, such as the extreme scarcity of male agricultural labour during the Civil War, was there a temporary rise in maidservants' wages.[138]

What was life like for young women in service? Accounts gleaned from court records tend to single out instances of cruel or exploitative employers and blatant cases of physical and sexual abuse. In contrast, contemporary memoirs and letters assumed that the generous and affectionate treatment of maidservants was the norm as well as the ideal. Since service was such a common experience, it is hardly surprising that the physical and psychological treatment of servants varied from one household to another. Nevertheless, certain characteristics of good and bad employers appear regularly in seventeenth-century records. Contemporary conduct books, domestic manuals, and female memoirs stressed what might be called the 'maternalistic' obligations of mistresses towards their maids, including their literate and religious education. But the responsibilities *in loco parentis* of the 'good mistress' went far beyond literacy and vocational training. These supererogatory duties could perhaps be summed up in young women's expectation of friendship from their employers. Thomas Tusser listed friendship between maidservant and mistress among his 'huswifely admonitions':

> Good servants hope justly some friendship to feele,
> And looke to have favour what time they do weele.[139]

Leonard Wheatcroft and his wife, visiting their daughters Anna and Esther in service at Glapwell and Routhorne, observed that their children were 'very much made of, to our joy and comfort'.[140]

Young women themselves voiced positive expectations about life in service. Indeed, many sought a berth in another household to escape problems at home. Sixteen-year-old Alice Smyth, plagued by her parents' attempts to force her to marry George Plant, begged her sister to let Alice stay with her 'til she did provide her self a service to live in whereby she might avoid the company of . . . George Plant with an intent to go home to her father & mother no more 'til . . . Plant had forsaken her'.[141] Alice Hayes suffered

[138] Best, *Farming and Memorandum Books*, 138; Bodl., MS Clarendon 48, fo. 308^{v}.
[139] T. Tusser, *Five Hundred Points of Good Husbandry* (Oxford, 1984), 166.
[140] Wheatcroft, 'Autobiography' (1899), 44.
[141] OA, MS Oxf. Dioc. papers c. 26, 1629–34, fo. 318.

under the 'sharp Government' of a stepmother after her own mother died, so she too left home at age 16 and went into service.[142]

Friendship between maidservant and mistress was expressed in many ways: as an employer's benevolent interest in maidservants' spiritual and material well-being, the care for servants' health, the bestowal of gifts and other perquisites. Fringe benefits of service—including cast-off clothing, tips, legacies, and other windfalls—might amount to several years' contractual wages in value. Some maidservants received substantial legacies from grateful mistresses. Alice Owen left legacies of £10 each to her two personal maidservants, twice as much as she bequeathed to the parson and schoolmaster.[143]

Many of the material profits that accrued to maidservants were the outward expression of an emotional bond rather than a cash payment for services rendered. Indeed, legacies and other perquisites were bestowed on a more egalitarian basis to the two sexes than annual wages. The mistress–maid relationship was an intensely personal one: employers' wills often mentioned the good qualities of those servants on whom they bestowed special legacies.[144]

Such 'maternalistic' assumptions helped justify young women's low rate of pay. Like waitresses nowadays, maidservants were allotted a meagre basic salary, with the rest of their earnings made up through perquisites which were rewards for merit and loyalty. Although the arrangement was flexible and personal, it could be autocratic and arbitrary. It may also have conditioned some maidservants' alleged propensity to take small amounts of food as part of their 'salary'. Concerning the hiring of maids, Henry Best warned farmers 'neaver to hyre such as are too neare theire freinds, for occasion is sayd to make a theefe, and being hyred yow are not to committe over much to theire trust, but to see into all things your selfe and to keepe as much as yow can under locke and key'.[145] As in other occupations where low rates of pay were the norm, some servants apparently regarded petty theft of food and supplies as an unofficial perquisite.

Maidservants expected their mistresses to show concern for their advancement in life, which might mean promotion in the service hierarchy, help in launching a vocation, or an advantageous marriage. In 1694, Mary Clarke conferred with her maidservant Rose about the latter's best options for a career on her departure from the Clarke household. While Rose suggested she might 'get up mantua making and head dressing at Taunton', Mrs

[142] A. Hayes, *A Legacy or Widow's Mite* (1723), 14.

[143] Guildhall, MS 6817, fo. 64.

[144] See, for example, the will of Mary Rich, fourth countess of Warwick (1678), PRO, Prob. 11/356, 316.

[145] Best, *Farming and Memorandum Books*, 140.

Clarke thought that service with her neighbour Mrs Sandford offered Rose a better opportunity. 'Providence that has so luckily guided her here will I believe send her a good husband, Mrs. Sandford being very fortunate in marrying her maids well.' Later, Mary Clarke proudly reported that she had found Rose 'a very good place where she is hired'.[146]

It was customary for employers to offer monetary contributions to valued maidservants on certain occasions, particularly upon their marriage. Such gifts could represent a sizeable investment. The rector of Myddle, who had 'adopted' the daughter of a poor parishioner as a domestic servant, gave her a dowry amounting to about £60 on her marriage to a farmer.[147]

While some young women benefited from a stint in service, others were less fortunate. In the hands of unscrupulous men and women, the quasi-parental authority wielded by employers could lead to economic, physical, or sexual abuse. Although the annual contract, which could be terminated at a quarter's notice from either party, offered women an escape route, even a few months' time gave some employers sufficient scope to persecute female servants under their governance.

Court records tell of young women who were sent away without being paid the wages due to them, while others were beaten beyond the 'moderate' level which authorities deemed necessary to maintain household discipline. A typical entry records Nathaniel Cole's appearance at the Bourne, Lincolnshire, sessions in 1677, 'for turning of Elizabeth Remmington his servant out of his house & service before the end of her terme without any reasonable cause showne [and] . . . withholding and deteyning from the said Elizabeth Rimmington the summe of 2 li. 1s. 10d. wages &c'.[148]

While complaints of financial double-dealing or physical mistreatment came from servants of either sex, maidservants had one problem which was not usually shared by their male counterparts. Sexual abuse was an ever-present hazard from masters, masters' sons, and fellow servants. In the case of Elizabeth Rimmington, her sexual vulnerability was probably the ultimate cause of her dismissal without wages. An earlier sessions minute required William Hakeman of Bourne to give a recognizance of £20 'pro bastardia Eliz. Rimington'.[149]

Many kinds of contemporary documents record the sexual abuse of

[146] Somerset RO, DD/SF 4515, nos. 24 and 25, Mary Clarke to Edward Clarke, 7 and 15 Sept. 1694.

[147] Gough, *Myddle*, 41.

[148] *Minutes of Proceedings in Quarter Sessions held for the Parts of Kesteven in the County of Lincoln, 1674–95*, 2 parts, ed. S. A. Peyton, Lincoln Record Society, 25–6 (1931), i. 62. This sum would have represented at least one year's wage.

[149] Ibid., i. 37. See also S. Amussen, 'Punishment, Discipline, and Power: The Social Meanings of Violence in Early Modern England', *JBS*, 34 (1995), 15–16.

maidservants. Their vulnerability to rape or seduction was a commonplace not only of court records, but of proverbs, jokes, anecdotes, conduct books, and private correspondence. Gouge warned masters to prevent male servants under their care from the 'too too frequent' sin of seducing female servants. Not only was the master's house dishonoured; 'the maid so defiled is oft disabled to doe her service well; nay many times the charge of the childe lieth upon the master. Thus the shame and dishonour, griefe and vexation, losse and dammage all meet together, the more to gall & pierce him to the very heart.'[150]

Masters often bore the blame for servants' pregnancies precisely because it was well known that they or their sons were as likely as menservants to be the guilty agents. Sir Nicholas Le Strange recorded the saying that 'crackt chambermaids are commonly the masters whore, the serving-mans wife'.[151] That this proverb reflected reality is illustrated by Sir Ralph Verney's request to a friend to find him a maidservant who would 'fit' him as a whore, as his former maidservant had done.[152]

Female servants' vulnerability to sexual abuse was sometimes exacerbated by family living arrangements. In small households, the maidservant might share a room or even a bed with an adult male. Whatever the household size, however, no social class offered maidservants a haven from sexual pursuit. Even when families provided segregated sleeping quarters, élite men still assumed that women of the labouring classes were sexually available. The most obvious variation between social classes was not men's attitude to female servants, but rather the extent to which wealthy masters could bribe or threaten their way out of a shameful predicament.[153] Both secular and ecclesiastical courts record numerous cases of masters and other males whose sexual exploitation of maidservants was discovered—usually when the woman became pregnant—and exposed to public censure.[154] Service in a household was supposed to be a refuge for young unmarried women; yet, for some, it was more hazardous than the life of a vagrant.

Although service could provide experience in industrial or agrarian skills, or increase the opportunities for finding a husband, it was unlikely to give women the formal qualifications which led to a professional occupational

[150] W. Gouge, *Of Domesticall Duties* (1622), 630.

[151] Le Strange, *'Merry Passages and Jeasts'*, 161 (615).

[152] M. Slater, 'The Weightiest Business: Marriage in an Upper-Gentry Family in Seventeenth-Century England', *Past and Present*, 72 (1976), 39.

[153] See, for example, *The Letter Book of Sir John Parkhurst*, ed. R. Houlbrooke, Norfolk Record Society, 43 (1974), 259.

[154] See, for example, Essex RO, Q/SR 88/84 [1584]; Q/SR 124/63, 63a; Q/SR 153/29, 30 [1601]; Q/SR 126/34, 34a; Q/SR 124/61, 62 [1593]; Norfolk RO, AYL 347.

identity. Instead, the flexible multi-occupational nature of female service or apprenticeship, with its core of housewifery, was intended to foster a woman's probable career as the wife of a labourer or artisan when service ended with marriage at about age 25. As will be seen, married women's work routine was very similar to that of maidservants in its motley character. The chief difference marriage made was to add supervisory responsibilities and 'sexual work'—child-bearing and child-rearing—to a young woman's domestic tasks.

Many women delayed marriage until their late twenties, and a significant proportion never married at all. The custom of late marriage was closely linked to the prevailing low rates of wages for maidservants. Women were expected to save out of their earnings for a dowry, but with maidservants' salaries at rock-bottom, they found it difficult to save anything at all. In church court interrogatories, most maidservants described themselves as 'little or nothing worth, their debts paid' or 'worth nothing except their apparel'. Hence the process of saving for marriage was liable to be a protracted one. Even by their late twenties, a substantial minority were financially unable (or temperamentally unwilling) to marry. For these women, life-stage service was likely to turn into a lifetime career.

COURTSHIP

Regardless of their social rank, women regarded courtship as a critical life phase, whose outcome would determine their future happiness and success as adults. In terms of their prescribed role in the courtship process, young women had more in common with those of their own sex than with the men who were their social equals. Nevertheless, courtship conventions of the gentry and nobility differed markedly from those of the labouring classes. Elite women married at a younger age than their plebeian counterparts, after a briefer courtship period. Compared with plebeian women, gentlewomen were permitted less privacy and physical intimacy with their suitors. Among the prosperous classes, parents and other kin played a more prominent role in initiating and concluding a match. And while all social ranks were concerned to some degree with the social and financial aspects of marriage, the upper classes were apt to place greater emphasis on economic matters, when weighed against young peoples' personal feelings.

In many respects, women of the labouring classes had more scope for independent action than their wealthier counterparts. Popular literature often contrasted the matrimonial slavery of daughters of the aristocracy

FIG. 11. Formal courtship. Woodcuts in popular ballads illustrate different aspects of courtship. Here an élite couple are depicted formally as though in a publicly sanctioned courtship

with the relative freedom of choice enjoyed by poor women. As the tragic heroine of the ballad *Loves Downfall* lamented,

> Would I had been a scullian-maid
> or a servant of low degree,
> Then need not I have been afraid,
> To ha' loved him that would love me.[155]

The class differences portrayed in ballads and other fictional genres are corroborated by other types of sources, such as the records of the ecclesiastical courts.

For the most part, our narrative will describe the experiences of the majority: the daughters of cottagers and labourers, artisans and shopkeepers and small landholders. Moreover, we shall try to interpret the evidence from the female point of view, showing the range of ways women intervened to influence the courtship process and promote their own interests. Our attempt to construct a female-centred analysis of courtship among the labouring classes raises historiographical as well as historical issues.

[155] *The Roxburghe Ballads*, ed. W. Chappell and J. Ebsworth, 9 vols. in 8 (London and Hertford, 1866–99), vi. 267.

Historians such as Laurence Stone have stressed the ideals and behaviour of the gentry; within this élite framework they have concerned themselves with men's activities, omitting any consideration of female agency.[156] This model posits a society in which parents—meaning fathers—controlled the match-making process on behalf of children. Although a son might help choose and court his prospective mate, a daughter was limited to a passive role, with at most a power of veto.[157] While several scholars have challenged Stone's model for its class bias, asserting that different courtship patterns were customary among the middling and plebeian classes, they have been slower to explore gender differences in courtship roles.[158]

If we turn to contemporary sources produced by and for young women, we find a paradigm which gives much greater scope to female agency. Indeed, the adolescent mythology of courtship was apt to run to the opposite extreme, fostering a romantic ideal which exaggerated female authority and control. According to literary models, which circulated among plebeian women as well as élite female readers, courtship was the only female life-stage in which the usual relations of dominance and subjection between the two sexes were inverted. While the transient process lasted, women were supposedly 'on top' of the gender hierarchy.[159]

For most young women, reality corresponded neither to the patriarchal ideal of parental control nor the literary pattern of romantic love. Although ordinary women did have some degree of agency, it arose not from an inversion of the gender hierarchy, but rather from structural factors that shaped the parameters of plebeian courtship. Moreover, the romantic ideal, which attributed immoderate powers and absolute control to women (and a corresponding degree of subjection in their suitor-servants), was a misleading model of power relations between the sexes during the courtship period. In real life, plebeian women's autonomy carried them into a minefield of hazards over which they had little or no control.

The most important structural factor that shaped female adolescence and

[156] The works of Laurence Stone contain the most extensive exposition of the élite 'patriarchal' view of courtship; see relevant sections of *The Crisis of the Aristocracy* (Oxford, 1965), *The Family, Sex and Marriage in England, 1500–1800*, *Road to Divorce: England, 1530–1987* (Oxford, 1990), and *Uncertain Unions: Marriage in England, 1660–1753* (Oxford, 1992).

[157] For a debate on agency in courtship among the élite, see Slater, 'The Weightiest Business', 25–54, and S. Mendelson, 'Debate: The Weightiest Business: Marriage in an Upper-Gentry Family in Seventeenth-Century England', *Past and Present*, 85 (1979), 126–35.

[158] K. Wrightson, *English Society, 1580–1680* (1982); R. Houlbrooke, *The English Family, 1450–1700* (1984), chapter 4; M. Ingram, *Church Courts, Sex and Marriage in England, 1570–1640* (Cambridge, 1987), chs. 6–7.

[159] For the 'romantic' paradigm, see Mendelson, 'Debate: The Weightiest Business', 128–31.

early adulthood was a relatively late age at first marriage.[160] Combined with the practice of sending young women out to service from approximately their mid-teens, one effect of this pattern was to remove most plebeian parents from their daughters' sphere of influence in initiating a match. Thus courtship comprised a major life-stage for the majority of the female populace, as women were left to their own resources for a lengthy period between puberty and marriage at about age 25 or 26. During the ten or more years of courtship, young women had many opportunities for varied experiences with different suitors, and a good deal of scope for personal choice.

In accord with this demographic pattern, young people created their own plebeian 'culture of courtship' which included unmarried youth of both sexes from about age 15 to 30. Diaries, popular literature, and church court depositions all refer to numerous group and individual venues for socializing between the sexes. Wakes, weddings, village dances, and other local ceremonials all provided courtship opportunities.[161] Lovers accompanied each other to markets and fairs, where suitors treated their female companions to food and drink, and presented them with 'fairings' or gifts. Several seasonal holidays, particularly Mayday and Whit Sunday, had specific associations with popular courtship rituals.[162]

Work was one of the commonest locales where plebeian young women might encounter potential suitors. Alice Hayes met her first husband while serving in the family of a justice of the peace.[163] Depositions in spousals disputes in the church courts often mention that the two parties had been domestic servants living in the same house, or agricultural servants working in the fields together.[164] Dairying was a well-known courtship venue: a popular saying referred to 'creampot love', defined as what 'young fellows pretend to dairy-maids, to get cream and other good things of them'.[165] Haymaking was also notorious as a site for young people's amorous activities. Indeed, the entire outdoors served as the theatre of plebeian

[160] For fluctuations in average age at first marriage in the early modern period, see Wrigley and Schofield, *Population History*, 423. Wrigley and Schofield's figures for 18th-cent. women have been questioned by B. Hill, 'The Marriage Age of Women and the Demographers', *History Workshop*, 28 (1989), 129–54.

[161] For Mayday and Sunday maypole dancing, see R. Baxter, *Reliquiae Baxterianae* (1696); J. Bunyan, *Grace Abounding* (1962), 14; see also J. Brand, *Observations on Popular Antiquities*, 2 vols. (1813), i, 193–204. For other venues see Martindale, *Life of Adam Martindale*, 16.

[162] For popular seasonal ceremonials connected with courtship customs, women's love divinations, and similar topics, see Brand, *Observations on Popular Antiquities*, i. 47, 179–93, 226–32, 264–7, 451–2; ii. 322–3.

[163] Hayes, *A Legacy*, 17.

[164] For example, OA, MS Oxf. Dioc. papers c. 27, 1634–40, fo. 11; OA, MS Archd. papers Oxon. c. 118, 1616–1620, fo. 2; Bodl., MS Rawlinson B. 382, fo. 294^{v}.

[165] J. Ray, *A Collection of English Proverbs* (1678), 69.

courtship: 'to give a woman a green gown' was a euphemism for rural lovemaking.[166]

In contrast, daughters of the aristocracy experienced courtship in a way that was much closer to the 'patriarchal' model. Although child marriages were the exception rather than the rule by the seventeenth century, some parents still arranged matches for daughters as soon as they reached puberty.[167] Because of their relative youth and their physical and financial dependence on parents and other kin, women from the highest ranks had least agency in courtship. In theory at least, they were continually chaperoned so as to prevent private meetings with suitors on their own initiative.[168] They might be allowed to veto a disliked match, but had very limited powers to insist on their own choice.[169]

Nevertheless, even among the nobility, women sometimes followed the same pattern as their plebeian counterparts. When Ann Hyde became pregnant by the future James II, her father's high political status ensured that the couple would marry despite parental disapproval, just as pregnancy frequently triggered marriage among the labouring classes. Mary Boyle eventually persuaded her father to let her marry a younger son, an unequal match for a daughter of the wealthy earl of Cork, but she was the only sibling among seven daughters who succeeded in frustrating her father's matrimonial plans for her.[170] Widows of the middling and upper ranks who contemplated a second marriage, however, had less to fear from the objections of family members, and consequently enjoyed more scope for independent choice than those women who had never been married.[171]

Mothers and other female relations among the aristocracy were as likely as fathers to play an authoritative role in regulating young women's matrimonial choices according to the tenets of patriarchy. Female memoirs and correspondence tell of many young gentlewomen like Lady Anne Delaval, who recounted in her diary how she was thwarted by her guardian in her desire to marry Lord Annesley, and later forced to wed Mr Delaval:

> Because I once disobey'd my aunt in not giveing my selfe to a young man that she had chose for me (who was indeed both hansome, rich, and great; yet one who being

[166] W. Smith (ed.), *Oxford Dictionary of English Proverbs* (Oxford, 1952), 266.

[167] Mendelson, *Mental World*, 67.

[168] For example, *Memoirs of Anne, Lady Halkett*, 14–15.

[169] See, for example, *Advice to Amabella. Sir Anthony Benn to His Daughter*, ed. B. Carroll (Clayton, Victoria, 1990), 3–4; S. Bufford, *An Essay against Unequal Marriages* (1692), 56–117.

[170] Mendelson, *Mental World*, 64–77.

[171] See, for example, Mendelson, 'Weightiest Business', 132; BL, Sloane MS 4454, Diary of Katherine Austen, fos. 40, 50, 68^{v}, etc.

off a contrary relighon to mine, my consience wou'd not suffer me to be ty'd too) she crosses me now out of revenge for my disobeydience to her.[172]

The deferential structures of class and age which governed élite courtship sometimes led women to play very different roles as marriageable daughters and as respectable matriarchs. When they were girls, both Mary Boyle and Lady Mary Pierrepont had defied their fathers and eloped with favoured suitors. But as parents and guardians, Mary Boyle (now the countess of Warwick) and Lady Mary Pierrepont (now Lady Mary Wortley Montagu) each insisted on controlling the matches of daughters and nieces who were in their care. Lady Mary Wortley Montagu strongly disapproved when her daughter copied her own youthful insubordination in marrying for love.[173]

For the middling ranks, the daughters of yeomen and prosperous urban tradesmen, the management of courtship fell somewhere between élite and plebeian ideals, sharing some characteristics with each. Young women often had a say in the choice between suitors, although parents insisted on becoming actively involved at an earlier stage than in the case of plebeian families. The ambiguities in the roles of both daughters and parents led to a good deal of familial negotiation and strife, which we find documented in numerous 'spousals' or betrothal disputes in the church courts.[174] In a York matrimonial cause, for example, 16-year-old Dorothy Cawton had promised Thomas Driffield, her uncle and guardian, that she would not marry contrary to his choice. Meanwhile, however, she had pledged her faith and troth in an exchange of vows with her own chosen suitor, William Hewytson. Moreover, she had sent him a 'silk point with silver tag' in token of her liking, and had allowed him to call the marriage banns.[175]

Litigants' depositions in *Hewytson* v. *Cawton* betray conflicting views not only about Hewytson's suitability as a marriage partner, but about the meaning of the courtship process itself. Driffield offered a commodified view of the affair, in which his niece Dorothy Cawton's dowry of about

[172] E. Delaval, *The Meditations of Lady Elizabeth Delaval*, ed. D. Greene, Surtees Society, 190 (1975), 112; see also pp. 166–74. For an example of a gentry family's matrimonial negotiations, see V. Larminie, *Wealth, Kinship and Culture: The Seventeenth-Century Newdigates of Arbury and their World* (1995), 67–77.

[173] See Mendelson, *Mental World*, 64–76, 111–12; M. Wortley Montagu, *The Complete Letters of Lady Mary Wortley Montagu*, ed. R. Halsband, 3 vols. (1965), i. 148, 156; ii. 128 n. 3.

[174] See, for example, OA, MS Oxf. Dioc. papers c. 26, 1629–34, fos. 9^v–12^v., 27–32, 61–2, 113–18, 120–5, 140–1, 296^v–297, 308–9^v, 315–17; OA, MS Archd. papers Oxon. c. 118, 1616–1620, fos. 1–2, 68–71; Bodl. MS Rawlinson B 382, fos. 1–21, 311–36, 361–96, 426–37, 438–512, 520–41.

[175] Borthwick Institute, CP, series H, Archiepiscopal Cause Papers 1–36, 1600–1, no. 3, *William Hewytson* v. *Dorothy Cawton*. In this series, documents are arranged as bundles of cause papers, rather than in bound deposition books.

£100, rather than her person, was the object of rivalry between William Hewytson and Driffield's own son. In her personal answer to court officials, however, Dorothy Cawton presented herself as the object of her lover's ardent quest, and as the semi-willing conspirator in a series of romantic episodes, including a clandestine rendezvous from which Hewytson carried her off on horseback for a weekend stay at his father's house.

In the space between the competing discourses of her uncle and her lover, Dorothy Cawton found scope for active agency, which she expressed through traditional modes of plebeian courtship. The revelations of her own feelings included her gift of a token to her lover, a lengthy visit to her suitor's house, the exchange of vows in the customary 'handfasting' ritual, and the acceptance of a 'gold or gilded ring' which she put on her finger. Despite her verbal pledges of obedience to her uncle, Cawton's actions reveal her grasp of a large repertoire of behavioural signals through which she could express her own choice, and exert some influence on the events that determined her future.

Other daughters of the middling ranks also steered a course between the managerial efforts of parents and guardians and their own desires to direct their matrimonial fate. Elizabeth Clarke allowed her parents to present a series of matches for her approval; after passively resisting them all, she eventually married her own choice. At this stage her mother apparently had come to feel that any match was better than none; Mrs Clarke commented that she hoped something would work out soon, because her daughter Elizabeth was getting to be 'past the best'.[176] Like Dorothy Osborne and other young women from the minor gentry and yeomanry, Elizabeth Clarke achieved her goal by patiently out-waiting her parents and friends.[177]

In plebeian society, most daughters had a wider scope for independent action than their counterparts among the middling and upper ranks. Forced marriage arranged by parents was a relatively rare phenomenon, although instances are occasionally found. The case of *Smith* v. *Plant*, a suit for annulment in the Oxford diocesan court, exemplifies the unusual circumstances in which forced marriage could occur at lower levels of society, and demonstrates the negative reaction of the community to an extreme case of

[176] *The Correspondence of John Locke and Edward Clarke*, ed. B. Rand (Cambridge, Mass., 1927), 594.

[177] For other examples from the minor gentry and middling ranks, see D. Osborne, *Letters from Dorothy Osborne to Sir William Temple, 1652–54*, ed. G. Moore Smith (Oxford, 1928); OA, MS Oxf. Dioc. papers c. 27, fos. 328–58; G. Holles, *Memorials of the Holles Family*, ed. A. Wood, Camden Society, 3rd ser., 55 (1937), 228–9.

parental coercion.[178] William and Joan Smith, a poor couple who ran the Cuddesdon mill, arranged a match between their 16-year-old daughter Alice and George Plant, a youth of about 20 who had just inherited a house and land worth £12 per annum. Alice's mother Joan used all possible means to put pressure on Alice, although the latter had already contracted herself to one Matthew Langston. Testimony reported that Joan Smith had shut her daughter up in the house, had beaten her and tied her to a table, and threatened that Alice would starve and beg if she continued to refuse the match with George.[179] Meanwhile Alice asked her married sister to take her in until Alice could 'provide herself a service to live in'. Because Alice's sister was just about to give birth, her husband vetoed the idea.[180]

On 1 February 1629, Alice was married to George Plant, weeping and pleading with her parents all the way to church, as witnesses reported. Her father was inclined to relent, but her mother replied that Alice was still young and might learn to love George. In the event, Alice allegedly left George after living with him for two or three months, and started cohabiting with her contracted lover, Matthew Langston. By the time the case reached the courts in 1633, witnesses reported that Joan Smith was condemned by the local community for forcing her daughter to marry against her will, that Alice had informed the entire neighbourhood that she 'had never suffered the said George to lie with her', and that Alice had had three children by Matthew Langston.[181] In her deposition, Joan Smith dramatically confessed her fault, and the courts apparently agreed to an annulment, since Alice married Matthew Langston in a church ceremony a few months later.[182] This attempt at plebeian forced marriage went as far as it did only because Alice was young and living at home, dependent on her parents. Nevertheless, the union was such an obvious failure and so universally condemned that Alice achieved something akin to a court-sanctioned divorce.

Forced marriage among the labouring classes was thus the exception that proved the rule. In conformity with plebeian attitudes, contemporary ballads invariably portray cases of forced marriage as the evil and tragic consequence of parental greed. The ballad narrative usually ends in universal slaughter, as the lovers die of suicide and their parents pine away from grief

178 OA, MS Oxf. Dioc. papers c. 26, 1629–34, fos. 316^{v}–18^{v}, 326^{v}–7; OA, MS Oxf. Dioc. papers c. 27, 1634–9, fos. 110^{v}–12^{v}, 114^{v}–15, 116^{v}–17.

179 Ibid., fos. 114^{v}–15.

180 OA, MS Oxf. Dioc. papers c. 26, 1629–34, fo. 318.

181 OA, MS Oxf. Dioc. papers c. 27, 1634–39, fos. 114^{v}–15.

182 Ibid., fos. 326^{v}–7; OA, MS Oxf. Dioc. papers c. 27, 1634–39, fos. 114^{v}–15.

and guilt. Moreover, just as in the actual case of *Smith* v. *Plant*, parents in the idealized scenarios of popular literature were condemned by society:

> None sought to remedy their pain
> nor to their sorrows give relief
> that had thus through their tyranny
> brought their own child to misery.[183]

For most women, courtship was more like a lengthy series of private negotiations than a *fait accompli* arranged by parents, or a one-way relationship of dominance and subjection between 'mistress' and 'servant'. Because the quest for a mate was spread out over many years, it usually included several sequences or episodes before the woman either settled upon a partner to marry, or failed to find such a partner. Throughout all the stages of this process, women were active in negotiation and choice, and in signalling and controlling their preferences. The repertoire of gesture through which women mediated the sequence of courtship was generally less overt—and indeed deliberately more ambiguous—than the forceful role allotted to men; nevertheless women's active participation in the process was equally important.

Whatever their social rank, women were not supposed to take the initiative in the first stages of courtship. Yet they had a part to play from the outset in judging the merits and fidelity of their suitors. In fact plebeian courtship involved testing rituals by both sexes. The male task was to solicit as vigorously as possible. 'Courting and wooing brings dallying and doing' as the proverb put it.[184] Women rated their suitors accordingly: the more laborious the process, the more honourable the courtship. Leonard Wheatcroft proudly tallied up his travels during his two-year courtship of his wife. 'If you would know how many times I went a wooing, you shall find so many slashes upon an Ash Tree at Winster Towne End: and how many miles I travelled for her sake: they were 400 and 40, and odd.'[185] During the courtship process, women considered daily visits their due, as ballads and other popular sources inform us.[186] Similar judgements were expressed by élite women. Lucy Hutchinson wrote of her courtship by John Hutchinson that it would make a 'true history of a more handsome management of love than the best romances describe'.[187]

Women's role was not passive, but active in a complementary way: their

[183] Bodl., Douce Ballads 1, fo. 117^{v}. [184] Ray, *Proverbs*, 57.
[185] 'Autobiography of Leonard Wheatcroft' (1896), 45.
[186] For example, *The Ingenius Bragadocio*, Bodl., Don. b. 13, fo. 41.
[187] Cited in Mendelson, 'Debate: Marriage in an Upper-Gentry Family', 130 n. 27.

FIG. 12. Informal courtship. Private courtship was commonly allowed among plebeian couples, but it could be hazardous for young women

task was to scorn, jeer, and generally discourage the advances of a suitor. There is much evidence that the 'art of scorning', as popular sources called it, was practised by women of every social rank. As Shakespeare's Juliet remarks, 'if thou thinkst I am too quickly won, I'll frown and be perverse and say thee nay'. But in its most energetic and bantering form, scorning was especially characteristic of plebeian women. The duchess of Newcastle observed that 'the Way or Manner of Courtship amongst the Inferiour sort of People in E.[ngland] is Scolding, they Scold themselves into matrimony'; proverbial wisdom noted that 'by biting and scratching, cats and dogs come together', meaning that 'men and maidservants that wrangle and quarrel most one with other . . . are often observed to marry together'.[188]

Feminine scorn and masculine diligence were two halves of a ceremonial trial by ordeal. The female role was the more difficult of the two, requiring a finely honed judgement to display the exact degree of scorn necessary to turn away undesirable suitors, while keeping a desirable suitor attracted long enough to test his sincerity and his fidelity. Courtship was generally a protracted process, often played out without parental interference and advice; consequently it involved many factors which women were unable

[188] M. Cavendish, duchess of Newcastle, *CCXI Sociable Letters* (1664), 87; Ray, *Proverbs*, 110.

to control. Thus, plebeian women's capacity for independent action entailed the fact that there was greater scope for matters to go wrong. Moreover, the process was far more hazardous for women than for men, because of women's sexual and economic vulnerability.

Given the circumstances of plebeian courtship, it is noteworthy that feminine collective wisdom expressed a preference for constancy over passionate sexual love: 'Love me little and love me long'; 'Hot love is soon cold'; 'Love of lads and fire of chats is soon in and soon out'; 'Lads love's a busk of broom, hot awhile and soon done.'[189] This female order of priorities made sense in view of the length of the average courtship, which might easily drag on for several years until a wedding at the church door was achieved.[190] Women were particularly at risk in the negotiation of their sexuality. Of course the dangers of men's sexual aggression were by no means limited to courtship; as we have seen, men regarded female servants as sexually available almost by definition. Yet the management of sexuality within the context of courtship was more problematic for women, because the boundaries between the forbidden and the permitted were much more ambiguous.

Although 'bundling' (a night of courting, fully clothed, which stopped short of intercourse) or its equivalent was widely practised by plebeian couples, and was tacitly condoned by society at large, women knew that the full expression of their sexuality during courtship was extremely hazardous.[191] Aside from the danger of pregnancy, young women who sued for their reputation in the church courts often mentioned that a sexual slander had damaged their matrimonial prospects.[192] To make matters more complicated, issues of sexuality had an equivocal status after the couple had gone through a ceremony of 'spousals' or engagement.

It is not a coincidence that the betrothal ritual which entailed the ceremonial exchange of vows in front of witnesses, termed 'spousals' or 'handfasting' by contemporaries, was also called 'to be made sure'. An account of the circumstances surrounding an Oxfordshire matrimonial case shows the extent to which the ritual was an integral part of female culture which could

[189] Ray, *Proverbs*, 54.

[190] For some of the social and legal ambiguities inherent in the period between 'spousals' (betrothal) and the solemnization of marriage at the church door, see Ingram, *Church Courts, Sex and Marriage*, 129–36.

[191] L. Wheatcroft, *The Courtship Narrative of Leonard Wheatcroft*, ed. G. Parfitt and R. Houlbrooke (Reading, 1986), 21; see also A. Macfarlane, *Marriage and Love in England, 1300–1840* (Oxford, 1986), 298; Stone, *Uncertain Unions*, 9; J. Gillis, *For Better, For Worse: British Marriages, 1600 to the Present* (Oxford, 1985), 30–1.

[192] See, for example, GLRO, DL/C 630, Consistory Court Depositions, 1632–4, fos. 8–8^{v}; see also Ingram, *Church Courts, Sex and Marriage*, 310–11.

serve as an instrument for female agency in the courtship process. Details of the ceremony were passed on from one woman to another; the rite could be invoked as a way of mediating the timing of marriage, or of deploying the moral force of the community to sanction a particular match, especially if there was opposition from parents.

In 1634 Jane Little, a married woman aged 34, described how Mary Simpson (who lodged with her), had 'privately asked her what she should do to be sure to John Jarvis, for she feared (as she then said) she was with child by him'. Mrs Little told Mary that when she had been 'contracted or made sure' to her own husband, they had performed the following customary rite: 'they did break between them a piece of silver before witnesses and take each other to be husband and wife and promised to marry each other and not forsake one another so long as they lived'. Mary then asked Mrs Little to lend her a groat (a silver coin worth 4*d.*) to give to John Jarvis 'to the end it might be broke between them, and that they might be made sure together'.[193] Mary gave the borrowed coin to John Jarvis, who was sitting by the fire talking to Jane Little's husband. When John asked Mary what she wanted him to do with the groat, she replied: 'to break between us and make all things sure that we may cross your mother'. They then went through the ceremony as Jane Little had outlined it, with Jane and her husband as witnesses.[194] The ritual in this case had at least two covert purposes, serving as a manœuvre to foil parental opposition to the union, and an attempt to ensure its solemnization in church, now a more urgent matter because of Mary Simpson's pregnancy.

In some cases, women appear to have regarded the spousals ceremony as itself a cue to initiate sexual relations. The morning after overhearing what appeared to be lovemaking between Agnes Bennet and George Pearse, William Hixe joked with Agnes about her amorous activities, telling her that she had had 'a great deal of good sport the night before'. Agnes replied 'that it was nothing between those that were in love . . . that they were assured together meaning [as William Hixe understood] in marriage'.[195] There is a good deal of evidence that popular opinion held the pre-contract to be the decisive act of marriage, with the wedding at the church door regarded merely as a tying-up of loose ends.

Such sentiments explain why pre-marital sex at this stage in courtship was viewed with so much ambivalence. Some couples saw themselves as man and wife once contractual vows had been exchanged, and began to behave

[193] OA, MS Oxf. Dioc. papers c. 27, 1634–9, fo. 73. [194] Ibid., fos. 73–73^{v}.

[195] Devon RO, Chanter 866, Consistory Court Depositions 1634–40 (not foliated or paginated), *Pearse* v. *Bennett*, testimony of William Hixe, 14 Jan. 1635.

accordingly. In the Oxfordshire case cited above, Mary Simpson moved in with John Jarvis and his mother for an extended visit and began calling him 'husband', as neighbours reported. When her father dragged her out of St Martin's parish church in the middle of her attempt to marry John Jarvis, she shouted at her father in front of the entire congregation that John 'was her husband . . . and . . . if she were hindered by her father from being married to him the said Jervase she would notwithstanding lie with him the night following'.[196] Neighbours often perceived and described a couple as a matrimonial unit after a contract had been made: 'There was a fame and report . . . that Elizabeth Marshall and Thomas Humphreys were contracted together in marriage and were man and wife.'[197]

There was in fact a wide spectrum of opinion on the question of sexual relations between espoused couples; we can chart substantial variations not only by age and social rank, but also by geographical region.[198] Parents, the élite, women, and inhabitants of lowland regions generally insisted that sexual relations were taboo before marriage. But their complementary counterparts—young men, the lower ranks, and those who lived in the highland regions of England—were considerably more tolerant of pre-marital intercourse, and tended to assume that pregnancy would serve as a cue for a church marriage.[199]

Nevertheless, negative feelings about pre-marital sexuality were frequently expressed. When a young man told his father he had no choice but to marry the woman he had seduced, his father replied, 'Why, man, cannot . . . a man fall into a turd but must bind him to his nose as long as . . . he liveth?'[200] Moreover, a woman might be subjected to her own trial by ordeal, in which a potential suitor tested her chastity or sexual control. The feminine 'chastity test' is a common theme in contemporary ballads, jests, and anecdotes. One example from a jest book reveals the element of 'gamesmanship', especially on the part of men:

> A miller had wooed abundance of girls, and did lie with them, upon which he refused to marry them. But one girl he did solicit very much, but all would not do. Then he married her, and told her on the marriage-night, if she would have let him do as the rest did he would never have had her. 'By my troth, I thought so', says she, 'for I was served so by half a dozen before'.[201]

[196] OA, MS Oxf. Dioc. papers c. 27, 1634–9, fo. 67. [197] Ibid., fo. 288.

[198] R. Adair, *Courtship, Illegitimacy and Marriage in Early Modern England* (Manchester, 1996).

[199] For the complicated interplay between these factors see Ingram, *Church Courts, Sex and Marriage*, 219–37.

[200] Ibid., 203. [201] J. Wardroper, *Jest Upon Jest* (1970), 54.

The male rationale behind the test is revealed in a ballad entitled *The Credulous Virgins Complaint*:

> Whenas I did urge his former vow
> He said I pleaded all in vain
> If I'd by him be tempted now
> Others when married might do the same.[202]

The low rate of illegitimacy and high rate of bridal pregnancy makes us ask to what degree women—both as individuals and as a collective cultural force—were taking an active role in negotiating this dangerous situation. Women were aware that the 'chastity test' could be used as excuse for male duplicity or desertion. Some became victims of their lovers' deceit, lured into a sexual relationship by a promise of marriage. In a Devon case, Agnes Barons described how she had been betrothed and had had the banns published in church, 'and the man left [me] and refused to marry [me] after he had abused [me] and brought [me] with child'.[203] Certainly it was more prudent for a woman to refuse sexual relations until after marriage, as Alice Wheeler did. When her suitor James Myntey tried to persuade Alice to yield to him on the grounds that they were contracted, and therefore man and wife, she replied, 'I know . . . that I am your wife and you my husband, yet until such time as we are married [in church] you shall not have the use of my body'.[204]

Although plebeian daughters had a considerable degree of autonomy compared to their élite counterparts, they were by no means isolated from the help and interference of the community, especially in its female guise. Mothers were well known to hold a key place in the courtship process, lending their experience and skill as mediators between their daughters and the male world. As the proverb put it, 'he that would the daughter win, must with the mother first begin'.[205] Church court disputes also record numerous instances of intercession by other female relations and associates—aunts, grandmothers, sisters, and female neighbours and friends. A defamation suit reportedly originated with Elizabeth Marshall's hostility to Norrice Burdit 'because he was poor and sought to marry the sister of the

[202] Bodl., Douce Ballads 1, fo. 40.

[203] Devon RO, Chanter 866, Consistory Court Depositions 1634–40 (not foliated or paginated), cited in S. H. Mendelson, '"To Shift for a Cloak": Disorderly Women in the Church Courts', in V. Frith (ed.), *Women and History* (Toronto, 1995), 16.

[204] Wilts. RO, B/Misc. Ct. papers 29/47 (unfoliated), quoted in Ingram, *Church Courts, Sex and Marriage*, 228.

[205] Ray, *Proverbs*, 58.

said Elizabeth against her mother's and other friends' mind and wills, and thereupon to disgrace him she uttered the words [spoken]'.[206]

Aid and protection might be expressed as communal sanctions imposed on a couple who violated social or sexual mores by consorting together in suspicious circumstances.[207] But we can also catch glimpses of women's agency in the courtship process in more practical ways. Female relatives and friends were often involved in helping to ease young women's economic transition from cashless maidservant to mistress of a well-stocked household.

In general, labouring women had a say in their own matrimonial decisions because of their critical position in the family economy. If a woman had access to capital or material goods, she was in a strong position to influence the timing of matrimony. In the ballad 'Heartless Harry, or Doll's Earnest desire to be married', Doll catalogues her possession of the wherewithal to start a household, and finally persuades Harry to speed up the wedding date:

> I have wealth enough in store, the sum of forty shilling,
> With Piggs Ducks Geese and household-stuff
> All left by my good old grannum,
> And if this be not wealth enough, I've a noble also per annum.
> Nay, besides a little hutch, for thee and I to sleep in,
> Everyone hath not so much, when they begin house-keeping.[208]

A number of other ballads depict young women begging, borrowing, or inheriting household goods from an assortment of female relatives, declaring their intention of using their labour power to make ends meet.[209]

Among the artisan and labouring classes, testamentary suits reveal the value of household goods in bringing the courtships of plebeian women to a successful conclusion. In one case, a good feather bed worth three pounds and a large kettle formed the centre-piece of a fierce battle in the church court between a new bride and her brother.[210] The ownership of such goods might represent the potential for consummating an engagement in church, rather than waiting for years trying to save capital on a maidservant's or day-labourer's wages. Both popular sources and church court depositions give the impression that young women had an image in mind of the minimal

[206] OA, MS Oxf. Dioc. papers c. 26, 1629–34, fos. 90^{v}–1.

[207] For an example of collective enforcement of morality by matrons of an Oxfordshire parish, see OA, MS Oxf. Dioc. papers c. 26, 1629–34, fos. 141^{v}–8^{v}.

[208] Bodl., Douce Ballads 1, fo. 94.

[209] See, for example, Bodl., Douce Ballads 1, 'The Downright Wooing of Honest John and Betty', fo. 63; Bodl., Douce Ballads 2, 'The Maidens Sad Complaint', fo. 145.

[210] OA, MS Oxf. Dioc. papers c. 26, 1629–34, fos. 296^{v}–300, 304–6, 322–5^{v}, 348–348^{v}.

amount of resources in cash and goods needed to set up a household appropriate to their social level. The timing of the church wedding then depended on their achievement of this goal; if they could not reach the goal, the church wedding might never materialize, despite the existence of a pre-contract. Of those women who were unable to gather together the capital or goods to stock a household of their own, the majority would spend the rest of their lives as single women, working in the households of others.

As we have seen, women's life choices varied a great deal, depending on the grid of status and geography. Moreover, for each woman, whatever her class position, individual circumstances and the contingencies of family life made a difference in her situation. Socialized as they were according to social level and gender, nevertheless many young women had considerable scope for personal agency in the life-stages from infancy to adulthood.

3

ADULT LIFE

How did women see themselves as having attained adult status? Women conceptualized female maturity mainly in terms of being married, with a household to run, and possibly with children to rear and servants to oversee. 'As I am a woman, so I am also mistress of a large family', wrote Susanna Wesley to her husband in 1712, identifying her responsibilities as 'a trust by the great Lord of all the families both of heaven and earth'.[1] Marriage marked a break with the dependence of childhood and the semi-dependence of adolescence and service. It was a life-stage, 'the hon[ou]rable estate of marriage' as Alice Thornton termed it.[2]

Early modern society recognized adult status in several different ways. In legal terms, men and women became adult at various ages; in practice, participation in the adult world was delayed for both sexes.[3] Since the age at marriage was generally late, most historians have concluded that 'the transition from semi-dependency to full adult status' and 'equal participation' in the adult world was deferred until well beyond the age of 20.[4] Yet, for a woman, 'equal participation' was actually denied if she married, since she lost her status as a legal individual through the doctrine of coverture.[5] No adult woman, whether married or single, participated as a citizen in the same way as a man did, with the exception of the queen regnant. Nevertheless, a woman who was married enjoyed greater social status than a single one; as adults, women were accorded different degrees of independence and responsibility.

Women's ideas about adulthood ran directly counter to legal discourse, which insisted that marriage turned a woman into a non-person, her husband's dependant with no real will of her own. Ideally, a woman was to her husband what she had been to her father or master, except that she

[1] *The Journal of John Wesley*, ed. N. Curnock (Epworth, 1912), iii. 32.

[2] *The Autobiography of Mrs Alice Thornton*, ed. C. Jackson, Surtees Society, 62 (1873), 234.

[3] K. Thomas, *Age and Authority in Early Modern England* (1976), 12–30.

[4] R. Wall, 'Leaving Home and the Process of Household Formation in Pre-Industrial England', *Continuity and Change*, 2 (1987), 87; P. Collinson, *The Religion of Protestants: The Church in English Society, 1559–1625* (Oxford, 1982), 229.

[5] *Pace* Thomas, *Age and Authority*, 12; see Ch. 1, 'Contexts: The Law and its Administration'.

possessed even fewer adult rights and privileges than she had had before her marriage.

Since the bulk of the female population married in their mid-twenties, we shall define female adulthood as beginning at about age 25. Probably less than half the female population was over 25 years of age. At this age, women's lives diverged at each social level depending on their marital status. Some adult women remained single, for a range of reasons. Of those who married, not all found that marriage provided them with economic support. Many were deserted or widowed; these women might live lives similar to those of single women. Thus the 'godly wife and matron' beloved of the Protestant propagandists represented only a small group. Although much of the historical literature refers to all females in early modern society as though they were married women with supporting husbands, in fact such women were numerically a minority of the total female population. Marriage was a stage in many women's lives, but it did not and does not encapsulate the female condition.

During their reproductive years, women's lives differed more markedly from those of men than at any other stage. Heterosexuality entailed greater physical and social consequences for women than men. Between the menarche and the menopause, heterosexual intercourse could lead to pregnancy and the hazards of childbirth. Furthermore, women who were sexually active outside wedlock risked pregnancy and community censure: labelled 'bastard bearers', they were liable to loss of employment, social ostracism, and physical punishment.

Whether she was single, married, or widowed, a woman's social and economic position affected the circumstances in which she lived. There were great material differences between the lives of wealthy, middling, and poor women. Aristocratic women enjoyed many elements of a common lifestyle with gentlemen and noblemen, just as the lives of the poorest women, like their male counterparts, were dominated by the struggle to survive.

Women's experiences of child-bearing were affected by their socio-economic position. An aristocratic woman was more likely to employ a wet-nurse, to conceive again quickly, and to bear more children than a poor woman who breast-fed her own infants. Queen Anne is an example from the apex of the social triangle: she experienced eighteen pregnancies, but died with no child of her own to succeed her.[6] In contrast, a poor woman was likely to see five or six of her babies baptized; she would be

[6] E. Gregg, *Queen Anne* (1980), 121.

unusually unfortunate if none of her children survived to adulthood.[7] Child-bearing could affect women's subsequent health, as could their experience of the menopause.

This chapter explores the factors which influenced the lives of adult women: their sexuality and matrimonial status; the attitudes of their communities towards them as women; their opportunities for economic survival; and their bodily changes. Women's subjective experiences were produced in a multiplicity of situations. The physiological differences between women and men may have mattered most when women were of child-bearing years, for becoming a mother was a biological as well as a social and cultural transition. Bodily difference may have been less significant as women aged and passed the menopause, but at every stage of adult life, gender shaped their experiences.

MARRIAGE

In this section we try to reconstruct what the day-to-day experience of marriage was like from women's point of view, and to show how women responded to social, economic, and demographic forces that affected them as wives. Expectations about marriage and its actual impact on daily life were different for women than for men. Although wedlock marked a significant *rite de passage* for both sexes, it was far more momentous for women: the metamorphosis from 'maid' to 'wife' transformed every aspect of their existence. Marriage was experienced in bodily as well as social terms. Husbands could demand sexual access to their wives, and could chastise them physically.

Seventeenth-century writers produced an enormous literature purporting to describe married life. Nearly all of it was written by men, who focused on the relationship between husband and wife from the husband's viewpoint. Diaries and memoirs by élite women, although valuable for the feminine perspective they provide, do not always represent the experiences of the majority of the female populace. And while literate women's correspondence offers vivid glimpses of married life, we must be attentive to the constraints of these genres, of women's awareness of their readers' expectations.

Women's testimony in matrimonial disputes, while including a wider cross-section in terms of social rank, generally portrays the negative side

[7] Estimates from E. A. Wrigley and R. S. Schofield, *The Population History of England, 1541–1871* (Cambridge, 1981), 254.

FIG. 13. Marriage. Marriage was a significant life stage for women. This woodcut depicts a stylized representation of the church ceremony

of wedlock. The relatively small number of wives who appealed to the courts for separation represents the most desperate cases. Indeed, all the surviving records from this period tend to scant or omit ordinary women's experience of marriage and family life. Moreover, although long-lived unions at this time apparently had their ups and downs, very few female memoirs cover the evolution of a marriage through the vagaries of its psychological and demographic phases. In short, we do not have enough direct evidence from the illiterate female majority to be confident we can describe marriage from the average woman's point of view.

We can, however, make intelligent conjectures through the careful use of diverse sources. Having explored the full spectrum of feminine behaviour in surviving documents, we can deduce what married life was like for the majority who presumably occupied the middle range between the best and worst scenarios. By considering the structural effects of class differences, we can develop hypotheses as to what was different about plebeian marriage compared to that of the élite, for which we have far better documentation.

Reading male or popular sources 'against the grain' enables us to set female memoirs, letters, and court records in context. For example, several popular proverbs advocated wifebeating: 'A spaniel, a woman, and a walnut tree, the more they're beaten the better still they be.' A sixteenth-century London by-law forbade wifebeating after 9 p.m. because the noise was disturbing to inhabitants.[8] Such evidence offers insights into a milieu in which wifebeating was common and habitual. Set in this framework, the horrific details presented in court cases do not appear aberrant, but rather one extreme of a spectrum in which men's routine violence against women was the norm.[9]

In portraying marriage, we need to stress a variety of female experiences. A combination of demographic and economic forces created diverse life patterns for women. Although in this section we focus on women's initial entrée into wedlock as a significant life-stage, not all marriages were first marriages. Many wives were widowed and remarried; others were deserted by their husbands but unable to remarry. Even those who spent a lifetime with the same partner still expected the relationship to change over time. A contemporary marriage wish underlined this notion of an evolving companionship, wishing the couple 'one year of joy, another of comfort and all the rest of content'.[10]

Wealth and social rank added another set of variations, affecting not only the age at which women married, but the number of children they were likely to bear, the size and constituents of their households, the range of tasks included in their daily responsibilities, and even their deportment towards husbands and in-laws. Child marriages had decreased among the upper ranks since preceding centuries, but brides of the nobility, gentry, and wealthy urban élite were still two to ten years younger than their

[8] J. Ray, *A Collection of English Proverbs* (1678), 59; R. Warnicke, *Women of the English Renaissance and Reformation* (Westport, Conn., 1983), 156.

[9] M. Hunt, 'Wife Beating, Domesticity, and Women's Independence in Eighteenth-Century London', *Gender and History*, 4 (1992), 10–33; S. D. Amussen, 'Punishment, Discipline, and Power: The Social Meanings of Violence in Early Modern England', *JBS*, 34 (1995), 13.

[10] Ray, *Proverbs*, 63.

counterparts among ordinary women. Although there was a 'scatter' around the average age at first marriage within each social group, plebeian women usually delayed wedlock until their mid- to late twenties. Moreover, the age at first marriage among labouring women was very sensitive to economic conditions, rising to new heights when times were hard.[11]

Whatever their social background, women saw marriage as a critical turning-point in life. This conviction was expressed in many ways, for example in feminine superstitions associated with the wedding day. Some female diarists noted in restrospect that the state of the weather on that day had foretold their future happiness or unhappiness. Elizabeth Walker recalled that providence had caused the sun to shine literally as well as figuratively upon her nuptials: 'thus God was pleased to condescend to my weakness.' Elizabeth Freke had eloped on a 'most dreadfull Raynie day, A presager of all my sorrows & Misfortuns to mee'.[12]

Women were liable to experience wedlock as a violent discontinuity. Such feelings did not conform to the dominant male discourse, in which nuptial rites were interpreted as symbolizing the woman's smooth transfer from paternal to spousal authority. The reason for giving the bride away, Hooker noted, was that the custom 'putteth wemen in mind of a dutie whereunto the verie imbecillitie of their nature and sex doth binde them, namely to be alwaies directed, guided and ordered by others'.[13] But for élite women in particular, the break with a previous life was felt in sexual, emotional, and physical terms. An atmosphere of prurient teasing pervaded contemporary wedding rites: undressing and putting the couple to bed, stealing the bride's garters, imbibing sack-posset with its allegedly aphrodisiac qualities, inflicting a mocking serenade or sexual interrogation on the pair the next morning. All these customs harped on the bride's mental and physical change of state. In *The Maid's Tragedy*, Evadne's loss of virginity is compared to the breaking in of a mare, causing manifest physical changes overnight: 'Let's see you walk, Evadne.'[14] Some young women were so repelled by the prospect of these rituals that they eloped in order to avoid a public wedding.[15]

[11] Wrigley and Schofield, *Population History*, 421–35; T. Hollingsworth, 'The Demography of the British Peerage', suppl. to *Population Studies* 18 (1964); P. Sharpe, 'The Total Reconstitution Method: A Tool for Class-Specific Study?', *Local Population Studies*, 44 (1990), 47–8.

[12] A. Walker, *The Holy Life of Mrs Elizabeth Walker* (1690), 27–8; E. Freke, 'Mrs Elizabeth Freke her Diary, 1671–1714', *Journal of the Cork Historical and Archaeological Society*, 16–18 (1910–13), 1.

[13] R. Hooker, *Of the Lawes of Ecclesiasticall Politie* (1597), v. 215.

[14] F. Beaumont and J. Fletcher, *The Maid's Tragedy* (1619), III. i. 95.

[15] M. Rich, countess of Warwick, BL, MS Add. 27357, fo. 15^{v}–16 ; D. Osborne, *Letters of Dorothy Osborne*, ed. G. Moore Smith (Oxford, 1928), 169; M. Cavendish, duchess of Newcastle, *The Bridals*, in *Plays Never Before Printed* (1668), 11–12 and 18–20.

FIG. 14. Wedding chamber. Family and neighbours were involved in the undressing and bedding of the couple on their wedding night. The rite of passage signalled the change in a woman's status from 'maid' to 'wife'

The sense of physical displacement, of being wrenched out of a sheltered environment and plunged into a hostile milieu, was most common among women of the upper ranks, where custom dictated that the couple live at first in the household of the husband's parents. Here the bride's difficulties were often increased by the potential for friction in the form of power struggles between mother- and daughter-in-law. After frequent quarrels between newly married Lady Elizabeth Mordaunt and her mother-in-law, Lady Mordaunt asked God's forgiveness for telling her husband 'sum things that may insence him against his mouther'.[16] Lower down the social scale, daughters might also be overcome by feelings of loneliness and displacement. When Sarah Savage said goodbye to her relations (after weeks of nuptial celebrations) to be left alone with her husband, she called it 'the saddest day that ever came over my head'.[17]

For labouring women, the break with parents and siblings was less traumatic, since most had already lived in other households as servants. Moreover, the majority deferred marriage until the couple could support

[16] E. Mordaunt, *The Private Diarie of Elizabeth, Viscountess Mordaunt* (Duncairn, 1856), 227, 231, 234; Marquis of Halifax, *The Lady's New Years Gift* (1688), 62.

[17] Chester City RO, Diary of Sarah Savage, D/Basten/8, fo. 13.

themselves in a separate dwelling. Among artisans and labourers, the household's structure was small, separate, and nuclear, composed of husband and wife, children, and perhaps a maidservant. Both age and household structure could have 'political' implications for family dynamics, enabling ordinary women to start married life on a more equal footing with their partners than brides of the upper ranks.

Women saw wedlock not only as a break with their former lives, but as an entrée into a different caste, marked by distinctive dress (of which the matron's 'scarf and hood' was the archetypal emblem) and deportment. As Lady Elizabeth Delaval noted, 'the gayety of my humour and the harmelesse mirth in my conversation was pleaseing to those I formerly kept company withall, and what was estimed by them to be wit . . . is look'd upon to be a gidynesse unbecomeing a wife'.[18] Marriage elevated women to a loftier rank in village as well as élite society. In church, matrons sat together in front of their single counterparts, to mark their higher standing in the community. Because matrimony conferred adult status on women, wives and widows assumed more respect and weightier responsibilities in the local power hierarchy.[19]

What did women hope for in their relationships with their husbands, and what sort of *modus vivendi* did they generally achieve throughout the vagaries of married life? While we consider these questions, we must be careful to avoid projecting our own assumptions about marriage into the seventeenth-century context. Modern couples are encouraged to seek happiness in the form of emotional and sexual compatibility as their highest priority. The possibility of romantic and sexual attraction was also prominent in the minds of early modern women, but they were not always free to rank it first. Because wives had no legal stake in the physical and economic resources of the household, no lawful way out of an unsatisfactory union, and few if any career options in lieu of marriage, they were more likely to feel impelled to make marriage work as a social and economic partnership, even when it was not viable as an emotional and sexual bond.

Another difference in our attitude to marriage relates to the connection between love and authority. Nowadays we do not see a contradiction in the notion that a loving relationship between husband and wife can involve an egalitarian sharing of power, resources, and decision-making. Although early modern women entertained the hypothetical possibility of marriage as a perfect friendship, they were apt to portray the real-life union of equals

[18] *The Meditations of Lady Elizabeth Delaval*, ed. D. Greene, Surtees Society, 190 (1975), 207–8.
[19] See, for example, OA, MS Oxf. Dioc. papers c. 26, 1629–34, fos. 144–8.

as the rare exception that proved the rule. Mary Beale noted that the curse of Eve's subjection to Adam had been entailed on all her female posterity, 'except a small number, who by Friendship's interposition, have restored the marriage bond to its first institution'.[20]

In society at large, an affectionate but hierarchical relationship was the dominant ideal. The question posed in prescriptive writings by either sex was not whether women were equal to their husbands, but rather what form of inequality was consistent with religion, equity, and the best interests of the family and state. Issues of love and power were regarded as separable in theory, although admittedly intertwined in day-to-day interactions.

With respect to matrimonial love, women's normal expectation was of a loving partnership based on personal affinity and mutual respect. In actual unions, a wide spectrum of behaviour existed, but we do not have enough data to calculate whether the range was substantially different from what we observe nowadays. Certainly there was no lack of display of love and affection, both of wives for husbands and vice versa, among the literate classes of every social rank. Mary Clarke wrote to her husband Edward that she could not 'possibly live any longer without the sight of him that is most dear to me'. Lady Apollina Hall confessed that her heart was 'immoderately let out' upon her husband.[21] While we cannot determine how typical such marriages were, we can at least infer that the subservient role which society imposed on women did not preclude the possibility of passionate love and devotion by wives as well as husbands.

Because of the scarcity of direct evidence, it is far more difficult to reconstruct what affective relations were like for plebeian wives. Historians such as Olwen Hufton, writing about early modern France, have suggested that the 'acid of poverty' undermined emotional ties in plebeian unions, and that labouring women could hope at best for a working partnership, but not for romantic love.[22] For England we see a variety of patterns, some of which do appear to fit Hufton's pessimistic scenario. Many women thought that marriage was still the best survival tactic even when it did not evolve from adolescent romance, but was simply a pairing of different gender-based skills

[20] Folger, MS V. a. 220, M. Beale, 'A Discourse of Friendship', fo. 3.

[21] Somerset RO, DD/SF 4515, 20 Aug. 1675; W. Typing, *The Remarkable Life . . . of Lady Apollina Hall* (1647), 13. For other examples see T. Alleine, *The Life and Death of . . . Joseph Alleine* (1672), 91–7; BL, MS Egerton 607, E. Egerton, countess of Bridgewater, 'Meditations', fos. 111^{v}–13; Folger, MS V. a. 166, fos. 27–8; Chester City RO, S. Savage, Diary, fo. 33^{v}; Walker, *Life of Elizabeth Walker*, 54–5.

[22] O. Hufton, 'Women and the Family Economy in Eighteenth-century France', *French Historical Studies*, 9 (1975), 1–22. For similar views about England, see L. Stone, *The Family, Sex and Marriage in England, 1500–1800* (1977), 362–3, 389; J. Gillis, *For Better, For Worse: British Marriages, 1600 to the Present* (Oxford, 1985), 98–100.

and a pooling of resources. Evidence for marriage as a subsistence strategy can be inferred from unusual age gaps among couples whose ages are recorded in sixteenth-century censuses of the poor.[23]

But the problem with our evidence is that illiteracy tends to filter out positive sources, leaving us the predominantly negative evidence of court records. While it is true that poverty made life harder for married couples, increasing the rate of desertion when family survival as a unit was no longer viable, it also made spouses more dependent on each other for companionable partnership. In fact we do have evidence that poverty did not preclude matrimonial love. The casebook notes of the astrologer Richard Napier reveal that poor women not only expected to be loved, but were distressed when husbands failed to show affection. There is also indirect evidence suggesting that plebeian wives expressed mutual love through the gendered tasks of everyday life.[24]

To what extent did women accept the patriarchal model of power relations in marriage, or follow its dictates in their own lives? Feminine views on this subject are not easy to disentangle from the dominant discourse in which they are embedded. It is hardly surprising that female litigants in matrimonial disputes affirmed the tenets of patriarchy while insisting they had conformed to its precepts, for they would have had little chance of winning their suits otherwise. In the courts as well as the home, the language of wifely love and obedience was often fused. Indeed, a wife's subjection was interpreted as a measure of her affection for her spouse; conversely, insubordination was taken as proof that she no longer loved him. In a 1604 case, a wife promised submission to her husband, a London alderman: 'I will not spare any pains nor neglect any duty to recover his love and favour again . . . I have sought his love upon my knees with tears.'[25]

It could be imprudent or even dangerous for a wife to rebel. In the course of a property dispute with her stepdaughter Lady Fenton, Dame Margery Norreys was accused of erupting with rage after her husband Sir John tried to prompt her about her wifely duties. According to the Fentons' testimony, Sir John had invited a minister to read a biblical text on 'the duty of women to their husbands' for Dame Margery's edification, after the couple had

[23] For examples, see *The Norwich Census of the Poor, 1570*, ed. J. Pound, Norfolk Record Society, 40 (1971), 23–4, 26, 30, 32–4, 36, 38, etc.

[24] M. MacDonald, *Mystical Bedlam: Madness, Anxiety and Healing in Seventeenth-Century England* (Cambridge, 1981), 102–4; Bodl. MS Rawinson. B 382, fo. 294^{v}.

[25] BL, Lansdowne MS 161, Caesar Papers, fo. 160. For a plebeian wife who begged her husband's forgiveness on her knees, see Bodl., MS Rawlinson B 382, fos. 126–46.

quarrelled about signing a deed. The plaintiffs' testimony reported that Dame Margery 'did most prophanely, impiously and irreligiously . . . tear the page in which the said chapter was written . . . and did in most heathenish manner tread and trample the same leaf under her feet and . . . most furiously . . . cast the same leaf into the fire, and did with most execrable oaths swear that . . . the minister that read the chapter was an arrant knave, and he that commanded him to read the same was a scurvy rascal'.

Dame Margery told a different story. The incident had occurred a decade before, after some 'small unkindness . . . in some domestical affairs, which nevertheless was presently appeased and ended'. At prayers afterwards, a servant (not a minister) had read a chapter of Ecclesiastes containing 'some things against women'.[26] Thinking that the servant was mocking her, Dame Margery had given him some 'angry words' and had torn a leaf out of the book, but had not trampled or cast it into the fire, nor used blasphemous or profane speeches. Sir John had treated the affair as a jest. Yet after his death, Dame Margery's brief outburst placed her in peril of being charged with blasphemy, an offence 'against the state of this kingdom'.[27]

Nearly all our evidence of wifely insubordination comes from male writers like William Gouge, who spoke of 'many wives, whom ambition hath tainted and corrupted within and without: they cannot endure to heare of *subjection*: they imagine that they are made slaves thereby.'[28] Very few first-hand sources preserve both wives' and husbands' versions of events. And as the Norreys case reveals, family members did not always agree on the facts (let alone their interpretation) when conflict occurred.

As for female sources, it is significant that even in their private meditations (where presumably they could adopt a more disinterested viewpoint), most women conceded the duty of wifely submission, whether this obligation was grounded on the consequences of Eve's sin, the laws of the land, or the contractual vow to 'love, honour and obey' a husband. Because its basis was religious, the countess of Bridgewater pointed out, a wife's status was not susceptible to rational dispute: 'we are commanded, by those that are above our capacity of reason, by God himself.'[29] Mary Astell, while contesting the general subordination of the female sex, had no doubts about the divine and consequently the coercive nature of wifely subjection: 'She . . . who Marrys

[26] Presumably Ecclesiastes 7: 26–9.

[27] PRO, STAC 8/138/18, *Thomas, Viscount Fenton et uxor Lady Elizabeth Fenton* v. *Dame Margery Norreys et al.* Many thanks to Felicity Heal for this reference.

[28] W. Gouge, *Of Domesticall Duties* (1622), 269.

[29] BL, MS Egerton 607, E. Egerton, countess of Bridgewater, 'Meditations', fos. 78^{v}–9.

ought to lay it down for an indisputable Maxim, that her Husband must govern absolutely and intirely, and that she has nothing else to do but to Please and Obey. She must not attempt to divide his Authority, or so much as dispute it.'[30]

At least in theory, women acknowledged that the powers granted them by their husbands were privileges to be negotiated, not rights to be defended. For those who set store by their piety or personal repute, the issue was not their subject status, but its character and limitations. At this point, however, women entered ambiguous and highly contested terrain. It is not a coincidence that female opinions on the topic of matrimonial rule bear a striking resemblance to the political debates of the time. The key question was exactly parallel: what was the true nature of wifely 'subjection', and how far did a husband's powers extend before his wife had the right to resist his authority?

On this issue, women's responses show a subtle change of focus compared to their male counterparts. While writers like Gouge dwelt on women's acceptance of subjection as the key component of the relationship, affirming that 'every dutie which they [wives] performe to their husband, their very opinion, affection, speech, action, and all that concerneth the huband, must savour of *subjection*',[31] women were apt to stress the wife's companionate role. Dorothy Leigh remarked, 'if she bee thy wife she is always too good to be thy servant, and worthy to be thy fellow'. The countess of Bridgewater thought women should not be in such awe of their husbands as a servant of his master, 'as not to speak, to contradict the least word he saith, but to have an affection, and love to him, as to a friend . . . if the wife be so meek, and low in spirit, to be in subjection for every word, she makes him fear he is troublesome . . . this is far from a companions way'.[32]

But no matter how earnestly they argued for companionate models of matrimony, women were aware of an inherent contradiction between the ideal of wedded comradeship and the compulsory nature of wifely subjection. By the late seventeenth century, this disparity was increasingly noted by female writers, who had begun to measure women's status by the yardstick of liberal political philosophies. As Mary Astell remarked: 'how much soever Arbitrary Power may be dislik'd on a Throne, not *Milton* himself wou'd cry up Liberty to poor *Female Slaves*, or plead for the Lawfulness of

[30] M. Astell, *Reflections Upon Marriage* (3rd edn., 1706), 56.

[31] Gouge, *Of Domesticall Duties*, 269.

[32] D. Leigh, *The Mothers Blessing* (1616), 55; BL, MS Egerton 607, E. Egerton, countess of Bridgewater, 'Meditations', fos. 79^v–80^v.

Resisting a Private Tyranny.'[33] The author of *The Female Advocate* (1700) conceded that the female sex was made for man's 'Comfort and Benefit', but protested that to require women to submit to men's every whim was a 'Tyranny . . . that extends farther than the most absolute Monarchs in the World'.[34] Lady Chudleigh's popular poem, 'Wife and Servant are the same, and differ only in the name', was copied by young women into their commonplace books.[35] In the age of Locke, some women expressed the view that wifely subjection was no different from slavery.

How could the two incompatible ideals of subjection and companionship be reconciled? Some women thought the problem should be resolved at an earlier stage: wives must choose a man they could obey, and 'inquire with themselves, whether or no they could esteem of such a person so as to value his Judgement; and in matter of consequence, to yield to his counsel'.[36] Clearly, a wife would have little trouble submitting to a man whom she genuinely considered her superior. But what if an unwise choice were made, by the woman herself or by relatives and friends who chose for her? What were her options if she found herself joined to a wastrel, a drunkard, a philanderer, or a petulant despot? Court records and female memoirs reveal a multitude of husbands who treated their wives with cruelty or neglect, subjecting them to what Ann Wentworth called 'the unspeakable tyrannies of an hard-hearted Yoak-Fellow'.[37] Of women unhappily married, Lady Chudleigh wrote,

> They are like Victims to the Alter [sic] led,
> Born for Destruction, and for Ruine bred;
> Forc'd to Sigh out each long revolving Year,
> And see their Lives all spent in Toil and Care.[38]

To comprehend the behaviour of women who found themselves in unsatisfactory marriages, we should begin by clarifying their goals. Those historians who have discovered with surprise that seventeenth-century wives were 'mostly not docile and passive'[39] have taken their bearings from men's rather than women's perspective. Women's writings reveal that their aim was not so much to escape 'due subjection' as to preserve self-respect, to avert moral and social disgrace, and to transform their unhappiness to some

33 Astell, *Reflections Upon Marriage*, 27.
34 [M. Chudleigh] *The Female Advocate* (1700), 20.
35 See Folger STC 22273 No. 23.
36 BL, MS Egerton 607, E. Egerton, countess of Bridgewater, 'Meditations', fos. 79–79^{v}.
37 A. Wentworth, *A Vindication* (1677), 1.
38 'Eugenia' [M. Chudleigh], *The Ladies Defence* (1701), 5.
39 A. Fletcher, 'Men's Dilemma: The Future of Patriarchy in England, 1560–1660', *TRHS*, 6th ser., 4 (1994), 63.

constructive end. Hence a common choice, especially among middling and élite women, was to turn to religion. 'If he be fickle and various, not caring much to be with his wife at home, then thus may the wife make her own happiness, for then she may give her self up to prayer . . . ; in his absence, she is as much God's, as a virgin.'[40]

The married female saint was a well-known type in seventeenth-century society, partly because feminine piety made a special scruple of 'relative duties'. For example, an anonymous female diarist berated herself for some 'unbecoming peevishness to my husband which though I approved not, I did not strive enough against'. It was said of Elizabeth Juxon that if her husband had commanded her the 'vilest drudgerie . . . she durst not have refused, in verie conscience of Gods Law'.[41]

Although the correlation between piety and wifely obedience was frequently observed, it is hard to discern which was the cause and which the effect. Some wives appear to have been socialized into submission through their understanding of theology. Having a small child and a new baby, Susannah Bell had resisted her husband's desire to emigrate to New England. But after her infant died, as she recalled, 'I begged earnestly of [God] to know why he took away my Child, and it was given in to me, that it was because I would not go to *New England*.' With the Scriptural verse on her mind, '*Wives submit your selves unto your own Husbands, as unto the Lord*', she told her husband she was now willing to go with him.[42]

Others turned to religion as a source of strength in an intolerable situation. Mary Rich, countess of Warwick, who saw her life as a chequerwork of mercies and 'sanctified afflictions', had identified her irascible invalid husband as one of the latter, referring to him in her diary as her 'cross'. Embracing a regimen of piety, the countess developed a mode of dynamic obedience that transformed the conflict between herself and her husband into a personal campaign for self-mastery.[43]

In her own terms, the countess of Warwick's behaviour was neither docile nor passive. On the contrary, she showed exceptional force of character which earned the respect and admiration of all around her, including the earl himself, for he knew that her obedience was to a higher power than that of a husband. To some wives, the moral victory achieved was more satisfying than a degrading struggle for the breeches, as Mary Astell remarked, 'when a Superior does a Mean and unjust Thing . . . [although] this does not

[40] BL, MS Egerton 607, E. Egerton, countess of Bridgewater, 'Meditations', fos. 82^v–3^v.

[41] Bodl., MS Rawlinson Q.e.26, fo. 7^v; S. Denison, *The Monument or Tombe-stone* (1620), 114.

[42] S. Bell, *The Legacy of a Dying Mother . . . being the experiences of Mrs Susanna Bell* (1673), 45–6.

[43] S. Mendelson, *The Mental World of Stuart Women* (Brighton, 1987), 101–10.

provoke his Inferiors to refuse that Observance which their Stations in the World require, they cannot but have an inward Sense of their own real Superiority . . . at the same time that they pay him an outward Respect and Deference'.[44]

Piety could be a double-edged sword. While some women became domestic saints, others were impelled by conscience to the opposite extreme, the courage to defy their husbands. In this they were occasionally supported by the law, which recognized limits to patriarchal excess when it entailed the violation of moral or judicial codes. Women knew that their duties did not include obeying a husband in wrongdoing. In 1688, Edward Harding was prosecuted for hindering his wife and daughter from receiving the Sacrament; he had asserted he was 'master of their consciences', and they should do what he thought fit.[45] While Harding's action was clearly unlawful, a large area of ambiguity remained: to what extent could a wife follow her own conscience against her husband's will? The issue was even more contentious when wives were drawn to communions different from those of their husbands, particularly those outside the Established Church. The divisive effects of religious dissension within the domestic sphere became particularly acute during the Civil War period, when it was intensified by other destabilizing forces.[46]

Piety was only one of many variables—social, financial, sexual, cultural, political, and personal—through which power might be negotiated in seventeenth-century marriages. The marriage of Anne Dormer, the second wife of Robert Dormer of Rousham, exhibits the interplay between a number of these elements. Through a remarkable series of autobiographical letters which Anne Dormer wrote to her sister, Lady Elizabeth Trumbull, we can explore her feelings about her marriage, and examine some of the psychological and structural forces which influenced the politics of matrimony.

Anne Dormer depicted her marriage as a cage.[47] Many factors appeared to her to contribute to her entrapment. She blamed her own 'natural softness of temper,' as well as her husband's extremes of misanthropy and sexual

[44] Astell, *Reflections Upon Marriage*, 49.

[45] Bodl., MS Rawlinson B. 382, fos. 121–7.

[46] See P. Crawford, *Women and Religion in England, 1500–1720* (1993), 52; ead., 'Public Duty, Conscience, and Women in Early Modern England', in J. Morrill, P. Slack, and D. Woolf (eds.), *Public Duty and Private Conscience in Seventeenth-Century England* (Oxford, 1993), 67–76.

[47] BL, Trumbull MS, D/ED c 13, Anne Dormer to Lady Elizabeth Trumbull, 25 July 1689 (St James Day). The 'cage' simile for marriage was a common one: the duchess of Newcastle wrote of women 'we are kept like birds in cages to hop up and down in our houses'; 'To the Two Universities', *Philosophical and Physical Opinions* (1655), sig. B2^{v}.

jealousy, which she concluded were a 'sort of madness'.[48] Yet these attributes merely exaggerated traditional gender-linked traits: the ideal wife was soft and submissive, repressing her anger; the ideal patriarch guarded the sexual honour of his wife and lineage.

Beyond quirks of personality, Dormer pondered the structural constraints that moulded her life, notably the conviction that she was absolutely dependent on her husband's will: 'I must not exasperate him, for I and my poor children are in his power.'[49] In her efforts to pacify her husband, she became increasingly isolated, both physically and socially. Dormer's jealousy had led his wife to resolve never to go beyond the garden; sometimes she did 'not see another face for 2 months'.[50] Nominally the mistress of a huge household staffed by 30 domestics, including several loving and loyal maids, she complained she had 'not a person to send', for the servants were likewise under her husband's dominion. Control of her own space had dwindled to the dimensions of her closet, which became her haven: 'my closet is a safe shelter but out of it is little quiet because he whose life is idleness is seldom from home.'[51] Her chamber and the nursery were constantly invaded: 'my chamber when he is up he is always passing to and fro and in the nursery if I stay ½ hour he is in a fury; in winter he broke the door when he fancied I was there but I was not.'[52]

Yet like the countess of Warwick, Anne Dormer was not docile. She fought against her husband's contempt, 'which I do by freely speaking my mind to him'. As if humouring a lunatic, she turned his foibles into jokes: 'I submit most cheerfully to his absolute dominion over me, and jest with it, for when he says I will do this and that I say as Sir Oliver Butler did 'twas his own house and should sh— in every room on it.'[53] Meanwhile, Dormer put her energies into the care of her children, her reading, her piety, and an epistolary network of female friends and relations: 'there is nothing but my friends that I set a value upon.'[54]

The dual character of the life Dormer had constructed as prison and refuge was betrayed in her response to widowhood. Friends thought she had 'cause to rejoice', predicting she should 'fly out as soon as the cage was broken', but she viewed her marriage differently. Anne Dormer had loved her husband, she insisted, for he 'though he never made me happy did passionately love me'. Moreover, even after his death, she was still under his domination. She felt remorse looking in boxes and trunks he had kept

[48] BL, Trumbull MS, 3 Nov. [1688?]. [49] Ibid. 20 July [1688?].
[50] Ibid. 28 Jan. [1689?]. [51] Ibid. 28 Aug. 1686. [52] Ibid. 3 Nov. [1688?].
[53] Ibid. 10 Mar. [1688?]. [54] Ibid. [1685?]; 9 Aug. [1686?].

locked; 'using such things as he would scarce suffer me to look upon I am like one haunted with an evil spirit or who has committed some crime.'[55]

Anne Dormer suffered psychological torments caused by her husband's obsessive jealousy. Other married women experienced a whole spectrum of mistreatment, ranging from verbal and psychological harassment and threats of violence, physical assault and attempted murder, to actual homicide. In some matrimonial cases which have been preserved in church and secular court records, we can document an escalating spiral of mental and physical cruelty.

In a plea for separation from her husband Jasper, a solicitor, Elizabeth Kynaston insisted she had been a good obedient wife. She had 'used all the ways and means she could think of or imagine whereby she thought she might have engaged and pleased' her husband, and was resolved 'to serve him and respect him as she always conceived it was her duty to do'.[56] Yet he had denied her the midwife of her choice, 'by reason of which . . . [she] had a very hard and difficult labour'. During her recovery from childbed, he would not allow her a servant to assist with household tasks. He refused her meat, drink, linen, apparel, and convenient lodging, so that she was forced to leave him, 'rather than perish for want of common diet'. He then locked her out, tricking her by a pretended arrest and threatened whipping at Bridewell. (The threat of institutional punishment was a frequent ploy, and was characteristic of men's greater familiarity with the legal system.)[57] In addition to verbal and physical abuse, Kynaston had forced his wife to sign away her widow's thirds, a deprivation of her legal rights.

Society tolerated a high level of violence against wives as a normal feature of domestic relations. The Scriptural and legal language about the patriarch's responsibility for 'lawful and reasonable correction' authorized men to beat their wives, children, and subordinates.[58] Domestic violence was not concealed, but was usually well known to the household and neighbours. Not only did servants talk about their employers' doings, but wood-and-plaster walls were so thin, especially in crowded cities and towns, that the community knew what was happening. In 1566, Judith Pollard brought witnesses to court to tell of beatings 'in the dead time of night' which disturbed the neighbourhood. Her husband had locked her out of the house on a cold January night; although she was pregnant and the neighbours had

[55] Ibid. 25 July 1689 (St James Day).

[56] Bodl., MS Rawlinson B. 381, fos. 5^{v}–10.

[57] See Hunt, 'Wife Beating', 19.

[58] R. Phillips, *Putting Asunder: A History of Divorce in Western Society* (Cambridge, 1988), 323–9; Hunt, 'Wife Beating', 18 and n. 27; T.E., *The Lawes Resolutions of Womens Rights* (1632), 128–9.

begged him to readmit her, he had refused, 'whereby [Margaret Jones] for pity did lodge her in her house the same night'.[59] Other women told similar stories of mistreatment by kicks and blows during pregnancy, and of being locked out of the house.[60] More than one wife spoke of being attacked with a drawn sword, a knife, or other dangerous weapons. Joanna Randall's friend Ellen Clarke had received 'two dangerous wounds in her wrist' while trying to prevent Robert Randall from murdering Joanna.[61] The tenets of masculine 'honour' supported the notion of justifiable homicide, a concept which did not usually apply to women.[62] Men were better able to wreak violence because they were usually larger and stronger; most carried some kind of weapon, whereas women did not do so. In 1686 Thomas Watson, a cashiered soldier, used his bayonet to murder his wife.[63]

Aside from habitual violence, there were other ways that husbands could brutally mistreat their wives. While women might tolerate a certain level of sexual infidelity, they did not expect a husband to be flagrantly unfaithful, to maintain a mistress at the expense of his own family, or to infect his wife with venereal diseases. In a 1684 case, Elizabeth Vesey appealed to the London consistory court for a separation from her husband James. Among other charges, witnesses for the plaintiff deposed that James Vesey had openly kept another woman as his mistress, and had said that she 'should never want, if his Wife and Child went a Begging'. He had also tried to rape the maidservants, and had infected his wife with a sexual disease.[64]

Confronted with male violence and with what was experienced as an intolerable situation, what were women's options? During the early modern period, wives were not permitted to initiate an action for divorce which allowed remarriage. Nor was divorce available to husbands, apart from a few wealthy peers who, after 1670, could secure a private act of Parliament to allow them to remarry.[65] Among the lower ranks, an unofficial substitute for divorce was the custom known as 'wife sale'. Although wife sales were normally prearranged, the 'buyer' being the wife's lover, the ceremony entailed the wife's appearance in the public market-place in the guise of a beast for sale, with a halter around her neck. No husband ever agreed to take

[59] Guildhall, MS 9056, London Archdeaconry, Depositions in Libel Causes 1566–7, fos. 16^{v}–21^{v}.
[60] GLRO, DL/C 241, Consistory Court Depositions, 1684–7, fos. 2–3, 13–14.

[61] Bodl., MS Rawlinson B. 382, 275^{v}; GLRO, DL/C/241, Consistory Court Depositions, 1684–7, fos. 23^{v}-24.

[62] G. Walker, 'Homicide, Gender and Justice in Early Modern England', unpublished paper, 1995. We are most grateful to Dr Walker for allowing us to cite her paper.

[63] *A Sad and True Relation of a most barbarous and bloody murder by one Thomas Watson* (1686), 5–6.

[64] GLRO, DL/C/241, Consistory Court Depositions, 1684–7, fos. 1–14.

[65] L. Stone, *Road to Divorce: England, 1530–1987* (Oxford, 1990), 309–12.

on this role.[66] For the woman, it was a humiliating end to her first marriage; nor did the symbolism of an animal displayed for sale put her in a strong position *vis-à-vis* her new, illegal husband.

Another option was flight, but since women usually accepted responsibility for children, they found both escape and economic survival difficult. Deserted wives were far more numerous than deserted husbands. In the 1570 Norwich census of the poor, apart from married couples, only two men had children, compared with 112 women.[67] Absconding or deserted spouses sometimes remarried bigamously: Stone estimates that thousands, 'probably tens of thousands', did so in the seventeenth and eighteenth centuries.[68] For some women, bigamy may have been a means of survival, but it did not necessarily remove them from the dangers represented by an unsatisfactory marriage.

A legal separation *a mensa et thoro* (from bed and board) granted a wife the right to live apart from her husband, although it did not permit remarriage. Sometimes the wife was awarded alimony, i.e. an allowance for maintenance while living apart from her spouse. In theory, obtaining a decree of separation was a straightforward matter, but in practice it could present insurmountable obstacles. A suit cost a minimum of £20 early in the eighteenth century, so only those of the middling and upper ranks could afford litigation.[69] Moreover, women who sought a separation found no sympathy from the judicial system. Court officials tended to ignore a woman's allegations if she was unable to prove excessive physical cruelty on her husband's part, or if the court suspected that she herself had failed in any detail of proper wifely subordination and conduct.

The barriers to a separation could be social and religious as well as legal. When the poet Anne Wharton told her spiritual adviser, Bishop Burnet, that she wished to leave her profligate husband, Burnet was offended. Separation, he told her, was 'a downright rejecting the yoke of God, and rebelling against his providence'. Any woman who contemplated the possibility 'must lay doune both religion, vertue, and prudence . . . unlesse they are really in danger of their lives'.[70] Even when a wife was thought to be at risk, officials did not always act on her behalf. Male authorities often disagreed with women as to what constituted a dangerous degree of violence, or failed to take women's fears seriously.

[66] S. P. Menefee, *Wives for Sale: An Ethnographic Study of British Popular Divorce* (Oxford, 1981).

[67] *Norwich Census of the Poor*, 18–19.

[68] L. Stone, *Uncertain Unions: Marriage in England, 1660–1753* (Oxford, 1992), 232.

[69] Hunt, 'Wife Beating', 13.

[70] 'Life of Mrs Anne Wharton', in P. Bayle *et al.*, *A General Dictionary* (1741), 10, 126.

Elizabeth Palmer had suffered years of brutality from a husband who was suspected of wanting his wife dead so that he could marry a former love. He had raped his wife, and had terrorized her with threats to 'rip open her belly' and murder her. When Elizabeth's mother told Dr Owen, a clerical acquaintance, of her plans to keep Elizabeth away from her husband for fear of her life, Dr Owen tried to dissuade her, saying 'it was a very hard thing to separate a man from his wife, and that he pitied her and was sorry for her . . . . And advised her to submit to God Allmighty's pleasure, and to take it patiently'.[71]

Even when friends, neighbours, or local officials were sympathetic to female victims of male brutality, their power to intervene was liable to be ineffective or too late. Judicial authorities had few ways of curbing male violence. A justice's usual procedure was to require the husband to give a bond for his good behaviour: in 1615 Sir Francis Ashley bound Henry Sea for £20 'for beating and dangerously wounding his wife with a paire of tonges in the hinder part of the head'.[72] But bonds to keep the peace were easy to ignore. Moreover, those friends and neighbours who tried to protect the wife were liable to put themselves in danger; they were frequently injured as well.

In the case of Elizabeth Samways, allegedly poisoned by her husband in 1624, neighbours and family members later reported that they had known of his cruelty: 'he beat his wife and [did] give her many blows with a cudgell.' Elizabeth's mother described how her son-in-law had mistreated his wife, 'beatinge her often with ropes and cudgells . . . and lodginge her in the lower part of his howse adjoyninge to his barne, uppon straw with a bolster of dust under her head'. Dying, her daughter had told her that 'she could not lyve for her heart was broken'.[73]

Partly because the concerns of legal and religious institutions ran counter to the woman's own interest of escape from a dangerous situation, marital breakdown tended to take the form of a slow deterioration in the relationship, rather than a quick and decisive break. Like the formation of marriage, its termination was generally a cumbersome and protracted process, for there were myriad obstacles in the way of the wife's efforts to leave a cruel or violent partner. Community authorities often forced the wife to return to her husband, in the belief that if her behaviour were sufficiently compliant, then the marriage could be patched up. Court documents record a number of cases of this see-saw movement between the wife's attempted separation

[71] GLRO, DL/C/241, Consistory Court Depositions 1684–7, fos. 15–29^{v}.

[72] *The Casebook of Sir Francis Ashley J. P. Recorder of Dorchester, 1614–1635*, ed. J. H. Bettey, Dorset Record Society, 7 (1981), 17.

[73] Ibid. 84–5.

and an officially imposed reconciliation, with the struggle sometimes lasting for years.

Although their options were limited, many wives fought either to improve or end their marriages. After a quarrel with her husband over the lack of beer, Lettice Kynnersly told her brother that her husband had taken charge of the household away from her and commanded her to stay in her chamber; 'good brother be good unto me: and either write, or get my brother Anthony to come and talk with him: if I may but have the rule of my children: and somewhat to maintain them and myself, I would desire no more.'[74] Others sought neighbours to witness for them. In 1618, Ursula Erdeswicke complained to her cousin, Walter Bagot (in his role as justice of the peace), that her husband had 'wronged' her, and pleaded with him to call her neighbours as witnesses: 'Good cousin send for the neighbours to come with me.'[75] A wife might turn to friends or relatives for sanctuary from violence. Since the husband in many cases had ceased to provide his wife with basic 'necessaries', she might be obliged to depend on friends and neighbours for food and clothes as well as a haven from her husband.

Even if the church courts agreed that a couple live apart, and granted the wife alimony, her troubles were not over. Margaret Henshall was awarded alimony in 1664, but returned to the courts, in theory seeking restitution of rights. The 'friends' of the couple had negotiated that they should live together again, but the relationship again deteriorated. John refused first to eat and then to sleep with Margaret. By February 1666 he had ceased to live with her and had denuded the house of goods. Not only had he refused Margaret and her children 'necessaries'; he had destroyed her spinning wheels and 'yarnwindles' so that she could not maintain herself by her own labour.[76]

Some unhappy wives ended a marriage through suicide, although the significance of gender in the recording of deaths is complex.[77] Others murdered their husbands. If a wife killed her spouse, her offence was deemed petit treason, a far more heinous offence than spousal murder, although much less common. If convicted, a husband guilty of spousal

[74] Folger, Bagot MS, L. a. 598; Lettice Kynnersly to Walter Bagot.

[75] Folger, Bagot MS, L. a. 454.

[76] Cheshire RO, Chester Consistory Court, EDC5/1664 no. 43. We are extremely grateful to Tim Wales for giving us a transcription of this case.

[77] M. Macdonald and T. Murphy, *Sleepless Souls: Suicide in Early Modern England* (Oxford, 1990), 247–8, 261–3.

homicide faced a charge of murder, which could be reduced to manslaughter.[78] Wives who murdered their violent and abusive husbands were more vulnerable to conviction because their acts appeared premeditated. Cases provide chilling evidence of domestic violence and of wifely resistance. In 1688 Mary Hobry, a French midwife, murdered her husband. For years he had refused to provide for her, demanding that she maintain him instead. He had beaten, reviled, and threatened to kill her, and had forced her to commit sexual sins, 'Villanies contrary to Nature'. After her husband came home drunk one morning, waking her with blows to her stomach and breast, and compelled her to 'the most Unnnatural of Villanies . . . as forc'd from her a great deal of blood', she strangled him while he slept, dismembered his body, and disposed of it about the city. The court convicted her of petit treason, and she was burnt to death.[79]

When marriages broke down, women at whatever social level had fewer choices than their male counterparts. Husbands had the physical and financial power to make their wives' lives unendurable. Wives could be deprived of the necessities of life, and could be violently 'corrected'. Contemporary documents reveal that women in unhappy marriages were not necessarily passive victims; but all too often they ended up as victims nevertheless.

Can we identify structural factors that influenced the way women in different social and economic contexts experienced marriage? Both contemporary commentators and modern historians have tried to formulate hypotheses which correlate class differences with the politics of married life. Brodsky has shown that daughters of wealthy London tradesmen married older, established men. Such wives were in a weaker position *vis-à-vis* their husbands than many London women who married men nearer themselves in age.[80]

In her classic study of seventeenth-century women, Alice Clark linked the relationship between husbands and wives to women's work roles in the family economy. Clark believed that those women who were actively employed in a direct or complementary partnership with their husbands were likely to enjoy more prestige and equality than those who did not,

[78] For petit treason, see J. Beattie, *Crime and the Courts in England, 1660–1800* (Oxford, 1986), 100; for 'excusable homicide' or manslaughter see ibid. 86, 95.

[79] *A Hellish Murder Committed by a French Midwife, on the Body of her Husband, Jan 27. 1687/8* (1688).

[80] V. Brodsky, 'Single Women in the London Marriage Market: Age, Status and Mobility, 1598–1619', in R. B. Outhwaite (ed.), *Marriage and Society: Studies in the Social History of Marriage* (1981), 81–100.

whether the failure to work was the effect of idleness or the forces of a capitalist labour-market.[81]

Seventeenth-century women also posited a connection between social class and the politics of gender roles. The anonymous author of the *Essay in Defence of the Female Sex* (1696) thought that there was far more equality between the sexes at the bottom of the social ladder, among those who subsisted on day labour: 'For amongst these, though not so equal as that of Brutes, yet the Condition of the two Sexes is more level, than amongst Gentlemen, City Traders, or rich Yeomen.'[82] In pondering the sources of her matrimonial unhappiness, Anne Dormer compared her circumstances unfavourably with that of her plebeian neighbours, implying that her own elevated social rank entailed a diminished freedom in the domestic context: 'a poor woman that lives in a thatched house when she is ill or weary of her work can step into her neighbour and have some refreshment but I can have none.'[83]

Dormer was right in thinking that the enforced seclusion she suffered was almost unknown among ordinary women. Economic necessity did not allow men to stay home all day guarding their wives' chastity, nor was it in a husband's interest to impede his wife from her work when this involved going forth on 'necessary occasions'. But structural differences were relative rather than absolute. Dormer's physical isolation from her network of female friends was uncommon even among women of the gentry and yeomanry, who generally bridged the geographical distance between households with frequent social visits as well as correspondence. In fact Dormer herself thought her situation abnormal: she told her husband that if all men behaved as he did, 'in a few years no woman of understanding would ever venture upon marriage'.[84]

In any case, the existence of structural differences between women of the upper and lower ranks does not prove that such differences affected the quality of relationships between husbands and wives. If labouring men were unable to safeguard their wives' chastity in person, the local community generally deputized for them, using such popular group rituals as charivari or Skimmington to punish both the erring wife and her weak and ineffective husband.[85] There was no context of seventeenth-century life in which

[81] A. Clark, *The Working Life of Women in the Seventeenth Century* (2nd edn., 1982), 38–41.

[82] [Judith Drake], *An Essay in Defence of the Female Sex* (1696), Preface, 15–16.

[83] BL, Trumbull MS, D/ED c 13, 5 Apr. [1688?].

[84] Ibid. 22 June [1687?].

[85] For popular shame rituals, see M. Ingram, 'Ridings, Rough Music and Mocking Rhymes in Early Modern England', in B. Reay (ed.), *Popular Culture in Seventeenth-Century England* (1985), 166–97.

women were free of moral and sexual surveillance of some kind. In terms of women's own modes of coping with matrimonial problems, women of the upper ranks turned to a different set of female relationships for the same function. Whereas plebeian wives relied on nearby friends and neighbours for help in a crisis, gentlewomen were more likely to appeal to female relatives who lived at a distance.

If we analyse elements in married life that were closely tied to the politics of matrimonial relations, such as the degree of violence wives suffered from their husbands, then it is not at all clear that one social group had the edge over any of the others. Certain aspects of marriage, including women's vulnerability to misery and violence if they were unlucky in their partners, appear to have been so overdetermined in this society that they persist as a pattern throughout the social spectrum. Wifebeating was rife among all social groups for which we have any evidence.

What of the influence of economics on the relations of power and prestige between wives and husbands? While we might guess that wives who had separate settlements would be accorded more power *vis-à-vis* their husbands because they controlled their own financial resources, this conjecture is not borne out by surviving evidence. In the matrimonial disputes analysed by Margaret Hunt, the existence of a separate settlement was instead the instigating cause of conflict and matrimonial violence in a high proportion of cases, because the husband felt he ought to own everything. Nor is there any clear indication that plebeian or middling women were more valued, or were treated more as equals in marriage, because of their labour. At this level of society, it was assumed that all women ought to work, and in fact a major ground for violent marital conflict was the husband's belief that his wife was not working to her full capacity.[86]

Marriage was a different kind of institution and experience for women and for men in early modern times. Women's experiences were so various, influenced by so many different factors, that generalization is impossible. Some women found in marriage their greatest happiness; others, the most abject misery. For some it could be the best chance for social and economic survival; for others, the single life seemed more free of care. While it might appear that wives higher in the social scale were more subject to patriarchal power, we cannot confidently point to strong correlations with class differences without thinking of a host of exceptions to each one. A woman's reproductive capacity and her society's construction of her—in other words,

[86] Hunt, 'Wife Beating', 16–18.

biology and gender—appear to have been more important than class differences in determining general patterns of marriage at this time.

MATERNITY

Becoming a mother, one of the greatest blessings of marriage for many women, was a life-stage with both biological and cultural meaning. During pregnancy, parturition, and lactation, a woman's body was at its most different from that of a man. But far from being a 'natural' experience, motherhood was socially and historically constructed.[87] Mothers' experiences differed according to their marital status, social level, and a range of personal factors. Motherhood was a job; but it was also a relationship with profound significance for the woman herself and for her children's development as women and men.[88]

The maternity of single women was very different from that of wives. Not surprisingly, records suggest that pregnant women had hoped for marriage and had been disappointed. Unmarried, they could expect to be stigmatized as 'bastard bearers' and punished as whores. In one London parish in 1639, the clerk recorded that money paid out for an unmarried woman's lying-in was for 'the whore and her bastard'.[89] In some areas, the justices ordered 'bastard bearers' to receive physical punishment or a year in the house of correction, with or without their babies.[90] In 1599, the Essex justices ordered that Frances Barker was to be carted and whipped until her blood flowed, for bearing a bastard.[91] Parish authorities tried to force mothers in labour to divulge the names of the father, so that he would maintain the child. Confronted with threats that the midwife would not assist her, one single mother swore that 'although she should be torn in pieces with wild horses she could accuse none other', while another, whose wealthy lover had reneged on his promises, 'cried woe to the bones of him that ever she knew him, but if he had kept promise with her she would never have betrayed him though she had been racked to death'.[92]

[87] S. de Beauvoir, *The Second Sex*, trans. H. M. Parshley (1972). For recent discussion see E. Grosz, *Sexual Subversions: Three French Feminists* (Sydney, 1989), 70–99, 119–26; L. M. G. Zerilli, 'A Process Without a Subject: Simone de Beauvoir and Julia Kristeva on Maternity', *Signs*, 18 (1992), 111–35. Maternity was not a popular topic in feminist research in the 1980s.

[88] E. Ross, *Love and Toil: Motherhood in Outcast London, 1870–1918* (Oxford, 1993).

[89] Guildhall, MS 7706, St Katherine Creechurch Overseers Account Book, fo. 1^{v}.

[90] M. Dalton, *The Country Justice* (1655), 40–2; R. Kilburne, *Choice Presidents . . . Relating to the Office and duty of A Justice of the Peace* (1685), 45–6.

[91] Essex RO, Calendar of Quarter Session Rolls, xvii. 129.

[92] Essex RO, Q/SR 117/61 (10 June 1591); Q/SR 153/29, 30 (1601).

While parishes might pay money to a widow[93] or a poor woman to help her to rear her child, they usually sent the child of an unmarried mother out to nurse. For example, at St Matthew Friday Street in 1592, the vestry paid 20*s.* for the lodging and diet of a 'poor woman that was delivered of a child in Friday Street', while in 1600 they paid to send Elizabeth Gayll's child from her, and put her 'unto nurse unto Judith Gilbert a widow woman dwelling in Hertford'. Although it might have been cheaper to have supported the mother in keeping her child, since she could have kept herself in spinning and other casual work, the vestry paid for the nurse as well as for the child's clothing.[94]

The crime of infanticide was one which single women were more likely to commit than any other group in society. A study of infanticide in the early seventeenth century showed that of sixty mothers, fifty-three were single, six were widows.[95] Should a single mother have kept her child, subsequently her material circumstances may have made it difficult or impossible for her to support it, in which case again the parish or poor law officials would intervene by taking her child away and placing it in another household.

The majority of women who became mothers were wives. Maternity followed soon after marriage for a significant proportion of women. In a sample of rural parishes, it has been calculated that about 21 per cent of brides were pregnant. The percentage was less in London: only 16 per cent.[96] What these figures represent in terms of women's pre-marital sexual practices and hopes we can only guess. For some, pregnancy may have been a failure in contraceptive efforts, so that marriage was the unplanned outcome. For others, the marriage ceremony may have been accelerated, when the woman's pregnancy resulted from the commencement of sexual relations after a formal betrothal had been concluded.[97]

After marriage, in most cases, women conceived quickly and bore babies within ten months. Those who did not do so began to worry, for barrenness

[93] Widow Acreman was given rent and the same allowance for her children 'as is given to other nurses for nursing and keeping the said children' in 1697; Guildhall, MS 1196/1, St Katherine Creechurch, Vestry Minute Book, 1639–1718, fo. 228^{v}.

[94] Guildhall, MS 3579, St Matthew Friday St Vestry Minute Book, 1576–1743, fo. 3.

[95] K. Wrightson, 'Infanticide in Earlier Seventeenth-Century England', *Local Population Studies*, 15 (1975), 12. The conviction rate between 1684 and 1714, of women charged and tried, was around a third or more; Beattie, *Crime and the Courts*, 118.

[96] P. E. H. Hair, 'Bridal Pregnancy in Rural England in Earlier Centuries', *Population Studies*, 20 (1966), 233–43; P. E. H. Hair, 'Bridal Pregnancy in Earlier Rural England Further Examined', *Population Studies*, 24 (1970), 59–70; R. Finlay, *Population and Metropolis: The Demography of London, 1580–1650* (Cambridge, 1981), 149.

[97] See Ch. 2 above, 'Courtship'.

was seen as an unhappy female condition, perhaps even, as the Bible suggested, a punishment for sin. Women's own memoirs reveal the unhappy feelings of barren wives.[98] Through the diary of Sarah Savage, for example, we can trace a pattern of her alternating hopes of pregnancy and disappointments. Married in March 1687, within a few months Sarah was praying that if God should delay or deny the mercy of children to her, 'still by his grace I will wait on him, and love him not one jot the less, though sometimes I can scarce quiet my spirit as I would'.[99] The higher the social level, the greater the importance attached to child-bearing, so that wives longed not just for children, but for sons.

Women tried to control their fertility, although they lacked effective means. From a range of different kinds of evidence, we know that those who were unmarried hoped not to become pregnant, and that many who were married but unable to conceive were trying to do so. Women's medical commonplace books contain remedies for barrenness.[100] There is no real evidence that women had any better knowledge than men about how to procure conception. In 1664, a group of women merrily gave Samuel Pepys ten remedies for infertility, but Elizabeth never bore a child.[101] Although we can have no direct evidence of poor women's attitudes, we may speculate from the poor law records that sometimes their problem was limiting fertility; too many children may have threatened the economic survival of the whole family unit.

In London, medical practitioners offered advice about 'women's disorders' which may have covered advice about abortion. Later in the seventeenth century, such services were advertised.[102] Nevertheless, the large number of women who faced penalties for pregnancy outside wedlock suggests strongly that many women lacked access to reliable methods of contraception. Perhaps in some regions women knew of herbal remedies, such as savin. The effects of lactation in delaying conception may have been known, but apart from total abstinence, no method of prevention was reliable. Women may have found that abortion and infanticide were more certain methods of controlling fertility. Successful abortion would by its very

[98] P. Crawford, 'The Construction and Experience of Maternity', in V. Fildes (ed.), *Women as Mothers in Pre-Industrial England* (1990), 19 and n. 99.

[99] Chester City RO, Diary of Sarah Savage (1686–8), D/Basten/8, 22 May 1687.

[100] Wellcome Institute Library, MS 4338, W.IIa (Johanne St John, 1680); Folger, MS V. a. 387, Book of Katherine Packer, 1639, 22.

[101] *The Diary of Samuel Pepys*, ed. R. Latham and W. Matthews, 11 vols. (1970–83) v.222.

[102] P. Crawford, 'Printed Advertisements for Women Medical Practitioners in London, 1670–1710', *Society for the Social History of Medicine, Bulletin*, 35 (1984), 66–70; P. Crawford, 'Sexual Knowledge in England, 1500–1750', in R. Porter and M. Teich (eds.), *Sexual Knowledge, Sexual Science: The History of Attitudes to Sexuality* (Cambridge, 1994), 99.

nature have left few records. Few married women were prosecuted for infanticide, but their situation was very different from that of the single woman. Married mothers whose babies died were not objects of suspicion.[103]

Women understood that they were pregnant by certain bodily signs. Usually, they viewed the cessation of menstruation as one of the first symptoms: 'her monthly termes stop at some unseasonable time that she lookt not for.'[104] Court cases relating to 'bastardy' provide some intriguing hints about women's ideas about the relationship between sexual activity and conception. Many of the women were very definite about the particular occasion on which conception had occurred, although they admitted to sexual intercourse on previous occasions. For example, Martha Bonnington conjectured 'by her quickening' that she had conceived a month before Easter 1651. She could not tell when she expected the child, but was precise about the duration of her pregnancy: 'that she had been quick three weeks and two or three days.'[105] Conversely, in a defence against infanticide in 1651, Anne Greene pleaded that as she was not long 'without the usual courses of women', she could not be guilty of the crime of infanticide.[106]

Most women showed anxiety about their pregnancies. They feared miscarriage, and kept 'remedies' in their commonplace books 'For such as are subject to miscarry'.[107] Would the baby be healthy or deformed? Women recounted the popular lore to each other, believing that their behaviour, diet, and imagination could contribute to the outcome of their pregnancies. Maternal longings were to be indulged. The story was told that Archbishop Abbott's mother had dreamed that if she should eat a jack rabbit, 'her Son in her Belly should be a *Great Man*'.[108] Women feared the consequences of unexpected mishaps: a hare crossing a woman's path might give her child a hare lip. A mother's imagination or dreams might produce a monster.[109] Sins, including failure to observe the taboo on sexual activity during menstruation, could lead to miscarriage or deformity: Elizabeth Turner confessed that she knew not what caused her to miscarry in 1662, 'But am

103 A. McLaren, *A History of Contraception from Antiquity to the Present Day* (Oxford, 1990), 141–77.

104 J. Sharp, *The Midwives Book* (1671), 103.

105 Devon RO, QSB Box 58, 1651, no. 16.

106 *Newes from the Dead* (1651), 9.

107 Folger, MS V. a. 425, Commonplace book of Sarah Long (1610), fos. 21, 22, 26; see also MS V. a. 396 (1675), Commonplace book of P. Jephson, 10, 34, 36.

108 J. Aubrey, *Miscellanies* (1696), 52.

109 P. Crawford, '"The Sucking Child": Adult Attitudes to Child Care in the First Year of Life in Seventeenth-Century England', *Continuity and Change*, 1 (1986), 27; Crawford, 'Maternity', in Fildes (ed.), *Women as Mothers*, 21.

jealous [i.e. worried] least it may be a punishment of some particular sin'.[110] Lady Bridgewater prayed that her child might be 'born without any deformity, so that I and its father may not be punished for our sins, in the deformity of our babe'.[111] Some pregnant women were haunted by dreams of the deaths of their babies. Alice Thornton dreamt of lying in childbed with a white sheet spread but sprinkled with drops of blood. She recalled, 'I kept [the dream] in my mind till my child died'.[112] A horrible image of a dead child haunted the dreams of Lady Eleanor Davis, who was imprisoned in the Tower: she saw the child's head was cut off, and women were trying to comfort the 'head that cryed'.[113]

During every pregnancy, each woman feared her own death. Although Schofield has estimated that the chance of a woman dying in childbirth was not great—no more than a 6 or 7 per cent chance in her procreative career—this was not how women themselves calculated the danger.[114] 'I am now near the time of my travail,' wrote Mary Carey in 1649, 'and am very weak, faint, sickly, fearful, pained, apprehending much suffering before me, if not death it self, the King of Terrors.'[115] Around 1688, Mrs Witton noted in her diary that she was often in child-bearing circumstances, 'which I hope is a means to keep me on my watch and so make me ready for life or death'.[116] Some pregnant women prepared winding sheets for themselves, like the famous Mrs Elizabeth Joceline, who expected and found her death in childbirth.[117] Each woman must have anticipated pain. While men expatiated on the inevitability of the sorrows of childbirth because of the transgression of Eve—'none other thing but a worthie cross laid upon us by thy godly ordinance', taught Thomas Bentley in his prayers for women in the Elizabethan period—women prayed, and tried to secure the services of

[110] Kent Archives Office, F. 27, Journal of Elizabeth Turner (unfoliated), Oct 1662; Crawford, 'Attitudes to Menstruation in Seventeenth-Century England', *Past and Present*, 91 (1981) 62.

[111] BL, Egerton MS 607, E. Egerton, countess of Bridgewater, 'Meditations', fo. 33; S. H. Mendelson, 'Stuart Women's Diaries and Occasional Memoirs' in M. Prior (ed.), *Women in English Society, 1500–1800*, (1985), 196.

[112] Thornton, *Autobiography*, 123.

[113] Quoted in E. S. Cope, *Handmaid of the Holy Spirit: Dame Eleanor Davies, Never Soe Mad a Ladie* (Ann Arbor, 1992), 22.

[114] R. Schofield, 'Did the Mothers Really Die? Three Centuries of Maternal Mortality in "The World We Have Lost"', in L. Bonfield, R. M. Smith, and K. Wrightson (eds.), *The World We Have Gained: Histories of Population and Social Structure* (Oxford, 1986), 259.

[115] Bodl., MS Rawlinson D 1308, fo. 2. (Mary Carey, wife of George Payler).

[116] DWL, Henry MS 91/18, Extracts from Grandmother Witton's diary, transcribed early 18th cent. (fo. 2).

[117] E. Joceline, *The Mothers Legacie to her Unborne Child* (1624 and subsequent edns.); see also Leigh, *The Mothers Blessing*.

good midwives whom they could trust to help them.[118] Girls grew up seeing adult women around them die in childbirth: even if the birth was successful, many women suffered illness afterwards. Some even lost their wits, like Lucy Hutchinson's grandmother, who lost 'her most excellent understanding after a difficult childbirth'.[119] Each successful birth was an occasion for rejoicing, prayer, and thanksgiving.

Childbirth within wedlock was a *rite de passage* in female adulthood. For the majority of women, giving birth took place within a female culture. Childbirth was women's business, although the licensing of midwives was controlled by the male ecclesiastical authorities, and, by the end of our period, male medical practitioners were increasingly popular.[120] Women had strong views about who should deliver them. In church court cases for separations, one frequent grievance listed by wives was that their husbands had not allowed them to have the midwife they wanted, and consequently they had experienced a difficult labour. A cause of dispute between Sir Richard Grenville and his wife was his refusal to allow her the midwife of her choice.[121] By the early eighteenth century, some aristocratic London women asked their husbands to hire male doctors to attend them. A number of ladies praised Dr Chamberlen, vowing that they owed their lives to him, insisting 'they would not for never so much have a woman, its so much more terrible with a woman'.[122]

Childbirth took place in a separate, darkened room. Only adult women were present at the beginning of our period, and even after the incursion of the male midwife, the majority of women gave birth in an all-female environment. In addition to the midwife, the woman's mother and female relatives had significant roles, and a number of other women were invited to be present.[123] The woman in labour was sustained by cordials, but no other anaesthetic was available.[124]

Giving birth was followed a month or so later by churching, a ceremony which the Protestant Church defined as a thanksgiving for a safe delivery.

[118] T. Bentley, *The Monument of Matrones: Conteining Seven Severall Lamps of Virginitie* (1582), iii. 95.

[119] L. Hutchinson, *Memoirs of the Life of Colonel Hutchinson*, ed. J. Sutherland (Oxford, 1973), 19.

[120] For the licensing of midwives, and the work of midwives, see Chs. 5 and 6 below. For birth as part of female culture, see Ch. 4 below.

[121] S. R. Gardiner (ed.), *Reports of Cases in the Courts of Star Chamber and High Commission*, Camden Society, NS 39 (1886), 265–7. See also Bodl., MS Rawlinson B 381, fos. 5^{v}–10.

[122] BL, Add. MS 62225, fos. 375–6; J. J. Cartwright (ed.), *The Wentworth Papers, 1705–1739* (1883), 314 and n. Thanks to Frances Harris for these references.

[123] Mendelson, 'Stuart Women's Diaries', 196–7.

[124] For further discussion of childbirth, see Ch. 4; A. Wilson, 'The Ceremony of Childbirth and its Interpretation', in Fildes (ed.), *Women as Mothers*, 68–107.

FIG. 15. Childbirth. Most births took place in a darkened chamber, with only female adults present. Note the swaddled newborn baby lying on the coverlet

Churching signalled the woman's status as a mother, her community's recognition of her experience, and her own thanksgiving for her survival.[125] In the London parish of Southwark, the majority of women did attend the ceremony.[126] But not all women found churching acceptable, and some were presented to the church courts for failing to be churched, others for coming 'undecently and unwomanly without any woman with her'.[127] Some women disliked the ceremony on religious grounds.[128]

After giving birth, a mother either fed her child herself, or employed a

[125] D. Cressy, 'Purification, Thanksgiving and the Churching of Women in Post-Reformation England', *Past and Present,* 141 (1993), 106–46.

[126] J. Boulton, *Neighbourhood and Society: A London Suburb in the Seventeenth Century* (Cambridge, 1987), 276–9.

[127] F. G. Emmison, *Elizabethan Life: Morals and the Church Courts* (Chelmsford, 1973), 159–61.

[128] Crawford, *Women and Religion*, 55.

FIG. 16. Wet-nurse at a lying-in. After giving birth, a mother of middling or élite status might be assisted by a wet-nurse to help feed and care for her infant

wet-nurse. The higher a woman's social status, the less likely she was to suckle her own child. Although we know that some aristocratic woman wanted to feed their own babies, they could be overruled by their husbands, whose preference may have been for the resumption of sexual relations and further pregnancies.[129] In godly families, a father was more likely to support his wife's breast-feeding, and, of course, poorer women could not afford to hire a wet-nurse. Women exchanged their own lore about breast-feeding. Some suffered sore breasts and difficulties in drying up their milk, and sought remedies.[130] In her commonplace book, Katherine Parker wrote instructions for 'A poultice to break any sore breast' and 'for to make a

[129] E. Clinton, *The Countesse of Lincolnes Nurserie* (1622); Crawford, 'Sucking Child', 29–35.

[130] Folger, Women's commonplace books: MS V. a. 456, M. Baumfylde (1626), fo. 31; MS V. a. 396, Penelope Jephson (1675), fo. 88; MS V. a. 215, Susannah Packe (1674), fo. 285; Carlyn [1660], p. 50, gives a receipt to dry up a woman's milk and endorses it 'probatum est'.

woman have milk': 'Give her juice of Veruen [vervain] to drink it will bring her milk again.' Lettice Pudsey recorded 'Mrs Okeover's Recipe of Balsom . . . I have also found it most excellent for [a] sore breast'.[131]

Because infant mortality was high, many mothers suffered the deaths of their children.[132] In much of earlier historical debate about parental attitudes to infant mortality, historians did not distinguish the feelings of mothers from those of fathers, but there is abundant evidence of maternal grief at the deaths of children.[133] Margaret Lucas's sister died soon after her infant daughter, allegedly of inconsolable grief.[134] The countess of Bridgewater remembered being overcome with sorrow 'when I lost my Dear Girl Kate who was as fine a child [as] could be'. It 'grieves my heart, even my soul', she wrote, to remember that 'the last word she spoke was to me, when in passion I asked if I should kiss her, she said yes, . . . and lay so sweetly, desiring nothing but her Lord Jesus'.[135] In 1647 Lady Mary Verney was so distressed at the deaths of two of her children 'that she spake idly for two nights and sometimes did not know her frends'.[136] In 1680 Elizabeth Stout 'was afflicted with great sorrow by the death of her two youngest sones . . . she continued in much sorrow for a long time'.[137]

While early modern historians have studied childbirth and the care of young children,[138] they have devoted less attention to the relationship of mothers with their older and adult children. At the time of their deaths, many women were responsible for children under 10 years of age, a significant difference from today's experiences of maternity in the West. The subject is too large for investigation here, but a few brief comments about significant issues may suggest questions for further research.

Maternity, a constantly changing relationship, aroused in each woman a range of intense and sometimes contradictory emotions. At the lowest social

[131] Folger, Commonplace book, Katherine Packer (1639), MS V. a. 387, recipes 2, 8; MS V. a. 450, Lettice Pudsey, unfoliated.

[132] On the basis of 12 parish reconstitutions, roughly one child in four died in its first year; and another one in four before the age of 10; Wrigley and Schofield, *Population History*, 248–50.

[133] P. Ariès, *Centuries of Childhood* (1962); L. de Mause (ed.), *The History of Childhood* (New York, 1974); Stone, *The Family, Sex and Marriage*; L. Pollock, *Forgotten Children: Parent–Child Relations from 1500–1900* (Cambridge, 1983); R. A. Houlbrooke, *English Family Life, 1576–1716* (Oxford, 1988); Crawford, 'Sucking Child', 23–52.

[134] Mendelson, *Mental World*, 88.

[135] BL, Egerton MS 607, E. Egerton, countess of Bridgewater, 'Meditations', fos. 119^{v}.–25^{v}.

[136] F. P. and M. M. Verney, *Memoirs of the Verney Family during the Seventeenth Century* (3rd edn., 2 vols., 1925), i. 382.

[137] *The Autobiography of William Stout of Lancaster, 1665–1752*, ed. J. D. Marshall (Manchester, 1967), 76.

[138] Fildes (ed.), *Women as Mothers* and bibliography; H. Marland (ed.), *The Art of Midwifery: Early Modern Midwives in Europe* (1993); A. Wilson, *The Making of Man-Midwifery: Childbirth in England, 1660–1770* (1995).

FIG. 17. A poor woman with her children. Contemporaries were suspicious of beggars, and preferred to relieve poor women through organized charity. Yet some mothers, particularly those whose husbands did not provide for their families, had no option but to beg for the survival of their offspring. One of the small children holds a toy

levels, much of a woman's mothering energy was devoted to ensuring the sheer physical survival of her children in adverse material circumstances. At various stages of her children's lives, she might be endeavouring to provide for them so that they would not be apprenticed out by the parish, or placed in service against her wishes. Impoverished mothers may have been especially anxious about their daughters living away from home. In 1701 the parish of Aldenham threatened to cut off the poor relief from Widow Dickenson if she 'doth not forthwith put her daughter to service'.[139] We can only guess at the widow's motives, which could include a pleasure at her daughter's company, a need for her physical help, or a fear of her fate in service.

Elite women were less directly involved in caring for their children; theirs was more a supervisory role. Even so, many busied themselves with their children's education. 'My dear Fanny and little Clem are all the pleasure that two sweet natured towardly children can be, but then teaching comes in, which is a toil to me now' wrote Anne Dormer.[140] From Somerset, Mary Clarke told her husband 'I am as much employed in the care of my 6

[139] W. Newman Brown, 'The Receipt of Poor Relief and Family Situation: Aldenham, Hertfordshire, 1630–90', in R. Smith (ed.), *Land, Kinship and Life-Cycle* (Cambridge, 1984), 418.

[140] BL, Trumbull MS, D/ED c. 13, Anne Dormer to Lady Elizabeth Trumbull, 10 Mar. [1688?].

FIG. 18. A mother teaching her daughter. Literate mothers of middling or élite status were often closely involved in their daughters' education. Here a contemporary print shows a mother instructing a girl

children as you are with all your business in Parliament and elsewhere'.[141] Lower down the social scale, mothers shared the tasks of child-care with their own older daughters.

Mothers frequently professed their love for their children. 'I feel the same love to thee', wrote one Quaker woman, just 'as I did when I dandled thee

[141] Somerset RO, DD/SF 4515, no. 35.

upon my knees, and sweetly hugged thee in my bosom.'[142] Indeed, any mother who confessed that she could not love her child was considered by physicians to be suffering from mental disorder.[143] To save her children's souls, will not a mother 'venture to offend the world', declared Dorothy Leigh. 'The love of a mother to her children, is hardly contained within the bounds of reason.'[144] Some literate mothers prepared advice books for their children as a token of their love; a few of these works were printed, usually posthumously.[145]

Mothers allowed themselves to voice a preference for a particular child. Some seem to have had no compunction about favouritism, demonstrating little effort to love all children equally. Lady Isabella Wentworth usually addressed her eldest surviving son as 'dearist and best of children'; 'never mother loved her only child more then I doe you.'[146] Jonathan Priestley recorded that 'Joseph, my brother, was my mother's darling', but when his uncle challenged her preference, 'She would say, "Alas, brother, you know if one have one child sickly in the family, one is more tender of it than of all the rest that are well." '[147] Daughters too could be favourites: Anne Dormer wrote of her dying sister-in-law's concern for Fanny, 'who is her beloved of all her children'.[148]

Women's style of child-rearing was based on observation and experience. Unlike fathers, who dealt less with their children on a day-to-day basis, and were more likely to approach their children with demands for obedience, mothers were more likely than fathers to rely on their observations of children's behaviour in order to suit the discipline to the individual temperament. Mary Rich observed of a mother watching her child learn to walk: 'Though she let it go in a plane way, yet when it came near any steep stair or stumbling block take it in her arms and lift it over . . . how pleasingly have I observed the care this tender mother takes by her watchful eye to preserve her child from falling.'[149]

During the 1670s, Elizabeth Turner regularly reviewed the state of her

[142] Quoted in P. Mack, *Visionary Women: Ecstatic Prophecy in Seventeenth-Century England* (Berkeley, 1992), 359.

[143] Macdonald, *Mystical Bedlam*, 3–4.

[144] Leigh, *The Mothers Blessing*, 11–12.

[145] Northampton RO, Book of Advices to the Children by several Ladies Westmorland, W(A) misc. vol. 35; Crawford, 'Published Writings', 221–2.

[146] Cartwright (ed.), *Wentworth Papers*, 111, and *passim*.

[147] 'Some Memoirs . . . by Jonathan Priestley, 1696', in *Yorkshire Diaries and Autobiographies in the Seventeenth and Eighteenth Centuries*, ii, Surtees Society, 77 (1886), 22–3. Other families in which a son was observed to be 'his mother's favourite' included the Norths; *The Lives of the Norths*, ed. A. Jessopp, 3 vols. (1890), ii. 2.

[148] BL, Trumbull MS, D/ED c. 13, Anne Dormer to Lady Elizabeth Trumbull, 8 Nov. 1689.

[149] BL, Add. MS 27356, fos. 48^{v}–9.

FIG. 19. Family life. Family life as depicted in this woodcut shows the mother with her children grouped around her, with the father standing slightly apart

children's souls on her wedding anniversary. As her eldest son was 'full of pride and self conceit and carried forth with expectation of applause', her endeavour was to convince him 'of the need for truthfulness'; a daughter Mary was 'graciously inclined', but bodily weakness had meant she was 'very much indulged and withheld from discipline'.[150] In marriage negotiations for their children, mothers showed a careful awareness of the multiple factors to be balanced out to secure their children's happiness. They shared the complex ideas of the rest of the family about marriage, but they were frequently more directly concerned with their children's aims.[151]

Mothers related to their adult daughters and sons differently. They offered help to daughters. Frequently, mothers were key figures in their daughters' lying-in, and assisted with child-care while the new mothers continued with their chores. Sarah Savage, for example, told her sister that she had to 'keep house many times while they milk. I have a great

[150] Kent AO, Journal of Elizabeth Turner (unfoliated), 14 Feb. 1673[4], 14 Feb. 1677[8].

[151] For examples from a range of social levels, see OA, MS Oxf. Dioc. papers c. 27, 1634–9, fos. 66, 328–43^{v}; Mendelson, *Mental World*, 111–12; Emmison, *Elizabethan Life: Morals and the Church Courts*, 150.

miss of my mother to nurse and rock.'[152] In turn, Sarah journeyed to help her daughters with their lyings-in by caring for the other children in the family.[153] Contacts between Jane Josselin and her daughters seem to have increased after their marriages; sometimes they came home to lie-in, at other times Jane travelled to be with them.[154] Some mothers tried to help their unhappily married daughters. Mothers' testimonies in the church courts tell of their attempts to restrain abusive sons-in-law, and to support their daughters' complaints. In their relationships with adult sons, however, mothers of gentry rank were more likely to defer to their sons and to rely upon them for assistance. Some used their sons as intermediaries with the patriarchal world. Brilliana Harley regularly urged her son Edward to ask her husband Sir Robert for the things she wanted. As she explained to Ned in 1641, she would 'be very glad, if your father would be pleased to bye a coach and haue horrses . . . . And good Ned, tell your father so, and let me pray you to put him in minde of it.'[155] One mother hoped that her son Nat 'will be a comfort to me and his father: and a staff to us in our old age'.[156]

Mothers, like fathers, resorted to physical punishment, but they also sought other means of exercising their authority. If a mother did not allow her children to be beaten, it seems to have occasioned remark. Princess Anne was reported to be 'the tenderest of mothers' for she would not permit her son be whipped.[157] Margaret Lucas recollected that her mother 'did strive, to please and delight her children, not to cross and torment them'.[158] In other families, however, mothers were the disciplinarians. Roger North remembered that his mother Anne 'maintained her authority', and reduced her argumentative children to obedience 'by the smart of correction'.[159] The best-known disciplinarian was probably Susanna Wesley who taught her children when they were a year old 'to fear the rod, and to cry softly'.[160] Evidence about the middling ranks would be worth exploring more fully. Ann Hulton told her mother, with whom her 4-year-old daughter was to stay for a time, to use the rod sometimes, as

[152] DWL, Henry MSS 4 no. 29. (*c.* 1700).

[153] Bodl., MS Eng Misc e 331, Diary of Sarah Savage, 1714–1723, 96–7.

[154] A. Macfarlane, *The Family Life of Ralph Josselin, a Seventeenth-Century Clergyman: An Essay in Historical Anthropology* (Cambridge, 1970), 113–17.

[155] *Letters of the Lady Brilliana Harley*, ed. T. T. Lewis, Camden Society, 58 (1854), 134 and *passim.*

[156] Folger, Rich MSS, X. d. 451, no. 168.

[157] J. Lewis, *Memoirs of Prince William Henry* (1789), 19–20.

[158] M. Cavendish, duchess of Newcastle, *Natures Pictures Drawn by Fancies Pencil to the Life* (1656), 370.

[159] *Autobiography of . . . Roger North* ed. A. Jesopp (1887), 4.

[160] Wesley, *Journals*, iii. 34.

the child required it.[161] Mary Clarke treated her children as individuals whose disparate personalities required different kinds and degrees of discipline.[162] Sarah Meadows in her 'Reflections on the education of her children', completed just before her death in 1688, urged 'the breaking their wills betimes'.[163]

Mothers' strong involvement with their children gave them claims to influence. Brilliana Harley was in constant and loving correspondence with her eldest son, Ned.[164] In the letters of Sir John Holles, later first earl of Clare, his wife Anne's deep concern for their eldest son John was manifest through the instructions and messages Sir John relayed: be guided by your mother in diet; obey your mother in all things.[165] When John travelled to France, his father rebuked him for not writing to her: 'your mother muche marvailed shee had no lyns from yow, which nevertheless lyk a mother shee layeth uppon accident.'[166] News of her son's illness so afflicted her that she 'thought and dreampt of nothing else'.[167] Later, when their daughter Arbella died in childbirth, Anne was devastated with grief: 'these three days shee hath not eaten one bitt of bread, and muche a doe have I with her, to gett down one spoonfull of brothe.'[168] Lady Petty's weekly letters from Ireland to two of her children in London later in the seventeenth century contained a stream of maternal admonitions about their health, behaviour, and social activities: 'My Dear children, . . . I would have you tell me every thing you hear, and where you go, and who comes to see you, and what clothes you have.'[169]

Nevertheless, conflicts did occur, particularly with adolescent children. No doubt skilful women negotiated successfully, but the records do tell of clashes. Brilliana Harley was unsympathetic to the 'fits' which her second son Robert experienced; he should learn that 'his stubborneness was not the way to gaine any thinge but reproufe'.[170] Different religious preferences could also precipitate divisions between mothers and children. In Queen Mary's reign, the bitter resentment shown by Julins Palmer's mother when he espoused the Protestant faith was memorably expressed:

161 BL, Add. MS 42,849, fo. 20 (Anne Hulton to Katharine Henry, 8 June 1697).

162 *The Correspondence of John Locke and Edward Clarke*, ed. B. Rand (Cambridge, Mass., 1927), 247–9.

163 E. Taylor (ed.), *The Suffolk Bartholomeans: A Memoir* (1840), 140.

164 *Letters of Brilliana Harley*, *passim.*

165 *Letters of John Holles, 1587–1637*, ed. P. R. Seddon, Thoroton Society, 3 vols., 31, 35, 36 (1975–86), i. 95, 98. John, b. 13 June 1595 (*DNB*).

166 Ibid., i. 80.

167 Ibid., i. 102.

168 Ibid., iii. 432.

169 BL, Sir William Petty's Papers, vol. 8, fos. 3–3^{v} and *passim.*

170 *Letters of Brilliana Harley*, 9.

'If thou be at that point' [of Protestant faith], saith she, 'I require thee to depart from my house and out of my sight, and never take me more for thy mother hereafter. As for money and goods I have none of thine, thy father bequeathed nought for heretics: faggots I have to burn thee.'[171]

In 1654, Prince Charles warned his brother Henry against the religious influence of their mother: obey her 'in all things, religion only excepted'.[172] Nevertheless, Henrietta Maria did her work of conversion very successfully, as all of her adult children died in the Catholic faith. In other cases, young people testified to the major influence which their mothers had upon their own religious choices.[173] Margaret Plowden's mother 'made a promise to God, that if one of her daughers would be religious she would willingly give her to God'. Margaret professed as an Augustinian nun in 1625.[174]

The very poorest mothers had fewer opportunities than wealthier women to develop close relationships with their adult children. Marrying later than gentlewomen, they were less likely to live until their children reached maturity. The poorer mothers were, the younger the age at which their children moved away from home.[175] Unlike wealthier, literate women, plebeian mothers could not correspond nor so easily travel to visit their children. Yet while studies of migration suggest that many people lived at a distance from their parents, we should not conclude from this demographic evidence that family ties were broken.[176] Other evidence shows that there were multiple connections between mothers and their adolescent or adult children. Even if women could not write, they paid others to write for them.[177] Furthermore, many people continued to live within walking distance of their parents. By the mid-seventeenth century, a special visit to mothers had developed into a regular custom. In Worcester, 'Every Midlent Sunday is a great day . . . when all the children and godchildren meet at the head and cheife of the family and have a feast. They call it the Mothering-day.'[178] The custom of seeking the mother's blessing was widespread.[179]

While most women's maternity began within their bodies, others became

[171] Foxe, quoted in S. Brigden, 'Youth and the English Reformation', *Past and Present,* 95 (1982), 58.

[172] Bodl., MS Clarendon 48, fo. 324.

[173] Crawford, *Women and Religion*, 60–1.

[174] H. Foley (ed.), *Records of the English Province of the Society of Jesus*, 7 vols. (1882), iv. 19.

[175] Pauper children were commonly apprenticed at 8 years of age; P. Sharpe, 'Poor Children as Apprentices in Colyton, 1598–1830', *Continuity and Change*, 6 (1991), 255.

[176] cf. P. Laslett, *Family Life and Illicit Love in Earlier Generations: Essays in Historical Sociology* (Cambridge, 1980), 65–75, 259–60.

[177] *The Diary of Roger Lowe, 1663–74*, ed. W. Sachse (New Haven, 1938), 24, 28, 42–3, 46, 48, 51, 53, 62–3; *Casebook of Sir Francis Ashley*, 7–8.

[178] *Diary of the Marches of the Royal Army . . . by Richard Symonds*, ed. C. E. Long, Camden Society, 74 (1859), 27.

[179] C. Hole, *British Folk Customs* (1976), 142.

mothers when they married widowers with children, took in orphans, or undertook fostering. Stepmothers had no easy role, for it was one to which many contemporaries expressed hostility. Folk tales and ballads of cruel stepmothers presented a negative image. A father who remarried was said to do nothing 'of better liking to his foes'.[180] Yet records show that some stepmothers consciously struggled against negative stereotypes. One who became a stepmother on her marriage could not bear to think of herself 'in that relation', because she believed it was generally the occasion of so much cruelty and wrong: 'She loved Children exceedingly, and could not bear their hard usage.'[181] The widowed Mary Wilson decided, when courted by the widowed Bulstrode Whitelocke, the father of ten children, that his children needed mothering: 'And in marrying him, I thought I might be in a capacity to do some good amongst those children.'[182] Mary Rich, countess of Warwick, endeavoured to care for her orphaned nieces 'as if they had been my own'.[183] Some children lived with relatives: Elin Stout and her brother Leonard always looked after two of their nephews and nieces as soon as they turned 2 years old, and Elin 'was as carfull to nurs and correct them as if they had been her own children'.[184] Fostering was another form of maternity which was widespread, especially in the London parishes. While fostering was paid work, many women undertook a maternal role towards the orphans or illegitimate children entrusted to their care. For example, in the accounts of St Alban Wood Street, Goody Hasell received payments for the care of a parish foundling, Ann Alban, from at least 1642 to 1650; to keep a foster child alive in London for over eight years suggests devotion and skill in mothering.[185]

Motherhood played a large role in constructing women's subjectivities. A woman's sense of herself as a mother changed over her lifetime, as her children developed. In this evolving process, the historical variables which structured women's experiences of motherhood were as important as the biological and physical elements.

[180] J. Newnham, *Newnams Nighcrowe. A Bird that Breedeth Brauls in many Families and Households* (1590), 23. On p. 32 Newnham says that stepmothers ought not to procure the disinheriting of their husband's eldest sons.

[181] *Conversion Exemplified* (1669), sig. A5^{v}.; see also, Crawford, 'The Construction and Experience of Maternity', 25–6.

[182] R. H. Whitelocke, *Memoirs, Biographical and Historical, of Bulstrode Whitelocke* (1860), 286.

[183] *Autobiography of Mary, Countess of Warwick*, ed. T. Croker, Percy Society (1848), 28–31.

[184] Stout, *Autobiography*, 142.

[185] Guildhall, MS 7674, St Alban Wood Street . . . Accounts, 1627–75.

SINGLE WOMEN

A marryd state affords but little Ease
The best of husbands are so hard to please . . .
A virgin state is crown'd with much content
Its allways happy as its inocent[186]

Katherine Philips's praise of the single life was echoed lower down the social scale in occasional ballads.

A single Life is void of Care,
For married Wives much pinch and spare.
. . . Besides my Mother she doth cry,
I shall have all when she doth dye.[187]

These were not, however, the dominant poetic voices. Since contemporary wisdom declared that woman was made for man, any adult woman without a husband was an anomaly. Mary Astell, herself single, remarked that many women were 'quite terrified with the dreadful name of Old Maid . . . the scoffs that are thrown on superannuated Virgins'.[188] Indeed, by ignoring the single woman and refusing to acknowledge her existence, contemporaries contributed to her invisibility. Historians have to a degree shared that contemporary bias. They have written as though all women were married, discussing single women in terms of their failure to marry. As Lawrence Stone wrote of a young woman of unspecified age in 1700, 'She was penniless and ugly, and if left a spinster was likely to become a burden to the family.'[189] Furthermore, feminist historians have concentrated on married women, since marriage has been seen as a site of female oppression. We have therefore sought to comment on some general features of single women's lives and to suggest some questions which need further research.

Terminology for the single woman has reflected social attitudes to her unmarried state. The term 'spinster' was ambiguous, referring both to a woman's matrimonial and occupational status. Since a number of court records include indictments of women as both 'wife' and 'spinster'—in

[186] K. Philips, untitled poem, written before 1648, in G. Greer *et al.*, *Kissing the Rod: An Anthology of Seventeenth-Century Women's Verse* (1988), 188–9.

[187] *The Roxburghe Ballads*, ed. W. Chappell and J. Ebsworth, 9 vols. in 8 (London and Hertford, 1866–99), iii. 652, 'The Crafty Maid'. See also Bodl., Douce Ballads 2, fo. 144, 'The Maidens Fairing'.

[188] M. Astell, *A Serious Proposal to the Ladies* (1694), 160. See also Ch. 1.

[189] Stone, *Uncertain Unions*, 136.

the form 'A.B. wife of C.D. spinster'—historians have inferred that the word 'spinster' does not always refer to a single woman.[190] The phrase 'unmarried woman' is a definition by an absence. The classification 'never married' should not, strictly speaking, be used until a woman has died. The term 'independent women' seems inappropriate since many single women were dependent on poor relief. Increasingly popular in the later seventeenth century was the derogatory term, 'old maid'. Although to be an old maid implied virginity, the sexual status of the single woman was unclear. Some were sexually active with men, others with women.

The sources are biased towards the obedient, pious single woman. Institutional records contain more information about the 'good' women who sought assistance because they lacked a man's support than about those who lived outside the patriarchal household. Independent single women, to whom their contemporaries referred variously as vagrants, criminals, or prostitutes, left few traces of their ideas about their lives and their choices.[191]

The difficulty of finding out about the lives of single women extends to uncertainty about their numbers. The proportion of single to married adult women is difficult to estimate. Gregory King calculated that of those over 25 only a small proportion, 2.5 per cent, remained unmarried.[192] Nevertheless, 2 per cent of the total population amounts to 11,200 unmarried women over 25. The proportion of single to married women fluctuated enormously over the early modern period. Wrigley and Schofield estimated that in the years 1560–1720, between 5 and 27 per cent of the population never married. (These figures do not distinguish between males and females.) Although the proportion of celibates rises to about 27 per cent of those born in the mid-seventeenth century, this may be an exaggerated figure because of an increasing number of clandestine marriages.[193] Recent revision suggests that

[190] *County of Middlesex. Calendar to the Sessions Records, 1612–1616*, ed. W. Le Hardy, 3 vols (1935), iii. 242; C. Z. Wiener, 'Is a Spinster an Unmarried Woman?' *The American Journal of Legal History*, 20 (1976), 27–31; J. H. Baker, 'Male and Married Spinsters', *The American Journal of Legal History*, 21 (1977), 255–9; V. C. Edwards, 'The Case of the Married Spinster: An Alternative Explanation', *The American Journal of Legal History*, 21 (1977), 260–5.

[191] S. Amussen, 'Elizabeth I and Alice Balstone: Gender, Class, and the Exceptional Woman in Early Modern England', in B. S. Travitsky and A. F. Seeff (eds.), *Attending to Women in Early Modern England* (Newark, NJ., 1994), 223–5.

[192] G. King, *Natural and Political Observations . . . upon the State and Condition of England* (1696), 40. It is worth noting that the number of unmarried females at any one time was a large proportion of the total female population, for the number under 25 who were unmarried was high, and we should include widows, and women 'between' marriages.

[193] Of those born around the mid-16th cent., the proportion never marrying was between 4–8%. However, of those born around 1600, the figures rose to about 24%. Wrigley and Schofield, *Population History*, 260–3.

of the birth cohort of 1666, which married mainly during the period 1680–1704, only 9.2 per cent remained unmarried.[194] Furthermore, the proportions varied at different social levels. Among the daughters of peers, only 5 per cent did not marry in 1600, but in the later period 1675–1724, the proportion increased, fluctuating between 20 per cent and 28 per cent.[195]

Both contemporaries and demographers have problematized celibacy, treating marriage as normal, and then 'explaining' single women's failure to marry. According to demographers' theories, several factors influenced marriage rates. First, sex ratios varied. More males than females were born, but the mortality rate among males was higher.[196] In London there was an increase in the proportion of single women over the seventeenth century, as apprenticeship for men declined in importance while the demand for female domestic servants grew.[197] Outside London, the sex ratios in individual towns varied; ratios of female to male heads of household differed from town to town, and the burial registers show that different proportions of women and men died of the plague.[198] More women than men migrated into large towns and cities, leading to a surplus of males in the rural areas, and of females in urban districts.[199] Single women had reduced chances of marrying in towns.[200] Migration out of England also affected the ratios; men outnumbered female emigrants by three to one by the early eighteenth century, and probably did so earlier.[201] Secondly, demographers have argued that the proportion of people never marrying rose as a response to a fall in real wages.[202] This was an ironic development for women: if fewer married, their chances of survival in bad times were even worse. While it may be that unfavourable sex ratios affected women's opportunities for marriage, we

[194] R. Schofield, 'English Marriage Patterns Revisited', *Journal of Family History*, 10 (1985), 14.

[195] Stone, *Family*, 43, 47. Stone calculated on the basis of those over 50 years of age who had never married.

[196] Wrigley and Schofield, *Population History*, 225, have a table for 1700+ ratios.

[197] R. Finlay, *Population and Metropolis* (Cambridge, 1987), 139–41 and table; J. Barry (ed.), *The Tudor and Stuart Town: A Reader in English Urban History* (1990), 23.

[198] P. Slack, *The Impact of Plague in Tudor and Stuart England* (1985), 179–81, 382–3. Slack observes that we do not yet know what the sex ratios in towns were before the plague.

[199] D. Souden, 'Migrants and the Population Structure of Later Seventeenth-Century Provincial Cities and Market Towns', in P. Clark (ed.), *The Transformation of English Provincial Towns, 1600–1800* (1984), 133–68.

[200] Boulton, *Neighbourhood*, 130.

[201] Wrigley and Schofield, *Population History*, 223–6.

[202] Schofield, 'English Marriage Patterns Revisited', 16.

cannot assume that all women wanted to marry; some may have deliberately chosen the single state.[203] Demography can mislead because it conflates statistical data with socially conditioned outcomes.

Not all women desired marriage. Many expressed reservations. John Evelyn's daughter Mary 'showed greate indifference to marrying at all'.[204] Elizabeth Stout advised her daughter Elizabeth, whose health was poor, 'to remain single, knowing the care and exercises that always attended a marryed life, and the hazerd of hapiness in it'.[205] Margaret Kennedy's servant, when asked 'if she would not be glad to see her lady marryed?', replied, 'truly . . . she would be sorry to know her such a foole as to quite [quit] a contented life to make her selfe a slave to any man's humour'.[206] We know too, of some women who chose to remain single for spiritual reasons. By the seventeenth century, these were chiefly Catholic women, some of whom entered convents abroad.[207] Others abandoned their dreams of the cloister in order to stay single and assist the missionary effort in England.[208] Some Anglican women considered celibacy for spiritual reasons, but were usually dissuaded by their spiritual advisers. In the 1630s, two of the Ferrar women at Little Gidding wanted to make vows of chastity, but Bishop Williams dissuaded them: 'Let the younger Women marry was the best Advice, that they might not be led into Temptation.'[209] In the 1670s Margaret Blagge initially resisted marriage to Sidney Godolphin for spiritual reasons: 'one day I fancy no life so pure as the unmarried.' Although she resolved on celibacy—'I will keep my Virgin, present it unto Christ, and not put myself into the temptation of loving anything in Competition with my God'—she nevertheless married in 1675.[210]

Happy single women provided counter-examples to the contemporary Protestant chorus praising matrimony. In 1688 Jane Barker celebrated

[203] One of the assumptions in the Cambridge Group's calculations about the proportion of the population never marrying is that people wanted to marry, and explanation is required for why they did not. However, it should be equally valid to explore why people marry: it is no more 'natural' than the single state.

[204] *Diary of John Evelyn*, ed. W. Bray, 4 vols. (1879), ii. 456.

[205] *Autobiography of William Stout*, 87.

[206] *Letters from Lady Margaret Kennedy to John, duke of Lauderdale*, Bannatyne Club, 24 (Edinburgh, 1828), 17–18.

[207] For a study of English women in convents abroad, see C. Walker, 'Contemplative Communities: English Catholic Convents in France and the Low Countries, 1598–1700', Ph.D. diss., University of Western Australia (1996). Walker suggests that their numbers may not have amounted to more than 2,000.

[208] G. Anstruther, *Vaux of Harrowden: A Recusant Family* (Newport, 1953), 191, 461.

[209] J. Hacket, *Memoirs of the Life of Archbishop Williams* (1715), 154.

[210] J. Evelyn, *The Life of Margaret Godolphin* (1904), 46–7, 50.

singleness in her poem 'A Virgin life', concluding with a positive view of her existence:

> Her whole lives business, she drives to these ends,
> To serve her god, her neighbour, and her friends.[211]

Joyce Jeffreys, who died in 1650, spent a busy life occupied with farming, market gardening, horse breeding, and money lending. Never married, she interested herself in her young relatives, her friends, religious duties, and pursuits such as gardening and duck-keeping.[212] Celia Fiennes travelled England for over thirty years, recording her observations. She recommended to her 'own Sex, the studdy of those things which tends to improve the mind and makes our Lives pleasant and comfortable as well as proffitable in all the Stages and Stations of our Lives'.[213] In the preface to her anonymously published work, Mary Chudleigh referred to herself as 'one who never came within the clutches of a husband'.[214]

The adult lives of single women were similar to those of married women and widows in several ways. Families of origin determined much of their social and material status. Their work opportunities as women were limited, and their pay was less than that of their male counterparts. Nevertheless, there were important differences between the single and married adult woman. First, a single woman could trade on her own account. She had a legal identity which allowed her to sue and be sued. Secondly, her sexual life and her maternal responsibilities differed. In any heterosexual relationship outside marriage, a fertile woman risked pregnancy and social disgrace. Thirdly, a woman's opportunities for independence varied according to her social rank. Elite single women had a greater chance of independence than any other adult women. At the lowest social levels, single women, deserted wives, and widows all suffered poverty, although the latter two groups were more likely to have children to support.

If a single woman succeeded financially, she achieved a measure of independence greater than that enjoyed by her married counterpart. As Amy Froide's work demonstrates, in Southampton a number of single women were able to trade on their own because they received bequests of

[211] Greer *et al.*, *Kissing the Rod*, 360–1.

[212] R. G. Griffiths, 'Joyce Jeffreys of Ham Castle', *Transactions of the Worcestershire Archaeological Society*, NS 10–12 (1933–5).

[213] C. Morris (ed.), *The Illustrated Journeys of Celia Fiennes, 1685–c.1712* (1982), 33.

[214] [M. Chudleigh], *The Female Advocate* (1700).

FIG. 20. Susanna Perwich, who died in 1661, age 25. John Batchiler's funeral sermon for Susanna Perwich, *The Virgins Pattern* (1661), commended the virtues of the young single woman. Perwich's training in music, mathematics, and calligraphy enabled her to earn her living as a teacher of girls in her parents' Hackney school

money and goods from their mothers and aunts. A number of women who had choices preferred to remain unmarried.[215]

Whatever their social level, single women were not expected to keep house on their own or together. At the upper levels of society, such women

[215] A. Froide, '"Passing the Buck": The Transmission of Trades Between Single Women in Early Modern England', unpublished paper presented to 1995 NACBS meeting. We are grateful to Dr Froide for allowing us to cite her paper.

usually lived with relatives or friends, although their position in the household could be an uneasy one. Paulina Pepys joined the household of her brother Samuel and his wife Elizabeth in London in 1661. Samuel insisted that she was to live there 'not as a Sister in any respect but as a servant', and refused to allow her to eat with them. Not surprisingly, given her anomalous situation, he soon found her 'proud and idle' and so dismissed her. Thereafter her family busied themselves in trying to find her a husband.[216] Higher up the social scale, Anne Halkett was on an extended visit to Sir Charles Howard and his wife at Naworth castle, when gossip made her believe herself unwelcome to Lady Howard because she was suspected of a sexual liaison with Sir Charles.[217] Stories of courtships suggest that single women were watched closely by their relatives. In some cases, women exercised ingenuity in evading their families' surveillance. Unmarried gentlewomen usually lived under the control of fathers or male relatives. For example, in the late seventeenth century, the orphaned Elizabeth Elstob was placed under the governance of her uncle 'who was no Friend to Womens Learning'; even as an adult, she lived with her brother.[218]

From the sixteenth century, Protestant single women planned various kinds of societies or colleges where they might live together, as men were able to do at institutions such as universities and the Inns of Court.[219] In the 1630s, the widowed Lettice, Viscountess Falkland, proposed Great Tew as a place where widows might retire and young women be educated. The most famous seventeenth-century proposal was that of Mary Astell, who in 1694 advocated the establishment of a college for unmarried women. Patronage was thwarted by men's fears that the college would be too much like a nunnery. Bishop Burnet, who opposed the scheme, may have been more worried about the prospect of independence for women than he was about the attractions of Roman Catholicism.[220]

At the middling social level, a single woman was likely to be a servant in someone else's household. If her family were wealthy enough, they might keep her at home. On the basis of probate documents, Erickson has estimated that about half of the population of single woman were living alone at their deaths, half in the households of others. In some areas, such as

[216] Pepys, *Diary*, i. 288, 290–1; ii. 4, 139, 153; iv. 366; v. 42–3 (and index entries).

[217] *Memoirs of Anne, Lady Halkett*, 32–50.

[218] Bodl., Ballard MS 43, fos. 57–61.

[219] B. Hill, 'A Refuge from Men: The Idea of a Protestant Nunnery', *Past and Present*, 117 (1987), 107–30.

[220] R. Perry, *The Celebrated Mary Astell: An Early English Feminist* (Chicago, 1986), 134, 502 n. 34.

Yorkshire, many single women had small holdings of land.[221] The poorest women were lodgers in the households of others.[222]

Neighbourhoods were unwelcoming to single women who were not in service. Parishes suspected that all such unmarried women would bear bastards, and thus increase the poor rates.[223] A case of 1704, in which a husbandman responded to a charge of assault brought against him by Joanna Box, a single woman, illustrates how prejudices were linked:

> The said Joanna & Mary Box are two lusty young wenches & fare well & plentifully, & will not go to service, but live with their said mother, in a little house & occupy no land, nor having any visible estate or stock to live upon in an honest way, except Spining wch is a miserable trade now since the wars; no man nor woman living with them, except when some men of no very good fame haunt & frequent their company.[224]

At the poorer levels, the alternatives to service were few, and single women, particularly in London, were involved in an economy of makeshifts which could include prostitution.[225] Although women's wages were lower and their employment opportunities more limited than those of men, they had similar subsistence costs for rent and food. They were restricted in the exercise of the skills they had learned. For example, in Elizabethan Manchester the Court Leet ordered in 1589 that no single woman was to keep any house or chamber, or sell ale or bread, or work at other trades.[226] The stated reason was the protection of the family economy of poor men: single women's trading was said to be 'to ye great hurtte of ye poore Inhabitants havinge wiefe & children'.[227]

Heterosexuality was dangerous for all single women. While contemporaries disapproved of illicit sexual activity by single men, there was a *de facto* tolerance of brothels and prostitution. The only 'safe' sex for single women (safe in that it carried no risk of pregnancy) was lesbian. We know little about women, married or single, whose sexual needs were met by other women. Cohabitation was difficult for single women, unless one disguised herself as a man.[228]

[221] A. L. Erickson, *Women and Property in Early Modern England* (1993), 191.

[222] Boulton, *Neighbourhood*, 132. [223] Ibid. 129 n. 28.

[224] Cited in E. P. Thompson, *Customs in Common* (Harmonsdsworth, 1993), 501.

[225] See Ch. 5 below.

[226] T. S. Willan, *Elizabethan Manchester*, Chetham Society (Manchester, 1980), 82.

[227] J. P. Earwaker (ed.), *The Court Leet Records of the Manor of Manchester* (Manchester, 1884–90), ii. 37–8. The order was reiterated in 1588.

[228] W. Hooper, 'The Tudor Sumptuary Laws', *EHR*, 30 (1915), 448–9; J. E. Howard, 'Cross-dressing, the Theatre, and Gender Struggle in Early Modern England', *Shakespeare Quarterly*, 39 (1988), 420–1. For a case of two women marrying, see Ch. 4 below.

FIG. 21. Young unmarried women carrying the coffin of their friend. At the funeral of a young single woman, it was customary for her unmarried female friends to serve as pallbearers, as depicted in this ballad woodcut

Unlike married women, who had no goods of their own, single women were permitted to make wills. The survival of wills varied. They were rare in Elizabethan Manchester.[229] Yet single women may have been uncertain of their rights. Susannah Perwich, a young woman who taught in her parents' school in Restoration London, was able to bequeath her few personal possessions to her friends only with the permission of her father.[230] Erickson has estimated that up to 20 per cent of surviving women's wills in the early modern period were made by single women. This group favoured female legatees more frequently than male testators did. Girls might therefore have had an unmarried sister or aunt as a benefactress.[231]

At the end of the seventeenth century, the negative stereotype of the 'old maid' was more commonly used as a bogey to frighten women; Mary Astell claimed that many women embraced dishonourable marriages lest they should become 'old maids'.[232] While Astell recognized that most women would marry, she had a positive view of the single state. She, and other

[229] Willan, *Elizabethan Manchester*, 97. [230] J. Batchiler, *The Virgins Pattern* (1661), 33.
[231] Erickson, *Women and Property*, 204–22.
[232] Astell, *Serious Proposal*, 160–1. See also Ch. 1, 'Contexts: Stereotypes', above.

women, may have chosen to remain single, perhaps preferring their own sex, or fearing pregnancy and childbirth. Some may simply have enjoyed the independence which the *feme sole* status allowed. Those who chose to be single made a primary commitment not to a man but to themselves.

WIDOWHOOD

Women perceived widowhood as a life-stage. As Alice Thornton observed, commenting on 'the first yeare of my widdowed condition', she had already 'passed through the two stages of my life of my virgin estate, and that of the hon[ou]rable estate of marriage'.[233] Widowhood could occur at any time after marriage. While each widow's experiences were different, certain factors affected them all: contemporary attitudes, their social and economic position, their age, and the number of their dependants. Widowhood could also be a transitory stage, for many widows remarried.

The number of women who were widows at any one time is difficult to estimate. Calculations about the marital status of heads of household do not necessarily distinguish between single women and widows.[234] Moreover, not all women who claimed to be widowed were truly so. Unmarried mothers could pass themselves off as widows, as a church court case of 1706 demonstrated. Phoebe Harrison nursed a child for a year or so at lodgings, claiming to be a widow, but was in fact supported by her lover, who passed as an uncle.[235] Nevertheless, demographers estimate that there were more than twice as many widows as widowers in the population.[236] Wives were usually younger than their husbands, and thus more likely to be widowed than husbands were to become widowers. Women's mortality rates improved after they passed the child-bearing years. At the end of the seventeenth century, Gregory King calculated that widows made up 4.5 per cent of the total population (compared with 1.5 per cent widowers) and were aged 60 years on average, compared with 56 years for widowers.[237] Widows were less likely to remarry than widowers.

A proportion of widows were heads of households. Historians have estimated these variously: Laslett has argued that 12.9 per cent of households were headed by widows; in London at the end of the seventeenth century, Glass has estimated around 9 per cent; Mary Prior, in her study of Oxford,

[233] Thornton, *Autobiography*, 234.
[234] An exception is Laslett, *Family Life*, 198–9.
[235] Bodl., Rawlinson B 382, fos. 442–90. [236] Laslett, *Family Life*, 198.
[237] King, *Natural and Political Observations*, 39.

found the proportion to be much smaller, around 6 per cent, probably because many widows were too poor to appear on taxation lists.[238] Erickson estimated that 84 per cent of widows either headed a household or lived alone.[239]

A widow found herself an anomaly in a society which expected all women to be either married or about to be married.[240] She knew that if she were old and pious, living in as self-effacing a way as possible, she would be respected and, if poor, be considered a proper recipient for Christian charity and relief. Widows at all social levels appealed to the stereotype of the poor, distressed, and weak individual: 'remember that the mercifull shall obtain mercy, and if the sighs and tears of a comfortless widow cannot move you to compassionate my miserable condition, then I can say no more.'[241] Some who were neither poor nor weak still deployed the same rhetoric to urge men to help them. Elizabeth Lock, a Yoxford widow, petitioned Sir Robert Rich to use his interest to remove a soldier quartered at her house in 1698: 'I am your humble petitioner; being a widow oppressed: though god hath promised he will be a judge of the widow's cause yet it is our duty to use the means of Relief.'[242]

Widows shared many experiences with other female adults who were without men: they were more likely to be poor, to be objects of suspicion, and were under pressure to live under male governance. Their social position was anomalous and their sexuality was ambiguous. There was one important difference, however: widows kept the social status, prestige, and dignity of their married state. They were more likely to be viewed as objects of compassion than other adult women without men. A further difference which set widows apart from deserted wives was their legal status, which left them freer to engage in certain economic activities.

From surviving evidence we know that women's own immediate reactions to the loss of their husbands varied. Feelings ranged from almost suicidal despair to barely disguised relief. Elizabeth Hatton's remark upon her late husband—'we shall never see his like again—praises be to God'[243]—was circulated as court gossip, but the more private mourning of women was

[238] P. Laslett, 'Mean Household Size in England Since the Sixteenth Century', in P. Laslett and R. Wall (eds.), *Household and Family in Past Time* (Cambridge, 1972), 147; M. Prior, 'Women and the Urban Economy: Oxford, 1500–1800', in M. Prior (ed.), *Women in English Society* (1985), 105–6; D. V. Glass (ed.), *London Inhabitants within the Walls*, London Record Society, 2 (1966), table 5, p. xxvii.

[239] Erickson, *Women and Property*, 187–8.

[240] See Ch. 1, 'Contexts: Stereotypes', above.

[241] Folger MS x. d. 451, no. 124, Elizabeth Civel to Sir Robert Rich, 12 Feb. 1697.

[242] Folger MS x. d. 451, no. 140, Elizabeth Lock to Sir Robert Rich, 21 Jan. [1699].

[243] S. E. Thorne, *Sir Edward Coke, 1552–1952* (1957), 4. (Thorne cites only BL Harleian MS 7193, fo. 16, which is a copy of Lady Hatton's will. We have been unable to trace the source of the comment.)

confided to their trusted correspondents or to diaries. 'I want him to talk with, to walk with, to eat and sleep with', wrote Lady Russell in 1683.[244] Mary Penington suffered deeply: 'my very heart-strings seemed ready to break and let my heart fall from its wonted place . . . . I wept not, but stood silent and amazed, frozen with grief.'[245] In 1675 William Lawrence found that his sister was so 'frighted and afflicted at her sudden loss' of her husband that she miscarried.[246] Some wealthier widows chose to retire from the world, signalling their state by more sober attire and lifestyle.[247]

Although lower down the social scale we lack women's own writings, indirect evidence exists. Between 1597 and 1634, over 700 people consulted the physician, Richard Napier, with symptoms of psychological distress. Of the 42 who were ill or in despair after the death of a spouse, women outnumbered men by more than three to one. The widowed Margaret Lancton, Napier noted, 'hath taken much grief touching the death of her husband . . . . Full of melancholy and ill thought and cannot rest day nor night. No comfort. Tempted to drown herself. Weepeth all the day long. Craveth God's help and grace.'[248] The death of a spouse altered women's lives more seriously than men's. As wives, women were encouraged in dependency; as widows, they were on their own, responsible for themselves and their families. Female diarists bemoaned their financial difficulties; certainly the financial consequences of a husband's death were more serious than those of a wife's death.[249] The loss of a husband was an economic catastrophe in most households.[250]

How widows fared depended upon the provisions governing their widowhood. Jointures, common law, and a husband's will were among the most significant variables. Among women of the gentry and aristocracy, marriage settlements governed the widow's economic situation. At her marriage, a jointure was negotiated on the basis of her dowry. By the end of the seventeenth century, a larger dowry was required for the same jointure, as families sought to consolidate their landholding to increase their political power.[251]

[244] *Letters of Lady Rachel Russell* (1773), 7 (30 Sept. 1683).

[245] *Some Account of . . . the Life of Mary Penington* (1821), 76.

[246] *The Diary of William Lawrence. Covering periods between 1662 and 1681*, ed. G. E. Aylmer (Beaminster, 1961), 28.

[247] R. Warnicke, 'Private and Public: The Boundaries of Women's Lives in Early Stuart England', J. R. Brink (ed.), *Privileging Gender in Early Modern England: Sixteenth Century Essays and Studies*, 23 (1993), 137–8.

[248] Macdonald, *Mystical Bedlam*, 159–60.

[249] Mendelson, 'Stuart Women's Diaries', 199; Macdonald, *Mystical Bedlam*, 73, 103–4.

[250] A. Laurence, 'Godly Grief: Individual Responses to Death in Seventeenth-Century Britain', in R. Houlbrooke (ed.), *Death, Ritual, and Bereavement* (1989), 64.

[251] H. J. Habakkuk, 'Marriage Settlements in the Eighteenth Century', *TRHS*, 4th ser., 32 (1950), 15–30.

Changes in legislation during this period saw the widow's financial position deteriorate to the advantage of the male heir.[252] In practice, the financial situation of the widow with a jointure depended upon additional factors. While a 'strict settlement' at her marriage appeared to safeguard a widow's financial security, wives could be 'persuaded' by husbands to surrender some of their rights. By the later seventeenth century, there are many examples of fathers and sons acting in collusion to break settlements.[253] Male heirs could make life difficult, as one widow's letter in the 1670s makes clear:

> My son keeps my land in his own hand and will give me no money nor any bond, but railed bitterly against me that he makes me tremble . . . . He hath broke my heart . . . He promised his father before he died, that he would never take nor meddle with my copyhold land . . .[254]

A widow's position was also affected by her husband's management of his affairs. Alice Thornton found herself in difficulties at her husband's death, despite the large dowry she had brought, because he had mismanaged his estate.[255] Many widows would, for the first time, be keeping accounts and managing estates at a time when they were personally distressed.[256] One argument for female education was to enable women to manage their own affairs as widows. Higher up the social scale, widows could and did take advice about their rights.

The extent to which women of the middling and poorer ranks knew of their legal entitlements is unclear. While Erickson presents a picture of well-informed widows who maintained or improved their economic position, Staves argues that most were ignorant of their legal rights to property.[257] Widows of middling and poorer men could rely upon their right at common law to one-third of a husband's land and goods after his death. In some regions widows held free bench rights, which made such widows significant in their communities as these rights gave access to land.[258] Wives might also receive land or goods at the deathbed transfer from their

[252] E. Spring, *Law, Land and Family: Aristocratic Inheritance in England, 1300 to 1800* (Chapel Hill, NC, 1993).

[253] L. Stone and J. C. F. Stone, *An Open Elite? England, 1540–1880* (Oxford, 1984), 77.

[254] Bodl., MS North c 10, fo. 61, M. Norbury to Lady Frances North, 24 Apr. [1672–8].

[255] Thornton, *Autobiography*, 261.

[256] Mendelson, 'Stuart Women's Diaries', 199.

[257] Erickson, *Women and Property*, 155, 193–5; S. Staves, *Married Women's Separate Property in England, 1660–1833* (Cambridge, Mass., 1990), 205.

[258] E. P. Thompson, 'The Grid of Inheritance: A Comment', in J. Goody, J. Thirsk, and E. P. Thompson (eds.), *Family and Inheritance in Rural Society in Western Europe, 1200–1800* (Cambridge, 1976), 349–50.

husbands.[259] Wives were treated generously in many husbands' wills, and, until 1670, the ecclesiastical courts were similarly favourable towards the widows of men who died intestate. After the statute of 1670, however, women's position deteriorated. A childless widow's right to her husband's goods was halved, and the courts strictly enforced the more restrictive widows' entitlement, reducing it to one-third.[260]

Below the level of the gentry, different conditions obtained. In her study of two Cambridgeshire villages, Margaret Spufford found two distinct patterns of provision for widows reflected in wills. In the village of Chippenham, while widows and sons inherited, the widow usually enjoyed a life interest in the house and land. At Orwell, on the other hand, the husband ordinarily left his widow the holding only until his son was 21. After the son reached his majority, the widow was to have carefully specified house-room. Because land usually passed immediately to the heir, if he was of age, the householder's will normally specified in detail how the widow was to be treated. Again, house-room was often clearly defined. However, maintenance of the widow 'almost always' ceased on her remarriage.[261]

Some widows managed to run their farms with the help of sons or servants. When Mary Bodley's husband died in the 1620s, her son was young, but as soon as George was capable, he helped his mother run the farm.[262] Elizabeth Stout, widowed in 1680, 'was advised to get some good servant well experienced in husbandry'. She hired William Jenkinson 'till her own sones were capable to manage the same'.[263]

In towns, the working widow running the family craft or trade with the help of apprentice or servant is a popular stereotype, but surviving evidence suggests that managing a business was more difficult than running a farm. Widows did not always inherit the tools of trade.[264] Some, like Alice Greenwood, whose husband died suddenly, had been so busied about her children and her household 'that she had little knowledge of his affairs or circumstances', and was forced to ask for help in selling up his wholesale grocery.[265] But there are many examples of widows continuing to run businesses. Detailed studies of particular trades provide examples of widows both

[259] R. Smith, 'The Manorial Court and the Elderly Tenant in Late Medieval England', in M. Pelling and R. M. Smith (eds.), *Life, Death, and the Elderly: Historical Perspectives* (1991), 57.

[260] Erickson, *Women and Property*, 29, 155, 174–86.

[261] M. Spufford, *Contrasting Communities: English Villagers in the Sixteenth and Seventeenth Centuries* (Cambridge, 1974), 88, 112–15.

[262] Devon RO, Chanter 878, Consistory Court Depositions 1679–81, fo. 49^{v}.

[263] Stout, *Autobiography*, 75.

[264] S. Wright, '"Churmaids, Huswyfes and Hucksters": The Employment of Women in Tudor and Stuart Salisbury', in L. Charles and L. Duffin (eds.), *Women and Work in Pre-Industrial England* (1985), 112–13.

[265] Stout, *Autobiography*, 132–4.

supervising businesses and of working in them. In some instances, widows were keeping a family business going for their children, but, in others, women continued to work for one or two decades. They might find men to assist them, or they might actually perform the work themselves. Their own knowledge and age affected their decisions. A plumber's widow in Chester who was clearly labouring herself in 1607 did not retire until around 1630.[266]

Lower down the social scale, widows' opportunities to be gainfully employed were limited by their training and by the lesser rates of pay for females. Like other poor women, they were forced to engage in multiple employments in order to survive.[267] Those with young children were at the highest risk for a life cycle of poverty. Children were a drain on the family income, and child-care, especially that of infants, precluded most types of work. Like the deserted London wife who pleaded with parish officers either to give her a larger pension or to take away her youngest child so that she could go out to work,[268] widows with dependent children were trapped at home in the lowest paid and most unreliable of occupations, spinning, knitting, and piece-work. Such women had no capital, and no control over whether they worked. Since they could get no continuous employment, they were reduced to knitting or spinning.[269] Parishes were unwelcoming. In Essex, the residence of one widow was disputed 'by reason of her charge of children'. In this case, the widow petitioned that an abiding place be appointed 'and that then she would labour for her living and not be burdensome in any place'. The court co-ordinated so that she and her children could stay together.[270] In other cases, the parish went to law to ensure that a widow's children would not be a charge, or that if she lacked the security, 'to get her and children removed out of the said parish'.[271] Debt could separate a widow from her child. Rebecca Bond was imprisoned for debt, and her six-year-old son put out in the parish.[272]

[266] D. W. Woodward, *Men at Work: Labourers and Building Craftsmen in the Towns of Northern England* (Cambridge, 1995), 84–91. In the 18th cent., printers' widows likewise responded in a variety of ways, including running the business themselves for many years; H. Barker, 'Women, Work and the Industrial Revolution: Female Involvement in the English Printing Trades, *c.*1700–1840', in H. Barker and E. Chalus (eds.), *Gender in Eighteenth-Century England* (1997).

[267] For further discussion see Ch. 5.

[268] Boulton, *Neighbourhood*, 126.

[269] T. Wales, 'Poverty, Poor Relief and the Life-Cycle: Some Evidence from Seventeenth-Century Norfolk', in R. Smith (ed.), *Land, Kinship and Life-Cycle* (Cambridge, 1984), 366–9.

[270] Essex RO, Q/SR 122/72, 73 [1592].

[271] Guildhall MS 952/1, St George Botolph Lane Vestry Minute book, 1600–1685, fo. 28 (10 Jan. 1672).

[272] Guildhall, MS 22,897 [St Olave, Southwark], 14 Aug. 1685.

A widow's need for support was recognized: widows and their children received the bulk of poor relief.[273] Hence they were less likely to be forced into crime than their impoverished male counterparts.[274] But charitable relief also kept women in a more dependent situation than men: the parish authorities scrutinized a widow's moral conduct, and withheld support if they disapproved of her behaviour. Impoverished old women might be despised as poor beggars.[275] The widow who quarrelled with her neighbours was vulnerable to accusations of scolding or witchcraft.

Relationships with families affected widowhood. Demographic studies suggest that girls were more inclined to stay at home with widowed mothers.[276] A daughter was generally expected to have a responsibility for the well-being of her widowed mother. In one case, early in the eighteenth century, a widow who had remarried was censured by one female correspondent because her daughter had done everything possible to help her in her widowhood. Lady Dallawaer [Delaware?] had taken her mother in, but the widow married her coachman: 'She had been much les to blame had she been slighted bye her Daughter, and not yoused with all this kindness.'[277]

The combination of widowhood and old age for wealthier women allowed the exercise of independence impossible in any other female condition: widowhood was a time of maximum female autonomy.[278] Clearly widowhood alone did not earn a woman independence. In old age, gender might be less important than wealth in affecting a woman's status. The Barrington correspondence of the 1630s reveals the deference accorded to the 70-year-old widow of a respected Puritan gentleman, Sir Thomas Barrington. Lady Joan enjoyed an average annual income of £1,237. She controlled her own household within the household of her son. She was consulted by a wide range of relatives, friends, and clients on important religious and social issues.[279] The dowager countess of Warwick was similarly influential at a later period.[280] Among early Quakers, there were several

[273] R. W. Herlan, 'Poor Relief in London During the English Revolution', *Journal of British Studies*, 18 (1979), 30–51; Wales, 'Poverty, Poor Relief and the Life-Cycle', 358.

[274] C. Z. Wiener, 'Sex Roles and Crime in late Elizabethan Hertfordshire', *Journal of Social History*, 8 (1975), 41.

[275] See, for example, Bodl., MS Rawlinson D. 18, fo. 81, Petition of Elizabeth Turner, Widow; Bodl., MS Tanner 104, fos. 319–20, Case of Sarah Coles, Widow.

[276] Wall, 'Leaving Home and the Process of Household Formation', 94–6.

[277] Cartwright (ed.), *Wentworth Papers*, 49.

[278] Nancy Roelker found a similar phenomenon among wealthy 16th-cent. French women; N. Roelker, 'The Appeal of Calvinism to French Noblewomen in the Sixteenth Century', *Journal of Interdisciplinary History*, 2 (1972), 391–418.

[279] *Barrington Family Letters, 1628–1632*, ed. A Searle, Camden Society, 4th ser., 28 (1983), 16–17 and *passim*.

[280] Mendelson, *Mental World*, 110–15.

independent-minded gentlewomen, apart from the well-known example of Margaret Fell.[281]

Contemporaries were well aware of widows' potential for religious independence. A Catholic writer, Jane Owen, begged widows to be charitable, 'when your states are in youre owne disposall', for future husbands 'will bridle you'.[282] At the beginning of the seventeenth century, widows nurtured the early Puritan movement, providing houses in which people could meet, and supporting ministers financially.[283] During the persecution of Nonconformity after 1662, several widows supported ministers as their chaplains, and allowed meetings at their houses. In 1672, they applied for licences for their meetings under the king's declaration of indulgence.[284] Ladies of high social status were effective protectors because of their friends among the local judiciary: as Thomas Brand, chaplain of Lady Roberts, explained, without a licence he would have 'met with trouble, had not one of them been my Ladys friend'.[285] Judging by the number of dedications of sermons to widows, and funeral sermons about them, ministers were appreciative of their support. Widows' financial contributions in religious matters are bound to be underestimated in surviving sources, because women were socialized to believe that they should make no public stir. We know of the support which Hester Shaw, a widowed London midwife, gave to her minister, Thomas Clendon, only because she believed that he had misappropriated some of her cash after a terrible fire.[286] Some widows were publishers, although their role in publishing Puritan and later nonconformist literature deserves further study.[287] Widows were also allowed to serve as deaconesses in the Baptist churches, provided that they promised not to remarry.[288]

Some widows with financial means had social and charitable goals which were not identical with those of the population at large. A study of charitable bequests for the period 1480–1660 suggests that the pattern of women's bequests differed from that of men. Overwhelmingly, widows gave money for the relief of the poor, putting into immediate and pragmatic effect the precepts of Christian charity. Unlike male testators, who usually

281 Mack, *Visionary Women*, 221.

282 J. Owen, *An Antidote against Purgatory* (1634), 185.

283 R. L. Greaves, 'The Role of Women in Early English Nonconformity', *Church History*, 52 (1983), 299–311.

284 G. L. Turner, *Original Records of Early Nonconformity* (3 vols., 1911–14), iii. 823–4, 741–56.

285 Ibid., iii. 775.

286 For Hester Shaw, see entry by P. Crawford in *The Europa Biographical Dictionary of British Women* (1983).

287 See Ch. 7 below.

288 Crawford, *Women and Religion*, 45 and see references.

made conditional bequests, widows' gifts were without any controlling purpose.[289]

Since widowhood might occur at any age, it could be a transitory stage, ending in remarriage. The speed at which widows remarried should not be interpreted, as it was by many jibing contemporaries, as the absence of grief. Remarriage could be a necessary survival strategy. Several factors affected the likelihood of a widow's remarriage: her age, her economic circumstances, the situation of her children, and, finally, her own inclination. Evidence about the likelihood of a widow's remarriage decreasing from the sixteenth to the end of the seventeenth century has been confirmed by local studies.[290] Barbara Todd's study of remarriage in Abingdon has shown that whereas, in the later sixteenth century, half of the widows remarried, only one-quarter did so in the later seventeenth century.[291] What these trends meant for women is difficult to interpret. Was it more difficult for widows to remarry because of economic circumstances, or were they increasingly choosing not to remarry?

Younger widows were more likely to remarry. From a study of the London licensing papers, Vivien Brodsky has concluded that widows of tradesmen and craftsmen were more likely to remarry than those of wealthy citizens or of the poorest men. Whereas widows under 45 years of age frequently chose single men as their spouses, those over 45 were more likely to marry widowers.[292] Erickson's work illuminates the variety of economic circumstances which influenced a widow's decision to remain single or to remarry.[293]

The interval before remarriage appears to have increased during the early modern period. In the late sixteenth century, widows' remarriages occurred after a longer interval than that of widowers, at nine months compared with four. Widows were less likely to be pregnant than other brides, partly because they had passed the high fertility of youth, and partly

[289] W. K. Jordan, *Philanthropy in England: A Study of the Changing Pattern of English Social Aspirations, 1480–1660* (1959) 253–4; id., *The Charities of London, 1480–1660: The Aspirations and the Achievements of the Urban Sector* (1960); id., *The Charities of Rural England, 1480–1660: The Aspirations and Achievement of the Rural Society* (1961), 27.

[290] Wrigley and Schofield, *Population History*, 258–9, 426.

[291] B. J. Todd, 'The Remarrying Widow: A Stereotype Reconsidered', in M. Prior (ed.), *Women in English Society* (1985), 57–61.

[292] V. Brodsky, 'Widows in Late Elizabethan London: Remarriage, Economic Opportunity and Family Orientations', in L. Bonfield, R. M. Smith, and K. Wrightson (eds.), *The World We Have Gained: Histories of Population and Social Structure* (Oxford, 1980), 130.

[293] Erickson, *Women and Property*, 196–200.

because social circumstances had kept them chaste.[294] Nevertheless, there may well have been wide regional variations. In Ludlow in the first half of the eighteenth century Wright found that there were much longer intervals before remarriage for both sexes: the average interval before a widow remarried was just under three years, compared with forty months for the widower. Poorer men were more likely to remarry, and that more speedily, than their wealthier counterparts, but the older and poorer the widows, the less likely they were to marry again.[295] In the Elizabethan period, despite popular disapproval of marriages disparate in age, the 1570 Norwich Census of the Poor shows that 72 per cent of such unequal marriages occurred among the elderly poor. For indigent older widows, remarriage to a younger spouse was a survival strategy tolerated both by the poor themselves and by the parish authorities.[296] Historians such as Houlbrooke, sympathizing with young men for whom 'marriages to older women were often the unavoidable price to pay for economic independence',[297] have overlooked the extent to which marriage and remarriage were the usual price which women themselves paid for survival.[298]

Women's greater longevity may help explain the smaller number of widows remarrying by the end of the seventeenth century. There may have been material factors as well. Men's growing desire to control the transmission of wealth to the family of the first marriage led to increasing financial penalties on women who remarried. Further studies may reveal whether this practice was a general trend. Hostility to widows' remarriage may have increased during this period.[299]

Widows contemplating remarriage were influenced by a number of considerations: love for a dead husband may have been offset by loneliness and the need for affection, and a desire for independence and autonomy may have been outweighed by anxiety over economic insecurity. Some women chose not to remarry lest their children should suffer. Margaret Cavendish's mother never forgot her father 'so as to marry again' and her grief for his

[294] Hair, 'Bridal Pregnancy in Earlier Rural England Further Examined', 59–70. R. Schofield and E. A. Wrigley, 'Remarriage Intervals and the Effects of Marriage Order on Fertility', in J. Dupaquier *et al.* (eds.), *Marriage and Remarriage in Populations of the Past* (1981), 216, 217, calculated that the mean interval for men remarrying in the first half of the 17th cent. was 22.9 months; for women, 26.6 months. In the second half of the 18th cent., it was 31.2 months for men, 40.3 months for women. See S. J. Wright, 'The Elderly and the Bereaved in Eighteenth-Century Ludlow', in M. Pelling and R. M. Smith (eds.), *Life, Death and the Elderly* (1991), 129 n. 16.

[295] Ibid. 106.

[296] M. Pelling, 'Old Age, Poverty, and Disability in Early Modern Norwich', in Pelling and Smith, *Life, Death and the Elderly*, 91–2.

[297] Houlbrooke, *English Family*, 222.

[298] Pelling, 'Old Age, Poverty, and Disability', 87–91.

[299] Todd, 'The Remarrying Widow', 83.

death 'was so lasting' she never spoke of him but with tears.[300] Others feared social scorn if they married younger men: a coachmaker's widow who maintained the business declined a suitor, fearing ridicule.[301] Katherine Austen vowed not to remarry, partly to honour her husband's memory, and partly to safeguard her children's inheritance.[302] As usual, our sources for the attitudes of poorer women are extremely limited. A story of a poor widow with seven starving children who survived on a burnt loaf and some windfall apples was recorded in several ballads.[303] Isolation, loneliness, poverty, and increasing dependence may have been the lot of many widows in seventeenth-century England; independence and autonomy were enjoyed by only a few.

OLD AGE

Growing old was perceived as a process in the seventeenth century. It was both a subjective experience, as a woman observed her body ageing and felt herself to be old, and one of social categorization, as she found herself numbered among the old.

The time at which society decided that a woman was old was variously defined. Some contemporaries linked female old age to the menopause, equating it with the cessation of menstruation, a part of ageing which was distinctive to women.[304] For example, in 1667 Thomas Willis wrote of 'old women after their flowers have left them'; earlier, Reginald Scot had discussed the fantasies of 'old witches' which increased 'upon the stopping of their monethlie melancholike flux'.[305] However, there was no common age at which menstruation ceased and the menopause could be deemed to have occurred.[306]

300 Cavendish, *Natures Pictures drawn by Fancies Pencil to the Life*, 375.

301 Stone, *Uncertain Unions*, 96–104.

302 BL, MS Sloane 4454, fos. 40, 68^{v}–9^{v}, 94^{v}, 110^{v}, etc.

303 Four ballads extant in *Roxburghe Ballads*, viii. 34–41.

304 The menopause may be one of the more defined stages of the 'climacteric', a term currently used for the process of ageing in women which involves the cessation of ovulation, and hormonal change. The term 'climacteric' in the 17th cent. usually referred to ages which were multiples of 7. The grand climacteric was 63; *OED*. For a comparison with men, see C. Gilber, 'When Did a Man in the Renaissance Grow Old?', *Studies in the Renaissance*, 14 (1967), 117–32.

305 Quoted in R. A. Hunter and I. Macalpine, *Three Hundred Years of Psychiatry, 1535–1860* (1963), 190; R. Scot, *The Discoverie of Witchcraft* (1584; Amsterdam, 1971), 54.

306 Medical texts, based on theories rather than observation, are an unreliable guide. Even now, medical theorists are no more precise than to estimate that the menopause occurs roughly between 45 and 55; G. Greer, *The Change: Women, Ageing and the Menopause* (1991), 167–75.

Here we will take the view that around 50 years marked the end of adult maturity and the beginning of old age, but our chronological measure will not be rigidly applied.[307] Fifty was commonly the age at which people were accepted as old in the medieval period,[308] and many early modern commentators agreed. For example, Gilbert Holles, third earl of Clare, thought that his wife's 'gadding usually from morning to night' was inappropriate given her age: 'I thought it not decent in a woman turned of fifty to be so much abroad but sometimes to retire herself within her own apartment.'[309] Nor was he alone in mentioning 50 as the crucial age. Lady Wentworth referred to the duchess of Cleveland at about 50 as 'This old lady'.[310] Lower down the social scale, the church court records refer to 'ancient women' in their fifties who were respected for their sobriety and wisdom.[311] We shall also take account of subjective judgements: if women thought themselves to be old, or if their contemporaries identified them as old, we shall include them in this section.

Some contemporaries defined old age in chronological terms. Gregory King distinguished those over 60 years of age, implying that they were old, and calculated that they were about 10 per cent of his estimated total population, a smaller proportion of the population than those over 60 comprise in Britain today[312]. Old women in their eighties seemed much more remarkable in the early modern period than they do nowadays.

Some old women seemed not to know how old they were: Sir James Whitelocke's elderly mother died after living 'a goodly time; the certeyne number of yeares she could not tell', but her family reckoned that she was 80.[313] There is some debate about whether people knew their ages accurately.

Studies suggest that women in third world countries cease to menstruate around 45, women in developed countries at around 50; J. G. Green, *The Social and Psychological Origins of the Climacteric Syndrome* (Aldershot, 1984), 3.

[307] Pelling, 'Old Age, Poverty, and Disability', 78; cp. R. Wall, 'Intergenerational Relationships Past and Present', unpublished paper, who says that the age of 65 'serves now as a standard threshold for defining the onset of old age'.

[308] S. Shahar, 'Who were Old in the Middle Ages?', *Social History of Medicine*, 6 (1993), 314–41.

[309] PCC 42 Ent (1689), Will of Gilbert Holles, earl of Clare.

[310] Cartwright (ed.), *Wentworth Papers*, 50.

[311] OA, MS Oxf. Dioc. papers c. 26, 1629–34, fos. 143–8^{v}.

[312] King, *Natural and Political Observations*, 40. King calculated the number of women over 60 at 330,000, men over 60 to be 270,000. The total was thus 10.7% of his estimated total population of 5,600,000. This proportion is similar to that calculated by Wrigley and Schofield, *Population History*, 528–9. They estimate the proportions at around 7% in the mid-16th century, rising to 9% at the end of the 18th cent. The proportion in 1676–80 was 9.95%. In the United Kingdom in 1985, the proportion was around 20.9%; L. Bonfield, 'Was there a "Third Age" in the Preindustrial English Past? Some Evidence from the Law', in J. M. Eekelaar and D. Pearl (eds.), *An Ageing World* (Oxford, 1989), 43.

[313] *Liber Familicus of Sir James Whitelocke*, ed. J. Bruce, Camden Society, 70 (1858), 16.

Census takers in the nineteenth century found that elderly people frequently exaggerated their age.[314] Keith Thomas has argued that women were less likely to learn arithmetic than men, and that, when asked their ages by the ecclesiastical courts, they offered rough estimates rather than precise figures.[315] From the records we have studied, this seems not universally true. Sometimes the church court records show that ages were rounded out, in other areas women's ages were recorded reasonably precisely.[316]

At about 50, most women would have experienced bodily changes associated with the menopause, which they may have seen as marking the onset of old age. Their experiences of the menopause were influenced by their own biology, health, and diet, and by social circumstances. The actual physiological changes may have varied in early modern times. Because the diets of the rich and poor differed, as did the amount of physical activity, the incidence of osteoporosis may have been more class specific. Women of the upper ranks may have had a calcium deficiency, since they despised drinking milk or eating cheese, claiming it to be 'the food of the poor'.[317]

Furthermore, if their society considered women of more value in old age, compared with late twentieth-century Western societies which have a negative view of women who are incapable of reproducing,[318] then it may be that the physiological changes were accompanied with less trauma. The end of their fertile years may have been experienced as a cultural event. There was no evidence of a taboo on sexual intercourse with a post-menopausal woman, as there has been in more recent times.[319]

Sources, especially those by women, are generally silent on the subject of menstruation. Women's silence makes it difficult for us to understand their experiences. Silence could mean that women were not interested in the menopause; but it could also signal a taboo or a trauma. Some women were pleased to cease child-bearing. More work on the health problems of

[314] Wrigley and Schofield, *Population History*, 109.

[315] K. Thomas, 'Numeracy in Early Modern England', *TRHS*, 5th series, 37 (1987), 113, 126.

[316] See, for example, Devon RO, Chanter 866, Consistory Court Depositions 1634–40 (not foliated or paginated), where women's stated ages include many more round numbers than would be statistically likely. In records from the Oxford Diocese, round-number ages are far less common, even among very old women like Katherine Rowland, who gave her age as '87'. See OA, MS Oxf. Dioc. papers c. 26, 1629–34, fo. 31 and *passim*.

[317] N. Le Strange, *'Merry Passages and Jeasts': A Manuscript Jestbook*, ed. H. Lippincott (1974), 114, 140. To date, there have been no studies of diet and menstruation in early modern times.

[318] See, for example, Greer, *The Change*, ch. 1 and *passim*.

[319] Crawford, 'Attitudes to Menstruation', 71.

older women in early modern times, for which there are sources, would contribute to our understanding of this subject.[320]

How did women view old age? In some cases, we can glimpse their sense of achievement. An 84-year-old widow in York proudly testified in court that she was not promised anything for testifying, that she was independent and had her own house and a cow.[321] Anne Docwra styled herself 'An Ancient Woman' in the title of one of her printed works, and boasted that at 67 years of age she could still walk the streets to visit her friends and the sick, 'and can see without spectacles still'.[322] Some planned ahead for their comfort. Elizabeth Freke objected to a match between her son and Lord Drogheda's daughter, whom she thought too far above her socially: 'I cared not to be a servant to any one in my Old Age.' Mrs Freke's comment suggests that she intended to be obeyed and respected.[323] Some Quaker women claimed that their age had given them authority: 'We which have been Mothers of Children and Antient Women in Our Families, do know in the Wisdom of God, what will do in Families.'[324] Old women, especially if they were married, gained authority over members of their own sex. As wealthy widows, old women might enjoy authority over younger men as well.

Health affected a woman's experience of old age. Aches, pains, and various ailments were the common lot of both sexes, but women's complaints, a legacy of childbirth, grew worse. Contemporaries usually distinguished levels of health in old age. In decrepit age, the old were like children, weak in both mind and body.[325] Whatever a woman's social level, if she enjoyed good health she was more likely to be independent of others and to take pleasure in life. Gervase Holles presented a delightful picture of his grandmother, Catherine Kingston, who lived to 89. She was

> of so healthfull and happy a constitution that hir long life seemed not in the least manner to be burthensome to her. . . . shee never took phisicke in hir life (as I have often heard her say) and to hir last did read wthout spectacles. All her life long to her last sicknes shee would rise at 6 of the clocke in winter, and before five in summer, and would order her house wth so much providence and move to and fro

[320] Sources such as literate women's correspondence, medical treatises, and physicians' case books would provide some material.

[321] Borthwick Institute, Consistory Court Records, Deposition Book 1676–78, fos. 107^{v}–11.

[322] A. D[ocwra], *An Apostate Conscience Exposed* (1699); Mack, *Visionary Women*, 317.

[323] *Mrs Elizabeth Freke her Diary*, ed. M. Carbury (Cork, 1913), 41.

[324] Mary Forster and others, *A Living Testimony From the Power* [1685], 2–3.

[325] J. Robinson, *The Birth of a Day* (1654), 18.

FIG. 22. 'Four for Six pence Mackrell'. In Laroon's London street scene, an old woman tries to sell her last remaining mackerel. As well as being old, she is both poor and ill: she has lost one eye, walks with a staff, and is dressed in mended rags

with so litle trouble yt no man could say yt either hir reason or spirits were empayred.[326]

Gervase thought that his grandmother might have lived twenty years longer had she not taken cold when she was out enjoying her garden. Another octogenarian had survived happily on a chiefly vegetarian diet.[327]

Women's economic position affected their experience of age. Some had amassed sufficient wealth through their work to live comfortably when they were old. Ellen Green 'got enough' by her employment at a trade over twenty or thirty years to keep her husband and herself 'in their Old Age'. She had used a bequest wisely, and was 'an Ingenious Industrious Woman'.[328] But if women had always been poor, and had worked at manual labour to support themselves, then old age and physical infirmity affected their ability to provide for themselves.

Although men might retire in old age, women were still expected to work. Even the wife who could afford to leave off her trade was still responsible for housekeeping and expected to earn whatever she could towards her keep by spinning or some other task. The Norwich Census of the Poor of 1570 lists many elderly women who were still working, including women 84 and 85 years old: 'Janis House, wedow, of 85 yeris, that spyn wolle, and have dwelt here ever' was deemed able and given no alms.[329]

At all social levels, elderly women were nurses of the sick.[330] Their services as nurses were recognized in the contemporary saying, that women were the delights of man's youth, but 'Nurses for the Sage'.[331] In the almshouses, women might be required to look after other old people, but we have found no examples of men looking after women.[332] Eventually, however, some economic activities ceased to be possible. The Carlisle quarter sessions in 1688 record that one woman was no longer able to travel with her husband selling small wares. A poor widow who was too old to beg from door to door could be said to have retired on to the parish rates.[333]

The parish was not the sole source of relief. Various localities and institutions had charitable bequests which they administered. For example, the

[326] G. Holles, *Memorials of the Holles Family, 1493–1656*, ed. A. C. Wood, Camden Society, 3rd ser., 55 (1937), 226.

[327] Lewis, *Memoirs of Prince William Henry*, 25.

[328] D[ocwra], *Apostate Conscience*, 38–9.

[329] *The Norwich Census of the Poor, 1570*, 56, 62, 64, 65, 80, 85, 86; for more detailed discussion, see Pelling, 'Old Age, Poverty, and Disability', 82–4.

[330] Boulton, *Neighbourhood*, 131.

[331] R. A[ylet], *A Wife Not Ready Made* (1653), 7.

[332] Guildhall, Grocers' Company, Warden's Accounts 1622–1633, MS 11571/11, fo. 289^{v}; Grocers' Company, Orders of the Court of Assistants, 1616–1639, MS 11588/3, fo. 397.

[333] Cumbria RO, Carlisle Quarter Sessions, 1688, no. 11; 1693, Michelmas no. 8.

FIG. 23. 'Buy a Fork or Fire Shovel'. Poor old woman street vendor. Even when they were old, society expected poor women to earn what they could. Laroon's *Cryes of the City of London* (1711) shows an old woman with wrinkled face, leaning on a walking-stick, who hawks fireplace implements on the London streets

London company of Fishmongers was not atypical in providing assistance for the elderly widows of company members. This included immediate relief, pensions, and places in their almshouses.[334] Usually the company increased pensions as the recipients grew older. Some objected to having to wear the clothing or badge of a pensioner.[335] Others lost their pensions if they remarried out of the company's ranks.[336] Retirement and maintenance contracts were one of many devices used by medieval people to secure their assets in old age.[337] Some similar transfers of assets in return for maintenance in old age or incapacity persisted during the early modern period.[338]

As women aged, they required increasing amounts of assistance. Parishes attempted to force relatives to care for the old. According to an Elizabethan statute (43 Eliz. c. 2) children were responsible for maintaining their elderly parents.[339] When this was impossible, parishes and other organizations offered pensions, support, and, finally, care in an almshouse. Although there were widespread expectations that children would care for the aged, in practice several factors militated against this model of family care. Many of the old were childless, or had no adult children living; in other cases, women lived at a distance from their families. In towns, Souden found that only 29 per cent of women over 60 had stayed in the same place all their lives.[340] Poverty could prevent children from caring for their aged relatives; an estate was sold for the subsistence of two widowed sisters in Lancaster, 'being old and infirme and no suport from children'.[341]

One way of understanding women's experience of old age is to examine their living arrangements. Old people who lived with their children had the possibility of financial assistance, care, and companionship, but women were less likely than men to do so. In one study, 16 per cent of elderly women were residentially isolated, compared with only 5 per cent of elderly men. In rural communities, one-third of elderly women had no relative living in their households.[342]

[334] Guildhall, Company of Fishmongers, Calendars of Court, Ledger 3, 524; Leger 5, 140 (charity); Ledger 3, 1631, 18 (pension and immediate relief).

[335] Guildhall, Calendar of Court Ledger, 1606, 509; Guildhall, Court Ledger 3, MS 5570/3, 547 (1641).

[336] Guildhall Fishmongers, Calendar of Court Ledger, 1609, p. 564.

[337] Smith, 'The Manorial Court', in Pelling and Smith (eds.), *Life, Death and the Elderly*, 39–61; E. Clark, 'Some Aspects of Social Security in Medieval England', *Journal of Family History*, 7 (1982), 307–20.

[338] Pelling, 'Old Age, Poverty and Disability', 86–7.

[339] Newman Brown, 'The Receipt of Poor Relief and Family Situation', 405–22.

[340] Souden, 'Migrants and the Population Structure', in Clark (ed.), *Transformation of English Towns*, 140.

[341] Stout, *Autobiography*, 126.

[342] R. Wall, 'Elderly Persons and Members of their Households in England and Wales from Pre-Industrial Times to the Present Day', unpublished paper, ESRC Cambridge Group for the History of Population and Social Structure.

Although women's lives were more structured around relationships than were men's, in their old age they were more likely to find themselves living alone.

Wealthy old women were more likely to have the support and companionship of relatives. Aristocratic daughters worried over whether they had done all they could to care for their aged mothers. Sarah, duchess of Marlborough, nursed her mother, Mrs Jenyns, devotedly after the latter suffered a stroke in 1693, but was troubled that she could have done more for her.[343] 'I am confident you never omitted ye least title of your Duty to your Mother while she was living', wrote Anne reassuringly, '& in her sickness you have shown your self ye best & tenderest daughter yt ever was.'[344] Some gentlewomen remained in the houses where they had always lived. Katharine Henry died aged 78 at Broad Oak, where she had remained for nearly eleven years after her husband's death.[345] Others hoped to live with younger kin. A widowed grandmother was so fond of her eldest granddaughter, whom she had cared for when the girl's parents fled to Hull at the outbreak of the war, that she planned to visit and live with her.[346]

One relationship which some women enjoyed in old age was that of grandmother. Gentlewomen who married young were more likely to live to see their grandchildren than were poorer women. In some cases grandparents looked after children, and women's letters reveal their pleasure in the young. Lady Anne North wrote charmingly of the family ceremony at which her grandson put on breeches for the first time, giving her 'the first salute' after he was dressed as a man.[347] Lady Browne and her husband were kept busy looking after their grandson Tommy. His one fault was neglect of his book, but his grandmother was soon able to report to his mother that he was 'now a very good Boy for his boock, . . . and delights to read [to his] Grandfather and I when he comes from schole'.[348] As always, we have more evidence about the emotions of the literate, but other sources suggest that women from different social groups enjoyed their grandchildren. Ballads provide a glimpse of grandmothers as significant in family life: 'grandam will give me' was a frequent refrain.

[343] F. Harris, *A Passion for Government* (Oxford, 1991), 70–1.

[344] BL, Additional MS 61,415, Blenheim Papers, fo. 81^{v}.

[345] From 1696 until 1707; see J. B. Williams, *The Lives of Philip and Matthew Henry* (1974).

[346] *Memoirs of the Life of Master John Shawe*, ed. J. Broadly (Hull, 1824), 30, 59.

[347] *The Autobiography of the Hon Roger North*, 215–16 (Anne, Lady North, to Francis North, 10 Oct. 1679).

[348] *The Letters of Sir Thomas Browne*, ed. G. Keynes (1931), 184–5 and *passim*.

My Gran'um will give me a Cradle,
which is both firm and strong[349]

A church court case tells of the widow Hulet, whose granddaughter Elizabeth was suspected of bearing an illegitimate child. The grandmother was allegedly willing to overlook the disgrace and support the child: 'why yes, I do love to dandle a child in my old age.'[350]

In theory, old age in both women and men was esteemed in English society. Keith Thomas has argued that age did not cancel class distinctions, but it did make for fewer differences between people. In old age a woman was respected more than at any other time of her life, approaching nearest in value to that of a man.[351] But there were negative stereotypes as well, and, in practice, many old women were scorned and neglected.

The main factors influencing a woman's experience of old age were her economic position and her personal moral prestige. The situation of poor old women was unenviable, as rate-paying parishioners granted them sufficient aid to keep them alive, but little more. For some women, authority may have increased in old age. How much this was the case depended on a woman's social status, health, wealth, power of patronage, and character. Mothers were deferred to for advice by their adult daughters and sometimes even by their daughters-in-law. Having survived, they could dispense reassurance to those preparing for childbirth, even if they could not be there themselves: 'you are in place where you have good neighbours . . . wch no doubt will be very kind and carefull of you' wrote Lady North to her daughter.[352] The authority of poor women may have been more dangerous to them, since their contemporaries were liable to suspect they were in league with the Devil. Such women were not necessarily victims; they had authority, albeit of an illegitimate and threatening kind.[353]

Gendered expectations did not disappear for old women, who were still under the same strictures with reference to the control of their sexuality as younger women. Marriages of elderly women—particularly to younger men—were condemned by both sexes as unfit, although a number of these marriages took place among the poorer sections of the population.

[349] *Roxburghe Ballads*, vii. 111. See also C. Cross, 'Northern Women in the Early Modern Period: The Female Testators of Hull and Leeds, 1520–1650', *Yorks. Archaeological Journal*, 59 (1987), 88.

[350] OA, Oxf. Dioc. papers c. 26, 1629–34, fo. 145.

[351] Thomas, *Age and Authority*, 33–4. See also E. Le Roy Ladurie, *Montaillou: village occitan de 1294 à 1324* (Paris, 1975), 287, for a similar conclusion.

[352] North, *Autobiography*, Appendix 1, 220, 2 Jan. 1681.

[353] K. Thomas, *Religion and the Decline of Magic: Studies in Popular Beliefs in Sixteenth and Seventeenth Century England* (1971), 520–3; C. Larner, *Enemies of God: The Witch-hunt in Scotland* (Oxford, 1981), 94–8.

Old women were expected to behave with gravity and sobriety, especially in dress: 'The duety of old wemen is, . . . in maners to be sober, sage, & auncient, to weare no lyte apparell, but suche rayment as become their age and professon.'[354] Lady Wentworth thought that old women who dressed youthfully were 'very ugly, as al old people ar' in such attire.[355] Actions which signified an enjoyment of life could provoke harsh censure: it was 'preposterous', declared the author of the *Ladies Dictionary*, to see an old woman delight in trifles, wearing spectacles to read love stories.[356]

Finally, some old women saw their last years as a time of preparing for death. Winifrid Thimelby, prioress of the English convent at the Louvain, acknowledged, when urging her niece to send her news of her relatives in England, that she should be 'busied with nothing but preparation for death: for age summons me quickly to my grave'.[357]

DEATH

At this period, women's life expectancy was on average two years longer than that of men.[358] Ideally, a woman died a good and pious death when she reached the biblical three score and ten, esteemed by her family and friends. Her death occurred from natural causes, after she had set her spiritual and temporal concerns in order. But death could occur at any age, and not all deaths were ideal. Some women died in desperate circumstances; others in childbirth. Although people were less likely to die of starvation compared with earlier periods, poverty and malnutrition still exposed women to infections which might prove fatal.[359] The life expectancy of the poor was shorter than that of the rich; but those of middling rank who lived in the countryside probably lived longest.[360]

Many women who knew that they were about to die saw the occasion as an opportunity to assert themselves. Most endeavoured to leave life as they had lived it: they were concerned about their souls and their fate after death, about their children and families, their material goods, and their funerals

[354] T. Becon, *The Principles of Christian Religion* [1552?], sig. [J5^v–J6].

[355] Cartwright (ed.), *Wentworth Papers*, 117.

[356] N.H., *The Ladies Dictionary* (1694), 487.

[357] *Tixall Letters; Or the Correspondence of the Aston Family*, 2 vols. (1815), ii. 108.

[358] S. R. Johansson, 'Welfare, Mortality, and Gender: Continuity and Change in Explanation for Male/Female Differences over Three Centuries', *Continuity and Change*, 6 (1991), 135–77.

[359] There is insufficient evidence to generalize about the effects of plague on the two sexes; Slack, *Impact of Plague*, 179–81, 382–3.

[360] In London, expectation of life at birth was 30–35 in wealthier parishes, 20–25 in poorer; Finlay, *Population and Metropolis*, 100.

FIG. 24. Woman on her deathbed, surrounded by her children. The deathbed was often the setting for a ceremonial occasion in which the dying woman gave her blessing to her children, bade goodbye to family and friends, and if single or widowed, disposed of her worldly goods

and burials. Death was a semi-public occasion. A woman's closest relatives—husband, children, and servants—as well as friends and neighbours might be assembled, to hear her last wishes, receive her blessing, and witness the manner of her death.

Deathbed scenes were dominated by women. It was women who watched with the dying and laid out the bodies after death. When a woman was ill, a relative, friend, neighbour, or nurse would be watching with her; if her death was expected, her closest relatives would be summoned to bid her farewell. There was nothing female-specific about this custom: the same attention would be provided for a male. But it meant that a dying woman was attended by members of her own sex, and, having seen others die, was likely to be knowledgeable about the procedures. Even well-born women were familiar with rituals for the laying out of the dead. An unnamed gentlewoman, dying in the 1660s, instructed her husband on how her body was to be laid out:

'I pray take care of this poor body of mine when I am dead. . . . Let my chin be kept from falling, by pinning the ends of my pinner under it. . . . When I am put in my Coffin, raise my head with a small pillow, and turn it to one side, that it may resemble sleep, and as little of ghastliness appear in it as may be.'[361]

[361] *Conversion Exemplified* (1669), sig. B. 2.

Lady Conway wanted 'to avoid the coming of any men about hir, but desired that only Her Woman with the two maids should lay her in the Coffin'.[362]

Women of all ranks sought to die well. As Lucinda Beier observes, women attended 'a veritable university course on the proper manner of dying'.[363] But the particular deathbed ritual varied according to women's religious beliefs. Before the Reformation, the majority were Catholic, and sought a priest to administer the last rites. A witness reported that the dying Winifrid Thimelby, prioress of the English Augustinian canonesses at the end of the seventeenth century, took leave of her friends, received the last rites, and 'being perfectly her selfe, and so overjoyed to dye, . . . wondred I could be troubled at what she so much reioyced at'.[364] Protestant women died with edifying texts upon their lips, and their relatives gathered around to receive the dying woman's blessing. The model of a good death was publicized by the Protestant clergy in their funeral sermons: women were praised for their piety and their 'good deaths'; men for their secular accomplishments.[365] A Quaker woman usually concerned herself with leave-taking before she died. The death of 15-year-old Susanna Whitrow was attended by Quaker women ministers; her experiences of terror and ecstasy were recorded by the by-standers.[366] Court testimony about the deathbeds of ordinary women relate chiefly to their material goods, but we should not assume from the absence of sources that only wealthier women were concerned with their souls.

Imminent childbirth often focused women's thoughts on death. The custom of pregnant women serving as 'Pall-bearers of their friends dead in Child-birth' was a grim reminder of the possibility.[367] Several women composed letters of advice for their unborn children, with directions about their upbringing. Elizabeth Joceline and Margaret Godolphin, who each died in childbirth, one in 1622, the other in 1678, both wrote letters poignantly expressing love for the child to be.[368] Sarah Meadows (1654–88) left rules for the governing of her seven children.[369]

[362] M. H. Nicolson (ed.), *Conway Letters: The Correspondence of Anne, Viscountess Conway, Henry More, and Their Friends, 1642–1684* (1930), 481.

[363] L. M. Beier, 'The Good Death in Seventeenth-Century England', in R. Houlbrooke (ed.), *Death, Ritual, and Bereavement* (1989), 46.

[364] *Tixall Letters*, ii. 112.

[365] J. L. McIntosh, 'English Funeral Sermons, 1560–1640: The Relationship between Gender, Death, Dying, and the Afterlife', M.Litt. diss., University of Oxford (1990), 108–79.

[366] Mack, *Visionary Women*, 391–6, 400–1.

[367] J. A. Blondel, *The Power of the Mother's Imagination* (1729), 38.

[368] E. Joceline, *The Mothers Legacie to her Unborne Child* (1624); Evelyn, *Life of Margaret Godolphin*, 104–7.

[369] E. Taylor (ed.), *The Suffolk Bartholomeans: A Memoir* (1840), 137–48.

Stories of good deaths circulated in families. John Evelyn's mother died at age 37 after summoning her family and servants, giving them Christian admonitions, gifts, and blessings.[370] A few days after giving birth in 1650, Catherine Aston asked her husband to call her children, saying she did not know how soon she would die: 'I must needs take my leave of them, and give them my blessing.'[371] Lower down the social scale, when Mary Hurll's married sister was dying, she sent a man and a horse fifteen miles to fetch Mary, saying 'if I would see her alive, I must come away strait'. Her sister told her 'that we must part, but she would not have me troubled, for we should meet together in a better Place, where we should never part'.[372]

In some cases, a dying woman focused the drama of the event upon her last will and testament. But while men's testamentary concerns were directed to the transmission of wealth to the next generation, women showed more interest in distributing material goods and personal possessions to friends and relations, especially those of their own sex.[373] Both unmarried daughters and married women were rare as testators, since each needed male permission—a father or husband, respectively—to dispose of personal property.[374] Married women required a husband's consent to dispose of personal property, apart from bequests of pin money. A few wives did leave wills with the permission of their husbands.[375] A widow's power to bequeath her possessions depended upon how much of the family wealth her husband had left to her.[376] A study of Nottingham widows found that those women who made bequests were likely to share their estate among their children.[377] Wealthier women frequently included charity to the poor in their last bequests: in 1705 a dole of 2*d*. was distributed to nearly 700 people at the death of Sir Walter Calverley's sister, Mrs Waide.[378] In many instances, wills include loving lists of personal property.[379]

Ordinary women had fewer possessions, but they still sought to bestow their goods according to their own will. Disputes over nuncupative wills show that many poor widows were concerned about the distribution of their

[370] Evelyn, *Diary*, i. 7. [371] *Tixall Letters*, i. 195.

[372] *An Account of the Remarkable Conversion and Experience of Mary Hurll* (3rd edn., 1719), 58.

[373] Brodsky, 'Widows in Late Elizabethan London', in Bonfield, Smith, and Wrightson (eds.), *World We Have Gained*, 148. [374] Erickson, *Women and Property*, 204–22.

[375] M. Prior, 'Wives and Wills 1558–1700', in J. Chartres and D. Hey (eds.), *English Rural Society, 1500–1800: Essays in Honour of Joan Thirsk* (Cambridge, 1990), 201–3.

[376] C. Shammas, *The Pre-Industrial Consumer in England and America* (Oxford, 1990), 203.

[377] S. Dunster, 'An Independent Life? Nottingham Widows, 1594–1650', *Transactions of the Thoroton Society of Nottingham*, 5 (1991), 35.

[378] *Memorandum Book of Sir Walter Calverley, Yorkshire Diaries and Autobiographies*, ii, Surtees Society, 77 (1886), 105.

[379] For example, Thornton, *Autobiography*, 335–8.

meagre possessions. With great ceremony, surrounded by friends, neighbours, and relations, they disposed of each item: a petticoat to one, a brewing pot to another.[380] Probate inventories reveal the desperate poverty of many old women. Yet the general impression we can glean from records relating to ordinary women is that such women were deeply concerned with both people and things at their deaths. More than men, they sought to complete a circle of relationships by their words and gifts at their dying moments.

Women were concerned with the arrangements for their funerals. However, the funerals of aristocratic women were subject to the control of the College of Heralds. Because the rituals were so complex, a woman's body would require embalming before the arrangements could be completed. Noblewomen disliked the idea of their bodies being exposed to the gaze and knife of strangers,[381] and sought to evade the process by expressing a preference for a speedy burial at night with a less hierarchically ordered ritual. In 1639 Frances, duchess of Richmond, specified that she should be buried on the first night twenty-four hours after her death. No great persons should be invited, but those who attended voluntarily should be respectfully treated.[382] Queen Mary II's request 'that her body might not be open'd' was found too late, after her state funeral.[383] In less politically significant cases, the dying woman's wishes were respected. Sir Walter Calverley recorded that when his beloved sister Bridget died in 1711, her second husband brought her body to Calverley church and, 'at her own request', interred her in the same grave with her first husband.[384] Women might specify the place of their burial, but no widow arranged her husbands around her monument, as a husband did his wives.

Some women chose the text for their own funeral sermon. The widowed Alice Thornton nominated hers in her will: 'Blessed are all the dead which die in the Lord.'[385] Margaret Sanderson selected Romans 8: 10, on the spirit as life.[386] Even a servant might take an interest in her funeral arrangements. In 1588 a Stepney servant asked in her will for all female attendants: 'four

[380] See, for example, OA, MS Oxf. dioc. papers c. 27, 1634–39, fos. 95–6[v]; F. G. Emmison, *Elizabethan Life: Home, Work and Land* (Chelmsford, 1976), 139, 144.

[381] L. Stone, *The Crisis of the Aristocracy, 1558–1641* (Oxford, 1965), 579.

[382] C. Gittings, *Death, Burial and the Individual in Early Modern England* (1984), 191.

[383] Evelyn, *Diary*, iii. 120 (8 Mar. 1695).

[384] *Memorandum Book of Sir Walter Calverley*, 129.

[385] Thornton, *Autobiography*, 338.

[386] Diary of Christopher Sanderson, *Six North Country Diaries*, Surtees Society, 118 (1910), 38.

maids' should carry her to the church, three of them her fellow servants, and the fourth, her mistress's daughter.[387] Young women took a special role in the funerals of their friends; in the early 1650s, at the obsequies of a merchant's sister in Chelsea, 'all the girls of the neighbourhood walked with the men, and 10 or 20 held the corners of the pall covering the bier'.[388]

Women also perpetuated certain traditional burial customs. Aubrey recorded that when anyone died in Yorkshire, women came to sing to the dead body. The song told of the journey that dead people had to undergo; if they had never given shoes to anyone, thistles would prick them to the bones. Finally, they would reach the fire of Purgatory:

> If ever thou gave either Milke or drinke
> every night and awle:
> The fire shall never make thee shrink
> and Christ receive thy Sawle.[389]

Widow Venables told Aubrey that in North Wales and nearby Cheshire, 'they doe sett Dishes of meate on the Coffin at a Funerall, and eate over the Defunct'. This may have been a relic of the Herefordshire custom of hiring poor people to eat the sins of the dead, a rite which was still ceremonially performed as late as the 1650s. One Hereford woman kept a bowl 'for the sinne-eater' for many years before her death. Another woman told of an animistic belief, of 'Men being metamorphosd into Trees, and Flowers'. If a tree or flower was planted on the grave, the soul of the deceased went into the plant.[390]

The very poorest women had least control over their burials. The parish usually paid for the funeral and burial: in some cases, officials spent more on a woman's death than on her relief in sickness. In 1679 the parish of St Katherine Coleman Street paid expenses of 20*s.* 6*d.* for nursing Widow Knight for a month; her burial costs amounted to £1. 12*s.* 6*d.* Wine, rosemary, and a coffin at the burial of Goodwife Hill in 1672 cost 22*s.* 5*d*; the parish paid 3*s.* for the appraisal of her goods which were then sold for 7*d.*[391]

Death focused women's minds on the meaning of life and the life to come. The Quaker, Mary Mollineux, who lay dying in 1695, told the

[387] Thanks to Vivien Brodsky for this example from her forthcoming book, *Londoners*. We are very grateful to Dr Brodsky for allowing us to read and to cite her work.

[388] A. G. H. Bachrach and R. G. Collmer (eds.), *Lodewijck Huygens: The English Journal, 1651–1652* (Leiden, 1982), 147. Aubrey recalled that at the funerals of young virgins, it was a custom for a garland of flowers to be placed on the corpse; J. Aubrey, *Remaines of Gentilism and Judaisme, 1686–87*, in *Three Prose Works* (Carbondale, Ill., 1972), 174.

[389] Ibid. 177–8. [390] Ibid. 175–80.

[391] Guildhall MS 1124/2, Accounts of St Katherine Coleman Street.

bystanders she 'had such a Dream, as I have seldom had; *it is an Emblem of my Life*'. Walking beside a broad river, she crossed with difficulty until she came to the final breach. 'How shall I get over this Breach? But yet she went on, and passed through it, and it was fair on the other side; and she awakened.'[392] Mary Mollineux found that the visual images of her dream symbolically represented the meaning of her existence. Through the recounted dream, she told of her passage through dangers to a better fairer state, thereby presenting the archetypal Christian soul's journey and reassuring the by-standers of her ultimate salvation.

CONCLUSIONS

Gender, class, and age were related through all of a woman's life. Her family of origin determined many aspects of her circumstances. For the poorest girls, childhood was frequently terminated prematurely: in their earliest years they were employed in begging, and from age 7 they could be placed as apprentices. While there was no mass exodus from their families at this age, the poorest girls confronted society's expectation that the sooner they could contribute to their upkeep, the better. By contrast, wealthier girls enjoyed a prolonged period of protection within their families. Adolescence, as a time of physical and psychological maturation, was frequently curtailed for aristocratic and wealthier girls, who were married relatively young. Conversely, adolescence was prolonged for the bulk of the female population, who did not marry until their mid-twenties. As girls grew to adulthood, regardless of their social level, they learned what was entailed in becoming a woman.

Gender mattered most during women's reproductive years. Physical maturity brought shared physiological experiences to women, although their bodily experiences varied with their levels of nutrition, age at marriage, and social customs relating to sexuality and lactation. In later years, women's experiences remained gendered, but perhaps difference of sex mattered less than earlier, especially for a small proportion who were wealthy widows. Gender and class interacted at all stages of women's lives.

In discussing women's life-stages, we have emphasized continuity during this period. While there were fluctuations in the illegitimacy rate, slight shifts in women's age at first marriage, and a small increase in the average number of children born to married women, we cannot see major changes in

[392] M. Mollineux, *Fruits of Retirement* (1702), sig. B 2.

the biological experiences of women's lives. There were no new ways for women to control their fertility and so to alter the significance of sexuality in the patterns of their lives. Throughout the early modern period, mothers reared their daughters in conventional ways to enable them to function in a patriarchal society.

4
FEMALE CULTURE

Did women have a culture of their own? Few scholars of early modern culture have thought the subject worth investigating. Initially, historians defined a broad division between two cultures, élite and popular. Recent scholarship has offered a critique of this simple dichotomy, positing a 'cultural pluralism' in which regional variation as well as a tripartite class structure played a role in producing diverse subcultures.[1] Yet despite the growing focus on a multiplicity of subgroups within the larger society, relatively little attention has been paid to fundamental differences between the cultures produced by women and by men.

Part of the problem stems from the models which have been employed to interpret popular culture. Male popular culture has been defined as the norm, with female culture consciously or unconsciously measured against it and found wanting. Although historians have increasingly acknowledged that women's role in popular culture is problematic,[2] few scholars have tried to tease out gender differences, or to examine the question of women's relationship to popular culture.[3] Nor have historians sought to construct a model that delineates an autonomous culture common to women which was not shared by men. One of the aims of this chapter is to demonstrate that such an independent female culture did in fact exist in early modern England.

By the term 'culture' we understand a system of shared meanings within which people lived their lives.[4] Female culture can be analysed in both a vertical and horizontal sense. There were common elements to women's activities which cut across social barriers and helped to define the entire female sex in binary opposition to the male sex. And at a particular social

[1] P. Burke, *Popular Culture in Early Modern Europe* (1978); R. W. Malcolmson, *Life and Labour in England, 1700–1780* (1981); B. Reay, *Popular Culture in Seventeenth-Century England* (1985); J. Barry and C. Brooks (eds.), *The Middling Sort of People: Culture, Society and Politics in England, 1550–1800* (1994); T. Harris (ed.), *Popular Culture in England, c. 1500–1850* (1995).

[2] Reay, *Popular Culture*, 10; Harris (ed.), *Popular Culture*, 4, 13.

[3] A recent exception is S. D. Amussen, 'The Gendering of Popular Culture in Early Modern England', in Harris (ed.), *Popular Culture*.

[4] C. Geertz, *The Interpretation of Cultures: Selected Essays* (New York, 1973).

level, women shared models of thought and behaviour which set them apart as a group from men of the same social class. For example, needlework has both a vertical and a horizontal meaning. All women were involved with sewing, but men were not, unless they had an occupational designation such as tailor or embroiderer. Needlework was just called 'work', it was something all women did. But ordinary women worked at bone-lacemaking, knitting, and plain sewing, while wealthier women and girls embroidered.[5] Each of these cultural traditions was transmitted within its own social grouping, either from mother to daughter, teacher to pupil, or friends helping friends.

To reconstruct the common culture of ordinary women, as distinct from that of the élite, is no easy task. Whereas élite women have left a rich variety of writings, little has remained of the mental or material culture of ordinary women. For the most part, we must glean what we can from indirect evidence which was produced or mediated by men. The difficulties are increased by the fact that social distinction played less part in female culture than in early modern culture generally. While élite men exerted a dominance in the culture of their society, the hegemonic power of élite women among their own sex was limited. Gentlewomen engaged in a separate literate culture to a much lesser extent than their male counterparts. Within the female population, knowledge came from experience and observation as much as from books. Central to the female world was the woman with knowledge, the midwife who was herself a mother. The majority of women, from the poorest to the most aristocratic, shared direct experience of maternity. Even a woman of high social status who had not borne a child could find herself on the periphery of a key aspect of female culture.

We see women's culture both as a phenomenon in and of itself and in its relation to the dominant culture or cultures. Women were not an isolated group; they always had diverse kinds of social relationships to men. Women who were educated shared in many aspects of élite culture, which was focused on literature. Elite women also had access to popular culture, while for the most part ordinary women had access to popular culture alone. The common culture was misogynistic, and popular sayings reflected widespread hostility to women.[6] 'To love a woman's soul whilst there are men, is as bad as bestiality whilst there are women'; 'None but fools were fit to bear children.' Even praise carried a sting: 'I like a thing that's excellent, though

[5] P. Crawford, '"The Only Ornament in a Woman": Needlework in Early Modern England', in *All Her Labours*, 2 vols. (Sydney, 1984), ii. 6–20.

[6] See Ch. 1, 'Contexts: Popular Notions'.

in an ill kind, as I like a good woman.' This particular set of saws actually comes from the commonplace book of a woman, Dame Sarah Cowper, showing us that women participated in perpetuating this misogynistic oral culture.[7] Women as well as men told jokes of female imbecility, cunning, and frailty: Sir Nicholas Le Strange's mother told stories such as that of an illiterate servant girl who, when asked to produce a testimonial, 'up she runns, and for her Testimonial, brings downe a very faire and formall warrant, signifying that she had lately had a Bastard'.[8] The Lady Spring was Le Strange's source for another story, about a wife who could not speak. Her husband took the advice of a physician, which proved so efficacious that he was troubled with her perpetual clamour before which the physician was helpless: 'God helpe the[e] now for I cannot; A woman that hath lost her speech, thou see'st may be recoverd; but if once her Tongue setts a running, all the Divells in hell cannot make it lye still.'[9]

Given that women ideally belonged to the household, and men claimed public space as their own, both élite and popular cultures recognized that women as women had concerns of their own. If the household was the proper place for women, then the household could sometimes become a female space. In this chapter we explore women's relationship to the spaces of early modern society, the places where they associated together, and where only women were likely to be found. Furthermore, we show how society encouraged women to spend time with each other. Yet although, since women were perceived as sexually unstable, men regarded them as being at risk in mixed company, men were also suspicious of women in all-female company, fearing their opportunities for gossip.

Perhaps too, we should speak of women's cultures rather than of culture in the singular. Social distinction, age, and geographical location all played a part in shaping women's bonds. Nevertheless, across these divisions there were aspects of a common culture which women shared. Their cultures and values connected them to fundamental concerns: giving birth, child-rearing, and sustaining life. From women's own perspective, they preserved a culture with important life-enhancing values. In comparison, men appeared to be preoccupied with politics, authority, and their masculine vanity and virility. Within their own culture, women shaped and

[7] Herts RO, Panshanger MSS, MS D/EP F37, Dame Sarah Cowper, Commonplace Book, 1673–*c.*1700, 373–5.

[8] N. Le Strange, *'Merry Passages and Jeasts': A Manuscript Jestbook*, ed. H. F. Lippincott (1974), 104, 120.

[9] Ibid. 120.

enhanced the lives of both sexes, across all ages. Women shared a female consciousness.[10]

SPACE

Separate cultures for women and men were closely associated with the gendering of space. In some contexts, segregation was imposed on the female sex by patriarchal edict, for women were barred from certain locations and institutions reserved for men. But women's role in the gendering of space was not merely negative. They created their own culture, in part, by demarcating and controlling their own space. When special female concerns were at stake, groups of women constructed private spaces from which they excluded men. Women might also exercise spatial and cultural dominance in spheres which were under men's nominal authority, such as the household or market. An investigation of the domains in which women lived and worked can help us to understand female culture as a multifaceted but organically linked whole.

From their own viewpoint, women enacted a mapping of space that was different from the normative strictures decreed by men. The sole context in which women deliberately cloistered themselves within the household was for the rites of childbirth, when they cordoned off an interior space to keep men and girls *out*, not to shut themselves in. But even in daily life, the household was a female-dominated milieu, offering women a secure yet flexible base of operations for their forays into the outside world. Unlike élite advice books, popular culture affirmed women's right to control household space, applying the derogatory term 'cotquean' to men who meddled with domestic concerns. Ballads like *The Woman to the Plow and The Man to the Hen-Roost* (1629)[11] vividly portray the catastrophes that ensued when the husband usurped his wife's charge of household affairs.

Another popular anecdote mocks a husband who tried to 'get the mastery' by testing his wife's compliance to his orders, ending with his command that she place some boiling stew in the hen-roost. Responding to his comment, 'now standeth the pot there-as I would have it', his wife poured the stew over his head, saying, 'And now ben the pottage there-as I would

[10] T. Kaplan, 'Female Consciousness and Collective Action: The Case of Barcelona, 1910–1918', *Signs*, 7 (1982), 545–50.

[11] *The Roxburghe Ballads*, ed. W. Chappell and J. Ebsworth, 9 vols. in 8 (London and Hertford, 1866–99), vii. 185.

FIG. 25. Women buying and selling at the market. Women kept market stalls. They were also buyers of foodstuffs and other commodities. Note female purchasers strolling with baskets, and stallholders proclaiming their wares or haggling with customers

have them!'.[12] Such ballads and tales implied that the household was women's proper realm of authority by virtue of knowledge and skill. In everyday life, women exercised *de facto* control of domestic space and its objects through their work. When they embarked on major enterprises such as laundry day, men might even shift their own agendas. Nehemiah Wallington failed to attend a fast day because 'it was a drying day and my wife would be forth a drying'.[13]

During the daytime, women treated their dwellings as fluid and open expanses, from which they surveyed the passing scene and emerged at will. They also freely resorted to each other's houses, making use of neighbours' dwellings much like a series of linked female spaces. Friends casually entered to eat and drink and chat, borrow domestic implements, give or receive charity, exchange information, visit the sick and dying, or share work and child-care. Incidental references reveal that women's habit of treating each other's dwellings and possessions as common property was so widespread as to be taken for granted. Sometimes we learn of these communal female mores when they led to abuse or discord. Edith Eyles, accused of stealing some rings from a neighbour's house, explained her presence at the scene of the crime by saying she 'came to borrow thread, and finding no one at home she went away'. Suspicions of infanticide directed against Elizabeth Lowes, a

[12] J. Wardroper, *Jest Upon Jest* (1970), 35.

[13] BL, Add. MS 40883, 'Nehemiah Wallington his Booke', fo. 6^{v}.

FIG. 26. Female space and speech from 'Tittle-Tattle; Or, the Several Branches of Gossiping'. Derived originally from a continental source, this 1603 woodcut illustrates many scenes which were characteristic of English women's workaday life and female *rites de passage*. Here the tableaux are manifestly satirical and moralistic in intent: rather than heeding their housewifely duties or higher concerns such as the preacher's sermon, women are shown idling, eating and drinking, gossiping and arguing, or even assaulting each other (fights are depicted in 'At the conduit' and 'Washers at the river')

maidservant, first arose because Wilmott Winterhay came to borrow a bowl and heard Elizabeth groaning. In other incidents, women claimed they had been inside a neighbour's house borrowing a basin or coals for their fire.[14]

Both the flexibility and liminal ambiguity of feminized household boundaries were embodied in women's habit of posting themselves at their doorsteps. Although the women who appear in church court records can be found in most locales, they frequently report themselves standing or sitting in doorways, either alone or in sociable groups of two or three.[15] Occasionally the 'doorway' stance was linked to women's work, since outdoor light was preferable for needlework or lacemaking. But most female witnesses spoke as if they assumed that the doorway was their rightful place as housewives and villagers.

The liminal stance of the doorway connected women in their economic role as overseers of the household to their social role as participants in village life. At her doorstep, a woman was technically within the bounds of her home without being enclosed within its walls. From this vantage point, she could observe the panorama of street life, and take part or remain aloof from her neighbours' affairs. In towns and urbanized areas like London, women also watched the spectacle of street life from open shop windows or house windows on upper floors. Living literally on top of each other, female neighbours carried on conversations and disputes, or observed others do so, while remaining inside their own houses and shops.[16]

The print and doggerel poem 'Tittle-Tattle; Or, the Several Branches of Gossiping' is ostensibly a satirical attack on women's propensity for idle and contentious chatter. But what the print incidentally depicts is women's custom of forming their own spatial groupings related to life-cycle events, work, and leisure, sociable gatherings, and religious observance. These categories were mixed rather than distinct, for women's work and the feminine rites of passage were treated as social and ceremonial as well as instrumental occasions.

In seventeenth-century society, the social dimensions of childbirth assumed almost as much prominence as its biological purpose. Women's

[14] *The Casebook of Sir Francis Ashley J. P. Recorder of Dorchester 1614–1635*, ed. J. H. Bettey, Dorset Record Society, 7 (1981), 73, 18.

[15] For some examples, see OA, MS Archd. papers Oxon. c. 118, fo. 67; OA, MS Oxf. Dioc. papers c. 26, 1629–34, fos. 18, 74–5, 138; Devon RO, Chanter 878, Consistory Court Depositions 1679–81, fos. 7, 25–25^{v}, 41^{v}; see also L. Gowing, 'Gender and the Language of Insult', *HWJ*, 35 (1993), 18.

[16] See, for example, Devon RO, Chanter 878, Consistory Court Depositions 1679–81, fo. 7^{v}; GLRO, D/LC/215, Consistory Court Depositions 1632–4, fo. 17; GLRO, DL/C/235, Consistory Court Depositions 1637–40, fos. 20^{v}, 27^{v}; Guildhall, MS 9189/2, fos. 27^{v}, 56; OA, MS Oxf. Dioc. papers c. 26, 1629–34, fos. 6^{v}–7, 41.

FIG. 27. Satirical street scene. This ballad woodcut represents both satirical and realistic elements of early modern street life. Two women are stationed near their doorsteps (one brandishes a staff at a man wearing cuckold's horns who stands in a doorway), a woman empties a chamberpot from an upper window, and children play in the street

creation of a ritual space on this occasion was an opportunity for defining relationships of female intimacy, for recognizing those relatives and neighbours held in friendship and esteem. Childbed was a site where different generations affirmed their bonds, particularly the mother–daughter bond. The ceremony also united women of different social classes. Gentlewomen might visit their plebeian neighbours to help with the birth, to bring gifts of childbed necessities or medicines and cordials, which were used as anaesthetics.[17] For those above the poorest classes, the lying-in period thus took on the aspect of a protracted party, with expectations of lavish hospitality, including abundant food and drink for the guests.[18] Christenings, too, were arranged much like a 'mini-childbed' where women assembled among their own sex for hospitality and sociability.[19]

Outside the household, some female tasks and occasions had developed into feminized milieux in their own right. The town conduit or public well, the bakehouse, and the riverbank where clothes were washed were patronized mainly by women, and treated by them almost as an extension of their dwellings.[20] Outdoor chores also led to sociable female gatherings,

[17] A. Walker, *The Holy Life of Mrs Elizabeth Walker* (1690), 173, 180.

[18] Bodl., MS Ashmole 36–7, fos. 232^{v}–3.

[19] OA, MS Oxf. Dioc. papers c. 26, 1629–34, fos. 342^{v}–3, incidentally describes a christening party; see also *The Diary of Samuel Pepys*, ed. R. Latham and W. Matthews, 11 vols. (1970–83), ii. 109, viii. 405.

[20] For conduit and river as feminized locales, personal communication by Mark Jenner.

such as women's custom of milking their cows in common.[21] Certain centres of economic activity, although technically under male jurisdiction, were apt to be colonized by female groups, including female vendors' informal control of market space. Although the allocation of stalls was supposedly dictated by male officials, women tried to establish their own territorial groupings within the shared domain of the market.[22]

Religious and neighbourly or charitable occasions also offered women opportunities to construct feminine spheres of social dominance. Visits to the sick and dying were women's special concern because of their nursing expertise. As records of testamentary disputes confirm, the deathbed was a 'feminized' locale. Church was another setting where women demarcated their own spatial and sociable terrain. Women's quarrels about 'place' were generally confined to their own sector of the church; only rarely did they publicly question their segregation from men. Yet while worshipping in the established church, they did not passively accept the places appointed for them by the clergy and churchwardens. Ecclesiastical court records document quarrels between female parishioners over seating and behaviour.[23] Among the Quakers, women's separate meetings extended their control of a female sacred space to the point where some men felt threatened.[24]

During daylight hours, the male ideal of encloistered femininity was irrelevant to most women's behaviour. Church court records show women interacting with each other and with men in the street, the church, the fields, markets and fairs, and sometimes in predominantly masculine domains such as the alehouse. In part this was a corollary of the gendered division of domestic labour. The need for wives and children to contribute to the family economy meant that many women in their daily work routine were obliged to overlap with men in male-dominated space.

Women's incursions into male territory varied with socio-economic status. Roughly speaking, the higher a woman's social position, the less likely she was to share or invade male physical or psychological space. At the top of the social ladder, access was restricted by both class and gender: the Privy Council and Houses of Parliament were off limits not only to élite women, but to plebeian classes of both sexes.[25] The lower the social level,

[21] OA, MS Archd. papers Oxon. c. 118, fos. 25–6, 49–53.

[22] *The Petition of the Oppressed Market People* [1699?].

[23] K. Dillow, 'The Social and Ecclesiastical Significance of Church Seating Arrangements and Pew Disputes, 1500–1740', D.Phil. diss., University of Oxford (1990), 129–42.

[24] For gendered political spaces in the Quaker Wilkinson–Story controversy see P. Mack, *Visionary Women: Ecstatic Prophecy in Seventeenth-Century England* (Berkeley, 1992), 293–302.

[25] For example, Queen Elizabeth's Privy Council included only one woman, the queen herself.

the more common it was for women to control their own cultural, physical, and ritual space, and to share, dispute, or invade space which was under the nominal control of men. The ceremony of childbirth remained an all-female preserve among labouring women, but saw the encroachment of men-midwives among the aristocracy towards the end of the seventeenth century. Mary of Modena gave birth in 1688 before male 'witnesses'.[26]

Ordinary women's need to share male space had its negative aspect. Female labourers who gleaned in the fields or worked there along with men were too poor to subsist on domestic labour alone. The lowliest maidservant was chosen to help with outdoor farming chores or go on errands, to haul water from the conduit, or to fetch her master from the tavern. Similarly, daughters of poor families were more likely to be found in male space, like the 12-year-old girl found working in the kitchen of her father's alehouse after midnight.[27] Such tasks were relegated to those who were powerless to refuse them, because male space was physically as well as morally dangerous to women.

For many women, indoor and outdoor space were equally hazardous environments. Women suffered numerous covertly sanctioned forms of violence within the household: wives, daughters, and maidservants were assaulted, robbed, or raped in their own homes.[28] And, even in peaceable households, the contradiction between female and male concepts of space was never resolved; conflict might surface among the happiest married couples. Moreover, women's custody of domestic space was always precarious. Since the husband was sole owner of his house and 'appurtenances' according to common law, some men utilized their property rights as a weapon during domestic disputes. In several church court cases, witnesses reported that the husband had locked his wife out of the house in her nightclothes in mid-winter.[29]

Their susceptibility to male violence helps explain why women often went about in pairs or groups during the daytime, for they were vulnerable to opportunistic forms of bodily harm when they ventured into outdoor or male-dominated space. Court records reveal that women were attacked

[26] R. Weil, 'The Politics of Legitimacy: Women and the Warming-Pan Scandal', in L. Schwoerer (ed.), *The Revolution of 1688–1689: Changing Perspectives* (Cambridge, 1992), 65–82.

[27] OA, MS Oxf. Dioc. papers c. 26, 1629–34, fos. 346^{v}–7^{v}.

[28] For example, see J. M. Guilding (ed.), *Reading Records*, 4 vols. (1895), ii. 340–1, for a husband's alleged rapes of girls aged 9, 11, and 14 who were in the care of his wife in their home; see also Ashley, *Casebook*, 17, 31, 49, 60, 65, 75, 79, 85, etc. Even in female space, maidservants were vulnerable to fatal beatings from masters or mistresses.

[29] For example, GLRO, DL/C/241, Consistory Court Depositions 1684–7, fos. 31–35^{v}; see also A. Wentworth, *A Vindication* (1677) and *The Revelation of Jesus Christ* (1679).

while walking to market, working in the open fields, serving in alehouses or inns.[30] At night, outdoor space was even more dangerous to women, for it was defined by society as both male and taboo, officially off limits to the female sex regardless of social status. Most women did not venture out alone at night; they rarely went out in female groups, because of the danger to life and reputation. Women who evaded the ban were taken to be 'nightwalkers', or prostitutes. Merely to walk unescorted at night rendered a woman liable to be arrested for immorality and sent to the local Bridewell. Women, but not men, were subject to a *de facto* curfew after dark.

Women had many practical reasons for demarcating separate spaces in a society in which work and life-stages were both strongly differentiated by sex, and the gender order was enforced by the threat of violence. But women also gathered together among their own kind for social or 'cultural' reasons. Within their own milieu, female collectivities sustained a rich heritage of oral and material traditions.

SPEECH

Arise earlie
Serve God devoutly
Then to thy work bustlie
To thy meat joyfully
To thy bed merilie
And though thou fare poorely
And thy lodging homelie
Yet thank God highly.

This little poem with its philosophy of life and work was a 'saying' of Katharine Dowe, a dairy-wife who kept seven score cows at Sibton Abbey, Suffolk. We know of it only because Katharine's son Bartholomew quoted it in his *Dairie Booke for Good Huswives*, 1588, a manual which drew its information from his mother's extensive experience.[31] Although women's oral traditions were one of the most fertile creations of seventeenth-century culture, they are an aspect of female life of which we can have very little direct knowledge.

Women's speech is hidden from us not only because it was liable to be negatively constructed by men, but because it was highly contextualized by

[30] Ashley, *Casebook*, 3, 32, 35, 60, 62, 65, 71, 75, 79, 86, 97, etc.

[31] Cited in J. Fleming, 'Writing Women in Jacobean England', *Huntington Library Quarterly* (1994), 203–4.

women themselves. Female discourse was often linked to places where women worked or gathered, such as childbed and church, dairy and bake-house, town conduit and market. Moreover, the utility and sheer spontaneity of women's rhetorical styles encouraged them to maintain these traditions within the privacy of a self-contained feminine world. The more vigorously women's oral culture flourished, the less need anyone felt to write it down or to display its treasures to an outside audience. In early modern Wales, where many women composed poetry and shared it with friends, the feminine bardic tradition was so robust that even those female poets who were *able* to write did not transcribe their poetry, but used literate skills for utilitarian purposes.[32]

Responses recorded in court depositions exhibit other connections between female speech and its locale. Women generally chose their topics, vocabulary, and rhetorical modes according to two axes of variation, the 'gender context' of the setting in which they found themselves, and the social status of speaker and audience. Both popular anecdotes and court records depict ordinary women as more direct, uninhibited, and 'vulgar' (by élite standards) than their aristocratic counterparts.[33]

Likewise, as far as the records can take us, all-female groups were relatively candid and free in conversation, whereas women in mixed or male-dominated milieux such as the law courts adapted their language to collective notions of feminine modesty. Interrogated at the quarter sessions about her mistress Rebecca Purcas, Mary Clarke mentioned that Rebecca had used 'such speeches . . . which she will not confess or utter to men but to women'.[34] A maidservant testifying in Sir Edward Moseley's trial for rape refused to repeat Moseley's obscenities, but instead reported he had said 'he would make me kiss his et cetera'. The plaintiff Mrs Swinnerton likewise modestly stated that Moseley had told her maid 'she should kiss something that was about him'. Finally, *Mr* Swinnerton quoted Moseley's actual words: 'he said he would make her kiss his arse.'[35]

Picaresque literature spawned some highly coloured accounts of what women talked about within their own private spaces.[36] Such depictions, which

[32] C. Lloyd-Morgan, 'Poets, Singers and Writers: Welsh Women in Eighteenth-Century Wales', unpublished talk, McMaster University, 4 Feb. 1993.

[33] See, for example, Le Strange, *'Merry Passages and Jeasts'*, 46, 57, 106.

[34] Essex RO, Session Papers 124/59, 60 [1592].

[35] *The Arraignment and Acquittal of Sir Edward Moseley, Baronet* (1648), 45. While the judge criticized the maid for being 'so nice', the trial reporter called her 'modest', surely the image she aimed to project.

[36] *Roxburghe Ballads*, vii. 210–11; *The Bagford Ballads*, ed. J. W. Ebsworth, 2 vols. (1878), ii. 68; T. H.[eywood], *A Curtaine Lecture* (1637); *Ar't Asleepe Husband? A Boulster Lecture* (1640).

were centred on the idea that women were obsessed with their husbands' sexual performance, tell us more about male anxieties in an atmosphere of misogyny and phallocentric sexuality than they do about female speech. Men knew what women talked about in mixed company, but were unable to supply the lacunae, the words and topics omitted because women were inhibited by the very presence of males. Men could not know what women said when they were secure in their own space, free of masculine supervision. Although Pepys assumed that his incursion into all-female space at a christening party gave him the right to ask for expert advice about the begetting of children,[37] we cannot be sure that sexual matters were an important concern for women when talking among themselves. Occasionally, topics of private discourse were mentioned in church court depositions, or in women's correspondence. In a defamation cause which originated at a christening party, there were 'many women there talking and discoursing merrily together of new married women and of singlewomen never married that were unlawfully begotten wth Child'.[38] Jane Pilkington wrote to Lady Elizabeth Rich to convey a mutual friend's invitation to her childbed: 'she sayeth she should be glad of your company when she lyeth in, if you can at that time forbear talking against her husband' (with whom Lady Rich was involved in a financial dispute).[39] Gossip about both sexes, unfettered by 'public' standards of female modesty and decorum, may have been one of the staples of women's private conversation. Yet other constraints continued to operate as ideals in all-female settings, including expectations of polite and socially harmonious behaviour.

Defamation causes between plebeian women show us the two extremes of verbal freedom and constraint confronting each other in a male and public setting. Female witnesses, knowing their own reputations were at risk, might refuse to repeat or to interpret for the court the abusive or prurient language with which their female neighbours had insulted each other from their doorways. In a London case, Alice Stere reported part of a neighbour's defamatory speech, then explained 'for that she was ashamed to hear such filthy words, [she] went immediately into her house and heard no more of their talk'.[40] Two married women deposing in an Oxfordshire suit claimed they did not know what Alice Hearne had meant in saying that Ursula Butler 'did hold up her coats three quarters of an hour to a young fellow . . . and that his thing . . . would not stand'.[41]

The rare glimpses of women's actual speech recorded by court officials

[37] Pepys, *Diary*, v. 222.
[38] OA, MS Oxf. Dioc. papers c. 26, 1629–34, fos. 342v–3.
[39] Folger, Rich MSS, X. d. 451, no. 46.
[40] Guildhall, MS 9056, London Archdeaconry Depositions 1566–7, fo. 4v.
[41] OA, MS Oxf. Dioc. papers c. 26, fos. 358v–9v.

tend to show us the negative side of plebeian female culture, where verbal skills served combatants as weapons in *ad feminam* strife.[42] Yet sometimes the literate élite saw sufficient merit in women's oral traditions to preserve them for posterity. The exchange of goods and information between women of different social rank, for example the sharing of a magical charm or medical recipe in return for alms at the door, might result in its being written down by the recipient. Male authors often made use of information gleaned from illiterate women, with or without acknowledgement, in their scientific, literary, and practical publications.[43]

The proverb 'words are women, deeds are men' reminds us that one of women's greatest strengths resided in discourse, which they were apt to employ as a mode of direct and vigorous action. Women censored their own speech and men disparaged feminine rhetorical prowess not because it was insignificant, but because it could be powerful and dangerous. The immense power of speech in this society was noted by Roger Whitby: 'It is safer to kill a great man; then to talk against him.'[44] The use of words as weapons found its epitome in the scold, whose repertoire of verbal belligerence was acknowledged in satire and punished by the secular courts.[45] But scolding was just one end of a wide spectrum of female rhetorical genres which offered modes of female agency in family, neighbourhood, and the world at large.

'Gossip', the exchange of information about people and events, had a respected function in the community as a means of enforcing canons of morality and neighbourliness. Its utility in deterring crime and sexual licence was acknowledged by church court officials, who often asked witnesses about the existence of a 'common fame', the gender-neutral term for a rumour spread through gossip. In a pre-industrial society of honour and shame, gossip rather than the judiciary was one of the most effective agencies for policing the community.

Women's verbal networks operated within the domestic sphere, between households, and farther afield. Maidservants and part-time labourers such as laundrywomen and charwomen were particularly noted for their ability to

[42] See Gowing, 'Gender and the Language of Insult'.

[43] For examples see below.

[44] Bodl., MS Eng. Hist. e. 312, fo. 22.

[45] S. Butler, *Characters*, ed. C. Daves (Cleveland, Ohio, 1970), 307. For different views of the social context of the scold, cf. Gowing, 'Gender and the Language of Insult'; D. Underdown, 'The Taming of the Scold: The Enforcement of Patriarchal Authority in Early Modern England', in A. Fletcher and J. Stevenson (eds.), *Order and Disorder in Early Modern England* (Cambridge, 1985), ch. 4; M. Ingram, '"Scolding Women Cucked or Washed"', in J. Kermode and G. Walker (eds.), *Women, Crime and the Courts in Early Modern England* (Guildford, 1994), 48–80.

acquire and disseminate information, especially of a clandestine or discreditable kind.[46] Female intelligence might extend to the larger community as well.[47]

Speech between women exposed the gulf between society's ideals and the individual's violation of those ideals. Wife-beating and male sexual immorality were secretly accepted among the fraternity of men, but condemned by the public standards of the community at large, and punished through loss of repute when perpetrators were exposed. One way women modified male behaviour was by broadcasting men's covert acts. In so doing, they also established a context of excessive male violence or immorality which might persuade the judiciary to act.[48] Thus female discourse constructed a collective view whereby accusations became a 'public' concern of which formal authorities were compelled to take notice.

The threat of publicity could be a powerful weapon in the hands of the betrayed wife. When Samuel Pepys persisted in pursuing his former maidservant Deb Willet, Elizabeth Pepys warned she would 'be gone herself this very night from me; and did there demand 3 or 400 l of me to buy my peace, that she might be gone without making any noise, or else protested that she would make all the world know of it.'[49] Husbands complained of wives who purposely made a row to draw friends and neighbours into their matrimonial battles.[50] Many defamation suits between women were in fact quarrels over the husband's sexual infidelity which had reached the publicity stage.[51]

Other female rhetorical genres were both useful and entertaining. It is not a coincidence that female witnesses in church court disputes were adept at fashioning coherent and persuasive narratives, for storytelling was considered women's special province. Although nursery rhymes and fairy tales were employed partly to amuse children, the audience for women's stories extended to all ages and both sexes. One of the wife's duties, listed in the rhyme 'I had a little hen . . .', was to tell 'many a fine tale'.[52] Guests, too, expected to be entertained by female narrative art. In *The Old Wives Tale*, visitors coaxed their plebeian hostess: 'a merry winters tale would drive away

[46] For example, see *HMC*, 77 (1966), De L'Isle and Dudley MSS, 6, Sidney Papers, 1626–98, 561–2.

[47] For examples, see S. D. Amussen, *An Ordered Society: Gender and Class in Early Modern England* (Oxford, 1988), chs. 4 and 5.

[48] Ashley, *Casebook*, 84–5.

[49] Pepys, *Diary*, ix. 367.

[50] Bodl., MS Rawlinson B 382, fo. 165.

[51] For example, GLRO, DL/C/235, London Consistory Court Depositions 1637–40, fos. 3^{v}–4, 27^{v}–8.

[52] 'Hen' was slang for a woman or wife. *Oxford Dictionary of Nursery Rhymes*, ed. I. and P. Opie (Oxford, 1951), 202.

the time trimly, come I am sure you are not without a score.'[53] Men recorded jokes and anecdotes told by female relatives and friends for their family commonplace books.[54]

Beyond their role as tellers of tales and anecdotes, women were repositories of oral traditions of all sorts: literary, musical, poetical, magical, pragmatic, mythical, and historical. Such tales, songs, and apothegms have come down to us in forms that trivialize their value, like the fairy tales and 'old wives' tales' which eighteenth-century antiquarians collected for their quaint folkloric interest. But the pejorative and childish connotations later given to these traditions veil the fact that in their original setting they were handed down as a useful stock of common knowledge. Speech was the primary medium for transmitting not only superstitions and magical lore, but collective feminine experience about housewifery, medicine (particularly gynaecology and obstetrics), gardening, cookery, childcare, textile and other work skills, and a host of philosophical as well as practical concerns.

Proverbs, for example, were valued as time-tested strategies for dealing with a situation. It is difficult to distinguish those proverbs which were composed or cited mainly by women. Ray identifies only one 'women's proverb' in his collection: 'That that's good sawce for a *goose*, is good for a gander.'[55] But other sayings which are clothed in feminine imagery or express the fruits of female experience may have had their origin in women's culture. Women were probably responsible for sayings like 'near is my *petticoat*, but nearer is my smock'.[56] The adage expressed a truth of which plebeian women had daily experience, the greater importance of immediate family and near neighbours compared to distant kin. A cluster of proverbs warns of the brevity of young men's sexual passion, a vital lesson for girls to learn: 'love of lads and fire of chats [i.e. chips] is soon in and soon out.'[57] The illiterate majority of the female populace may have acquired much of their practical knowledge for everyday survival from this communal store of female wisdom.

Female oral and musical traditions were also utilized by contemporary scientific and medical writers, as well as by antiquarians, historians, and musicians. Authors of herbals obtained their empirical information from

[53] G. Peele, *The Old Wives Tale* [1595] (Scolar Facsimile, 1969), sig. B. (The goodwife's tale then becomes the play itself.)

[54] Le Strange attributes many of his anecdotes to specific women, either family or friends. Le Strange, *'Merry Passages and Jeasts'*, *passim*. See also Francis Fane's commonplace book of anecdotes, Folger, MS V. a. 180.

[55] J. Ray, *Proverbs* (1678), 148.

[56] Ibid. 189.

[57] Ibid. 54.

'highly expert old women', a mode of transmitting botanical knowledge which was carried on into the mid-eighteenth century.[58] Labouring women preserved a living legacy of songs and ballads which they used to entertain each other while working. Spinsters, knitters, and 'free maids that weave their thread with bones' were the source of the 'old and plain' song requested by the Duke in *Twelfth Night*.[59] Isaac Walton spoke admiringly of a young milkmaid named Maudlin who could sing over fifty ballads, for she had a 'notable memory'.[60] Women's extensive repertoire of traditional narratives and ballads was also quarried by collectors and antiquarians. When searching for historical traditions at Otterburn, Defoe 'could not but enquire of the good old women everywhere, whether they had heard of the fight at Chevy Chace'. To his pleasure, 'They not only told us they had heard of it, but had all the Account of it at their Fingers end'.[61]

Historians, like their seventeenth-century male counterparts, have tended to assume that women were culturally impoverished because of their exclusion from élite literate culture. In some respects women certainly were disadvantaged by their illiteracy, notably when dealing with the courts and other institutions, for example in probating a will. Ordinary women's lack of writing skills also hampered (although it did not prevent) communication at a distance, in contrast to élite women, who could maintain bonds of friendship and family relationship through correspondence.[62] But in a plebeian society based on sociability, neighbourliness, and mutual interdependence, oral genres were often more useful and effective than literate skills. Like their spatial groupings, women's speech was the 'glue' that held female collectivities together, facilitating a culture of co-operation and exchange.

MATERIAL CULTURE

While the dominant discourse acknowledged (however reluctantly) that women had created private spaces and distinctive rhetorical genres, the

58 A. Arber, *Herbals: Their Origin and Evolution* (Cambridge, 3rd edn., 1986), 319–20.

59 Act II, sc. iv.

60 I. Walton, *The Compleat Angler* (1653), cited in L. Shepard, *The Broadside Ballad* (1962), 63–4.

61 D. Defoe, *A Tour thro' the Whole Island of Great Britain*, ed. G. Cole, 2 vols. (1927), ii. 634, 662.

62 Plebeian women often paid to have letters, accounts, and other documents written for them. For examples see Ashley, *Casebook*, 7–8; R. Lowe, *The Diary of Roger Lowe, 1663–74*, ed. W. Sachse (New Haven, 1938), 24, 28, 42–3, 46, 51, 53, 62–3.

whole tenor of the common law opposed the notion that married women controlled their own material possessions. Aside from a tiny group who traded under *feme sole* status, wives had no legal right to dispose of the commodities they produced, nor to spend the cash they had inherited or earned. And like male minors and servants, unmarried female household dependants generally stated in court records that they were 'of little or nothing worth' aside from their wearing apparel. Wills and inventories, while they can tell us a great deal about the possessions of men and of wealthy widows, were very rarely produced by married women, or by plebeian women of any matrimonial condition.[63]

Female production and exchange economies were not necessarily covert, but they were liable to leave few evidentiary traces. Incidental remarks in court records reveal that women exchanged such commodities as textiles, household goods, and garden plants with each other privately, as friendly or neighbourly transactions. But we rarely find a written record of these informal arrangements, nor do we have any basis for calculating their extent. Much of ordinary women's activity in the material realm has remained hidden from historians.

Yet while it is almost impossible to amass a complete quantitative picture, we can use a range of sources to build up a qualitative 'anthropology' of women's material life.[64] Scattered comments in church court depositions, for example, offer valuable clues to women's actual use and circulation of their possessions. Although the evidence is anecdotal, its fortuitous quality, often immaterial to the issue in dispute, makes it more likely to be accurate.[65] Moreover, the kind of information we find attached to defamation cases or tithe or testamentary disputes offers a vivid picture of the linkages between material possessions and other aspects of women's everyday life. By comparing the testimony of plebeian women to the detailed information recorded in personal accounts by gentlewomen, we can explore the ways in which social and economic rank influenced women's relations to the material world and to each other.

Within the framework of a female culture, several elements provided a basis for women's intimate relationship to the world of material goods. Women of every social and matrimonial status assumed a kind of 'psycho-

[63] See M. Prior, 'Wives and Wills, 1558–1700', in J. Chartres and D. Hey (eds.), *English Rural Society, 1500–1800: Essays in Honour of Joan Thirsk* (Cambridge, 1990), 201–25.

[64] For a quantitative approach to the study of 17th-cent. women's material possessions, see L. Weatherill, 'A Possession of One's Own: Women and Consumer Behaviour in England, 1660–1740', *JBS*, 25 (1986), 131–56; C. Shammas, *The Pre-Industrial Consumer in England and America* (Oxford, 1990).

[65] Inventories, in contrast, were liable to over- or under-valuation of goods, usually the latter.

logical' or 'moral' proprietorship of goods and possessions through their knowledge, labour, and customary use. The clothes women wore, the objects they made or transformed, the food and drink they prepared, the wares they bought and sold, the household goods they inherited or brought to a marriage, the herbs and foodstuffs they grew, the tools and utensils they used in daily life were all linked in myriad ways with female domains of use and skill. When friends commended Anthony Walker on his cider, saying it was the best they had ever drunk, his wife Elizabeth would sometimes reply half jokingly, 'His Sider! 'tis my Sider: I have all the Pains and Care, and he hath all the Praise who never meddles with it.'[66]

There is much evidence of women's unofficial control of those possessions and profits which pertained to the feminine sphere. At the top of the social hierarchy, husbands often granted wives a proportion of the family income for household management, clothing, and charitable activities. Wives might also retain earnings from their own labour, with 'egg money' the archetypal example. Among gentry and middling ranks, we can glimpse a complex perception of women's areas of control through custom and use. In a Devon tithe dispute, a Mr Hocking was sued for the tithe on his produce and fruit. But because both fruit and charity were in his wife's domain, it was *Mrs* Hocking of whom witnesses reported that 'when poor people did come to Mr Hocking's house and beg apples . . . Mrs Hocking [would] give them money, and tell them that her apples were not [yet] tithed and therefore she would [not] give nor dispose of any till the tithe were set out'.[67] Even maidservants might arrogate a form of custodianship through use and expertise, especially of foodstuffs and domestic objects.[68]

Court records confirm women's intimately detailed knowledge of objects and commodities, particularly of household goods and implements, linens and clothing, and foodstuffs. Feminine expertise about goods and their value applied not only to their own households, but to the possessions of friends, relatives, and neighbours. Their encyclopaedic knowledge of material objects helps explain why women were often called as witnesses in testamentary and tithe disputes, despite a strong misogynistic bias against them among an all-male judiciary.

Like women's demarcation of space and speech, their material culture was strongly linked to their work routine and to the life-cycle events that united

[66] Walker, *Life of Elizabeth Walker*, 89.

[67] Devon RO, Chanter 866, Consistory Court Depositions 1634–40 (not foliated or paginated), 6 July 1637, testimony of Abraham Vanston.

[68] See S. Mendelson, '"To Shift for a Cloak": Disorderly Women in the Church Courts', in V. Frith (ed.), *Women and History: Voices of Early Modern England* (Toronto, 1995), 9–17.

them as a sex. And as with all facets of female existence, women's relationship to material objects was embodied in a collectivity of social and economic exchange. Although we can categorize the products of women's skills in the form of lists—clothing and textiles, cookery and gardening and the like—such inventories fail to illuminate the multiple connections between different domains in which women functioned. Nor does a list convey the dynamic quality of female activities, the continual transformation of objects from one form to another, the constant circulation of possessions and commodities from one woman or household to another.

In the female world of material goods, the official market economy was only the visible tip of a large iceberg of diverse kinds of transactions, many of them structured by informal bonds of female friendship and neighbourhood. On the one hand, women had developed an intricate structure of 'horizontal' exchange. The canons of female neighbourliness imposed a kind of collective regime in which food and drink, clothing, and household implements were constantly shared or bartered, loaned or given. Women's charity at the door frequently involved the donation of food or linens or cast-off clothing in exchange for labour or services or information. Even petty theft was part of the female web of material transactions.[69]

We also need to consider the 'vertical' circulation of goods from women of older to younger generations, from mistresses to their maidservants, and from the wealthy élite to plebeian female acquaintances. Sometimes a pattern of female inheritance networks stretching through several generations can be discerned from the wills of ordinary women. The widow Dorothy Fletcher made a will by word of mouth 'wherein she gave her goods to her daughter Bridget Branche saving that out of them she gave and bequeathed one feather bed and the bolster to it and a rug to her grandchild Dorothy Branche'.[70]

Analysis of an Oxfordshire testamentary dispute, *Elizabeth Buller alias Busby* v. *William Buller* [1633], reveals many connections between the world of material possessions and the complex of feminine interests and activities arising from life-stage concerns and the family economy.[71] It also allows us to explore specific circumstances which influenced women's social and economic interactions with material objects. In the course of a dispute between Mrs Elizabeth Busby and her brother William Buller, mainly about the value and ownership of a feather bolster and 'great brass kettle', the

[69] See, for example, B. Lemire, 'The Theft of Clothes and Popular Consumerism in Early Modern England', *Journal of Social History*, 24 (1990), 255–76.

[70] OA, MS Oxf. Dioc. papers c. 26, 1629–34, fo. 165.

[71] OA, MS Oxf. Dioc. papers c. 26, 1629–34, fos. 297^{v}–300, 304–6, $322–5^{v}$, $348–348^{v}$.

court learned minute particulars about the family household goods and linens which Elizabeth had inherited. In their depositions, relatives and neighbours listed these possessions with their market value in exhaustive detail. They also affirmed that Elizabeth had sold the brass kettle in question to her brother John for 18*s.* in order 'to buy herself apparel withall'.

Finally, witnesses described exactly what Elizabeth Busby had done with the bequest of linens, which were kept locked in a coffer. As Elizabeth's sister-in-law Anne Buller told the court,

> Elizabeth did in [my] sight unlock the said coffer . . . and take out thereof one christening sheet which she pawned to goodwife Clark of Sandford, one waistcoat which she did sell to the wife of Thomas Hitchman, one facecloth whereof she made an apron, one tablecloth [with] which she made smocks, and two ruffs, part whereof she cut for herself, and part whereof she sold to the said Hitchman's wife, as also a biggin [hood] which she converted to a coif, and another piece of linen which she made a neckcloth of.

Elizabeth had also 'received from the said Buller one blanket' which she had cut into a petticoat for her own use.[72]

If we consider Elizabeth Buller's specific concerns at this point in life, we can deduce why she first decided to convert her legacy into cash and apparel, and later sued her brother for a kettle and feather bolster. Since her initial goal was marriage, she was in urgent need of attractive clothes, and indeed the engagement and wedding to William Busby followed shortly after she had received and transformed her inheritance. An obsession with the acquisition of beautiful and flattering clothes was a leitmotif of many young women's memoirs at this period, regardless of social rank.[73] But once Elizabeth Busby had become mistress of a household, she must have regretted her sale of the 'great brass kettle', an essential implement of housewifery.

The detailed catalogue of clothing and linens which figured in *Busby* v. *Buller* hints at the profound importance of textiles in female social and economic interactions. Because all women were trained in needlework, textiles were almost as fluid as money as a medium of exchange. As Elizabeth Busby's use of her legacy demonstrates, textiles could be traded or sold (either in their original or modified forms) among a personal network of

[72] OA, MS Oxf. Dioc. papers c. 26, 1629–34, fos. 323–4. For another example of women's informal sale of linens, in this case recorded only because the goods in question were thought to have been stolen, see Guilding, *Reading Records*, ii. 437–9.

[73] See, for example, E. Stirredge, *Strength in Weakness Manifest in the Life . . . of . . . Elizabeth Stirredge* (3rd edn., 1772), 12–15; M. Penington, *Some Account of Circumstances in the Life of Mary Penington* (1821), 16–17; OA, MS Oxf. Dioc papers c. 26, 1629–34, fos. 298–9^{v}, 322–5^{v}; S. H. Mendelson, *The Mental World of Stuart Women*, (Brighton, 1987) 15, 72.

female friends and neighbours, without recourse to commercial markets. Linens and clothes were easily transformed into cash and back again; indeed women frequently treated their clothes as another form of cash, bringing them to an extensive second-hand market, or pawning them in cases of dire need.[74] In 1707, a destitute woman named Priscilla Parr begged her parish for relief, having used up this last resource: 'I have bin Very ill A Long time which forced mee to borrow Mony upon my cloths to the Valieu of tenn shillings to keep mee from starving . . . Grant mee ten shillings to gett my Cloths to keep me warm.'[75]

Women's textile creations formed the basis of social and cultural as well as economic networks. Elite and middling women often presented the products of their own labour (including items like embroidered purses or book-covers) to female friends as gifts.[76] The love-tokens which young women gave to favoured suitors were also likely to be in the form of textiles which they had made themselves, such as knitted stockings. One of the main perquisites maidservants and female labourers received from employers was their cast-off but still highly valued clothes. Among many items of clothing and linen mentioned in her will, Celia Fiennes made several bequests to female servants: 'Let my washer woman have my cotton night gown and one paire of my ordinary couch sheets and ordinary apron.'[77]

Some of the meanings embedded in material objects expressed class as well as gender differences. Although women were united in a number of ways through common cultural interests, each social level had its own particular associations with objects of female use and skill. While women of every rank showed an interest in clothes and textiles, the apparel and linens of the élite were made of richly coloured silks and satins, adorned with exquisite lace and cloth-of-gold, in contrast to the coarse grey and brown homespun of the labouring poor.[78] Gentlewomen cultivated an interest in a wide range of aesthetic objects, including jewellery, paintings and furniture, books and musical instruments, and even landscaping and architecture.[79] Yet

[74] B. Lemire, 'Consumerism in Preindustrial and Early Industrial England: The Trade in Secondhand Clothes', *JBS*, 27 (1988), 1–24.

[75] Guildhall, MS 11, 280A, Parish Papers, St Dionis Backchurch, quoted in S. MacFarlane, 'Studies in Poverty and Poor Relief in London at the End of the Seventeenth Century', D.Phil. diss., University of Oxford (1982), 256.

[76] For example, Northants RO, IC 265 (with thanks to Sarah Jones for this reference); T. Hughes, *English Domestic Needlework, 1660–1860* (n.d.), 95–101, 216–20.

[77] C. Morris (ed.), *The Illustrated Journeys of Celia Fiennes* (1982), 25.

[78] See, for example, the 1614 inventory of Lady Jane Stanhope's apparel, Folger, MS X. d. 522, nos. 1–2.

[79] Norfolk RO, WKC 6/12–14, Katherine Windham personal accounts; Mendelson, *Mental World*, 114; A. Laurence, *Women in England, 1500–1760: A Social History* (1994), 152–62.

within their own social setting, élite women still experienced material objects in a gendered way. For example, the female sex was associated with certain musical instruments, especially the lute and the virginals; but other instruments were forbidden women, such as the cello, which could only be played in an 'immodest' and unfeminine posture.

Women's proficiency in transforming material objects allowed them to capitalize on the connections between different areas of household production and consumption. For example, the housewife had charge of the dairy, as well as small domestic animals such as poultry and pigs. Eggs and poultry fed the family, or were turned into cash (the proverbial 'egg money'). Raw materials could be converted to profitable consumer items like speciality cheeses, pies, or cheesecakes, while waste products such as skim milk fed the animals. Feathers were plucked to make feather beds, a product linked not only to women's care of household goods and linen, but to the obligation for successive female generations to provide their part of the marriage dowry, since the female half of the couple contributed the bed and bedding in plebeian families. These associations between women and small domestic animals extended to the upper ranks as well as plebeian society. The countess of Warwick described how her young niece had made a pet of a hen, which followed her everywhere.[80] There were also symbolic reflections in the perception of gender. Women were associated with hens and geese, as in the rhyme 'I had a little hen' (hen = wife) and in the many proverbs identifying alleged feminine traits with those of poultry.

Another web of interconnections related women's responsibility for food preparation and medical care, the tending of both ornamental and kitchen gardens, and female expertise in the use of plants grown or gathered for foodstuffs and medicine.[81] To these tasks some women added the market gardening of soft fruit and salads, and the production or use of flax for linen, straw for bedding, rushes for floor coverings, and herbs for cookery and housewifery. Gardening, whether utilitarian or decorative, was generally women's province regardless of social status. Some women collected seeds and raised seedling plants not only for their own use, but for sale or exchange with other women.[82]

Female expertise in the cultivation, collection, and preparation of edible

[80] BL, MS Add. 27356, fos. 109–110.

[81] For female social and cultural interactions involved in the exchange of medical recipes, see J. Stine, 'Female Sociability and the Circulation of Medical Advice in Seventeenth-Century England', paper presented to the North American Conference on British Studies, Chicago, 1996. We are grateful to Dr Stine for allowing us to cite her unpublished work.

[82] See OA, MS Oxf. Dioc. papers c. 96, 1606–1720, fo. 13; Devon RO, Reynall Family Papers, MS 4652 M/F3, 3.

and medicinal products was reflected in many areas of life, including poor families' staples of subsistence like beans and bacon, or the gift of foodstuffs and home-made medicines and cordials in sociable and neighbourly exchanges. There was the legacy of cookery, household, and medical recipes transmitted from one female generation to the next;[83] the plebeian female occupation of 'wise woman' or herbalist; the ceremonial use of symbolic flowers and herbs, such as gilded rosemary to decorate a wedding cake, or plain rosemary to embellish an old woman's coffin.[84] The female world of objects carried not only functional connotations, but a heavy weight of social meanings and relationships.

THE PRACTICE OF PIETY

If we think of female culture in terms of beliefs and activities that linked women as a group, shaping their lives in distinctive patterns which set them apart from men, then religious devotion was one of its most significant expressions in the early modern period. To some extent the communal character of feminine religiosity has been ignored by historians, partly because Protestant historiography has depicted such a stark contrast between the collective ceremonials of medieval Catholicism and the 'individualistic' spirit of the Reformation. Admittedly, there is some substance to the comparison. The Reformation eliminated most of the formal linkages between religious ritual, female collectivities, and the yearly cycle of village life which had been a feature of medieval life. Although ceremonies such as hocktide survived well into the seventeenth century in attenuated form, nearly all the rites which called for women's collective religious organization had disappeared.[85] Apart from informal settings—private gatherings for childbirth, prayers at each other's houses, and separate rooms at christenings—there were no female religious associations in England after the Reformation until the separate Quaker Women's Meetings of the 1670s. Catholic women who wished to join a convent were forced to go abroad,

[83] The large collection of women's cookery and medical commonplace books at the Folger Shakespeare Library offers many illustrations; see, for example, Folger, MS A2254.5; Folger, MS V. a. 235; Folger, MS X. d. 469; Folger, MS V. a. 387; Folger, MS V. a. 388; Folger, MS V. a. 20; Folger, MS V. a. 215; etc.

[84] J. Brand, *Observations on Popular Antiquities*, 2 vols. (1813), ii. 49–50, 146–8, 203–12; Guildhall, MS 1124/2, St Katherine Coleman Street, Account Book, p. 24.

[85] For the survival of hocktide, see, for example, OA, MS Oxf. Dioc. papers c. 27, 1634–9, fo. 50. For general social effects of the Reformation on women see P. Crawford, *Women and Religion in England, 1500–1720* (1993), 40–56.

until a small group of women in Mary Ward's Institute returned to England in 1669 under the guise of a school.[86]

Yet religion was gendered in significant ways in early modern England.[87] Although the practice of piety was never the exclusive province of the female sex, there are many signs that private godliness and public morality were labelled as feminine concerns, especially towards the end of the seventeenth century. Even before the Civil War, both sexes assumed that a pious lifestyle naturally pertained to the female domain, and that women were more inclined than their male counterparts to religious duties and personal devotions: 'The weaker sexe, to piety more prone.'[88]

Contemporaries acknowledged that feminine modes of piety sprang from impulses that were intimately connected to female experience. John Featley's *A Fountaine of Teares*, a series of prayers for women structured around the trials and tribulations of female life-stages, was composed at the request of Elizabeth Keate, 'who much complained that her *sexe* was so much *neglected* by *Divines*, that they had not *penned devotions* for all their *severall sufferances* that are common to many', i.e. common to women but not to men.[89] As Frances Widdrington advised her sister, women had to adjust their own religiosity to the sequence of life-stages:

> Now in your single estate must be the time for you to store up knowledge and experience of the corruption or grace that is in you, and so also it is your best time to get an acquaintance with God. For when you come to have a family to care for your heart will be much taken up with those things . . . aye too much too if you have not stored up better cares in your heart . . . I speak by too much experience.[90]

Many women saw the religious life as a self-imposed regime, an all-encompassing lifestyle, a private vocation that transformed every facet of existence, including daily activities, social and familial relationships, and the space in which they lived and worked. For those like the countess of Warwick who could set aside several hours each day for godly exercises, the practice of piety entailed a lengthy routine which included private prayer, the reading of Scripture and other devotional works, several hours of meditation on divine subjects, the scrutiny of one's spiritual condition, the confession of sin, and the keeping of a diary to log one's spiritual

[86] Crawford, *Women and Religion*, 46, 64, 85; Laurence, *Women in England*, 189–90.

[87] See Crawford, *Women and Religion*, 1–17.

[88] Earl of Stirling, *Recreations with the Muses* (1637), 107.

[89] J. Featley, *A Fountaine of Teares* (Amsterdam, 1646), 'To the Reader'; see also T. Bentley, *A Monument for Matrones* (1582); S. Hull, *Chaste, Silent and Obedient: English Books for Women, 1475–1640* (San Marino, 1982).

[90] Bodl. MS Add. A. 119, fo. 22, 10 Feb. 1637.

progress.[91] Women of the middling and lower ranks might also cultivate a regime which comprised as many of these elements as they could fit into their overburdened work schedules, incorporating morning and evening prayer and Scripture reading into their daily routine.[92] In order to do so, some made a habit of rising several hours before the rest of the household.[93]

While the full panoply of spiritual exercises could be practised only by the leisured few, plebeian women found ways of infusing a sacred meaning into even the most mundane activities. Even with little or no leisure at their disposal, they imposed a spiritual dimension on the drudgery that made up their daily routine, singing psalms or meditating on spiritual concerns as they worked.[94] Like their upper-rank counterparts, they tried to transform their environment into a sacred space in which they could be alone with God. During her time as a servant, Alice Hayes would 'seek some secret Place' to fall on her knees and beg God's mercy.[95] Agnes Beaumont spent a cold winter's night communing with Jesus in the barn: 'the word "Beloved" made such a melody in my heart as is not to be expressed.'[96] Plebeian women shared the same need for a secluded space for divine communion that was felt by well-educated diarists like Elizabeth Bury, who remarked that the Lord had 'made my Chamber his Presence-Chamber'.[97] Frances Widdrington assured her sister that the Lord 'when he will not reveal himself to the world, will yet be pleased to meet you in a corner sometimes'.[98]

Although past studies of Protestant modes of thought have emphasized the individual's private quest for salvation, we need to recognize the environment of collective feminine endeavour in which women's personal struggles were set. Piety could lead women in two contradictory directions. Some became socially isolated, engrossed in a self-absorbed quest for individual salvation. Susanna Hopton's *Daily Devotions*, published anonymously, portrays her in the fronstispiece in the guise of an anchorite.[99] But others were animated to greater involvement in group activities, becoming part of a collectivity of female friends and relations, of activists within their own parish or community, or members of an independent sect. Whether as

[91] Mendelson, *Mental World*, 82–108; Crawford, *Women and Religion*, 34–40.

[92] A. Hayes, *A Legacy or Widow's Mite* (1723), 25–6; Walker, *Life of Elizabeth Walker*, 34–40.

[93] See S. H. Mendelson, 'Stuart Women's Diaries', in M. Prior (ed.), *Women in English Society, 1500–1800* (1985), 189.

[94] Hayes, *Legacy*, 17, 26.

[95] Ibid. 16.

[96] A. Beaumont, *The Singular Experiences . . . of Mrs Agnes Beaumont* (1822), 12.

[97] S. Bury, *An Account of the Life and Death of Mrs Elizabeth Bury* (Bristol, 1720), 140, 18 Oct. 1695. Thanks to Mary O'Connor for this reference.

[98] Bodl. MS Add. A. 119, fo. 6, 28 June 1638.

[99] [S. Hopton], *Daily Devotions* (1673).

individuals or as members of groups, women expressed subtle but important differences from men in their approach to the godly life.

Much like needlework or housewifery, feminine piety had evolved into a body of expertise which mothers taught daughters and mistresses their maidservants. Once acquired and perfected, the religious discipline became a storehouse of experience to be shared with female friends, neighbours, and relations in the course of everyday work and socializing. Secular tasks and religious concerns were often combined in the same milieu, as women conversed about godly topics over their sewing. Many women chose biblical scenes for their needlework patterns.[100]

Letters between female relations contain advice about the practice of piety interspersed with family gossip and recipes for treating children's teething pains.[101] Although the illiterate could not record their communal activities, we do have accounts from observers such as John Bunyan, whose own sense of religiosity was first awakened when he eavesdropped on some plebeian women's conversation:

> I came where there was three or four poor women sitting at a door in the Sun, and talking about the things of God . . . their talk was about a new birth, the work of God on their hearts; also how they were convinced of their miserable state by nature: they talked how God had visited their souls with his love in the Lord Jesus, and with what words and promises they had been refreshed, comforted, and supported against the temptations of the Devil . . . and told to each other by which they had been afflicted, and how they were borne up under his assaults . . . they spake with such pleasantness of Scripture language, and with such appearance of grace in all they said, that they were to me as if they had found a new world . . .[102]

Religious sympathies could also provide the basis for rapport between women of different social ranks. Elizabeth Walker, the wife of a clergyman, shared pious concerns with her aristocratic neighbour, the countess of Warwick.[103] Similarly, Sarah Henry found that religious affinities could bridge the distance between her and her social superiors. In 1717, Sarah spent weeks reading over the religious reflections of her old friend, Mrs Hunt, a gentlewoman who had recently died.[104] Within the household, a mistress and her maid dissolved the social barriers between them for the

[100] For some surviving examples of women's needlework panels, purses, and other decorated objects using pious or biblical themes, see Victoria and Albert Museum, T.86–1913; T.85–1913; T.448–1990; T.55–1927; T.117–1936.

[101] For example, Bodl. MS Add. A. 119, *passim.*

[102] J. Bunyan, *Grace Abounding to the Chief of Sinners*, ed. R. Sharrock (Oxford, 1962), 14–15.

[103] Walker, *Life of Elizabeth Walker*, 8.

[104] J. B. Williams (ed.), *Memoirs of the Life and Character of Mrs. Sarah Savage* (1818), pp. xii–xiii; Bodl. MS Eng. Misc. e. 331, 147, 154.

time of their pious conversation together. Lady Elizabeth Brooke, when consulted by a maidservant about spiritual matters, 'required her for that time, to forget that she was a Servant'.[105]

After the Reformation, women could not enter a religious order in England. They were always members of the laity, unless they joined a movement outside the Established Church, such as the Quakers, in which the distinction between clergy and laity did not exist. Nevertheless, women sought a special relationship with the divine when performing public duties. Although clergy and churchwardens decided how the church was to be organized and furnished, wealthy women tried to domesticate the sacred space. Elizabeth Jenyson's bequest to Heighington church in 1604 included 'a carpet for the communion table, a pulpytt clothe, and quishions all of greene velvett ready to be furnished and made upp with lyninges and fringe'.[106] In 1705, the widowed Alice Thornton confirmed gifts of pulpit cloths and cushions to Stonegrave parish church, and bequeathed to the chapel at East Newton a large tablecloth embroidered with gold flowers marked with her initials, as well as her 'new salvo of silver for a pattent'.[107] While plebeian women had no property with which to furnish the place of worship, they provided labour to keep the building clean. Churchwardens' accounts regularly note small payments to poor women for cleaning the church and washing the linen. Wealthier women might arrange for housekeeping duties: in 1705, Dame Mary Calverley left money in her will for the recipients of her benefactions to dust the monuments.[108]

One strand of women's religio-political engagement during the decades preceding the English Civil War begins with the household context of feminine piety.[109] The expression of spiritual convictions through family or 'relative' duties was perhaps the commonest form of female activism at this time, since household piety could (at least in theory) be reconciled to the old-fashioned passive feminine virtues approved by men. Aristocratic and middling women expressed their allegiance to what they believed was a more authentic and 'purified' Protestantism through personal and family discipline: Bible-reading and private prayer, attendance at weekday lectures

[105] N. Parkhurst, *The Faithful and Diligent Christian Described* (1684), 59. For further examples, see Crawford, *Women and Religion*, 88.

[106] *Wills and Inventories . . . Durham*, iv, ed. H. Wood, Surtees Society, 142 (1929), 6.

[107] *The Autobiography of Mrs. Alice Thornton*, ed. C. Jackson, Surtees Society, 62 (1875), 336.

[108] *Lancashire and Cheshire Wills and Inventories, 1563–1807*, ed. J. P. Rylands, Chetham Society, NS 37 (1897), 64.

[109] See D. Willen, 'Women and Religion in Early Modern England', in S. Marshall (ed.), *Women in Reformation and Counter-Reformation Europe* (Bloomington, Ind., 1989), 140–63; Crawford, *Women and Religion*, ch. 4.

and sermons, rejection of infant baptism, the choice of moral or biblical names for offspring, the godly education of children and servants, twice-daily family prayers, the enforcement of strict sabbath observance, and charitable activities among pious friends and relations. The 'regime of piety' extended beyond the household to the neighbourhood at large.[110]

Such a pious regime was not confined to Protestant women: Catholic women engaged in their own regime which depended similarly on time for prayer and reflection. While the specifics of their practices differed—Catholics prayed with rosary beads, read different kinds of devotional literature, and were more dependent on the rituals offered by the priests—they shared with other pious women of middling social rank a desire to shape their own lives and that of their households and children around the tenets of godliness. In so doing, they hoped to attain spiritual benefits for themselves and their families. Because women accepted responsibility for such religious goals, and for the spiritual good of their families, this household form of piety was distinctively female.

Private religiosity might lead to a form of semi-public authority. Like her medieval predecessors, the woman famed for her piety cultivated an energetic retreat from the world. Yet her focus on the inner life of the soul stimulated the life of the group, as her perceptions were shared with other women and her example became a well-known model to be emulated.[111] Some women went beyond personal and 'household' piety to express their dissatisfaction with the Established Church by forming separate religious groups. From the earliest days of Christianity, women had been prominent in religious reform movements. During the sixteenth and seventeenth centuries, they were persecuted as sectaries and separatists. Nevertheless, they found religious forms which suited their spiritual needs, in some cases questing from one group to another. As the Quaker Martha Simmonds explained, she had sought the Lord for many years, 'from one idols temple to another'.[112] Within the new separatist churches, women were numerically prominent, and were more likely to have significant roles. Yet even within these groups, women found that many conventional notions about the gender order still obtained.[113]

Women's exclusion from the formal church hierarchy directed them into

[110] Mendelson, 'Stuart Women's Diaries', 194–5; Mendelson, *Mental World*, 113–15.

[111] D. Willen, '"Communion of the Saints": Spiritual Reciprocity and the Godly Community in Early Modern England', *Albion*, 27 (1995), 19–41.

[112] M. Simmonds, *A Lamentation for the Lost Sheep* (1655), 5–6; see also Crawford, *Women and Religion*, 161–2.

[113] Ibid. 119–82; A. Laurence, 'A Priesthood of She-Believers: Women and Congregations in Mid-Seventeenth-Century England', *Studies in Church History*, 27 (1990), 345–63.

personal modes of worship that transcended parochial and other institutional boundaries. In addition to private devotions and public duties, women were present in great numbers at lectures, at sermons outside their own parishes, as members of new sects, as vocal participants in the crowds who came to support persecuted religious leaders, and as patrons of a range of extra-mural activities for which they contributed moral and financial backing. In some instances, women's collective traditions of religiosity laid the groundwork for their political radicalism during the Civil War years.

FEMALE FRIENDSHIP

As Virginia Woolf remarked in 1929, relationships between women are 'that vast chamber where nobody has yet been'.[114] For the early modern period, we must confront major problems with evidence. Most female friendships were based in activities and oral traditions rather than in literary culture; as we have argued, we shall probably never know what women said among themselves when no men were present. Moreover, the sources for female friendship are qualitatively different depending on social level, ranging from glimpses of poor women sitting companionably chatting, to literary protestations of love in which one aristocratic woman may refer to her female beloved as 'her dearest husband'. We should be wary of concluding that female friendship was merely functional at the lowest levels of society, grounded in mutual help and co-operation, and more affective among the upper ranks, fostered by the leisured cultivation of the finer feelings.

Indeed, the evidence that does survive allows us to argue that women had a strong sense of a shared condition. They possessed what Temma Kaplan has called 'female consciousness', an awareness of themselves as a social entity distinct from men.[115] Women's consciousness of themselves as a discrete group is hardly surprising, given that men put so much energy into telling women that they were different, because they shared inferior characteristics. But this 'female consciousness' was not simply a negative response. Women needed to co-operate with each other in sustaining life; hence they evolved ways of working together, from which they gained a degree of collective power. Bonds of friendship could, and did, cross class barriers.

[114] V. Woolf, *A Room of One's Own* (1963), 84.
[115] Kaplan, 'Female Consciousness and Collective Action', 545–50.

Female relationships should be viewed within their cultural and social setting.[116] While women shared certain biological experiences which formed the basis of common interests, we need to take account of social distinctions. Friendship followed specific patterns which were shaped by women's access to other cultures: élite women were influenced by literary models of friendship, the mass of women by their own traditions. Female friendships might take different forms, depending on social level, kinship, propinquity, religion, age, and individual temperament.

Young and unmarried women spent most of their time with members of their own sex. Bonding between women probably occurred early in life. Among the upper ranks, sons were educated separately, leaving daughters with female companions. Heterosexual socializing of young women was closely supervised. Elite women had intimate friendships among female relatives, including those related by marriage as well as by birth, and sustained their sociable ties by correspondence and frequent visits. During the second half of the seventeenth century, increasing numbers of single women and aristocratic widows with education and leisure shared their lives, forming friendships based on the leisured pursuit of literary interests. In 1651 Katherine Philips established a 'Society of Friendship' for both sexes,[117] but her poetry celebrated female friendship.[118] Mary Astell, who lived and worked mainly among women, argued in her writing for women's opportunity to contract 'the purest and noblest Friendship'.[119] In the 1690s Astell tried to establish a college where women might pursue learning and religious contemplation in retired seclusion.[120] By the eighteenth century, companionate relationships between women were a more recognized form of sociability among the upper ranks of society.[121]

While some women reflected upon the nature of friendship, others shaped relationships by their daily social interactions. For example, when Anne Murray went to stay with Lady Anne, wife of Sir Charles Howard, she heard that her friend was jealous of her. Believing that friends should clarify

[116] C. Smith-Rosenberg, 'The Female World of Love and Ritual', in her *Disorderly Conduct: Visions of Gender in Victorian America* (New York, 1985), 54.

[117] G. Greer *et al.*, *Kissing the Rod* (1988), 192–3.

[118] K. P[hilips], *Poems* (1664; further editions, 1667, 1669, 1682). For a selection, Greer *et al.*, *Kissing the Rod.* See also E. Hobby, *Virtue of Necessity: English Women's Writing, 1646–1688* (1988). Philips has been claimed as a lesbian poet by Hobby; E. Hobby, 'Katherine Philips: Seventeenth-Century Lesbian Poet', in E. Hobby and C. White (eds.), *What Lesbians Do In Books* (1991), 183–204; Perry, *The Celebrated Mary Astell* (Chicago, 1986), 503 n. 46.

[119] *A Serious Proposal to the Ladies* (1696), printed in B. Hill (ed.), *The First English Feminist. Reflections on Marriage and other writings by Mary Astell* (Aldershot, 1986), 163.

[120] Perry, *Mary Astell*, 129–34.

[121] B. Rizzo, *Companions without Vows: Relationships Among Eighteenth-Century British Women* (Athens, Ga., 1994).

misunderstandings, Anne used all opportunities to talk of 'love and friendship and jealousy', telling her friend that if she had any suspicion of 'any person that I thought worth my friendship, shee should bee the first person her selfe that I would declare itt to'. The two women did talk through their difficulties, which they attributed to a malicious minister in the household, but Anne still felt uncomfortable at Naworth castle, so she left for Edinburgh soon after.[122] In this case, the two adopted a creative approach to their relationship, attempting to define its terms for themselves.

Female monarchs and courtiers mingled friendship with the ties of patronage and clientage. Same-sex bonds were socially acceptable, and from these relationships, which were often intimate and even passionate, some gentlewomen gained enormous political power for themselves and their male kin. The political effects of the celebrated friendship between Queen Anne and Sarah Churchill, duchess of Marlborough, will be discussed in Chapter 7; here, however, our purpose is to analyse the dynamics of the relationship.[123]

The friendship between Anne and Sarah was formed in the early 1680s, and cemented by the political crisis of 1688. Anne allowed a breach with her sister Mary rather than dismiss Sarah from her service in 1693. The two corresponded for years, choosing the pen-names of 'Mrs Morley' and 'Mrs Freeman' to bring more equality into their relationship. There are difficulties in interpreting the relationship. For the most part, only Anne's side of the daily exchange of letters survives,[124] and Sarah's caustic comments on Anne after the two had quarrelled suggest that little true intimacy had ever existed. Yet even from Anne's letters alone, we can deduce sympathy and affection between the two women. In 1691, Anne confided in Sarah, saying 'your having trusted me formerly with your most secret thoughts makes me so impertinent'.[125] In the 1690s Anne wrote of her children, of mutual acquaintances, and of remedies for illness ranging from piles to children's convulsions. She confided her worries about daily matters, including her conjectures about possible pregnancy when 'Lady Charlotte' did not appear.[126] These were not subjects which either woman offered for general

[122] *The Memoirs of Anne, Lady Halkett*, ed. J. Loftis (Oxford, 1979), 32–50.

[123] Historians have recognized the political significance of the friendship between Queen Anne and Sarah, duchess of Marlborough, but some have been uncomfortable with its emotional content. For example, David Green, *Queen Anne* (1970), 72, refers to Anne's 'infatuation' and suggests that her letters may have been embarrassing to Sarah.

[124] Sarah asked both Anne and her husband to destroy all her letters. She chose to reproduce some of her own in her memoirs, *An Account of the Conduct* (1742).

[125] BL, Blenheim papers, Add. MS 61414, fo. 147.

[126] BL, Blenheim papers, Add. MS 61414–6, *passim*.

court gossip. Anne and Sarah shared an intimacy which was not unusual between women, but was atypical in that it linked a monarch to one of her subjects.

For years Anne professed her love to Sarah: 'I am sure you have not a faithfuller friend on earth nor [one] that loves you better than I do'; 'tis impossible for any body to have a more real passion for her, than her faithful Mrs Morley'; 'I am more yours than can be expressed & had rather live in a cottage with you than reign Empress of the world without you.'[127] Sarah must have responded warmly, for Anne regularly thanked Sarah for her 'dear kind letter'. Anne admired Sarah for the quality of her friendship: 'as I have often said,' she wrote in 1697, 'I do really believe there never was nor will be, such a friend as dear Mrs Freeman.'[128] Anne's correspondence can be read as part of the dialogue by which the two endlessly negotiated their relationship. Literary models informed some of their concepts. When Sarah discovered that Anne had not told her that her cousin, Abigail Hill, had married, she reproached the queen with a literary allusion, 'putting her in mind of what she often used to say to me out of Montaigne, that it was not breach of promise of secrecy to tell such a friend anything, because it was no more than telling oneself'.[129]

When Anne and Sarah did quarrel in 1708, the bitterness and hurt were irreparable, in part because the friendship had been so close for thirty years. Yet Frances Harris, Sarah's biographer, has shown that the friendship was always an unequal one, for, try as they might, the two could not forget their respective positions. Anne wanted companionship; Sarah wanted power. Had Anne not been queen, it was unlikely that the brilliant, witty, and entertaining Sarah would have bothered with her.[130] Nevertheless, Sarah may have underestimated the emotional significance of the friendship and later have regretted its demise for more than political reasons.

The comfort of a woman friend was a trope of female correspondence. After the Restoration, women's language was often more fulsome than at earlier times. Mary Stuart, Mary Astell, and others were warm and passionate in their expressions of love. Such relations might best be described as 'sentimental friendship', in which feeling and its refined expression were

[127] BL, Blenheim papers, Add. MS 61414, fo. 3 [1683?], fo. 167 [1692]; Add. MS 61415, fo. 10.

[128] BL, Blenheim papers, Add. MS 61414, fo. 23 [7 July 1685]; Add. MS 61615, fos. 135^{v}–6.

[129] W. King (ed.), *Memoirs of Sarah, Duchess of Marlborough* (1930), 130. The citation from Montaigne: 'The secret that I have sworn to reveal to no other, I may without perjury communicate to him who is not another—but is myself'; M. de Montaigne, *Essays*, trans J. M. Cohen (Harmondsworth, 1958), 101.

[130] F. Harris, *A Passion for Government* (Oxford, 1991), 77–8, 91, 139–60.

paramount.[131] One important component was companionship: women enjoyed each other's company, and the opportunity to trust each other with their thoughts. Elizabeth Burnet confessed that she was miserable after her friend Sarah Churchill had left after a visit in 1708: 'I am just like one that has lost the sunshine that makes everything cheerful.'[132] Lady Rachel Russell referred to 'a delicious friend'.[133] Sisters were sometimes very close. Mary Rich, countess of Warwick, was usually depressed after a visit from her sister had ended.[134] Anne Dormer wrote regularly to her sister over several years, their relationship deepened by Anne's disclosures of her marital difficulties: 'You know so well that I love you dearer than my own life that it is needless for me to tell you so', she wrote.[135] Elizabeth Turner eulogized her dead sister and mourned her own loss of 'my true and cordial friend'.[136] Lower on the social scale, a tradesman's wife sorrowed for the death in childbirth of her 'dear friend whom I loved as my own soul'.[137]

Friendship implies a feeling of sympathy and some equality within the relationship, although not necessarily of social level or age. Friendships could be of many kinds. Among the middling sort, some literate women's friendships were similar to those of the aristocracy; they shared their joys and sorrows in correspondence. Friendships also involved mutual aid of various kinds. Depending on their social level and financial resources, women offered each other material and practical help as well as sympathy.

One example of a range of friendships among the middling ranks comes from the records of a Nonconformist woman, Sarah Henry (later Savage), in the late seventeenth and early eighteenth centuries. Sarah and her sisters, who lived in and around Cheshire, were isolated from many of their neighbours by their religious beliefs. Yet Sarah's diary entries about her daily life show a range of interactions with female kin and sympathetic neighbours. Closest to Sarah were her relatives, mother, sisters and sisters-in-law, and daughters, but she also records visits to neighbours. In June 1716 when she was visited by her married daughter, Sarah Lawrence, they both went 'to see our old neighbours'.[138] Shortly after, she saw 'my old friend Mrs Husbands' who had formerly been a servant at the household of a neighbouring gentry family, and had subsequently married a tanner.[139] Sarah and her female neighbours helped each other when they were ill. In 1717, Sarah 'had relief

[131] J. Todd, *Women's Friendship in Literature* (New York, 1980), 305–7.
[132] Quoted in Harris, *Passion for Government*, 148.
[133] *Letters of Lady Rachel Russell* (1773), 37. [134] Mendelson, *Mental World*, 106.
[135] BL, Trumbull MS, D/ED c. 13, [1685?], and *passim*.
[136] Kent AO, Journal of Elizabeth Turner, unfoliated, 25 Mar. 1675.
[137] Williams, *Memoirs of the Life and Character of Mrs Sarah Savage* (1818), 286.
[138] Bodl., MS Eng. Misc. e. 331, Diary of Sarah Savage (1714–23), 106. [139] Ibid. 109.

by something that my neighbour Mrs Voyce sent me'.[140] She valued her 'friend' Mrs Braddock who came to visit or to stay, sometimes for weeks at a time.[141]

Piety was an important element in Sarah Savage's female friendships. When 'poor old Mary Robinson' visited, the two prayed together. Sympathy was no doubt also exchanged, for Mary had domestic troubles which Sarah always pitied.[142] Nonconformity distanced Sarah from other women who were nearby: in August 1717 she noted that 'our neighbours censure us as schismatics & the like'.[143] Yet Sarah's religious views did not exclude her from all the neighbourhood female rites, for in December of the same year she was called up early 'to work of mercy', namely attendance at a neighbour's childbed.[144]

Friendship could cross class barriers as well as those of age and marital status. Mistresses and maids might sometimes empathize very closely with each other's joys and sorrows. When Anne Murray's maid Miriam first heard that Anne's former lover, Thomas Howard, had married a wealthy bride in 1646, 'shee lifted up her hands and said, "Give her, O Lord, dry breasts and a miscarying wombe"'.[145] During the crises of the early modern period, some women trusted their maids with their lives, using them to convey dangerous messages. In 1584, for example, Lady Throckmorton sent her servant Joane Morley to warn a priest in the Tower that his religious status was known.[146]

Servants could be privy to the family dramas and secrets. Alice Thornton, a gentlewoman, described her mother's maid, Dafeny Lightfoot as 'my good freind', and indeed this was what Alice's autobiography reveals her to have been over the years.[147] At various crises in Alice's life, Dafeny was there. She attended Alice's dying sister, and reported her last words.[148] She was party to a scheme of Alice's mother, Lady Wandesford, to leave some of her wealth to Alice (who as a married woman could not inherit). Dafeny attended Alice's mother when she was dying,[149] and secretly conveyed some of her mother's gold and money to Alice.[150] It was Dafeny who identified the goods which Alice claimed were her mother's, and thereby exempted them from loss for her husband's debts.[151] Loyalty may have been the key element in the bond between these women of unequal social status, but loyalty could

[140] Ibid. 159. [141] Ibid. 154, 145 (1716). [142] Ibid. 127, 159.
[143] Ibid. 161. [144] Ibid. 169. [145] *Memoirs of Anne, Lady Halkett*, ed. Loftis, 22.
[146] Crawford, *Women and Religion*, 62.
[147] *The Autobiography of Mrs. Alice Thornton*, 239.
[148] Ibid. 52. [149] Ibid. 109, 115, 242. [150] Ibid. 122.
[151] The legal arrangements by which Lady Wandesford had secured an inheritance to her daughter Alice, while the latter was a married women, were complicated.

FIG. 28. A young lady and her maid. Although they were divided by social class, mistresses and their maidservants could develop friendships. The young woman and her maid depicted here are similarly dressed, and about the same age

be interpreted as an essential element in friendship. Yet this evidence about friendship across social divisions needs to be interpreted with caution, for we know, from Rosemary Pringle's work on friendship between female secretaries and their female bosses in the late twentieth century, that there may be a different perspective on the relationship from the woman who is in the subordinate position.[152] In the case of Alice Thornton, we have Alice's words, but none from Dafeny.

This friendly concern of superiors for their servants made it difficult for either party to see the relationship in purely economic terms. In contrast to apprentices, servants found it more difficult to see themselves as a group with common interests in opposition to those of their masters. Personal relationships between women could mask some of their social differences.

When we consider the friendships of ordinary women, the evidence we can find is of a very different kind. Since the majority was neither literate nor

[152] R. Pringle, *Secretaries Talk: Sexuality, Power and Work* (North Sydney, 1988), 57–83.

wealthy enough to travel, relationships at a distance were harder to sustain. Most women found that they relied more upon their neighbours than upon kin. Such friendships were based in speech and actions, both of which are more difficult to trace. For rural and urban women of the lower ranks, relations with their neighbours were the most significant for daily life. Their friendships were more focused on propinquity than on kinship.

Because the bulk of the female population was illiterate, we must infer their social interactions from a range of indirect evidence. Witnesses in church court cases were required to explain their relationships with the litigants, thus offering some general statements about what friendship meant. Joan Gotobed testified that she had known the deceased for two years: 'either Jane Kitchen came to this deponent's house every day or else this deponent went to her who lodged' at a house nearby. She became 'familiarly acquainted with the deceased [Jane Kitchen] . . . by her coming to this deponent about 3 years since when she this deponent lay in [that is, in childbirth]'.[153] Elizabeth May referrred to her aunt as being 'an intimate acquaintance' of Mrs Pattison, a tobacconist.[154] In a 1635 Devon church court case, Agnes Hull explained that she was not a close friend of the litigant, Susan Richardson: 'she never drank in her company a long time nor was never a gossip to her nor familiar with her.'[155] Records involving women before the courts for crimes and misdemeanours also reveal hints of female networks. At the Devon quarter sessions in 1658 three women were charged with sheep stealing; the presentment states that Abigail Lee and Elizabeth Wood stole the sheep one Saturday night, and salted some away in earthen pots. Elizabeth Wood knew of it, and shared part of the mutton.[156]

Wills are another source of evidence about social relationships. In London widows' wills, Vivien Brodsky found a high proportion of unrelated female legatees, reflecting the importance of neighbourly relationships among women.[157] A Nottingham study showed that even if kin received the bulk of widows' estates, female testators nevertheless gave a number of small bequests to mark their friendships.[158] Testamentary disputes also reveal female friendships. Women were frequently called to testify about the goods

[153] Guildhall, MS 9057/1, London Archdeaconry Depositions 1632–8, fos. 35, 36^{v} (*Baker* v. *Kitchen* 7 Dec. 1633). [154] Bodl., MS Rawlinson B 382, fo. 444.

[155] Devon RO, Chanter 866, cause *Richardson* v. *Blight*, 24 Mar. 1635.

[156] Devon RO, QSB, Box 62, Epiphany 1657/8, 25.

[157] V. Brodsky, 'Widows in Late Elizabethan London', in L. Bonfield, R. M. Smith, and K. Wrightson (eds.), *The World We Have Gained* (Oxford, 1986), 150–1.

[158] S. Dunster, 'An Independent Life? Nottingham Widows, 1594–1650', *Transactions of the Thoroton Society of Nottingham*, 5 (1991), 35.

in question. Their familiarity with each other's property came from time spent in each other's houses.[159]

Friendships were forged in the common spaces which women shared. The records tell of women working or travelling together: maids winnowing corn together;[160] or walking home from Woodstock market.[161] Two sisters-in-law laundered together, one washing, the other starching.[162] Working together provided companionship: it also offered protection from the dangers to which women working alone were exposed. As they walked together, they confided their secrets; Anne Bennet later remembered that her 'familiar acquaintance' Mary Blunt had told her that she had promised to marry Stephen Fowlkner.[163] Common geographical origins could provide another bond between women. A London maid stayed in a house for six weeks with a married woman 'for that she was her country woman'.[164]

Friends shared a physical intimacy as they relied upon each other for help in obstetric and gynaecological matters. During pregnancy, trusted women would be invited to feel the belly or examine the breasts. A woman might be assured that she was pregnant because other women had examined her and told her so.[165] Even Queen Mary of Modena in 1687 and 1688 allowed several women, from countesses to chamber women, to feel her belly, and see her breasts and smock wet with milk.[166] Since menstruation, pregnancy, and lactation were not subjects fit for mixed company, at least not outside the family circle, women's bonds were strengthened by their shared bodily experiences.

Ordinary women benefited from the common culture of female neighbourliness which provided not only day-to-day companionship, but an emergency safety net in time of marital difficulties. In the courts, some maltreated wives alleged they would have had nothing to eat or wear except for what friends had donated. Anne Wilson testified that even while she was with child, her husband had provided nothing for her and taken no care of her; 'had it not been for the charity of several neighbours and other friends she must have perished.'[167] One of Elizabeth Vesey's maidservants smuggled

159 See, for example, Devon RO, Chanter 866, Consistory Court Depositions, 1634–40 (not foliated or paginated), 3 July 1635, 27 Apr. 1636; OA, MS Oxf. Dioc. papers c. 26, 1629–34, fos. 298–300, 304, 323–5.

160 OA, MS Oxf. Dioc. papers c. 26, 1629–34, fo. 90v.

161 Ibid., fo. 63.

162 Ibid., fos. 45–45v.

163 OA, MS Oxf. Dioc. papers c. 27, 1634–9, fo. 377v.

164 Guildhall, MS 9056, London Archdeaconry Depositions, 1566–7, fo. 4 (1566).

165 OA, QS 1690 Easter 16.

166 *The Declaration . . . concerning the birth of the Prince of Wales* [1688], 7, 8, 12, 17.

167 Bodl., MS Rawlinson B 382, fos. 93–93v; for another case see Cheshire RO, Chester Consistory Court, EDC5/1664, no. 43 (thanks to Tim Wales for his transcript).

clothing to her mistress when her husband threw her out in the snow; Elizabeth's aunt and sister rescued her by taking her in.[168]

Friends offered other kinds of assistance, of which we learn from husbands' complaints. According to John Sabin, whenever he struck or provoked his wife Sara she would summon the neighbours by 'raising a tumult about the door which was her common practice', a tactic she had utilized against her former husband as well. Moreover, Sabin complained, his wife had 'by advice of several lewd women that she converses with put me to a great deal of trouble and charge unjustly'; she relied particularly on one, 'a noted woman of the town who used to instruct her in what she should do'.[169]

Women also tried to save each other from male violence. Maria Wilder spoke against Sam Baxter for beating his wife in his shop. Baxter called her a whore.[170] Women's efforts to help each other against male violence were liable to fail tragically, as the harm they sought to prevent recoiled on themselves. Joanna Randall told of a friend, Ellen Clarke, who had tried to protect her from the fury of her husband Robert. Clarke had received 'two dangerous wounds in her wrist' from the knife Robert Randall was using to try to murder Joanna.[171] An even more poignant case was that of Eliza Neale, who was murdered on 13 July 1687 by a male neighbour while 'endeavouring to make peace between him and his wife': she was commemorated on her tomb for her heroic intervention:

> To save her neighbour she has spilt her blood
> and like her Saviour died for doing good . . .[172]

Daily associations and contacts between women led to friendships, but they could also precipitate conflicts and enmities. Evidence about breaches between women can be interpreted to reveal the emotional significance of daily associations. Some disputes involved family groups, but others were generated within the female community. By discussing the occasions for these quarrels among women, we can measure something of the strength and importance of female bonds.

High expectations of female friendship were in themselves a source of tension. If there were failures in friendship or neighbourliness, conflict

[168] It would be difficult to imagine a more damaging case. Witnesses told of the mistress James Vesey kept, and of his giving his wife venereal disease. He had also spoken contemptuously of salvation. GLRO, DL/C/241, Consistory Court Depositions, 1684–7, fos. 1–13^{v}.

[169] Bodl, MS Rawlinson B. 382, fos. 165—165^{v}.

[170] OA, MS Oxf. Dioc. papers c 29, 1679–86, fo. 125.

[171] Bodl., MS Rawlinson B. 382, fo. 276^{v}.

[172] Bodl., MS Rawlinson C. 800, fo. 78^{v}.

ensued. Among the physician Richard Napier's patients early in the seventeenth century, several women reported that they were ill or bewitched because of breaches in custom or obligation. Some sufferers complained that certain neighbours were angry that they had not been invited to their childbirths or other hospitable occasions.[173] Others believed that they had been cursed by disgruntled neighbours.[174] Witchcraft was an unusually common explanation for children's complaints.[175]

The phenomenon of witchcraft can be interpreted in part as another manifestation of the darker side of female sociability. While breaches in neighbourliness have been used to explain witchcraft accusations in England, little attention has been paid to witchcraft as a failure in female friendship,[176] although many cases clearly involved conflicts between women.[177] Lyndal Roper's analysis of cases in early modern Germany suggests that fear and anxiety over the birth of children could lead to accusations between women.[178] Jealousies and tension about maternity were powerful solvents of female friendships. Just as maternity was one of the primary links uniting women, so the absence of maternal experience could exclude some women from female circles. Wet-nurses, stepmothers, and barren women were marginal figures.

Quarrels between women reveal networks, for frequently other women took sides in disputes. Mary Mooreton abused her neighbours as whores and thieves, so she found no support from them when she was indicted before the Cheshire quarter sessions in 1684. In another quarter sessions case, female neighbours testified against Margaret Kennerly, saying she acted 'out of some spite and malice she had to the poor persons . . . bound over'.[179]

Women quarrelled about apparently minor matters, but their disputes stand witness to the significance of appropriate behaviour among women. Aglentine Browne rejected Margaret Neate's proffered gift of food, and abuse followed when Margaret said she would see her choked.[180] An

[173] F. Heal, *Hospitality in Early Modern England* (Oxford, 1990), 366–7.

[174] M. Macdonald, *Mystical Bedlam* (Cambridge, 1981), 107–11.

[175] R. C. Sawyer, 'Patients, Healers, and Disease in the South-east Midlands, 1597–1634', Ph.D. diss., University of Wisconsin-Madison (1986), 327, 321.

[176] K. Thomas, *Religion and the Decline of Magic: Studies in Popular Beliefs in Sixteenth and Seventeenth Century England* (1971); A. Macfarlane, *Witchcraft in Tudor and Stuart England: A Regional and Comparative Study* (1970).

[177] J. Sharpe, 'Witchcraft and Women in Seventeenth-Century England: Some Northern Evidence' *Continuity and Change*, 6 (1991), 179–99.

[178] L. Roper, *Oedipus and the Devil* (1994).

[179] Cases quoted in T. C. Curtis, 'Quarter Sessions Appearances and their Background: A Seventeenth-Century Regional Study', in J. S. Cockburn (ed.), *Crime in England, 1550–1800* (1977), 139–40, 149–50.

[180] OA, MS Oxf. Dioc. papers c. 26, 1629–34, fo. 152.

allegation of cheating was made against a woman when she lent money at what was said to be an exorbitant rate of interest.[181]

Sexual reputation and jealousy were major sources of conflict. Mary Aldworth accused Elizabeth Adam of being a parson's whore, saying 'I have a black Gown as well as thou, but I did not get it with my Arse as thou didst'.[182] Elizabeth Parker denied that she had pawned her 'silver lac'd petticoat' and called Dorothy Butcher an 'impudent brash fac'd Jade' for suggesting that she had.[183] Robert Oliver's wife and her children had called Elizabeth Potts 'whore', so Elizabeth had gone into her house and soundly beaten her.[184] Wives frequently fought with other women whom they suspected of 'stealing' their husbands.[185] In January 1638, two women quarrelled publicly in the street, Joan Kettle accusing her neighbour in front of witnesses of being her husband's whore.[186] Friendships and animosities were revealed by the groups of witnesses each woman brought to the courts.

Daily association between women in their neighbourhoods led to both friendships and enmities. Sociable exchanges were important in women's lives, and to a degree distinct from those with men. Women, when they inhabited 'female spaces', developed their own bonds and codes of conduct. Friendships mattered to women at all social levels. Through their daily associations, their common tasks of creating and preserving life, women developed a shared consciousness and a different set of priorities from those of men.

PASSIONATE FRIENDS AND LESBIAN RELATIONSHIPS

Some women expressed passionate feelings for each other. How should we interpret their love, as erotic, sexual, or 'lesbian'? Is there any evidence, aside from that found in literary texts, of sexual passion between women?

There are many difficulties in interpreting the evidence. The poetry of Katherine Philips is one example of the problem. In her poems, such as *To My excellent Lucasia, on our Friendship*, Philips celebrated a woman's love for her female friend:

[181] Anne Parker took 20*s.* interest for a £5 loan, but the duration of the loan was not specified; OA, MS Oxf. Dioc. papers c. 29, 1679–86 (1679).

[182] Ibid., fo. 8.

[183] OA, MS Oxf. Dioc. papers c. 30, 1686–94, fo. 30 (1686).

[184] Devon RO, QSB, Epiphany 1655/6, unnumbered.

[185] GLRO, DL/C/235, Consistory Court Depositions 1637–40, fos. 3^{v}–4^{v}.

[186] Ibid., fo. 27^{v}.

I did not live until this time
Crown'd my felicity,
When I could say without a crime,
I am not thine, but Thee.[187]

While some scholars have argued that Philips's poetry can be read as a portrayal of lesbian sexuality, others point to its significance in establishing a discursive space in which erotic love between women could be expressed.[188]

Confronted with extravagant professions of love between nineteenth-century American women, Smith-Rosenberg argued that women's friendships were emotionally sustaining; whether they were sexual as well was not significant.[189] Similarly, Adrienne Rich redefined the term 'lesbian', celebrating the primary intensity of feelings between women. All female friendship, she argued, should be seen on a lesbian continuum, by which she meant a range of woman-identified experience. Women's friendships were emotionally important, and not to be defined in terms of physical sexual contact.[190] Janice Raymond, Harriette Andreadis, Elaine Hobby, and others have criticized the approaches of Smith-Rosenberg and Rich, arguing that the latter fail to distinguish relationships which have a sexual component from those which do not. Eroticism between women should not be obscured. Emma Donoghue argues persuasively that we should distinguish between different kinds of passionate feeling between women. While there were intense friendships of an exclusive and important kind, there were also erotic and sexual relationships.[191]

Should we label erotic relationships as 'lesbian'? While the term 'lesbian' can be used of sexual relationships between women, its meaning needs to be established in a particular historical context. In the early modern period, it would be mistaken to refer to women as 'lesbians', but we use the term 'lesbian' to speculate about sexual activity between women, to distinguish this kind of relationship from a non-sexual or erotic friendship. During the

[187] G. Saintsbury (ed.), *Minor Poets of the Caroline Period* (Oxford, 1905), i. 537.

[188] 'Katherine Philips' poetry, then, is "closet" lesbian verse'; Hobby, 'Katherine Philips', 183–204.

[189] Smith-Rosenberg, *Disorderly Conduct*, 33–76.

[190] A. Rich, *On Lies, Secrets, and Silences: Selected Prose, 1966–78* (New York, 1979), 201, 202. Sheila Jeffreys also desexualized women's intense relationships, suggesting that lesbianism should be understood as a passionate commitment to women, and as a political alternative to male supremacy. S. Jeffreys, 'Does It Matter If They Did It?', in Lesbian History Group, *Not A Passing Phase: Reclaiming Lesbians in History 1840–1985* (1989), 24.

[191] J. Raymond, *A Passion for Friends: Toward a Philosophy of Female Affection* (1986), 14–18; H. Andreadis, 'The Sapphic-Platonics of Katherine Philips, 1632–1664', *Signs*, 15 (1989), 58; E. Donoghue, *Passions Between Women: British Lesbian Culture, 1668–1801* (1993).

early modern period, different discourses ascribed different meanings to sexuality between women.[192]

The problems which present themselves in our attempting to assess the sexual element in women's culture extend beyond those of terminology. Certainly the evidence is limited, but documents do exist, although to date much of the evidence relates more to the later seventeenth and eighteenth centuries, rather than to earlier periods.

Literary sources contain many references to women's passionate friendships. Apart from the well-known work of Aphra Behn and Mary Delarivier Manley, Donoghue analyses a wide range of literary texts which can be read to refer to lesbian relationships, including work by women. In a collection of stories published in 1723, Jane Barker recounted a tale of a wife and a mistress who together left their husband/lover. Barker, however, makes no comment upon the relationship between the two women.[193]

Women's letters to friends offer another group of sources whose meaning remains ambiguous. These 'romantic friendships' (as historians have termed them),[194] did not elicit adverse contemporary comment unless there was an explicit reference to sexual activity. It is not our intention to desexualize all female friendships; yet to assume a sexual dimension in every passionate friendship is to go beyond the evidence, and devalues the non-physical or emotional aspect of women's intense relationships. Two examples from correspondence, one from the 1630s, the other from the 1670s and 1680s, illustrate the difficulties in interpreting the evidence about women's passionate friendships.

In the 1630s, Constantia Fowler became acquainted with Catherine Thimelby through her brother, Herbert Aston, to whom she wrote of her new friend:

> I canot hide from you the many, and great obligations, that I have receaved from Mrs Thimelby: truely, I never gained so much by the acquaintance of any, as of her; therefore a thousand times have I blest, and allmost adored the time, that first I saw her.[195]

Constantia's love blossomed as her correspondence with Catherine developed: 'I have bin most deadly in love with her as ever lover was.' 'For never creture was more fortunat then I in gaining afection from her. For I beleeve

[192] See Ch. 1 above.

[193] J. Barker, *Patchwork Screen* (1723; Garland repr. 1973), 97–106; see Todd, *Women's Friendship*, 324, 327.

[194] L. Faderman, *Surpassing the Love of Men: Romantic Friendship and Love between Women from the Renaissance to the Present* (New York, 1981), 15–20.

[195] *Tixall Letters*, 2 vols. (1815), i. 100 (11 Feb. 1637).

I am blest with the most perfectest and constant lover as ever women was blest with.'[196] Catherine married Herbert, and died in childbirth in her fortieth year. Clearly the two sisters-in-law were open about their love. Constantia, married at the time, felt comfortable using the language of romantic heterosexual passion to express her intense feelings.

More ambiguous and intriguing was the friendship between Mary Stuart, later Queen Mary II, and Frances Apsley, later Lady Bathurst. When she was about 9, Mary began a friendship with Frances, and the two exchanged letters for over two decades. Mary adopted the persona of Mary Clorine, wife to Aurelia; Frances, Aurelia, was Mary's husband.[197] (Mary's correspondence was probably preserved for many years under the mistaken notion that it was to her husband William.) Their friendship and their intimate style of address survived both their marriages. When Mary wrote to Frances to tell her that she was pregnant in 1678, she still referred to herself as Frances's wife, confessing in an elaborate charade that 'though I have played the whore a littell I love you of all things in this world'.[198] Unlike nineteenth-century female friends, who elevated their love as surpassing the love of men, these two women measured their love by the standard of a woman's love for a man. In a letter full of exaggerated language to her 'dearest, dearest, dear' in 1679, Mary defined her love for Frances as beyond the love of woman:

> I love mrs Apsley better then any woman can love a woman but I love my dear Aurelia as a Wife should doe a husband nay more then is able to be exprest.[199]

Yet if the language was of matrimony, it was the comfort of female friendship which Mary found in her correspondence with Frances. Worried at William's departure for the Army in 1678, Mary confided that 'tis a great comfort that I have a friend in the world' to whom she could confess her fears.[200]

While these friendships apparently were not sexual, intense relationships between women were open to being labelled as such. Once the loving friendship between Queen Anne and Sarah, duchess of Marlborough, ended, Sarah's charges of lesbianism levelled at Anne's preference for her new favourite, Abigail Masham, surely contributed to making the breach irreparable. Adopting the persona of the true friend who pointed out

[196] Ibid. 109, 108. This letter, which probably dates from 1637, the editor considered 'one of the greatest curiosities in the epistolary style that I ever met with'. (107).

[197] B. Bathurst (ed.), *Letters of Two Queens* [1924], 30.

[198] Ibid. 91.

[199] Ibid. 62. Green, *Queen Anne,* 25, had difficulty with these 'charming ridiculous letters' and invokes 'a doctor' to explain that intimacy between women was possible 'without implying any homosexual basis at all'.

[200] Bathurst, *Letters of Two Queens*, 89.

unpleasant truths,[201] Sarah told Anne that her reputation was lost 'after having discover'd so great a passion for such a woman'.[202] Anne's character could not be maintained, Sarah charged, while Anne retained 'noe inclenation for any but of one's own sex'. References to 'the disagreeable expressions of the dark deeds of the night' in the popular press, and to the Queen's passion for 'a dirty' chambermaid were highly insulting.[203] Anne may have blushed and turned her head away when Sarah mentioned passion between two women, but rather than guilt, as Sarah concluded, her emotion may have been anger at the rudeness of her former friend.[204]

Mary Astell, a prominent late seventeenth-century feminist writer, freely expressed passionate feelings for other women, 'having by Nature strong Propensity to friendly Love'. She confessed, however, that such feelings were a threat to her spirituality, coming between her and her love of God.[205] How Astell's passionate friendships should be interpreted is problematic. Ruth Perry suggests that the significant point is that Astell found emotional support from her friends.[206] She lived her life in a network of women, who tried to support and educate their own sex, including female servants and impoverished women.[207] In proposing 'a *Religious Retirement*' for women, Astell argued that women would find there the pleasure which excelled all others, 'a Noble Vertuous and Disinteress'd Friendship'.[208]

Early modern women may have been more candid in their words of love for each other, without becoming overly concerned about the discourses which labelled same-sex relationships as unnatural. The language of passionate love did not always have a sexual meaning; but historians of lesbian sexuality have rightly pointed out that sometimes it did.

Singleness was one aspect of an erotic culture between women, but evidence about single women who cohabited is also difficult to interpret. Those who lived in an all-female household were objects of suspicion. Women lower down the social scale who lived in all-female groups were liable to prosecution under the Statute of Artificers, as were a number of Quaker

[201] *Memoirs of Sarah*, 157–8.

[202] Sarah to Queen Anne, printed in Green, *Sarah, Duchess of Marlborough*, 318–21.

[203] Harris, *Passion for Government*, 147. It was Sarah herself who later stressed the degrading manual part of Abigail's work. She claimed that she had hesitated about introducing her young relative into the queen's service because Abigail had worked as a manual servant; *Memoirs of Sarah*, 126; Harris, *Passion for Government*, 60–1.

[204] Harris, *Passion for Government*, 160.

[205] Perry, *Astell*, 137.

[206] Hill (ed.), *First English Feminist*; Perry, *Astell*, 140–1.

[207] Ibid. 233–81; see also, I. Q. Brown, 'Domesticity, Feminism, and Friendship: Female Aristocratic Culture and Marriage in England, 1660–1760', *Journal of Family History*, 7 (1982), 406–24.

[208] Astell, *A Serious Proposal*, in Hill (ed.), *First English Feminist*, 150–1.

women after 1660. Four women of South Milton who had kept themselves comfortably 'by their own honest employment of spinning which they followed many years' were told to put themselves into service.[209] Jane and Anne Wright, 'both single persons living only upon their labour' were taken from home.[210] Women of higher social status and conforming religious behaviour could more easily cohabit without questions being asked. A widow enjoined two of her daughters to dwell together after her death, making the elder daughter responsible for the portion of her younger stepsister.[211] Small communities of women were attacked if they threatened patriarchal authority; the spectacle of women living together disturbed the notion that woman was made for man, and suggested sexual possibilities which undermined heterosexuality. But even though some cohabiting women may have been involved in sexual relationships with each other, we have no means of discovering this from court records alone.

One way in which women disguised their relationships with each other was by cross-dressing. Popular literature usually framed such stories in terms of heterosexual passion: women dressed as men to be united with their husbands or lovers who were in the Army or Navy.[212] Another reason commonly adduced was ease of travel. Nevertheless, some women may have offered spurious reasons for their masculine disguise in order to conceal a lesbian relationship. Although the sources baffle our enquiries, we must remember that yet another dimension to female cross-dressing could be sexual. A woman might dress as a man for her own and her lover's erotic pleasure.[213]

We are just beginning to realize the extent to which censorship has affected the survival of documents about women's friendships. The convents of Catholic Englishwomen abroad were an obvious space in which woman-to-woman relationships could develop, but Church officials' sensitivity to the 'scandal' of same-sex friendships has made them wary about preserving such material, and about allowing unrestricted access to convent archives.[214] Moreover, families as well as the clergy could censor material. As we have

[209] LF, The Great Book of Sufferings, 331. [210] Ibid., 109.

[211] *Wills and Inventories from the Registry at Durham*, iv. 169 (1635).

[212] A. Fraser, *The Weaker Vessel: Woman's Lot in Seventeenth-Century England* (1984), 195–201. R. M. Dekker and L. C. van de Pol, in *The Tradition of Female Transvestism in Early Modern Europe* (1989), discuss love for another woman as only one motive for cross-dressing.

[213] Donoghue, *Passions Between Women*, 87–108.

[214] J. C. Brown, *Immodest Acts: The Life of a Lesbian Nun in Renaissance Italy* (Oxford, 1986).

seen, Mary II's letters to Frances Apsley probably survived because they were mistakenly believed to be the expression of wifely affection.[215]

In the light of these problems in finding and interpreting sources, a diocesan court case of a marriage between two women in London in 1680 offers a rare glimpse of two women involved in what may have been a sexual relationship.[216] While the case leaves many questions unanswered, nevertheless it offers a different perspective on the issue of lesbian sexuality, for it documents a story about known women.

On 12 September 1680, in the parish of St Martin-in-the-Fields, Amy Poulter, 'representing herself to be a man' named James Howard, was married to 18-year-old Arabella Hunt. When Arabella later suspected that her husband 'went under the suspition of one of a double gender (being usually called an Hermaphrodite)', she forsook the marital bed and appealed to the Court of Arches for an annulment. The case came to court in 1682, when a jury of five midwives examined Amy Poulter and found her to be 'a perfect Woman in all her Parts'. The court annulled the marriage, and declared that either woman was free to remarry with any suitable man.[217]

In 1680 Amy had for eight years been the wife of Arthur Poulter, the eldest surviving son of a prominent Hertfordshire family.[218] She had courted Arabella in the guise of a young man, an heir not yet of age.[219] By day she went about the city disguised as a woman. Amy's cross-dressing allowed her to sustain her role as a wife, and subsequently a widow, and as a male heir. If her partner had been content, the situation could have continued indefinitely, and no evidence of the disguise would have come to light.[220] The case came to court only because Arabella sued for annulment of the union.

Arabella Hunt was to become a famous lutenist and soprano at the court of Queen Mary II. She may have been the 'Mistress Hunt' who appeared in the court masque *Calisto* with the Ladies Mary and Anne in

[215] At a later period, the diaries of Anne Lister, 1791–1840, which contain a record of her lesbian relationships, were at risk of destruction in the interests first of family pride and later, civic propriety; J. Liddington, 'Anne Lister of Shibden Hall, Halifax (1791–1840): Her Diaries and the Historians', *HWJ*, 35 (1993), 45–77.

[216] For a fuller discussion, and for some of the documents, see P. Crawford and S. Mendelson, 'Sexual Identities in Early Modern England: The Marriage of Two Women in 1680', *Gender & History*, 7 (1995), 362–77.

[217] Bodl., Rawlinson B 378, fos. 259–67. The names are spelt variously through the case.

[218] R. Clutterbuck, *The History and Antiquities of the County of Hertford*, 3 vols. (1845), iii. 518.

[219] Although we have been unable to find her date or place of birth, she was probably in her late twenties.

[220] M. Garber, *Vested Interests: Cross-dressing and Cultural Anxiety* (New York, 1992), 67–8, for some 20th-cent. cases.

1675.[221] Her portrait, painted later by Kneller, shows her to be a beautiful woman. What her understanding of her 'marriage' was remains unclear. She presented herself as an innocent deceived, a possible role, since her mother and two of her friends bore witness to the marriage. (It is unlikely that so large a group of witnesses would have connived at a lesbian marriage.) But it is equally probable that Arabella knew that Amy was not a man.

One of Amy Poulter's motives could have been financial, although this is an unlikely possibility, since her jointure as the widow of Arthur Poulter was at least £300 p.a. The most plausible reading of Amy's behaviour is that she wanted to be in Arabella's bed. In her court testimony Amy claimed that she had married Arabella 'not seriously but rashly and unduly and in a frolic jocular or facetious manner'. Yet since she had courted Arabella for some months, and cohabited for a period (it is unclear from the court testimony whether for a few weeks or for six months), her excuse of a jest would be hard to sustain. A month after the court pronounced the marriage null, Amy was buried in the parish church at the manor of Cottered in Hertfordshire. Arabella lived on until 1705, but she died single, leaving all her goods to her mother.[222]

Aphra Behn's play of 1682, *The False Count*, appears to allude to a lesbian meaning in the Poulter/Hunt case. In the play, an elderly husband is troubled at his wife's relationship with her sister and her maid, saying, 'I have known as much danger hid under a Petticoat, as a pair of Breeches. I have heard of two Women that married each other—oh abominable, as if there were so prodigious a scarcity of Christian Mans Flesh.'[223] Given what we know from other incidents about the speed at which news passed around London, it is likely that Behn was alluding to the Poulter case.[224] While the comment suggests that contemporaries thought that only a shortage of men could explain the motivation of women who turned to each other for sexual passion, Behn was publicly airing the possibility of lesbian marriage.

Most popular literature around this date gave a heterosexual reading to tales of relationships between women. For example, the ballad *Comical News from Bloomsbury* (*c*.1690) told of an impoverished prostitute, Mary Plunket, who masqueraded as 'Captain Charles Fairfax'. To maintain the

[221] E. Boswell, *The Restoration Court Stage (1660–1702)* (New York, 1932), 199, 201 n., 327.
[222] PRO, Prob. 11/486/40/310.
[223] A. Behn, *The False Count* (1682), 16.
[224] V. Pearl, 'London Puritans and Scotch Fifth Columnists: A Mid-Seventeenth-Century Phenomenon', in A. E. J. Hollaender and W. Kellaway (eds.), *Studies in London History Presented to Philip Edmund Jones* (1969), 320–4.

FIG. 29. Arabella Hunt, lutenist and soprano. Arabella Hunt, who later became a renowned musician at the court of Queen Mary, was courted by another woman, Amy Poulter, and married her in a church ceremony in 1680, during which Amy disguised herself as a man. The couple lived together 'at bed and board' for about six months; the marriage was annulled by the London Consistory Court in 1682

deception after the wedding, she employed a blown-up sheep's gut as a dildo.[225] In this and other popular narratives, phallic sexuality was represented as the universal feminine desideratum.

Clearly there was a discursive space, a silence, about the subject of lesbian relationships at this period. The story of Amy Poulter and Arabella Hunt allows us to glimpse two women in bed together. At least one of the two—perhaps both women—took advantage of society's inability to conceptualize the reality of lesbian desire.

FEMALE CONSCIOUSNESS AND FEMINISM

Most historians of feminism have concentrated on the evolution of feminist thought, and on the development of arguments about women's rights and status in society. Some have asserted that 'feminism' did not exist before the word entered the English language[226] during the late nineteenth century, when it was borrowed from the French.[227] Indeed, by writing of 'first wave' and 'second wave' feminism in the twentieth century, historians imply that no feminist consciousness was present at earlier times. We argue that the term 'feminism' can be used in the early modern period, since feminism is not a series of defined goals, but rather takes different forms depending upon the cultural and historical context in which protests about the female condition are expressed. Feminism, as Barbara Caine has argued, 'is necessarily bound by the preoccupations of the society in which it develops and by the terms in which the situation of women there was currently being discussed'.[228]

Literary feminists, such as the duchess of Newcastle and Mary Astell, have been among the most extensively studied of all early modern women.[229] Any

[225] *Comical News from Bloomsbury. The Female Captain: Or, the Counterfit Bridegroom* [*c.*1690], W. G. Day (ed.), *The Pepys Ballads: Facsimile* (Woodbridge, 1978), v. 424.

[226] See, for example, N. Cott, *The Grounding of Modern Feminism* (New Haven, 1987), 3–6.

[227] See K. Offen, 'Defining Feminism: A Comparative Historical Approach', *Signs*, 14 (1988), 119–57.

[228] B. Caine, *Victorian Feminists* (Oxford, 1992), 17.

[229] H. Smith, *Reason's Disciples: Seventeenth-Century English Feminists* (Urbana, Ill., 1982); M. Ferguson (ed.), *First Feminists: British Women Writers, 1578–1799* (Bloomington, Ind., 1985); Perry, *Mary Astell*; Mendelson, *Mental World*; Hill, *The First English Feminist*; M. J. Ezell, *The Patriarch's Wife: Literary Evidence and the History of the Family* (Chapel Hill, NC, 1987); Hobby, *Virtue of Necessity*; J. Todd (ed.), *A Dictionary of British and American Women Writers, 1660–1800* (1987); C. Jordan, *Renaissance Feminism: Literary Texts and Political Models* (Ithaca, NY, 1990).

woman who published her work defied contemporary ideals of the silent woman and helped establish a tradition of female authorship.[230] Women translators compelled respect. Ann, Lady Bacon's translation of Bishop Jewel's *Apologie . . . in defence of the Church of England* was acknowledged to be the standard translation.[231] Female authors suggested alternative views of the single and married conditions, rewrote the stories of the Fall, and participated in the *querelle de femmes*, the literary dispute over the nature of woman. By the sixteenth century, arguments for the social equality of the sexes were common throughout Europe.

Feminists emphasized certain arguments based on reason. Authors such as Bathsua Makin, Mary Astell, and Judith Drake were social determinists: we are 'Education's more then Nature's fools'.[232] By the end of the seventeenth century, even if the quality of scholarship among élite women had declined—neither of the Stuart queens, Mary nor Anne, could match their Tudor predecessors Mary and Elizabeth—women's education had improved in general terms.[233] Furthermore, by the late seventeenth century, circles of learned women fostered women's serious pursuit of intellectual goals.[234] Women scholars from the time of the Cooke sisters in the Elizabethan period to Elizabeth Elstob early in the eighteenth century corresponded with each other and with learned men.

While historians have studied the developed arguments of literate feminists, they have paid less attention to the wider social context in which these ideas were expressed. This context was one of shared tasks in which bonds between women were important. Although most middling and educated women did not themselves perform the household tasks necessary to sustain life, they too accepted responsibility for supervising the household and for the care of children. A consciousness of themselves as a sex developed from women's shared spaces, tasks, and conversation. The majority never challenged the gender order; they accepted the sexual division of labour, and derived from it a sense of rights and obligations. Much of the time, women identified with their families of origin or their own nuclear family, forming their closest friendships with female kin. By comforting and supporting each

[230] P. Crawford, 'Women's Published Writings', in M. Prior (ed.), *Women in English Society, 1500–1800* (1985), 231–64, 268–9.

[231] *STC* 14591.

[232] A. Finch, *The Introduction*, in J. Goulianos (ed.), *By a Woman writt. Literature from Six Centuries by and about Women* (Baltimore, 1974), 72. Educational observations in Crawford, 'Women's Published Writings', 215–16, 228–9; see also Ezell, *The Patriarch's Wife*, 111–91.

[233] M. Reynolds, *The Learned Lady in England, 1650–1760* (1920; Gloucester, Mass., 1966).

[234] S. H. Myers, *The Bluestocking Circle: Women, Friendship, and the Life of the Mind in Eighteenth-Century England* (Oxford, 1990).

other, women helped each other to live in a male-dominated world, and so indirectly supported patriarchal power.

Yet if woman was made for man, then any female-only, or female-directed activities were potentially subversive. Bonds between women could threaten patriarchal control. Certainly early modern popular culture reveals great hostility to women's bonds. Satire about women's gossip, such as *The Parliament of Ladies*, illustrates men's conviction that women talking together undermined male authority.[235] There was some substance to men's fears; women *did* discuss sexual matters and their husbands' behaviour among themselves. Hélène Cixous has alerted us to the subversive quality of female laughter:[236] women who joked together about men undermined the notion that woman should be silent and obedient.

'Female consciousness' had revolutionary potential because it politicized everyday life.[237] Female interests could be activated for 'class' purposes, for example when rural women banded together in defence of common rights, against the interests of the gentry. As we shall argue in Chapter 7, long-standing communal female traditions could and did lead to political action in early modern England. While the women who led demonstrations in London during the Civil War were not feminists in the modern sense of the word, they did share a consciousness of themselves as women. Female consciousness could also serve women's own interests as women.[238] It was crucial not only to women's political activism in the seventeenth century, but to the evolution of feminism in the long term.

Religious belief, piety, and spirituality were central to early modern feminism. Educated women wrote about women's need for literacy so that they might study the Scriptures, read their prayers, and record their spiritual condition. While most women accepted the doctrine of female inferiority, with its concomitant duties of obedience and subordination, they wrote of women as worthy of salvation, and of their value as individuals. Most significantly for our argument here, women used religious justifications to resist or subvert the dominant ideology. On the basis of their own spiritual truths and conscience, they defied religious authorities, some even to the death as heretics or martyrs.[239]

Any theorizing from a feminist viewpoint below the level of female

[235] See Ch. 1 above, 'Popular Notions'.

[236] H. Cixous, 'Castration or Decapitation?', *Signs*, 7 (1981), 41–55.

[237] Kaplan, 'Female Consciousness and Collective Action', 545–51.

[238] See in particular Mary Moore's essay, 'The Womans Right', printed in Ezell, *The Patriarch's Wife*, 191–203.

[239] Crawford, *Women and Religion*, 82, 163–4.

literacy has not survived. The women who pulled down hedges were punished, and the woman who led a grain riot was hanged.[240] Yet there is evidence that feminism extended beyond the literate minority. Some remnant of feminist theory survives in female Levellers' petitions and in some Quaker women's writings. Reading these texts, we can discern connections between women's bonding in normal social circumstances, and the development of female groups which expressed a collective consciousness. As women, some groups developed their own philosophical basis for feminist argument. They claimed to be a disadvantaged social group, and appealed to common Christian values. Some women theorized a religious space in which they transcended the specific disadvantages of the female condition. Quaker women claimed that since they had been born anew, their original prelapsarian equality was restored, as a sign of which Eve's punishment of pain in childbirth had disappeared. An account of a woman who gave birth without suffering was circulated as proof.

In the long term, historians have attributed changes in women's social position to various intellectual developments, such as the effects of the Protestant Reformation and the ramifications of liberal thought, implying that women's position in society was determined by men's thoughts and activities.[241] Such histories deprive women of agency and distort some elements of feminist thought. In writing the history of feminism, and of women's movements of emancipation, historians have given insufficient attention to women's own bonding and feelings of solidarity. From their sense of shared oppression, women undertook political action. Protests such as those about food supplies or trade were important to women, as they showed what collective action could achieve. Female consciousness and women's culture added another element to the tradition of women's collective action.

Women's friendships and traditions of protest were fundamental to later feminist movements which attempted to alter women's condition in society. A shared culture offered a space where women could support each other, develop their own ideas, resist the assumptions of patriarchy, and, in some cases, challenge their subordinate social position.

[240] See Ch. 7 below.

[241] K. Thomas, 'Women and the Civil War Sects', in T. Aston (ed.), *Crisis in Europe, 1560–1660: Essays from Past and Present* (1965), 339.

CONCLUSIONS

To dwell for a little in the realm which only women inhabited is to add a dimension to our understanding of the complex interrelationships between the diverse cultures of early modern England. While the concepts of élite and popular cultures, and the relationships between the two, have engaged the interest of historians, little attention has been paid to the spaces in which women interacted, the words they exchanged, their traditions of communal work and leisure, and the friendships and passions which they shared.

Women's culture was closely connected to the forces of life and death, to sexuality, and to the communal life of society. In order to survive in difficult circumstances, women had to develop co-operative behaviour, and work with as well as alongside other women. Early modern women were creative in their friendships, loves, and strategies for survival. Although many of their concerns were ignored by the dominant culture of their time, women could choose to inhabit a female culture of rich and complex meaning.

5

THE MAKESHIFT ECONOMY OF POOR WOMEN

WORK AND GENDER

In early modern England there were sexual divisions of labour; some work was considered women's work, other men's. Although these divisions might vary regionally—for example, in a few areas women undertook ploughing, although mostly this was men's work—yet in all places there were types of work deemed proper solely for women or for men. The gender order of society was both expressed and defined in terms of work. Contemporaries were troubled at any disturbance of the division of labour.[1] Ballads such as *The Woman to the Plow and the Man to The Hen-Roost* mocked reversals of work roles and implied that such reversals turned the world upside-down.[2] One hypothesis to be tested here is that the higher the social level, the more rigid were the divisions between men's and women's work. The lower the status, the more likely it was to find men and women engaging in similar tasks.

Class or social divisions were also reflected and reinforced by the nature of work which individuals performed. No ladies could engage in manual labour and retain their status. Yet while noblewomen and poor labouring women performed different kinds of work, there were nevertheless some common features. Irrespective of social status, wives were responsible for housekeeping and child-care.

A history of women's work requires that we consider what work they performed at different social levels. This chapter focuses on what Hufton has termed the 'makeshift economy' of that large proportion of the female population who were poor;[3] the next, Chapter 6, on the work of the

[1] Although Bridget Hill, citing Alice Clark, *The Working Life of Women in the Seventeenth Century* (1982), 5, believes that 17th-cent. men did do housework, the evidence suggests that this was highly unusual; B. Hill, *Women, Work and Sexual Politics in Eighteenth-Century England* (Oxford, 1989), 120.

[2] *The Woman to the Plow and the Man to The Hen-Roost*, in *The Roxburghe Ballads*, ed. W. Chappell and T. Ebsworth, 9 vols. in 8 (London and Hertford, 1866–99), vii, 185–7.

[3] O. Hufton, *The Poor of Eighteenth-Century France, 1750–1789* (Oxford, 1974).

middling and upper ranks of women. We discuss why women's labour assumed the patterns it did, and the common features of female labour across social divisions, so that we can consider the connections between gender and class.

Early modern England was largely an agrarian society, and location affected labour. The bulk of women lived in the countryside, producing food for sale as well as for consumption. Variations in soil types and agriculture, between woodland and pasture, influenced patterns of production and so female labour. Manufacture in town and countryside also affected women's economic opportunities.

At all social levels, much of women's labour has been hidden by a range of factors. First, women's identity as workers was obscured by contemporary preoccupations with their marital status as spinsters, wives, and widows. (Only the term 'spinster' implies a work identity, and that not always.)[4] A woman's legal status as worker was certainly affected by her marital status. As a *feme covert*, a wife was incapable of trading on her own account, although by the custom of certain cities, she might be granted permission to trade as a *feme sole*. (In London, a wife who exercised her own craft 'wherein her husband doth not intermeddle' was permitted to trade and to take apprentices.)[5] But while contemporaries recorded the occupations of men, acknowledging their work identities, usually they recorded women's marital status only.[6]

Secondly, historians' preoccupation with 'the family economy' has contributed to the invisibility of women's labour, subsuming all women within the household.[7] We argue that women must be viewed as individuals. Sometimes they were involved in family economies, at other times they were not. A significant proportion of the female population was single, dependent on themselves, as were those who worked as servants. Even after marriage, 'the family economy' was not always functional for women, because men were not always present to provide material support. Deserted wives could find themselves working to support their families; widows were responsible for themselves and their children.

[4] C. Z. Wiener, 'Is a Spinster an Unmarried Woman?' *The American Journal of Legal History*, 20 (1976), 27–31; J. H. Baker, 'Male and Married Spinsters', *The American Journal of Legal History*, 21 (1977), 255–9; V. C. Edwards, 'The Case of the Married Spinster: An Alternative Explanation', *The American Journal of Legal History*, 21 (1977), 260–5.

[5] W. Bohun, *Privilegia Londini; Or the Laws, Customs, and Privileges of the City of London* (1702), 123–4.

[6] Sometimes London church courts enquired about women's occupations.

[7] See for example P. J. P. Goldberg, *Women, Work and Life-Cycle in a Medieval Economy: Women in York and Yorkshire, c. 1300–1520* (Oxford, 1992).

Thirdly, women were individuals whose occupations could change over their lifetime. This made their working lives disjointed, and an occupational designation hard to sustain.[8] Even middling women, who were more likely than the poorest to have some occupational designation such as nurse or midwife, had domestic responsibilities. Most women had multiple work identities, which any record of a single occupation obscures.[9] Sometimes men would list two occupations, although one was the wife's. (Leonard Wheatcroft, a yeoman farmer, took out the licence for what was clearly his wife's brewing.)[10] Contemporary recording practice thus complicates even further the difficulty of quantifying any pattern of women's work in crafts and trades. Furthermore, occupational identities for women were blurred because similar tasks could be performed for pay or for nothing, depending upon their marital status. A wet-nurse or a parish nurse was paid for child-care, and housework was performed for wages when a woman was an unmarried servant: similar work for her family at other life-stages was not paid. Since there was a tendency to define work only as paid labour, women's unpaid labour tended to be invisible.

Fourthly, early modern discourse about 'work' obscured much of women's economic activity. Women's work was taken for granted, something which they 'naturally' did. Child-bearing, child-rearing, and house-keeping were rarely dignified with the term 'work'. Popular sayings such as 'women's work is never done' implied that women were continuously doing things, but never completing any tasks. At the upper levels of society, embroidery was referred to as 'her work' implying that gentlewomen were engaged in decorative pursuits only, while men at the same level might have a vocation or a calling.[11] Since contemporaries viewed whatever work women did as being of intrinsically less economic value than what men did, women's wages or pay was nearly always less than that of men for the same kind of work. Such differentials reinforced female dependence, and the poverty of labouring women without men. Men spoke of the household as a private sphere, and claimed the more public areas of paid labour as their

[8] N. Z. Davis, 'Women in the Crafts in Sixteenth-Century Lyon', *Feminist Studies*, 8 (1982), 47–80.

[9] M. Pelling, 'Occupational Diversity: Barbersurgeons and the Trades of Norwich, 1550–1640', *Bulletin of the History of Medicine*, 56 (1982), 484–511.

[10] L. Wheatcroft, 'The Autobiography of Leonard Wheatcroft', *Journal of the Derbyshire Archaeological and Natural History Society*, 18 (1896), 58, 'The Ale-draper's Petition to the Honorable Bench at Chesterfield Aprill 20, 1677'.

[11] For sewing as 'work', H. Wolley, *A Supplement to the Queen-like Closet* (1674), 80–2; M. Roberts, '"Words They are Women, and Deeds They are Men": Images of Work and Gender in Early Modern England', in L. Charles and L. Duffin (eds.), *Women and Work in PreIndustrial England* (1985), 130–6.

own. Thus the problem of the invisibility of women's work has been compounded, for few records survive of work within the household. Accounts of the female economy of barter and exchange probably never existed, although we may infer from scattered references that such transactions were important to survival. Women's work outside the household was frequently a combination of wages and various kinds of perquisites and informal exchanges.

Finally, modern historians have compounded the invisibility of women's work, for while early twentieth-century historians saw it as crucial in the changing economy of the seventeenth and eighteenth centuries, recent revisionist theories have taken little account of women's labour.[12] Housework, reproduction, and child-rearing were always women's work. Essential in any society, they are rarely included in histories of work.

Here we seek to consider all aspects of women's work, paid and unpaid, over the course of their lifetimes. We have turned to many different kinds of source material in order to demonstrate the omnipresence of working women. The picture we present is frequently based on tiny glimpses of female labour, and on a multitude of examples.

In attempting to consider all aspects of women's work, we have departed from the framework adopted by Alice Clark in her important pioneering account of women's work in seventeenth-century England. Bearing and rearing children was central to women's working lives, although Clark deliberately excluded both.[13] Moreover, continuities in women's work may be as important as change. Clark believed that the seventeenth century was a watershed in the history of women's work, arguing that the effect of capital accumulation transformed the busy Elizabethan housewife, preoccupied with her productive role, into either the idle bourgeois woman or the drudge of poor men. Certainly there was a change during the early modern period; by the end of the seventeenth century, many of the goods which women had produced by their labour, such as food and clothing, were more likely to be purchased. But Clark's thesis does not explain the working situation of *all* women in early modern society; only those at the middling level were affected by the changes she described. Neither poor women nor aristocratic women were engaged in production for the use of their

[12] For a discussion of this exclusion, see M. Berg, 'Women's Work, Mechanization and the Early Phases of Industrialization in England', in R. E. Pahl (ed.), *On Work: Historical, Comparative and Theoretical Approaches* (Oxford, 1988), 61–6.

[13] Clark, *Working Life of Women*, preface, p. lviii. Clark's work has been reissued three times. The recent edition (1992) contains a valuable introduction by Amy Erickson and a useful bibliography.

households during the Elizabethan period; the poor lacked the resources and were dependent on cash, and aristocratic women were in situations of dependence; if élite households produced for use, it was not the gentlewomen themselves who laboured. Secondly, Clark's preoccupation with the contrast between the medieval and eighteenth-century economy led her to ignore significant continuities. As Judith Bennett has argued, the most important characteristics of women's work over the medieval and early modern periods were low skill, low status, and low pay.[14] Enduring characteristics as well as changes in women's work must be considered.

POVERTY

Who were the poor women who were engaged in a lifetime's economy of makeshifts? Basically, there were two groups of impoverished people at any one time. The first were those who were employed, but who still struggled to provide themselves and their dependants with food, clothing, and housing. They were the daughters and wives of labourers, small-scale artisans, and poor 'husbandmen'. Female labourers depended on wages; as small-scale artisans they worked at various trades which required minimal capital equipment and stock. Those who were poor farmers had insufficient land to support themselves without recourse to some paid labour. There was little difference between those who were struggling as small tenant-farmers and those who depended on wages.[15] All of these female workers—labourers, artisans, and cottagers—were too poor to be required to pay subsidies or taxes, or rates for poor relief, but not so poor as to need relief themselves. In a society characterized by underemployment and unemployment, their poverty was relative, but structural factors and personal misfortune rendered them always vulnerable to absolute poverty. The second group of poor was the destitute, who needed assistance to find food, clothing, and housing. Although destitute women lived in what could be called real or absolute poverty, not all were given relief. Beggars and vagrants were among those in absolute poverty.

Over their lifetimes, women could move from relative to absolute poverty. Girls who started life on a baseline of poverty were unlikely to improve

[14] J. M. Bennett, '"History that Stands Still": Women's Work in the European Past', *Feminist Studies*, 14 (1988), 278 (269–83).

[15] A. Everitt, 'Farm Labourers', in J. Thirsk (ed.) *The Agrarian History of England and Wales*, iv. *1500–1640* (Cambridge, 1967), 397.

their status. Their levels of poverty fluctuated for both personal and societal reasons; their socio-economic status was always affected by that of their fathers and husbands, as well as by their own life-stages and health. While a marriage might improve a woman's economic situation initially, usually her position worsened: increasing numbers of growing children required food and clothing, while their care restricted her own opportunities for waged labour. Her economic situation usually deteriorated in old age as she was more likely to be widowed and physically incapable of work. Any economic crisis, such as a series of bad harvests or fluctuations in the cloth trade, could precipitate poor women from the ranks of those who could manage to the group of those who needed relief. Occasionally it is possible to glimpse the life cycle of poverty. In 1712 Elizabeth Williams was a widow with three young children 'in a mean & Poor Condition'. Her husband had been poor, starting life presumably as a foundling or orphan in Christ's Hospital, from whence he was put out as an apprentice to an apothecary of St Dionis parish. There was little chance that Elizabeth's children would find a more secure future than that of their parents.[16]

What proportion of women were poor? Contemporaries took a keen interest in the question of the numbers of the poor. At the end of the seventeenth century, Gregory King calculated that cottagers, labourers, servants, and vagrants comprised about two-thirds of all households.[17] Historians have generally agreed that labourers made up roughly half the rural population, although the proportion varied from region to region.[18] Most of the labouring population were poor, paying neither rates nor taxes. Yet we cannot assume that the female population in poverty was simply half the total. Not all those within the same family enjoyed equal access to resources. Wives and children could be in even greater poverty than the male labourer who was the chief wage-earner. At any one time, perhaps half the female population was poor. Furthermore, probably two-thirds experienced poverty at some stage of their lives.

Most poor women worked at whatever they could from a very early age until death. Their existence was based on a whole set of expedients, ranging from the legal to the illegal, including marriage, service, day-labour, piece-work, formal and informal charitable help, gleaning, begging, and theft. Typically, the work of poor women was labour intensive and ill-paid.

[16] Guildhall, MS 11280A/5, Removal orders and settlement papers.

[17] J. Thirsk and J. P. Cooper (eds.), *Seventeenth-Century Economic Documents* (Oxford, 1972), 780–1.

[18] Everitt, 'Farm Labourers', 397–400; K. Wrightson and D. Levine, *Poverty and Piety in an English Village: Terling, 1525–1700* (New York, 1979), 7.

Ordinary women were 'partial wage-earners'; that is, the paid work that they were able to find was intermittent and therefore inadequate for their support. Even in areas of newly developing industries, there was limited employment.[19] Although historians have discussed female work in terms of 'income supplements', what was a supplement from the male point of view was often, or usually, a woman's basic wage. Much of women's work was by nature part-time, low-paid, and insufficient for subsistence for more than one person, even at the best of times. At the worst, full-time work, such as spinning, could be performed all day, six days a week, and still not provide enough to cover subsistence. As one contemporary observed at the end of the seventeenth century, 'now a poor Woman, perhaps a Mother of many children, must work very hard to gain Three Pence, and Three Pence Farthing per Day. The Misery of these Poor Creatures and their Families, is inexpressible.'[20]

Men of the lower ranks also had multi-occupations and were partial wage-earners. Yet women of the lower ranks were more vulnerable to poverty than men. All of the factors which influenced the patterns of female work discussed above operated at the lowest levels of society: women bore children and reared them, were expected to be dependent, and were paid lower wages. Those without men, single women in particular, were vulnerable to misfortunes such as illness, unemployment, or old age. Parishes were always anxious to move single women out so that they did not become a charge on the poor rates. Typically, in 1619 the London parish of St Saviours, Southwark, directed their officers to search out newcomers, and to remove single women.[21] Widows, or wives with absent husbands who had children to support, were at risk of poverty. From the Norwich Census of the Poor of 1570, Pound calculated that 8 per cent of poor women between the ages of 31 and 40 were deserted wives. Another 15 per cent were widows.[22] Surviving records show that female-headed households were more likely to be poor; in Southwark, in 1631, only 8 per cent of such households were assessed for the poor rate compared with 15.6 per cent of male-headed

[19] T. Wales, 'Poverty, Poor Relief and the Life-Cycle: Some Evidence from Seventeenth-Century Norfolk', in R. Smith (ed.), *Land, Kinship and Life-Cycle* (Cambridge, 1984), 352; D. Levine and K. Wrightson, *The Making of an Industrial Society: Whickham, 1560–1765* (Oxford, 1991), 265–7.

[20] *A Second Humble Address from the Poor Weavers and Manufacturers to the Ladies* [*c.*1690].

[21] The parish surveyor reported finding a woman vagrant and her child. She claimed to be mute but was punished as a fraud, and sent to Suffolk; H. Raine, 'Christopher Fawsett Against the Inmates: An Aspect of Poor Law Administration in the Early Seventeenth Century', *Surrey Archaeological Collections*, 66 (1969), 82.

[22] *The Norwich Census of the Poor, 1570*, ed. J. F. Pound, Norfolk Record Society, 40 (1971), 95.

households; and female householders were overrepresented among those considered poor.[23]

Gender affected degrees of poverty within a family. The wife of the keeper of the Lincoln Bridewell, the wife of a respectable civic employee, was arrested for begging with her seven children in Norwich.[24] A male bread-winner could receive his own food as part of his wages, while his wife and children went hungry. Even when female labourers received food as part of their wages, the rate was less. The Norfolk wage assessment of 1616 allowed the male reaper, clipper of sheep, and harvest worker 6*d.* for his diet, but the female reaper, woman clipper of sheep, and woman labouring in the harvest, 4*d.* Her diet allowance was certainly larger than that of other women workers, such as weeders, but we have found no female agricultural workers who were allowed the same food (or calories) as males.[25] Kitchen accounts from the Bacon estate in the late sixteenth century suggest that larger amounts of meat and drink were provided for male workers than for female.[26] The reasons for this differential are nowhere justified, but perhaps it was assumed that the smaller size of the female required less nourishment, and that she was weaker and therefore did not work as hard. Wives may have contributed to the differing distribution of food resources, deliberately denying themselves food so that their husbands, whose wages were higher, could continue working. But we should remember that higher esteem for the adult male and his labour was already well entrenched. This seemed so obvious no one bothered to justify it. The great estimator of England's population, Gregory King, valued men and women as roughly the same in terms of reproduction, 'yet as to Labour & Industry and the Qualifications of the mind which [with?] respect the Publick the men are more valuable than the women'.[27]

MAKING A LIVING

The working lives of poor girls started when they were young. If girls were orphaned or deprived of one parent (especially of a father), in infancy, or born into a family already burdened with too many children, they could be

[23] J. Boulton, *Neighbourhood and Society* (Cambridge, 1987), 127–8.

[24] She and the three eldest were sent to Bridewell to be set to work, and the other four children were to be returned home; Norfolk RO, Mayor's Court Book, 1624–34, fo. 111.

[25] Clark says that wage assessments allowed 6*d.* or 8*d.* for women's diet if their labour was hard, but she gives no dates or sources; *Working Life*, 72–3. Norfolk RO, AYL 1/1.

[26] L. Campbell, 'The Women of Stiffkey', MA diss., University of East Anglia (1985), 31.

[27] G. King, Notebook, 248, reproduced in P. Laslett (ed.), *The Earliest Classics* (1973).

apprenticed or put into service from the age of 7. However, the access of poor girls to training for employment in their youth was restricted. Service was the most important training and was the main source of employment for poorer women until marriage. While girls may have learned various domestic skills in service, they were not prepared for a specific occupation, profession, or work outside a household.

The status of apprenticeship as a form of training for girls is problematic in the early modern period. While it could be an opportunity for training, in many cases we know that apprenticeships were no more than a useful stratagem by which institutions and parishes transferred responsibility for the very poorest children in their care. The authorities' object was to relieve ratepayers and to put the children in the way of earning their keep. For a fixed sum of money, girls could be trained in some means of earning their own living. In 1573, for example, Christ's Hospital put out 11-year-old Elizabeth Towerhill, who had been in their care for ten years, as a covenanted servant to a widow for seven years.[28] In 1697 the Bristol corporation gave £5 to a joiner to take Rachel Keen, 'a girl now chargeable to this Corporation', as an apprentice.[29]

Apprenticeship for girls was not necessarily a means of training them in skills; nor were they all better off than they would have been in domestic service. Any training in service was posited on the notion of the complementarity of the female role. Whether this training was appropriate to the reality is another question. Even where a woman acquired a specific skill it did not open an avenue of lucrative employment. Lacemaking is an example. In 1625 the council in Chester clearly believed that bone-lace weavers, about two-thirds of whom were women, were synonymous with poor people. Apprenticeship in this trade was to a lifetime of arduous toil for little return.[30]

In many cases, poor girls were actually apprenticed to housewifery, or husbandry, which in terms of the work tasks they performed was similar to that of servants, although the terms of employment differed. Apprentices were bound to serve one master or mistress for a fixed number of years. Parishes also placed poor children in apprenticeships. According to the statute of 1577, beggars' children could be bound as apprentices until

[28] *Christ's Hospital Admissions, 1554–1599*, ed. G. A. T. Allen (1937), 47.

[29] *Bristol Corporation of the Poor. Selected Records, 1696–1834*, ed. E. E. Butcher, Bristol Records Society, 34 (1932), 58–9.

[30] *Calendar of Chester City Council Minutes, 1603–1642*, ed. M. J. Groombridge, Record Society of Lancs and Cheshire, 106 (1956), 134, 221. In 1625 the council enquired after poor people 'and of all bonelace weavers'.

they were 24 years of age; girls, to 21.[31] Fairly typical is the indenture from the Devon parish of Abbotswell in 1697 of Grace Hutchins, one of the poor of the parish, bound apprentice 'in ye art of husbandry'.[32] Examples abound, particularly in London, where foundlings and orphans were numerous. In 1644, officials at St Christopher le Stocks gave Humphery Blundon £3 and clothing to take Ann Christopher, a parish foundling, to serve him 'after the manner of apprentice', while a couple of weeks later they apprenticed a male foundling, John Christopher, to a draper for £4.[33] In practice, apprenticeship for poor girls did not necessarily provide better training or working conditions than service. Although Snell argues that parish apprentices had extra legal protection, on a day-to-day basis in a household the master's authority and influence was considerable, as women's complaints witness.[34]

Poor single women might have little choice of employment. By the 1563 Statute of Artificers, all unmarried women between 12 and 40 could be ordered into service. Subsequently, all over England, civic authorities worked at putting the statute into effect.[35] In Norwich in the 1630s, Cecily Robinson was sent to Bridewell until she was put into service or her father fetched her.[36] In 1654, Mary Plumstead was ordered to find herself a master within the month or be confined to the House of Correction until she was hired.[37]

Service was thus the expected occupation of unmarried women; it could be in husbandry, housewifery, or in the developing by-employments. The different economies followed by rural and urban households generally entailed diverse sets of tasks for servants. Yet a number of town-dwellers owned some land and livestock, and many multi-occupational artisanal families were located in the countryside as well as the city. In either context, maidservants might perform feminine chores such as brewing, baking, and milking, combined with a subsidiary role in male farming tasks, such as harvesting. Regardless of geographical locale, maidservants also worked along with female family members in textile production, such as spinning, knitting, and plain sewing.

[31] P. Sharpe, 'Poor Children as Apprentices in Colyton, 1598–1830', *Continuity and Change*, 6 (1991), 253–70.

[32] Devon RO, MS 2954A add. 2, PO 76.

[33] Guildhall, MS 4425/1, Minutes of the Vestry . . . St Christopher le Stocks, 1593–1731, fos. 37–37v.

[34] K. D. M. Snell, *Annals of the Labouring Poor* (Cambridge, 1985), 284–5.

[35] See Ch. 2, 'Service', above.

[36] *Minutes of Norwich Court of Mayoralty, 1632–1635*, ed. W. L. Sachse, Norfolk Record Society, 36 (1967), 164, 186, 224.

[37] *Norfolk Quarter Sessions Order Book, 1650–1657*, ed. D. E. Howell James, Norfolk Record Society, 26 (1955), item 624.

Perhaps the most important factor which determined the servant's work routine was the size and wealth of the household. At one extreme, large noble households exhibited the kind of specialization described in Hannah Wolley's manuals for women, with a host of live-in female personnel: house-cleaning, laundry, cooking, child-care, and different types of personal service.[38] The wealthy yeoman's manor or farm might practise similar specialization in husbandry. At the lowest level, the artisan or labouring family employed a single maid-of-all-work for the full range of household tasks. She might, however, receive help from family members and from casual labourers, such as washerwomen and scourers or charwomen.

As a form of employment, service was thus an enormously varied experience, but had some advantages compared with other work. It provided food and lodging, sometimes clothing, as well as pay. In service women could save towards marriage, or, more importantly, be in employment while they waited for whatever small portion they would receive from the deaths of parents or relatives. Basic subsistence needs were usually met.

Although women servants moved frequently from one household to another, their mobility did not enable them to command the same wages as their male counterparts. While servants of either sex were not permitted to negotiate their wages in a free market economy, custom and law guaranteed that the market in women's labour was even less free than that for young men. Maximum rates of pay were fixed by justices at the quarter sessions, and rates for maidservants were set at lower levels than for males of equal standing in the domestic hierarchy. In Norfolk in 1613, the annual wage of a common male servant was fixed at 42*s.*, while that of female servants over 20 years of age was assessed at 30*s.*[39] In the 1590s in Yorkshire, 'A woman servant that taketh charge of brewing, baking, kitching, milk-house, or malting, thayt is hired with a gentleman or rich yeoman, whose wife doth not take the pains and charge upon her' was to be paid no more than 13*s.* with meat and drink, with livery (clothing), 4*s.*[40] Although amounts varied from one region to another, women were usually permitted to earn only one-half to two-thirds as much as men.

Actual rates of pay may have differed, as they did in the later seventeenth-century household of a Norfolk gentlewoman, Katherine Windham. In her account book, one of the few women's account books surviving, she recorded rates of pay for nurses ranging from £16 to £6 per annum. One

[38] H. Wolley, *The Gentlewomans Companion; Or, a Guide to the Female Sex* (3rd edn., 1682).

[39] Norfolk RO, AYL 1/1, Wage assessments 1613.

[40] *The House and Farm Accounts of the Shuttleworths*, ed. J. Harland, Chetham Society, 4 vols. (1856–8), ii. 351.

was to be paid £6 for a quarter of a year, but only £10 if she stayed for half a year.[41] Even if these were no higher than the wages fixed for Norfolk at that date, in practice servants were likely to receive more than their legal wages if they were satisfactory.

Service could offer additional benefits. First, many servants received legacies on the death of a master or mistress. Around a quarter of Manchester wills in the Elizabethan period mentioned bequests to servants. One clothier left 10*s.* to every servant in his employ at this death, while Alice Gee received 40*s.* and a gown at the death of her master, and £5 at the death of her widowed mistress.[42] Usually bequests were more equal between male and female servants than were wages. Servants could expect cast-off clothing and household goods, as well as cash perquisites at the death of their employer. Secondly, masters might help with marriage celebrations. When two of Giles Moore's servants married in 1676, he contributed generously to their wedding: 'gratis Spent at theire wedding 20s, Fiddlers 1s, Giv'n them a Large Cake All their fewell & the free use of my House & stables for 2 dayes, with a Quart of white wine with Resbeecyes'. In all, he spent not less than 40*s.* 'or one years wage'.[43] Masters and institutional employers might also provide dowries or payments to women on marriage.On 16 July 1619, the matron's maid at Bridewell hospital in London was given a benevolence of 20*s.* for her marriage the following day.[44] In 1630 the Grocers' Company paid a marriage benevolence of £8 to their beadle's maid, 'who hath served him very honestly for the space of 11 years'.[45] The Reading municipality administered a sum of money for dowries for maidservants.[46]

While service may have had advantages over other employment available to poor women, it was not available to women at all stages of life. Usually, householders preferred young single women. Wives might go into service;[47] but they may have disguised their marital status, since contemporary wisdom decreed that a woman could not serve two masters, her husband and her employer.

Employment as servants had particular hazards for women. Apart from

[41] Norfolk RO, WKC 6/12, Katherine Windham personal accounts, 1669–89.

[42] T. S. Willan, *Elizabethan Manchester* (Manchester, 1980), 98, 99.

[43] *The Journal of Giles Moore*, ed. R. Bird, Sussex Record Society, 68 (1971), 178; Pepys also contributed to the wedding of Jane Birch and Tom; *The Diary of Samuel Pepys*, ed. R. Latham and W. Matthews (1970–83), ix. 526.

[44] A. J. Copeland, 'Extracts from Bridewell Court Books', *Under the Dome*, 12 (1903), 118.

[45] Guildhall, Grocers' Accounts, MS 11588/3, fo. 42^{v}.

[46] J. M. Guilding (ed.), *Reading Records*, 4 vols. (1895), ii. 123, 180.

[47] See, for example, L. Stone, *Road to Divorce: England, 1530–1987* (Oxford, 1990), 219.

the general risk of bad employers who starved, beat, and otherwise cruelly treated their servants, women were vulnerable to sexual harassment and rape by their masters or fellow servants. Furthermore, they were trapped by the doctrine of obedience to male authority, and were more likely than the perpetrators of the offences to be the ones punished. Deb Willett, the object of Samuel Pepys's persistent sexual harassment, was dismissed for his offences and last glimpsed by Samuel as she trudged through London in her old clothes. Pepys was well aware that she was a sacrifice to his domestic peace, and that her economic situation was adversely affected.[48] Anne Barker was before the Devon justices for bastardy in 1651. John Reeve, her master, had arranged that she sleep in a truckle bed at the foot of his own bed for three and a half years. In the middle of the night, he came into her bed and 'used' her every week for a couple of years.[49] Sarah Gant, another Devon servant, was ordered by her master Giles May to go to a furze break, where he announced his intention of having sexual intercourse with her. Despite her struggles and protests—'how can you do such a thing against God, and against my good Gammer [mistress]'—he raped her, 'which being over, her said master left her, and she lay there until the cold forced her into his house'. The only person in whom she confided her pregnancy was her mistress.[50]

Pregnant maidservants were usually dismissed, and might be forced to join the vagrant population on the roads, where they were liable to find the doors of charity closed to them. Parish officials were determined that no 'bastards' drained their poor rates. No woman with child was to be admitted to the London hospital of St Thomas, which was declared to be for the relief 'of honest persons and not of harlots'.[51] Dismissal from service could reduce a woman to poverty very quickly. Pregnant single women found it difficult to gain other employment, and could be forced to turn to prostitution, an illegal form of work, in order to survive.

Given the limited options for self-sufficiency open to single women, marriage could be an attractive economic option, one of the expedients for survival open to poor women at certain ages and stages. Ironically, it could also lead to poverty. Once married, a woman relied heavily on the pay of her husband. As a *feme covert* she did not command her own wages; the law offered no recourse if her husband spent her wages on drink or anything else. Furthermore, should the male worker fall ill, then she was expected to

48 *Diary of Samuel Pepys*, ix. 346, 518, and 337–543, *passim*.
49 Devon RO, QSB Box 58, 22 Apr. 1651.
50 Devon RO, QSB Box 61, Epiphany 1656, unnumbered.
51 E. M. McInnes, *St Thomas's Hospital* (1963), 36.

provide for the family on less than male wages. In 1679 in Warwick, a wife petitioned for relief, stating that her husband 'is very poor and lame and hath been so for the last twelve weeks and is not able to get anything to maintain himself, his wife and five small children'. The overseers were to pay 2*s.* 6*d.* per week until he recovered.[52] Many poor mothers and widows lived in systemic poverty.

As married women in the town and countryside, women engaged in housewifery. As wives they performed many tasks similar to those for which as single women they had received wages. All housewifery was labour intensive. Many jobs, such as carrying water, gathering wood, lighting fires, gardening, and caring for small domestic animals, were so taken for granted that they were never mentioned as work. While basic housewifery varied according to the region and whether the household was rural or urban, certain themes were common to all. Married women usually combined housewifery with other work, including child-care and waged labour. Wives might perform a wider range of household tasks than they had been paid to perform as servants in the households of others. In the poorest households, tasks were more basic and less specialized than in wealthier ones. Household tasks were part of the basic struggle for survival. Wives, mothers, and widows were required to be adaptable, to juggle ways and means of keeping the family fed, clothed, and sheltered.

The poor had limited land and animals and were therefore less able to produce their own food. By the later Tudor period they were not producing their own breadcorn. Many were already consumers, purchasing much of their food. Gregory King estimated that, in the countryside, many of the poorer sort were 'living in a manner wholy upon Roots or Plants with ye help of Oatmeal and Rye or Barley bread'. By the eighteenth century, many families bought their entire diet.[53] Most of the calories in the diet of the poor came from women's work, from the kitchen garden, and from scavenging. Kitchen gardening could produce legumes which were easy to cook as pottage without an oven. Cooking was therefore limited, as the staple diet in many areas was probably porridge and pottage.[54] The poor begged skim milk which their more prosperous neighbours usually fed to their pigs.[55] Cheese, described as 'white meat' was

[52] *Warwick County Records. Quarter Session Records Easter, 1674, to Easter, 1682*, 7 (1946), 152.

[53] G. King, Notebook, 213, reproduced in Laslett (ed.), *The Earliest Classics*; Everett, 'Farm Labourers', 416, 450; C. Shammas, *The Pre-Industrial Consumer in England and America* (Oxford, 1990), 145.

[54] C. Howell, *Land, Family, and Inheritance in Transition: Kibworth Harcourt, 1280–1700* (Cambridge, 1983), 165.

[55] Wolley, *The Gentlewomans Companion* (3rd edn., 1682), 302.

important, but despised by the rich as a 'food of the poor'.[56] Some families sold chickens, eggs, butter, cheese, apples, and pears, saving for themselves only what was not vendible. Kerridge claimed that the diet of labourers improved by the end of the seventeenth century, but he does not discuss the diet of women separately.[57] Shammas, relating calorific intake to daily requirements for manual labour and pregnancy and lactation, concluded that most of the English labouring population suffered from chronic malnutrition.[58]

What could make a difference between subsistence and the need for relief, between poverty and indigence, was often a cow. Milk, cream, butter, and cheese could either be consumed at home or marketed.[59] In the poorest households, dairy products were probably sold to pay for rent, fuel, clothing, and miscellaneous expenses such as burials. This left indigent families with little nourishing food for themselves. In the 1690s Richard Baxter claimed that rents were so high that poor tenant farmers could not afford to eat their own produce and lived on curds and whey.[60]

Wives of poor cottagers might regularly supply large households with some foodstuffs. The accounts of the Bacons in Stiffkey show frequent payments to women for eggs and chicken. (Larger suppliers of eggs, and of smaller animals, such as ducks and pigs, were the wives of men with some land.) Daughters were occasionally employed as carriers of wildfowl. Poorer women also gathered and sold the shell-fish along the Norfolk coast. They sold their cockles and mussels to wealthier households in the area.[61] Provisioning required many female suppliers. The 1678 domestic accounts of the family of Seymour of Berry Pomeroy in Devon included payments from 5*s.* 6*d.* to around £1 to the herb-woman, to the milkwoman for 3*s.* 7*d.*, and to a Mrs Gardner for two pecks of peas.[62] In addition to similar routine payments, the Shuttleworths' farm accounts include money for maids bringing the 'wassell-boule' (the spiced ale in which healths were drunk).[63] Domestic accounts include records of casual sales which may indicate that women were also acting as petty chapwomen. In 1695, Katherine Windham 'bought

[56] N. Le Strange, *'Merry Passages and Jeasts': A Manuscript Jestbook*, ed. H. Lippincott (1974), 114, 140.

[57] E. Kerridge, *The Agricultural Revolution* (1967), 332–3.

[58] Shammas, *Pre-Industrial Consumer*, 121–56.

[59] S. D. Amussen, *An Ordered Society: Gender and Class in Early Modern England* (Oxford, 1988), 16–17. Shammas argues that those with only one cow had little surplus for sale; Shammas, *Pre-Industrial Consumer*, 33–4. See also Wrightson and Levine, *The Making of an Industrial Society*, 264–5.

[60] R. Baxter, *'The Poor Husbandman's Advocate to Rich Racking Landlords'*, 1691 (1926), 25.

[61] Campbell, 'The Women of Stiffkey', 45–7, 58; see also A. H. Smith, Bacon Database (Centre for East Anglian Studies). We are grateful to Professor Smith for his kindness in allowing PMC to consult his database.

[62] Devon RO, 1392 M/L1678/1, Seymour of Berry Pomeroy, domestic accounts, 1678.

[63] *House and Farm Accounts of the Shuttleworths*, 179.

FIG. 30. Dairy work: maids carrying milk pails. Although the romanticized image of the 'merry milkmaid' was a trope of contemporary rural life, in reality all phases of dairy work were skilled, labour-intensive, and physically demanding. Here two milkmaids are shown carrying heavy wooden milk pails balanced on their heads

of Mrs Pooly' soap, apples, eggs, butter, and a shoe brush. Yet the money was not delivered to Mrs Pooly, but to her husband, for it was signed 'Jery: Pooly his mark'.[64]

Just as women produced food for both consumption and for sale, so their textile work could be used either to clothe their families or sold for cash wages. Increasingly women extended their spinning and sewing for cash as they found employment in the hand production of cloth. Women were the main spinners of wool; men were more likely to be weavers, requiring the work of roughly four spinners to keep their looms occupied. Spinning was supplementary work only. Among the other manufacturing tasks performed at home by poor women and their children was the preparation of flax and hemp into thread for linen and canvas.[65] Women and their children provided a cheap labour force; they were dependent on monotonous and repetitious labour for very low pay. As the centres of the cloth trade shifted during the seventeenth century, poor women in areas

[64] Norfolk RO, WCK 6/15, Katherine Windham kitchen accounts, 1695–6.

[65] V. Skipp, *Crisis and Development: An Ecological Case Study of the Forest of Arden, 1570–1674* (Cambridge, 1978), 57.

FIG. 31. Woman spinning outdoors. Women of all ages and nearly all social classes occupied their 'leisure' time in useful labour. Even the old and infirm who were incapable of heavier work could always spin. Although the economic rewards were small, spinning enabled women to avoid idleness, contribute to their own keep and add to the family earnings

such as Wiltshire lost employment, while others in parts of East Anglia, where the new draperies were produced, found work.

Clothes formed a significant part of the economy of the poor. Women could pawn or even sell their clothing in time of hardship. Others were involved in the second-hand clothes trade. In the 1620s Marian Burrough was in trouble because she 'doth run into infected houses' and 'buyeth clothes from them'.[66] Those who accepted clothes illegally for pawn could be accused of stealing.[67] Since the poor possessed few clothes, wives spent little time on family laundry, but washing linen was an area of employment in which their assistance was always required in larger households.

[66] Devon RO, Quarter Sessions Order Book 1625–1633, fo. 47.
[67] Devon RO, QSB Mich. 1627, no. 17.

Poor women sold their labour to those of higher social status. Large households required a range of miscellaneous and seasonal labour. The Shuttleworths paid wives and a maid to clip sheep. From 1585 to 1610, 'Birchall wife' was paid for washing, for being in the kitchen for a month, and for providing fifty-one meals for labourers.[68] Labouring women could combine a range of miscellaneous employment with housekeeping and child-care. A large household usually had women come in to help with washing, as, for example, appears in the household accounts of the earl of Ailesbury in 1678: 'Paid for 6 bush: of ashes [used for washing] and 2 washerwomen 4 days—8s.'[69] A washmaid in Sir William Becher's household in the 1680s was paid £2. 10*s*. 0*d*. per annum, 10*s*. above the county assessment.[70] Katherine Windham's kitchen accounts in 1695 included 26 April 'Goody Green for washing' 6*d*.[71] The Seymours' accounts included payments for a week's 'board wages' for three laundry maids amounting to 18*s*.[72] Kitchen labour might provide partial relief for a widow; in Nathaniel Bacon's house at Stiffkey, 'Mother Alnwick' was paid a regular retainer in the 1690s for scouring duties in the kitchen.[73]

Much of the casual work in the countryside was given to the female relatives of male workers. Such women were within the penumbra of paternalism. They were given an option on opportunities to labour, which was a benefit when work itself was hard to find. The opportunity to work was restricted, and most of the poor were only partial wage earners.[74] Although wages were inadequate, women already employed were around when extra work, perquisites, or charity was doled out. The farmer Henry Best allowed the wives and children 'of those that work with us' at 2*d*. or 3*d*. per day to glean at certain times during the harvest, but he never allowed anyone to glean who was able to work but refused.[75] Elsewhere, specific women had gleaning rights; a retirement contract might mention the transfer of a woman's gleaning right.

Household accounts reveal a series of miscellaneous payments to women workers. Giles Moore, a Sussex clergyman-farmer, recorded payments to various women in his accounts from 1655 to 1679; to Bes Falconer one

[68] *House and Farm Accounts of the Shuttleworths*, 24, 131, 179, 187, 200.

[69] *Domestic Expenses of a Nobleman's Household*, ed. the earl of Cadogan, Bedfordshire Record Society, 32 (1952), 125, 133.

[70] *A Bedfordshire Wage Assessment of 1684*, ed. T. S. Willan, Beds. Record Society, 25 (1957), 133.

[71] Norfolk RO, WCK 6/15, Katherine Windham kitchen accounts, 1695–6.

[72] Devon RO, MS 1392M/1678/1, Seymour of Berry Pomeroy household accounts [1678].

[73] Campbell, 'The Women of Stiffkey', 16.

[74] Wales, 'Poverty, Poor Relief and the Life-Cycle', 352.

[75] *The Farming and Memorandum Books of Henry Best of Elmswell, 1642*, ed. D. Woodward (Oxford, 1984), 46.

shilling 'for ending her spinning before Esther'; to Goodwife Ward one shilling 'towards the New-making of the Rosemary Border'. Women received small payments for weeding, sales of seeds, picking and setting strawberries, and relieving a servant who was sick. The same weeding women were often employed for three or four years at the usual rate of 5*d.* per day. Widow Weller was paid for cleaning a pond, ploughing a piece for oats, carrying fifteen loads of hay, and bringing in a load of loam. Another widow helped Moore to move 630 new bricks. What emerges chiefly from his accounts is the omnipresence of women in an immense variety of economic activities, including watching the sick, selling spices, and sewing.[76]

In the countryside, women were employed in seasonal work which complemented that of men. Estate accounts at Stiffkey show that women ranged in age from around 14 to the early fifties, when physical fitness may have declined. Such women were usually related to the male labourers—wives, daughters, or even mothers—who had little or no land of their own. Female labour was especially important in harvesting and haymaking. The Bacon accounts show that the same local women were employed for whatever work the manor needed. Women turned their hands to relieving in the dairy, helping with Christmas in the household, or gathering rushes and other preparations for a wedding. The majority of women workers were employed for less than twenty-five days per annum, and earned less than £1.[77] Their pay was less than that of men. In Bedfordshire in the 1680s, Sir William Becher employed the wives and daughters of his men at 6*d.* per day, while men were paid 1*s.*, which was 2*d.* over the assessed rate.[78]

One avenue opening up in the countryside and towns during the seventeenth century was a range of by-employments. Stocking-knitting was an important occupation for poor women. Joan Thirsk has calculated that this craft may have employed around 13 per cent of the labourers and paupers, so perhaps one woman in every fourth labouring household was so employed by the end of the seventeenth century.[79] Like bone-lacemaking, knitting required little in the way of capital equipment. Indeed, lacemaking and dairying together supported a spinster subculture in Devon towns from

[76] *The Journal of Giles Moore*, 51, 175, 193, 195, 198–201, 293–4.

[77] Campbell, 'Women of Stiffkey', 14–24, Appendix F; A. H. Smith, 'Labourers in Late Sixteenth-Century England: A Case Study from North Norfolk', *Continuity and Change*, 4 (1989), 29–30.

[78] *A Bedfordshire Wage Assessment of 1684*, ed. T. S. Willan, Beds. Record Society, 25 (1957), 134.

[79] J. Thirsk, *Economic Policy and Projects: The Development of a Consumer Society in Early Modern England* (Oxford, 1978), 175.

the mid- to late seventeenth century.[80] Some London women managed to survive on bone-lace work alone: the 58-year-old Margaret Cramp stated that 'she maintaineth herself by making of bone lace and that she is little worth besides her household goods'.[81] Others combined lacemaking with other textile work: 'Elizabeth Phillipps . . . hath been brought up in making of bone lace and in sewing and hereby she getteth her living and sometimes by making and selling of bone lace and sometimes by her needle and she saith she hath so lived and maintained her self at least six years last past.'[82]

Boundaries between country and town were flexible in early modern times. Marketing, one of women's weekly jobs, brought women from the country to sell in the town. A series of petitions from the poor market women at Newgate market in London in 1699 gives a picture of one aspect of the working lives of labouring women. All the petitioners were poor women, who sold 'small Provisions . . . viz. Lamb, Pork, Butter, Eggs, Oat-cakes, Hogs-Pudding, Sausages' and such like, none of them bringing more than one horse load. They did not trade daily, only a couple of times each week. Anne Milbourne, wife of a farmer, 'for divers years' had kept the market twice each week with two small 'dossars' (panniers or baskets) of small provisions. Some had marketed over a long period of time. The widowed Joan Laxton 'hath kept the same Standing [stall] in the said Market . . . for about eighteen Years last past'. The trading was small-scale, and not very lucrative. Mary Palmer, a weaver's wife from St Botolph Bishopsgate, sold small provisions from a moveable board: 'the cost of all the provisions she sold in market that week did not exceed 10*s*.' Furthermore, if married market women were not selling their own produce, they were not necessarily the sellers of their husbands' produce or labour; a carpenter swore that his wife sold 'small Butchers meat'.[83] Marketing was only one of these labouring women's multiple work identities.

Many poorer women moved between the town and countryside, as work was available in the countryside in the summer, while chances of survival were better in the town in winter. Later in the seventeenth century, female employment was much more abundant in the towns and cities than in the countryside, as more households employed women servants. In the

[80] P. Sharpe, 'Literally Spinsters: A New Interpretation of Local Economy and Demography in Colyton in the Seventeenth and Eighteenth Centuries', *Economic History Review*, 44 (1991), 46–65.

[81] Guildhall, Liber responsarum 1635–1644, MS 9065A/7, nf, case 30 Sept. 1637.

[82] Guildhall, MS 9187/2, London Consistory Court Examinations 1627–8, fo. 8.

[83] *The Petition of the Oppressed Market People* [1699?], 10–14.

countryside, agricultural labour became more and more exclusively male. In towns, women who had been live-in servants in their youth could find drudgery work, such as charring, in their old age. Laundry work was often mentioned in censuses of the poor as a small supplement to women's income.[84] Churchwardens' accounts show payments to women for cleaning and washing the church and its linen.[85] London city companies paid women to clean and scour.[86] Even for apprentices needing to have their shoes cleaned, 'there are poor women attending at the Shop-Doors, to do these things'.[87]

Women in the towns had a similar economy of makeshifts to those in the countryside, combining housekeeping and child-care with whatever paid employment they could find. Typically, they were servants in youth, earning their best wages as needleworkers in middle age, and charring, washing, nursing, and hawking in old age.[88]

Accommodation was more expensive and crowded in towns. The wife of one poor labouring man in London who was managing—they neither paid taxes nor received charity—said that they lodged in a room over a coal warehouse and 'that she hath four children living with her'.[89] Some poor women provided lodging for other poor people.[90] However, most towns' authorities were suspicious of those taking 'inmates', fearing that they would be a burden on the poor rates, and passed laws against the practice. In 1602 the Manchester civic authorities ordered that no one should let rooms to 'any strangers suspected to be poore and not hable to maynteane themselves'. Constant reiteration suggests that the laws were not observed.[91]

Compared with rural women, urban women had less access to scavenging for food, such as berries from hedgerows, or nuts and fruit from trees. Even water was a commodity in the towns and was more expensive and more inaccessible. On the other hand, in the towns street vendors offered easier access to prepared food. There were different pickings in the town.

[84] *Norwich Census of the Poor*, Appendix iv.

[85] *Accomptes of the Churchwardens of the Paryshe of St Christofer's in London, 1575 to 1662*, ed. E. Freshfield (1885), 39.

[86] For example, B. Marsh and J. Ainsworth (eds.), *Records of the Worshipful Company of Carpenters*, vii. *The Wardens Accounts, 1592–1614* (1968), 350, 471; G. Parsloe (ed.), *Warden's Accounts of the Worshipful Company of Founders of the City of London* (1964), 250, 251, 273.

[87] D. Defoe, *Great Law* (1724), 13.

[88] P. Earle, 'The Female Labour Market in London in the Late Seventeenth and Early Eighteenth Centuries', *Economic History Review*, 2nd ser., 42 (1989), 343.

[89] Guildhall, MS 9731/101, Papers re matters in the peculiar jurisdiction of St Catherine, deposition no. 8.

[90] Boulton, *Neighbourhood*, 85–7.

[91] J. P. Earwaker (ed.), *The Court Leet Records of the Manor of Manchester*, 12 vols. (Manchester, 1884–90), i. 197, 227; ii. 178.

FIG. 32. 'Hott Bak'd Wardens Hott', woman selling cooked pears. In this London street scene, a woman has prepared stewed wardens (a variety of cooking pear) and is selling them, still warm, from a heavy earthenware pot balanced on her head. Women prepared and sold a great variety of 'fast foods' on city streets, catering to an increasing demand for prepared foods in large urban areas like London

Scavenging for clothing and miscellaneous items was probably more profitable in a densely populated city such as London.

Marketing and street vending occupied many town and city women. Around 1700 in London, Anne Keene, the 26-year-old wife of a ship's armourer, a witness at a court case, said that she 'uses the Market and quays and sells Garden ware'. She paid no taxes, and expected to receive a total of 3*s.* 6*d.* for her loss of time over three-and-a-half days, which suggests that she may have hoped to earn a shilling a day.[92] Poor women sold perishables, such as fish and fruit. The profit margins were small, and there was always the risk of loss if the goods were not sold.

Women workers in towns and cities were vulnerable to changes in fashion. An unusually detailed poor law settlement dispute allows us to glimpse the effects of vagaries in fashion on the working life of a single woman in Elizabethan and Jacobean London. Annis Cowper, the daughter of an embroiderer, was born about 1560. Her father died when she was young, so she lived with her stepfather, a cap-maker. At around 11 or 12 years of age, she was apprenticed in the same trade to William Giblett, with whom she served nine years, then worked for another cap-maker for eleven years. When Annis was about 30 years old, 'the trade of capping then decaying', she lived in London with another woman, a costard monger (an apple seller), for twelve years. Subsequently she worked in an unspecified occupation with a Dutchman for six or seven years till he went abroad. A single woman aged 50, Annis then laboured as a charwoman for two or three years, moving to live with an almswoman of the Salters' Company, Goodwife Goose. Later she worked with a poulterer, who ran away after a week leaving the rent unpaid. Witnesses' accounts did not confirm all the details of this history; some claimed that she had begged daily with the poulterer's wife. Nevertheless, the picture is still one of vulnerability and recourse to a series of expedients.[93]

Detailed evidence from female witnesses in court cases provides further information about the working lives of poor women. In one case before the court of St Catherine's in London, Isabel Dodd, a 31-year-old widow, named three occupations she followed: 'she winds silk and knits and washes and scours whereby she maintains herself'. She rented a room from another widow. A sixty-year-old widow, Jane Steere, stated that she herself had lived in the same alley for nearly twenty years and 'that she buys fruit and sugar and brandy from Seamen and their wives and sells the same again and winds silk'. In addition to her stated occupations of retailing and silk winding, she

[92] Guildhall, MS 9731/101, deposition no. 13.

[93] Raine, 'Christopher Fawsett', 83–4.

FIG. 33. Street vendors. This depiction of the range of London street vendors in 1655 illustrates the great variety of foodstuffs, small wares and other consumer items which women hawked through the streets. Note that the woman selling card matches (the precursor to modern matchbooks) carries her swaddled baby on her back

FIG. 34. 'Buy any Wax or Wafers'; pregnant woman selling letter-writing supplies. Weighed down by advanced pregnancy, this street vendor is a walking stationery shop, hawking supplies used for writing and sealing letters. Although the profits of street selling were small, the work could be combined with pregnancy (as is the case here) and the care of small children

may also have worked as a laundress. From all of this work she claimed to be worth little but was not in debt. Not all of this evidence about occupations was unchallenged. The defendant in the case argued that Jane Steere's evidence was to be discounted because she was very poor, received alms (which Jane herself did not mention), and was of mean character and reputation. Opinions about how Christian Applebury gained her livelihood were similarly divided. While witnesses agreed that she and her husband kept a brewing house, some accused her of keeping a bawdy house and soliciting, while another thought her 'a very industrious carefull woman and endeavouring to maintain her family'.[94]

Poorer women specialized in finding things that were useless or uneconomic to their richer contemporaries. In the countryside, there was scavenging of both a formal and an informal kind. The labour of a family could be useful; in 1659 in Norfolk, 'poor people draw home to them their children and others to glean'.[95] Women and children gathered medicinal and cooking herbs, nuts, and windfall apples. Tithe cases sometimes refer to tithes of 'no commercial value—taken by the poor and children'.[96]

Poor women had few possessions. Ownership was precarious. They went to constables for a pair of lost shoes, for a missing petticoat, or an absent kettle. Work was hard, and only on Sunday was there some relief from toil. Yet still some women exercised choices. A deserted wife, tempted by her lover to flee to London, 'where she should be so well provided for That there her friday should be better then her Sunday', refused to abandon her two children for a less arduous life.[97]

INDIGENCE AND DESTITUTION

Misfortunes reduced many women to indigence. Although poverty was endemic for many women, others who were born into better material circumstances were vulnerable to poverty in sickness or old age. Widows, or wives whose husbands were ill or absent, could be quickly reduced to poverty and the need for relief. Those who were poor through no fault of their own and were of good reputation were eligible for poor relief and some charity; those whose lifestyles were disapproved of by the parish authorities received nothing. Facing destitution, many poor women who were denied relief turned to a range of illegal expedients in order to survive.

Contemporary authorities were less concerned about whether women's indigence was caused by personal misfortune or economic crises. They knew that there were structural factors in life which produced poverty, such as decrepitude or too many children, but their understanding of the

[94] Guildhall, MS 9731/101, deposition 10, 16, 20, 22.
[95] Amussen, *Ordered Society*, 94.
[96] See, for example, OA, MS Oxf. Dioc. papers c. 26, 1629–34, fos. 23–6^{v}, 52–4, 75–7; Devon RO, Chanter 866, Consistory Court Depositions 1634–40 (not foliated or paginated), 6 July 1637, testimony of Abraham Vanston.
[97] Norfolk RO, AYL 347, Doughty papers, unnumbered, 7 Oct. 1662.

wider causes of wealth and poverty were limited.[98] Thus they focused on the particular rather than the general, and sought to distinguish between women whose need for assistance was thought to be legitimate, because they were 'good' women, and those whose poverty was thought to be a consequence of their own moral failings. The chief aim of officials was to force the poor to provide for themselves, and they worried endlessly about what they saw as rooted idleness (rather than underemployment) in the poor. The fear that such habits would be perpetuated justified the removal of children from their parents.[99]

Poor relief bodies were sympathetic, although not generous, if sickness or age had incapacitated the male or female breadwinner in a family. Authorities might also assist if demographic disasters, such as too many children, had put the whole family group at risk. But they were not sympathetic to catastrophes such as befell wives of husbands who failed to provide, drank all the resources, or disappeared. Contemporaries saw no reason to provide assistance for wives whose husbands, they believed, were shirking their responsibilities.

A system of relief developed during the Elizabethan period, culminating in the Poor Law of 1601, whereby parishes collected rates from the wealthier inhabitants which they distributed to those who were distinguished as the 'impotent' poor: the sick, the very young, the old, and the incapacitated. Those willing and able to labour were to be given work; the unwilling were to be punished and forced to labour. Formal relief could be temporary or long-term. Parishes gave small supplements for immediate crises and payments over a long period of time for the destitute.

Poor relief, provided informally by individual charity, continued after the Reformation. Individuals distributed personal charity, such as small alms, food, or clothing, to those whom they deemed worthy; or they provided for perpetual and organized charity through bequests in their wills which they might ask parish authorities or other institutions to administer. No 'unworthy' poor would receive any kind of formal charity.

The basic principle underlying relief was that the parish was intended as the last recourse. Authorities sought to make family members provide for their own poorer relatives. A woman who petitioned the Fishmongers' Company for a pension was refused, 'she having a husband', although they did grant a sum of money for her immediate relief.[100] Parishes expected widows to provide for their children, even grandmothers to labour to

[98] See, for example, *An Ease for Overseers of the Poore* (1601), 23–6.
[99] J. Keble, *An Assistance to Justices of the Peace* (1683), 479–80.
[100] Guildhall, MS 5570/3, Fishmongers' Company Court Ledger, p. 54.

Shee layeth her Hand to the Spindle and
her hands hold the distaffe: Pro: 31. 19.

FIG. 35. Poor women were taught to spin. The neatly-dressed young woman at the spinning-wheel forms the frontispiece for Thomas Firmin's tract, *Some Proposals for the Imploying of the Poor* (1681). Reformers like Firmin urged that girls and women be taught to spin in order to enable the poor to provide for themselves. The biblical verse (Proverbs 31:19) was part of a well-known passage beginning 'A virtuous woman who can find?' (Proverbs 31:10), linking female diligence and industry with religious morality

provide for orphans. Often we know about family assistance only when relatives petitioned for help which they were no longer able to provide. In 1698 Janet Jackson petitioned the Carlisle quarter sessions for assistance in supporting a 4-year-old orphan: she 'is a poor servant tho scarce able to maintain [herself] yet with her endeavours has contributed to his main[-tenance]'.[101]

Parishes sought to enable a woman to provide for her own family by her own labour, even if they disapproved of her. If a woman with dependants was in prison for fornication, for example, a parish might intervene for her release. West Lynn parish petitioned for the release from Bridewell of a widow who had borne a second illegitimate child; she supported not only her illegitimate child, but also her mother, and a legitimate child.[102] The Bristol Corporation sought the discharge of Mary Jones from prison 'in order to enable her to provide for her Children'.[103]

Midwifery among poor women was a form of relief both for the midwife and her impoverished patients. Churchwardens were required to present all unlicensed midwives to the bishops' courts, but, in the case of many poor unlicensed midwives, they asked that women be permitted to continue when their practice was restricted to the poor. The inhabitants of the town of Acle in Norfolk pleaded on behalf of a widow who 'is so poor that she was never able to purchase a licence'. Deprived of a livelihood, a poor midwife would herself become a burden on poor rates, as another parish explained of a poor widow 'with seven small children to maintain and hitherto she out of her midwifery has provided for her said Children without being Chargeable to our said parish'.[104] In 1666 parish officials of Hammersmith supported Joan Maxley, an impoverished gentlewoman, in her application for a licence because she 'has undertaken that office for the better relief and livelihood both of herself and two of her grandchildren, whose parents are dead'.[105] Another parish pleaded on behalf of an excommunicated midwife, 'she being a very poor woman and hath seven children and that her whole livelihood doth consist therein'.[106]

Poor women were employed in a range of 'caring' tasks. They were to be 'keepers' of mothers in childbed.[107] Some tended the old; Margaret Nicholls

[101] Cumbria CRO, Quarter Sessions Midsummer 1698, no. 25.

[102] Amussen, *Ordered Society*, 136. [103] *Bristol Corporation of the Poor*, 59.

[104] Norfolk RO, TES 8, Elizabeth Barber, 28 July 1693; Mary Hendry, 4 Jan. 1702.

[105] Guildhall, MS 10,116/4. [106] Ibid.

[107] Wales, 'Poverty, Poor Relief and the Life-Cycle', 382.

was paid regularly in 1698 for her care of widow Browne.[108] Others worked as unlicensed medical practitioners among the poor. Although some scorned them—'every self-conceited shee-physician'[109]—parish authorities might plead for such workers, as they did for poor midwives, because their practice was limited and they would otherwise become a burden on the parish.

Child-care provided regular paid employment for many poor women, especially in the towns and cities, where parishes placed foundlings and orphans in the care of poorer mothers or widows. The rates of pay varied, and it is unclear to what extent they covered the barest minimum for the child, or included a supplement for the woman's labour. In the later seventeenth century, the parish of Westbury-on-Trym made various payments; 6*s*. 4*d*. per month for some children, 4*s*. for others, and 1*s*. 6*d*. for three days' diet for another.[110] The London parishes' rates also varied. In the 1630s, St Christopher's usually paid around £5. 6*s*. 8*d* per annum for nursing a child.[111] By 1673 their standard rate for children being 'nursed', schooled, and clothed was £7. 17*s*. 0*d*. Expenditure differed because clothing and schooling were variable costs.[112] Several foster mothers worked for many years. St Alban Wood St paid Goody Hasell to care for a series of parish orphans from 1642 to 1650. In 1644 she received £8. 5*s*. 0*d*. for keeping two parish children at 3*s*. per week, and money for 'necessaries' for them. Nurse Crouch was employed for several years from 1650 onwards. (The churchwardens there usually paid 2*s*. weekly for the care of a nurse child.)[113]

Parish records frequently hide women's presence as workers. St Christopher's paid John Sawyer for 'nursing' two children for thirty-one weeks. The term is ambiguous because it can refer both to breast-feeding and caring for a child, but in both instances, nursing was women's work, even though the husband was the one paid.[114] As a married man, Sawyer was, of course, legally entitled to his wife's earnings. Whether the payment was made to the husband or to the wife depended on the whim of the clerk. St Alban parish in London regularly employed a Mrs Hayward during the 1650s and 1660s to care for young children. Some clerks recorded a payment to 'Mrs Hayward',

[108] *Transcription of the 'Poor Book' of the Tithings of Westbury-on-Trym . . . 1656–1698*, ed. H. J. Wilkins (Bristol, 1910), 275–6.

[109] Baxter, *'Poor Husbandman'*, 28.

[110] *'Poor Book' Westbury-on-Trym*, 130–5.

[111] *Accomptes of the Churchwardens of St Christofer's*, 81, 85.

[112] *The Account Book of the Parish of St Christopher Le Stocks . . . London 1662–1685*, ed. E. Freshfield (1895), 20–1.

[113] Guildhall, MS 7674, St Alban Wood St Churchwardens' and Overseers' accounts, 1642–3, 1643–4, 1645–6.

[114] *Account Book of St Christopher Le Stocks 1662–1685*, 5.

or 'John Hayward's wife'; others paid 'Goodman Hayward'.[115] Such a confusion of entries masks the fact that Mrs Hayward worked as a foster mother for over fifteen years.

The very poorest mothers might even receive payments for nursing their own infants. In 1642, St Martin Ludgate paid goodwife Tucker 2*s.* weekly to nurse her child and 20*s.* per annum towards the rent.[116] St Christopher's paid widow Harwood £7. 4*s.* 0*d.* for nursing two of her own children in 1684.[117] Christ's Hospital occasionally recorded such payments.[118]

Towards the end of the seventeenth century, some cities and towns placed orphans and foundlings in institutions, thereby decreasing employment opportunities for the poorest women. In 1696, Bristol Corporation erected a new workhouse for destitute children where a mistress was paid £10 p.a. plus diet, and a reading teacher 5*s.* per week. There were four tutoresses, each responsible for twenty-five girls, a seamstress who was to come in when needed to both sew herself and teach the girls, and two women servants.[119] A case such as this illustrates the hierarchy of labour among women; the very poorest women would have found employment in manual drudgery, such as scouring and cleaning.

Poor women might also keep elementary schools for the instruction of young children. As with midwifery, schoolteaching employed women at various social levels, but our concern here is with teaching as a form of poor relief. Schoolteachers were licensed by the bishop, but we have found no references to women who had licences. Instead, the normal return to the bishops' visitation enquiries stated that a woman did teach, but that she was poor, taught only young children, and conformed to the Anglican Church: she is 'a poor woman a pensioner who is conformable that teacheth a few small children'.[120] Some teachers were presented because they did 'not do what is required by the Church'.[121] Early in the eighteenth century, a number of poor women were employed, sometimes in a charity school, but sometimes simply in conjunction with a parish church or chapel; 'The children are taught to read and learn the church Catechism by a poor woman.'[122]

[115] Guildhall, MS 7674, St Alban Wood St Churchwardens' and Overseers' accounts, 1652–67. Note that the spelling of her name also varies.

[116] Guildhall, MS 1311/1, fo. 137.

[117] *Account Book of St Christopher Le Stocks 1662–1685*, 44.

[118] *Christ's Hospital Admissions, 1554–1599*, 114, 117, 208, 218.

[119] *Bristol Corporation of the Poor*, 48, 54–8.

[120] Guildhall, MS 9583/2, pt. i, St Mary Woolchurch.

[121] Ibid., pt. ii, fo. 144, pt. vi, fo. 84.

[122] D. Busby (ed.), *The Bedfordshire Schoolchild: Elementary Education before 1902*, Bedfordshire Historical Record Society, 67 (1988), 14.

Women teachers of the poor had a tutorial and disciplinary role, ensuring that the poor kept at their work and that they did not steal materials on which they were employed. As we have seen, on many occasions it suited a parish to allow a woman to earn her living, provided she was conformable, rather than see her a burden on the poor rates. Teaching could provide employment for women of middling status who had fallen on hard times.

Even care of the destitute poor could provide employment for poor women. Both parishes and institutions employed indigent women to care for the sick and the old. The Grocers' Company paid 2*s.* per week to a poor woman 'for her pains in tending upon the Almshouses at Oundell . . . helping the said Almsmen upon all occasions'.[123] Widow Webster 'a poor woman' was employed at the same rate from 1628 to 1630.[124] In 1641 the parish of St Alban Wood St paid the nurse who cared for a sick widow for three weeks £1. 1*s.* 0*d.*; in 1649, 6*s.* 6*d.* to a nurse for looking after widow Smith; and 4*s.* to Goody Hunt and Goody Pott for 'watching' with Goody Reynolds who died in 1657.[125] The parish paid a woman 1*s.* 6*d.* to appraise a joiner's widow's goods.[126]

Communities still had expectations of those who were employed to care for the poor. In 1683 Goody Davies was paid £12 per annum to lodge several poor pensioners in her house in St Dionis Backchurch. Some parishioners refused to sit next to her in church because she was living 'of[f] the poor'. Moreover, she had defied the unwritten custom of the parish by refusing, as a beneficiary, to help clean the church.

> And whereas it is a Custom when the Church is to be made clean that the poor women are to help that are able or send another in her place, This goody Davies gave her answer that she would not come, nor send any in her place.[127]

Old women and others incapable of heavy work would be set to spinning, working hemp, or whatever else was available. One old woman kept a town herd. Others earned 4*d.* per day spinning.[128] The poorest women could be forced to undertake some of the most unpleasant and dangerous work. At the embalming of a body, there was 'a woman to attend the surgeons with water, mops, cloths and other things'. Women dressed the corpse after

[123] Guildhall, MS 11588/3, fo. 397.

[124] Guildhall, MS 11571/11, Accounts Grocers, fo. 298^{v}, fo. 335. Another poor woman, Margery Taylor, was employed in 1631; ibid., fo. 423^{v}.

[125] Guildhall, MS 7674, St Alban Wood St Churchwardens' accounts, 1641–2, 1649–50, 1657–8.

[126] Guildhall, MS 7674, St Alban Wood St Churchwardens' accounts (upside-down at end).

[127] Guildhall, MS 11280A/1, 23 June 1683.

[128] OA, MS Oxf. Dioc. papers c. 26, 1629–34, fos. 245–49^{v}; Wales, 'Poverty, Poor Relief and the Life-Cycle', 376.

embalming.[129] In 1577 almswomen in one London parish were ordered to look after any sick people, with 'any disease soever, upon pain of losing their parish payments'.[130] Equally dangerous work was that of 'helper and keeper' of plague victims for the town of Colchester in 1626.[131] In Norwich in 1630 the mayoralty appointed a married woman to carry water to the poor daily for the fee of 7*d.*, good pay for a woman, but heavy and risky work.[132] A nurse employed to tend a patient with smallpox infected her own child in turn.[133]

The task of searchers was dangerous, for their job was to examine bodies during epidemics of plague to discover the causes of deaths so that appropriate health measures, such as quarantine, could be taken. There is at least one reference to male searchers, but the majority were women. Contemporaries were contemptuous about searchers, the 'old blind women, whose judgment is as dim as their eyes',[134] but those who were old were those most likely to be coerced.[135] City authorities attempted to regulate the work by requiring searchers to swear to do their work carefully and report truly. At the time of the Great Plague of 1665, officials required the searchers to be women 'of honest reputation, and of the best sort as can be got in this kind'. Searchers became pariahs whose other economic activities were restricted. They were forbidden to engage in 'any publick work or imployment, or keep any shop or stall, or be imployed as a Laundress, or in any other common imployment whatsoever'. The pay in the 1620s varied from region to region. In Reading in 1625, a plague year, searchers were paid 4*s.* weekly. Given that around 1650 a labourer earned 10*d.* to 12*d.* per day, the rewards were meagre.[136] Although the pay was good compared with the usual female labouring rates, which were more like 5*d.* per day, a woman had to be desperate to undertake it. Afterwards, she might be shunned as a carrier of infection, and end up as a vagrant. Parish officials frequently compelled individuals to be searchers, threatening them with expulsion from the almshouse or suspension of their dole.[137] Perhaps this was the case in Norwich

[129] C. Gittings, *Death, Burial and the Individual in Early Modern England* (1984), 167.

[130] *The Vestry Minute Books of the Parish of St Bartholomew Exchange in the City of London, 1567–1676*, ed. E. Freshfield (1890), 5.

[131] I. G. Doolittle, 'The Plague in Colchester, 1579–1666', *Transactions of the Essex Archaeological Society*, 3rd ser., 4 (1972), 141.

[132] *Minutes of the Norwich Court of Mayoralty, 1630–1631*, 62 (26 June 1630).

[133] *'Poor Book' Westbury-on-Trym*, 246.

[134] Quoted in P. Slack, *The Impact of Plague in Tudor and Stuart England* (1985), 275.

[135] *Accomptes of the Churchwardens . . . of St Christofer's*, 85.

[136] T. S. Forbes, 'The Searchers', *Bulletin of the New York Academy of Medicine* (1974), 1031–8.

[137] Slack, *Plague*, 274–5.

where two widows in the hospital were appointed 'to continue their place of Scavengers of the infected poor'.[138]

Employment was the first form of relief for poor women; the second was charitable relief of immediate need. Parishes, guilds, and hospitals all administered bequests, some of which were of sums of money to be distributed to the 'most deserving' poor each year; others were gifts of fuel, such as coal or wood.[139] A few gifts were female specific; in Leicester, a bequest of £100 was distributed in the form of ten gifts of 12*d.* to 'ten Antient single persons widdows or maids'.[140] Surviving records of parishes and other bodies show the conscientious administration of many different forms of aid. Each year the parish of St Alban Wood Street distributed 40 sacks of sea coals, a legacy from Mrs Hill;[141] they contracted with a baker to bring 8 penny wheaten loaves every Sabbath morning to give to the poor, from the Embroiderers' Company's gift of £1. 6*s.* 0*d.*;[142] on Christmas day they distributed Mr Keates's gift of £5, and at other times Mrs Roberts's gift of £1. 11*s.* 0*d.*, and Mrs Rudyerd's gift of £1.[143] In 1653 St George Botolph Lane distributed Mrs Hough's gift of two smocks and two bushels of coals.[144] The good poor woman could also expect that her parish would pay for her burial, if she lacked relatives. A fairly typical payment from St Alban Wood St was for Goody Reynolds in 1658: 9*s.* 8*d.* for burial and 3*s.* 6*d.* for her coffin.[145]

Poverty also attracted the Christian charity of wealthier neighbours. Elizabeth Walker gave poor women a penny per day for attending her family's prayers.[146] Mary Rich, countess of Warwick, was always giving casual alms to local poor widows and to poor weeding women whom she met on country walks. A number of poor received daily relief at the houses of inhabitants of Norfolk. Poor women in the countryside may have received more charity from the rich in the countryside than in the city; the wealthy in a city were more anonymous, less approachable. Informal charity may have decreased by the end of the seventeenth century when householders believed that they already contributed through poor rates.[147]

The third form of relief was the regular support of the indigent based on

[138] Norfolk RO, Mayor's Court Book, 1624–34, fo. 84^{v}.
[139] E. M. Leonard, *The Early History of English Poor Relief* (Cambridge, 1930), 212.
[140] *Records of the Borough of Leicester . . . 1603–1688*, ed. H. Stocks (Cambridge, 1923), 304.
[141] Guildhall, MS 7673/1, Churchwardens' accounts, St Alban Wood St, 1626–7.
[142] Guildhall, MS 7673/1, Churchwardens' accounts, St Alban Wood St, 1626–7, 1630.
[143] Guildhall, MS 7674, Churchwardens' accounts, St Alban Wood St, 1641–2.
[144] Guildhall, MS 952/1, St George Botolph Lane Vestry Minutes, fo. 75.
[145] Guildhall, MS 7674, Churchwardens' accounts, St Alban Wood St, 1657–8.
[146] A. Walker, *The Holy Life of Mrs Elizabeth Walker* (1690), 35.
[147] Wales, 'Poverty, Poor Relief and the Life-Cycle', 357, 360.

the Poor Law of 1601. Basically the parish collected the poor rates and then paid small sums of money, first as immediate aid, and in more serious cases as a weekly pension, for care in sickness and old age. All over England, parishes disbursed relief to worthy recipients. In 1666, a single woman who usually worked at drawing coals was injured and confined to bed, unable to help herself. Her parish relieved her, she 'being a very poor woman ever endeavouring to get her a livelihood by her own labour and pains'.[148] Tim Wales has shown how the amount and number of payments to women gradually increased towards the end of their lives as they became incapable of labour. Parishes provided supplementary assistance as well as money; poor women were permitted to live rent-free in broken down cottages, or to dwell in cottages with less than the minimum land. There could be hand-outs of food or fuel. The only way women ceased to be on poor relief was if they remarried (which was less likely if they were poor), or died.

In cases of extreme age and chronic illness, a fortunate few might find places in almshouses. Established by individual or corporate charity, almshouses were administered by parishes and by corporate bodies, such as the livery companies of London. There sick and old women might find board, lodging, and medical care, provided they behaved properly, which for women usually meant that they remained single, led a chaste and sober life, and wore the gown and badge prescribed. Women were required to bring a certificate from their parish at their admission to ensure that, if they misbehaved, their parish would relieve the almshouse of their presence and would take them back.[149]

Even in an almshouse women could experience extreme poverty. When there was a dispute over the management of the hospital of St Katharine by the Tower in 1697, one of the issues was the treatment of the beadswomen. Hester Bartlett, resident for thirteen years, claimed to be satisfied because she had received her salary, half a crown for the sealing of every lease, twelve bushels of coals at Christmas, and her share of the profits of renting out the pall, which amounted to *6d.*[150] Others alleged that her statement was prompted by fear, and testified to terrible hardship. They claimed that pensioners had been forced to pawn their clothes in order to buy medicine,

[148] A. Fessler, 'The Official Attitude Towards the Sick Poor in Seventeenth-Century Lancashire', *Trans. of the Historic Society of Lancs. and Cheshire*, 102 (1950), 99.

[149] Guildhall, MS 5570/3, Fishmongers' Court Ledger, 1631–46, p. 32.

[150] Guildhall, MS 9740, St Katharine by the Tower, Depositions at Lord Somers Visitation, fo. 21.

and in one desperate case a bedridden woman 'cut off her grey hairs and sold them to buy her meat and drink'.[151]

Gender affected the economy of the old. The pension allowed to men and women was usually the same, suggesting initially that contemporaries were more concerned about survival needs rather than gender stereotypes. But gender could never be ignored. (Old men were not usually required to remain unmarried.)[152] A wife was expected to care for her husband, thereby relieving the almshouse administrators of paying a woman to care for him. There were perquisites for almsmen which were not open to women; male pensioners were allowed to wait on the members of the Fishmongers' Company at their dinners, and were provided with a special dinner afterwards.[153] One of the almsmen at the Bray house administered by the Fishmongers was appointed reader of prayers and gatekeeper and received an extra pension.[154] Only in an all-female almshouse, such as St Katharines by the Tower, did women share the perquisites.[155]

A reputation for being a hard-working and honest female was the prerequisite for relief from misfortune. Women acquired their pensions and places by their good behaviour and through the offices of influential friends, who told them when pensions were available and spoke in their support. From the records of the Fishmongers' Company, a picture emerges of a hierarchy of the poor relief which a company provided. From casual gifts at Christmas or Easter, deserving poor women could proceed to payments for immediate relief and then to weekly pensions. Finally, they might be permitted to occupy a place in one of the company's almshouses at Bray or at Holt. Even then, women petitioned to change from one house to another, or for extra benefits or concessions.[156] Women could try to manipulate the relief systems. In the 1620s, Salisbury charwomen refused to work for the wives of town officials unless they were put on the list of poor rates. The long-term effect of this practice was that the poor rates acted as a

[151] Guildhall, MS 21,041 B, An Account of St Catherines, 1595–1699, written 1803, unfoliated.

[152] There are instances of men required to be celibate; see A. Laurence, *Women in England, 1500–1760: A Social History* (1994), 106.

[153] Guildhall, Calendar of Fishmongers' Court Ledger, 1691–9, v, pt. v, p. 1137. PMC acknowledges the kindness of the Worshipful Company of Fishmongers who allowed xerox copying from the typed calendar.

[154] Guildhall, MS 5570/3, Fishmongers' Court Ledger, 1631–46, p. 576.

[155] They shared the profits from the hire of the pall at burials, which was 2*s.* 1*d.* per time; C. Jamison, *The History of the Royal Hospital of St Katharine by the Tower of London* (Oxford, 1952), 119.

[156] Guildhall, Calendar of Fishmongers' Court Ledger, 1691–9, v, pt. i, p. xli.

subsidy to wages of servants of town officials, thus undermining the whole system of poor relief in the eighteenth century.[157]

Formal and informal relief was for the good poor only, and goodness was always defined in gendered terms. Religious conformity was exacted; in 1681 the Devon justices ordered that those who failed to attend church every Sunday should forfeit their allowance.[158] Sexual reputation was crucial. In 1634 in Warwick, a widow who was pregnant 'by a young fellow who would marry her' had her payment cut off when she refused to regularize her relationship.[159] Suitable gratitude was demanded; in 1633 in Warwick, Margaret Doughty had her 8*d.* pension reduced to 4*d.* because she had 'grown very clamorous and behaveth herself in a very peremptory manner as if she were careless of the benefit . . . or at leastwise altogether unthankful for the same'. Even the 4*d.* was to be paid only so long as she behaved herself 'peaceably and orderly and shall show herself thankful for the same'.[160]

Denied relief, many poor women engaged in illegal activities in order to survive. Sometimes their economic activities were illegal because society refused them the necessary permission. If they could not obtain licences, because of either their poverty or their behaviour, then they had little choice but to work illegally.

Many poorer women were unlicensed ale-sellers. They required little in the way of capital resources, for they could use their front room or even part of a room, furnished, perhaps, with a bench. Alehouses were a meeting place for illegal activities, such as trading in stolen goods, and illicit sex. Civic authorities regularly took action against unlicensed houses. In January 1646, two men informed the Norwich mayor's court that they had found three men and three wenches drinking at the house of Anne Salt. The court suppressed Anne Salt's alehouse 'for misdemeanors'.[161] Many unlicensed female alehouse keepers were suspected of bawdry. There were prosecutions in Middlesex of women for keeping a bawdy house.[162] In 1681, the mayor of Norwich attempted to reduce the number of alehouses, 'most of them, 'tis said, bawdy houses too', but was opposed by the brewing interests.[163]

[157] *Poverty in Early-Stuart Salisbury*, ed. P. Slack, Wiltshire Record Society, 31 (1975), 114.

[158] A. H. A. Hamilton, *Quarter Sessions from Queen Elizabeth to Queen Anne* (1878), 185.

[159] *Warwick County Records. Quarter Sessions Order Book, Easter, 1625 to Trinity, 1637*, ed. S. C. Ratcliff and H. C. Johnson (1935), i. 200.

[160] Ibid., i. 172.

[161] Norfolk RO, Mayor's Court Book, 1634–46, fo. 467^{v}.

[162] *County of Middlesex. Calendar to the Sessions Records, 1612–16*, ed. W. Le Hardy, 3 vols. (1935), i. 20, 84, 85.

[163] P. Corfield, 'A Provincial Capital in the Late Seventeenth Century: The Case of Norwich', in P. Clark and P. Slack (eds.), *Crisis and Order in English Towns, 1500–1700* (1972), 288.

Contemporaries distinguished various degrees of depravity in illegal work. Some they ignored; others, they attacked spasmodically. Lowly social status usually attracted harsh penalties; poor women were whipped for prostitution while the mistresses of kings were rewarded with titles and sinecures. All illegal and criminal activity was dangerous to women, for it risked their reputations and made it less likely that they would find regular work. Some could find themselves with no option but crime at certain stages of their lives.

In the countryside, petty agrarian crime was rife.[164] Some of women's scavenging efforts shaded off into illegal activity and were viewed by their contemporaries as stealing. Henry Best notes that he gave poor people a handful of the worst wool each, as charity, but that theft was common.[165] Some women stole firewood and gleaned on land where they were not entitled to be. In a defamation case in Oxford, women who were accused of illegally gleaning wheat claimed that they were only gathering mustard.[166] In 1603 a labourer's wife in Hertford went to glean in a corn field 'as is usuall for all pore to doe'. When she was found on land where no gleaning was allowed, she was so beaten by a man with a pitchfork that she could do nothing 'to sustain her and her children and do her business for her husband'.[167]

Some poor women were opportunistic thieves, stealing drying clothes from hedges and bushes. In 1658 Margaret Field, a servant, gave bread and beer to a beggar, Mary, the wife of Nicholas Preston. When Margaret checked her clothes drying in the field, she found a sheet worth 6*d.* missing. She caught Mary, whom she found begging at another house, and although Mary initially denied the theft, she confessed, offered to return the sheet, 'and fell on her knees and prayed this Informant [Margaret Field] to forgive her'.[168] While threshing, some of the poor stole grain.[169] Women milked their neighbours' cows and took their straying poultry. They stole fruit and vegetables, and wool for clothing. One, accused of sheep stealing, claimed that on her way home from binding oats, she had found a dead sheep which

[164] For a valuable discussion of women's thefts, see G. Walker, 'Women, Theft and the World of Stolen Goods', in J. Kermode and G. Walker (eds.), *Women, Crime and the Courts in Early Modern England* (1994), 81–105.

[165] Best, *Farming and Memorandum Books*, 21, 25.

[166] OA, MS Oxf. Dioc. papers c. 27, 1634–9, fo. 104.

[167] *Hertford County Records: Notes and Extracts from the Session Rolls, 1581 to 1698*, ed. W. J. Hardy (Hertford, 1905), i. 35–6.

[168] Devon RO, QSB Box 63, Midsummer 1658, 17.

[169] *The Casebook of Sir Francis Ashley J. P. Recorder of Dorchester, 1614–1635*, ed. J. H. Bettey, Dorset Record Society, 7 (1981), 33, 48.

she brought home.[170] Even if men were more involved in sheep-stealing cases than women,[171] it was always women who cooked the mutton or who salted away the pieces in earthen pots.[172]

Some women pleaded absolute necessity for their misdeeds. In 1651 one woman was before the quarter sessions in Wiltshire for a theft of beans; she confessed that she had stolen for pure hunger for her children. Earlier, she had been in trouble for alleged witchcraft, telling people where lost goods could be found. Her activities illustrate how an impoverished woman might try every possible expedient to support herself and her children.[173]

Women as well as men participated in minor thefts. They were prosecuted at the quarter session for thefts of wool. In 1656 at the Devon quarter sessions, Evelyn Mineffee, a married woman, was charged that 'being hired as a spinster' by the wife of Edward Clode, a yeoman, 'having a good quantity of wool intrusted wth her did very much abuse us therein by withholding much of the yarn'. She or some of her family had sold some yarn of the same colour.[174] A reputation for dishonesty in work endangered a woman's opportunities for legitimate labour.

Opportunistic theft was also rife in towns and cities. A spinster in Crediton, Devon, confessed that she had gone into a shop around candle-lighting time and had taken four penny loaves. 'And being asked why she did so saith that it was for need.'[175] The development of retail shopping in the towns and the consequent opportunity for shoplifting led to harsher laws against shoplifting at the end of the seventeenth century.[176]

Servants had even greater opportunities for stealing, but the law viewed their offence very harshly compared with other types of theft. Quarter session records reveal charges that female servants had stolen money, clothes, and food.[177] Some maids stole food to give to their own needy friends, or stole expensive food and drink for themselves.[178]

Prostitution was work performed by some women at all social levels and was an important part of the livelihood of poor women at certain stages of

[170] Devon RO, QSB Mich. 1625, unnumbered.

[171] There are cases in the Devon quarter sessions of women stealing sheep; for example, Devon RO, QSB Epiphany 1657/8, 25.

[172] Devon RO, QSB Epiphany 1626, 15; Epiphany 1657/8, 25; Epiphany 1658/9, 56.

[173] *HMC Various*, i. 120.

[174] Devon RO, QSB, Epiphany 1655/6, 8.

[175] Devon RO, QSB Epiphany 1625, 38.

[176] J. M. Beattie, *Crime and the Courts in England, 1660–1800* (Oxford, 1986), 178–9; Walker, 'Women, Theft and the World of Stolen Goods', 81–105.

[177] See, for example, QSB, Box 63, Epiphany 1658/9.

[178] Best, *Farming and Memorandum Books*, 26, 140.

their lives.[179] The language employed about sex as a service justifies writing about it as work: 'he had the use of the body' of a woman, or he procured or kept her.[180] Urban prostitution was of various types ranging from casual sex for small payments or favours to the employment of women as both prostitutes in brothels and keepers of them.[181]

Sometimes it is unclear whether women were engaged in casual prostitution or simply illicit sexuality. In 1699 Mary Thomas, spinster, was taken during a search of an unlicensed alehouse for being in bed with a man. She was known as disorderly for 'refusing to put herself to service though often ordered to do so'.[182] The record does not distinguish whether she was working as a prostitute so that she could stay out of service, or enjoying a night at the alehouse with a man. An unhappy tale of a poor widow sentenced to death for infanticide told of how she had succumbed to an illicit sexual liaison with her neighbour in order to buy food for her children.[183] In London in the 1690s there were frequent prosecutions for 'nightwalking', sometimes combined with the suspicion of pick-pocketing.[184] Again, women could be engaging in opportunistic prostitution as well as theft.

In London, some prostitution was organized. The London Bridewell governors referred to brothels where up to nine prostitutes worked.[185] Most of the information about prostitution from the Elizabethan period indicates that brothels were establishments where women paid from 4*s.* to 6*s.* a week rent.[186] The average fee which men paid in brothels was 4*s.* 3*d.*, but it is not clear how much the keepers took.[187] Women tried to make money while they were young and pretty, but in old age they had to turn to procuring or keeping a brothel.

Among those charged for keeping 'a common house of bawdry' were single and married women, widows, and couples.[188] If a husband and wife

[179] R. Shoemaker, *Prosecution and Punishment: Petty Crime and the Law in London and Rural Middlesex, c. 1660–1725* (Cambridge, 1991), 183–7.

[180] Essex RO, Quarter Session Rolls, Q/SB, 61, 62.

[181] *Middlesex Sessions Records*, iii. 4, 242, 288.

[182] *Hertford County Records: Notes and Extracts from the Session Rolls, 1699 to 1850*, ii. 1.

[183] *Fair Warning to the Murderers of Infants Being an Account of the Trial . . . of Mary Goodenough* (1692).

[184] Corporation of London Record Office, Waiting Book, 15, 1690–6, fos. 83^{v}, 90^{v}, and 29 Jan. 1693.

[185] I. Archer, *The Pursuit of Stability: Social Relations in Elizabethan London* (Cambridge, 1991), 211–13.

[186] I. W. Archer, 'Governors and Governed in Late Sixteenth-Century London, *c.* 1560–1603: Studies in the Achievement of Stability', D.Phil. diss., University of Oxford (1988), 306.

[187] P. Griffiths, 'The Structure of Prostitution in Elizabethan London', *Continuity & Change*, 8 (1993), 46–8.

[188] Mary Greening was committed on this charge, for want of sureties; Corporation of London Record Office, Waiting Book, 15, 1690–6, fo. 126^{v}.

were accused, the court might commit the husband first, but the 'bawdy house' might still be operating months later.[189] Two wives were sent to the Norwich Bridewell in 1645 'for keeping a bawdy house',[190] although this may have meant the lodging of an unmarried mother. Any woman running a lodging house was potentially at risk of neighbours complaining that she kept a brothel, as did those of the widow Mary Ferries in 1615, who alleged that Ferries lodged men and women suspected of incontinency.[191] In 1630 the Norwich mayoralty committed a woman to Bridewell for entertaining three men at her house after midnight.[192]

The occupational hazards of prostitution were serious: disease and punishment. Women could be infected with syphilis or gonorrhoea. They were labelled 'whores' and could be whipped or imprisoned. Their clients seem to have been invisible to the authorities, and to have escaped punishment altogether (unlike the men who fathered bastards, who would be pursued for maintenance).[193] Prostitutes paid with bodily pain and public humiliation; in 1582 in York Barbara Sympson 'for misuseinge of her bodie' was ordered to be set on a barrel on the pavement in the open market for an hour, her head was to be shaven, she was to have a superscription of her offence on her head, and then to be whipped out of the city.[194] Contemporaries were aware of some injustice; in criticism of Bridewell in the Elizabethan period, it was alleged that 'the beggarly harlottes are punished, and the riche eskape'.[195]

Reputation was crucial for a woman's success in surviving in employment and in securing relief. Public accusations of sexual offences—whoredom and bastardy—seriously damaged a woman's reputation as a worker, which partly explains why victims of slander were quick to take their cases to the church courts to clear their names.[196] Trading in the market, selling in the streets, gaining employment as a charwoman, all these economic activities

[189] The editor of *Westminster City Fathers* suggests, of a 1614 case, that the man apparently transferred the business to his wife. Probably she kept the house all the time, but he was liable for her offence; W. H. Manchee, *The Westminster City Fathers (The Burgess Court of Westminster), 1585–1901* (1924), 115.

[190] Norfolk RO, Mayor's Court 1634–46, fo. 443^{v}.

[191] *Middlesex Sessions Records*, iii. 3, 4, 242, 288.

[192] *Minutes of Norwich Court of Mayoralty, 1630–1631*, 11.

[193] *HMC Various* 1, Wiltshire Quarter Sessions, 98. A vicar was to pay 18*d*. weekly to support his child till it was 8 years old.

[194] *York Civic Records*, vii [1570–8], ed. A. Raine, Yorks. Archaeological Society Record Series, 119 (1952), 58. Further examples are numerous; *Somerset Quarter Sessions*, i. 277.

[195] Bridewell court book, quoted in Archer, 'Governors and Governed', 322.

[196] S. H. Mendelson, '"To Shift For a Cloak": Disorderly Women in the Church Courts', in V. Frith (ed.), *Women and History: Voices of Early Modern England* (Toronto, 1995), 3–10; L. Gowing, 'Gender and the Language of Insult in Early Modern London', *History Workshop Journal*, 35 (1993), 18–19.

could be adversely affected by talk of a woman being 'before the courts'. The public punishments which women suffered could make it difficult for them to earn a living. In 1624 Sara Seele, who was unable to pay a hefty 5*s.* fine for being drunk in church, was publicly shamed by being set in the stocks.[197] No parish or charitable authorities would give relief to a disorderly woman.

Female vagrants were a typical case of the disorderly woman outside the bounds of assistance. The contemporary stereotyped picture of female vagrants enjoying a free life is quite mistaken.[198] Life on the roads was dangerous and women were vulnerable to sexual exploitation as well as the usual hazards of hunger and cold. Female vagrants were usually women in desperate circumstances. Some took to the roads as an escape, as did 20-year-old Mary Bryce, 'going in a mixt Say wastcoate wth a greenishe clothe petticoate', who was wanted for leaving a child in Norwich.[199] Some were seeking absent husbands, as may have been the case of Kathleen, the wife of Francis Tomson, who was punished in Norwich and sent to Cambridge with a pass for herself and a boy of 6 and a 'suckling child' of three months old.[200] Joan Roberts may have been escaping from her domestic responsibilities when she left her husband in Derby and abandoned her child in Warwick in 1649.[201]

Women had few occupations which would justify an itinerant existence. Since they were expected either to be in service or at home with their husbands, women's pleas of being employed on the roads did not impress the justices. Vagrants were sometimes whipped at the post and sent home with a pass.[202] A petty chapman and his wife were punished at the whipping post in Norwich in 1624.[203] In 1697 two women from London, one of whom was married, 'confessed that they are Ballad singers and were taken singing lewd Ballads' in Bristol.[204] Other harsh treatment included marking the vagrants with a brand. In 1638 at Pontefract twelve people, including three women, all over 14, were convicted of vagrancy and branded because

[197] Norfolk RO, Mayor's Court Book 1624–34, fo. 8.

[198] J. Mikalachki, 'Women's Networks and the Female Vagrant: A Hard Case', in S. Frye and K. Robertson (eds.), *Women's Alliances in Early Modern England* (forthcoming). We are grateful to Dr Mikalachki for allowing us to cite her paper. See also P. Griffiths, *Youth and Authority: Formative Experiences in England, 1560–1640* (Oxford, 1996).

[199] Norfolk RO, Mayor's Court Book 1624–34, fo. 79.

[200] Ibid., fo. 102.

[201] *Warwick Quarter Session Order Books, 1637–50*, ii. 232.

[202] For example, Norfolk RO, Norwich Mayor's Court, 1643, fo. 390^{v}, 1645, fo. 460^{v}, 463.

[203] Norfolk RO, Mayor's Court Book 1624–34, fo. 15^{v}.

[204] *Bristol Corporation of the Poor*, 57.

they were able-bodied but had 'no art, land, or master'.[205] Some were committed to Bridewell where they were expected to work. In London in 1642 the Lord Mayor sent Martha Maddoxe to labour at Bridewell because 'she is a vagrant woman is out of service and can give no good account'.[206] Some Bridewell women were put out to service; four girls were apprenticed to a knitter in 1598, and in 1604 a hatmaker was to have six boys and girls to work for *2d.* per day. In the 1570s, Maryon Colley was ordered to keep the poor in Bridewell at work and to teach them card making.[207] Destitute women begged on the streets of towns and cities. By definition, they were not fulfilling any of their expected roles. Although they might find charity, they also risked punishment, usually a whipping.[208] Yet they may have had no other option.

CONCLUSIONS

The early modern period has been seen as a time of major economic upheaval, but little changed in the working lives of poor women.[209] Women who were born into labouring families, whether in the town or countryside, spent most of their lives labouring in turn. With minimal training and skill, their employment was in low status jobs. Whether single or married, they were chronically underemployed; little of the work which might have paid them better was available. Sometimes they could get no work at all. Vulnerable to a range of economic fluctuations and personal misfortunes, and lacking resources to see them through the bad times, labouring women could be reduced to indigence very quickly.

The 'family economy' was not a universal system of production through early modern society, yet the very concept worked against poor women. So far as the overseers of the poor were concerned, 'the family' provided for all of its members. Officials refused to recognize that not all women were married, or supported by their husbands. Poor women usually lived in smaller households than those of prosperous members of society, and so were less able to absorb economic or personal crises. If a single woman was

[205] *West Riding Sessions Records 1611–1642*, ed. J. Lister, Yorks. Archaeological Society, 54 (1915), 62–3.

[206] Guildhall, Microfilm 515, Bridewell Royal Hospital, Court Minutes, vol. 8, 1634–42, p. 25.

[207] Copeland, 'Extracts from Bridewell Court Books', *Under the Dome*, 11 (1902), 83, 86; 12 (1903), 3, 72.

[208] Norfolk RO, Mayor's Court Book, 1624–34, fo. 64.

[209] Cf. M. Kowaleski, 'Women's Work in a Market Town: Exeter in the Late Fourteenth Century', in B. A. Hanawalt, *Women and Work in Preindustrial Europe* (Bloomington, Ind., 1986), 155–7.

FIG. 36. Woman begging with her children. Laroon's inclusion of this ragged trio in his *Cryes of the City of London* (1711) underlines the fact that begging was a means of livelihood for many poor women whose parishes had granted them insufficient (or no) relief. Sometimes begging was combined with the selling of small wares; sometimes it was the sole occupation of the destitute, although it left them liable to punishment for vagrancy

physically incapable of work, she was vulnerable to absolute poverty. If the male breadwinner was sick, absent, or dead, his wife received no assistance until the whole group was reduced to destitution. A widow's petition for relief poignantly illustrates the process of material decline:

> by reason of her late husband lying sick on her hands two years and in regard of her two small children which she hath had no means at all to relieve, except only her own labour, [she] is now fallen into great extremity and want and likely to suffer most miserable calamity and affliction.[210]

Although a more organized system of poor relief developed during the period, and women and their children received a larger share of it than did men, nevertheless the Poor Laws created a new kind of dependence in women. Only the 'good' poor received relief, and they were forced to comply with the expected norms of female dependence: to be content with little, conform to patriarchal authority, and be grateful. Moreover, as we saw in Chapter 3, poor mothers were liable to lose their children earlier to various kinds of servitude. Even in old age, the parish provided small relief, and women were expected to labour at whatever miserable drudgery was available so long as they were physically able.

From their earliest years until death, getting a living was the major preoccupation of labouring women. Their work was characterized by low status and low rewards. Although labouring men shared women's economic vulnerability and low status, even they were better paid than their female counterparts.

[210] Quoted in Boulton, *Neighbourhood and Society*, 128.

6

OCCUPATIONAL IDENTITIES AND SOCIAL ROLES

In the previous chapter we discussed the basic strategies by which poorer women survived over their lifetimes. At the middling and upper levels of society, where taxes and rates were paid, life was obviously less desperate, and women's work involved less drudgery. This chapter discusses the main features of women's work at these higher levels.

The work of women of the middling and upper ranks shared certain common features with that of poorer women. Women's work always included responsibility for a household and, if they were mothers, the care or supervision of children. Compared with men of the same social rank, they had limited choices of occupations and professions, and less access to training. There were few occupations exclusive to women, compared with a large number monopolized by men. The economic rewards of women's labour were usually smaller than those of men. Whatever work women performed was likely to be less highly valued. All women, whether single or married, were affected by the expectation that they would bear children; reproduction was their main 'labour', and if they did have children, their responsibilities affected their capacity to engage in work on the same terms as men. Women's roles as wives and mothers influenced their employment choices. Regardless of whether they lived in countryside or town, child-care responsibilities made them comparatively less mobile than men, which in turn affected their opportunities for paid employment. Women's marital status, unlike that of men, affected their economic rewards: the single woman was paid for work which the married woman was expected to perform as a duty, and the married woman did not own the economic rewards of her work.

Similarly, the concept of 'the family economy' is as problematic for middling and élite women as for the mass of the female labouring population. Undoubtedly, a woman's family of origin affected her life chances. But women were individuals. Not all married. Of those who married, many had independent work identities. Not all wives enjoyed the economic contributions of their husbands. When husbands were absent or dead, wives and widows could be forced to provide for themselves and their families by their own labour.

If we compare women as workers at the middling and upper levels of society with those below them, we can perceive some differences. First, middling and upper rank women had more economic options. The greater affluence of their families of origin provided them with better education. They could be trained for a trade, craft, or profession. They married men of better economic position. But paradoxically, at the upper levels of society, there was more work from which women were excluded because of their sex than at the poorest levels of society. And while middling women enjoyed a more secure economic position than their plebeian counterparts, they were not invulnerable to hardship. The death of a husband could reduce his wife to the poorer ranks of society.

Secondly, the reproductive work of women higher up the social scale was more important. At this level, patriarchal patterns of inheritance were most significant. The main duty of a queen—regnant or consort—was to produce an heir, preferably of the male sex. Aristocratic women bore children more frequently than their lower status counterparts. They married younger and, since they were more likely to employ wet-nurses rather than feed their babies themselves, they conceived again more quickly.

Thirdly, the higher a woman's social rank, the less likely she was to engage directly in the manual work of housewifery. The households of the wealthiest were more complex than those further down the social scale, and women's supervisory duties consequently more extensive. We know more about the housewifery of women of the upper and middle ranks who were literate and kept accounts. From those records and from probate inventories we can deduce that women of the middling and upper ranks were more likely to be involved in the household production of food and clothing than their lower status counterparts.

Fourthly, women of the middling ranks were more likely to have an occupational or professional identity than were any other women. Apart from midwifery, medical practice, and schoolteaching, women ran businesses and were providers of services. They ran inns, kept shops, and engaged in a range of crafts and trades. Women of the middling ranks were more likely to follow a single occupation full-time than were poorer women who engaged in multiple occupations. Unmarried women and widows were legally freer to follow certain trades and occupations than their married counterparts.

Differences in the nature and types of work performed by women were significant in establishing and maintaining the class divisions between them. The social status of a gentlewoman or a wealthy citizen depended upon her ability to employ the labour of other women. Without a maid-of-all-work to perform the household drudgery and a servant to help her to dress and arrange her hair, a woman would find it hard to maintain the appearance of a gentlewoman.

This chapter focuses on the diversity of the work performed by women of the middling and upper ranks. Although such women were more likely to develop a professional occupational identity than poorer women, the work of married women was frequently a taken-for-granted component of their husband's employment. While some aristocratic women were appointed to posts at court in their own right, most wives were expected to contribute to the economic activities of their husbands.

After discussing women's roles in running a household, which they performed irrespective of their other work, we consider women's professional and skilled work, female occupations in crafts and manufacture, and, finally, the work of aristocratic women.

RUNNING A HOUSEHOLD

Housework and child-care were always women's work, but the higher the social level, the more complex and specialized the tasks, and the larger the body of servants.

Housewifery was fundamental to the working life of women at the middling level of society. The archetypal Elizabethan housewife, well described by Alice Clark, was employed in the countryside in growing food, brewing, baking, and marketing. She and her female servants manufactured clothing. She came closest to achieving a closed system of production: that is, her labour satisfied most of her household's needs for food and clothing. Most is known about this group of women workers, yet it is important to stress at the outset that those who were engaged in rural farming production, the wives of prosperous farmers, were a more limited proportion of the female population than Clark implied. Clark believed that, by the end of the seventeenth century, these productive women workers had been displaced. But while the size of farms did change during the century, some becoming

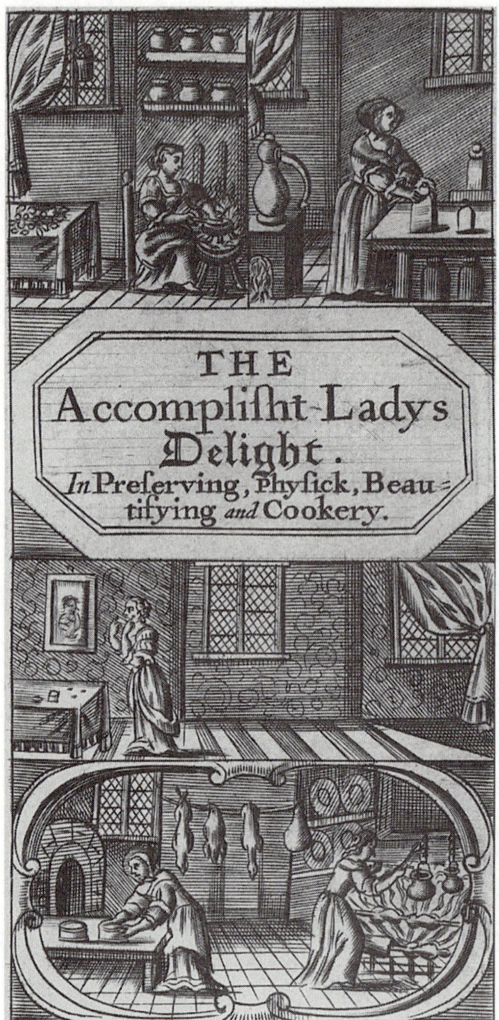

FIG. 37. Housewifery. This decorative title-page of *The Accomplisht Ladys Delight* (1675) reveals that housewifery involved women of middling and élite social status in a multitude of highly skilled tasks. Brewing and distilling, cooking and baking, and even the practice of medicine ('physick') were part of the labour performed by the mistress of the household as well as by her female servants

larger, others smaller, and fewer remaining at the middling level, wives in larger farms continued to produce food and clothing.[1]

The basic work of women farmers in the countryside was the production of food, drink and clothing for their households. From account books, diaries, and contemporary treatises we can document their labour. Farming wives tended small livestock, such as hens and ducks. They planted kitchen gardens, and processed the fruit from orchards. From their kitchens farm

[1] C. Shammas, *The Pre-Industrial Consumer in England and America* (Oxford, 1990), 26–7.

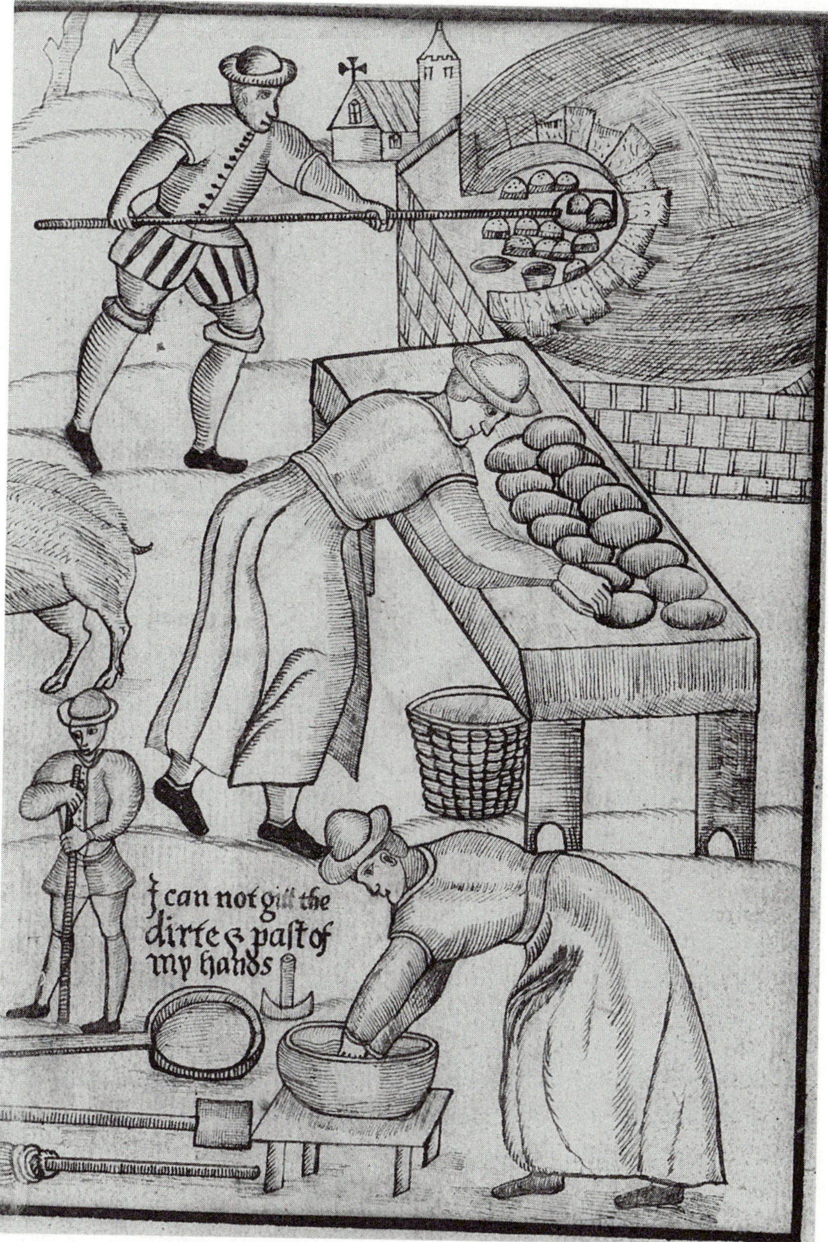

FIG. 38. Making bread. In rural households which were large enough to include an oven, many women baked their own bread rather than purchase it. Those who lacked ovens often prepared the loaves and brought them to the baker's oven to be baked, as was probably the case in this contemporary depiction of seasonal occupations. The woman kneading dough in the foreground complains, 'I cannot get the dirt and paste off my hands'

This hurtleſſe beaſt with meeke moode yelds his woll
And ſkin. to cloth our naked clotte of claye
He giues his fleſh to feede our bellies full
Nought for him ſelfe he bringe but for our ſtaye
June
Cancer
mayd milke cleane

FIG. 39. Rural work: sheep shearing and milking. Among both middling and plebeian classes, women were involved in a full range of outdoor rural tasks

labourers and servants were fed; without women's labour, cash for the purchase and preparation of food and clothing would be needed. Clothing was manufactured largely by female labour. Spinning-wheels were more likely to be listed in the probate inventories of wealthier households where there was surplus female labour.[2] During the seventeenth century, women participated in what Margaret Spufford has described as 'the great reclothing of rural England'. Increasingly, a wide range of material and patterns were available from chapmen all over England. More people had more clothing; this reclothing was the work of women.[3]

In the country, women were responsible for various specialized forms of work, such as dairying. Dairying was a profitable occupation for women. It involved them in a daily routine of rising to milk at 5 or 6 a.m. in summer and again in the evening, and tending to cows in the byre in winter. Since in some counties, markets were customarily held on Wednesdays and Saturdays, women would churn cream into butter on Tuesdays and Fridays ready for sale.[4]

In the towns, many women in middling households had kitchen gardens, and so they and their servants were involved in both growing and preparing food and medicinal herbs. Urban probate inventories show an increasing range of household goods in middling level households, much of which was the product of female labour, and all of which required further female labour to maintain. Linen sheets, pillow covers, bed hangings, cushions, towels, napkins, and table cloths represented the accumulated labour of generations of women, and, if handled carefully, could be passed on from one generation to the next. One of the Manchester widows whose personal property was above the median in the reign of Elizabeth left linen valued at £26, including thirty-four pairs of sheets.[5] Women's inventories were more likely than men's to mention linen.[6]

Women of the upper ranks took their household duties seriously. They were involved in supervising the efficient running of large households, sometimes in both London and the counties, for many gentry families had more than one house. Wives had duties of hospitality and sociability, and daughters were trained to function as hostesses.[7] Mistresses of households were responsible for provisioning, and they organized the purchase of more specialized goods. Sarah Fell's account book shows her active in planning kitchen gardens, making and caring for her own clothing and that of children, and overseeing the production or purchase and care of household goods. She

[2] Ibid. 31–3.

[3] M. Spufford, *Great Reclothing of Rural England: Petty Chapmen and their Wares in the Seventeenth Century* (1984).

[4] G. Markham, *Country Contentments* (1615), 107.

[5] T. S. Willan, *Elizabethan Manchester* (Manchester, 1980), 113.

[6] L. Weatherill, 'A Possession of One's Own: Women and Consumer Behaviour in England, 1660–1740', *JBS*, 25 (1986), 143.

[7] F. Heal, *Hospitality in Early Modern England* (Oxford, 1990), 178–83.

FIG. 40. Woman on horseback with panniers going to market. Women of middling social status, like the prosperous-looking rider depicted in this contemporary drawing, could afford to travel on horseback when bringing their surplus farm produce for sale at local markets

also supervised the dairy.[8] The care of a large household could be exhausting. Katherine Austen wrote of her 'mother's strong nature worn out by too much stirring . . . And the many cares and businesses which a great family gave occasions to her'.[9] The widowed Katherine Windham kept a series of regular accounts for her own pin money, her children's money as her husband's executrix, and the kitchen. A sample entry for the kitchen accounts of 31 August 1695 indicates her careful supervision of daily management: she recorded money for peas, a pig, paste, oatmeal, salt, 'petties', yeast, six chickens, eggs, five turkeys, wheat, sheep, and lamb.[10] Anne Brockman, a gentlewoman in Kent, kept similar accounts in the early eighteenth century.[11] Some women also developed expertise in the care of farm animals.

[8] S. Fell, *The Household Account Book of Sarah Fell of Swarthmoor Hall*, ed. N. Penney (Cambridge, 1920). See also Cumbria CRO, Lowther accounts, D Lond/L3/1/6.

[9] BL, MS Sloane 4454, fo. 57, Diary of Katherine Austen.

[10] Norfolk RO, WCK 6/15, Katherine Windham kitchen accounts, 1695–96.

[11] BL, Accounts of Anne Brockman, Add. MS 45,208, Add. MS 45,209, Add. MS 45,210.

Anne Glydd had a number of treatments for animal ailments, such as 'for a bullock that is Hide-bound'.[12]

Tasks were more complex in larger households, and servants were more specialized. Even a countess was expected to supervise the washing of the laundry at home; the second earl of Clare included a lengthy tirade in his will about his wife's lazy habit of sending the laundry out, thereby shredding the labour of generations of his female ancestors.[13] The care of linen was labour intensive. To wash lace, for example, involved a series of activities spread over several days.[14] Needlework was so pervasive an activity for a gentlewoman that it was frequently referred to as her 'work'. Pillows, cushions, and bed-hangings were produced by female labour.[15] Recipes to preserve textiles from moths were exchanged and included in the compendiums of household hints which literate women compiled.[16]

Many mothers of the middling and upper ranks were closely involved with the care and education of their children. Their correspondence reveals their anxieties about their children's health and development. If children were nursed away from home, mothers supervised and gave directions about matters of health.[17] They were involved in the schooling of sons as well as the instruction of daughters. In the 1680s, Mary Woodforde's diary recorded the progress of her sons' education at Eton, and Mary Evelyn corresponded frequently with her son's Oxford tutor.[18] Ladies might also oversee the welfare of relatives' children. Lady Petty told her niece Blundell that she had visited 'her boys': 'I see them often, they shall want no care of mine.'[19]

Duties towards dependants occupied wives. The higher the social level, the more likely was the mistress of the household to be involved in the supervision and resolution of personal conflicts among household members. Many godly mistresses took seriously their responsibilities to their servants, trying to educate their maids in basic literacy and piety.[20] In urban house-

[12] BL, Brockman papers, Recipe Book of Anne Glydd, 1656, Add. MS 45,196, fo. 3^v.

[13] PCC, 42 Ent (1689), Will of Gilbert Holles, earl of Clare.

[14] See, for example, Folger MS V. a. 20, Constantia Hall, her Book of Receipts, 1672, and Folger MS ADD 931, Mary Hookes, Receipt Book, 1680, no. 128.

[15] Embroidery as 'work': Ann Clifford, Cumbria CRO Kendal, Letters from Anne Clifford, Box 44, 1615, to her mother; P. Crawford, '"The Only Ornament in a Woman": Needlework in Early Modern England', in *All Her Labours, ii. Embroidering the Framework* (Sydney, 1984), 7–20.

[16] BL, Brockman papers, Recipe Book of Anne Glydd, 1656, Add. MS 45,196, fo. 14.

[17] See, for example, BL, Harley papers, Portland loan 29/76, 3.

[18] New College, Oxford, Mary Woodeforde Booke (1684–1690). Mary Evelyn's letters now BL, MS Additional.

[19] BL, Petty MS 5, 25 Oct. 1684, Lady Petty to her children, fo. 45^v. For another example, see BL, Harley papers, Portland loan 29/76, 3, 8 Nov. [16]80, Abigail Harley to her husband.

[20] P. Crawford, *Women and Religion in England, 1500–1720* (1993), 88.

holds, especially in London, an increasing number of servants required supervision. Maidservants might be off on errands and have an opportunity to socialize, an annoyance to the mistress responsible for the work of the household. In addition, many mothers trained their daughters who worked at home. Gregory King believed that there were more females in wealthier London parishes because daughters were not sent out to service, but kept at home, while sons were sent away to learn marketable skills.[21]

In addition to caring for a husband and children, the mistress of a household was responsible for providing board and lodging for servants, whether they worked in husbandry or at her husband's trade or craft. Depending on her husband's occupation, her duties could be extensive. The wives of schoolteachers provided board for wealthy pupils. 'To Mrs Snellinge upon a bill for Charles and Robin', for a year £4. 9*s.* 11*d*, noted their father in 1634.[22] Parents of Eton boys around 1700 could pay about £30 per annum for 'Mrs procters bill' for school board, shoes, and books.[23] 'Mrs proctor' performed the tasks which would later become that of matron; as a wife, she as well as her husband was working at the school.

Wives were responsible for estate management, while men were away attending to legal business or at court or Parliament. They usually arranged for the collection of rents, supervised the accounts, and oversaw the activities of stewards, all with some confidence. Wives' letters to their husbands usually reported what they had done; they did not solicit advice about what they might do. During the Civil War and Interregnum, when many more men were absent from home, fighting or in exile, wives' work in estate management was intensified. Even in normal times, as widows and guardians of heirs, women could be solely responsible for the preservation and improvement of the family estates. Katherine Windham presented elaborate accounts to her son when he came of age, documenting her financial transactions as his guardian.[24]

Another group of hard-working housewives whose labour supported that of their husbands were the wives of the Anglican clergy and Nonconformist ministers. Their status ranged from those who, like Jane Josselin, were married to clergy of roughly yeoman status, to wives of bishops who could

[21] Quoted in M. Prior, 'Women and the Urban Economy: Oxford 1500–1800', in M. Prior (ed.), *Women in English Society, 1500–1800* (1985), 100.

[22] BL, Add. MS 27,399, Household Accounts of Framlingham Gawdy, 1626–39, fo. 221.

[23] Norfolk RO, WCK 6/13, Katherine Windham domestic accounts; WCK 6/16, An account made by Katherine Windham, as executrix of the will of her husband, William, with her son Ashe Windham, 1696.

[24] Norfolk RO, WCK 6/16, Account made by Katherine Windham, executrix of the will of her husband William, with her son Ashe Windham, 1696.

be the friends of aristocratic women. Their activities are more fully documented because admiring relatives or ministers saw these wives and mothers as exemplifying the godly ideal of good womanhood. But, in the spiritual scales, worldly things were always found wanting. Many wives had internalized the clergy's negative views of their labour: 'she that is married careth for things of the world.' The Presbyterian minister Christopher Love refused to 'entangle himself with the business of the world', and committed the care of his family and household to his wife, renting a separate establishment so that he could work undisturbed.[25] Elizabeth Walker slept fewer hours so that she could be up at 4 a.m. to spend time at her private prayers before her busy daily round of supervising children and servants and assisting neighbours.[26] While they prided themselves in running their households smoothly and sparing their husbands from trouble and anxiety, godly women were under no illusions: their work was of secondary importance. Moreover, some wives could find their own spirituality impeded by their worldly roles. At the end of the seventeenth century, the wives and daughters in the Nonconformist families of the ministers Philip and Matthew Henry were constantly troubled at their domestic duties: 'through the necessity of my outward affairs, my secret duties are commonly limited', wrote Sarah Savage. 'I have been ready to fear that I have declined in grace.'[27]

At the upper levels of society, the boundaries between duties and work were frequently blurred. Public roles were discharged by women of the upper ranks. Queens consort and regnant promoted various religious causes; both Queen Anne, the wife of James I, and Queen Henrietta Maria, the wife of Charles I, were Catholic, and the latter, in particular, laboured for the conversion of England to her faith. Queens consort or dowager were responsible for the patronage of the Hospital of St Katharine by the Tower, and in the 1690s the Dowager Queen Catherine was required to arbitrate, through her council, over the alleged mismanagement of the governor.[28] As rulers, Mary, Elizabeth, Mary II, and Anne worked hard at the defence of the realm and domestic peace. (A fuller discussion of the roles of queens in early modern England is found in Chapter 7.)

Gentlewomen, especially when widowed, could be powerful religious

[25] BL, MS Sloane 3945, fo. 105.

[26] A. Walker, *The Holy Life of Mrs Elizabeth Walker* (1690), 33.

[27] J. B. Williams, *Memoirs of the Life and Character of Mrs Savage* (1821 edn.) 296–7, 285; P. Crawford, 'Katharine and Philip Henry and their Children: A Case Study in Family Ideology', *Transactions of the Historic Society of Lancashire and Cheshire*, 134 (1984), 49–57.

[28] C. Jamison, *The History of the Royal Hospital of St Katharine by the Tower* (Oxford, 1952), 63–4, 96–103.

patrons, furthering the godly cause by their choices. In this they had no more 'work' identity than a man who performed a similar role. In the late 1620s, Joan Barrington's correspondence reveals that she was at the centre of a powerful East Anglian Puritan group. The earl of Warwick acknowledged to Lady Barrington that in a matter of ecclesiastical patronage, 'I had soner taken your recomendation then all the bishops in this kingdome.'[29] Wives of bishops and ministers recognized their public responsibilities. The widowed Elizabeth Berkeley, who married Bishop Gilbert Burnet, hoping that she might have 'more power to do good in a more public part', thought it her duty to promote piety by writing a number of religious works, including *A Method of Devotion.*[30] Led by Queen Mary II, great ladies were increasingly important as patrons of charitable work, such as the foundation of schools. Yet their role as public philanthropists was restricted; for example, they could be subscribers but not voting members of the Society for Promoting Christian Knowledge.[31]

Gentlewomen engaged in charitable work among their poorer neighbours, assisting in sickness and in childbirth. Elizabeth Walker's example, celebrated by her husband in his *Life*, was not atypical:

> Another object of her Painfull Charity . . . was, Women Labouring with Child, whom she would rise at any hour of the Night to go too, and carry with her what might be usefull to them, having good Skill, and store of Medicines always ready by her for such occasions; and there was scarcely ever any difficulty in that case round about, but recourse was made to her, both for Advice and Medicines; and, if might be with Convenience, for her Presence, which was always very acceptable and comfortable to the distressed Women when the distance was such that she could afford it.[32]

Financial management preoccupied many wealthy women. By the later seventeenth century, marriage settlements gave wives an annual income which women referred to as their 'pin money'. Although wives were legally prevented from owning real and personal estate, some husbands allowed their wives to inherit and manage money. Sarah, duchess of Marlborough,

[29] *Barrington Family Letters, 1628–1632*, ed. A. Searle, Camden Society 4th ser., 28 (1983), 220–1 and n.

[30] Bodl., MS Rawlinson D. 1092, fo. 136, fo. 136^{v}. Elizabeth thought herself capable of preventing the hasty errors which another might have engaged in. Elizabeth Blake, 1661–1709, was the third wife of Burnet.

[31] L. W. Cowie, *Henry Newman: An American in London, 1708–43* (1956), 100.

[32] Walker, *Holy Life of Mrs Elizabeth Walker*, 180.

amassed a large personal fortune with her husband's permission, inheriting her mother's estate and using an investment adviser.[33] More usual was the widow who was responsible for her own and her children's finances. A Norfolk gentlewoman, Katherine Windham, managed her investments with the help of her father.[34]

The range of skills involved in the household tasks of preserving and distilling meant that women in wealthier households were involved with some of the early developments in scientific experiments. Lady Ranelagh's book of medical recipes was probably shared by her brother, Robert Boyle, and it was at her house that he conducted experiments. The boundaries between women and science were not yet established, as they would later be. Lady Ranelagh herself, however, was more interested in religion and in healing the sick.[35]

Whatever other work they performed, all women, including those of aristocratic and middling status, were responsible for child-care and housewifery. The time and energy involved in these daily tasks was extensive when water was to be fetched, fires were wood, and clothes were washed by hand. Although wealthier women engaged in little manual work, they oversaw the labour of those who did. Furthermore, their households were larger, and contained a multitude of material possessions, all of which required care and maintenance.

PROFESSIONAL AND SKILLED WORK: MEDICAL, EDUCATIONAL, AND CULTURAL

In early modern times, a work identity for a woman was comparatively rare. Professions were most common among women of the middling ranks. Their opportunities for education and training allowed some to develop careers as medical practitioners, midwives, teachers, and civic functionaries. But since all women of the middling and upper ranks were expected to be knowledgeable about childbirth and health care, especially of children, and to teach their children as well as instruct their servants, such general female knowledge militated against the professional identities of women who did

[33] F. Harris, *A Passion for Government: The Life of Sarah, Duchess of Marlborough* (Oxford, 1991), 73–4.

[34] Norfolk RO, WKC 6/12, Personal account book of Katherine Windham, 1669–89.

[35] BL, Lady Ranelagh's Medical Receipts, MS Sloane 1367, fos. 81–3, refers to 'Our abbreviations'.

such work for pay. In this section we discuss women's work in medical, educational, and cultural areas.

Medical practitioners: midwives, surgeons, physicians, and healers

Women across all social strata were involved in nursing, treatment of the sick, and healing, providing within their households most of the health care of early modern society. Those who were paid as midwives, physicians, surgeons, specialists, and nurses had an occupational identity. While female medical practitioners are not usually described as professionals, the work of those with training and experience can be categorized as such, like that of their male counterparts. As with many other occupations which would today be termed professional, women in these professions lacked a formal institutional structure to control their practice. But since there was no agreed contemporary definition of a profession, the claims of female medical practitioners to be termed professional are as reasonable as those of other groups.[36]

Midwifery provides one of the best studied examples of a female occupation in early modern times.[37] The practitioners are a good example of women whose work was professional but whose occupation was not normally recognized as such by their contemporaries. Stigmatized by later doctors who sought to enhance their own status by denigrating that of women, the midwives of early modern Europe possessed skill and a professional identity. Although, as we have shown in Chapter 5, not all midwives should be classified as professional, because some were too poor to purchase the necessary licence and practised only among their poorer neighbours, the majority were trained, skilled, and shared a group identity.

What midwives lacked, compared with male professionals in other areas, was the power to control their own conditions of work; they were licensed by the ecclesiastical authorities. The bishops were concerned chiefly with women's characters and their conformity to the Anglican Church. Usually midwives were married or widowed, although there were some single women.[38] There was no

[36] W. R. Prest (ed.), *The Professions in Early Modern England* (1987), 1–21.

[37] J. H. Aveling, *English Midwives: Their History and Prospects* (1872); J. Donnison, *Midwives and Medical Men: A History of Inter-Professional Rivalries and Women's Rights* (1977); H. Marland (ed.), *The Art of Midwifery: Early Modern Midwives in Europe* (1993). D. Evenden-Nagy, 'Seventeenth-Century London Midwives: Their Training, Licensing and Social Profile', Ph.D. diss., McMaster University (1991).

[38] Harley has found a few examples of young licensed midwives in Lancashire and Cheshire from the late 17th and 18th cent. who were single; D. Harley, 'Provincial Midwives in England: Lancashire and Cheshire, 1660–1760', in Marland (ed.), *Midwifery*, 34.

provision for their formal education. The system of training was an informal apprenticeship; those who became midwives usually practised for several years under the supervision of a licensed midwife.[39] The testimonials in support of applications for licences commonly include certificates from a licensed midwife to the effect that the applicant has served as her deputy for three, four, or more years.[40] Some testimonials refer to 'several years instructed' by a sworn midwife, and in one case the arrangement was a more formal one, as a woman 'did article and covenant with Alice Herbert, an ancient and skillfull Midwife to become her Deputy', and the time period, unspecified, was said to have ended.[41] There are instances where midwifery was professed by at least two generations of women. In her will of 1712, one London midwife bequeathed her 'midwifes-mantle' to her granddaughter, provided she follow her mother and practise in London too.[42] This system of training by apprenticeship may have been typical of a very narrow range of women's occupations by the end of the early modern period.

Midwives could be among the better paid women workers. The range was enormous: from £300 for attendance on a queen, £31 for the daughter of Sir Thomas Throckmorton in 1609, to 1*s.* 6*d.* for the midwife of a poor woman.[43] The overseers of the poor usually paid between half a crown and five shillings.[44] A midwife's diary from Kendal for the years 1665–75 documents the earnings of a rural midwife. In 1665 she earned 19*s.* and in 1674, her most profitable year, £26. 18*s.* 2*d.*[45] An anonymous midwife's diary from Oxford from 1695 to 1722 includes annual earnings, and records of births. Her maximum earnings rose to over £44 in 1706 and 1715.[46] In 1652 Hester Shaw, a London midwife, claimed that she had lost around £3,000 in a fire, the fruit of 'forty years toilesome gleaning in the way of my labourious calling'.[47]

Women's work identity was weak even in this well-established and

[39] This is the view we have reached in the course of our research; it is confirmed by the chapters by Evenden, Harley, and Hess in Marland (ed.), *Midwifery*. Cf. Wilson in R. Porter (ed.), *Patients and Practitioners: Lay Perceptions of Medicine in Pre-Industrial Society* (Cambridge, 1985), 136, who claims that most midwives practised on the basis of a few deliveries and purchased a book.

[40] Guildhall, MS 10,116/4, file 7.

[41] Guildhall, MS 10,116/4, file 7, 31 May 1671.

[42] Evenden-Nagy, 'Seventeenth-Century London Midwives', 372.

[43] A. Clark, *Working Life of Women in the Seventeenth Century* (1919; 2nd edn., 1982; 3rd edn., 1992), 279–81; Donnison, *Midwives and Medical Men*, 10–11; R. C. Sawyer, 'Patients, Healers, and Disease in the South-East Midlands, 1597–1634', Ph.D. diss., University of Wisconsin-Madison (1986), 176.

[44] Harley, 'Provincial Midwives', in Marland (ed.), *Midwifery*, 34.

[45] Kendal RO, MS WD/Cr, Transcript of a midwife's diary, 1665–75.

[46] Bodl., MS Rawlinson D. 1141, Diary of a London midwife.

[47] H. Shaw, *A Plaine Relation of My Sufferings* (1653), sig. A2. *The Europa Biographical Dictionary of British Women* (1983), P. Crawford, entry for Hester Shaw.

reasonably well-paid female calling. A large element of charitable mutual self-help weakened the 'professional' identity of the midwife. Women of higher social status were often summoned to attend at births, but they were amateurs. In a small parish the churchwardens might report that no woman took 'the profession of a midwife' but that women have 'done the office for a neighbour'.[48] There was an incredible range among practitioners of midwifery: in addition to those who worked steadily, there was the case of one midwife who wanted to be licensed but was not willing to take the oath, or to go out at night.[49] Midwives' own histories demonstrate that they combined their work with child-care and housekeeping; in the 1650s and 1660s, a Quaker midwife worked while her children were young and her husband in and out of gaol.[50] Moreover, since all midwives were involved in the usual range of female occupations, this further blurred their work identity, making it sometimes difficult to define who was a midwife.[51]

During the seventeenth century, midwives, like other professionals, sought to improve their skill and status. In the 1630s, Mrs Whipp and Hester Shaw tried unsuccessfully to improve the training of midwives; in the 1670s, Elizabeth Cellier likewise failed to establish a College of Midwives.[52] The opposition of male medical practitioners, the women's rivals, was in part responsible for their lack of success. Men resented attempts at female organization and feared the prospect of a female professional group; controlling birth was too important to be left in female hands, even if under ecclesiastical supervision. Men's own status as professionals involved a separation from 'ignorant' practitioners. The ill-defined work identity of midwives made it more difficult for them to organize. By the end of the seventeenth century, women of the middling social levels seem to have been less interested in training as midwives.[53]

By the early eighteenth century, the preferences of some aristocratic women and their husbands had altered in favour of male accoucheurs, for reasons which remain contentious. Male conspiracy seems too simple a view, although part of the identity of male professionals depended upon distancing themselves from those they categorized as ignorant and foolish women.[54] Undoubtedly, the status of licensed medical practitioners

[48] Guildhall MS 9583/2/pt. 3, 24. David Cressy kindly referred us to this volume.

[49] Guildhall, MS 10,116/14, 16 Oct. 1697.

[50] A. G. Hess, 'Midwifery Practice among the Quakers in Southern Rural England in the Late Seventeenth Century', in Marland (ed.), *Midwifery*, 61.

[51] Sawyer, 'Patients, Healers, and Disease', 171.

[52] Donnison, *Midwives and Medical Men*, 13–20.

[53] Harley, 'Provincial Midwives', in Marland (ed.), *Midwifery*, 42–3.

[54] Donnison, *Midwives and Medical Men*.

FIG. 41. Angel pushing woman back from bed of sick man. During the seventeenth century, male professional physicians sought to distance themselves from female practitioners. Here an angel is shown pushing a woman back from the bed of a sick man while ushering a physician forward

increased in the early modern period. Given the network of women praising male midwives, gentlemen who were in a position to 'let' their wives exercise choice may have been happy to concur with this prejudice in favour of men.[55] The employment of a male was negotiated not by the mother-to-be, but by her husband: the male accoucheur Hugh Chamberlen demanded a fee of 100 guineas and refused to attend 'any body except the husband writes to him'.[56]

Female physicians and surgeons continued to practise during the sixteenth and seventeenth centuries.[57] In York in 1572, Isabel Warwike was permitted to practise because she had 'skill in the scyens of Surgery and hath done good therin'.[58] Women's skills were respected and were not restricted to a practice of women and children. In London, women surgeons were employed by St Bartholomew's Hospital; in 1598 Alice Gordon was paid 20*s.* on 20 January, and 10*s.* twice more in the same year.[59] When in 1691 Margaret Neale petitioned for a licence; 'for her better security from any peevish disturbance', responsible clergymen and laymen attested to her training and skill: 'By the instructions from an Artist in surgery and by her own practice (with good success) [she] hath attained to much expertness in blood-letting as also to a dextrousnes in pulling out teeth and is reasonably well versed in dressing and healing all sort of common and ordinary sores.'[60] Both women and men attested to Ann Dover's skill: 'I have had my Child's arm twice out of the Joint and she have set it both times very well', stated Thomas Flynn.[61] Like midwives, physicians and surgeons were licensed by the bishops, although the licensing was patchy. As in other areas of skilled female work, while the norm was the woman of middling status, women of other ranks were involved. One woman who petitioned for a surgeon's licence in Gloucester claimed that she was poor, her husband was aged, and her son incapable of labour.[62]

Formal records relating to female surgeons and physicians are hard to find, but there are hints that more women were involved than the licensing

[55] BL, Add. MS 62225, fos. 375–6. See Ch. 3 above, 'Maternity'.

[56] J. J. Cartwright (ed.), *The Wentworth Papers, 1705–1739* (1883), 314.

[57] A. L. Wyman, 'The Surgeoness: The Female Practitioner of Surgery, 1400–1800', *Medical History*, 28 (1984), 22–41; D. E. Nagy, *Popular Medicine in Seventeenth-Century England* (Bowling Green, Ohio, 1988).

[58] *York Civic Records*, vii [1570–78] ed. A. Raine, Yorks. Archaeological Society Record Series 115 (1950), 48. Further examples, see OA, MS Oxf. Dioc. papers c. 26, 1629–34, fo. 158^{v}; BL, MS Sloane 4047, fo. 38, fo. 158^{v} (thanks to Isobel Grundy for this reference); Norfolk RO, Bishops' Licensing Papers, TES 3; Prest (ed.), *Professions*, 101, 109, 112, 124 n., 127 n.

[59] London, St Bartholomew's Hospital, Account Book, HB 1/3, 1599.

[60] Norfolk RO, Bishops' Licensing Papers, TES 8.

[61] Ibid., TES 3.

[62] Gloucs CRO, GDR c 8, petition of Silvester Ship, wife of John, 1 Sept. 1708. Her petition was supported by JPs, minister, and churchwardens.

papers indicate. The churchwardens of a London parish presented an unlicensed female surgeon to the ecclesiastical authorities in 1664.[63] We know of one woman in Norwich who was a surgeon, as were her husband and son, but there was no sign of her profession in her will.[64] A 1679 presentment for recusancy in Warwick mentions a woman as 'doctris', and a 1631 Oxford church court suit referred in passing to a 'female physician that dwelt at Burford'.[65] A few female medical practitioners published advice for other women. In 1675 Mary Trye's work *Medicatrix, or the Woman-Physician* was printed. Some female almanac writers included medical information, and the midwife Jane Sharp published a book to help other midwives.[66] Female medical specialists were employed by St Bartholomew's Hospital, London. In the early seventeenth century, Alice Sworden was paid for cures at a rate of 15*s.* per person.[67] In 1623, Frances Holcombe was paid £27, and later the very large sum of £135 under her married name.[68] In 1656 Mrs Frances Worth was paid £85 for a year's work in curing scaled heads, and similar sums in 1662 and 1663. She may have been the 'Frances Waller' who was paid in 1665. Subsequently, the hospital employed Mrs Ingram for the same work. Some of these fees appear considerable, although costs for ingredients for medicines may have been involved. Smaller fees were paid to other specialists; in 1704 Elizabeth Bond contracted to clear the beds of bugs in the sisters' room for 40*s.*[69]

Many women who engaged in health care and healing were unlicensed. Excluded from formal medical training in universities, and usually from formal apprenticeships as well, they learned their skills from their female and male relatives and friends. We know of daughters, such as Mary Trye, and Percival Willughby's daughter, working alongside their medically trained fathers. Such women practitioners had had only an informal apprenticeship, without a statutory right to practise, and were liable to prosecution. Between 1580 and 1610, twenty-nine unlicensed female practitioners were prosecuted by the College of Physicians.[70] Nevertheless, a certain level of

[63] Guildhall, MS 9583/2/pt. 4, no. 60.

[64] Thanks to Margaret Pelling for this comment.

[65] *Warwick Quarter Session Records*, vii. 157; OA, MS Oxf. Dioc. papers c. 26, 1629–34 fo. 158^{v}.

[66] S. Jinner, *An Almanack or Prognostication for . . . 1658* [1658] (also for 1659 and 1664); J. Sharp, *The Midwives Book* (1671); M. Trye, *Medicatrix, or the Woman-Physician* (1675);

[67] London, St Bartholomew's Hospital, HB 1/3, Account books, fos. 569^{v}–570^{v}.

[68] Ibid. HB1/7, p. 12.

[69] N. Moore, *The History of St Bartholomew's Hospital*, 2 vols. (1918), i. 353.

[70] M. Pelling, 'Knowledge Common and Acquired: The Education of Unlicensed Medical Practitioners in Early Modern London', in V. Nutton and R. Porter (eds.), *The History of Medical Education in Britain* (1995), 250–79.

small-scale and comparatively unremunerative medical practice was tolerated by the episcopal licensing authorities and the College. In post-Restoration London, several women advertised services in female disorders, children's ailments, and beauty treatments. Many claimed to be related to medical professionals. Some women had specialized, such as Margaret Searl, who cured deafness.[71] Dorothy Dury, the wife of the educational reformer John, distilled medicinal drinks for profit.[72] A poor Norwich widow in the Elizabethan period was curiously described as one who 'worketh not but stylleth [distills] aqua vitae'.[73]

Wealthier women who engaged in healing as a form of charity for the poor further weakened women's professional identity as physicians. The mother of Samuel Benion, a medically trained Nonconformist minister, 'us'd to be serviceable to her poor Neighbours, sometimes in the charitable curing of those that were hurt, or sore'.[74] Leonard Wheatcroft's elegy on his mother Anne Wheatcroft praised her charitable surgery:

> Who e're was hurt, if this ould matron knew
> Haste would she make, and presently them view
> Either in head or foot, or armes, or shoulder;
> A rare Chirurgeon and the poores' upholder.
> All that she did was done for charitee:
> Come poor or rich, they all to her were free.[75]

Some of the remedies in wealthier women's commonplace books involved elements of magic, such as taking fox's blood, but, unlike their poorer sisters, gentlewomen were not usually in danger of prosecution for witchcraft. Even indigent old women were unlikely to be prosecuted so long as they were not too visible, that is, not too successful.

Nursing was women's work, frequently a part of their customary roles. During the Civil War, women of all ranks nursed wounded soldiers. While gentlewomen might act from charity, poorer women were paid.[76] During the seventeenth century, women were employed as nurses in London hospitals, such as St Bartholomew's, St Thomas's, Christ's, and St Katharine

[71] P. Crawford, 'Printed Advertisements for Women Medical Practitioners in London, 1670–1710', *Society for the Social History of Medicine, Bulletin*, 35 (1984), 66–70.

[72] G. H. Turnbull, *Hartlib, Dury and Comenius: Gleanings from Hartlib's Papers* (1947), 260–1.

[73] *Norwich Census of the Poor*, 29.

[74] Through helping her, Benion decided to go to Glasgow to beome a doctor of physic. M. Henry, *A Sermon preach'd at the Funeral of Dr Samuel Benion* (1709), 47–8.

[75] 'The Autobiography of Leonard Wheatcroft', *Journal of Derbyshire Archaeological and Natural History Society*, 18 (1896), 80.

[76] A. Laurence, *Women in England 1500–1760: A Social History* (1994), 137–8.

by the Tower, but not until the 1650s were they actually identified as 'nurses' rather than by the monastic term 'sisters'.[77]

Wet-nursing was work which married women could combine with housewifery and maternal duties. A degree of respectability was required for those employed by the gentry and the hospitals, and nurses generally came from more prosperous families.[78] The pay was comparatively high (for female work), and a number of women were employed in the countryside, especially around London. Although wet-nursing was thought of as a 'lazy' female job which contemporaries said was overpaid and spoiled women for 'real' work,[79] in fact it required skill and dedication to nurture a child through the first year of life. Mothers frequently made enquiries about possible nurses. In 1692 Mary Browne reported to Mrs Le Neve that two of those she thought suitable had sore breasts, 'but I hear of a very tidy woman . . . that hath a Child about a quarter old . . . the woman is very much commended'.[80] Wet-nursing could be hazardous work; syphillitic children infected their nurses. In one case, a man was given 40*s.* to pay for the cure of his wife who had been infected with a 'foul disease' by her parish nursling, Matthew Dionys.[81]

Teachers

A second major area of paid employment for women of the middling and upper ranks was teaching. Here again, women's traditional role as educators of their families blurred the professional category. Yet in contrast with the difficulties which women faced as professionals in health care areas, women's employment in education increased during the early modern period, with the proliferation of schools, especially boarding schools, for girls, the increasing employment of governesses for the education of the daughters of the wealthy at home, and the need for teachers in the growing number of charity schools for children of both sexes.

Middling and upper level women had educative roles as mistresses of servants and also as mothers. A few gentlewomen published advice for

[77] Moore, *St. Bartholomew's.* The duties of the matron and sisters were specified in *Orders and Ordinances for the Better Government of the Hospital of St Bartholomew the Lesse* (1552; rep. 1580, 1652).

[78] V. Fildes, *Wet Nursing: A History from Antiquity to the Present* (Oxford, 1988); F. Newell, 'Wet Nursing and Child Care in Aldenham, Hertfordshire, 1595–1726: Some Evidence on the Circumstances and Effects of Seventeenth-Century Child Rearing Practices', in V. Fildes (ed.), *Women as Mothers in Pre-Industrial England* (1990), 131–4.

[79] J. Ray, *A Collection of English Proverbs* (1678), 182.

[80] Norfolk RO, MC 44/20, 500 X. I.

[81] Guildhall, MS 11280A/3, indentures.

others; many more were actively engaged in instructing their children and servants in godliness. A few gentlewomen saw a role for themselves as educators of their own sex, chiefly in religion and piety. Before the Civil War, several women published maternal advice books, of which the countess of Lincoln's treatise urging mothers to breast-feed their own babies was the most specific.[82] While the educative work of wealthier women blurred occupational boundaries, during this period many women were paid to teach and to run schools.

Employment in teaching ranged from the informal, casual, and low-paid, to higher paid categories: governesses and gentlewomen who tutored the daughters of royalty. As in midwifery, training was informal; girls who were themselves educated could learn to teach by working in a school. The young Susanna Perwich was a teacher in her parents' school for girls at the time of her death in her twenties.[83] During the seventeenth century, girls' schools increased in number. Some were partnerships between husband and wife: Mr Twiford taught the neighbours' children to read, while his wife taught young women to sew and do needlework.[84] Other schools were established as businesses by women. The Perwich establishment was large, with over a hundred gentlewomen and their attendants in residence.[85]

Many schools had a brief history; they did not necessarily continue beyond the lifetime of the women involved. Thus the history of girls' schooling is difficult to trace, and more systematic study is needed to establish a better understanding of the profession of school teaching. We know from casual references in correspondence in the first half of the seventeenth century that girls' schools existed: Brilliana Harley wrote of her niece whose hatred of embroidery made her unwilling to return to Mrs Friend's school at Stepney.[86] Municipal records are another source: those of Leicester refer to a payment of £20 to Mr Hargrave towards building a loft in a church 'for the Gentlewomen schollars to his Wife'.[87] These seventeenth-century girls' schools were potentially profitable and employed trained professional staff. After the Restoration, boarding schools for young gentlewomen were more visible, and attracted visitors, Elizabeth Pepys among them.[88] Some were advertised in newspapers: 'Mrs Woodcock

[82] E. Clinton, *The Countesse of Lincolnes Nurserie* (1622).
[83] J. Batchiler, *The Virgins Pattern* (1661).
[84] R. Gough, *The History of Myddle*, ed. D. Hey (Harmondsworth, 1981), 61.
[85] Batchiler, *Virgins Pattern*, 14.
[86] BL, Harleian MS 382, D'Ewes correspondence, fo. 82.
[87] *Records of the Borough of Leicester, . . . 1603–1688*, ed. H. Stocks (Cambridge, 1923), 587.
[88] *The Diary of Samuel Pepys*, ed. R. Latham and W. Matthews, 11 vols. (1970–83), iv. 45.

FIG. 42. Woman school teacher. Women were increasingly employed in the education of young children. Although it was more usual for women to teach both sexes in a dame-school, here a female teacher is shown instructing a class of grammar-school boys

(Mrs Salmon's Daughter) who has kept school . . . near the Royal Exchange, is removing to a great house at Islington, for the air, to keep a boarding school.'[89] Girls' boarding schools developed more extensively in the eighteenth century.[90]

During the Civil War, there were dreams of educational reform and better schools, but limited interest in improvement of girls' education.[91] Dorothy Dury, whose second husband was one of the leading reformers,

[89] *Domestick Intelligencer, or news both from City and Country*, no. 75 (23 Mar. 1679).

[90] J. H. Plumb, 'The New World of Children in Eighteenth-Century England', *Past and Present*, 67 (1975), 64–95.

[91] F. Watson, *Encyclopaedia and Dictionary of Education*, 4 vols. (Bath, 1921), ii. 711; D. Gardiner, *English Girlhood at School: A Study of Women's Education through Twelve Centuries* (1929), 231; C. Webster, *The Great Instauration: Science, Medicine and Reform 1626–1660* (1975), 219–20.

was highly critical of the content of girls' schooling, as was Bathsua Makin.[92] But there are few examples of interest in serious education for girls. Later, Mary Astell was involved with an attempt to establish a college for ladies, but the proposal was thwarted by influential men who mistrusted an all-female institution, and damned it as a nunnery.[93]

Female teachers increased in numbers during the seventeenth century. Bathsua Reynolds, a gentlewoman, had a career in girls' schooling, first in the early seventeenth century as a teacher whose known skill drew pupils to the school of her father, Henry Reynolds, then as a tutor to Princess Elizabeth in the 1640s, and finally as the proprietor of a school at Tottenham High Cross around 1673.[94] Mrs Theodosia Alleine was a schoolmistress with around eighty pupils, twenty or thirty of whom were boarders.[95]

Some female teachers were specialists. Language teaching was one skill in demand for the daughters of the gentry. Brilliana Harley's sister Pelham had 'a frenchwoman for her daughters'.[96] Women taught mathematics and writing: Sarah Cole's arithmetical exercise book of 1685 survives, in which she has written 'scholar to Elizabeth Beane . . . mistress in the art of writing'.[97] In 1678, an anonymous woman wrote a treatise instructing women how to keep accounts.[98] Some teachers specialized in the fancy needlework which young gentlewomen were required to learn.

Scholarly gentlewomen were not always able to find suitable employment. Elizabeth Elstob, an Anglo-Saxon scholar, was reduced to keeping an ordinary school for children. Her educational principles, she ruefully confessed, were unappreciated:

> if I would teach to make Artificial flowers, a bit of Tapestry and the like, I should get more than I shall by instilling the Principles of Religion and Virtue, or by improving the Minds of Young Ladies, for those are things little regarded.[99]

[92] D. Dury, 'On the Education of Girls', in Turnbull, *Hartlib, Dury and Comenius*, 120–1; [B. Makin], *Essay to Revive the Antient Education of Gentlewomen* (1673).

[93] B. Hill, 'A Refuge from Men: The Idea of a Protestant Nunnery', *Past and Present*, 117 (1987), 107–30.

[94] V. Salmon, 'Bathsua Makin: A Pioneer Linguist and Feminist in Seventeenth Century England', in B. Asbach-Schnitker and J. Roggenhofer (eds.), *Neuere Forschungen zur Wortbildung und Historiographie der Linguistik* (Tubingen, 1987), 303–18.

[95] T. Alleine, *The Life and Death of Mr Joseph Alleine* . . . (1672), 91.

[96] PRO, SP 16/316/87, 21 Mar. 1636.

[97] Folger, MS V. b. 292.

[98] *Advice to the Women and Maidens of London* (1678).

[99] Bodl., MS Ballard 43, fo. 57; J. Nichols, *Literary Anecdotes of the Eighteenth Century*, 6 vols. (1812), iv. 127–39.

Not until late in life did Elstob find employment as a tutor to the duchess of Portland's children, where her friends hoped that she would find the time and energy to pursue her scholarly work.[100]

At the end of the seventeenth century, charity schools for the education of poor children provided more employment for female teachers. The women and men who founded the Society for Promoting Christian Knowledge (SPCK) in 1699 established nearly 900 charity schools before 1720.[101] The SPCK sought teachers with moral as well as educational principles. Of special note was the school in Chelsea under the direction of Mary Astell, initially for thirty poor girls. Wealthy women funded the school, and determined that it was 'always to be under ye Direction of Women'.[102]

Schoolteachers were licensed by bishops in seventeenth-century England, and, as in the case of midwives, unlicensed practitioners were investigated. Conformity to the Established Church and current political orthodoxy was expected. Several Nonconformist teachers were presented to the ecclesiastical authorities during the 1660s and 1670s, as was Elizabeth Loveman in 1665, teaching 'not licensed & Excommunicate'.[103] Quaker women who taught school in Essex were cited to the church courts for teaching without a licence and for refusing to teach the catechism.[104] At the time of the Jacobite uprisings in 1716, charity school governors imposed tests of loyalty to the Hanoverian regime. Mary Harbin, who had been a good teacher for sixteen years, 'an indefatigable mistress to the school, admirably qualified', refused to teach the children to pray for the Hanoverian monarchy and was dismissed.[105]

Although we have found no records of women being formally licensed, the visitation returns show that many women were instructing children, usually with the approval of their parishes. Increasingly, women teachers were employed in the charity schools, both to care for and to teach the children. In Bedfordshire, the bishop of Lincoln's visitations of 1717 and 1720 revealed that women were teaching in a number of charity schools: at Ampthill, about twenty-six children were 'taught to read write & cast

[100] Bodl., MS Ballard 43, fos. 1–89; V. Blain, P. Clements, and I. Grundy (eds.), *The Feminist Companion to Literature in English* (1990).

[101] M. G. Jones, *The Charity School Movement* (Cambridge, 1938), 351–2.

[102] R. Perry, *The Celebrated Mary Astell: An Early English Feminist* (Chicago, 1986), 233–43.

[103] G. L. Turner, *Original Records of Early Nonconformity*, 3 vols. (1911–14), ii. 1168, 1267–94.

[104] T. A. Davies, 'The Quakers in Essex, 1655–1725', D.Phil. diss; University of Oxford (1986), 187.

[105] Jones, *Charity School Movement*, 107.

accounts by a Master and two Dames'.[106] The school-dame retained something of the image of an ignorant old woman.

In evr'y Mart that stands on Britain's Isle,
In ev'ry Village less reveal'd to Fame,
Dwells there, in Cottage known about a Mile,
A Matron old, whom we School Mistress-name;
Who boasts unruly Brats with Birch to tame.[107]

Schoolteachers were, however, of varied abilities and qualifications. At the top end of the scale, the occupation of teacher was comparatively well paid. In 1673, Elizabeth Bowyer, a schoolmistress of West Ham, bequeathed her husband four houses and her sister one.[108] By the early eighteenth century, schoolmistresses in the charity schools could make up to £25 p.a., and often had a house provided.[109] Such pay was good for women, but men were usually paid more. At the Tiverton charity school, the master received £40 p.a. while the schoolmistress received £20, while in Bath a master was paid £30 p.a. with housing to teach fifty children, and a matron £10 'to look after teaching' and employ some of the children in knitting and sewing.[110] Rewards varied according to the woman's own social status—which determined her point of entry into the profession—and that of the pupils whom she was employed to instruct. In Norwich in 1570 a teacher of knitting was employed to teach the poor; in York in 1590 Janet Alderson was allowed 20*s.* for an unspecified period for teaching eight poor children to knit.[111]

Opportunities for other professional work were limited, and did not always provide a woman with a professional identity. Writing is one example. During the seventeenth century, women writers increased in number and published in a wider number of genres, yet few gained the title of author.[112] In the 1670s, Aphra Behn published plays, poems, and pamphlets, and developed a new form of writing in her prose fiction; she was probably the first woman to earn her living by her pen.[113] Female

[106] D. Busby (ed.), *The Bedfordshire Schoolchild: Elementary Education before 1902*, Bedfordshire Historical Record Society, 67 (1988), 12.

[107] W. Shenstone, *The School Mistress* (1742), sig. A3^{v}.

[108] PRO, PCC, Prob. reel 342, fos. 451–2, 6 Sept. 1673.

[109] Jones, *Charity School Movement*, 107.

[110] SPCK archives, CR1/6, Abstract Letters 1715–16, 23 Mar. and 2 May 1715.

[111] *The Norwich Census of the Poor, 1570*, ed. J. F. Pound, Norfolk Record Society, 40 (1971), 16; *York Civic Records*, ix [1588–90], ed. D. Sutton, Yorks. Arch. Society Record Series, 138 (1978), 86.

[112] P. Crawford, 'Women's Published Writings, 1600–1700', in M. Prior (ed.), *Women in English Society, 1500–1800* (1985), 265–74.

[113] S. H. Mendelson, *The Mental World of Stuart Women: Three Studies* (Brighton, 1987).

astrologers published almanac books.[114] While women writers have been intensively studied in recent times, we need more understanding of the economics of their work and of their relationships with printers and booksellers.[115]

Female artists, musicians, and actresses all found professional employment during the seventeenth century. Mary Beale ran a successful studio which also employed her husband and sons.[116] Women appeared on the stage from Restoration times onwards. They had a significant cultural impact and have attracted historical as well as contemporary interest.[117] Sopranos sang in Purcell's operas, and one, Arabella Hunt, taught singing and performed for Queen Mary II.[118] Some careers were comparatively unusual. Esther Inglis was a calligrapher, examples of whose exquisite work survive in the British Library, the Bodleian Libary, and the Folger Library.[119]

CRAFTS, TRADES, AND MULTIPLE OCCUPATIONS

Many wives of the middling rank worked with their husbands, when the occasion demanded. A contemporary ballad, 'The Good Wife's Fore-cast: or, the Kind and Loving Mother's Counsel to her Daughter after Marriage', set out the choice facing wives with reference to their economic contribution to the household: was it better for a wife to have her own occupation

[114] Astrologers include Mary Holden (1688, 1689); Sarah Jinner (1658, 1659, 1660, 1664); Dorothy Partridge (1694).

[115] A. Goreau, *The Whole Duty of a Woman: Female Writers in Seventeenth-Century England* (New York, 1984); M. P. Hannay (ed.), *Silent But for the Word: Tudor Women as Patrons, Translators and Writers of Religious Works* (Kent, Ohio, 1985); Crawford, 'Women's Published Writings'; M. Ferguson (ed.), *First Feminists: British Women Writers, 1578–1799* (Bloomington, Ind., 1985); Mendelson, *Mental World*; E. V. Beilin, *Redeeming Eve: Women Writers of the English Renaissance* (Princeton, 1987); E. Hobby, *Virtue of Necessity: English Women's Writing, 1649–1688* (1988); B. K. Lewalski, *Writing Women in Jacobean England* (Cambridge, Mass., 1993).

[116] Bodl., MS Rawlinson 572, Diary of Charles Beale, cited in C. Reeve, *Mrs Mary Beale, Paintress, 1633–1699* (Bury St Edmunds, 1994), 5–6, records her commissions and payments. See also, R. Jeffree and E. Walsh, *The Excellent Mrs Mary Beale* (1975).

[117] J. H. Wilson, *All the King's Ladies: Actresses of the Restoration Stage* (Chicago, 1958); A. Fraser, *The Weaker Vessel: Woman's Lot in Seventeenth-Century England* (1984), 418–39; E. Howe, *The First English Actresses: Women and Drama, 1660–1700* (Cambridge, 1992).

[118] O. Baldwin and T. Wilson, 'Purcell's Sopranos', *The Musical Times* (Sept. 1982), 602–9; *DNB*.

[119] See A. H. Scott-Elliot and E. Yeo, 'Calligraphic Manuscripts of Esther Inglis (1571–1624): A Catalogue', *The Papers of the Bibliographic Society of America*, 84 (1990), 11–63; Bodl., MS Bodl. 987.

and be paid wages, or run the household well and not delegate her responsibilities?

> Daughter, for those that has been brought up to a trade,
> When they are marry'd, what use can be made
> Of that imploy, when as they have a Family,
> To guide and govern as it ought to be?
> Then if that Calling, and work, it be done,
> All things beside that to Ruin must run . . .
> Maids by their trades to such a pass do bring,
> That they can neither brew, bake, wash, nor wring,
> Nor any work that's tending to good housewifry;
> This amongst many too often I see;
> Nay, their young children must pack forth to nurse,
> All is not got that is put in the Purse.[120]

Urban women of the middling rank were engaged in a variety of trades and occupations. Despite the myth of the omnipresent craft workshop, where the wife was assumed to share the husband's occupation, recent research indicates that women did not always pursue the same occupations as did their husbands as their main source of cash income. Instead, by the late seventeenth and early eighteenth centuries women were involved in a wide range of occupations, combining paid work with child-bearing and child-rearing.[121] Diversity and a willingness to turn to a variety of tasks characterized female labour in the town as well as in the country.

Formal apprenticeship was the standard means of training for a craft, and, in many cases, only those who had completed their apprenticeships and were free of their company or guild could work at a particular trade. After serving apprenticeships, women traded and could themselves take apprentices. In Reading in 1626, a widowed feltmaker took a male apprentice to learn the trade 'which she useth'.[122] The London company records listed women of varied marital status who participated in trades: widows who took apprentices, married women exercising their craft or trade as *femes sole*, and single women.

Although 'housewifery' and 'husbandry' were the two most commonly mentioned occupations in indentures, young women of the middling classes

[120] *The Good Wife's Fore-cast*, in *Roxburghe Ballads*, ed. W. Chappell and J. Ebsworth, 9 vols. in 8 (London and Hertford, 1866–99), vi. 349–50.

[121] Earle lists only one occupation for wives, although he recognizes that many had more. For example, he cites the case of one woman who used to take in washing and keep a herb shop; P. Earle, 'The Female Labour Market in London', *Economic History Review*, 2nd ser., 42 (1989), 339, 345 n. 50.

[122] J. M. Guilding (ed.), *Reading Records*, 4 vols. (1895), ii. 425.

were apprenticed to many other trades during the sixteenth and seventeenth centuries: carpenter, draper, mercer, capper, weaver, plumber, whittawer, cordwainer, silversmith, baker, fringe-maker, sieve-maker, housepainter, and pipe-maker.[123] There was an enormous range of occupations, beyond those listed here.[124] There were also regional differences in female apprenticeship: in York, unlike Coventry, no women were apprenticed to baking.[125]

During the early modern period, as the economy diversified and new industries developed, the guilds with their system of apprenticeship declined in importance. Within this changing structure, fewer female apprentices enrolled than male. Furthermore, as Alice Clark argued, their numbers declined compared with the medieval period. No one has yet quantified this assertion, although our impression from lists of apprentices is that Clark was correct.[126] Women were apprenticed to a more limited range of occupations than had been the case in the earlier periods. They were most likely to be apprenticed to occupations connected with the female work role, especially housewifery.[127]

A full study of women's participation in guild business has yet to be undertaken. In Coventry, no ordinances forbade women to hold offices. Although there is no evidence to prove that women did not vote in the election of officers,[128] it is difficult to argue from this absence that women did vote, and it seems unlikely that they participated in guild or company business in the early modern period. Prior's study of Oxford shows that sometimes women were not even listed as guild members, although widows were known to have been trading. No records suggest that women did attend guild meetings.[129] In some cases, however, women shared in the corporate rites of their companies: those in the Merchant Taylors had the right to dine quarterly with other company members.[130]

Most trading, unlike guild crafts, could be undertaken by single women

[123] Martha Andrews was apprenticed to a pipe-maker in 1686; *Transcription of the 'Poor Book' of . . . Westbury-on-Trym, 1656–1698*, ed. H. J. Wilkins (Bristol, 1910), 194.

[124] L. Fox, 'The Coventry Guilds and Trading Companies', in *Essays in Honour of Philip B. Chatwin*, Birmingham Archaeological Society (Oxford, 1962), 13–26; T. R. Forbes, 'Case of the Casual Chirurgeon', *Yale Journal of Biological Medicine*, 51 (1978), 583–8. See also K. D. M. Snell, *Annals of the Labouring Poor*, (Cambridge, 1985) 270–319.

[125] D. Willen, 'Guildswomen in the City of York, 1560–1700', *The Historian*, 46 (1984), 209; Fox, 'Coventry Guilds and Trading Companies'. 19.

[126] M. Kowaleski and J. M. Bennett, 'Crafts, Gilds, and Women in the Middle Ages: Fifty Years after Marian K. Dale', *Signs*, 14 (1989), 474–88; C. Barron, 'The "Golden Age" of Women in Medieval London', *Reading Medieval Studies*, 15 (1989), 35–58; Clark, *Working Life*, 150–235.

[127] For an example of apprenticeship to housewifery: Devon RO, Axminster parish, R7/2/2 no 9, 1697.

[128] Fox, 'Coventry Guilds and Trading Companies', 26.

[129] Prior, 'Urban Economy', 103.

[130] Clark, *Working Life*, 179.

without a formal apprenticeship. In this brief discussion of the trades in which women were engaged, our main purpose is to show the diversity of female work, as well as the ways in which gender constrained female employment. Women did not engage in the work-force as equals of men, although obviously many of the middling women in trade earned more from their labours than did poor men. But, in these middling trades, women were less likely than men to have served an apprenticeship, and less likely to have pursued their trade without interruption. Many were wives and mothers, responsible for a household and children. The structure of work was inimical to their full participation. Tools, equipment, and stock needed for trades was often bequeathed to sons and servants rather than to widows.[131]

Single women could trade on their own account. By the custom of London, a married woman who pursued a trade separate from that of her husband could trade legally as a *feme sole*; if she worked in the same trade, 'she doth it as a Servant'.[132] Craft work by women was not necessarily linked with their husbands' work.[133]

Many widows of middling status were able to make a living either at their own or their husbands' trades. In some cases, widows continued a husband's business, either on their own, or with male assistance. Sometimes they worked as widows for many years; in other cases they seem to have continued only until sons could take over.[134] The Fishmongers' Company accounts over the course of the seventeenth century include payments to widows of various tradesmen, including a plumber, plasterers, founders, and painters.[135] One widow kept the company's 'Engine' for five years,[136] another was responsible 'for keeping the company's armour clean and serviceable',[137] while yet another looked after the Fishmongers' barge.[138] In 1604 the Grocers' Company paid widow Chaunton 6*s*. 'for mending &

[131] S. Wright, ' "Churmaids, Huswyfes and Hucksters": The Employment of Women in Tudor and Stuart Salisbury', in L. Charles and L. Duffin (eds.), *Women and Work in Pre-Industrial England* (1985), 112–3.

[132] W. Bohun, *Privilegia Londini; Or, the Laws, Customs, and Privileges of London* (1702), 124–5.

[133] Cf. medieval Havering, where McIntosh found that at least two-thirds of the married women in craft activities were the wives of farmers; M. McIntosh, *A Community Transformed: Havering, 1500–1620* (Cambridge, 1991), 174.

[134] S. J. Wright, 'The Elderly and the Bereaved in Eighteenth-Century Ludlow', in M. Pelling and R. M. Smith (eds.), *Life, Death, and the Elderly: Historical Perspectives* (1991), 112–19.

[135] Guildhall, MS 5561/1, Fishmongers' Accounts, 1638, to widow Barley.

[136] Guildhall, MS 5561/1, Fishmongers' Accounts, 1648.

[137] Guildhall, MS 5561/1, Fishmongers' Accounts, 1656, 1658.

[138] Guildhall, MS 5570/5, Fishmongers' Court Ledger 5, p. 812 (1696).

trimming' the company's muskets.[139] None of this work was specifically female labour. In other cases widows were also employed in more conventionally female areas: Isabell King was paid for removing rubbish from the Hall,[140] and widow Garland kept the company garden.[141] Sometimes it is clear that the widows did not actually perform the work themselves; appointing a widow their plumber, the Grocers' Company stipulated 'so as she find and provide a sufficient man from time to time to attend the master wardens, as occasion shall require'.[142] While the records show a number of patterns, rarely do we gain insight into the widows' motives.

Widows who ran businesses kept the profits. After the Fire, rebuilding work was lucrative. The Fishmongers paid the widows of a plumber and a painter comparatively large sums: £127 and £46. Further payments to both show that their employment (and businesses) continued.[143] The last payment to a woman in the Fishmongers' building accounts for the seventeenth and early eighteenth centuries was Mrs Dutton: £4. 10*s.* 0*d.* for the company's arms in painted glass for the hall in 1686–8.[144]

The textile trades occupied many women. Most women could spin, work which was comparatively poorly paid. Weaving required a loom and was more often men's work, but some women worked as weavers. A widow arguing against eviction after twenty-eight years' residence claimed that she needed the house so that she might follow 'her trade of a weaver'.[145] Millinery was female specific, but subject to the vagaries of fashion. Needleworkers and seamstresses could earn up to £1 weekly. Earle suggests that such jobs as mantua (loose-gown) maker, milliner, and seamstress were practically the only ones which contemporaries though suitable for the daughters of respectable people.[146] Girls were more likely to be apprenticed to needlework by their families than they were by a parish.[147]

Trading and dealing were pursued by women as well as men. Again, the evidence is scattered. An Elizabethan widow in Manchester who traded as a dealer in yarn and cloth was probably the wealthiest woman in the city.[148]

[139] Guildhall, MS 11571/9, Grocers' Accounts, fo. 106^{v}. Our thanks to Joe Ward for this and other references to the Grocers' Company, and for much useful discussion of women's participation in the London livery companies.

[140] Guildhall, MS 5561/2, Fishmongers' Accounts, 1660.

[141] Guildhall, Fishmongers' Company, Calendar to the Minutes, vol. 1 (1592–1600), 5.

[142] Guildhall, MS 11588/2, Orders of the Court of Assistants, Grocers' Company, p. 310.

[143] Guildhall, MS 5561/2, Fishmongers' Accounts, 1668–70, p. 201.

[144] Guildhall, MS 5561/3, Fishmongers' Accounts, 1682–1706, p. 60.

[145] *Warwick Sessions Order Book, 1657–1665*, 216.

[146] Earle, 'Female Labour Market in London', 342, 344.

[147] Snell, *Annals*, 291–4.

[148] Willan, *Elizabethan Manchester*, 93.

Katherine Chidley was a supplier of textiles to Cromwell's army.[149] There were female 'middlemen' or intermediaries in corn. The Norwich mayor's court records that Mary, wife of Robert Uttinge, bought corn, ground it at Trouse mill, and sold meal in the market.[150] Before the water-way of Wiveton was obstructed in 1639, Margaret Williams had a profitable trade which allowed her to be charitable to the poor. She exchanged beer for her coals 'to her great advantage' and then sold beer to strangers in the port and coals to the poor. When the water-way was blocked, transport costs halted all her business.[151] The same obstruction wrecked the trade of a widowed naval supplier: 'her profit by vending of her bisket for Ireland have been worth to her £10 per annum to 3 ships.'[152] Although the evidence is fragmentary, it confirms a pattern already discerned of the diversity of female workers. Their marital status varied, from single to married and widowed.[153]

Wives who engaged in their husbands' trades risked prosecution. The wife of a Chester cooper who bought and sold a ton of whale oil was pardoned because she had acted innocently and without her husband's consent.[154] The London carpenters forbade wives to go to the wharves to collect timber when their husbands were present in the city.[155] Although it may seem that a husband and wife ran a business together, in many cases wives were so busy with their children and households that they did not know how to manage the trade when they were widowed. The widow of Augustin Greenwood in Lancaster knew nothing of his affairs, 'nor had ocation, only to govern the famely'. In another Lancaster case, a husband fled leaving his wife with five small children, so she was reduced to making candles and soap.[156]

Femes sole and widows could trade as printers. Moreover, widows could transfer their right to a second husband.[157] There are hints that journeymen in England, like those in Germany, attempted to limit women's participation

[149] *BDBR*.

[150] *Minutes of the Norwich Court of Mayoralty, 1630–1631*, ed. W. L. Sachse, Norfolk Record Society, 15 (1942), 91.

[151] PRO SP6/424/53.

[152] Ibid.

[153] Earle suggests that widows were more successful in trade than *femes sole*; P. Earle, *The Making of the English Middle Class: Business, Society and Family Life in London, 1660–1730* (1989), 167.

[154] *Calendar of Chester City Council Minutes, 1603–1642*, ed. M. J. Groombridge, Record Society of Lancs and Cheshire, 106 (1956), 60 (22 Dec. 1612).

[155] *Records of the Worshipful Company of Carpenters*, ed. B. Marsh (Oxford, 1915), iii. 15, 31.

[156] *The Autobiography of William Stout of Lancaster, 1665–1752*, ed. J. D. Marshall (Manchester, 1967), 125, 132.

[157] Clark, *Working Life*, 161–7; M. Bell, 'Mary Westwood', *Publishing History*, 23 (1988), 5–66.

in printing. In 1635, the Stationers' Company agreed to restrict juvenile labour at the petition of younger printers; no master printer was permitted to allow 'any Girles, Boyes or others to take off anie sheets from the tinpin of the presse, but hee that pulleth at the presse shall take off every sheete himself'.[158]

As the retail trades developed in London later in the seventeenth century, an important avenue of work opened up for women. Indeed, work opportunities in shops may help explain the attraction of London for a growing female work-force. Female participation in the retail and brokerage trades can be documented through the probate inventories of widows and single women.[159] Women also ran the second-hand clothing trade.[160]

By the early eighteenth century, single women were responsible for about 10 per cent of London businesses. In the 1720s, about one-third of the London women who had fire insurance policies were in the food and drink trades; another third were in the textiles and clothing trades. Pawnbroking was the registered occupation of about 10 per cent of the women.[161] Following Alice Clark, we would stress the omnipresence of female economic activity. There were female coach manufacturers, licencees of hackney coaches, housepainters.[162] In London, comparatively few widows ran inherited businesses. More common were women with their own occupations of a distinctively female character, such as providing lodgings, food, and services.[163] Few were businesses in which women were likely to make large profits.

One expanding area of economic activity in which women were prominent was that of providing services. During the seventeenth century, the growth of English towns and cities stimulated a demand for accommodation and food. Women, who had always been providers of lodgings, food, and drink, took advantage of growing trade. Middling women were victuallers and innkeepers. A widow, Maud Ringall, said that when the Wiveton was obstructed in 1639, she was almost wholly impoverished by the bank, 'for she was wont to make 7 or 8 beds in one night and now she make

[158] Clark, *Working Life*, 166.

[159] Weatherill, 'A Possession of One's Own', 148.

[160] B. Lemire, 'Disorderly Women and the Consumer Market: Women's Work and the Second-Hand Clothing Trade in England, 1660–1800', in *Dress, Culture and Commerce: The English Clothing Trade before the Factory* (1997), ch. 4. We are grateful to Dr Lemire for allowing us to read her chapter before publication.

[161] Earle, *English Middle Class*, 169–70.

[162] Bodl., MS Rawlinson D. 28, fo. 22; MS Eng. misc b. 31, fo. 167, Wardrobe accounts (furniture seller, joiner); M. Pelling, 'Medical Practice in Early Modern England', in Prest (ed.), *The Professions*, 106 (housepainter).

[163] Earle, *English Middle Class*, 173.

not one in one night for strangers'.[164] Female innkeepers could be among the upper ranks in the city of London; Mary Young, the widowed daughter of a brewer, whose second husband was Isaac Penington, Lord Mayor of London in 1642, kept an inn at Whitefriars at which many Puritan clergy lodged before the Civil War.[165] During the Civil War, women provided accommodation and nursing for soldiers. The Manchester records list many payments over the period 1643–5, such as to a widow for providing beds for sick soldiers.[166] Sometimes we learn incidentally that women were involved in the business of accommodation; two Manchester women whose probate inventories mentioned nine or ten-room houses probably kept inns or lodging houses.[167] Such work could extend over a long period; a case in 1680 referred to a deceased sailor, Robert Curtis, who had lodged at Alice Beck's house whenever he returned from the sea for twenty years.[168] By around 1730, many London widows owned houses and so could take in lodgers or rent out rooms.[169]

Women's position as brewers in early modern England is currently the subject of debate. Brewing in the medieval period was an activity women could take up as the family's situation demanded. In Havering, Marjorie McIntosh found that one wife brewed commercially when her husband was getting established, retired in his prosperous middle years, and resumed when he ceased work in his late fifties.[170] In the early modern period, however, women were increasingly excluded from the brewing trade. Those who brewed ale and those who sold it were attacked as dishonest and disorderly in a wide range of popular literature. Judith Bennett argues that, as the licensing scheme extended, the authorities, whether church or civic, assumed that the market would be better if run by men.[171] Bennett has also contended that a major factor in women's exclusion was misogyny. Although misogyny may well have been a factor, we need a history of misogyny which explains why it takes specific forms at certain periods. In early modern times, it does appear that, at the middling level of society, the

[164] PRO, SP 424/53.

[165] *DNB*; V. Pearl, *London and the Outbreak of the Puritan Revolution* (1961), 179.

[166] PRO, Commonwealth Exchequer Papers, SP 28/10, fo. 378; Indemnity Papers, SP 24/4, fo. 26^{v}; J. P. Earwaker (ed.), *The Constables' Accounts of the Manor of Manchester . . . 1612 to 1647* (Manchester, 1891–2), ii. 102, 120, 123, 115, 121.

[167] Willan, *Elizabethan Manchester*, 107.

[168] Corporation of London RO, MC 6/394 A, 21 Feb. 1680. When he was ill she took care of him, spent money, then paid for his funeral. No relatives ever visited.

[169] Earle, *Making of the English Middle Class*, 169–70.

[170] McIntosh, *Havering*, 132–4.

[171] J. M. Bennett, 'Misogyny, Popular Culture, and Women's Work', *History Workshop*, 31 (1991), 166–88.

active participation of women in various kinds of public work was becoming socially unacceptable.

One of the most significant female occupations in early modern times was that of alewife. While many women who held licences themselves were widows and indeed poor, wives of middling status might work in alehouses for which licences were held by their husbands. Thus alehouses kept by middling status women were often hidden from the records, although it is clear from other evidence that women did the actual work of drawing beer and serving customers. For women of all ranks, keeping an alehouse was an occupation frequently pursued in conjunction with other housewifery tasks or even with prostitution. Not surprisingly, keeping an alehouse or inn was not an altogether respectable female occupation: an Oxford clergyman refused to proceed with marriage because his betrothed was forced to keep an inn in order to survive after her father's death.[172]

A London court case illustrates several features of women's work in alehouses. Around 1700, ale was being sold in the house of Christopher Bannister of East Smithfield when a brawl broke out which put the parties into court. Bannister himself was nominally the keeper of the public house, but gave two other occupations: officer of the Marshalsea court, and the keeping of a gunlock maker's shop, 'and thereby gets a livelihood'. In practice, Bannister had nothing to do with the public house trade. His daughter Anne explained that her father 'never concerns himself with the drinking trade in his house and never draws any drink for any persons within or without his house'. Anne declared that it was her mother who 'manages the drinking trade', although, in her own deposition, Mary Bannister had stated in conventional terms that 'her husband keeps a victualling house', thereby obscuring her own role. Anne herself, although she was noted as maintained by her father, clearly worked in the alehouse and was washing in the cellar when the dispute broke out.[173] Work in the Bannister household shaded off into the disreputable. One woman working at prostitution had requested a private room for herself and a man. Her fee of 5*s.* for the sexual encounter was higher than many women would earn in a week.[174] The episode raises interesting questions about the doctrine of coverture, suggesting that perhaps it was more necessary in the later seventeenth century than earlier.

Prostitution provided employment for women of varying social ranks. The more organized work in brothels usually involved women above the

[172] OA, MS Oxf. Dioc. papers c. 29, 1679–86, fos. 83^{v}–8.

[173] Guildhall, Papers re matters in the peculiar jurisdiction of St Katharine, MS 9731/101, no. 6, 26 depositions.

[174] Ibid. Deposition 9.

poorest. Although the fees charged were higher than for casual prostitution, the women who worked in brothels could pay 4*s.* to 6*s.* per week rent, and might hand over up to three-quarters of their earnings to the brothel-keeper. Some brothel-keepers, around half of whom were women, would move the prostitutes between their houses to cater for demand. The rewards for keeping a house were alleged to be considerable. One 'May's wife without Aldgate' was said to have earned £300 over three years 'by bawdrye'. Some of the male brothel-keepers who were on the subsidy lists paid sums which put them in the upper third of London society.[175] In this culture, where Sir Horatio Palavicino sent his servant searching London and Guildford for 'some mayden to abuse who had not been dealte with all before',[176] women were a commodity for male consumption whose value diminished after they were used. Prostitution in women of the middling and upper ranks also restricted their opportunities in other social situations.

By whatever means earnings were accrued, another service provided by widows and single women was the investment of capital. Widows especially were a significant source of rural and urban capital. Studies from probate inventories indicate that widows, together with well-endowed single people, were the most important providers of sums of money for lending from 1660 to 1800.[177] Among the Norwich money lenders were many widows with cash to invest.[178] Widows and single women were centrally important in the economies of village life. Widows on average had lent more than two-thirds of their moveable assets at the time of death. A single woman, Elizabeth Parkin, had a mixed portfolio of investment; during the Restoration, female investors were among the first to finance the public debt.[179] Yet London bankruptcy records suggest that women were twice as likely to be investors in businesses run by men, rather than act as independent traders.[180]

[175] I. Archer, *The Pursuit of Stability: Social Relations in Elizabethan London* (Cambridge, 1991), 211–15; id., 'Governors and Governed in Late Sixteenth-Century London, *c.* 1560–1603: Studies in the Achievement of Stability', D.Phil. diss., University of Oxford (1988), 305–30.

[176] Bridewell court book, quoted in Archer, 'Governors and Governed', 321–2.

[177] B. A. Holderness, 'Credit in a Rural Community, 1600–1800: Some Neglected Aspects of Probate Inventories', *Midland History*, 3 (1975), 100–2; B. A. Holderness, 'Widows in Pre-Industrial Society: An Essay upon their Economic Functions' in R. M. Smith (ed.), *Land, Kinship and Life-Cycle* (Cambridge, 1984), 423–42.

[178] P. Corfield, 'A Provincial Capital in the Late Seventeenth Century: The Case of Norwich', in P. Clark and P. Slack (eds.), *Crisis and Order* (1972), 295–6.

[179] B. A. Holderness, 'Credit in English Rural Society before the Nineteenth Century, with Special Reference to the Period 1650–1720', *Agricultural History Review*, 24 (1976), 105.

[180] Earle, *Making of the English Middle Class*, 167–8.

ROYAL, CIVIC, AND INSTITUTIONAL EMPLOYMENT

Women of the middling and upper ranks were employed as public office-holders by royal households, civic institutions, charitable bodies, city companies, and parishes. In this significant category of female employment, work was defined by a familiar grid: the duties of the office, the woman's marital status, and her behaviour. The labour was similar to work women might perform elsewhere, but their status differed because they held office in their own right; at court, the Groom of the Stole served as a female companion, but was a member of the royal household. Depending on the nature of the work, women were required to be married or single; a hospital matron was expected to be a wife or widow, but a maid of honour at court must be single. Office-holders took oaths, and held their posts on good conduct; a maid of honour would be dismissed in disgrace if she were pregnant. Subject to good behaviour, however, women could be employed in certain offices for many years. Some female office-holders were responsible for the behaviour of others; a hospital matron supervised the nurses or sisters.

Especially in the reign of a female monarch, the royal household offered the richest rewards for female office-holders. Noblewomen competed for posts for themselves and their female relatives. Although their wages were small, and court dresses expensive, royal servants enjoyed lucrative perquisites. In addition to board, lodging, and salaries, female office-holders had opportunities for patronage.[181] Royal servants also received customary rewards, such as pensions,[182] and dowries on their marriages or those of their daughters; Princess Anne contributed £5,000 when Sarah Churchill's daughter, Henrietta, was married.[183]

Ladies in the royal households had duties and responsibilities. For example, the mistress of the robes in Elizabeth's chamber was responsible for the care of the queen's vast wardrobe, and for overseeing the labour of those who made, cleaned, mended, and altered it.[184] No special training was necessary for such an office, beyond that which any aristocratic young woman might receive, and some instruction in the specific requirements of the household. Furthermore, court ladies performed important functions

[181] See C. Merton, 'The Women who Served Queen Mary and Queen Elizabeth: Ladies, Gentlewomen and Maids of the Privy Chamber, 1553–1603', Ph.D. diss., University of Cambridge (1991).

[182] PRO, Book of Warrants (Charles II), PRO LS 13/252; thanks to Gerald Aylmer for this reference.

[183] Harris, *Passion for Government*, 78–9.

[184] J. Arnold, *Queen Elizabeth's Wardrobe Unlock'd* (Leeds, 1988), 104.

for their families. They kept an ear out for news, and corresponded with distant kin.

Female courtiers were well placed to ask for and to dispense patronage and support. The terms of their power was influenced by the character of the monarch. In the reigns of Charles II, James II, and William III, the monarchs required sexual services. Royal mistresses were sometimes appointed to offices; Charles II made some of his mistresses ladies of the bedchamber to his queen. But the benefits mistresses received came from their informal services to the Stuart kings rather than their formal duties at court. Mistresses were recognized as powerful politicians and patrons.[185] To a similar degree, close personal friends of the monarch could profit. In Elizabeth's reign, clients sought the queen's support through her female friends; in the 1590s the Fishmongers' Company tried unsuccessfully to present the countess of Warwick with three gilt bowls to secure her support for a suit.[186] In the reign of Queen Anne, female courtiers exercised considerable patronage, although the extent of their political power remains debatable.[187]

Outside the court, various civic bodies and institutions employed middling women. Cities and towns appointed female prison warders. Women were keepers of gaols and houses of correction.[188] The matron of Bridewell was paid a salary, given a maid, and paid various sums for prisoners' meals and the use of her beds. She was responsible for keeping secure all the prisoners committed to her, and occupied an intermediate position in the prison hierarchy. In 1608 when benevolences were paid to the Bridewell employees, the clerk received £5, the matron, steward, and porter 30*s.* each, and the beadle 20*s.*[189]

Institutions for the care of the aged, the sick, and orphans governed by civic authorities or separate boards all employed women. One London institution for the care of the aged, the Hospital of St Katharine by the Tower, was under the governance of a master, three sisters, and some brothers. The sisters were poor gentlewomen, usually widows, who were appointed by the patron, usually at the suit of relatives or powerful neigh-

[185] Their role is the subject of the doctoral thesis of S. Wynne, 'The Mistresses of Charles II, 1660–1685', Ph.D. diss., University of Cambridge (forthcoming).

[186] Guildhall, Fishmongers' Company, Calendar to the Minute Books, 1592–1600, 24 Sept. and 1 Oct. 1594.

[187] R. O. Bucholz, *The Augustan Court: Queen Anne and the Decline of Court Culture* (Stanford, Calif., 1993), 156–72. See also Ch. 7, below.

[188] *Quarter Sessions Order Book, 1642–1649*, ed. B. C. Redwood, Sussex Record Society, 54 (1954), 89.

[189] A. J. Copeland, 'Extracts from Bridewell Court Books', *Under the Dome*, 12 (1903), 7–8, 107, 120.

bours.[190] During the seventeenth century, the sisters and brothers were paid the same salaries, namely £8 p.a.,[191] and shared in the distribution of fees from christenings, marriages, or burials in their church.[192] The governor's wife was not directly employed but was expected, like the wives of other high-ranking office-holders, to perform a charitable role. In 1697 there were extensive complaints against St Katharine's governor, Sir James Butler, but several beadswomen averred that his wife 'was a very charitable and kind woman'. His housekeeper, a 40-year-old widow, said that Butler's wife had sent cordials and chickens to the almswomen.[193] In other localities, women served as officials administering medical poor relief.[194]

The records of St Bartholomew's, a London hospital, provide a case study of one employer of women from the middling to the plebeian level. Some positions, such as that of the matron, nurses, and cook, were salaried, while other specialist work was paid by item, as was the healing of scaled heads. Some employees were paid by contract, including the woman butcher who supplied the hospital.[195]

The matron, whose position was 'an Office of great Charge and Credit', was responsible for overseeing all the women and children in the hospital, and the work of the sisters, nurses, laundry staff, and cook. She was paid an annual salary, which in 1642 was £6. 8*s.* 4*d.*, plus 40*s.* for a servant. (In comparison, the physician was paid £33. 6*s.* 8*d.* and the surgeon £40.)[196] In 1599, the matron had been paid £3. 6*s.* 8*d.*, while the female cook was paid £8. The cook's higher wage may have included responsibility for some provisioning, or the matron's lower cash wages may have been balanced out by her perquisites.[197] The matrons appear to have been of the middling social level; many served for long periods. Elizabeth Collston was matron for over twenty-five years from 1597.[198] (Since Henry Collston was paid as a porter, the couple may have been a husband-and-wife team.) Margaret Blague, matron from 1643 to 1675, was the widow of a barber-surgeon when she was appointed.[199] Matrons enjoyed perquisites in addition to

[190] BL, MS Lansdowne 161, fo. 166, petition on behalf of widow Webb (1597).

[191] Jamison, *History of St Katharine*, 85–6, 89–90.

[192] Ibid. 90.

[193] Guildhall, MS 9740, St Katharine by the Tower, Depositions at Lord Somers Visitation, fos. 15, 21–21^{v}.

[194] D. Willen, 'Women in the Public Sphere', *Sixteenth Century Journal*, 19 (1988), 559–75.

[195] London, St Bartholomew's, MS HB1/3, 1609, fo. 430.

[196] London, St Bartholomew's, MS HB1/6.

[197] Payments for cloth for the hospital's liveries were at the rate of 8*s.* per yard for the matron, 7*s.* for beadles, and 7*s.* for sisters in 1589.

[198] Ellen Smyth was employed from 1559 to 1584, Margaret Blague from 1643 to 1675, and Mary Sanders from 1679 to 1714.

[199] N. J. M. Kerling, 'A Seventeenth Century Hospital Matron: Margaret Blague', *London and Middlesex Archaeological Society Transactions*, 22 (1970), 30–6.

formal gratuities and pensions; in 1665 Matron Blague, 'for her constant great paynes' at the time of the plague, was given an extra ten years on the twenty-one year lease on a house occupied by her son-in-law.[200]

A sister's (or nurse's) place was worth wages, clothing, and food. (The term 'nurse' was mentioned first in 1652.)[201] Nurses might even receive pensions: in 1589 St Bartholomew's granted a pension to a sister, with the proviso that she was 'allwaies to give good wordes to the governers'.[202] Several hospital appointees were initially on probation in their places; in 1661 Elizabeth Culpitt, widow, a helper at the Lock hospital, was 'upon trial of her merits & demeanor' at Kingsland hospital.[203] In 1654 St Bartholomew's dismissed a buttery woman for marrying,[204] as, earlier, St Thomas's hospital had dismissed a female employee suspecting she *would* marry.[205] A widow appointed as a nurse was required to give a bond of £40 to discharge the house for her two children, and to give a true account of items with which she was entrusted. In 1665, the year of the plague, there were fifteen nurses and several sisters working at St Bartholomew's.

How did women get places? The records suggest the usual mix of patronage, service, and bribery. At St Bartholomew's in 1662, a widow was recommended to a sister's place by Mr Hall, one of the court present at the meeting.[206] In 1652 a nurse and helper who had served for five years was promised the next vacant sister's place.[207] At the hospital of St Katharine by the Tower, a place seeker complained of corruption; Mrs Burman alleged that she had paid £44 to a middleman for a sister's place, but, when a position fell vacant, the governor Sir James Butler appointed someone else. The middleman claimed that he had spent all the money treating Sir James at the tavern on her account. When Mrs Burman finally gained the place, she found that she had no lodgings and was forced to pay 30*s.* for six months' accommodation. Sir James declared that she was an 'ungrateful rebel and told her he was Governor of Bedlam and he would put her there'.[208]

The hospital's supervision of its employees was not sex specific, but there was a gender component. The governors enforced what they thought were proper forms of womanly behaviour. In 1662, when the buttery woman and five or six sisters were in trouble for their uncivil language to each other and

[200] Moore, *St Bartholomew's Hospital*, ii. 327. [201] Ibid. 764. [202] Ibid. 761.
[203] A buttery woman, Anne Spender, was admitted on trial in 1659.
[204] Moore, *St Bartholomew's Hospital*, ii. 764.
[205] E. M. McInnes, *St Thomas' Hospital* (1963), 36.
[206] London, St Bartholomew's, Minutes of the Board of Governors, MS H1/5, fo. 303.
[207] Moore, *St Bartholomew's Hospital*, ii. 764.
[208] Guildhall, MS 21,041B, An account of St Catherines 1695–1699, written 1803, unfoliated.

for creating a disturbance, they were admonished and told not to be 'bitter and Unwomanly'.[209] The hospital demanded celibacy of unmarried female employees: one woman was to be retained 'so long as she shall continue a single woman of a good life & Conversation'.[210]

PUBLIC HOUSEWIFERY

Thus far, women's work has been surveyed in terms of occupations. Such an approach is frustrating, because it includes only a small part of the work women performed. We know that women were working in massive numbers, even though there are very few clues in the official records. If we look carefully, however, we can trace women's omnipresence along the lines of men's formal professional work roles.

In addition to the possibility of employment in their own right, married women of the middling and higher ranks were frequently assumed to be part of the 'team' which was hired for various kinds of urban civic employment. Women's roles as housekeepers, overseeing servants and children, were extended into a further category of economic activity, as various institutions assumed that the men whom they employed had wives who would contribute to the work involved. Because this wifely contribution was taken for granted by men, it has been invisible in discussions of work in the early modern period. More was involved than is implied in the discussion of a 'family economy': aristocratic and middling wives actually performed a significant proportion of the labour for which their husbands were paid. In this sense, women's housewifery became public work.

Even gentlewomen, such as the wife of the lieutenant of the Tower of London, could be called upon to work. The supervision of certain exalted female prisoners was delegated; James I permitted either the wife or daughter-in-law of Sir George More to be present when the countess of Somerset received visitors.[211] The wives of hospital employees, such as those of the sexton and the beadles, were also routinely employed, judging from entries in St Bartholomew's accounts 'to the Steward and his wife', and from the purchase of items related to female textile and cleaning work, such as flax and ashes.[212] Occasionally the wives of parish officials were paid

[209] London, St Bartholomew's, Minutes, fo. 292.
[210] London, St Bartholomew's, Treasurers' ledgers, H1/5, fo. 6 (18 Dec. 1649).
[211] A. J. Kempe (ed.), *The Loseley Manuscripts* (1836), 398.
[212] London, St Bartholomew's, HB 1/7, fo. 13.

directly; St Christopher's, London, paid the wife of the sexton 3*s.* for keeping a foundling until the nurse arrived.[213]

More frequently, the records obscure the work of wives. When the Grocers' Company paid a widow 18*s.* 4*d.* owed to her husband for miscellaneous work, including the provision of three garlands and nine dozen nosegays, we can infer that the making of garlands and nosegays was actually her own work.[214] Beadles' wives were often employed on the occasion of company feasts, or for miscellaneous jobs. The Fishmongers usually paid a gratuity rather than a wage; it followed that the wives were constantly dependent on good will. In 1638, the beadle's wife was given 20*s.* to mend the company's banners and streamers. On other occasions, when the beadle himself was named as being paid a similar sum for the same work, we can assume that his wife was still mending the banners.[215] Similarly, in the Founders' Company, the wife and children of John Falkener the clerk had long careers in the service of the company.[216] Widows of company officers might be required to serve in lieu of their husbands; should the accountant of the Fishmongers die during his two-year term of office, his widow as executrix was required to present the accounts.[217] Even if wives were neither directly nor indirectly employed, their own working opportunities might be restricted because of their husbands' work. The wife of a Norwich man hired to care for the infected poor in 1625 was forbidden to go out unless she retired from company, walked with a white wand, and observed a candle-lighting curfew.[218]

Some work seems of lower status, but it may have been performed by women of middling rank who had fallen on hard times. Civic bodies employed the widows of their former employees, thereby saving the payment of pensions. The 'Company Scourers' employed to clean the Fishmongers' Hall usually served for many years; the widow Joan Crouch worked for twenty years 'in scouring the vessells and Pewter and washing and cleaning the rooms at the hall and garden', retiring with a pension and further relief in 1641. At this point she was 'in her old age taken on the leftside wth a lameness that she cannot stir or feed herself without help' and

[213] *The Account Book of the Parish of St Christopher Le Stocks . . . London, 1662–1685*, ed. E. Freshfield (1895), 39. She was paid again in 1682–3; ibid. 41.

[214] Guildhall, MS 11571/9, Grocers' Accounts 1607–8, fo. 271.

[215] Guildhall, MS 5561/1, Fishmonger's Accounts 1638 and 1648. In 1657 Whiting was paid 40*s.* The work included the repair of the banners and streamers and she was paid for making a new silk curtain.

[216] G. Parsloe, *Wardens' Accounts of the Worshipful Company of Founders of the City of London, 1497–1681* (1964), pp. liii, 291–333. In 1641 the wife of a company officer was paid 2*s.* 6*d.* for dressing dinners for the year; ibid. 313.

[217] Guildhall, MS 556/2, p. 246.

[218] Norfolk RO, Mayor's Court Book 1624–34, fo. 66.

was paying 2*s.* weekly to another woman to help her 'in this her great extremity'.[219] Ellen Webb, the next scourer who worked for twenty years, was another poor widow dependent on the Fishmongers' charity and her own 'hard labour of washing and scouring'. She was given the place because she 'hath always been an honest painfull [i.e. painstaking] woman'.[220] Another widow, Alice Chamlett, took the place after Webb.[221] Similarly, at the Founders' Company, widow Judrey, the beadle's widow, scoured from 1611 till her death in 1622, and another scourer served for at least seventeen years.[222]

A similar pattern obtained in parishes, which had less money at their disposal than either companies or institutions. The wives of sextons performed numerous services. As we have seen already, the parish preferred to provide employment as a form of relief to deserving cases, placing parish nurslings and orphans with women in the parish to whom they then paid a stipend.

Ultimately, civic employers acknowledged the contribution of wives by providing for relief for the widows of employees. In 1660 the beadle's widow, Mary Baldwin, was allowed £3 as a gratuity as well as a proportion of his wages in regard of 'her poverty and great charge of Children, with her husband's faithfull service'.[223] As in the case of poor relief generally, the woman's own character and behaviour were monitored.

CHANGES OVER THE PERIOD, 1550–1720

If we consider changes in middling women's employment over a range of professional occupations in the early modern period, we can point to both gains and losses. In some ways, those of middling rank are the most interesting group of workers, for, unlike the very wealthiest and the poorest women, their working lives did change. While élite women retained their roles as wives and mothers, and while the poorest women still laboured to make a living, middling women were affected by the emergence of new opportunities as well as the closing off of some avenues. As educators of

[219] Guildhall, MS 5570/3, Fishmongers', Company Court Ledger 3, p. 503.

[220] Guildhall, MS 5570/3, Fishmongers', Company Court Ledger 3, p. 459; MS 5561/1, Fishmongers' Accounts, 3 May 1648, 27 May 1650, 6 May 1651. In 1652 Ellen Webb was paid 18*s.* 2*d.* Some of the company's officers, such as beadles, were provided with accommodation. Ellen Webb may have been so provided also.

[221] Guildhall, MS 5561/2, Fishmongers' Accounts, p. 140.

[222] Parsloe, *Wardens' Accounts Founders*, 250–78, 291–322.

[223] London, St Bartholomew's, Treasurers' ledgers, H1/5, fo. 160.

girls, women had a growing role as the demand for teachers and governesses increased.

Middling women were found in increasing numbers in service roles as the population in towns and cities grew. Their status, like that of aristocratic ladies, depended in turn upon their employment of other women as their servants. In both town and countryside, the archetypal busy housewife of the Elizabethan period continued to run her servants, family, and household.

Yet there were losses in the sectors of midwifery and health care. Male professionals claimed some areas of practice, and, more puzzlingly, a declining number of women from the upper social strata practised midwifery. Such women may have considered that an independent work identity and the maintenance of their social position constituted incompatible goals, but we still have a problem explaining why the change occurred.

Furthermore, although women of the middling and upper ranks continued their traditional roles in health care, unlicensed women practitioners who were paid for their services faced increasing restrictions as male professionalism developed. Physicians protected their own interests by proceeding formally against unlicensed practitioners of either sex, and by incorporating themselves into professional bodies, a development which further disadvantaged women. At the same time, paid work of any kind was becoming socially taboo for women of the minor gentry and above, a process which may explain why those of the middling rank who aspired to higher status were less likely to engage in work which gave them an occupational identity. Social status at this period came more from a woman's family position in the social hierarchy than from her own skills as a professional.

Many questions remain to be answered in our survey of women's work in the early modern period. Perhaps the greatest changes occurred for women of middling status. Yet more than the rise of capitalism seems to have been involved, for the shift away from paid work was not typical of the poorer women, for whom an economy of cash and exchange remained vital.

Continuities as well as change characterized women's status as workers: at the middling and upper levels, as at the lowest levels of society, child-care and housewifery remained invisible as work. At all social levels, reproduction was simply something women did, of no economic value.

7

POLITICS

Gender was deeply significant to matters of government and rule in early modern society, although its importance has been seriously underestimated by most historians. In this chapter, our main purpose is to argue that the study of early modern political history should be rethought, to take account of the presence and influence of women. We cannot here include a comprehensive discussion of women and politics from the mid-sixteenth to the early eighteenth century, for it needs a study in itself. Yet we question the tradition of political history which has been written as a narrative excluding women. We aim to restore women to politics, and politics to women.

Historians rarely define their notion of 'the political' for the early modern period. While feminists have sought to expand its scope, arguing 'that the personal is political', early modern historians have taken a more limited view. Politics, they insist, was men's business, encompassing the monarch and the institutions of government: Parliament, the patronage system, and the conflicts in the counties between rival families. Thus Peter Laslett, in *The World We Have Lost*, writes of England in 1640 as an association between the heads of families: 'Almost no woman ever belonged to England as an individual, except it be a queen regnant—scarcely a woman in the ordinary sense—or a noble widow and heiress or two, a scattering of widows.'[1] Laslett at least asked the question about women's participation in 'England'; others never raise the matter. Even popular politics has a typology which places women at the bottom: E. P. Thompson has argued that it is difficult to see food riots in which women were involved as being '"political" in any advanced sense'.[2]

Political power was fluid in early modern society. Beyond the institutions of government—the monarchy, parliaments, courts of law—as sources of power and places where it was exercised, was the court.[3] And beyond the

[1] P. Laslett, *The World We Have Lost* (2nd edn., 1971), 20.

[2] E. P. Thompson, 'The Moral Economy of the English Crowd in the Eighteenth Century', *Customs in Common* (Harmondsworth, 1993), 188.

[3] D. Starkey (ed.), *The English Court: From the Wars of the Roses to the Civil War* (1987).

court, extending the boundaries still further, were the households of the élite where much of the political negotiation over policies and patronage took place. Where political power was exercised in informal ways, women's roles should be examined more specifically.

Like other scholars, historians have assumed that political categories are sexually neutral and therefore universal. Most historians have asked no questions about how and why women as a sex were excluded from the exercise of public power, claiming that because a few women, by accidents of birth or inheritance, came to political power, the gender neutrality of historical categories is assured. However, the categories of political analysis are not neutral, but constantly being constructed. What historians in general have ignored are questions about the power which men had over women, and about men as sexual beings with an interest in controlling women. Their histories disembody men as well as women, making both gender and sexuality peripheral.

Throughout this book, we have sought to analyse questions of power between women and men, and to understand women's situation in society. In this sense, we would argue that we have a broad view of 'the political'. Yet while elsewhere we argue for a wider definition of the subject-matter of politics, here we propose to make our arguments by the more difficult cases, those of 'high politics' and 'mass politics', the territory which has been marked out as 'men's own'. We shall show that even at the heart of élite male politics and of popular protests, gender was of central significance. Questions about who was to participate in the political process, who might exercise authority, had implications for women and men as social beings.

Although contemporaries believed that politics was ideally confined to men, and that the greatest political power rightly rested in an élite group recruited largely on the basis of birth and wealth, they feared that women were involved in politics at all levels of society. If we examine the evidence about religious and political protests from women's point of view, especially in the period before and during the Civil War and Interregnum, we can see that their activities were an expression of their religious and political consciousness. As we argued in Chapter 4, women accepted a responsibility for their families' survival; thus they sought food at affordable prices, they defended their livelihoods, and they demanded peace and an end to the wars.

Several points need to be made about the evidence for women's religio-political protest activities during the period. First, there was a great diversity of responses, documenting the involvement of women at every social level.

Although religious commitment crossed socio-economic and ideological lines, it took different forms depending on women's social and financial resources or limitations. Wealthy women could patronize radical preachers, hold sectarian meetings in their homes, fund lecture series, bully male relatives about their political allegiance using property as a goad or threat; but those of the upper ranks were debarred from manual tasks or the politics of the street. Ordinary women found themselves in the opposite position: they could and did join political riots and street demonstrations or donate their manual labour to their chosen cause; but they lacked private financial resources to divert to political ends.

Secondly, evidence about women's activism during this period tends to be obscured by its informal nature. Many women formed political associations outside the family group, but their opposition to particular religious regimes still tended to take unofficial forms, especially in the years before 1640. Although women's activities had vital consequences for contemporaries, yet their modes of resistance cannot be measured statistically, in contrast to male activities such as voting or office-holding which were formally recorded.

Thirdly, we must allow for the fact that the dominant perception of female nature led contemporaries to minimize or ignore the political implications of women's protest movements, just as most modern historians have done. Women's expressions of political consciousness were unlikely to be noted in official documents unless such women were considered unusually threatening by authorities, in which case they were branded as instigators and given exemplary punishment. While we can sometimes cite individual examples of female leaders, we cannot accurately gauge the overall extent of female involvement.

Some women did try to register their convictions through official channels, but the sparse documentation for their activities has survived only by chance. Since votes even of males were recorded only in the case of a dispute, it is remarkable that we have some anecdotal accounts of women's attempts to vote in several seventeenth-century parliamentary elections. The women's votes were noted only to be challenged and rejected, but such instances serve to warn us that our knowledge of the limits of female political behaviour is very fragmentary. We cannot be certain that there were no elections in which single women's votes were accepted in some form rather than disqualified. In an election at Richmond in 1678, women were prevented from voting directly, but were conceded the right to assign their votes to males who would deputize for them.[4]

[4] R. Fieldhouse, 'Parliamentary Representation in the Borough of Richmond', *Yorks. Archaeological and Topographical Journal*, 44 (1972), 208.

Thus, at the outbreak of the Civil War in 1642, women were deeply involved, as men were, in choosing sides, in trying to influence their male relatives, in petitioning, and in taking on the role of prophets. The conflicts were more total and caused more trauma than has been realized. When people expressed fears later in the century that 'the days of '41 are come again,'[5] they alluded to more than a crisis between Crown and Parliament: by March 1642 everyone had seen how the populace at large was pursuing political issues, and how some women had moved out of their households into visible public roles, tumultuously petitioning Parliament, and even preaching to small religious groups.

There were three avenues by which women entered politics in the early modern period. The first was through birth; by inheritance women came to the throne, by birth and patronage women enjoyed places at court, and moved in social circles in which politics was discussed. Secondly, as citizens women claimed participatory rights, sometimes as individuals, on other occasions as a group in defence of common rights.[6] Thirdly, religious beliefs motivated many women to engage in mass political movements, especially during the 1640s and 1650s. During the Civil War, Leveller women claimed rights as both citizens and Christians.

The basis of politics was shifting from the medieval household of the monarch to the modern liberal oligarchy/property model. By the end of the seventeenth century, a new basis of political rights had been enunciated. The development of the political theories of John Locke has been regarded in the historiography as a progressive development, a good thing for 'mankind'. We question this assumption. In the matter of voting for Parliament, at the end of the seventeenth century, it was made explicit for the first time that women were debarred because of their sex; gender was a disqualifying factor for political power. Even more significantly, as Carole Pateman has shown, men's right to comprise the political nation entailed the exclusion of women.[7]

Not all women accepted their exclusion from the public political sphere at the end of the seventeenth century, any more than they had accepted the earlier view that all women belonged to the household under male governance. Furthermore, some had a sophisticated understanding of the implications of new theories of political power. Mary Astell attacked the very basis of contract theory, demanding 'How if all men are born free are all women

[5] N.B. As the year began on 25 Mar., 'the days of 41' included the first 3 months of 1642 by our calendar.

[6] See Ch. 1 above.

[7] C. Pateman, *The Sexual Contract* (Stanford, Calif., 1988).

born slaves?' Her profound question was neither heeded nor answered for over two centuries.

The sources for this chapter are widely varied. All the standard sources for political history—state papers, Parliamentary diaries, correspondence of men and women, printed treatises and broadsheets—can be reinterrogated with questions about women's activity. Here we seek to show how our questions can provide a new perspective on political history, by discussing women as active participants. We indicate some of the possibilities of the sources through a case-study of the period 1640–60.

FEMALE MONARCHS

In early modern Europe, issues of gender were everywhere regarded as vital to the workings of monarchy. In a society which assumed that females were naturally inferior to males and were subject to them by divine law, the prospect of female rule aroused men's deepest anxieties. Europe's intellectual élite had inherited a belief in women's incompetence for state affairs from classical writers such as Aristotle, who declared that women's involvement in politics was unnatural.[8] Contemporary statesmen echoed Aristotle's opinion: Sir Thomas Elyot noted the common belief that 'in the partes of wisedome and civile policy, [women] be founden unapt, and to have litell capacitie'.[9]

The problems entailed by female rule were legal and practical as well as psychological and symbolic. Female heirs to the throne were aware that men foresaw intractable difficulties for a queen regnant in both political and religious spheres. How could a woman lead troops in battle, manage Parliament, or negotiate with foreign kings? If women must not speak in church, as Paul had instructed the Corinthians, how could the queen command her bishops as head of the Anglican establishment? This was not an issue in 1553, since, as a Catholic, Mary I simply restored the pre-Reformation state of affairs. But later, when Parliament defined Elizabeth's position *vis-à-vis* the Anglican Church, they gave her the title 'supreme governor' rather than head, in the belief that no woman could be head of the Church.

[8] I. Maclean, *The Renaissance Notion of Woman* (Cambridge, 1980), 60.

[9] T. Elyot, *The Defence of Good Women* (1545), sig. B7^{v}; J. Goldsmith, 'All the Queen's Women: The Changing Place and Perception of Aristocratic Women in Elizabethan England, 1558–1628', Ph.D. diss., Northwestern University (1987), 23. See also John of Salisbury, 'Policraticus', *Cambridge Texts in the History of Political Thought*, ed. C. J. Nederman (Cambridge, 1990), 131. Many thanks to Judith Richards for this reference.

Marriage was central to the problems of all four English queens regnant during the period 1553–1714. Each encountered different circumstances, and adopted a different solution. If a queen remained unwed, like Elizabeth, she could not produce legitimate heirs. But if she married, her dependent status as wife might negate her magisterial powers as head of state. Political theorists debated whether queens were liable to the same punishment as the rest of Eve's daughters: subjection to their husbands. If the queen's consort was of royal status, it was argued that her political dominion reverted to him, just as a wife's property belonged to her husband.

The issue of queens' rights to inherit was central to the politics of the sixteenth century. Before Mary's reign, there had been no English example of female governance to serve as a favourable legal precedent. The only candidate for queen regnant had been Maud or Matilda, whose 'reign' (1135–67) had failed to materialize.[10] In later centuries, women of royal lineage promoted their sons' claims, rather than assert their personal right to rule. Although Margaret, dowager countess of Richmond, might have claimed the succession for herself, she chose instead to help establish her son Henry VII, who claimed the throne by right of conquest.

As late as Henry VIII's reign, no statute law existed to settle the key question defining the nature of the English crown: was the English monarchy an estate or a title? If an estate, the heir general should have succeeded regardless of sex. But if the crown was a title, it was entailed on male heirs, and even females in the direct line of succession were barred from inheritance. In the fifteenth century, the Lord Chief Justice of the King's Bench, Sir John Fortescue, had argued that a woman could not act as queen regnant under any circumstances. Meanwhile, men feared that the dubious rights of a female successor might provoke civil war, as Matilda's claims had done in the twelfth century.

Women's ambiguous status and unsuccessful history as royal heirs helps explain Henry VIII's desperate concern to beget a male heir. Indeed, the English Reformation can be understood in part as the consequence of Henry's efforts to avoid a female heir. Henry did not doubt women's practical ability to govern: he depended on his wife Catherine's advice, and left home rule to her management when he was at war abroad. But no counter-example could refute the perceived disadvantages of a queen regnant.

[10] Although Matilda asserted her right to the throne as sole heir of her father, Henry I, she failed to gain recognition for her claim. Instead, the crown passed via Matilda to her son Henry of Anjou, who reigned during her own lifetime.

In sixteenth-century debates about queenship, the paradoxical status of female monarchs was rationalized in theoretical terms as an instance of the medieval principle of the monarch's 'two bodies'.[11] According to this doctrine, even if the king's personal body was defective, as in the case of an under-aged or senile male heir to the throne, the monarch's 'body of state' was secured against human weakness through God's grace, with the aid of privy counsellors and the rest of the political nation. In the case of females, the notion of the queen's 'two bodies' was extended to reconcile the incongruity between women's subordinate role and the requirements of sovereignty. As Sir Thomas Smith remarked, such considerations explained why a queen by 'blood and progenie' had the same authority as a male monarch.

> For the right and honour of the blood, and the quietnes and suertie of the realme, is more to be considered, than either the base age as yet impotent to rule, or the sexe not accustomed (otherwise) to intermeddle with publicke affaires, being by common intendment understood, that such personages never do lacke the counsell of such grave and discreete men as be able to supplie all other defaultes.[12]

England's initial resolution of the gender issue was embodied in two documents of Henry VIII's reign, the third Parliamentary succession statute and Henry's own will. Both documents specified that any male heir was to be given precedence; if none existed, first Mary and then Elizabeth was to succeed to the throne. When Edward died, constitutional uncertainty lay not in who was his rightful successor, but on what terms and with what powers a female monarch would rule.

In 1553 Mary I succeeded to the English crown as its first acknowledged queen. By the time Elizabeth I died in 1603, England had experienced half a century of female rule. Although there were several unsuccessful rebellions during each reign, none had focused directly on gender as the grounds of the queen's unfitness to rule. Because of its relatively peaceful advent, most historians have dismissed the inauguration of female governance as an unremarkable event, a mere accident of demography. Others have argued that female rule was inevitable in 1553 because there were no 'serious male claimants'.[13] Yet the events preceding Mary's accession were deeply con-

[11] C. Jordan, 'Woman's Rule in British Political Thought', *Renaissance Quarterly*, 10 (1987), 439.

[12] Sir T. Smith, *De Republica Anglorum*, ed. Mary Dewar (Cambridge, 1982), 64–5.

[13] M. Levine, 'The Place of Women in Tudor Government', in D. Guth and J. McKenna (eds.), *Tudor Rule and Revolution* (1982), 109; R. Warnicke, *Women of the English Renaissance and Reformation* (Westport, Conn., 1983), 47.

cerned with gender, as Northumberland's faction made use of a female figurehead, Lady Jane Grey, to block the opposing faction which supported Mary.

Historians have also discussed the accession of Elizabeth in 1558 as though it raised for the first time the issue of a female ruler. In fact, Mary I was the first queen regnant of England, and many of the complex issues of gender and authority had been confronted already. At Mary's accession in 1553 there was general uncertainty about what her status would be. How would her powers be affected when she married (as everyone assumed she would)? Although Elizabeth subsequently evaded some of the problems of reconciling constitutional and divine law by remaining single, at the end of the seventeenth century, when another Mary came to the throne, the question of the respective authority of a queen regnant and her husband was still an unsolved problem.

On the ceremonial public occasions marking the accession of Mary I as the new monarch, symbolism was confused between her roles as a female king and as a woman. On previous occasions, before his coronation, a king rode through the City of London, and for the corresponding occasion, a queen, dressed in white, was carried in a litter, with her hair down, like a bride. Accounts of Mary's entry into London and her coronation were contradictory. Some reported that Mary had been dressed in white and carried in a litter, others depicted her as magnificently dressed, while others still described her as dressed in blue, with the heavy crown upon her head. As Judith Richards argues, contemporaries were uncertain about what they saw, because they were unclear about the nature and role of a female monarch.[14]

Mary and most of her councillors assumed that she should marry so that she could produce an heir and also have someone to help her to rule. The constitutional implications of her marriage were unclear. When it was known that she would marry Philip, a Catholic Habsburg prince, Parliament and Council were especially concerned to preserve her authority. They sought to prevent Philip from treating England as his own property, particularly in the sphere of foreign affairs. Nevertheless the Spanish ambassador reported a rumour that some lawyers thought that 'by English law' Mary would lose her title to the crown on marriage. The marriage treaty stipulated that Mary remain queen, that Philip's duty was to assist, and that England

[14] This, and the following three paragraphs, owe much to J. Richards, 'Mary Tudor as "Sole Quene"? The Gendering of Tudor Monarchy', forthcoming, *Historical Journal*. We are most grateful to Judith Richards for allowing us to cite her article before publication.

would not be drawn into war on Philip's behalf. Thus the idea of the queen's 'two bodies' was extended to account for the possibility that Mary's public role as monarch might supersede her private duties as a wife under certain conditions.

In 1554 Parliament passed acts to assert that Mary's power as queen was identical to that of a king, as absolute as it had been in any of her predecessors. At the marriage ceremony, Mary's superiority as monarch was asserted—she was on the right hand, and the sword of state was carried before her—but contemporaries also saw that she had become a wife, with duties of subordination. Although Philip was never crowned, he was given the title of king, and acts were issued in the names of the joint monarchs.

Equal power was hard to sustain, and Mary's monarchical power was eroded while her husband's greater authority was asserted. When Mary thought that she was pregnant, Parliament had to decide about arrangements for a possible regency, in case the queen should die. Despite the marriage treaty, Parliament agreed that Philip's power as a father would have to be acknowledged, and that he should rule for his child. The constitutional implications of this decision were never tested, since the queen proved not to be with child. Yet, in the short period of her marriage, the limitations upon Philip's power were already undermined, and only Mary's death prevented further challenges to her marriage treaty. During the reign of the first female monarch, everyone had found the issue of woman as ruler vexed and difficult. Nevertheless, Mary herself had pursued her own Catholicizing policies, and had married against the wishes of some of her male advisers.

The events of Mary's reign confirmed anxieties about the equivocal status of queens who were married. Nevertheless, through an extraordinary series of contingencies, the sovereign powers of the queen regnant had been settled by statute for all future female heirs, thus removing one contentious issue from the debate over Elizabeth's accession. Moreover, gender issues in 1558 were overshadowed by the attractions of a monarch whose Protestantism was guaranteed by the circumstances of her birth, especially since the only alternative prospect was the Catholic—and female—Mary, queen of Scots.

Elizabeth, although immediately acknowledged as queen regnant, was seen initially as an inexperienced young woman who would be guided by male advisers, whether by her privy counsellors or the man she chose to marry. But gradually Elizabeth came to see herself as an extraordinary woman, a 'phoenix, matchless and unique' as emblem books were later to portray her.[15] Because she was a Protestant, and chose not to take a husband to share her rule, Elizabeth was the first English queen to confront head-on all the paradoxes created for the English Church and State by an independent female monarch. Although her pioneer role provoked tension with male counsellors, who continually urged her to marry and bear an heir, the novelty of her situation gave Elizabeth the opportunity to experiment, to forge an individual solution to the problems of female power.

Elizabeth founded her personal supremacy over Church and State on traditional, non-gendered grounds: her God-given right by inheritance, a prerogative to which all her subjects must swear allegiance. Going beyond the notion of divinely ordained rule, however, Elizabeth strengthened her authority and promoted popularity among her subjects by manipulating contemporary images of monarchy and gender. Elizabeth dealt with her subjects' anxieties, and with the weaknesses and ambiguities of her position, by pushing the notion of the monarch's 'two bodies' to its symbolic and psychological limits, representing herself as both queen and king. To express her unique status, the queen employed rhetoric and imagery appropriate to both sexes, describing herself alternately in feminine and masculine terms.

In masculine milieux like the battlefield, Elizabeth portrayed herself as repressing her female aspect to allow 'male' qualities to emerge. The queen's famous remarks allegedly addressed to the troops at Tilbury in 1588, just prior to the Armada crisis, highlighted her manly attributes: 'I may have the body of a weak and feeble woman, but I have the heart and stomach of a king.' On this occasion she further dramatized her male persona through visual imagery, appearing in breastplate and helmet, mounted on a charger. In general, without surrendering her femininity, she stressed those mental and physical traits she shared with her father Henry VIII, such as her bravery and her linguistic proficiency. In the religious realm, like the other three Tudor-Stuart queens, Elizabeth continued the kingly tradition of 'sacred monarch', whose healing powers confirmed her divine and majestic status.

As 'sacred monarch' and virgin queen, Elizabeth also creatively elaborated upon a repertoire of female images.[16] Her virginity served as a potent symbol

[15] H. Diehl, *An Index of Icons in English Emblem Books, 1500–1700* (1986), 162 (cites Godyere no. 3).

[16] C. Levin, *The Heart and Stomach of a King: Elizabeth I and the Politics of Sex and Power* (Philadelphia, 1994); P. Berry, *Of Chastity and Power: Elizabethan Literature and the Unmarried Queen* (New York, 1989).

FIG. 43. Queen Elizabeth I, here shown very richly dressed, crowned and holding a sceptre, surrounded by symbols and mottoes highlighting her regal powers and her role as defender of the Protestant faith

of female power, enhancing the magical and religious aura that surrounded her. Such imagery was initiated with her accession portrait, in which Elizabeth was shown with her hair down, attired as a virginal maiden. At times depicting herself in the guise of the Virgin Mary, the queen appropriated those divine attributes that could be embodied in a woman. Similarly, in her persona as Diana the chaste goddess and as the Fairy Queen, Elizabeth created a stage setting in which her subjects' obedience was translated into the romantic language of chivalry. 'Courtly love' rendered male subservience to a woman acceptable to noble courtiers; in any other context, subjection would have been experienced as demeaning or even unmanning.

Elizabeth also capitalized on her 'feminine' characteristics to achieve well-defined goals of statecraft. For a sixteenth-century regime, her reign saw very few executions, and the queen agonized over those to which she was obliged to consent. Elizabeth's preference for 'mild and merciful rule' towards her political rivals, in contrast to the ruthless policies of her father and sister, was seen as an expression of her feminine compassion. The queen's legendary meanness was represented as the frugality of the conventional housewife applied on a national scale. Elizabeth carefully deployed her alleged vanity, sexual jealousy, and passionate temper to manage her councillors and suitors. Cultivating the myth that she could 'never keep a secret', she played her councillors against each other in a strategy of 'divide and conquer'.

Elizabeth's manipulation of contemporary assumptions about gender attributes is shown clearly in her management of her official courtships. Courtship had complex significance for the queen as a game, a strategic political tactic, and an entire social and cultural milieu.[17] As a strategy, courtship became the queen's method for sidestepping the choice between two equally problematic alternatives, wedded subservience and barren virginity. Elizabeth appealed to the feminine quality of 'shamefastness' to delay and ultimately to avoid matrimony. At the same time, her advisers' construction of female sexuality, encouraged by Elizabeth's ambiguous behaviour towards unofficial suitors like the earl of Leicester, seemed to confirm the queen's right to choose or reject each potential suitor.[18]

Elizabeth's outstanding political skills were employed not only to run the

[17] Levin, *Heart and Stomach of a King*, 39–65. For a specific instance see S. Doran, 'Religion and Politics at the Court of Elizabeth I: The Habsburg Marriage Negotiations, 1559–1567', *EHR* (1989), 908–26; S. Doran, *Monarchy and Matrimony: The Courtships of Elizabeth I* (1996).

[18] Levin, *Heart and Stomach of a King*, 66–90.

kingdom, but also to demonstrate that she was an exception who was superior to the usual disabilities that afflicted ordinary women. Paradoxically, her success as a female ruler depended on putting a distance between herself and all other women, because of the central problem of female authority.[19] Although some historians have labelled Elizabeth patriarchal or even misogynistic, it is anachronistic to attribute her behaviour to an anti-female bias. The queen could not afford to be receptive to other women's claims for power, for fear of undermining her own position. Moreover, Elizabeth's apparent 'hostility' to other women's political pretensions was not necessarily inconsistent with female friendship on a personal level, or royal favour and bounty in the form of patronage.

Although relatively less popular in the final years of her reign, Elizabeth evoked a good deal of sentimental regret during the first half of the seventeenth century, especially when her prudence and parsimony were contrasted with Stuart excess and misjudgement.

> The honor, wealth, and glory of the nation, wherein Queene Elizabeth left it, were soone prodigally wasted by this thriftlesse heire, the nobillity of the land utterly debas'd by setting honors to publick sale . . . Then began Murther, Incest, Adultery, drunkennesse, swearing, fornication, and all sort of ribaldry to be no conceal'd but countenanc'd vices . . . because they held such conformity with the Court example.[20]

The enduring popularity of Elizabeth's image as monarch can be traced in the seventeenth-century nostalgia for a mythical 'Merrie England' in which England's honour and prosperity as a nation had reached their greatest heights.[21]

Yet even with Elizabeth as a successful exemplar of female monarchy, the belief persisted that women as a sex were naturally unfit for political rule. While we might have expected Elizabeth's achievements to have transformed the axioms of misogyny into more positive notions about the potentialities of queenship, it is clear from contemporary commentaries on her reign that notions about female political rule were not tied to the empirical performance of any particular queen. On the contrary, even her warmest female admirers discounted evidence of Elizabeth's independent

[19] A. Heisch, 'Queen Elizabeth and the Persistence of Patriarchy', *Feminist Review*, 4 (1980), 45–56.

[20] L. Hutchinson, *Memoirs of the Life of Colonel Hutchinson*, ed. J. Sutherland (Oxford, 1973), 42.

[21] Elizabeth's legendary image was already current as early as 1611, when the King James Bible referred in its Epistle Dedicatory to the 'setting of that bright Occidental Star, Queen Elizabeth of most happy memory'.

abilities. In denouncing Henrietta Maria for her 'fatal' influence on her husband Charles I, Lucy Hutchinson interjected a general condemnation of female political power. No place is ever happy, she remarked, 'where the hands that are made only for distaffes affect the management of Sceptres'. And if anyone objected the recent counter-example of Queen Elizabeth, 'let them remember that the felicity of her reigne was the effect of her submission to her masculine and wise Councellors'.[22]

Whereas the inheritance of the two Tudor queens was not challenged on the right of their sex, the situation of the first Stuart queen was different. Politicians in 1688 were concerned that Mary's rights were abrogated by her marriage to William; and they set aside Anne's rights to allow William to rule alone should Mary die, although his heirs by any subsequent wife were placed after Anne's heirs in the succession. The settlement of 1689 was confused, for by both denying and acknowledging women's hereditary rights, it had profound implications for women's position as heirs, as subsequent political disputes would show.

Gender was central to the revolution of 1688, as some historians have acknowledged.[23] First, the rights of married women and female heirs caused major debate.[24] Some Tory politicians thought that Mary alone, by hereditary right, should succeed to the crown, and decide what power or dignity she proposed for her husband. Although Danby was confident that, if Mary decided to be sole monarch, he and his allies could carry her claim, Mary allegedly rejected the option, saying 'she was the prince's wife, and would never be other than what she should be in conjunction with him and under him'. William was opposed to his wife succeeding her father as sole monarch, reportedly saying that 'a man's wife ought only to be his wife'; 'he could not think of holding any thing by apron-strings' or 'to be his wife's gentleman usher'. Unless he were made joint monarch, with power to rule after Mary's death, William threatened to take his troops and return home.[25]

[22] Hutchinson, *Memoirs of Colonel Hutchinson*, ed. Sutherland, 48.

[23] L. G. Schwoerer, 'Women and the Glorious Revolution', *Albion*, 18 (1986), 195–218; L. G. Schwoerer, 'Images of Queen Mary II, 1689–1695', *Renaissance Quarterly*, 42 (1989), 717–48; R. Beddard, *A Kingdom without a King: The Journal of the Provisional Government in the Revolution of 1688* (Oxford, 1988), 11; R. Weil, 'The Politics of Legitimacy: Women and the Warming-Pan Scandal', in L. G. Schwoerer (ed.), *The Revolution of 1688–1689: Changing Perspectives* (Cambridge, 1992), 65–82.

[24] See esp. L. G. Schwoerer, *The Declaration of Rights, 1689* (Baltimore, 1981); L. G. Schwoerer, 'The Queen as Regent and Patron', in *The Age of William III and Mary II: Power, Politics and Patronage, 1688–1702* (Washington, DC, 1989).

[25] G. Burnet, *Bishop Burnet's History of His Own Time*, 2nd edn. enlarged, 6 vols. (Oxford, 1833), iii. 391, 393–5 and notes; Schwoerer, 'Women and the Glorious Revolution', 212.

FIG. 44. Queen Mary II. This portrait of Queen Mary II emphasizes her feminine charms (underscored by the miniature of the 'Three Graces' below her portrait) while downplaying her sovereign powers. Note that the crown and sceptre are not worn by the queen, but rest almost unnoticed beside the oval frame

Thus the debates in the Convention in 1689 began with the proposition that the crown, as an hereditary possession, should descend to the Princess of Orange, but in the end granted full rights to William.[26] Some invoked the legal doctrine of the *feme covert*, arguing that the crown was part of the property of a woman, and therefore belonged to her husband after marriage. Mary, as a *feme covert*, had already given the crown to William as an estate, Halifax argued. Others thought that if the crown were an estate, Mary and William could be joint tenants.[27] Ultimately, the administration was vested singly in William, although contemporaries were aware that in the reign of Mary Tudor no such power had been given to Philip.[28]

The settlement of 1689 which allowed William to rule after Mary's death had the effect of diminishing the rights of Anne. Although friends to Anne protested, according to Burnet she gave them no support.[29] Other sources more plausibly allege that Anne claimed that nobody had spoken to her of it, and that she would do nothing to disadvantage herself or her children.[30] Thus, for pragmatic reasons, Mary's and Anne's rights were curtailed; but the rationale for the denial of their rights as married women gave theoretical support to a general diminution of the rights of all married women. What was agreed upon at the insistence of William was couched in terms of a general principle. Contemporaries were uneasily aware that the rules of inheritance for both the monarchy and 'private families', based as they were on the law of God, ought to be consistent.[31]

The second issue in the politics of the later seventeenth century, and of 1688 in particular, related to women's allegiances. In a conflict between her family of origin and that of her husband, which should a woman choose? Shakespeare had dramatized the issue earlier in the century in *Antony and Cleopatra*, as Octavia bemoaned her unhappy fate, torn between her husband and her brother.[32] In December 1688, when James considered his options, some advised that he should go north to join Anne who had fled: 'Your daughter will receive you, or she will not.' If the latter, 'all will cry out on her'. It was assumed that a good daughter could not refuse her

[26] A. Grey, *Debates of the House of Commons . . . 1667 to 1694*, 10 vols. (1763), ix.

[27] Ibid., ix. 73, 75–6. [28] Burnet, *History of His Own Time* (1833), 392–3.

[29] Ibid. 392.

[30] S. W. Singer (ed.), *The Correspondence of Henry Hyde, Earl of Clarendon*, 2 vols. (1828), ii. 246–7.

[31] T. Craig, *Concerning the Right of Succession to the Kingdom of England* (1703), 99, 110–11.

[32] William Shakespeare, *Antony and Cleopatra*, III. iv: 'A more unhappy lady, If this division chance, ne'er stood between, Praying for both parts'.

father her support; and a bad daughter would be supported by no one. In the event James did not test Anne, but he felt the betrayal of his daughters very keenly.[33] Mary's position as an usurping daughter was a particularly unpleasant one, hence William instructed her that when she succeeded to her father's position and possessions on her arrival, she should show a cheerful demeanour.[34] Some observers considered her undutiful behaviour in her early days at Whitehall 'very strange and unbecoming'.[35] In her memoirs, Mary confessed to being deeply troubled at her conflicting loyalties. While she comforted herself with the reflection that the Lord had guided her in her duty 'when Religion was at stake', she interpreted her later quarrels with her sister Anne as 'a punishment for the irregularity by us committed upon the revolution'.[36] Members of Parliament continued to be worried about Mary's loyalties. When William proposed to go to Ireland in 1690, Parliament debated whether Mary had power in her own right, or from William. MPs pondered the terrible consequences of vesting authority in Mary, since if William should die, 'and the Queen be Regent, what if, out of Duty to her Father, if he land, she should not oppose him?'[37] In all of these debates, assumptions about the nature of women's duties as women featured prominently.

As Mary had not involved herself in the day-to-day dealings with the Council, she was at a disadvantage when William was away fighting in Ireland. As a submissive wife she had allowed William to decide whether the government in his absence was to be in her name or that of the Council: 'I only desired he would take care I should not make a foolish figure in the world. I told him that the thing in effect was the same, for I being wholy a stranger to bussiness, it must be the Privy Council must do all things.'[38] In her correspondence with William, Mary was deferential: 'if I do any thing that you dont like, 'tis my misfortune, and not my fault; for I love you more than my life, and desire only to please you.'[39] Similarly, in her *Memoirs*, Mary constructed herself as a dutiful wife, a woman limited by nature: 'My sex was not able to bear those violent passions, those fears, those joys.'[40] Her own preference was for a retired life, and, in taking responsibility in William's absence, she feared only her ignorance of politics (which she termed

[33] J. S. Clarke, *The Life of James the Second*, 2 vols. (1816), ii. 226–9.
[34] Burnet, *History of His Own Time* (1833), iii. 406–7.
[35] *Memoirs of Sarah, Duchess of Marlborough*, ed. W. King (1930), 18–19.
[36] *Memoirs of Queen Mary II (1689–1693)*, ed. R. Doebner (Leipzig, 1886), 3, 45.
[37] Grey, *Debates*, x. 108. [38] *Memoirs of Queen Mary*, 21–2.
[39] Sir John Dalrymple, *Memoirs of Great Britain and Ireland*, 3 vols. (1773), ii. 129.
[40] *Memoirs of Queen Mary*, 47.

stupidity), and rejoiced in her husband's approval. Invested with executive power, Mary refused to exercise the monarch's (and woman's) prerogative of mercy; she was deaf to the pleas of a poor, unfortunate mother for her son's life, and comforted herself with the Scriptural text about the Lord's wrath against a land defiled with blood. 'Women should not', she thought, 'medle in government.' Her own role as a wife was to divert her husband from his cares of state.[41]

A third issue in the politics of the 1680s and the revolution was women's sexual honour, and the consequent questions of hereditary right and legitimacy. As Algernon Sidney observed, much in England was left to 'the faith of women, who besides their other Frailties have bin often accused of suppositious Births'.[42] In 1680, when the exclusion of James from the throne was proposed, questions were raised about the possible legitimacy of Charles's son, the duke of Monmouth. The marital status of his mother, Lucy Walter, was crucial.[43] In 1688, doubts about the legitimacy of the Prince of Wales, which impugned the chastity of Mary of Modena and the integrity of James II, featured in the invitation to William to invade. As Rachel Weil has shown, the debate about Mary of Modena's pregnancy and childbirth had implications for the relationship of women to political authority.[44]

Queen Mary of Modena's pregnancy and parturition in 1687–8 must be one of the best documented of the early modern period. Enormous political significance attached to the sex of the child: a son would displace James's two adult Protestant daughters in the succession. Mary gave birth before a large mixed audience, an unusual situation, for normally only women attended a birth. Several of the male observers felt uncomfortable at so unfamiliar a scene, and later professed that they lacked the appropriate language—'he does not know the proper expression'—to describe what they saw. Another male witness was so distressed at the queen's cries that he blocked his ears with his fingers to avoid 'hearing more of the like'.[45] While James himself seemed comfortable in explaining the stage of labour to one of his councillors, 'You are a married Man, and so may know these Matters', the earl of Mulgrave thought that 'it was not to be expected one

[41] *Memoirs of Queen Mary* 22–3, 25, 28, 33, 40; see also Schwoerer, 'Images of Queen Mary', 717–48; M. Zook, 'History's Mary: The Propagation of Queen Mary II, 1689–1694', in L. O. Fradenburg (ed.), *Women and Sovereignty* (Edinburgh, 1992).

[42] A. Sidney, *Discourse* (1698), 340.

[43] Clarke, *Life of James II*, ii. 312; H. Nenner, *By Colour of Law: Legal Culture and Constitutional Politics in England, 1660–1689* (Chicago, 1977), 58.

[44] Weil, 'The Politics of Legitimacy', 65–82. For further discussion, see below.

[45] *The Declaration . . . concerning the birth of the Prince of Wales* [1688], 30, 40.

of his sex should be able to give full Evidence in such a Matter'.[46] Among the testimonies enrolled were those of Mary's female attendants through her pregnancy, and women who had witnessed or assisted at the birth. None was sufficient to authenticate that the child was truly the son of King James. Only by claiming that the baby was illegitimate or spurious (smuggled in in a warming-pan) could many people acquiesce in the accession of James's daughter. Mary's acceptance of the crown, as a daughter displacing a son, had implications for all families.

Queen Anne, the fourth of the Tudor-Stuart queens regnant, was, like her sister Mary, already married on her accession to the throne. Unlike Mary, whose husband was made joint monarch and given executive power, Anne allowed her husband George no share in her authority. Anne retained full power as a monarch, including executive power, although as a woman she could not exercise military leadership.[47] She made George the generalissimo of 'all her forces by sea and land', but he was never given the title of king.[48] She was perhaps the most successful of the four queens regnant in negotiating both her inheritance and marriage. She even bore a male heir, although her son, the duke of Gloucester, died before her, as did all her daughters. From the outset, Anne emphasized maternal qualities, choosing for her coronation the text from Isaiah 49: 23, 'Kings shall be thy nursing Fathers, and their Queens thy nursing mothers'. Throughout her reign she sought to promote national unity, and expressed her dislike for parties in politics. Although she was aware that various political leaders would try to coerce her, like Elizabeth I before her, she was determined to resist: if the Whigs should think 'I am to be Heckter'd or frighted into a Complyance tho I am a woman, [they] are mightey mistaken in me. I thank God I have a Soul above that.'[49] Aware of the belief that women were peace-loving and compassionate, she showed her dislike of conflict in religion. There were no political executions during her reign.

By the end of the seventeenth century, gender had intruded more into the public ceremonies attaching to the monarchy. At the funeral of Mary Tudor, her body was exempted from the normal heraldic rule that the emblems of war were unsuitable for women: the full set of the emblems—gauntlets, spurs, a horse, and battleaxe—were displayed. At Elizabeth's funeral, the gauntlet and spurs were omitted, and at the funeral of Mary II there was no military paraphernalia at all, only her crown and sceptre.[50] All four queens

[46] Ibid. 29, 26. [47] E. Gregg, *Queen Anne* (1980), 130–60.

[48] N. Luttrell, *A Brief Historical Relation of State Affairs, 1678–1714*, 6 vols. (Oxford, 1857), v. 164. [49] Gregg, *Queen Anne*, 137–8.

[50] C. Gittings, *Death, Burial and the Individual in Early Modern England* (1984), 184, 222.

FIG. 45. Queen Anne depicted on her seal. On one side of her official seal, Queen Anne is shown with full ceremonial regalia, crowned and enthroned, holding the monarch's globe and sceptre; on the other side, still crowned, she is mounted on horseback

regnant negotiated differently through their reigns on the issues of power and gender.

ARISTOCRATIC WOMEN: QUEENS CONSORT, FEMALE COURTIERS, AND MATRIARCHS

A comparatively small group of women, most of whom were of aristocratic birth, exercised political influence as the wives, mistresses, mothers, daughters, kin, or friends of the monarch and of men who held political power. Political influence was diffuse in the sixteenth and seventeenth centuries. While the apex was the sovereign, who was the fount of the patronage system, there were numerous points along the pyramid where power was distributed. At all levels, success depended on knowledge of the dispositions of those above. To obtain their objectives, people needed to know how best to recommend themselves to a patron, and what considerations would move their patron to grant favours or petitions. Gossip, the gathering of news and information, or networking, as we might term it, were all vital. In this process, women played a crucial part. Although their opportunities varied depending on their social position and access to patrons, their own abilities played a part. There were many maids of honour at the court of Mary of Modena, but only Sarah Jenyns used her place to gain the friendship of Princess Anne.

Our object in this section is to suggest some of the ways in which political power could be wielded by women around the monarch and around powerful courtiers. Women's political influence has been both overestimated and underestimated. Men felt threatened by the power and influence which some women wielded, and so exaggerated the power of court women such as Barbara Villiers or Sarah Churchill, but they underestimated the political influence of women such as Lady Ranelagh who worked very quietly behind the scenes. (Preaching her funeral sermon in 1692, Burnet admitted 'she made the greatest Figure in all the Revolutions of these Kingdoms for above fifty years, of any Woman of our Age'.)[51] Individual women, such as Henrietta Maria or various of Charles II's mistresses, became 'bogeys' in popular eyes as female devils with power to do evil.[52] Historians have reacted in not

[51] Printed in M. Hunter (ed.), *Robert Boyle by Himself and his Friends* (1994), 52.

[52] N. K. Maguire, 'The Duchess of Portsmouth: English Royal Consort and French Politician, 1670–85', in R. M. Smuts (ed.), *The Stuart Court and Europe* (Cambridge, 1996). We are grateful to Dr Maguire for allowing us to read her chapter prior to publication.

dissimilar ways, dismissing the quiet influence of some ladies, and ignoring questions which impugn the sagacity of the men. Contemporaries alleged that Charles II was led chiefly by his sexual impulses.

> His sceptre and his p—k are of a length
> And she may sway the one who plays with t'other
> And make him little wiser than his brother.[53]

Yet many historians have written as though the king was ruled by what they define as 'rational' as opposed to 'baser' instincts. Even those historians who acknowledge the importance of the sexual politics of the Restoration court find the subject uncomfortable, fearing 'It may seem unnecessarily prurient to dwell on the sexual mores of Charles and his court'.[54] Nevertheless, literary scholars have, in important ways, shown how contemporary writers were preoccupied with the relationship between the king's sexual conduct and his political decisions.[55]

There is no doubt that some aristocratic women influenced the patronage system and culture. But whether they had real policy-making power remains an open question. How did women, compared with men, gain a position in which they could influence the policies of the monarch, courtiers, or, increasingly, Members of Parliament? First, like men, they found that aristocratic birth helped. Birth and wealth brought young women to the attention of monarchs and courtiers. Combined with other qualities, such as beauty and talent, they might enter the court and marry well. Sexuality was a factor. A maid of honour at court gambled on whether or not to embark on a pre-marital sexual relationship. If she were fortunate, like Anne Hyde, her lover would marry her when she became pregnant.[56] Less happy was the maid of honour, Mary Trevor, whose lover refused to marry her, and who was removed in disgrace from the court.[57] Once married, a wife's political influence might depend on a range of factors: her relationship with her husband, whether or not she had sexual rivals (as the wives of many

[53] G. de F. Lord (ed.), *Poems on Affairs of State: Augustan Satirical Verse, 1660–1714*, 7 vols. (New Haven, 1963–75), i. 424.

[54] J. Miller, *Charles II* (1991), 97. Others write as though the personal can be separated from the public; eg. J. R. Jones, *Charles II: Royal Politician* (1987), 1: 'This is a political study . . . consequently his private life will not be discussed, except when it impinged on his public attitudes and performance of his duties as sovereign.'

[55] S. Zwicker, *Lines of Authority: Politics and English Literary Culture, 1649–1689* (Ithaca, NY, 1993); R. Braverman, *Plots and Counterplots: Sexual Politics and the Body Politic in English Literature, 1660–1730* (Cambridge, 1993).

[56] In Anne's case the duke of York married her despite the unanimous opposition of his family; Gregg, *Queen Anne*, 2–3.

[57] F. Harris, *A Passion for Government* (Oxford 1991), 24–5.

kings did), and her interest and ability. Even if they professed no desire to exercise political power, the wives of monarchs and powerful courtiers were the cynosure of attention.

Secondly, women could exploit their sexuality another way, and become mistresses.[58] This was an avenue also open to men, but such opportunities depended upon the sexual proclivities and sex of the monarch. None of the early modern queens regnant ever installed a lover in the way that kings felt free to do. (There was gossip about Elizabeth's relationship with Dudley, but the danger to her of a sexual relationship with any man was enormous. People might frown at the open sexual relationships of Charles II, but his political position was not seriously threatened.)

Thirdly, unlike a man aspiring to political influence, a woman found the way less open to demonstrated talent and ability. Women had no opportunity to shine in the service of some great man, no chance to recommend themselves to a patron by their loyal service in Parliament. All women with political power were more akin to favourites than to the men who rose by talents, or whose birth conferred an office upon them. Like a male favourite, a wife, friend, or mistress might be given some office as a colour for her presence at court,[59] and a title to give her some position in the court hierarchy.

Ultimately, a woman's political influence depended on her intelligence and skills. Ironically, the more skilful a woman was, the less likely was it that the object of her attentions would realize that he or she was being influenced and manipulated. Abigail Masham, who replaced Sarah Churchill as Queen Anne's favourite, may have been a more successful politician in influencing the queen than her more famous relative.

With these general points in mind, we shall now discuss some examples of the political influence of queens consort, mistresses, courtiers, and the wives of prominent gentry.

First in importance were the queens consort, whose duty in a society dominated by primogeniture was to produce a male heir, or, failing a son, a daughter. Henrietta Maria, who bore prolifically, enjoyed the love and esteem of her husband; Catherine of Braganza, who did not, was treated with unkindness, scorn, and was even threatened with divorce.[60] Since the

[58] The term 'mistress' was used at the time. We have kept it since it refers to a relationship of power between a woman and her sexual partner. He provided money and other benefits, in return for access to her body. In theory, her sexuality belonged to him alone.

[59] For example, Charles II insisted that Barbara Palmer be a lady of the queen's bedchamber; Miller, *Charles II*, 98.

[60] For a nasty satirical attack, see 'The Queen's Ball' (1670), *Poems on Affairs of State*, i. 421–2; Miller, *Charles II*, 106, 149–50, 299–300.

king was the apex of the social world of the court, his attitude to his wife affected her position, and her opportunities to influence policy.

Queens consort used their position to support their own religious goals. Earlier, in the reign of Henry VIII, Catherine of Aragon, Anne Boleyn, and Catherine Parr had all aspired to influence the king's religious policy. With varying degrees of success, they employed direct persuasion, patronage, and indirect support of various clergymen. In the seventeenth century, all the queens consort—Anne (the wife of James I), Henrietta Maria, Catherine of Braganza, and Mary of Modena—tried to support Catholicism, the first three in opposition to the public religious policies of their husbands. Henrietta's religious influence and its political consequences were particularly damaging to her husband in the events leading up to the outbreak of civil war in 1642.[61] Ironically, Charles resisted his wife's Catholicizing policies, although she was widely blamed for his religious policy. The religious influence of the other queens remains to be studied.

Of all the queens consort during the period, Henrietta was probably the most significant in political terms. She replaced the duke of Buckingham in Charles's affections at the end of 1628, and has been seen as heir to the favourite's political influence. Initially, she was not interested in politics, but after 1629 she was recognized as a significant adviser to her husband.[62] She was attacked throughout the 1630s, and 1640s, as one of the king's evil counsellors. Historians have blamed her for the king's pro-Catholic religious policies, although Malcolm Smuts has convincingly argued that her policies during the 1630s have been misunderstood.[63] However, Smuts himself is uncertain about the queen's political influence, for on the one hand he sees the French ambassador Chateauneuf as 'the architect of the queen's party', and agrees that the queen herself was 'a frivolous young woman' who never realized the 'potential implications of her policy'; on the other hand Smuts argues that it was Henrietta who isolated those courtiers who 'might possibly have reached an accommodation with the parliamentary leadership and avoided revolution'.[64] In the absence of a recent study of Henrietta, who was clearly a significant figure in political life, we can make only a few comments. One of the main difficulties in assessing her influence in the 1630s lies with

[61] C. Hibbard, *Charles I and the Popish Plot* (Chapel Hill, NC, 1983); C. Hibbard, 'The Court and Household of a Queen Consort: Henrietta Maria, 1625–1642' in R. G. Asch and A. M. Birke (eds.), *Princes, Patronage and the Nobility: The Court at the Beginning of the Modern Age c. 1450–1650* (1991); see also M. Smuts, *Court Culture and the Origins of a Royalist Tradition in Early Stuart England* (Philadelphia, 1987).

[62] K. Sharpe, *The Personal Rule of Charles I* (New Haven, 1992), 172.

[63] R. M. Smuts, 'The Puritan Followers of Henrietta Maria in the 1630s', *EHR*, 93 (1978), 26–45.

[64] Ibid. 28, 31, 38, 45.

the nature of the source material. The weekly reports of foreign ambassadors are a major source: yet the men who wrote them were seeking to demonstrate to their home governments their own influence and power. Imbued as they were with a belief that women should keep out of politics, they were hardly likely to be sensitive to the initiatives or skills of the queen or of any of the female courtiers. Yet, even in these sources, there are hints which would justify further questioning; in the mid-1630s the earl of Holland was said to consult with a council of women.[65] Many witnesses observed Henrietta's attempts to influence the king, although they found it difficult to estimate the extent of her power with Charles. In 1639, the countess of Carlisle told her brother that she had heard the queen 'usse straing violent perswations' to the king which would lead to quarrels with France.[66] During the Civil War, Charles confided his plans in his wife. Although the Parliamentarians had accused her of being an evil counsellor, they were shocked when they read the captured royal correspondence at Naseby in 1645. There Henrietta warned her husband not to trust himself 'in the hands of those people' during the peace negotiations. Whatever concessions he might make, 'Above all have a care not to abandon those who have served you, as well the bishops, as poor Catholick'.[67] After her husband's death, Henrietta continued to attempt to influence royal policy, and was still perceived by her contemporaries to be a malign influence.[68]

Other favourites, both female and male, were rivals to queens consort. Political power fluctuated with the monarch's sexual interest, and frequently with the woman's fecundity. A mistress usually gained greater financial rewards if she produced children. Historians have suggested that the 'wise' wife learned to live with the mistress, and the sensible mistress to cope with her jealousy of rivals.[69] What is significant is that the power of the monarch forced women to disguise their emotions in order to pander to the desires of their lovers. The ways in which royal wives gained or lost influence over their husbands' policies by their manipulative behaviour has yet to be explored.

The second group of influential women were the mistresses of kings whose access to power was, like that of queens, via their sexuality, but, unlike that of queens, was illicit. To become the mistress of a king or other courtier was dangerous. While successful women gained patronage,

[65] Ibid. 32. [66] *HMC De L'Isle and Dudley*, vi. 208.

[67] *The King's Cabinet Opened* (1645), in *The Harleian Miscellany*, 10 vols. (1811), vii. 561–3.

[68] Jones, *Charles II*, 28.

[69] A. Fraser, *The Weaker Vessel: Woman's Lot in Seventeenth-Century England* (1984), 402.

influence, financial rewards, or titles, they were always threatened by rivals and enemies. Like male favourites, mistresses depended upon royal favour. She who ceased to please could be discarded and supplanted.

Some aristocratic women became mistresses through their proximity to the monarch while they held a court office; others, such as Barbara Villiers, were given places at court as a colour for their presence. A few young women who were not nobly born came to their monarch's attention through the renown of their beauty, or their talents in acting or singing, as did Nell Gwyn. Any woman who was the sexual partner of a monarch or powerful courtier could find herself the object of people's requests. Regardless of whether she aspired to political influence, she found that she was assumed to possess power. Furthermore, she found that she was attacked for the monarch's policies, whether or not she had intervened.

The sexual power of royal mistresses has fascinated popular historians, but very little has been written about the mistresses of Charles II and James II in more recent times.[70] The succession of major and minor mistresses of Charles II formed one of the chief topics of political satire, and frequently of serious political commentary as well. Attention focuses in particular on the king's French Catholic mistress, Louise de Kerouálle, who was widely blamed for the king's pro-French and pro-Catholic policies.[71] From the 1660s, contemporaries observed that the duke of York was susceptible to female influence, first of his wife, later his mistress. Pepys thought that James was 'led by the nose by his wife', 'in all things but in his codpiece'.[72] Catherine Sedley, mistress of James II, was said to be a tool of the Protestant faction to influence the king.[73] She herself denied any political influence in 1689—'I never ded meddle in any busenesse knowing myselve very unfit for it'—but this was to be expected.[74] We lack a study of her political career and influence.

Thirdly, there were the women who held formal offices at court. They were appointed to places with salaries, and took oaths to serve. They had access to the monarch, depending upon their position in the hierarchy, the sex and personality of the monarch, and their own talents. Not all in the

[70] M. Gilmour, *The Great Lady: A Biography of Barbara Villiers, Mistress of Charles II* (1944); C. H. Hartmann, *La Belle Stuart . . . Frances . . . duchesss of Richmond and Lennox* (1924); B. Bevan, *Nell Gwynn* (1969); id., *Charles II's French Mistress* (1972); J. H. Wilson, *Nell Gwynn* (1952); Fraser, *Weaker Vessel*, ch. 20. For a recent scholarly treatment, see Maguire, 'The Duchess of Portsmorth'. Restoration women and politics are the subject of the current doctoral study of Sonia Wynne, 'The Mistresses of Charles II, 1660–1685', University of Cambridge.

[71] Maguire, 'The Duchess of Portsmouth'.

[72] *The Diary of Samuel Pepys*, ed. R. Latham and W. Matthews, 11 vols. (1970–83), ix. 342.

[73] J. Miller, *James II: A Study in Kingship* (Hove, 1978), 151, dismisses claims to her influence. For Sedley, see Fraser, *Weaker Vessel*, 399–408.

[74] *HMC Finch*, iii. 346.

royal household were nobly born; for example, Bridget Holmes, who had acted as nurse to Charles II, enjoyed a post as mop woman at court for many years.

The sources for an understanding of women's political roles as courtiers are better than for many other aspects of women's history. Courtiers were formally appointed to their salaried positions. Court ladies were more likely to be literate, and accounts of their activity survive in a range of other sources, including letters by their families, patrons, and clients. In what follows, we have attempted to ask questions about courtiers' own political and religious goals, to see if these can be separated from those of their families. We also ask about their religious and cultural aspirations, so that we may estimate their power and influence.

From the sixteenth century onwards, the aristocracy increasingly found that attendance at court was a necessity, since the court was the place where offices, favours, and titles were distributed.[75] In obtaining and distributing patronage, women as well as men had roles. Depending on the sexual proclivities and personal character of the monarch, women might have opportunities as wives, lovers, or friends, from which men by their sex were debarred. Ladies obtained their places at court through their lineage, kinship alliances, and the favour of the monarch; once at court, their success depended to some degree on their own talents. Being married did not debar women from offices at court. Indeed, a suitable marriage could give them access to favour. Even if, as married women, they were under a husband's aegis, they might still work for goals of their own setting.

Women courtiers were office-holders, and like other office-holders they took oaths of office. They might take extra oaths of allegiance in a political crisis. For example, in 1696 a Parliamentary association was organized after a Jacobite assassination plot against William III. It is interesting to observe how historians have written of this incident. Gregg observed that 'even lady Marlborough and the other ladies of the Princess's household took the oath'.[76] But Frances Harris points out that the diplomatic newsletter from which the information was derived makes it clear that Sarah insisted that she and all the princess's servants should sign.[77] In so doing, she asserted that female office-holders were responsible individuals, as men were. Even if women courtiers were married they could be empowered to act as *femes*

[75] L. Stone, *The Crisis of the Aristocracy, 1558–1641* (Oxford, 1965), 402–3.

[76] Gregg, *Queen Anne*, 108.

[77] F. Harris, 'Women at Court, 1660–1714', paper delivered at North American Conference on British Studies, Chicago, 19 Oct. 1996. Many thanks to Dr Harris for allowing us to cite her unpublished work.

sole. Queen Anne gave Abigail Masham a warrant to allow her to give legal discharge when she received money on the queen's behalf, 'notwithstanding coverture'.[78]

In the discussion of female friendship in Chapter 4, we have shown how friendship between women at the highest levels of monarch and courtier could serve political purposes and overlap with political clientage. While friendships had an emotional significance, here we are interested in their instrumental functions. Friendship and clientage could shade into each other. Women at court were dependent on others for favours; in this sense, any friendship was unequal. Furthermore, the obligations were mutual, for while a courtier had expectations from her patron, her patron in turn was obliged to reward the loyal services of a client. And if the friendship between the two women failed, then the formal relationship of patron and client collapsed.[79]

Courtiers served queens consort and royal daughters as well as female monarchs throughout the period. Aristocratic women eagerly sought places at court for a variety of reasons: for the salaries, for patronage opportunities, for their families, and for themselves. Their motives and roles have been discussed by several historians at different periods.[80] Salary *per se* was not the main goal of female courtiers, for the wages were small compared with the opportunities for conferring patronage and gaining other benefits. As Groom of the Stole to Princess Anne, Sarah Churchill had the power to appoint the pages, selling the first two places for £1,200 in 1685.[81] A queen would usually contribute generously to the dowries of her maid of honour, and even to the daughters of her female servants. Anne gave £3,000 to maids of honour who married with her approval, sufficient to supply a modest dowry even if the family provided little more.[82] At the beginning of Queen Anne's reign, Sarah Churchill's income from four offices amounted to £6,000 p.a.[83]

Female courtiers enjoyed their greatest influence on the patronage system

[78] Harris, 'Women at Court'.

[79] For insights into the client–patron relationship, see S. Kettering, 'Friendship and Clientage in Early Modern France', *French History*, 6 (1992), 139–58.

[80] C. Merton, 'The Women who Served Queen Mary and Queen Elizabeth: Ladies, Gentlewomen and Maids of the Privy Chamber, 1553–1603', Ph.D. diss., University of Cambridge, (1993); P. Wright, 'A Change in Direction: The Ramifications of a Female Household, 1558–1603', in D. Starkey (ed.), *The English Court* (1987); Smuts, *Court Culture*; L. Peck, *Court Patronage and Corruption in Early Stuart England* (1990); F. Harris, '"The Honourable Sisterhood": Queen Anne's Maids of Honour', *The British Library Journal*, 19 (1993), 181–98. We are grateful to Dr Harris for allowing us to read her papers before publication. R. O. Bucholz, *The Augustan Court: Queen Anne and the Decline of Court Culture* (Stanford, Calif., 1993).

[81] Harris, *Passion for Government*, 41.

[82] Harris, 'Maids of Honour', 184–5.

[83] Harris, *Passion for Government*, 87.

when a woman was on the throne. The organization of the royal residences gave women rather than men access to the more intimate space around the monarch and controlled access to her person.[84] While some contemporaries belittled the women's power—Sir Robert Cecil advised one friend that the queen would give the women good words 'yet they should never effect suit'[85]—in fact the successful male politicians made sure that they had a woman friend on whom they could rely. Robert Beale, who served as Principal Secretary to Elizabeth when Walsingham was away, prepared a memorandum of advice about the post in 1592, in which he made clear the importance of the women courtiers:

> Learne before your accesse her Ma[jes]tie's disposic[i]on by some in the Privie Chamber w[i]th whom you must keepe creditt, for that will stande you in much steede . . .[86]

To know the queen's mood was vital for her ministers.[87] Access to the queen was crucial for others, especially those in disfavour, who sought to plead their case with Elizabeth directly.[88] Although female courtiers may not have participated in the factional politics of Elizabeth's reign, that is not to conclude that they lacked political influence.[89] In a personal monarchy, knowledge about the monarch's disposition was useful for many kinds of political transactions, both to themselves and their male kin and friends. Some kept abreast of international affairs by their correspondence with members of the ambassadors' trains. Others accompanied their husbands on various duties.[90] Merton concludes that female courtiers' power, like much other political power, was of the moment, ceasing when a woman left the chamber, although she could call on her contacts at a later date.[91] Over a century later, even the politicians who doubted the power of Queen Anne's female attendants to give political advice still liked to have a female friend close to the queen. Harley found a way to a relationship with Anne through her chambermaid, Abigail Masham.[92]

The ladies close to Elizabeth gave their advice to men in confident terms. What is striking about some of the correspondence is the absence of female deference; women engaged with men on some kind of equal terms. In 1589,

[84] Wright, 'A Change of Direction', 159–63; Bucholz, *Augustan Court*, 152–201.
[85] Wright, 'A Change of Direction', 160.
[86] *A Treatise of the Office of . . . Principall Secretarie*, printed in C. Read, *Mr Secretary Walsingham and the Policy of Queen Elizabeth* (1925), 3 vols. (Cambridge, Mass., 1967), i. 423–43.
[87] Merton, 'The Women who Served Queen Mary and Queen Elizabeth', 171.
[88] Ibid. 157–63. [89] Wright, 'A Change in Direction', 160–1.
[90] Merton, 'The Women who Served Queen Mary and Queen Elizabeth', 165–71.
[91] Ibid. 191, 245. [92] Bucholz, *Augustan Court*, 162–6.

Lady Abigail Digby, a Gentlewoman of the Privy Chamber, warned Sir Arthur Heveningham that, if he acted illegally, he would lose the commission of the peace, and it would be beyond her power to help him.[93] Lady Dorothy Edmonds, Lady of the Privy Chamber, declined £100 for a suit, observing that 'for so smale a matter to employe her credyt and forces she will not'.[94] In some cases, the tone is of a superior to an inferior. The Dowager Lady Russell wrote critically to her nephew, Sir Robert Cecil, of various episcopal appointments, giving her advice 'as your good friend', and wishing him not to proceed 'for fear of afterclaps by her Majesty's indignation'.[95] The extent to which similar patterns continued into the early eighteenth century is not clear. Sarah Churchill certainly gave advice in no uncertain terms, but others may have adopted a more deferential style. The whole subject of the influence of aristocratic women in the early modern English court milieu awaits further investigation.

Even in the reign of a male monarch, female relatives of male courtiers could gain informal influence, as did those of James I's powerful favourite, George Villiers. The Villiers ladies provided a comfortable family environment for the ageing king. Chatting with him about domestic matters such as the weaning of children, they had opportunities to make requests. Charles retained the same favourite, but was less amenable to the ladies' persuasion, unless it was exercised through their brother, the duke of Buckingham. Buckingham's sister, Lady of the Bedchamber to the queen, importuned Charles on Henrietta's behalf when Charles had ordered her nurse return to France. After Charles refused her pleas, Lady Denbigh enlisted her brother's assistance. The duke obtained from the king the concession he had denied his wife. The extent to which the Villiers women could pursue their own political goals was, of course, limited. Placed in high favour by the influence of their brother, they were at court to look after family interests. Nevertheless, they developed loyalties of their own to the mistress whom they served. Susan Denbigh held on to her post after her brother's assassination, and died in exile with the queen in Paris in 1652.[96]

One of the roles of women courtiers and those whose male kin were in public office was networking. In a political system which was open to

[93] Merton, 'The Women who Served Queen Mary and Queen Elizabeth', 201–2.

[94] Ibid. 174.

[95] *HMC Salisbury*, v. 121–2; Merton, 'The Women who Served Queen Mary and Queen Elizabeth', 217.

[96] J. Grose, 'A Study of the Political Role of Aristocratic Women at the Court of Charles I, 1625–1640', honours dissertation UWA, 1987.

personal influence, they retailed the news and the information necessary for skilled political operations. Women around the court heard the men's talk, and used their female alliances for further information. Ann, Lady Fanshawe, recorded her own involvement at the royalist court during the Civil War. Arriving in Oxford, where her father was commander, she and her sister 'had the perpetuall discourse of losing and gaining of towns and men'. One of her kinswoman, Lady Rivers, encouraged Ann to wheedle confidential news out of her husband, and 'I might tell her'. While Ann naïvely believed that such political activity 'would make me more beloved of my husband', she ultimately accepted her husband's notion of what it was honourable for him to disclose.[97] Nevertheless, it is clear from her memoirs that Ann was an intelligent observer with her own views of the political crises of the period.

Women around the court networked and kept their male kin informed of the gossip. When Lord Raby was ambassador in Berlin, first his mother and later his wife sent him news. His wife apologized for the trivia of her content, but clearly her husband had requested it:

> I fancy you'll think me very rediculouse to pretend to send you any news of this kind, but you bid me send you all the Chatter-Chitter I heard, so like an obedient wife I'll obey your commands.[98]

Ladies within the ambit of court gossip were aware that their male relatives might not approve of their taking politics too seriously, and consequently adopted a placatory or self-deprecatory style. Lady Westmorland, who had some perceptive comments on the political crisis of 1639, nevertheless offered her views humbly.[99] In 1710, commenting on the Sacheverell case, Lady Wentworth acknowledged to her son that political views were inappropriate for her: 'I know you will laugh at me and say polleticks is not soe fitt for me as to speake in commendation of your most wunderfull prety table.'[100] Lady Russell, applying to King William for the Garter for her son in 1700, deployed the weak woman stereotype: 'I presume on your goodness to forgive a woman's troubling you.'[101]

Work for the family's advancement, the achievement of her own goals,

[97] *The Memoirs of Ann, Lady Fanshawe*, ed. J. Loftis (Oxford, 1979), 111, 115–16. For another example of an aristocratic woman's information seeking, see Dorothy Sidney, dowager countess of Sunderland to her son-in-law, *Some Account of the Life of Rachel Wriothesley Lady Russell* (1819), pt. 2, 109–150.

[98] J. J. Cartwright (ed.), *The Wentworth Papers, 1705–1739* (1883).

[99] PRO, SP 16/420, Countess of Westmorland to Secretary Windebanke, 6 May 1639, fo. 70. Many thanks to Sarah Jones for her transcription of this letter.

[100] Cartwright (ed.), *Wentworth Papers*, 118.

[101] *Life of Lady Russell*, 93.

finding a husband or a lover, could go together. Early in the eighteenth century, Lady Isabella Wentworth wrote steadily to her eldest son of her desire that her youngest daughter Betty would find a place at court: if only Betty could be a maid of honour, 'She would soon gett a good husband, she is now hansom, but will soon fayde, she is not a lasting buity.'[102]

Cultural policies of queens and noblewomen could have political ramifications. At early modern courts, a number of prominent ladies were patrons of the arts. Some, patrons of literature, have been studied by literary historians, especially during the reign of Elizabeth.[103] Queen Henrietta Maria built up a musical establishment, and enjoyed masques and dancing.[104] Her court theatricals were significant beyond the moment of performance, for her participation aroused great contemporary ire. William Prynne, who published an attack on women actors as 'notorious whores', was by many regarded as a martyr when he suffered the savage punishment of the loss of his ears. The women courtiers in England, unlike their counterparts in France, seem not to have formed salons, or any such female-dominated social meeting places.[105] Many wives and widows of the peers and gentry acquired honour and reputation through their pious and charitable hospitality in the countryside.[106]

Some women were genuinely interested in politics and attained considerable power. Among those whose influence requires further study is Lucy Hay, the countess of Carlisle, who competed with the Villiers kin in the 1620s for influence with the queen. By the 1630s, foreign ambassadors noted that she had great favour with Henrietta, and male courtiers wrote poetry to her to ingratiate themselves.[107] At the crisis in relations between Crown and Parliament in 1640–2, she transferred her allegiance to the Parliamentary party. It was later alleged that it was she who had alerted the five Members of Parliament to the king's disastrous attempt to arrest them in the House of Commons. (She had no doubt heard of the plan from the queen, who later blamed herself for urging Charles to execute it.)[108] Subsequently, the countess acted as an intermediary between the Parliamentarians Holles and Stapleton, who led the peace party, and the royalists. She was known as a

[102] Cartwright (ed.), *Wentworth Papers*, 61, 84.

[103] M. P. Hannay (ed.), *Silent but for the Word: Tudor Women as Patrons, Translators and Writers of Religious Works* (Kent, Ohio, 1985).

[104] Smuts, *Court Culture*, 124–5.

[105] For a discussion of women in France, see C. C. Lougee, *Le paradis des femmes: Women, Salons, and Social Stratification in Seventeenth-Century France* (Princeton, 1976).

[106] F. Heal, *Hospitality in Early Modern England* (Oxford, 1990), 178–83.

[107] Smuts, *Court Culture*, 189, 194.

[108] S. R. Gardiner, *History of England*, 10 vols. (1884–1904), x. 135–7; E. Hyde, earl of Clarendon, *History of the Rebellion and Civil Wars in England*, ed. W. D. Macray, 6 vols. (Oxford, 1888), i. 481.

supporter of the Presbyterian party against the Independents. In 1647 one of the articles of impeachment against the Presbyterian leaders was that they had met at the countess's house to correspond with the queen.[109] All the evidence suggests that she was a keen politician with considerable influence, one whose career would repay study.

One of the most successful courtiers for many years was Sarah Jenyns, later duchess of Marlborough, whose political influence both enraged and fascinated her contemporaries. Her 'Passion for Government' has been brilliantly analysed by Frances Harris in a recent biography.[110] Throughout her life Sarah repined that she was not a man to fight for liberty or to take a seat in Parliament: 'I am confydent I should have been the greatest Hero that ever was known in the Parliament Hous if I had been so happy as to have been a Man.'[111] At the end of her life, in her Memoirs, she enunciated both her credo and her sense of defeat at her sex and her age:

> I am and ever shall be of the opinion that nothing is so much worth struggling for as liberty; . . . But alas! what can it signify, the endeavours of an old woman.[112]

Sarah belied her influence in such a comment. Hers was a political influence which neither her contemporaries nor historians have been able to ignore. While Sarah wished that she had been a man, in fact her political influence depended upon her emotional friendship with Anne, an intimacy which would have been impossible for a male courtier.

The fourth group of aristocratic women with political influence consisted of the wives and widows of gentlemen. From their country houses, many kept abreast of affairs at Westminster through a network of correspondents. Their influence was particularly marked in religious policies. In some cases, their roles appeared most clearly when they were widowed. The Dowager Lady Montague, who held masses at Battle Abbey for over a hundred people in the 1590s, took advantage of her social position to avoid prosecution.[113] Similarly, a few noblewomen enjoyed political influence although they had no formal places at court. In the counties, some literate gentlewomen kept up to date by correspondence with their relatives in London who respected their interest in politics. As we shall see, noblewomen and gentlewomen were actively engaged in proselytizing for their respective causes during the Civil War.

[109] P. Crawford, *Denzil Holles 1598–1680: A Study of his Political Career* (1979), 109 n.
[110] Harris, *A Passion for Government.* [111] Ibid. 194–5.
[112] *Memoirs of Sarah, Duchess of Marlborough*, 302.
[113] Crawford, *Women and Religion*, 61.

FIG. 46. Sarah Churchill, duchess of Marlborough. The duchess of Marlborough exercised political power through her friendship with Queen Anne. Sarah's charm, beauty, and influence are symbolized by the two cupid figures, one of whom nudges a crown (placed beside an overflowing bag of gold coins) with his foot; the other holds a bow

Parliamentary politics became increasingly important in the later seventeenth century, and aristocratic women engaged in electoral contests. In 1668, Anne Clifford, dowager countess of Pembroke, determined that the borough of Appleby would return one of her Tufton grandsons. Although Joseph Williamson's friends assured him that the town and gentry were supporting him, they reported that success was unlikely unless the 'old lady' also supported him, for she 'is as absolute in that borough as any are in any other'. Even when the powerful politician Lord Arlington was enlisted on Williamson's side, the countess was unmoved: he could easily find his client a seat elsewhere, she wrote, 'without doing wrong or discourtesy to a widow that wants but 2 years of four score'.[114] She carried the day, and, on her death, the Tuftons inherited her interest.[115] Other women likewise involved themselves in Parliamentary elections, although their activities in the later seventeenth century have been comparatively little studied, apart from those of the duchess of Marlborough, whose electioneering was on a grander scale than many commanded.[116] In the bitterly fought by-election for Clitheroe in Lancashire in 1693, the widow of the deceased member was among those implicated in attempts to bribe electors.[117] In 1705, Elizabeth Isham oversaw her husband's campaign in Northamptonshire, distributing material and reporting on progress,[118] while, in Newcastle-under-Lyme in Staffordshire, Lady Gower campaigned for a candidate who, she hoped, would maintain her family's interest for the future benefit of her sons.[119]

Throughout the period, élite women took an interest in certain public trials. In 1619 when the countess of Exeter appeared in the Star Chamber on a poisoning charge, over thirty prominent ladies accompanied her in their coaches.[120] Charles I issued a proclamation forbidding all women from attending the trial of the earl of Castlehaven for sodomy and rape 'upon pain of ever after being reputed to have forfeited their modesty'.[121] Women attended Charles I's trial in 1649. When the name of Fairfax was called, a lady reputed to be his wife, declared 'he had more wit than to be there'.[122] At the

[114] *Calendar of State Papers Domestic, 1667–8*, 174, 190–1, 195, 196, 219. Thanks to Gerald Aylmer for these references.

[115] B. D. Henning (ed.), *History of Parliament: The House of Commons, 1660–1690* (1983), 435.

[116] F. Harris, 'The Electioneering of Sarah, Duchess of Marlborough', *Parliamentary History*, 2 (1983), 71–92.

[117] History of Parliament Trust, draft constituency article, Clitheroe. We are grateful to the Trust for allowing us to cite this and other material.

[118] History of Parliament, Sir Justinian Isham, draft biography.

[119] History of Parliament, draft constituency article, Newcastle-under-Lyme, Staffs.

[120] PRO, SP 14/105/96, fo. 30^{v}.

[121] Quoted in Sharpe, *Personal Rule*, 190.

[122] Clarendon, *History*, iv. 486 (Bk. xi. 235).

trial of Sacheverell in 1710, since all the ladies wanted 'to see and be seen at the Tryal', they all became great housewives so they could be there each morning at 7 a.m.[123] Later, in 1788, women were forbidden to sit in the galleries of the House of Commons.[124]

From many letters, political writings, and satires, we can see that women who exercised political power were hated and feared by their contemporaries. Influential noblewomen were deeply resented during the 1630s, and during the 1640s and 1650s, popular satires manifested a similar hostility to the wives of prominent Parliamentary politicians. Henry Neville recounted sexual gossip, and mocked a 'Parliament of Ladies', an assembly in which the wives and alleged lovers of several Parliamentary leaders debated their sexual requirements. By constituting the ladies as Members of Parliament, and attributing to them the stereotypical lusts of insatiable women, Neville sought to render the ladies' power ridiculous.[125] Nevertheless, although women's political influence was satirized and attacked, it was an ever-present factor in Tudor and Stuart political life.

POPULAR POLITICS BEFORE 1640

There are two main points to be made about ordinary women's involvement in politics. First, they had some access to information about the political world, including news about the monarch, the court, Parliament, and elections. Secondly, women had their own views about priorities, and might engage in public political action in defence of what they saw as their moral and communal obligations.

To discover what ordinary women knew about politics and public affairs is a difficult task. In the twentieth century, historians have become more interested in the 'political nation', but the answers about levels of knowledge of county or national politics are far from clear. We would suggest that, among the élite, the gentry, the well-educated, the wealthy, women were better informed about politics than the mass of the population, even the male portion. Although women were less likely to be literate than men of the same social level, they heard political news being discussed. Women of middling social rank who lived in cities could observe public events and participate in discussion, much like their male counterparts. In London,

[123] Cartwright (ed.), *Wentworth Papers*, 112–13.

[124] L. Colley, *Britons: Forging the Nation, 1707–1837* (New Haven, 1992), 248–9.

[125] [H. Neville], *A Parliament of Ladies* (1647); [H. Neville], *Newes from the New Exchange, or the Commonwealth of Ladies* (1650).

particularly, there were wide networks of news exchange. People heard news in shops, in the streets, and at church. Probably those in the rural communities, both women and men, had less information, although they may have had views about daily political events. Literate women had their own networks of correspondents.

Although women were not so directly involved in political matters as men were, nevertheless they were aware of changes in government and religion in a similar fashion to men of the same social rank. Their sources of information may have been no different from men's. Yet they were expected to respond differently to public and political events. Various stereotypes were available to categorize their involvement. Women were seen as weak and fearful, fainting or miscarrying at news of disasters; or they were portrayed as viragos, fighting and unnatural. But whatever the stereotypes, many individual women had political views, and expressed their ideas in ways which were influenced by their social level as well as their gender. A noblewoman was unlikely to participate directly in a street demonstration, although she might be involved in organizing one;[126] a countrywoman was unlikely to dine with a courtier.

Furthermore, as Colley argues for a later period, the political interests of women should not be seen in terms of protest alone. In the wars with France at the end of the eighteenth century, some women showed patriotism in contributing to the war effort.[127] Women as child-rearers participated in the shaping of the next generation. They taught their children about Christianity and the importance of obedience to the powers that be. The majority of women of middling social status were not religious dissidents, but instead inculcated conformity and intolerance. In so far as families were the nurseries of Church and State, women were engaged in political work in rearing their children to be good citizens and subjects. There are also signs that they were conscious of themselves as patriotic Englishwomen. By thanking God that they were born in 'a Land of Light (what Land like England)', they promoted concepts of nationalism.[128]

When we consider the political activities of the mass of ordinary women, we confront a number of difficulties with sources. There is the by now familiar problem of sources which were not written by women themselves. Nor is the problem simply that women's words have been refracted through

[126] When women demonstrated for peace in Aug. 1643, one allegation was that they had met at the house of Lady Brouncker where they had been given white ribbons; Crawford, *Holles*, 96.

[127] Colley, *Britons*, 250–62.

[128] Bodl., MS Rawlinson D 1308, Mary Carey, 'A Dialogue betwixt the soule and the body', 11 Feb. 1649[50], fo. 180.

the lenses of other perspectives; observers experienced particular problems when confronted with public political activity which was sometimes violent. Commentators were more likely to magnify the presence of women than to ignore them. If women were throwing down hedges or massing for a demonstration outside Parliament, then their outraged contemporaries were likely to comment on their unwomanly behaviour, castigating them for departing from the usual modesty of their sex. By an optical illusion, active women became Medusas, Hecubas, Amazons, or even quasi-men, 'of a gallant and true Masculine Spirit'.[129]

Yet the problem is also one of magnitude: there are too many sources about women's involvement in mass politics during the early modern period. Ralph Houlbrooke alluded to this problem in a valuable pioneering survey of women's involvement in 'common action' from the fifteenth century to the outbreak of the Civil War. He used a sample of protests from the records of the court of Star Chamber, but pointed out that 'a systematic examination of all possibly relevant Star Chamber bills would undoubtedly reveal a very much larger number'.[130] Further research needs to be undertaken in the records from the towns, cities, and countryside of early modern England before we can map out the parameters of women's involvement in public protests.

If we are to understand women's involvement in mass politics, we need a different starting-point from that dictated by a study of general popular movements in which a few female participants can be identified. We can gain more insight by starting with women themselves, with their goals, and then going on to consider the kinds of action open to them. If we acknowledge that women's values and consciousness were on occasions different from those of men, we can recognize that they had their own objectives in political action. Their task was to sustain life, both in the world they inhabited and in the one to come. In pursuit of material and spiritual goals, their most common forms of collective action were protests over the price of food, over fluctuations in trade, against war, and about religious matters.

All women had religious views of some kind, and were affected by the doctrinal and institutional changes of the sixteenth and seventeenth centuries. Closer than men to the daily events of sickness and death, many

[129] Examples cited by P. Higgins, 'The Reactions of Women, with special reference to Women Petitioners', in B. Manning (ed.), *Politics, Religion and the English Civil War* (1973), 179–80.

[130] R. Houlbrooke, 'Women's Social Life and Common Action in England from the Fifteenth Century to the Eve of the Civil War', *Continuity and Change*, 1 (1986), 339–52.

women depended upon their faith. Consequently, changes in religious beliefs disturbed and distressed them. We know, from the work of Margaret Spufford, about the religious debates of ordinary people in the country-side.[131] Alterations in religious rituals and practices impelled some women to object; others believed that further changes were necessary, and were active from the late sixteenth century in promoting new forms of worship.

Women's reactions were often different from those of men, and contemporaries and historians have understood them differently. Here we shall focus on the differences. What choices did women have in the form their protests might take? To what extent could they turn to direct action to achieve their goals?

Women's comparative social dispossession has been suggested as an explanation for their attraction to public action. Weber argued that since women, like poorer men, had no property, they turned to protest because they had nothing to lose.[132] This theory mistakenly assumes that women as a sex were universally deprived, and denies women any positive goals. Other historians have seen women as solely concerned about their domestic affairs. In the typology of political action, food riots and protests over common lands and wastes have been rated as unimportant. They were not 'the great issues' of the 1640s and 1650s.[133] But while their social superiors did not usually view the priorities of ordinary people very seriously—commanders were contemptuous of the country soldiers who abandoned their posts in September 1642 to gather the harvests—food was fundamental to economic life. Responsible for feeding others, women claimed the right to protest about food prices, about unjust authorities, and ultimately about the wars which did so much damage to a subsistence economy.

Female participation in rural protests and street politics was disturbingly visible to contemporaries, if not to subsequent historians. Most historians have not discussed gender questions explicitly, so that women are likely to end up in their accounts as bit-part players, or else to be ignored altogether.[134] Yet contemporaries could not avoid gender issues. Apart from the involvement of women, which to widespread perception was a different legal matter from mixed groups rioting, some riot leaders might take on a

[131] M. Spufford, *Contrasting Communities: English Villagers in the Sixteenth and Seventeenth Centuries* (Cambridge, 1974).

[132] M. Weber, *The Sociology of Religion* (4th edn., 1965).

[133] B. Sharp, *In Contempt of All Authority: Rural Artisans and Riot in the West of England, 1586–1660* (Berkeley, 1980), 220.

[134] J. Sharpe, *Crime in Early Modern England, 1550–1750* (1984).

female persona. In cases such as that of 'Lady Skimmington' in the Western Risings of 1626–32, three male leaders were disguised under this feminine appellation.[135] (Riding Skimmington in the west country, however, was a charivari against rebellious wives who were rumoured to be unfaithful or to beat their husbands.)[136] In other cases, such as that of Captain Dorothy, a married woman served as leader.[137]

Here we propose to discuss four main forms of public political protest: food riots, riots over common rights, Parliamentary petitions, and religious protests. The context of the first two forms of rural protests was the growing impoverishment in the countryside. Common rights on which poorer people depended for their livelihood were threatened by landowners' attempts to enclose land or to mine for minerals. All of these protests had a basis in claims to rights: the rights of people to make their wants known, their legal rights to land, their rights as aggrieved subjects to petition the monarch, and their responsibility as Christians to defend their faith. Formal rights could, in a crisis, expand, and so establish new bases for action, and new political traditions of protest. Women saw themselves as having special responsibilities. They claimed the right to protest, and established or continued diverse modes of common female action. Before the crises of the 1640s and 1650s, therefore, women had already established traditions of collective political protest.

Food riots were the first form of protest in which women were active. Social historians have illuminated the role of ordinary people in effective protest against the prices of food in times of scarcity. The populace, working from an agreed sense of morality, appealed to officials for assistance. Their threat was of uncontrollable disorder; their rulers were able, through concessions, to appease their grievances. As E. P. Thompson showed many years ago, the crowd in riots had various legitimating notions.[138] Moreover, by dispersing when the price of grain was lowered, the protesters legitimated the moral authority of the governing class. Other historians have discussed food riots in early modern England as a regular phenomenon which legitimated rather than challenged the structures of

[135] Sharp, *In Contempt of all Authority*, 97–100, 104–5; D. Underdown, *Revel, Riot and Rebellion: Popular Politics and Culture in England, 1603–1660* (Oxford, 1985), 110–11.

[136] D. E. Underdown, 'The Taming of the Scold: The Enforcement of Patriarchal Authority in Early Modern England', in A. Fletcher and J. Stevenson (eds.), *Order and Disorder in Early Modern England* (Cambridge, 1985), 129–32.

[137] R. B. Manning, *Village Revolts: Social Protest and Popular Disturbance in England, 1509–1640* (Oxford, 1988), 281.

[138] Thompson, 'The Moral Economy', 188.

authority.[139] They have noted that women were conspicuous in food riots, but conclude that not until the nineteenth century should the food riot be seen as a female province.[140]

If we consider early modern riots in terms of the relationship between rulers and ruled, then it is plausible to argue that women's position in riots was useful to men because women could exploit the ambiguity in the law. Women enjoyed a certain immunity, and it was widely believed, although sometimes mistakenly, that they were less likely to be severely punished.[141] If we look at riots from women's perspective, as an example of their participation in political life, the risks then seem more a matter of serious calculation: after some riots women were hanged. In food riots they had particular goals which they hoped to achieve by collective action, sometimes as women alone with their children, sometimes in concert with men. The point about leadership was not so much whether it was a woman or a man, but whether the riot achieved its objective for the group.

Women played a prominent role in grain riots. At Maldon in 1629 a crowd of over a hundred women and children boarded a ship to prevent grain from being shipped away. The rioters were subsequently tried, and, from those records, Walter has pieced together a picture of some of the women activists. Living an impoverished and tenuous existence, they were regularly in trouble with the town authorities for breaches of regulations. When questioned about the reasons for their actions, most alleged their poverty and want of food, but others alluded to wider issues. Initially, the authorities reacted reasonably leniently, purchasing grain for the poor, but later riots led to harsher proceedings. The May riots had involved crowds of up to 200 to 300 people, including clothworkers. Ann Carter assumed the title of Captain, employed a man to write for her, and toured the clothing towns to raise support. She attempted to arouse the inhabitants of Maldon, saying 'Come, my brave lads of Maldon, I will be your leader for we will not starve.' Her alleged motive for her actions, 'the Crie of the Country and Hir owne want', showed her consciousness of public duty.[142] She and

[139] P. Clark, 'Popular Protest and Disturbance in Kent, 1558–1640', *Economic History Review*, 2nd ser., 29 (1976), 365–81; J. Walter and K. Wrightson, 'Dearth and the Social Order in Early Modern England', *Past and Present*, 71 (1976), 22–42; J. Walter, 'The Social Economy of Dearth in Early Modern England', in J. Walter and R. Schofield (eds.), *Famine, Disease and the Social Order in Early Modern Society* (Cambridge, 1989).

[140] J. Bohstedt, 'Gender, Household and Community Politics: Women in English Riots, 1790–1810', *Past and Present*, 120 (1988), 88–122.

[141] Clark, 'Popular Protest', 376–7. See Ch. 1.

[142] J. Walter, 'Grain Riots and Popular Attitudes to the Law: Maldon and the Crisis of 1629', in J. Brewer and J. Styles (eds.), *An Ungovernable People* (1980), 72.

two male rioters were hanged.[143] In other parts of the country, women took public action over corn prices. In 1630 at Dorchester market when the price of corn had risen too high, a group of women cut the sacks of corn open. The following year they seized corn which was being taken out of the town.[144] On other occasions women objected to the quality of the grain; for example, in Kent in 1631, a riot of fifty to sixty people, most of them women, protested about the coarse quality of the bread-meal offered for sale.[145]

Secondly, women as well as men defended common rights against enclosures or fen drainage. As in food riots, it was widely believed that women enjoyed some special legal privileges. They might throw down hedges and banks with less danger of punishment than men. Although this view was probably mistaken, it encouraged women to participate in violent protests.[146] Thus, in riots, some women turned the doctrine of legal coverture on its head, claiming 'that women were lawlesse, and not subject to the lawes of the realme as men are but might . . . offend without drede or punishment of law'.[147] In the 1606 Rotherham riots, most of the women thought that they were 'lawless because they were women'. Similarly in Dorset in 1619, the rioters assumed there was no legal remedy against women and boys.[148]

Women were active in the conflicts over the drainage of the fenlands in the seventeenth century, although only rarely did they appear as leaders, or make up the majority of protesters. Frequently those throwing down hedges and banks were said to be women and boys, and sometimes men and women acted together.[149] How are we to understand these women rioters? Although Lindley's impression was that women participated 'at the dictate, and under the direction, of their menfolk',[150] equally likely, in view of the legal situation, was that women took a leadership role in some of the fenland riots.

From the point of view of the women whose whole complex economy was being destroyed by the drainers, there were few choices. Rights to graze a cow on the fen common could be worth 30*s.* or 40*s.* p.a., and might make all

[143] Walter, 'Grain Riots', 47–84; K. J. Lindley, 'Riot Prevention and Control in Early Stuart London', *TRHS*, 5th ser., 33 (1983), 109–26; Sharp, *In Contempt of All Authority*, 26–7.

[144] D. Underdown, *Fire From Heaven: Life in an English Town in the Seventeenth Century* (1993), 87.

[145] Clark, 'Popular Protest', 370.

[146] For the legal situation, see Ch. 1.

[147] Cited in Walter, 'Grain Riots', 63.

[148] Cited in K. Lindley, *Fenland Riots and the English Revolution* (1982), 254.

[149] E. Kerridge, 'The Revolts in Wiltshire against Charles I', *Wiltshire Archaeological and Natural History Magazine*, 57 (1958), 64–75; Higgins, 'Women Petitioners', 182–3.

[150] Lindley, *Fenland Riots*, 63.

the difference between poverty and destitution.[151] Those with legal rights went to law, and those without, who were in dire poverty, threw down the banks. In 1637 there were riots over the drainage of the Great Level in Norfolk and in Cambridgeshire. The investigating civil lawyer found that those involved were 'so miserable and base' that they were not worth bothering about, but a woman accused of being 'the first mover of this mutiny' was imprisoned, perhaps because she had a reputation as a witch and had allegedly used magic against the drainers' servants. Women also defended the rioters; a crowd threw stones to drive off the messengers who went to Wicken to make arrests in 1638.[152]

Many women who were involved in public protests during the sixteenth and seventeenth centuries were forthright in their views. Sometimes they showed contempt of the civil authorities and their processes of law. Cited for offences including drunkenness in the 1620s, Dorothy Berry, one of the Maldon rioters, told the constable 'she wold bring her dogg for one of her suerties [*sic*] and her Catt for the other'.[153] Reading against the grain of the sources, we can see women active about their own concerns.

A third form of communal protest was petitioning. From medieval times, women had petitioned the monarch and the courts for redress of various grievances. The situation of the married woman at law was anomalous, and, although Tudor and Stuart courts on occasions dismissed the rights of married women to petition, other courts at other times entertained their petitions. The state papers of the Tudor and Stuart periods indicate that the more usual course was to petition the monarch or a powerful councillor,[154] but at the opening of the Long Parliament, on 7 November 1640, Sarah Burton and Susannah Bastwick petitioned Parliament on behalf of their imprisoned husbands.[155]

The religious impetus for female activism

The most significant impetus for political participation among ordinary women was religious. Yet their religious activism differed in many respects

[151] J. M. Neeson, *Commoners: Common Right, Enclosure and Social Change in England, 1700–1820* (Cambridge, 1990), 316.

[152] Lindley, *Fenland Riots*, 92–3, 97, 100. In these two cases the women were widows, but in other riots their status was given as wives.

[153] Cited in Walter, 'Grain Riots', 57–8.

[154] Barbara Harris counted 56 petitions which noblewomen made to Wolsey and Cromwell; B. J. Harris, 'Women and Politics in Early Tudor England', *Historical Journal*, 33 (1990), 271.

[155] For much of the information about the history of women petitioners, we are indebted to the work of Frances Kelly (Cambridge University) and Amanda Whiting (University of Melbourne) who have kindly shared their unpublished work with us.

from the patterns of women's participation in secular protest movements. While food and enclosure riots played out a form of class conflict whereby labouring women fought for economic survival, religious radicalism was not tied to a specific social class or geographical context. On the contrary, it tended to cut across class lines, and to manifest itself in both urban and rural settings. Female religious activism also embraced many different doctrinal contexts: Catholic as well as Protestant women from a wide range of denominations felt impelled to act on their convictions.

From the standpoint of politics, female collectivities are like icebergs whose greatest bulk remains hidden from view. As we have seen, bonds between women were woven into the very fabric of village life, formed and strengthened in the course of neighbourly sociability and female interdependence. The potential for communal action always existed, because women were socially linked for local occasions such as the all-female rites of childbirth. But women's personal religiosity did not emerge into the political arena (and thus intrude into the chronicles recorded by men) except at times of acute crisis. Just as economic distress supplied the fuse that kindled female agrarian protest, women's apprehensions of a general crisis in Church and State provided the stimulus which transformed individual godliness into public, political, and communal modes of action.

Seventeenth-century women could point to a long history of participation in radical religious movements stretching back to the Middle Ages and earlier. Women had been prominent in the Lollards and in separatist groups such as the Family of Love. More immediately, the sixteenth-century Reformation (or the Counter-reformation in the case of Catholic women) gave an epic dimension to seventeenth-century female protest movements. The vivid accounts of female martyrs in Foxe's *Acts and Monuments* were widely circulated among women of all ranks, exerting a strong influence on seventeenth-century female ideals.

The well-known story of the deepening crisis in the English Church and State which led to civil war will not be retold here. Our concern with the general narrative is limited to its relevance as the cause and context of women's political activism. We shall describe the evolution of women's engagement in the political realm, with the main emphasis on the ways in which women's behaviour in this sphere differed from that of men.

Women's political participation in the decades preceding the Civil War began as an extension of their personal religiosity. The female paragon of piety had become a well-known type by the 1620s, delineated not only in adulatory funeral sermons, but in letters and memoirs by female friends and relations.[156] Yet the very notion of 'personal' or family devotions was inherently ambiguous. Women's spiritual efforts could be interpreted either as private and innocuous or as public and contentious, depending upon the broader context of their beliefs and behaviour. Certain forms of personal piety were thought to have political agency at the time, although nowadays we do not recognize them as either efficacious or political. Women's extemporaneous prayers, for example, could be directed to specific political ends; as Wallington noted, 'by prayer the Queen Mother was sent out of this Land'.[157] As early as 1625, Lady Eleanor Davies used prophecy as a medium for broadcasting her political views. A few years later, a Huntingdonshire woman named Jane Hawkins delivered ecstatic visions of the downfall of the bishops and the Anglican Church before a large congregation.[158]

Moreover, even intimate family decisions could have implications for the community at large. Lucy Hutchinson's scruples about infant baptism, which arose during her first pregnancy during the 1630s, led her to persuade her husband that paedo-baptism was contrary to Scripture. A meeting of ministers convened to debate the issue failed to convince the Hutchinsons, who decided not to baptize their child. As a consequence, they were reviled as extremists and ostracized by the neighbourhood.[159]

Family roles of wifely obedience and subjection could be a framework and springboard for political activism. During the 1620s and 1630s, women served as their husbands' religio-political 'helpmeets', suffering martyrdom at second hand. During the gruesome punishment for seditious libel meted out to Henry Burton, John Bastwick, and William Prynne in 1637, in which their ears were cut off, Burton asked his wife to fortify his morale by showing the same heroism: she should not 'blemish the glory of this day with one teare, or so much as one sigh'. She replied in significant imagery that she was 'more cheerefull of this day, then of her wedding day', an answer which 'exceedingly rejoyced his heart'. Burton said of his wife, 'Shee is but a young Souldier of Christs, but shee hath already endured

[156] J. McIntosh, 'English Funeral Sermons, 1560–1640', M.Litt. diss., University of Oxford (1990); D. Willen, '"Communion of the Saints": Spiritual Reciprocity and the Godly Community in Early Modern England', *Albion*, 27 (1995), 19–41; for an example see Folger, MS V. a. 166, 'An Account of the Lady Lucy . . . to a Particular Friend of Hers, Mrs. Moore'.

[157] BL, MS Add. 40883, fo. 26. For examples of female political prayers see D. Pakington, Prayers, Bodl., MS Add. B. 58, fos. 2–4^{v}, 36–52; E. Mordaunt, *The Private Diarie of Elizabeth, Viscountess Mordaunt* (Duncairn, 1856), 33–4; BL, MS Add. 40883, fo. 129^{v}.

[158] P. Mack, *Visionary Women* (Berkeley, 1992), 15–18; K. Thomas, *Religion and the Decline of Magic* (1971), 162–4.

[159] Hutchinson, *Memoirs of the Life of Colonel Hutchinson*, ed. Sutherland, 169.

many a sharpe brunt.'[160] When portrayed as matrimonial loyalty, female political dissent was especially problematic for contemporaries, since wives could claim they were fulfilling their marital vow to serve and obey their husbands.[161]

Church courts during the 1630s also cited ministers' wives along with (or sometimes instead of) their husbands for the women's outspoken criticism of Laudian innovations. The rector of Twistledon confessed his wife had spoken against the reading of the Book of Sports, saying that 'we may not do evil that good may come of it'. She had also denounced the contention that sabbath sports kept men out of the alehouses, for it was like the Pope 'allowing stews to avoid fornication'.[162]

In religious activism, as in women's work and culture, marriage was merely one of many different contexts that defined female life. Even in the midst of marriage and child-bearing, women could turn to alternative social, cultural, and economic interactions. Some of these collectivities were composed solely of their own sex; others crossed gender as well as family boundaries. This pattern of diverse kinds of associations also characterized women's religious and political activities. While many women expressed their convictions through 'relative' duties which harmonized with the partisan aims of husbands and sons, some developed views which clashed with those of family members, or expressed their convictions independently of male associations. Through their actions, these women challenged contemporary assumptions about women's passive and subordinate role in the political domain.

In their attendance at communal religious observances, women contested the boundaries between the personal and the political. During the polarized climate of the 1630s, women's presence at lectures and sermons outside their own parochial boundaries was taken as a critique of the establishment doctrine expounded in their parish churches. Puritan weekday lectures were so likely to be frequented by women that they were described by the Laudian vicar of Godalming, Nicholas Andrewes, as 'good for nothing but for women to make gossiping matches'. Because it was perceived as politically threatening, women's behaviour was labelled

[160] J. Bastwick, *A Briefe Relation of certain speciall and most materiall passages, and speeches in the Starre-Chamber* (1637), 28; BL, MS Add. 21,935, fos. 59–63.

[161] P. Crawford, 'Public Duty, Conscience, and Women in Early Modern England', in J. Morrill, P. Slack, and D. Woolf (eds.), *Public Duty and Private Conscience in Seventeenth-Century England* (Oxford, 1993), 70–1.

[162] Northants RO, Correspondence Book, 65/79. Many thanks to Julian Davies for this reference.

by the technical term 'gadding', and punished in the ecclesiastical courts.[163]

Moreover, by ranging beyond their own parishes, even the illiterate could procure a sophisticated education in political as well as theological issues. In radical London districts such as the parish of St Stephen Coleman Street, those who attended sermons and lectures were exposed to a wide range of current political theory.[164] Contemporaries were well aware of the rabble-rousing potential of a preaching clergy to incite the illiterate masses. As Roger Whitby remarked, 'A violent preacher that hath the ear of the people, will lead them which way he pleases . . . Preachers doe commonly blow ye bellows of popular commotions.'[165] Few historians have noted, however, that women were as likely as men to use this route to acquire political information. Women were also prominent members of the London political crowds of the 1630s, where they were reported as expressing approval for the leaders they endorsed.[166]

Beyond their role as frequenters of sermons, lectures, and other communal gatherings, women with financial means harboured the lecturers and preachers whom they favoured for their political views. Women founded lectureships, provided moral and financial support for persecuted ministers, and intervened in parish politics to promote candidates of their choice. One patroness of the 1620s had allegedly beggared her lawyer husband by entertaining divines; she was also reported to have rejoiced at the duke of Buckingham's assassination.[167] Wealthy noblewomen like the countess of Chesterfield sheltered suspended ministers by employing them as private chaplains or as lecturers.[168] Lady Mary Vere advanced several important protégés during the 1620s and 1630s, including radical clerics John Davenport and John Goodwin.[169] During the same period, Lady Jane Barclay patronized the Puritan minister Samuel Gardiner.[170] Lady Elizabeth Clare not only made bequests to Puritan ministers, but served as a carrier of seditious letters in 1635.[171] Women's charitable activities at this time created

[163] J. Davies,'The Growth and Implementation of "Laudianism" with Special Reference to the Southern Province', D.Phil. diss., University of Oxford (1987), 139–40.

[164] D. Kirby, 'The Parish of St Stephen's Coleman Street, London', B.Litt. diss., University of Oxford (1971).

[165] Bodl., MS Eng. Hist. e. 310, R. Whitby, MS notes, fos. 12, 74.

[166] Bastwick, *Briefe Relation*, 27.

[167] T. Raymond, *Autobiography of Thomas Raymond*, ed. G. Davies, Camden Society, 3rd ser., 28 (1917).

[168] R. Porter, *The Life of Mr John Hieron* (1691), 4, 6.

[169] BL, MS Add. 4274, fo. 32; BL, MS Add. 4275, fos. 32, 41, 158–74; T. Edwards, *Gangraena* (Exeter, 1977 repr.), ii. 16–17; D. Willen, 'Godly Women in Early Modern England', *Journal of Ecclesiastical History*, 43 (1992), 574–5.

[170] Kirby, 'St. Stephen's Coleman Street', 32.

[171] Ibid. 51.

a religio-political patronage network outside the Established Church, through which they wielded a good deal of influence.[172]

Years before the outbreak of war, women from a range of social ranks engaged in more radical forms of rebellion. Some removed themselves from the religious and political establishment, either by forming separatist churches within England or through migration abroad. Expanding separatist activity among women during the first half of the seventeenth century is shown by increasing numbers cited in the courts of High Commission. A higher level of indictments also betrays a perception on the part of the authorities that female separatists had become a political threat, despite the fact that they were 'mere women'.

An alternate form of resistance within the Established Church was women's illegal or obstructive protests against what was perceived as proto-Catholic ritual. Church court records for the 1630s show an increase in female acts of resistance and even sabotage against the entire spectrum of Laudian innovations. Women refused to bow at the name of Jesus, protested against the reading of the Book of Sports, tried to move the communion table back to its former position, rejected the cross at baptism, declined to wear a veil at churching, tore up surplices, prevented the removal of ministers they favoured, and agitated against those of whom they disapproved.[173] In some cases, individual women were singled out, like Lady Strode, who was opposed to bowing at the name of Jesus.[174] Elsewhere there are hints that the women of a community had organized themselves into groups for a specific purpose. The women of Beaconsfield were reported to have 'barred and cursed Sir John Lambe to the pit of hell' for suspending two ministers they favoured; the women were instrumental in having them restored to their places.[175] Several pregnant women of Saffron Walden petitioned the church court against the moving of the communion table. Troubled by its position at the east end, they moved it back to its original place.[176]

If we survey the range of social classes engaged in religio-political activities before the war, we find nearly the whole of the social spectrum represented, from gentlewomen like Lady Strode, Lady Elizabeth Clare, or Lady Eleanor Davies, to anonymous groups such as the 'women of Beaconsfield'

[172] For other examples see Willen, 'Godly Women', 569–79; R. Greaves, 'Foundation Builders: The Role of Women in Early English Nonconformity', in R. Greaves (ed.), *Triumph over Silence: Women in Protestant History* (Westport, Conn., 1985), 78–81; P. Seaver, *The Puritan Lectureships* (Stanford, Calif., 1970), 41–2, 158–63, 217–19.

[173] Davies, 'Laudianism', 173, 201, 262–3; M. Cary, *The Little Horns Doom and Downfall* (1651), 9.

[174] Wilts. RO, D5/28/34. Many thanks to Julian Davies for this reference.

[175] Davies, 'Laudianism', 201.

[176] Som. RO, D/D/Ca 309/227.

cited by the church courts for their defiance of Laudian ritual. Among middling, artisan, and labouring classes, we can point to women activists of the 1630s who later became well-known leaders in the separatist movement, like Dorothy Hazard, who sat sewing in her grocer's shop on Christmas day as a 'witness for God', or the Leveller leader Katherine Chidley, who proselytized for separatist congregations throughout the 1620s and 1630s.[177]

Before the Civil War, officials were more likely to cite upper-rank women by name as individuals, whereas lower down the social scale there are more frequent references to female groups, treated by the courts as if they had acted in concert. Some of this apparent class contrast in women's modes of behaviour may have been an artefact of the records, since officials were more likely to perceive propertied gentlewomen as individuals with a distinct social and political identity. Yet Star Chamber was capable of targeting plebeian women for exemplary punishment, as in the case of Agnes Clarke, executed for her leadership role in the 1629 Maldon grain riots.[178] The case for co-operative action by middling and plebeian women is even more striking during the 1640s and 1650s, when we can cite direct evidence of organization on the parochial level. But, even before 1640, action by groups of women was apparently a structural feature of plebeian society. In other words, female social and cultural patterns tended to be replicated in the various forms of political organization. Upper-rank women were more likely to act as individuals or within family alliances, whereas plebeian women had evolved collective modes of participation in both secular and religious contexts, organized by the locality of parish and neighbourhood, and the propinquity of friends.

Although female secular and religious protest movements had thus emerged several decades before the Civil War broke out, women were to engender new forms of political activism in the course of the Civil War and Interregnum. Modes of participation constantly evolved in response to changing conditions, and as a consequence of the increased intellectual sophistication that accompanied women's exposure to new theories of citizenship and natural rights. Like their male counterparts, women also learned about political realities from the experience of disillusion with a succession of governmental authorities who failed to address their concerns.

177 E. Underhill (ed.), *The Broadmead Records* (1897), 10; I. Gentles, 'London Levellers in the English Revolution: The Chidleys and Their Circle', *Journal of Ecclesiastical History*, 29 (1978), 281–309.

178 For a contemporary account which relates how Clarke was targeted for her leadership role in the Maldon riots, see Bodl., MS Firth c. 4, p. 503.

In a crisis, it is difficult to disentangle motivation. Sometimes we lack evidence; at other times, the evidence is difficult to interpret. Ann Carter was hanged for her part in the Maldon grain riots: was she protesting about social justice or did she have other motives? Although we have distinguished food riots, common right riots, petitioning campaigns, and religious protests for purposes of discussion, in practice the categories of protest were not rigidly separated. We do know that women's participation was voluntary. Women chose to act, not because they were constrained by the duties of formal office, but because they had a sense of common rights and public responsibility, as men did. As the women petitioners told MPs in 1649, 'Are we Christians, and yet must we sit still and keep at home?'[179]

What emerges clearly from the evidence is the presumption that women will be involved in public protests. Although both contemporary and modern commentators may refer to 'viragos' and 'amazons', finding themselves uncomfortable with those they term 'redoubtable' females, women themselves participated in protest movements as part of their traditional social role. This is not to say that women were unconscious of their female identity when they engaged in protest; on the contrary, in many instances they exploited their special status as women, their archetypal role as wives and mothers. The range of issues over which they protested came from their recognition of their social obligations as women, from their female consciousness.

WOMEN AND REVOLUTION, 1640–1660

War, whether foreign or civil, was thought to be men's business. That the Civil War was a masculine affair was underscored in countless ways during the conflict, perhaps most blatantly in a royalist standard portraying a naked soldier with an unsheathed sword and an erect penis, with the motto 'ready to use both' blazoned in Latin.[180] While it was recognized that women suffered from the impact of war on their own lives, men envisioned the female role as a passive and subordinate one. Women were to carry on with domestic tasks as best they could, supporting the efforts of fathers, husbands, brothers, and sons while bearing their own losses with pious

[179] *To the supreme authority* [5 May 1649].

[180] I. Gentles, 'The Iconography of Revolution: England 1642–49', in I. Gentles, J. Morrill, and B. Worden (eds.), *Writers, Soldiers and Statesmen* (Cambridge, 1998). Many thanks to Ian Gentles for allowing us to cite his forthcoming work.

fortitude. At most, women were urged to contribute financial aid, or direct their prayers towards a godly resolution of the conflict.[181]

Yet, during the course of the war, women from every sector of society challenged the assumption that their endeavours were irrelevant to the outcome of the struggle. In this section we explore the diversity of their responses to the events of the Civil War and Interregnum. In what ways did their political beliefs and behaviour differ from that of men? Can we identify any common attitudes to the conflict which women shared as a group? What theories of gender and citizenship did they evolve to justify their encroachment into the public political space?

As we have seen, some women had energetically opposed the Laudian regime several decades before the outbreak of civil strife. Moreover, women were already aware of each other's activities as a collective female response, grounded in their common interests as a sex. As the countess of Westmorland wrote to Secretary Windebanke in 1639, in a letter offering advice on the king's strategy, 'they say the women in Scotland are chief stirrers of this war, [I] think it not so shameful for women in England to wish well to the peace of these nations'.[182] While admitting that 'to meddle in things above us is dangerous', the countess excused her intrusion into state affairs on the grounds of extreme urgency, pleading that her concern for 'the children unborn, enforceth me to utter my mind'.[183] For such women, what distinguished the politics of the 1640s was their perception of a cataclysmic crisis whose effects threatened the destruction of everything they valued.

The existence of a state of emergency in which normal rules of political behaviour did not apply was identified early in the 1640s by Parliamentary theorists and by radical clergy. Termed the 'law of necessity' by militant preachers like John Goodwin, the doctrine was employed throughout the war years to justify everything from Parliamentary resistance to regicide.[184] What has not been recognized by historians is that women had grasped the relevance of the 'law of necessity' and applied it to their own circumstances. Women were as ready as men to see a plot against their own lives and

[181] For example, BL, MS Add. 4275, John Davenport to Lady Vere, fo. 158; *The Most Humble Petition of the Gentlewomen, Tradesmens Wives, and many others of the Female Sex* (1642), 6 (TT. E. 134 [17]); J. Featley, *Fountaine of Teares* (Amsterdam, 1646), 669.

[182] PRO, SP 16/420, countess of Westmorland to Secretary Windebanke, 6 May 1639, fo. 70.

[183] PRO, SP 16/420, fo. 70, cited in Crawford, 'Public Duty, Conscience, and Women in Early Modern England', 67.

[184] See, for example, W. Prynne, *The Sovereign Power of Parliaments and Kings* (1643); J. Goodwin, *The Butcher's Blessing* (1642) and *Right and Might Well Met* (1649); Cary, *The Little Horns Doom*, 36; and (for an argument *against* Goodwin), J. Geree, *Might overcoming Right or a Cleer Answer to M. John Goodwin's Might and Right Well Met* (1649).

liberties in the Irish rebellion of 1641, the attempt on the five Members of Parliament, and the rest of the series of incidents that triggered the outbreak of civil war. Some had come to believe that the very survival of English Protestantism hung in the balance, that they themselves must serve as makeweights to shift the balance in favour of true religion.[185] Throughout the war years, women on both sides of the struggle were to appeal to the 'law of necessity' to justify unprecedented activities and political agendas.[186]

When conflict assumed a specific form in the 1640 elections to Parliament, some propertied women voiced their partisanship directly by attempting to vote. Because electors' names were entered only in the case of a dispute, we do not know how many jurisdictions saw female bids for suffrage at this time. Contemporaries mentioned at least two instances of women's involvement in elections for the Long Parliament. In Worcestershire, opponents of Sir Thomas Littleton protested that his 'companie gott in first and filled the [polling] place, and many of them weere boyes, women and poore people'.[187] In Suffolk, some women's votes were at first accepted by the clerks before being disallowed and struck out by the High Sheriff.

For the Suffolk election, we have a personal account by Sir Simonds D'Ewes, who served as invigilating sheriff:

> . . . by the ignorance of some of the clerks at the other two tables the oaths of some single women that were freeholders were taken without the knowledge of the said High Sheriff who as soon as he had notice thereof instantly sent to forbid the same, conceiving it a matter very unworthy of any gentleman and most dishonourable in such an election to make use of their voices although they might in law have been allowed.[188]

In a memorandum, D'Ewes added more details:

> upon Tuesday morning some women came to be sworn for the two foresaid knights & Mr Robert's clerk did suddenly take some of them but as soon as Mr High Sheriff had intelligence of it we had word brought to our table where Mr Clerk & my self wrote that Mr Sheriff would have us take no women's oaths & both the knights

[185] Women were aware that theologians had speculated that in the hypothetical case that all men strayed from the true church, a pious woman might lead them back. Analogously, in civic office, if there were no qualified male candidates, a woman might serve.

[186] For examples, see Bodl., MS Clarendon 23, Lady Katherine Ranelagh to Edward Hyde, 3 Mar. 1644, fo. 114; Cary, *The Little Horns Doom*, 35–6, 41–2; M. Cary, *A New and More Exact Map* (1651), 62, 123–5, 170; Geree, *Might overcoming Right*. Geree's pamphlet arguing *against* the 'law of necessity' was dedicated to two prominent Parliamentarian women, Lady Vere and her daughter Lady Fairfax.

[187] D'Ewes, *The Journal of Sir Simonds D'Ewes*, ed. W. Notestein (New Haven, 1923), 463.

[188] BL, MS Harl. 158, Papers of Sir Simonds D'Ewes, fo. 285^{v}.

desired that those that were taken might be put out & that we should take no more, & so we refused the rest of the women after that notice from Mr High Sheriff & when Mr High Sheriff cast up the books he cast out the women out of the general sum.[189]

Significantly, the High Sheriff's objection was not on the score of illegality; as D'Ewes remarked, single women's freehold votes 'might in law have been allowed'. What did the High Sheriff mean by condemning women's suffrage as 'dishonourable'?

Even single women, if allowed to vote, would have exercised a form of magisterial authority over men, a dishonour associated with inversion of the 'natural' hierarchies of class, gender, and age. A female franchise was 'dishonourable' because it threatened to upset the gender order, just as Leveller proposals for manhood suffrage endangered the class order.[190] To the female freeholders of Suffolk, their cause was sufficiently important to warrant testing their rights as property owners. But, to male officials, the taint of female dominion rendered women's votes unacceptable, no matter how crucial the issues at stake.

Women of the middling and lower ranks found other ways of expressing partisan views. During the early 1640s, some women were recorded in the lists of those who pledged a series of loyalty oaths to the government, including the Protestation Oath (1641) and the Solemn League and Covenant (1643). Throughout the decade, individuals and groups of women petitioned Parliament about religious, political, and economic issues. Women also made financial contributions, and canvassed relatives and friends on behalf of favoured causes. In all these contexts, women infused new political meanings into the exercise of customary civic and property rights.

Oath-taking as an expression of civil status was more ambiguous than Parliamentary suffrage in its implications for women's engagement in politics. The Protestation Oath of 1641 and the Solemn League and Covenant of 1643 were intended not as a species of manhood suffrage but as litmus tests for the loyalty of the populace. Both the 1641 and 1643 oaths presented a perfect blend of religion and politics, framed as they were to unmask traitors to the Church as well as the State.[191]

[189] BL, MS Harl. 165, fo. 8.

[190] See, for example, A. S. P. Woodhouse (ed.), *Puritanism and Liberty* (1974), 53–4, 57–9, 63–4, etc.

[191] For context and wording of the 1641 Protestation Oath, see A. Whiteman, 'The Protestation Returns of 1641–2', *Local Population Studies*, 55 (1995), 14–25. For some contemporary reactions, see, for example, H. Burton, *Protestation Protested* (1641); *The Plain-meaning Protestant, or, An honest Defence of the taking of the Covenant* (1644).

How should women's civic status be interpreted in the process of separating sheep from goats? Was it positive, active, and direct, by virtue of women's spiritual equality? Or was it negative, passive, and vicarious, because of women's exclusion from state affairs? In fact, women's covenantal responsibilities were hotly debated during the 1640s. Presenting the conservative view, John Brinsley claimed that females were excused from formal obligations such as the Solemn League and Covenant, yet were not exempt from obedience: 'Even as it was in Circumcision; The Females were Circumcised in the Males . . . The Females Covenanted in the Males, Women in their Husbands.'[192] But Brinsley needed to convince women of the vicarious nature of their duties precisely because there was no consensus on this issue either in theory or practice.

Although some modern editors of the 1641 Protestation returns have erroneously stated that oaths were imposed only on males,[193] Parliament's actual instructions specified the gender-neutral category of 'inhabitants' over 18. What this meant in terms of women's civil status was interpreted in diverse and contradictory ways. Returns from different localities display a gamut of options, ranging from total exclusion of the female sex at one extreme, to the full inclusion of adult women at the other. Many parishes imposed the oaths only on males over 18. Some tendered the oath to both sexes, but included only male names in returns of oath-takers. Names of female recusants who had rejected the oath, however, might be recorded separately along with those of men who had refused to swear, a clear instance of women's status as 'negative citizens'.[194] Some localities included adult men plus a handful of females identified as widows.[195] Elsewhere, women's names (although not labelled as to status) correspond to the proportion of unmarried female adults.[196]

A minority of jurisdictions recorded names of both sexes in roughly equal numbers.[197] Adult women in these localities apparently claimed active status

[192] J. Brinsley, *A Looking-Glass for Good Women* (1645), 37.

[193] See, for example, 'The Protestation Oath Rolls for Middlesex, 1641–2', ed. A.J.C.G., *Supplement to Miscellanea Genealogica et Heraldica* (1920); 'The Dorset Protestation Returns Preserved in the House of Lords, 1641–2', ed. E. Fry, *Dorset Records*, 12 (1912); 'The Westmorland Protestation Returns of 1641/2', ed. M. Faraday, *Cumbria and Westmorland Antiquarian and Archaeological Society*, 18 (1971), p. viii.

[194] For examples, see W. F. Webster (ed.), *Lincolnshire Protestation Returns, 1641–2* (Nottingham, 1984), 34, 44, 50; Faraday, 'Westmorland Protestation Returns', 4, 9, 17.

[195] For examples, see W. F. Webster (ed.), *Nottinghamshire and Derby Protestation Returns 1641/2* (Nottingham, 1980), 69; Webster, *Lincolnshire Protestation Returns*, 48.

[196] For examples, see A.J.C.G., 'Protestation Oath Rolls for Middlesex', 51, 69, 72; Webster, *Lincolnshire Protestation Returns*, 49; Whiteman, 'Protestation Returns', 20.

[197] See Guildhall, MS 4458/1, St Stephen Coleman Street Vestry Book, fos. 873–9 (analysed below). For other examples see Whiteman, 'Protestation Returns', 20; Webster (ed.),

in the church-state, regardless of matrimonial condition. A notable example of female 'covenantal suffrage' is the 1643 return for St Stephen Coleman Street, a radical London parish which harboured John Goodwin's independent congregation, numerous sects, female preachers like Mrs Attaway, and (later in the 1640s) Fifth Monarchists like Mary Cary.[198] Anne Glover, who headed the list of female oath-takers, was a leading member of the parish who had earlier displayed her Parliamentary allegiance with a £40 contribution to the fund for suppressing the Irish rebels in 1641.[199] In this context, women's oaths evidently represented a self-conscious assertion of covenantal citizenship, one aspect of their multifaceted commitment to the Parliamentary cause.[200]

We can only speculate about the motivation of those women who pledged their names to the various loyalty oaths. It is a different story with the increasingly large and militant groups of women who petitioned Parliament throughout the 1640s and early 1650s, defending their views with sophisticated arguments adapted from current political and constitutional debates. Some female petitioners can be traced to other radical connections, including secular reform movements like the Levellers, and religious interest groups like the Independent churches. For a few leaders, we can glean personal details of marital status and social and economic rank: Mrs Anne Stagg, 'a Gentlewoman and Brewer's Wife', presented one of the first collective female petitions to Parliament on 4 February 1642.[201]

While in theory anyone, regardless of sex or status, might solicit Parliament in its equitable and paternalistic guise,[202] the mass political petitions of the 1640s and 1650s were a new departure.[203] Indeed, women's defensiveness about this unprecedented mode of political expression led them to preface their petitions with detailed justifications for their behaviour. Regardless of partisan allegiance, these apologia express an acute fear of imminent destruc-

Nottinghamshire and Derby Protestation Returns, 84, 85; T. L. Stoate, *Cornwall Protestation Returns, 1641* (Bristol, 1974), 189, 195.

[198] Kirby, 'The Parish of St Stephen's Coleman Street, London'.

[199] Guildhall, MS 4458/1, St Stephen Coleman Street Vestry Book, fos. 145, 876. Such contributions were recognized as a political touchstone. St Stephen Coleman Street lists 52 names of contributors, with amounts ranging from £5 to £50; one other woman, Rose Wood, gave £20.

[200] For another example of married women apparently pledging loyalty as 'covenantal citizens', see J. Alsop, 'Revolutionary Puritanism in the Parishes? The Case of St Olave, Old Jewry', *London Journal*, 15 (1990), 35.

[201] *Petition of the Gentlewomen, Tradesmens Wives, and many others of the Female Sex*, 6.

[202] Women had long petitioned Parliament as private individuals for personal causes; see Ch. 1. See also A. Whiting, 'Deference and Difference: A New Look at the Women Petitioners of the English Revolution', unpublished conference paper, AHMEME (Melbourne), 1989.

[203] Higgins, 'Women Petitioners', 179–221.

tion, not so much of the women themselves but more often of their families, as the impetus for women's actions. In one of the first examples of mass female petitions to Parliament, women thronged the Palace Yard, proclaiming 'We had rather bring our children, and leave them at the Lords' door, than have them starve at home'.[204]

In February 1642, following exaggerated reports of Catholic atrocities in Europe and the 'savage usage and unheard of rapes' committed upon their sex during the 1641 Irish rebellion, some English women became caught up in anti-Catholic hysteria, foreseeing the prospect of mass slaughter in their own country: 'our Husbands and Children . . . cut in pieces before our eyes . . . our Children dashed against the stones, and the Mothers milke mingled with the Infants blood, running down the streets.'[205] A year later, petitioners asserted that the 'utter desolation of this Kingdome' as well as 'our bleeding Sister Kingdom of Ireland which hath now almost breathed her last gasp' had impelled them to ask Parliament to settle the Kingdom in the 'true Reformed Protestant Religion' despite the fact that the writers were of the 'weaker sex'.[206] Similar forebodings of wholesale destruction were featured in women's peace protests in 1643, and in female Levellers' petitions of the late 1640s.[207]

Another theme which runs through female petitions of the 1640s and 1650s is women's assertion of spiritual equality. Invoking the example of sixteenth-century female martyrs, petitioners placed themselves in a tradition of godly protest against a corrupt establishment.[208] In the earliest petitions, women appealed to the doctrine of 'equal souls' in a modestly subordinate manner, stressing their weak and dependent nature, and insisting they were merely following the lead of husbands and other male authorities. As the petitioners of 4 February 1642 explained,

> We doe it not out of any selfe conceit . . . as seeking to equall our selves with Men, either in Authority or wisdome: But according to our places to discharge that duty we owe to God, and the cause of the Church . . . following herein the example of the Men . . .[209]

[204] Higgins, 'Women Petitioners', 185.

[205] *Petition of the Gentlewomen, Tradesmens Wives, and many others of the Female Sex*, 2.

[206] Bodl., MS Tanner 64, fo. 190.

[207] For example, see Higgins, 'Women Petitioners', 193; *The Humble Petition of divers well-affected WOMEN . . . Affecters and Approvers of the Petition of Sept. 11. 1648*, TT 669 f. 4 (27) [5 May 1649].

[208] For example, *The Humble Petition of Divers Well-affected Women* [23 Apr. 1649], 4–5, TT E. 551 (14); *The humble Petition of divers afflicted WOMEN, in behalf of M: John Lilburne* (25 June 1653), TT 669 f. 17 (26). See also Higgins, 'Women Petitioners', 214.

[209] *Petition of the Gentlewomen, Tradesmens Wives, and many others of the Female Sex*, 6.

By the late 1640s, however, female Levellers had begun combining the argument of 'equal souls' with claims for secular civil rights as English subjects; at this point, women's petitions had evolved from their origins as humble supplications into rousing manifestos which expressed new theories of female political rights.

Like men at the same social level, many women made pledges of financial and personal support to king or Parliament throughout the 1640s. During the war years, both sides were heavily dependent on voluntary contributions by female donors like the 'virgins of Norwich', who 'readily contributed so much money, as hath raised and armed a goodly troop of horse for their defence which is styled the Maiden Troop'.[210] Both royalist and Parliamentary sympathizers donated jewellery, plate, and money.[211] After 1660, Butler's *Hudibras* was to recall the many ordinary women who had offered their humble possessions for the Parliamentary cause:

> Women, that left no stone unturn'd
> In which the cause might be concern'd;
> Brought in their children's spoons and whistles,
> To purchase swords, carbines, and pistols . . .
> All they could rap, and rend, and pilfer,
> To scraps and ends of gold and silver . . .[212]

On both sides of the struggle, the war also burdened women with involuntary contributions, including heavy taxation, the quartering of soldiers, and other added expenses.[213]

Some women had already declared for one or the other faction before the calling of the Long Parliament in 1640; others were driven by the outbreak of military hostilities in 1642 into vigorous debates with relatives, friends, and neighbours about the merits of royalist and parliamentarian positions. Among the upper ranks, women's correspondence reveals details of the process whereby they chose sides and promoted their views through personal influence. In a long letter written in 1643, Lady Elizabeth Felton argued with her son-in-law in an effort to convert him to her own pro-Parliamentary stance:

[210] BL, Add. MS 21,935, N. Wallington, Historical Notes and Meditations, 1588–1646, fo. 231^{v}.

[211] Higgins, 'Women Petitioners', 219, and references cited therein. Women of varied social rank and geographical locale contributed to political causes: for example, Margery Holmes of Wilsthorpe, Lincolnshire, donated one shilling for 'reliefe of the Distressed Protestants in Ireland'; Webster, *Lincolnshire Protestation Returns*, 30. For other examples, see Guildhall, MS 4458/1, St Stephen Coleman Street Vestry Book, fo. 145.

[212] S. Butler, *Hudibras*, part II, canto II, lines 777–90.

[213] For examples, see I. Gentles, *The New Model Army* (Oxford, 1992), 129–39.

I suppose the great matter you stumble at, is an erring conceit, that arms are taken up against the king. It is a riddle to me, that a Parliament and those that adhere unto them should be enemies to his Majesty; assure your self they esteem his person sacred and pray heartily for his life.[214]

Lady Felton went on to invoke the 'evil counsellors' theory to explain the breach between king and Parliament. She then cited historical precedents as the basis for Parliament's legitimate opposition to the monarch:

the king is abused when he hearkens to the counsels of such, as are known traitors and ill-affected both to our religion and the state: and such as would delight to see the Protestant blood as plentifully shed in England, as it hath been in Ireland . . . in former times the nobility have attempted the like[215] upon like occasion, and their posterity not blaming them for so doing: I have heard . . . of Parliaments that have been their precedents for so doing: whose acts have been ratified by following Parliaments.[216]

In other families, wives disputed with husbands. Sir Hugh Cholmley recalled that his wife, 'not understanding the causes why I quitted the Parliament, or the true state of the difference between king and Parliament, was very earnest and firm for their party; but, after I had unmasked to her the Parliament's intent . . . she then was as much against them, and as earnest for the King'.[217]

While most women chose one side or the other, a significant number opted for a neutral or anti-war stance. Women from every social level urged male relatives to avoid involvement in the war. When Samuel Priestley enlisted as a soldier under Fairfax, his mother 'went along with him a quarter of a mile . . . she besought him with tears not to go', but to no avail.[218] The countess of Warwick was always 'much averse' to her husband's 'ingaging in the wars'.[219] Middling and ordinary women carried out personal acts of resistance against the army.[220]

Moreover, large numbers supported the peace initiatives of 1643–5. Although women were highly visible in the petitions and demonstrations of 1643, their exact role is difficult to assess. The peace party was viewed as

[214] Bodl., MS Tanner 69, Lady Elizabeth Felton to John Hobart, 27 Nov. 1643, fo. 108.

[215] i.e. taking up arms against the king; Lady Felton mentioned that she had been reading Speed.

[216] Bodl., MS Tanner 69, fo. 108.

[217] H. Cholmley, *The Memoirs of Sir Hugh Cholmley* (1787), 68.

[218] 'Some Memoirs concerning the Family of the Priestleys', in *Yorkshire Diaries and Autobiographies*, ii, Surtees Society, 77 (1886), 26.

[219] S. H. Mendelson, *Mental World of Stuart Women* (Brighton, 1987), 79.

[220] For examples, see Gentles, *New Model Army*, 126, 133–6; R. Gough, *The History of Myddle*, ed. D. Hey (Harmondsworth, 1981), 73–4.

a threat by the dominant group in the House of Commons, and consequently the 1643 peace protests were a source of intense anxiety for some MPs, who interpreted the demonstrations in terms of conspiracy theories in which women served as the ignorant cat's-paws of opposing factions.[221] On the other hand, the female sex was culturally constructed as timid and compassionate; partly for this reason, women believed it was natural for them to be actively disposed towards pacifism. Men, in contrast, were constrained to appear brave, virile, and warlike, or run the risk of impugning their masculinity. Women's social identity thus gave them greater freedom to appeal for the cessation of armed conflict, and to play an active role in urging warring male factions to negotiate with each other. In fact, there is a good deal of evidence of women's independent involvement in a number of peace initiatives during the 1640s, whether as individuals or as members of organized groups.[222]

The most common site of women's political engagement during the 1640s and 1650s was in the religious sphere. Some were occupied with parochial politics, including clerical appointments and ejections. At Great Maplestead in Essex, '16 women of [the] parish, some of the good sort, came to the committee to desire a godly minister, affirming Mr. Shepard [the incumbent] altogether unfit to be a minister'.[223] Others abandoned their parish churches to join independent sects, where a few became lay preachers within the more radical of the gathered congregations.

Contemporaries believed that women as a sex were more forward than men in joining groups outside the Anglican communion. Male critics denounced this alleged feminine propensity as an expression of women's desire for inordinate power over men, whether in the religious, matrimonial, or sexual sphere.[224] Yet women in the sects were liable to confront the

[221] For the 1643 demonstrations and the response of authorities see Higgins, 'Women Petitioners', 189–98; Crawford, *Denzil Holles, 1598–1680*, 96.

[222] Group demonstrations of 1643 are described by Higgins, 'Women Petitioners', 189–98. For individual women's involvement in peace initiatives and negotiations in various contexts throughout the 1640s, see, for example, Bodl. MS Clarendon 23, fo. 114; Bodl. MS Clarendon 24, fo. 22; Bodl. MS Clarendon 26, fo. 167; P. Crawford, 'The Savile Affair', *English Historical Review*, 110 (1975), 76–93.

[223] J. Sharpe, 'Scandalous and Malignant Priests in Essex', in C. Jones, M. Newitt, and S. Roberts (eds.), *Politics and People in Revolutionary England* (Oxford, 1986), 270.

[224] K. Thomas, 'Women and the Civil War Sects', *Past and Present* 13 (1958), 44–49; D. Ludlow, 'Shaking Patriarchy's Foundations: Sectarian Women in England, 1641–1700', in R. Greaves (ed.), *Triumph over Silence: Women in Protestant History* (Westport, Conn., 1985), 93–9; Edwards, *Gangraena*, i. 79–80, 84–9, 119; iii. 26–7, 80, 170, 188.

same opposition to female autonomy which they had experienced in the Anglican establishment.[225]

Typical of the mixed signals women received even from sympathetic males was the advice of the sectarian leader John Rogers. Seeking to prove that all church members, 'even Sisters as well as Brothers', had a 'right to all Church-affairs', Rogers demonstrated women's equal spiritual privileges with a plethora of scriptural texts.[226] Yet having urged women to defend their liberty 'even to the *life*', Rogers counselled female readers to be 'cautious too, (festina lente) not too fast . . . your silence may sometimes be the best advocate of your *orderly liberty*, and the sweetest evidence of your prudence and modesty'.[227]

Later in the 1650s, questions of gender and authority split Peter Chamberlen's separatist congregation, just as such issues had led to 'bitter contentions' in John Rogers's Dublin congregation. Although female members outnumbered males, the congregation allowed only male leaders to participate in a public debate in 1654 in which the congregation argued over the interpretation of 1 Corinthians 14–34, 'whether the sisters are excluded from speaking in the church'.[228] The debate was concluded with a compromise: 'a woman (maid, wife, or widow) being a prophetess (1 Cor. 11) may speak, prophecy, pray, with a veil. Others may not.'[229]

Female members of Chamberlen's congregation continued to challenge their subordinate role, and to defect from the church in protest. Anne Harriman boycotted the meeting because 'she could not walk where she had not liberty to speak'.[230] A lengthy letter from Elizabeth More explained why she, like her husband, was leaving the congregation. Although she had stayed all night to watch and pray while 'big with child', she had not found the presence of God amongst the group. Moreover, some of the men kept 'most wicked and lascivious company'.[231]

Meanwhile, male leaders tried to curb the spirit of autonomy among female congregants wherever it emerged, whether in church meetings or in women's own households. Chamberlen ordered Eliza Monck to 'turn to ye common rule of maidens' education (to be seen and not heard, and to

[225] A. Laurence, 'A Priesthood of She-Believers: Women and Congregations in Mid-Seventeenth-Century England', *Studies in Church History*, 27 (1990), 350–61; Crawford, 'Public Duty, Conscience, and Women', 73–4; Mack, *Visionary Women*, 293–304. For denial of female suffrage by Presbyterians and Independents in favour of 'head of household' suffrage, see B. Manning, 'Puritanism and Democracy, 1640–1642', in D. Pennington and K. Thomas (eds.), *Puritans and Revolutionaries* (Oxford, 1978), 158.

[226] J. Rogers, *Ohel or Beth-Shemesh* (1653), 463 (misprinted as 563).

[227] Ibid. 476.

[228] Bodl., MS Rawlinson D. 828, fos. 28–32.

[229] Ibid., fo. 32.

[230] Ibid., fo. 28.

[231] Ibid., fos. 121–4.

speak only when spoken to)', even though Monck had been engaged in defending his views. Sister Smith was admonished for 'miscalling her husband (dog etc)'; the censure provoked a debate between those men who advised Smith to bear it, and Chamberlen himself, who thought Smith 'might bear with offences to him: but not to God'.[232]

In general, men preferred to view female political activists in their relationships to others—as dutiful wives and daughters, 'tender' mothers, or submissive members of groups piloted by male leaders. Yet numerous women emerge from the mass of Civil War documentation as independent individuals who moved, self-impelled, through a web of complex alliances. We can trace patterns of female autonomy within a context of multiple affiliations in the activities of women like Katherine Chidley and Mary Cary, each of whom was linked to several radical reform groups. Both women progressed towards political engagement as a result of their religious concerns, and both became respected spokeswomen for the movements they espoused. But Katherine Chidley and Mary Cary envisioned different means for effecting radical change; hence each woman evolved her own concept of women's political role in the new order.

Katherine Chidley's career exemplifies both the opportunities and the dilemmas which participation in secular reform movements represented for female activists. Chidley had been involved in political struggles since the 1620s, as a proselytizer and apologist for the separatist churches. During the 1640s, she was part of a group that founded what became known as the Leveller party; Chidley had had various connections with male Leveller leaders through the Independent churches, and through her personal and financial associations with radical elements within the New Model Army.[233] Katherine Chidley became a leader in the female Levellers' petitioning campaigns, one of a number of women who were conspicuous for their energetic endeavours on behalf of the Leveller movement.[234]

Female Levellers' petitions and mass demonstrations reached a climax during the spring of 1649, focusing on a defence of the imprisoned Leveller leaders. Women's efforts show evidence of independent organization,

[232] Ibid., fos. 130–1.

[233] Gentles, 'London Levellers', 281–309. See also K. Chidley, *The Justification of the Independant Churches of Christ* (1641), *Good Counsell to the Petitioners for Presbyterian Government* (1645). Both Gentles and Higgins suggest that Chidley may have been the author of *The Humble Petition of divers well-affected WOMEN . . . Affecters and Approvers of the Petition of Sept. 11. 1648* (5 May 1649); see Higgins, 'Women Petitioners', 218.

[234] Gentles, 'London Levellers', 292–3; Higgins, 'Women Petitioners', 199–209; A. Hughes, 'Gender and Politics in Leveller Literature', in S. Amussen and M. Kishlansky (eds.), *Political Culture and Cultural Politics in England: Essays presented to David Underdown* (1995), 162–3.

particularly in the way parochial or sectarian bonds were used to recruit female adherents. The women's petition of 23 April 1649, for example, had been 'promoted at Severall Congregationall Meetings in and about the City of London' on the previous Sunday.[235] And, unlike their meek and submissive predecessors of the early 1640s, female Levellers in 1649 were in opposition to the government. The spectacle of women's political initiative was thus doubly offensive to Members of Parliament, who told presenters on 23 April 1649 that they, as women, had no political role: 'the matter you petition about, is of an higher concernment then you understand . . . the House gave an answer to your Husbands; and therefore . . . you are desired to goe home, and looke after your owne business, and meddle with your huswifery.'[236]

In response, the women devised more powerful arguments for their right to petition Parliament. On 5 May 1649 they returned with a manifesto which combined the argument of 'equal souls' with claims based on their secular civil rights as English subjects:

> we are assured . . . of an interest in Christ, equal unto men, as also a proportionable share in the Freedoms of this Commonwealth . . . Have we not an equal interest with the men of this Nation, in those liberties and securities, contained in the Petition of Right, and other . . . Laws of this Land? are any of our lives, limbs, liberties or goods to be taken from us more than from Men, but by due processe of Law?[237]

For female Levellers, it was essential to appeal to the religious doctrine of 'equal souls' in order to bolster their claim to a share in natural political rights. In their purely secular guise, women were ignored by the entire spectrum of radical male factions who fought over the meaning of 'natural rights' during the Civil War period. Nor did male Levellers plan to grant women political privileges in the secular republic for which they proposed a series of detailed constitutions. The issue of gender did not arise, partly because male Levellers envisioned political rights in terms of households rather than male and female individuals, and partly because the rationale justifying women's inclusion in the political nation was not analogous to the arguments developed by plebeian men. Male Levellers offered historical explanations such as the so-called 'Norman Yoke' to account for the loss of their ancient rights as freeborn Englishmen. Parliamentary apologists posited covenants between male householders at the dawn of history to

[235] Higgins, 'Women Petitioners', 217. [236] Quoted ibid. 212 n. 232.

[237] *The humble Petition of divers well-affected WOMEN . . . Affecters and Approvers of the Petition of Sept. 11. 1648* (5 May 1649).

TO THE

SUPREME AUTHORITY OF ENGLAND

The Commons Aſſembled in Parliament.

The Humble Petition of divers well-affected WOMEN, of the Cities of London and Weſtminſter, the Borough of Southwark, Hamblets, and Parts Adjacent. *Affecters and Approvers of the Petition of* Sept. 11. 1648.

Sheweth,

THat ſince we are aſſured of our Creation in the image of God, and of an intereſt in Chriſt, equal unto men, as alſo of a propoitionable ſhare in the Freedoms of this Common wealth, we cannot but wonder and grieve that we ſhould appear ſo deſpicable in your eyes, as to be thought unworthy to Petition or repreſent our Grievances to this Honourable Houſe.

Have we not an equal intereſt with the men of this Nation, in thoſe liberties and ſecurities, contained in the Petition of Right, and other the good Laws of the Land? are any of our lives, limbs, liberties or goods to be taken from us more then from Men, but by due proceſſe of Law and conviction of twelve ſworn men of the Neighbourhood?

And can you imagine us to be ſo ſottiſh or ſtupid, as not to perceive, or not to be ſencible when dayly thoſe ſtrong defences of our Peace and wellfare are broken down, and trod under-foot by force and arbitrary power.

Would you have us keep at home in our houſes, when men of ſuch faithfullneſſe and integrity as the FOVR PRISONERS our friends in the Tower, are fetcht out of their beds, and forced from their Houſes by Souldiers, to the affrighting and undoing of themſelves, their wives, children, and families? Are not our husbands, or ſelves, our children and families by the ſame rule as lyable to the like unjuſt cruelties as they?

Shall ſuch men as Capt. *Bray* be made cloſe Priſoners, and ſuch as Mr *Sawyer* ſnatcht up and carryed away, beaten and buffetted at the pleaſure of ſome Officers of the Army; and ſuch as Mr *Blanck* kept cloſe Priſoner, and after moſt barbarous uſage be forced to run the Gantlop, and be moſt ſlave-like and cruelly whipt; and muſt we keep at home in our houſes, as if we our lives and liberties and all, were not concerned?

Nay, ſhall ſuch valiant religious men as Mr *Robert Lockyer* be lya-ble to Law Martial, and be judged by his *Adverſaries*, and moſt unhumanly ſhot to death? *Shall the blood of War* be ſhed in time of Peace? doth not the word of God expreſly condemne it? doth not the Petition of Right declare, that no perſon ought to be judged by Law Martial (except in time of Warre) and that all Commiſſions given to execute Martial Law in time of Peace, are contrary to the Lawes and Statutes of the Land? Doth not Sir *Ed. Cook* in his chapter of Murder in the third part of his Inſtitutes, hold it for good Law (and ſince owned and publiſhed by this Parliament) that for a General or other Officers of an Army in time of Peace, to put any man (although a Souldier) to death by colour of Marſhal Law, it is abſolute murther in that General? And hath it not by this Houſe in the caſe of the late Earl of Strafford been adjudged high Treaſon? And are we Chriſtians, and ſhall we ſit ſtill and keep at home, while ſuch men as have born continual teſtimony againſt the unjuſtice of all times, and unrighteouſneſſe of men, be pickt out and be delivered up to the ſlaughter, and yet muſt we ſhew no ſence of their ſufferings, no tenderneſſe of affections, no bowels of compaſſion, nor bear any teſtimony againſt ſo abominable cruelty and injuſtice?

Have ſuch men as theſe continually hazarded their lives, ſpent their eſtates and time, loſt their liberties, and thought nothing too precious, for defence of us, our lives, and liberties, bin as a Guard by day, and as a Watch by night; and when for this they are in trouble and greateſt danger, perſecuted and hated even to the death; and ſhould we be ſo baſely ungrateful, as to neglect them in the day of their affliction? No, far be it from us: Let it be accounted folly, preſumption, madneſs, or whatſoever in us, whilſt we have life and breath, we will never leave them, nor forſake them, nor ever ceaſe to importune you (having yet ſo much hopes of you, as of the unjuſt Judge mentioned *Luke* 18. to obtain Juſtice, if not for Juſtice ſake, yet for Importunity) or to uſe any other means for the enlargement and reparation of thoſe of them that live; and for Juſtice againſt ſuch, as have bin the cauſe of M. *Lockiers* death: Nor will we ever reſt until we have prevailed, that We, our Husbands, Children, Friends, and Servants, may not be liable to be thus abuſed, violated, and butchered at mens Wills and Pleaſures. But if nothing will ſatisfie but the bloud of thoſe juſt men, thoſe conſtant undaunted Aſſerters of the Peoples Freedoms will ſatisfie your thirſt, drink alſo, and be glutted with our bloud, and let us all fall together: Take the bloud of one more, and take all: Slay one, ſlay all.

And therefore again, we entreat you to review our laſt petition in behalf of our Friends above mentioned, and not to ſlight the things therein contained, becauſe they are preſented unto you by the weak hand of VVomen, it being an uſual thing with God, by weak means to work mighty effects: For we are no whit ſatisfied with the anſwer you gave unto our Husband's and Friends, but do equally with them remain lyable to thoſe ſnares laid in your Declaration, which maketh the Abetters of the Book laid to our Friends charge, no leſs then Traytors, when as hardly any diſcourſe can be touching the affairs of the preſent times, but falls within the compaſs of that Book: So that all liberty of Diſcourſe is thereby utterly taken away, then which there can be no greater ſlavery.

Nor ſhall we be ſatisfied, however you deal with our Friends, except you free them from under their preſent extrajudicial impriſonment and force upon them, and give them full Reparations for their forceable Attachment, &c. And leave them from firſt to laſt, to be proceeded againſt by due Proceſs of Law, and give them reſpect from you, anſwerable to their good and faithful Service to the Common-wealth.

Our houſes being worſe then Priſons to us, and our Lives worſe then death; the ſight of our Husbands and Children, matter of grief, ſorrow, and affliction to us, until you grant our deſires, and therefore, if ever you intend any good to this miſerable Nation, harden not your hearts againſt Petitioners, nor deny us in things ſo evidently juſt and reaſonable, as you would not be diſhonourable to all Poſterity.

FIG. 47. 1649 Leveller women's petition, 'To the supreme authority of England'. This appeal by female Levellers on behalf of imprisoned Leveller leaders begins by arguing for women's legal and moral right to petition Parliament. Presented to the House of Commons in early May, 1649, it was also circulated as a broadsheet

explain the origins of civil society, imaginative reconstructions which later evolved into the contract theories of Hobbes and Locke.

But no one suggested that women as a group had ever had the same political status as men in the historical past (unless they considered Eve's prelapsarian state), or that women, too, had been enslaved by the 'Norman Yoke'.[238] Indeed, some radical republican theorists argued precisely the opposite view, that female dominion was part of the burden of an hereditary monarchy. John Cook, Solicitor at the king's trial and executed as a regicide in 1660, contended that hereditary monarchy was wrong because it was 'against the Law of God and nature to make Millions of men subject to the commands of a woman'.[239]

Thus, although some Independent congregations with which the Levellers were allied had granted full rights of church government to their female members, no reformer suggested extending the parliamentary franchise to female subjects of the secular republic.[240] Instead, despite women's prominent role in the Leveller movement, male leaders constructed their female allies as dependent beings. In their tracts, Lilburne and his colleagues represented wives and other female associates as 'meet helps' who had been instructed in their husbands' ideological convictions, and who obediently followed (or sometimes mutinously rejected) their husbands' orders.[241]

As an account from a 1653 newsletter reveals, onlookers appear to have cast Katherine Chidley, too, in the mould of a wife or dependent family member:

> On Wednesday there came to the Parliament about 12 women, with a petition in the behalf of John Lilburne [the imprisoned Leveller leader], it was subscribed by above 6000 of that sex, the chief of these twelve was wife to one Chidley a prime Leveller, they boldly knocked at the door, and the House taking notice that they were there, sent out Praise-God Barebones to dissuade them from their enterprise, but he could not prevail; and they persisting in their disturbance another Member came out and told them, the House could not take cognizance of their petition, they being women, and many of them wives, so that the Law took no notice of them.[242]

[238] For the theory of the 'Norman Yoke' see C. Hill, *Puritanism and Revolution* (1958), 50–122.

[239] J. Cook, *Monarchy No Creature of God's Making* (1652), quoted in G. Aylmer, 'Collective Mentalities in Mid-Seventeenth-Century England: III. Varieties of Radicalism', *TRHS*, 38 (1988), 15.

[240] B. Manning, 'Puritanism and Democracy, 1640–1642', in D. Pennington and K. Thomas, *Puritans and Revolutionaries: Essays in Seventeenth-Century History Presented to Christopher Hill* (Oxford, 1978), 158; see also Higgins, 'Women Petitioners', 216–18; Thomas, 'Women and the Civil War Sects', 53–5.

[241] Hughes, 'Gender and Politics', 169–74.

[242] Bodl., MS Clarendon 46, fos. 131^{v}–2.

But Katherine Chidley was a widow, not a wife; the male Chidley to which the newsletter referred was Katherine's son Samuel (also a prominent Leveller). Indeed, on this occasion Chidley and her female colleagues were reported as maintaining their right to petition Parliament in their own persons on precisely these grounds, namely that 'they were not all wives'. Moreover, the women threatened that if Parliament refused to receive their petition,

> they should know that they had husbands and friends, and they wore swords to defend the liberties of the People etc. and withall admonished them . . . not to persecute that man of God, lest they were also destroyed, as the late King, Bishops, Parliament, and all others that ever opposed him.[243]

If Katherine Chidley conformed to any stereotype, it was not that of the submissive 'meet help', but rather the London freewoman whose sturdy independence derived as much from her economic self-reliance as her intellectual and political sophistication. Like Katherine Chidley, many female activists of the 1640s and 1650s were business entrepreneurs of the middling sort, involved in the textile or provision trades. Chidley herself supplied stockings for the New Model Army; the Baptist preacher Mrs Attaway was a lace-seller, and the pamphleteer Mary Pope inherited and managed her husband's salting business, using the profits to finance her publications.[244]

A different pattern of radical female activism is exemplified by the career of Mary Cary. Like Katherine Chidley, Mary Cary became involved in politics through her association with the Independent churches. But whereas Chidley strove for secular reform on the Leveller model, Cary moved from independency to millenarianism along Erastian lines, eventually joining the Fifth Monarchist movement. By 1649, both Chidley and Cary supported the removal of the king, but each advocated a different method to accomplish this aim. Katherine Chidley fought for a democratic republic whose formation would be guided by mass ratification of the Leveller constitution, with government placed in the hands of 'the people'. Her own energies were thus devoted to promoting the Leveller platform, making full use of whatever secular civil rights she might legally claim, notably her 'undoubted right' to petition Parliament.[245]

[243] Ibid.

[244] Gentles, 'London Levellers'; R. Greaves and R. Zaller, *Biographical Dictionary of British Radicals in the Seventeenth Century* (Brighton, 1992–4); Mack, *Visionary Women*, 96.

[245] *Unto every individual member of Parliament; the . . . Representation of . . . women . . . on behalf of Mr John Lilburn* (1653), TT 669 f. 17 (36), cited in Higgins, 'Women Petitioners', 216.

More militant than Katherine Chidley in her opposition to monarchy, Mary Cary was one of a very few prominent female radicals who supported regicide.[246] Cary's extensive studies of Scripture had led her to conclude that such a total transformation would be effected by the military, who with the help of Providence would introduce the Millennium to England. Although Cary was deeply interested in social and economic reforms,[247] she believed that God (using the army as his instrument), rather than the general populace, had the power to enact fundamental changes in society. Consequently, Cary saw her role not as mass activist, but as an intellectual theorist who could best facilitate revolutionary change by explaining to political initiates the reasons why such change was inevitable. In aid of this scholarly purpose, Cary had made comprehensive studies of mathematics and world history, as well as of the Bible itself.[248]

Cary's prophecies were logically and clearly expressed, learned and precise rather than spontaneous and ambiguous; her works were given a courteous reception by male as well as female contemporaries.[249] Her defence of the Parliamentary 'doctrine of necessity', of the execution of Charles I, and of the activities of the radical republican wing of Parliament were published in a series of pamphlets during the late 1640s and early 1650s. The most well known of these, *The Little Horns Doom and Downfall* (1651) appeared under the patronage of Elizabeth Cromwell, Bridget Ireton, and other wives of Parliamentary leaders and army grandees. It was with this inner coterie, rather than the rank-and-file army agitators who were Katherine Chidley's associates, that Cary formed her political and social alliances.

While academic theorists like Mary Cary were protected by the patronage of the political élite, female millenarians from lower social strata were liable to meet with a hostile reception. Mary Gadbury, who turned to millenarian prophecy at about the same time as Mary Cary published her chiliastic theories, had developed her convictions within the same political milieu as Cary, the radical separatist groups of the St Stephen Coleman Street district.[250] But differences of class, education, and matrimonial status led

[246] Cary, *Little Horns Doom*, 46, cited in Mack, *Visionary Women*, 101.

[247] Mack, *Visionary Women*, 103.

[248] Cary, *Little Horns Doom*, sigs. A3–A6^v.

[249] Ibid., including laudatory prefaces by Hugh Peters, Henry Jessey, and Christopher Feake. An answer to one of Cary's earlier pamphlets, entitled *The Account Audited* (1649), respectfully acknowledged Cary's scholarship, while debating her interpretation of mathematical and historical data.

[250] H. Ellis, *Pseudochristus, Or, a True and Faithful Relation* . . . (1650), 8; Kirby, 'St. Stephen's Coleman Street', 117, 128–9, 166.

to a situation in which Mary Gadbury was persecuted rather than patronized by authorities.

Our main source for the events of Gadbury's career is a pamphlet by Humphrey Ellis, who interpreted Gadbury's behaviour through the lens of familiar misogynistic stereotypes.[251] Although Mary Gadbury had been deserted by her husband, she was blamed as though she had been the active party. After Gadbury joined forces in a missionary partnership with William Franklin (who had left his own spouse and children), the resulting sexual scandal aroused further suspicions about Gadbury's motives and morals. Although Mary Gadbury protested she had had no 'carnal copulation' with Franklin, and had accompanied him 'but as fellow-feeler of her misery', Ellis's comment was a sneering sexual innuendo: 'yea . . . fellow-feeler indeed'. Much like Mary Overton, activist wife of Leveller leader Richard Overton, Gadbury was punished with the double infamy of imprisonment in Bridewell, the abode of 'bawds, whores and strumpets'. Thus she was disgraced as an immoral woman rather than acknowledged as a serious political voice.[252]

Like Mary Cary and Mary Gadbury, a number of female prophets emerged during the 1640s and 1650s, bearing urgent political messages which they claimed had been entrusted to them by God. Some were mocked as lunatics; others were taken seriously by local community leaders, or even by Parliament itself. As Phyllis Mack has shown in a brilliant recent study, the supposed irrational qualities of the female sex offered a fluid cultural framework either for acceptance or for derogation of the female prophet, depending upon the content and the context of her utterances.[253] Women's acknowledged affinities with the spiritual realm appeared to give them a direct line to God, at least in certain instances. Elizabeth Poole's political commentaries found favour with Parliamentary soldiers because her prophecies appeared to offer a supernatural endorsement of Cromwell's views.[254] But those who meddled in politics risked contempt or worse, especially if they backed the wrong party. During a lengthy career, Lady Eleanor Douglas Davies suffered several terms of imprisonment for her views; she encountered the full spectrum of reactions ranging from

[251] Ellis, *Pseudochristus*, 52.

[252] Ibid. 52; see also Crawford, *Women and Religion*, 136; for Mary Overton, see M. Overton, *To the Right Honorable, the Knights, Citizens and Burgesses, the Parliament of England* [1647], cited in Hughes, 'Gender and Politics', 179–80.

[253] Mack, *Visionary Women*, 87–124.

[254] Gentles, *New Model Army*, 301; Mack, *Visionary Women*, 78–9.

veneration to infamy, depending on the way in which her commentaries were interpreted by contemporaries.[255]

Some female prophets were the subjects of laudatory biographies, such as 11-year-old Martha Hatfield, whose life and visions were described by her uncle James Fisher in his tract *The Wise Virgin* (1656). Others appear briefly (and usually anonymously) in contemporary newsletters, private correspondence, and polemical tracts. For one such woman, our information is limited to a newsletter report of 29 July 1653:

> on Saturday last a woman of Chancery Lane (that hath been always against the King) attended the rising of the Parliament, and on her knees desired them as the chosen of the Lord to carry on his work to the destruction of the ministry, and pulling down the prophane temples built with hands, to the abolishment of tithes and such stuff, but in the midst of her pious exhortations, she was struck dead in the place, and so carried away.[256]

During the 1640s and 1650s, increasing numbers of women disseminated their opinions in the public political space. We know a good deal about the views of Eleanor Douglas Davies, Katherine Chidley, Mary Cary, and a host of others who committed themselves to print.[257] But for those who communicated their ideas verbally, we must glean our information from sporadic references by hostile observers. Robert Baillie called the Baptist preacher Mrs Attaway 'the mistresse of all the she-preachers in *Colemanstreet*', and denounced her for her radical views on paedo-baptism. In *Gangraena*, Thomas Edwards wrote of Mrs Attaway's alleged personal interest in Milton's doctrine of divorce.[258]

Another group whose activities take shape from scattered documents and references are those women who served as intermediaries and diplomatic envoys between the two warring sides, or as spies for one faction or the other. At the top of the social spectrum, noblewomen were employed in dangerous negotiations between royalist and Parliamentary leaders. Some time before November 1645, the Prince's Council entrusted Lady Paulet with a list of articles concerning possible peace negotiations. She was instructed to present their substance to the commanders of the Parliamen-

[255] E. Cope, *Handmaid of the Holy Spirit* (Ann Arbor, 1992). See also Mack, *Visionary Women*, *passim*.

[256] Bodl., MS Clarendon 46, fo. 130.

[257] P. Crawford, 'Women's Published Writings, 1600–1700', in M. Prior (ed.), *Women in English Society* (1985), 211–82; Mack, *Visionary Women*, chs. 3–5.

[258] R. Baillie, *Anabaptism the True Fountaine of Independency* (1647), 53; Edwards, *Gangraena*, iii. 26–7.

tary forces, with assurance 'as from [her] self' of the royalists' 'sincere desires of peace upon tolerable terms'.[259]

Lady Paulet's own private mandate was to 'endeavour to discover whether there be any reality in their professions of peace'; and if so, 'what evidence they will or can give of it'. This general directive was accompanied by a detailed list of queries, ending with the plea 'that if they can or will contribute nothing else to peace, that they will give their opinion and advise which way it is to be pursued by the King and his adherents . . . in order to this you are desired to discover where the civil power of the Parliament lies, and in what persons [and] what party is like[ly] to prevail amongst them, and what government they aim at in church and state'.[260] The document betrays a high opinion of Lady Paulet's sagacity and discretion as a diplomatic agent, a sentiment which appears to contradict the contemporary stereotype of women as frivolous and irrepressible gossips. Yet it was precisely the conventional perception of women's social and intellectual qualities which made them so useful to men as emissaries, mediators, and spies. In the unstable conditions of wartime, women were more adept than men at transmitting intelligence through informal channels. For example, women could convey information in the low-key setting of kin group interactions, which maintained their social ties despite partisan political differences.[261]

Not only were women able to circumvent formal roles which limited male politicians' flexibility; female intermediaries were unhampered by male codes of honour and chivalry, which were considered irrelevant to the female sex. Women's supposed humoral characteristics—their slippery, liminal qualities—rendered them useful when normal rules of male political negotiation did not apply, as in the chaos of the mid-1640s. Indeed, it was Lady Paulet's task to try to find out what the rules were, and to identify the key male players, so that royalists might glean enough information to hazard a male emissary at a later stage.

Women's reputation for indiscretion made them especially serviceable in negotiating the shifting alliances of the 1640s. Some, like Lady Paulet, served as trusted agents who hid behind the innocuous façade of a female body. Others took on the role of flirtatious gossips who could be relied on

[259] Bodl., MS Clarendon. 26, fo. 167.

[260] Ibid. For details of the Savile affair, of which Lady Paulet's negotiations were probably a part, see Crawford, 'The Savile Affair', 76–93.

[261] For some illuminating examples, see D. Freist, 'The King's Crown is the Whore of Babylon: Politics, Gender and Communication in Mid-Seventeenth-Century England', *Gender & History*, 7 (1995), 457–81.

to spread information. Some women functioned in both roles: Lucy Hay, countess of Carlisle, whose considerable political influence earned her a place in Hyde's list of numerical secret ciphers, was both celebrated and reviled for her indiscriminate associations with all the different factions.[262] In 1654, Edward Nicholas complained of the countess that she 'hath been (throughout the whole story of his late Majesty's sad misfortunes) a very pernicious instrument & she will assuredly discover all things to her gang of Presbyterians who have ever . . . betrayed all they know to the ruling Rebels'.[263] Yet the countess was invaluable for her ability to serve as a connecting link between men who had no viable means of communicating with each other.

Even without a code-name of their own, many women discovered that expectations about gender offered the perfect disguise for every type of risky or clandestine enterprise. A letter of intelligence in a 'woman's hand' was not seized, because officials did not expect to find any 'business' in it.[264] When Lady Dalkeith made a hazardous escape to France with 3-year-old Princess Henrietta, she eluded pursuit by disguising herself as a 'ragged boy'.[265] It is not a coincidence that men, too, found it an effective ploy to hide behind the mask of gender, for example in devising female code names for such vital personages as Charles II.

In other contexts, however, assumptions about the attributes of gender did not necessarily protect women from the consequences of their political actions. Governments were particularly severe in punishing seditious words, one of the commonest political crimes committed by women during the Civil War years.[266] At Henley in 1646, a newsletter reported that

> a woman taking notice of the unwonted taxations imposed upon her and others by this Parliament, expressed (yet in civil terms) some dislike thereof, which made known to a committee there, she was by them ordered to have her tongue fastened with a nail to the body of a tree, by the highwayside on a market day, which was accordingly done, and a paper in great letters (setting forth the heinousness of her fact) fixed to her back to make her the more notorious.[267]

Undoubtedly this was a royalist atrocity story, aimed at discrediting the Parliamentary cause. Yet it is significant that people believed women were capable of making damaging criticisms of public policies, and that they were

[262] Bodl., MS Clarendon 19, fos. 200, 219, 221. Among other notable women who rated a cipher were the queen, the countess of Denbigh, Lady Savile, and Lady Stanhope.

[263] Bodl., MS Clarendon 48, Nicholas to Hyde, 16 Apr. 1654, fo. 120^{v}.

[264] Ibid. fo. 256.

[265] A. Collins, *The Peerage of England*, 9 vols. (1812), see under 'Morton 1648'.

[266] See, for example, Bodl. MS Rawlinson C. 366, fos. 116^{v}–117. See also Freist, 'Politics, Gender and Communication', 458–60.

[267] Bodl., MS Clarendon 28, fo. 199.

as liable as men for savage punishment when they did so. In accord with their status as 'negative citizens', women were thought to be strictly accountable for acts of disloyalty to the government, even though they did not enjoy the privileges of 'freeborn Englishmen'.

Although we have offered only a small selection from the many types of evidence which illuminate women's responses to the Civil War and Interregnum, it is clear that the interplay between gender and political crisis presents a picture of great complexity. In certain contexts, gender appears to have had some influence on women's political views, either in their substance or their mode of expression. But, in other situations, there is no obvious connection between the cultural construction of gender roles and the behaviour of individual women.

Some aspects of war apparently called forth what contemporaries considered an appropriate 'feminine' response. As befitted their reputation as the more pious sex, women were likely to appeal to moral or religious grounds to justify their partisan views. Explaining why she championed the Parliamentary side, Lady Elizabeth Felton capped her arguments by pointing out that

> the most religious, and conscientious men amongst the nobility, gentry, clergy and commonalty do generally take that way. I condemn not all on the other side: but take from them all papists, and delinquents . . . nay further bishops, and their prelatical faction: men of decayed fortunes, or such as hope to rise to preferment by their subtle insinuations into the kings favour, and then judge what number will be left . . .[268]

Women as a group expressed strong views in favour of peace, a bias which was acknowledged by contemporaries. Even when hopes for reconciliation were reluctantly abandoned, women were still inclined to appeal for moderation, to counsel against bloodshed. Although Elizabeth Poole was critical of the king, she advised Cromwell in 1649 that Charles's life must be spared, 'for he is the father and husband of your bodies'.[269] Mary Pope wrote several tracts urging the Parliament and Army to restore the king to his throne. She reminded readers that the grievances of which people complained in 1642 were as nothing compared to those of 1649. Mary Pope deployed familiar metaphors about the body politic, seeing Parliamentary rule as monstrous:

[268] Lady Elizabeth Felton to John Hobart, 27 Nov. 1643, Bodl., MS Tanner 69, fo. 108.

[269] E. Poole, *A Vision, Wherein is Manifested the Disease and Cure of the Kingdome* (1648), quoted in Mack, *Visionary Women*, 100.

'now instead of having one Head to make up the body with the members compleat, wee have had a preposterous Body without a Head.'[270]

Likewise, many women expressed views which implied that the king's trial and execution held a peculiar horror for the female sex. A number of ladies attended the trial in Westminster Hall, and publicly interjected remarks into the proceedings. At the reading of the charge, in the name of 'all the good people of England', a woman's voice declared 'No, nor the hundredth part of them!'[271] Some women seemed more sensitive to the oaths of loyalty and the divinity of monarchy than to vengeful arguments about expiating blood guilt. Elizabeth Cellier ascribed her conversion to Catholicism to her horror at the killing of the king.[272] The Puritan countess of Warwick became ill when she heard of the king's execution.[273] Two weeks after the event, Oliver Cromwell's sister Katharine Whitstone wrote to a female relative, 'Alas! dear cousin, I am very dark and know not what to judge of such high things.' While confessing that such matters were 'far above my capacity', nevertheless she articulated a profound disquiet: 'I was very much troubled at that stroke which took the head of this poor kingdom from us, and truly had I been able to have purchased his life, I am confident I could with all willingness have laid down mine.' Because of her response to the king's execution, neighbours had begun calling her 'royalist'.[274]

Yet, as we have shown, there was no simple correlation between the cultural construction of gender and variations in political behaviour. While Lady Fairfax understood female compassion in terms of sparing the king's life, Lucy Hutchinson and Mary Cary had a different perception of the political situation in 1649, in which regicide was seen as merciful, or at least the lesser evil, rather than monstrous. Indeed, the most striking characteristic of women's political engagement at this time is the diversity of forms in which it was manifested. Female adherents were widely and apparently randomly distributed throughout all the secular and religious movements for which we have evidence. At the left end of the spectrum, we can cite significant proportions of female Diggers, Levellers, and Fifth Monarchists; on the right, there were female monarchists of every shade of opinion.

It is difficult to find a political position of any description which did not have its female constituents or partisans. Yet we cannot explain female diversity by positing that women automatically aligned themselves with the views of husbands, fathers, or other male family members. On the

[270] M. Pope, *Behold, here is a word or, an Answer to the late Remonstrance of the Army* ([24 Jan.] 1649), 5.

[271] Clarendon, *History*, iv. 486 (Bk. xi. 235).

[272] E. Cellier, *Malice Defeated* (1680), 1.

[273] Mendelson, *Mental World*, 79.

[274] Folger, MS Add. 974.

contrary, there are numerous instances of women who felt constrained to choose between a divided allegiance, when family loyalties pointed in one direction, and their own inner convictions in another.[275] Moreover, whatever choice women made, it was influenced by their own awareness that, as women, they might be expected to respond differently from men.

Nor was women's activism confined to the traditional feminine modes of participation. Of course some women did conform to gendered paradigms, but others managed to break through the psychological and physical barriers separating them from the public political space. As the stronghold of the élite male nation, Parliament became the focus of many of these women's political initiatives. Some tried to vote in the elections for Members of Parliament; others thronged the Palace yard or stormed the very doors of Parliament with their collective petitions and demonstrations. Occasionally, a female prophet was permitted to deliver a message to representative MPs, who might bring her communication to the attention of the House.[276]

The only male space women failed to penetrate was the army itself. Yet, even here, documents record exchanges of various kinds between women and soldiers. In December 1648, the prophet Elizabeth Poole was given two separate days to present her views on monarchy to the Council of Officers; senior officers made a point of showing her respect.[277] We also read of hostile confrontations, physical as well as verbal, in which women sometimes got the better of their male opponents. When John Coxe tried to enter the house of royalist constable William Stephens, Mrs Stephens came out

> with a great stick in her hand and ran and struck John Coxe under the elbow and called him rogue and kicked him [in] the [privy] members, and swore that she would run a knife in his guts . . . and never left striking at him in despite of all the men that were there, and they could all hardly keep her from doing him a further mischief . . .[278]

Clearly, gender by itself was not the only influence on women's political behaviour. Yet we cannot single out any other factor as the sole explanation for patterns of female allegiance. Women's partisan choices, and the expression of these choices in diverse modes of action, must be understood as the result of a complex interplay between many different elements, including gender, class, family loyalties, and other contingent factors. Which of these

[275] Crawford, 'Public Duty', 70–5.
[276] Mack, *Visionary Women*, 79, 99.
[277] Gentles, *New Model Army*, 301.
[278] Ibid. 126.

factors finally became paramount in a particular case varied with the individual. Rather than a clear-cut division between the two sexes, we can observe a colourful mosaic of choices. From every social sector, from Henrietta Maria down to the female participants in impromptu street demonstrations, women manifested their vital interest and active engagement in the politics of the Civil War.

WOMEN IN POLITICAL MOVEMENTS, 1660–1720

In 1660, amidst general sentiments of horror at the events of the preceding twenty years, Charles II was restored to the English throne and the Anglican Church re-established. What were the consequences for women of England's retreat from revolution? Our knowledge of women's participation in political movements during the second half of the seventeenth century is still fragmentary and provisional, partly because of the nature of the documentation for this period, and partly because scholars have paid relatively little attention to women's political roles after the Restoration, in comparison to their activities during the Civil War and Interregnum. Rather than offer an exhaustive account of the relationship between gender and politics for the period 1660–1720, our aim in this section is to suggest what the main features of an historical narrative might include, once scholars have completed the archival work on which such a narrative should be based.

When monarchy and the Anglican Church were reinstated in 1660, women who had been engaged in the public political sphere suffered under a double handicap. First, in common with men, they were objects of a reactionary backlash directed against all the secular and religious reform movements that had achieved prominence during the Civil War period. Efforts to crush popular political participation in general, and the Nonconformist sects in particular, can be seen in much of the legislation of the early 1660s. By limiting groups of petitioners to twenty or fewer, the Act Against Tumultuous Petitioning (1661) aimed at curbing mass political demonstrations, one of the most effective vehicles developed by women and other disenfranchised groups to promote their political views during the Civil War period. The Licensing Act (1662) restricted freedom of the press, another avenue used extensively by women to disseminate theological and political ideas during the Civil War and Interregnum. The Act of Uniformity (1662) and subsequent statutes criminalized membership in the Independent churches, imposing harsh civil and financial penalties on those who failed to conform to Anglican belief and ritual.[279]

We should interpret these repressive statutes not as an indication of women's failure to influence the male political nation, but as a measure of how profoundly the efforts of both sexes had challenged the gender as well as the class hierarchy. A forceful recoil by newly re-established political and religious institutions proclaimed their determination to hit back correspondingly hard against what was still understood as a significant threat to their stability. That this was to some degree a correct perception is borne out by women's own endeavours during the latter decades of the seventeenth century. Throughout this period, women continued to join partisan movements at both ends of the political spectrum, to publish their views on matters of common concern, to petition Parliament on political and economic issues, and to take a leading role in churches outside the Anglican communion.[280]

Secondly, women were affected not just as members of groups targeted by the forces of reaction, but *qua* women, as members of the female sex. 'Restoration' implied a return to order and normalcy, including the customary gender order. While the 'doctrine of necessity' helped justify novel forms of female political engagement during the Civil War years, the same doctrine had the effect of reinforcing the *status quo ante* once the crisis was over. Indeed, women's visible presence in male domains was itself taken as a touchstone for abnormality. As a 1648 ballad had expressed it, female political power was one of the primary causes of anarchy, of the 'world turned upside down':

> Come clownes and come boyes
> Come hober de hoyes
> Come Females of each degree,
> Stretch your throats, bring in your Votes,
> And make good the Anarchy.[281]

Conversely, women's exclusion from the political realm became one of the defining conditions for normality once order had been restored. This is why even the most meritorious female actions of the Civil War years did not carry over into the structures of ordinary life at the Restoration. In wartime, men

[279] 14 Charles II, c. 4; 14 Charles II, c. 33; 16 Charles II, c. 4.

[280] For women's role in both Anglican and non-Anglican churches after 1660, see Crawford, *Women and Religion*, 185–208. A useful glossary of contemporary religious terms is found on pp. 212–13.

[281] *The Anarchie* (1648), TT. 669 f. 11 (114). 'Clown' was a derisive term for a peasant or rural labourer, and 'hobbledehoy' for an adolescent youth.

had given credit to women for their heroic behaviour;[282] but no one wanted sacrificial heroines in everyday life. On the contrary, women were expected to relinquish extraordinary roles as their contribution to what everyone presumably desired, a return to normality. Male politicians, for their part, continued to be judged by their ability to keep inferiors (including the women of their households) under patriarchal control. As Roger Whitby noted in his commonplace book, a man who could not govern his own family was not fit to govern the state.[283] At the Restoration, the duchess of Newcastle acknowledged that her attempted interference in state affairs in 1658 had damaged her husband's credibility among the inner ranks of the royalist party.[284]

Women who had been active in radical movements during the Civil War and Interregnum were thus assailed on two fronts. Like their male associates, they were engaged in a continuous struggle for survival in a climate of persecution. The shared effort to uphold their beliefs encouraged women to turn inward to the fellowship of the group. But even within Nonconformist congregations, female members were hard pressed to maintain the rights they had claimed in more revolutionary times. These twin facets of the spirit of reaction forced women into a defensive stance after 1660. The effects on women's social and political autonomy in the decades after the Restoration can be illustrated by the experiences of Quaker women.

Like other Nonconformist women, female Quakers played a major role in the survival of the Society of Friends during a period of intense persecution. When imprisonment and loss of property became a 'virtual way of life', women were as conspicuous for their heroism as men in the annals of the Quaker 'Books of Sufferings' compiled in the early decades of the movement.[285] But while leaders like George Fox continued to affirm women's authority within the framework of the church, other men questioned women's right to control their own social, political, and spiritual associations. A committee of 'male worthies' was formed to censor Friends' prophecies and printed works; as a result, women found fewer opportunities to publish their views.[286] Women's separate meetings became the focus of a bitter dispute about the nature and limits of female authority, eventually splitting the movement into open schism during the Wilkinson–Story

[282] See, for example, Clarendon's comments about his wife's heroic 'courage and magnanimity' in 1646 in Bodl., MS Clarendon 28, fo. 292.

[283] Bodl., MS Eng. Hist. e. 311, fo. 59.

[284] Mendelson, *Mental World*, 39–40.

[285] Mack, *Visionary Women*, 266–9.

[286] Ibid. 274–5.

controversy of the 1670s.[287] Meanwhile, the character of Quaker social and familial life became more patriarchal with each passing generation.[288]

The consequences of society's retreat from revolutionary ideals can be discerned in the historiography as well as the history of women's engagement in radical causes after 1660. While comparative freedom of speech during the Civil War years had opened a window into the world of the disenfranchised majority, including women as well as men, the repressive legislation of the 1660s muted both dissident and female voices. As a result, it is far more difficult for historians to gain first-hand information about those women who continued to be active in the political sphere. Yet there are materials to provide the basis for a narrative, even if the evidence is apt to be indirect or ambiguous. While their numbers were somewhat diminished after 1660, female authors continued to publish their political views in a wide range of genres, including polemical tracts and pamphlets, apologetic narratives, squibs and satires, and fictionalized treatments of the partisan issues of the day.[289] Moreover, although censorship and persecution drove female activists underground, the apparatus of repression created its own documentation. Among the State Papers and in published accounts of trials, we can find records of women's encounters with those authorities who sought to detect and suppress their activities.[290]

Even after 1660, women continued to circulate subversive views through preaching, prophecies, and written works. In 1666 Katherine Johnson urged the king to repent, assuring him that the people cursed him and longed for Cromwell. 'The nation ar redie with every puf of wind to rise up in armes because of the opressition that is Laid upon them.'[291] Some women served as couriers, intermediaries, or intelligence agents for the Fifth Monarchists and other revolutionary groups. An informant's account of a planned uprising in 1664 reported that women were 'now almost wholy employed' as rebel agents, especially to convey intelligence.[292] Women were also mainstays of the radical underground press throughout this period, both as printers and

[287] Ibid. 293–302.

[288] R. Vann, *The Social Development of English Quakerism, 1655–1755* (Cambridge, Mass., 1969).

[289] Crawford, 'Women's Published Writings', 265–71.

[290] Richard Greaves's series of volumes on British radicals and Nonconformists after 1660, *Deliver Us From Evil* (Oxford, 1986), *Enemies Under His Feet* (Stanford, Calif., 1990), and *Secrets of the Kingdom* (Stanford, Calif., 1992), contain useful information on many female radicals and Nonconformists, much of it gleaned from the State Papers and other government sources. For an example of a published trial record, see *The Tryal and Sentence of Elizabeth Cellier For Writing Printing and Publishing a Scandalous Libel called Malice Defeated* (1680); Cellier's rhetorical strategies are analysed in R. Weil, '"If I Did Say So, I Lyed": Elizabeth Cellier and the Construction of Credibility in the Popish Plot Crisis', in Amussen and Kishlansky (eds.), *Political Culture and Cultural Politics*, 189–209.

[291] Greaves, *Enemies Under His Feet*, 21.

[292] Ibid. 9.

FIG. 48. 'Londons Gazette Here'; woman selling broadsheet. Popular participation of both sexes in seventeenth-century political movements was promoted by the circulation of pamphlets, broadsheets, and newsletters. This female news-vendor hawks the London Gazette, a popular newsletter in broadsheet form

as distributors of unlicensed books, pamphlets, and broadsheets. Elizabeth Calvert, one of the most celebrated of the radical female printers, suffered repeated terms of imprisonment, returning to the publication and distribution of illegal works as soon as she was released from gaol.[293]

For the 1670s and 1680s, the years of the Popish Plot and the duke of Monmouth's rebellion, we have scattered evidence of women's activities at both ends of the political spectrum. Some women dispensed financial and moral support for political rebels and religious Nonconformists. In Edinburgh, Lady Gilkerscleuch was imprisoned in 1681 for aiding the rebels and for going to conventicles, the illegal meetings held by Nonconformist congregations.[294] Others continued to work as couriers for radical groups; an informant referred to prominent female agents like Elizabeth Gaunt or Jane Hall as a 'Nurseing Mother or Messenger'.[295] Another crucial but exceedingly dangerous function provided by female activists was the sheltering of their radical associates both in England and abroad. Lady Alice Lisle, wife of regicide John Lisle, was executed during the Monmouth rebellion for harbouring a fugitive. The radical courier Elizabeth Gaunt was also convicted of harbouring a Monmouth rebel, for which crime she was burned at the stake.[296] Her valiant scaffold speech was printed in both English and Dutch in 1685, and later reprinted in full in Whig martyrologies.[297]

Contemporary ballads and newsletters hint at various forms of commitment by the female populace during the duke of Monmouth's rebellion in 1685, particularly in the context of the western rising. A satirical ballad, *The Glory of the West, or, The Virgins of Taunton-Dean. Who ript open their Silk-Petticoats, to make Colours for the late Duke of Monmouth's Army* (31 July 1685), mocked women's devotion to the cause by portraying female actions in what were intended as grotesque masculine images: 'they learned the Discipline of War, to exercise Musquet or Pike.' But like the satires directed against women's partisan activities during the Civil War period, such ballads reveal the extent to which women in the western rising had ignored the barriers which supposedly divided them from the public political space.

[293] *BDBR*, entry on Elizabeth Calvert; Greaves, *Deliver Us From Evil*, 139, 267 n. 57; Greaves, *Enemies Under His Feet*, 168–79, 228; Greaves, *Secrets of the Kingdom*, 46, 48.

[294] Greaves, *Secrets of the Kingdom*, 77.

[295] Ibid. 415 n. 99; see also 271, 301.

[296] Ibid. 293.

[297] *Mrs. Gaunt's Last Speech who was burnt at London, October 23, 1685*. For Elizabeth Gaunt and Alice Lisle, see M. Zook, 'The Bloody Assizes: Whig Martyrdom and Memory after the Glorious Revolution', *Albion*, 27 (1995), 382, 389–90, 393–4. We are grateful to Dr Zook for allowing us to read her work before publication. Despite Gaunt's justly celebrated activities for radical causes, she has not been given an entry in the *BDBR*.

There are also traces of a reprise of the collective female campaigns of the 1640s: women were associated with mass petitions like *The Humble Petition of the Widdows and Fatherless Children in the West of England* (1689), allegedly brought by more than a thousand petitioners.[298] Presented to the 1689 Convention, the petition recalled the brutal punishments and 'Tyrannical and Illegal Sentences' which Judge Jeffreys had imposed on the petitioners' husbands and fathers, who had been 'so Tyrannously Butchered, and some Transported'.[299]

At the time of the Popish Plot in the early 1680s, female activists emerged from the Catholic Tory right as well as the Nonconformist Whig left. In 1680, the Catholic midwife Elizabeth Cellier was tried on a charge of treason for printing and publishing a pamphlet entitled *Malice Defeated* (1680), in which she claimed that witnesses' testimony about the alleged 'Popish Plot' had been obtained through torture; thus she implied that the so-called 'Popish Plot' was a fabrication invented by the Presbyterian faction. Although acquitted on the charge of treason, Cellier was nevertheless convicted of libel for defaming the English legal system. As her punishment, she was fined £1,000 and sentenced to stand 'three different days' in the pillory; in addition, parcels of her books were burnt.[300]

The playwright Aphra Behn, a fervent Tory and a secret Catholic, expressed her partisan views through a diversity of literary genres: comedies like *The Roundheads* (1681) and *The City-Heiress* (1682); lengthy political essays prefixed to the printed versions of her plays; fictionalized burlesques of the lives of Whig grandees and their associates; and miscellaneous poems, stories and, satires. As she summed up her own career as Tory propagandist in 1681,

> Twas long she did maintain the Royal Cause
> Argu'd, disputed, rail'd with great Applause
> Writ Madrigals and Dogerel on the Times
> And charg'd you all with your Fore-fathers crimes[301]

Behn's literary partisanship thus developed into a species of Tory journalism

[298] Although it is not certain that *The Humble Petition of the Widdows and Fatherless Children* was actually composed and presented by women, it is noteworthy that the style and the sentiments of the work are reminiscent of female Levellers' petitions of the 1640s and 1650s.

[299] See Schwoerer, 'Women and the Glorious Revolution', 200–01.

[300] *The Tryal and Sentence of Elizabeth Cellier For Writing Printing and Publishing a Scandalous Libel called Malice Defeated* (1680), 35–7.

[301] A. Behn, Prologue to *The False Count* (1681), cited in Mendelson, *Mental World*, 147. For Behn's political activities, see *Mental World*, 146–51.

Malice Defeated:

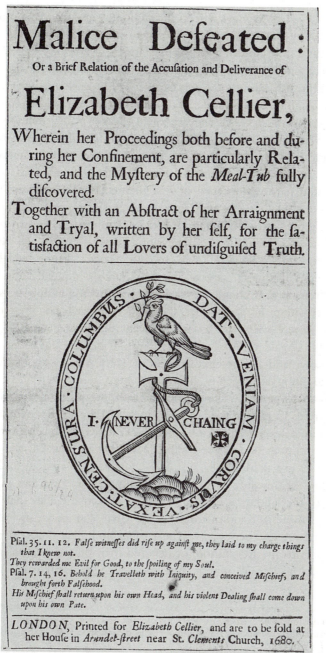

Or a Brief Relation of the Accuſation and Deliverance of

Elizabeth Cellier,

Wherein her Proceedings both before and during her Confinement, are particularly Related, and the Myſtery of the *Meal-Tub* fully diſcovered.

Together with an Abſtract of her Arraignment and Tryal, written by her ſelf, for the ſatisfaction of all Lovers of undiſguiſed Truth.

DAT · VENIAM · CORVUS · VEXAT · CENSURA · COLUMBUS ·
I· NEVER CHAING

Pſal. 35. 11. 12. *Falſe witneſſes did riſe up againſt me, they laid to my charge things that I knew not.*
They rewarded me Evil for Good, to the ſpoiling of my Soul.
Pſal. 7. 14, 16. *Behold he Travelleth with Iniquity, and conceived Miſchief, and brought forth Falſehood.*
His Miſchief ſhall return upon his own Head, and his violent Dealing ſhall come down upon his own Pate.

LONDON, Printed for *Elizabeth Cellier*, and are to be ſold at her Houſe in *Arundel-ſtreet* near St. *Clements* Church, 1680.

FIG. 49. Elizabeth Cellier, *Malice Defeated* (1680), title-page. *Malice Defeated*, Elizabeth Cellier's account of her trial and acquittal for her suspected involvement in the Meal Tub Plot, was not only written and printed by her, but sold at her own house, as the title-page proclaims

which achieved its strongest effects through satire and scandalous innuendo, rather than by a frontal attack on the opposition.

This was a new kind of activism for women, one which was adopted by subsequent female authors as a potent medium for political expression. Early in the eighteenth century, the *romans-à-clef* of Delarivier Manley employed the same techniques of fictionalized biography that Aphra Behn had used for *Love Letters between a Nobleman and his Sister* (1684), Behn's novelistic exposé of the Whig leader Forde, Lord Grey. Despite their literary trappings, the political satires and pseudo-chronicles of both female authors were treated seriously by government officials. In 1682, Behn was taken into custody and narrowly escaped imprisonment for her contribution to the anonymous play *Romulus and Hersilia*, an epilogue which was interpreted as libelling the duke of Monmouth.[302] Likewise, in 1709, Delarivier Manley was arrested for seditious libel for writing *Secret Memoirs and Manners of Several Persons . . . From the New Atlantis*, a mock allegory which libelled prominent Whigs, with a special focus on Sarah Churchill, Lady Marlborough. (Ironically, although Manley was interrogated about her suspected complicity with prominent Tories, she pleaded innocence on the ground that she was a mere writer of fiction.)[303] Even the partisan writings of more respectable female authors, such as the pro-Williamite poems of Elizabeth Singer Rowe and the polemical tracts of Mary Astell, owe something to rhetorical forms developed by Behn for political purposes.[304]

As Lois Schwoerer has shown, women from every sector of society found political roles to play in the events of 1688–9. Elite women worked within ties of kinship and lineage to influence male relatives who were at the centre of power on each side of the conflict. Rachel, Lady Russell, widow of the Whig leader executed in 1683, was closely involved in strategy and arrangements for the revolutionary settlement in 1688–9.[305] At the same time, women of the labouring classes turned to collective tactics that had been employed by female radicals during the Civil War years, including mass demonstrations and petitions.[306] Those of the middling ranks offered financial support to the Revolution, or devoted their professional talents to the cause, like the female printers and booksellers who circulated tracts and

[302] Mendelson, *Mental World*, 150–1.

[303] C. Gallagher, 'Political Crimes and Fictional Alibis: The Case of Delarivier Manley', *Eighteenth-Century Studies*, 23 (1990), 502–3.

[304] See E. Rowe, *Poems on Several Occasions* (1696), 27–32; M. Astell, *Moderation Truly Stated* (1704); *A Fair Way With the Dissenters* (1704); *An Impartial Enquiry into the Causes of Rebellion* (1704).

[305] Schwoerer, 'Women and the Glorious Revolution', 210.

[306] Ibid. 196–201.

other propaganda pieces.[307] Both Whigs and Tories had their champions among female writers who took part in the pamphlet wars of the late seventeenth and early eighteenth centuries. Quaker women like Anne Docwra and Joan Whitrowe pleaded for the rights of Dissenters, while female monarchists, including the prolific authors Elinor James and Mary Astell, argued the case for the Tory point of view.[308]

Female participation in the political mass movements of the 1690s appears to have focused mainly on economic and subsistence concerns, perhaps because women as a group were particularly hard hit by the wartime economy of William's reign.[309] Women were prominent in food riots, at times engaging in violent confrontations with grain retailers.[310] Following bad harvests in 1693, women in Northamptonshire led October attacks on corn dealers, coming to market with knives 'to force corn at their own rates'. In Oxford, in the same year, poor women in the market protested at the price of corn, 'pelting millers, mealmen, bakers etc. with stones'.

Women also participated in mass demonstrations about trade or industrial issues that affected their ability to earn a subsistence.[311] They presented a number of collective petitions throughout the 1690s, including complaints against imported calico printed gowns. In January 1697, a crowd of between 4,000 and 5,000 women besieged the House of Commons to promote the passage of a bill prohibiting the wearing of East India silks, whose imports had harmed the silk weavers' trade.[312] It was a woman who rang a bell in Spitalfields to call silk weavers together to go to Parliament.[313] On that occasion, the MPs who favoured the bill were allowed to come and go freely; although the women eventually agreed to leave, one MP thought that members who had opposed the bill were 'in great fear'.[314] Some petitions related to the economic hardship caused by new taxes. The 1697 petition of the poor glass-makers was presented to Parliament by the 'Work-

[307] Ibid. 202–3.

[308] Ibid. 204–8; Crawford, 'Women's Published Writings', 213, 216, 223, 248–9; R. Perry, *The Celebrated Mary Astell* (Chicago, 1986), 170–209.

[309] It is highly significant that nearly 50% of those tried for felonies in London during this decade were female. See J. Beattie, 'Crime and Inequality in Eighteenth-Century London', in J. Hagan and R. Peterson (eds.), *Crime and Inequality* (Stanford, Calif., 1995), 124.

[310] E. Thompson, 'The Moral Economy of the English Crowd in the Eighteenth Century', *Past and Present*, 50 (1971), 115–17.

[311] R. Shoemaker, 'The London "Mob"', *JBS*, 26 (1987), 278–9, 283, 285–6, 301–2; T. Harris, *London Crowds in the Reign of Charles II: Propaganda and Politics from the Restoration until the Exclusion Crisis* (Cambridge, 1987).

[312] M. Beloff, *Public Order and Popular Disturbances, 1660–1714* (Oxford, 1938), 82.

[313] Luttrell, *A Brief Relation of State Affairs*, iv. 174–5.

[314] *HMC Le Fleming*, 346.

ing Glass makers Wives, on behalf of themselves, Husbands and Children, who by reason of the said duty are almost redy to Perish'.[315]

As electoral contests became more regular by the late seventeenth and early eighteenth centuries, new patterns of political protest evolved. During the 1705 elections, Southwark women took exception to a Tory JP who had declared 'that he had rather see a Sow and Pigs, than a Woman and her children'; the women turned up to shout 'No Sow and Pigs'. In Coventry, 'Captain Kate' made a speech to the electoral crowd in support of a Tory candidate. According to *The Observator*, she clapped the candidate on the back, and declared 'Now, boys, or Never, for the Church.'[316] Women were also participants in political crowds, street demonstrations, and riots throughout the eighteenth century.[317]

By the 1690s, women's relationship to the political sphere had changed in many respects compared to their position in earlier centuries. Broadly speaking, the formal rights of propertied women which were under male institutional control, such as officeholding and parliamentary suffrage, suffered a relative decline; this downward trend continued over the course of the eighteenth century.[318] Nor did the prerogatives of Queen Mary II and Queen Anne represent an advance on those of their Tudor predecessors. Indeed, because Mary's husband William was in a strong position to negotiate the terms of his acceptance of the English crown, Mary's monarchical powers were somewhat diminished compared to those of the unmarried Elizabeth I.

CONCLUSIONS

By the end of the century, both political theory and political institutions were more clearly defined as male. After 1690, women were explicitly excluded from parliamentary suffrage because of their sex. In the eighteenth century, women were barred from listening to debates in the House of Commons. However, such developments do not necessarily indicate that women played fewer or less active roles in politics. Male-centred political theory may have been in part a response to women's greater participation

[315] *The Miserable Case of the Poor Glass-Makers and Families* (1697).

[316] *The Observator*, iv, no. 4, 11–14 Apr. 1705; T. Harris, *Politics under the Later Stuarts: Party Conflict in a Divided Society, 1660–1715* (1993), 191.

[317] Shoemaker, 'London "Mob"', 283–6; N. Rogers, 'Crowds, Gender, and Public Space in Hanoverian Politics', in *Crowds, Culture and Politics in Hanoverian Britain* (Oxford, 1998, forthcoming). We are grateful to Dr Rogers for allowing us to cite his forthcoming work.

[318] See Ch. 1 above.

and an attempt to contain it. Throughout the eighteenth century, aristocratic women continued to possess power and influence in elections. Those of the middling ranks, prohibited from joining male clubs, formed their own separate clubs and debating societies, where they displayed as much interest in the political and social issues of the day as their male counterparts.[319] Ordinary women continued to demonstrate and to protest over food prices, infringements of common rights, industrial and trade issues, and a wide range of religio-political concerns.[320]

Furthermore, we should not see women's political activity solely in its oppositional mode.[321] The doctrine of separate spheres for men and women, which was so powerful during the eighteenth and nineteenth centuries, was already influential in the aftermath of the Reformation. In so far as woman's domain was defined as the family, she had some power and authority there. Early modern women used that power in educating their children, and in protesting over policies which appeared to them to interfere with their ability to sustain their families' economic and moral well-being. At the end of the seventeenth century, warfare entailed a new emphasis on the separate roles of men and women. By their support of the Hanoverian monarchy, by inculcating the virtues of obedience and godliness in their children, eighteenth-century women were engaged in political activity.

Throughout much of the seventeenth century, a few adult women continued to perform civic and public duties, despite the disabilities entailed on their sex as a whole. In a society in which rights and privileges were derived chiefly from birth and inheritance, the possession of property could matter more than gender in certain circumstances, allowing élite women to claim some formal rights. The fact that women's political participation varied according to social rank alerts us to a paradoxical aspect of early modern society. The dominant ideal constructed women as wives and mothers, subordinate to husbands. Yet although female participation in politics seemed unimaginable according to this domestic ideology, in practice women were active in the public political sphere in a variety of ways.

What seems to have undermined women's formal participation by the end of the seventeenth century was the changing paradigm of political theory. From the Civil War onwards, when seventeenth-century political writers and

[319] D. Andrew, 'Women's Debating Societies', in V. Frith (ed.), *Women and History* (Toronto, 1995), 165–88.

[320] J. Bohstedt, 'Gender, Household and Community: Women in English Riots, 1790–1810', *Past and Present*, 120 (1988), 98–9; Neeson, *Commoners*, 198, 200–1; Shoemaker, 'The London "Mob"', 286, 302; Rogers, 'Crowds, Gender, and Public Space in Hanoverian Politics'.

[321] Colley, *Britons*, 372.

theorists considered questions of political rights, they conceptualized the citizen more clearly than before as male. Democratic paradigms of the rights of men and brothers excluded women more decisively than did patriarchal discourses, in which lineage and inheritance provided grounds for the formal political privileges of élite property-holders of both sexes.

EPILOGUE

> Our wedding Day 38 year Since, never yet kept with any Ceremony, but now is remarkable, for on it, Sir William hath yielded we shall Dine at One a Clock . . . 'tis the first time I ever did prevail . . . sure 'tis an Omen of my approaching death or perhaps, happening in the Reign of Queen Ann 'tis a Sign the power of Women will encrease.[1]

What changes can we observe in women's experiences of life and the world from the sixteenth to the eighteenth century? How should we draw the true contours of a chronological curve in which women are at the centre of our focus? The search for significant trends within the narrative sequence of women's history has become a particularly vexed issue in current historiographical debates. Indeed, some historians have suggested that there are intrinsic difficulties with the very notion of a fundamental transformation in women's condition over the centuries, given the 'chilling' persistence of so many basic components of the gender order, such as the defining characteristics of women's work. For scholars such as Judith Bennett, women's history is best depicted in terms of the 'problematic of continuity' rather than the problem of change.[2] Other scholars have suggested variations in the stability of the gender order, notably David Underdown, who has hypothesized a crisis in gender relations in the early seventeenth century, leading to the hardening of patriarchal attitudes.[3]

Most historical accounts have characterized the Stuart age as a century of revolution, an epoch of dramatic political, economic, and intellectual

[1] Herts. RO, D/EP/F29, Dame Sarah Cowper, Diary, i. 203, 11 Apr. 1702.

[2] J. Bennett, 'Medieval Women, Modern Women: Across the Great Divide', *Culture and History, 1350–1600: Essays on English Communities, Identities and Writing*, ed. D. Aers (1992), 158, 165. See also B. Hill, 'Women's History: A Study in Change, Continuity or Standing Still', *Women's History Review*, 2 (1993), 5–22; J. Bennett, 'Women's History: A Reply to Bridget Hill', *Women's History Review*, 2 (1993), 173–84.

[3] D. Underdown, 'The Taming of the Scold: The Enforcement of Patriarchal Authority in Early Modern England', in A. Fletcher and J. Stevenson (eds.), *Order and Disorder in Early Modern England* (Cambridge, 1985), 116–36. For different views, see M. Ingram, '"Scolding Women Cucked or Washed": A Crisis in Gender Relations in Early Modern England?', in J. Kermode and G. Walker (eds.), *Women, Crime and the Courts in Early Modern England* (Guildford, 1994); A. Fletcher, *Gender, Sex, and Subordination in England* (New Haven, 1995).

transformation which set Western society on a new course of development. Yet causal patterns of continuity and change in women's history do not correspond either to the Whig ideal of political and economic progress under an evolving capitalist democracy, or the socialist interpretation which posits social and economic decline under the same regime. An attempt to interpret significant developments in women's lives to fit one scenario or the other, for example to presume that propertied women achieved political gains as a result of the Glorious Revolution, or that labouring women shared exactly the same economic interests as labouring men, leads only to paradox when such assumptions are confronted with the evidence.

On the contrary, our findings suggest that the 'shape' of women's history is different from that of the traditional male-centred paradigms which have dominated the conventional narrative. Whatever their social class or matrimonial condition, women in early modern England had certain experiences in common. They did not respond to political, intellectual, and cultural change in the same way as their male counterparts. Whether wealthy or poor, matrons or maidens, women acted the parts of women, not of men, on the historical stage. And despite considerable variation in the beliefs and behaviour of women from different social backgrounds, we can observe an inexorable consistency in the reactions of the dominant society to women's endeavours. In every case, the elemental patterns of gender relations were preserved or re-established. One of the most fundamental insights which has emerged from our study is the remarkable degree of stability sustained by the patriarchal gender order throughout the whole of our time-period.

Stability here does not denote stasis—the state of nothing happening—but rather the dynamic ability to compensate for change, to adapt the gender order to a new equilibrium position. Such an adjustment in the dominant discourse and its institutions entailed alterations in the values of cultural, political, and economic parameters: certain elements acquired more importance as others declined in significance. Nevertheless, the system as a whole retained its hierarchical structure, its underlying beliefs about gender differences and gender roles. A persuasive model for women's history should be capable of explaining such a high degree of stability in the gender order, in contrast to what historians have interpreted as changes in society at large.

As we have seen in preceding chapters, the question of persistent continuities in gender roles cannot be answered for a hypothetical monolith called 'woman'. There is no single female narrative that comprehends the disparate experiences of women from diverse social, economic, geographical, and ideological subgroups. Even as we have paid due attention to the biological and cultural parameters that shaped women's lives *qua* women, we have followed the strands of many different female narratives, while charting their interactions with each other and with the conventional account that comprises our knowledge of early modern England.

Even the crudest starting-point must take account of differences in material circumstances. Although plebeian women certainly participated in the social and political upheavals of the sixteenth and seventeenth centuries, alterations in the composition of the political nation were of little relevance to their struggle for subsistence. For most women, the cyclical pattern of periodic mortality crises, such as those which affected England during the last three decades of the seventeenth century, were far more important in defining the conditions of everyday life. Women employed an extensive repertoire of individual and collective modes of response to subsistence crises, from food and trade riots to the adjustment of the parameters controlling nuptuality and fertility: during the early 1680s, women's age at first marriage rose to its highest point for the entire century, and the proportion of single women also reached new heights at this time.

While high politics had only limited significance for the majority of the female populace, the incidental consequences of changes in government sometimes impinged more directly on women's lives. The Glorious Revolution did not produce political gains for the female sex; but the war economy of William's reign did affect women as a group by exacerbating social and economic distress, in particular for urban single women. In London, many more women were forced to add crime to their repertoire of strategies for coping with economic disaster: during the 1690s, half of those tried for felony in the capital were female.[4] Parliament's first response in 1691 was a statute which included women among those allowed benefit of clergy (branding instead of the death penalty) for some offences. Although this statute appears to represent progress for the female sex, it was actually intended in the opposite sense, as a means of overcoming juries' reluctance to convict women—constructed as weak and dependent—on capital charges for minor property offences.

Alterations in the lives of élite women followed a very different pattern during these same decades. If we assume that the factors that produced changes in women's condition were parallel to the causes that acted on other historical variables, then propertied women's relationship to the political world of the 1690s and early 1700s presents us with a baffling paradox. In the aftermath of the Glorious Revolution, the triumph of Lockian

[4] J. Beattie, 'Crime and Inequality in Eighteenth-Century London', in J. Hagen and R. Peterson (eds.), *Crime and Inequality* (Stanford, Calif., 1995), 124.

liberalism accompanied by the rule of two female monarchs should have produced an intellectual and cultural milieu that affirmed women's equal political status as citizens of the state. Instead, the period of Whig ascendancy saw a decline rather than an increase in women's civic rights and privileges.

Elite educated women like Mary Astell were well aware of the fact that Lockian faculty psychology had laid the philosophical basis for a new theory of gender. In 1693, for example, an anonymous female author writing for *The Lady's Journal* asserted that women were as capable as men of intellectual achievements:

> The Mind acting in the same manner in both Sexes is equally able to effect the same things in either of them. This yet appears more evident if we do but examin the Head, which is the only Organ of the Sciences, the Mind performing all its functions there. Now the most accurate anatomists do not observe any difference between Man and Woman in that part, their Brains being altogether alike . . .[5]

Even more subversive were the political consequences which some women derived from Lockian liberalism. By arguing that the precepts of a democratic society applied to the family as well as the state, Mary Astell struck deep at the heart of the patriarchal gender order:

> If Absolute Sovereignty be not necessary in a State, how comes it to be so in a Family? or if in a Family why not in a State; since no Reason can be alledg'd for the one that will not hold for the other? . . . Nor is it less, but rather more mischievous in Families than in Kingdoms, by how much 100,000 tyrants are worse than one.[6]

There is a deep analogy between Parliament's punitive response to the rise in urban female criminality, and the increasing tendency of political theorists to construct civic rights as exclusively male. The legislative efforts to control female felons were directed at those women who, by becoming victims of the failure of patriarchy to provide for them, revealed the gap between paternalistic ideals and the desperate reality of women's lives as dependants. Similarly, the erosion in propertied women's political rights represented an attempt to discount the implications of glaring inconsistencies which had emerged in the political debates of the 1690s. As the contradictions inherent in patriarchy were exposed to view, and reasons were advanced to give women magisterial power in the state, men felt increasingly threatened at the very centre of patriarchal power—the family. Women's rights as citizens were the Achilles' heel of democratic theories of government. In order to

[5] *The Lady's Journal* (1693), 355.
[6] M. Astell, *Reflections Upon Marriage* (3rd edn., 1706), 'Second Preface'.

save the theory for men without sacrificing male power within the family, it became necessary to define propertied women's political rights out of existence.

What of women themselves? How did they see the world differently at the turn of the seventeenth century? In most of the contexts we have surveyed, women were apt to conserve the traditions embodied in female culture, rather than adopt masculine innovations. This was a perspective which made sense in terms of female survival. The informal control of sexual morality through the collective influence of matrons of the parish worked to protect women far more effectively than the harsh physical punishment of bastard-bearers after the fact by the secular courts, an increasing trend among the eighteenth-century judiciary.[7] Midwives attempted to sustain women's control of their own physiology, but their efforts were undermined by the rise of the man-midwife, part of a general movement towards male medical professionalism. Women of all social ranks perpetuated the patterns of piety which had been part of the common culture of both sexes before the Civil War, but were abandoned by many educated men as both politics and society became more secularized at the end of the century.[8] Yet in the economic sphere, where adaptation to new trends was favourable to survival, women were among the vanguard of proto-industrial and entrepreneurial creativity, particularly in the swiftly evolving textiles and service sectors.[9]

Women's preservation of certain traditional attitudes and customs, while men felt they were moving towards a more secular and 'enlightened' vision of society, tended to widen the cultural gap between the two sexes. The construction of the female sex as ignorant, pious, and irrational fed into the notion of 'complementary' spheres which so dominated eighteenth-century ideas about gender difference. Yet from women's own point of view, they were guardians of the things that mattered: a world governed by common rights and communal responsibilities, linked by bonds of religion and morality, family and friendship.

Some of the priorities which women expressed through their common culture thus offered a critical commentary on the conflicting messages of other discourses, an alternative view to oppose to their certainties. As it was with women's voices in early modern England, so it is with our book. Our

[7] A. E. Wrigley and R. S. Schofield, *The Population History of England, 1541–1800* (Cambridge, 1981), 266, 430. P. Laslett, *Family Life and Illicit Love in Earlier Generations* (Cambridge, 1980), ch. 3; R. Shoemaker, *Prosecution and Punishment: Petty Crime and the Law in London and Rural Middlesex, c. 1660–1725* (Cambridge, 1991), 20, 55, 286.

[8] P. Crawford, *Women and Religion in England, 1500–1720* (1993), 204–7.

[9] Papers delivered by J. Thirsk, P. Sharpe, S. Mendelson, at Achievement Project Conference, 'Women's Initiatives in Early Modern England, 1500–1750', London, June 1994.

meta-narrative is just one of many possible interpretations of women's experiences in early modern times. We offer our account not as the definitive answer to our original questions about women's lives, but rather as an open and sociable conversation with our readers, one which invites and indeed welcomes the rich diversity of other contributions to an ongoing inquiry.

Select Bibliography

PRIMARY SOURCES

Manuscripts (England)

BODLEIAN LIBRARY, OXFORD,

MS Add. A. 119, Letters of the Fairfax family.

MS Add. B. 58, D. Pakington, Prayers.

MS Ballard 43.

MSS Clarendon 19–49, Clarendon state papers, 1640–54.

MS Eng. Hist. 312, R. Whitby MS notes.

MS Eng. Misc. e. 331, Diary of Sarah Savage, 1714–23.

MS Eng. Misc. e. 479, H. Townshend, MS notes on *The Compleat Justice* (1661).

MS North c 10.

MS Rawlinson 8vo 572, Diary of Charles Beale.

MS Rawlinson B. 378, Ecclesiastical court papers.

MS Rawlinson B. 381–3, Ecclesiastical court papers.

MS Rawlinson C. 800.

MS Rawlinson D. 18, Petitions, temp. Charles II.

MS Rawlinson D. 421, 'Mulieres non Homines . . .'.

MS Rawlinson D. 828, Minute book of a Puritan Congregation, 1654.

MS Rawlinson D. 1092.

MS Rawlinson D. 1141, Diary of a London midwife.

MS Rawlinson D. 1308, Mary Carey, 'A Dialogue betwixt the soule and the body'.

MS Rawlinson Q. e. 26–28, Religious diary.

MS Tanner 104, Tanner papers.

BORTHWICK INSTITUTE

CP. series H, Archiepiscopal Cause Papers.

Consistory Court Records, Deposition Book 1676–8.

BRITISH LIBRARY

Additional MS 21,935, N. Wallington, Historical Notes and Meditations, 1588–1646.

Additional MS 27,399, Household Accounts of Framlingham Gawdy, 1626–39.

Additional MSS 27,351–5, M. Rich, countess of Warwick, Diary.

Additional MS 40,883, 'Nehemiah Wallington his Booke'.

Additional MS 42,849, Henry Letters.

Additional MS 45,196, Recipe book of Anne Glydd, 1656.

Additional MS 45,208, Additional MS 45,209, Additional MS 45,210, Accounts of Anne Brockman.

Additional MSS 61,414–16, Blenheim Papers.
Egerton MS 607, E. Egerton, countess of Bridgewater 'Meditations', *c.*1648–63.
Harleian MS 158, D'Ewes MSS.
Harleian MS 165, D'Ewes MSS.
Harleian MS 379, D'Ewes MSS.
Harleian MS 382, D'Ewes MSS.
Petty MS 5.
Portland Loan 29/76, Harley Papers.
Sir William Petty's Papers
Sloane MS 1367, Lady Ranelagh's Medical Receipts.
Sloane MS 4454, Diary of Katherine Austen.
Trumbull MS, D/ED c 13.

CENTRE FOR EAST ANGLIAN STUDIES, UNIVERSITY OF EAST ANGLIA
Smith, A. H., Bacon Database (Centre for East Anglian Studies).

CHESTER CITY RECORD OFFICE
Diary of Sarah Savage, D/Basten/8.

CORPORATION OF LONDON RECORD OFFICE
Waiting Book, 15, 1690–6.

CUMBRIA RECORD OFFICE (CARLISLE)
Quarter Session Records.
Carlisle Quarter Sessions, 1688, 1693.
D Lond/L3/1/6, Lowther Accounts.

CUMBRIA RECORD OFFICE (KENDAL)
MS WD/Cr, Transcript of a Midwife's Diary, 1665–75.
Letters from Anne Clifford, Box 44, 1615.

DEVON RECORD OFFICE
1392 M/L1678/1, Seymour of Berry Pomeroy, domestic accounts, 1678.
Chanter 866, Consistory Court Depositions, 1634–40.
Chanter 877, Consistory Court Depositions, 1676–8.
Chanter 878, Consistory Court Depositions, 1679–81.
MS 2954A Add. 2, PO 76.
QSB, Quarter Sessions Records.
Quarter Sessions Order Books.
Reynall Family Papers, MS 4652 M/F3.

DR WILLIAMS'S LIBRARY
Henry MS 91/18, Extracts from Grandmother Witton's Diary, transcribed early 18th cent.

ESSEX RECORD OFFICE
Q/SB, Quarter Sessions Rolls.

Q/SR, Quarter Sessions Records.
Calendar of Quarter Sessions Rolls.

FRIENDS' LIBRARY, LONDON

The Great Book of Sufferings.

GREATER LONDON RECORD OFFICE

DL/C/630, Consistory Court Depositions, 1632–4.
DL/C/235, Consistory Court Depositions, 1637–40.
DL/C/241, Consistory Court Depositions, 1684–7.

GUILDHALL LIBRARY, LONDON

Company of Fishmongers, Calendars of Court, Ledgers 1–5.
Microfilm 515, Bridewell Royal Hospital, Court Minutes, vol. 8, 1634–42.
MS 204, N. Wallington, His Booke, 1630.
MS 952/1, St George Botolph Lane Vestry Minute Book, 1600–85.
MS 1196/1, St Katherine Creechurch Vestry Minute Book, 1639–1718.
MS 2423/1, St Peter le Poor, Vestry Minute Book, 1687–1755.
MS 3579, St Matthew Friday St Vestry Minute Book, 1576–1743.
MS 4425/1, Minutes of the Vestry . . . St Christopher le Stocks, 1593–1731.
MS 4458/1, St Stephen Coleman Street Vestry Book.
MSS 5561/1–3 Fishmongers' Accounts.
MS 5570/3, Fishmongers' Court Ledger, 1631–46.
MS 7673/1, St Alban Wood St Churchwarden's accounts, 1626–7.
MS 7674, St Alban Wood St Churchwardens' and Overseers' accounts, 1652–67.
MS 7706, St Katherine Creechurch Overseers' Account Book.
MS 9056, London Archdeaconry Depositions, 1566–7.
MSS 9057/1–2, London Archdeaconry Depositions, 1632–8, 1686–92.
MS 9187/2, London Consistory Court Examinations 1627–8.
MS 9583/2, pt. i, St Mary Woolchurch.
MS 9731/101, Papers re matters in the peculiar jurisdiction of St Catherine.
MS 9740, St Katharine by the Tower, Depositions at Lord Somers Visitation.
MS 10,116/4.
MSS 11,280A/1–3, Indentures.
MS 11,280A/5, Removal Orders and Settlement papers.
MSS 11,571/9–11, Grocers' Company, Warden's Accounts, 1622–33.
MSS 11,588/2–3, Grocers' Company, Orders of the Court of Assistants.
MS 21,041 B, An Account of St Catherines 1595–1699, written 1803.
MS 22,897, St Olave, Southwark.

HERTFORDSHIRE RECORD OFFICE

Panshanger MSS, D/EP/F29, Dame S. Cowper, Diary, vol. i, 1700–2.
Panshanger MSS, D/EP/F36, Dame S. Cowper, Commonplace Book, 1673–1700.

KENT ARCHIVES OFFICE
F. 27, Journal of Elizabeth Turner.

JOHN RYLANDS LIBRARY, MANCHESTER UNIVERSITY
Legh of Lyme Correspondence.

NEW COLLEGE, OXFORD
Mary Woodeforde Booke (1684–90).

NORFOLK RECORD OFFICE
AYL 829, Notes of Quarter Session Proceedings by Robert Doughty, 1662–5.
AYL 1/1, Wage Assessments, 1613.
Mayor's Court Book, 1624–34.
TES 8, Bishops' Licensing Papers.
WCK 6/15, Katherine Windham Kitchen Accounts, 1695–96.
WKC 6/12, Katherine Windham Personal Accounts, 1669–89.

NORTHAMPTONSHIRE RECORD OFFICE
W(A) misc. vol. 35, Book of Advices to the Children by several Ladies Westmorland.

OXFORD ARCHIVES
MS Archdiaconal Papers Oxon. c 118, 1616–20.
MS Oxf. Dioc. Papers c 26, 1629–34.
MS Oxf. Dioc. Papers c 27, 1634–9.
MS Oxf. Dioc. Papers c 29, 1679–86.
MS Oxf. Dioc. Papers c 30, 1686–94.
MS Oxf. Dioc. Papers c 96, 1606–1720.
QS Quarter Sessions.

PUBLIC RECORD OFFICE
LS 13/252, Book of Warrants (Charles II).
SP 6/424/53.
SP 24/4 Indemnity Papers.
SP 28/10, Commonwealth Exchequer Papers.
STAC 8/138/18, Star Chamber.

SOMERSET RECORD OFFICE
DD/SF 4515, Clarke Letters.

ST BARTHOLOMEW'S HOSPITAL
HB 1/3–7, Account Books.
Minutes of the Board of Governors, MS H1/5.

WARWICKSHIRE COUNTY RECORD OFFICE
CR 2017/C1.

WELLCOME INSTITUTE LIBRARY, LONDON
MS 4338, W.IIa, Medical Commonplace Book, Johanne St John, 1680.

Manuscripts (USA)

FOLGER SHAKESPEARE LIBRARY

Collections: Bagot, Rich.

MS Add. 931, Mary Hookes, Receipt Book, 1680.

MS V. a. 20, Constantia Hall, her Book of Receipts, 1672.

MS V. a. 215, Susannah Packe, 1674.

MS V. a. 396, Commonplace Book of P. Jephson.

MS V. a. 425, Commonplace Book of Sarah Long, 1610.

MS V. a. 456, M. Baumfylde, 1626.

MS V. a. 387, Book of Katherine Packer, 1639.

MS V. a. 450, Lettice Pudsey.

MS V. a. 220, M. Beale, 'A Discourse of Friendship'.

MS V. a. 166, 'An Account of the Lady Lucy . . . to a Particular Friend of Hers, Mrs. Moore'.

Printed Primary Sources

Place of publication is London, unless otherwise stated.

A Kingdom without a King. The Journal of the Provisional Government in the Revolution of 1688, ed. R. Beddard (Oxford, 1988).

Account Book of the Parish of St Christopher Le Stocks . . . London, 1662–1685, ed. E. Freshfield (1895).

Accmptes of the Churchwardens of the Paryshe of St Christopher's in London, 1575 to 1662, ed. E. Freshfield (1885).

Advice to Amabella. Sir Anthony Benn to His Daughter, ed. B. Carroll (Clayton, Victoria, 1990).

Advice to the Women and Maidens of London (1678).

Albertus Magnus, *De Secretis Mulierum* (trans. 1725).

Alleine, T., *The Life and Death of . . . Joseph Alleine* (1672).

An Account of the Remarkable Conversion and Experience of Mary Hurll (1708; 3rd edn., 1719).

An Ease for Overseers of the Poore (Cambridge, 1601).

Aristotles Masterpiece (1690; 1710).

Ar't Asleepe Husband? A Boulster Lecture (1640).

Astell, M., *A Serious Proposal to the Ladies* (1694).

—— *A Serious Proposal to the Ladies*, pt. 2 (1697).

—— *Reflections upon Marriage* (3rd edn., 1706).

Aubrey, J., *Brief Lives*, ed. R. Barber (1975).

—— *Miscellanies* (1696).

—— *Remaines of Gentilism and Judaisme, 1686–87*, in *Three Prose Works* (Carbondale, Ill., 1972).

Autobiography of Mary, Countess of Warwick, ed. T. Croker, Percy Society (1848).

Bacon, F., *The Historie of Life and Death* (1638).

A Banquet of Jests (1634).

Barret, R., *A Companion for Midwives, Child-Bearing Women and Nurses* (1699).

Barrington Family Letters, 1628–1632, ed. A. Searle, Camden Society 4th ser., 28 (1983).

Batchiler, J., *The Virgins Pattern* (1661).

Bateson, M., *Borough Customs*, Selden Society, 2 vols. (1904, 1906).

Bathurst, B. (ed.), *Letters of Two Queens* [1924].

Baxter, R., *'The Poor Husbandman's Advocate to Rich Racking Landlords', 1691* (1926).

—— *Reliquiae Baxterianae* (1696).

Bayle, P., *et al.*, *A General Dictionary* (1741).

Beaumont, A., *The Singular Experiences . . . of Mrs Agnes Beaumont* (1822).

A Bedfordshire Wage Assessment of 1684, ed. T. S. Willan, Bedfordshire Record Society, 25 (1957).

Bell, S., *The Legacy of a Dying Mother . . . being the experiences of Mrs Susanna Bell* (1673).

Bentley, T., *Monument of Matrones: Conteining Seven Severall Lamps of Virginitie* (1582).

Bernard, R., *Ruths Recompence* (1628).

Best, H., *The Farming and Memorandum Books of Henry Best of Elmswell, 1642*, ed. D. Woodward (Oxford, 1984).

Blackstone, W., *Commentaries on the Laws of England* (4th edn., Dublin, 1771).

Bohun, W., *Privilegia Londini; Or the Laws, Customs, and Privileges of the City of London* (1702).

Borde, A., *The Breuiary of Helthe* (1547).

Brand, J., *Observations on Popular Antiquities*, 2 vols. (1813).

Brinsley, J., *A Looking-Glasse for Good Women* (1645).

Bristol Corporation of the Poor. Selected Records, 1696–1834, ed. E. E. Butcher, Bristol Record Society, 34 (Bristol, 1932).

Brownell, M., *Diary* (1688), in *North Country Diaries,* second series, ed. J. C. Hodgson, Surtees Society, 124 (1914).

Bufford, S., *An Essay against Unequal Marriages* (1693).

B[unworth], R., *The Doctresse: A Plain and Easie Method of Curing those Diseases which are Peculiar to Women* ([30 May] 1656).

Bunyan, J., *Grace Abounding to the Chief of Sinners*, ed. R. Sharrock (Oxford, 1962).

Burn, R., *The Justice of the Peace and the Parish Officer*, 2 vols. (1755).

Burnet, G., *Bishop Burnet's History of His Own Time*, 2nd edn., enlarged (Oxford, 1833).

Burton, R., *The Anatomy of Melancholy* (Oxford, 1621).

Bury, S., *An Account of the Life and Death of Mrs. Elizabeth Bury* (Bristol, 1720).

C., F., *A Present for the Ladies* (1692).

Calendar of Chester City Council Minutes, 1603–1642, ed. M. J. Groombridge, Record Society of Lancs and Cheshire, 106 (1956).
Calendars of State Papers, Domestic.
Cartwright, J. J. (ed.), *The Wentworth Papers, 1705–1739* (1883).
Cary, M., *A New and More Exact Map* (1651).
—— *The Little Horns Doom and Downfall* (1651).
The Casebook of Sir Francis Ashley J. P. Recorder of Dorchester, 1614–1635, ed. J. H. Bettey, Dorset Record Society, 7 (1981).
Cavendish, M., duchess of Newcastle, *CCXI Sociable Letters* (1664).
—— *Natures Pictures Drawn by Fancies Pencil to the Life* (1656).
—— *Philosophical and Physical Opinions* (1655).
—— *The Life of William, duke of Newcastle* (1667).
—— *The Worlds Olio* (1655).
Chamberlayne, T. *The Compleat Midwifes Practice* (1656).
—— *The Complete Midwifes Practice Enlarg'd* (1659).
[Chapone, H.], *The Hardship of the English Laws in Relation to Wifes* (1735).
Chidley, K., *Good Counsell to the Petitioners for Presbyterian Government* (1645).
—— *The Justification of the Independant Churches of Christ* (1641).
Child, J., *A New Discourse of Trade* (1693).
Christ's Hospital Admissions, 1554–1599, ed. G. A. T. Allen (1937).
[Chudleigh, M.], *The Female Advocate* (1700).
—— *The Ladies Defence* (1701).
Clarke, J. S., *The Life of James the Second*, 2 vols. (1816).
Clinton, E., *The Countesse of Lincolnes Nurserie* (1622).
Cogan, T., *The Haven of Health* (1584).
Coke, E., *First Institute of the Laws of England* (1628).
[Comber, D.], *A Companion to the Temple* (1684).
The Compleat Justice (1661).
Constant, T. (pseud.), *An Essay to Prove Women have no Souls* [*c.*1712].
Conversion Exemplified (1669).
County of Middlesex. Calendar to the Sessions Records, 1612–16, ed. W. Le Hardy, 3 vols. (1935).
Coventry Constables' Presentments, 1629–1742, ed. L. Fox, Dugdale Society (Oxford, 1986).
[Cragg, W.] *The Widowes Joy* (1622).
Craig, T., *Concerning the Right of Succession to the Kingdom of England* (1703).
Crooke, H., *Microcosmographia: A Description of the Body of Man* [1615] [1631].
Culpeper, N., *A Directory for Midwives* (1651).
Culpeper's School of Physick ([Oct.] 1659).
Dalrymple, Sir J., *Memoirs of Great Britain and Ireland*, 3 vols. (1773).
Dalton, M., *The Countrey Justice* (1618).
—— *The Country Justice* (1655).
Day, W. G. (ed.), *The Pepys Ballads: Facsimile* (Woodbridge, 1978).

Declaration . . . concerning the birth of the Prince of Wales [1688].

Delaval, E., *The Meditations of Lady Elizabeth Delaval*, ed. D. Greene, Surtees Society, 190 (1975).

de Loyer, P., *A Treatise of Specters* (1605).

D'Ewes, S., *The Autobiography and Correspondence of Sir Simonds D'Ewes*, ed. J. O. Halliwell, 2 vols. (1845).

—— *The Journal of Sir Simonds D'Ewes*, ed. W. Notestein (New Haven, 1923).

Diaries and Letters of Philip Henry of Broad Oak, Flintshire, A. D. 1631–1696, ed. M. H. Lee (1882).

Diary of John Evelyn, ed. W. Bray, 4 vols. (1879).

Diary of Roger Lowe, 1663–74, ed. W. Sachse (New Haven, 1938).

Diary of the Marches of the Royal Army . . . by Richard Symonds, ed. C. E. Long, Camden Society, 74 (1859).

Diary of William Lawrence. Covering periods between 1662 and 1681, ed. G. E. Aylmer (Beaminster, 1961).

Digby, K., *A Late Discourse* (3rd edn, 1660).

Dillingham, F., *Christian Oeconomy, or Household Government* (1609).

D.[ocwra], A., *An Apostate Conscience Exposed* (1699).

Drage, W., *A Physical Nosonomy* (1665).

Drake, J., *Anthropologia Nova; Or a New System of Anatomy*, 2 vols. (1707).

[Drake, Judith], *An Essay in Defence of the Female Sex* (1696).

E., T., *The Lawes Resolutions of Womens Rights* (1632).

Earwaker, J. P. (ed.), *The Court Leet Records of the Manor of Manchester*, 12 vols. (Manchester, 1884–90).

Ellis, H., *Pseudochristus, Or, a True and Faithful Relation . . .* (1650).

Elyot, T., *The Defence of Good Women* (1545).

Emmison, F. G., *Elizabethan Life. Morals and the Church Courts* (Chelmsford, 1973).

The English Reports, 179 vols. (Edinburgh, 1900–32).

Evelyn, J., *The Life of Margaret Godolphin* (1904).

Fair Warning to the Murderers of Infants: Being an Account of the Tryal . . . of Mary Goodenough (1692).

Fell, S., *The Household Account Book of Sarah Fell of Swarthmoor Hall*, ed. N. Penney (Cambridge, 1920).

Filmer, R., 'The Anarchy of a Limited or Mixed Monarchy', in *Patriarcha and other Political Works* (Oxford, 1949).

Foley, H. (ed.), *Records of the English Province of the Society of Jesus*, 7 vols. (1882).

Fontanus, N., *The Womans Doctour* ([8 Nov.] 1652).

Fox, G., *The Journal of George Fox*, ed. J. Nickalls (Cambridge, 1952).

Freke, E., 'Mrs Elizabeth Freke her Diary, 1671–1714', *Journal of the Cork Historical and Archaeological Society*, 16–18 (1910–13), reprinted ed. M. Carbery (Cork, 1913).

Gardiner, R., *Englands Grievance Discovered* (1655).

Gardiner, S. R. (ed.), *Reports of Cases in the Courts of Star Chamber and High Commission*, Camden Society, NS 39 (1886).

Geree, J., *Might overcoming Right or a Cleer Answer to M. John Goodwin's Might and Right Well Met* (1649).

[Gibson, T.], *The Anatomy of Humane Bodies* (1682).

Glass, D. V. (ed.), *London Inhabitants within the Walls*, London Record Society, 2 (1966).

G[oodcole, H.], *Heavens Speedie Hue and Cry* (1635).

Gouge, W., *Of Domesticall Duties* (1622).

Gough, R., *The History of Myddle*, ed. D. Hey (Harmondsworth, 1981).

Goulianos, J. (ed.), *By a Woman Writt. Literature from Six Centuries by and about Women* (Baltimore, 1974).

Graunt, J., *Natural and Political Observations* (1662), in *The Earliest Classics*, ed. P. Laslett (1973).

Greene, R., *Pinder of Wakefield*, English Reprints, ser. 12 (Liverpool, 1956).

Greer, G., *et al.*, *Kissing the Rod: An Anthology of Seventeenth-Century Women's Verse* (1988).

Grey, A., *Debates of the House of Commons . . . 1667 to 1694*, 10 vols. (1763).

Griffiths, R. G. (ed.), 'Joyce Jeffreys of Ham Castle', *Transactions of the Worcestershire Archaeological Society*, NS 10–12 (1933–5), 1–32, 1–13, 1–17.

Guilding, J. M. (ed.), *Reading Records*, 4 vols. (1895).

Guillimeau, J., *Child-birth or the Happie Deliverie of Women* (1612).

H., N., *The Ladies Dictionary* (1694).

Hale, M., *Historia Placitorum Coronae*, 2 vols. (1736).

Halifax, marquis of, *Advice to a Daughter* (1688), *Halifax: Complete Works*, ed. J. P. Kenyon (Harmondsworth, 1969).

—— *The Lady's New Years Gift* (1688).

Hamilton, A. H. A., *Quarter Sessions from Queen Elizabeth to Queen Anne* (1878).

Harley, B., *Letters of the Lady Brilliana Harley*, ed. T. T. Lewis, Camden Society, 58 (1854).

Harris, W., *An Exact Enquiry into . . . the Acute Diseases of Infants* (1693).

Hart, J., *Klinikh, or the Diet of the Diseased* (1633).

Harvey, G., *Morbus Anglicus: Or the Anatomy of Consumption* (1672).

Hawkins, W., *A Treatise of the Pleas of the Crown*, 2 vols. (1716).

Hayes, A., *A Legacy or Widow's Mite* (1723).

A Hellish Murder Committed by a French Midwife, on the Body of her Husband (1688).

Herbert, G., *Outlandish Proverbs* (1640).

Hertford County Records: Notes and Extracts from the Session Rolls, 1581 to 1698, ed. W. J. Hardy (Hertford, 1905).

H.[eywood], T., *A Curtaine Lecture* (1637).

Hic Mulier; Or, The Man-Woman (1620).

Highmore, N., *The History of Generation* ([28 Oct.] 1651).

Hill, B. (ed.), *The First English Feminist. Reflections Upon Marriage and other writings by Mary Astell* (Aldershot, 1986).

Holles, G., *Memorials of the Holles Family*, ed. A. Wood, Camden Society, 3rd ser., 55 (1937).

Holles, J., *Letters of John Holles, 1587–1637*, ed. P. R. Seddon, Thoroton Society, 3 vols, 31, 35, 36 (1975–86).

Hooker, R., *Of the Lawes of Ecclesiasticall Politie* (1597).

House and Farm Accounts of the Shuttleworths, ed. J. Harland, Chetham Society, 4 vols. (1856–8).

Hutchinson, L., *Memoirs of the Life of Colonel Hutchinson*, ed. J. Sutherland (Oxford, 1973).

Jinner, S., *An Almanack or Prognostication for . . . 1658* [1658] (1659 and 1664).

Joceline, E., *The Mothers Legacie to her Unborne Child* (1624 and subsequent eds).

Jones, J., *The Arte and Science of preserving Bodie and Soule in Healthe* (1579).

Jorden, E., *A Briefe Discourse of a Disease called the Suffocation of the Mother* (1603).

Josselin, R., *The Diary of Ralph Josselin, 1616–1683*, ed. A. Macfarlane (1976).

Journal of Giles Moore, ed. R. Bird, Sussex Record Society, 68 (1971).

Keble, J., *An Assistance to Justices of the Peace* (1683).

Kempe, A. J. (ed.), *The Loseley Manuscripts* (1836).

Keynes, G. (ed.), *The Letters of Sir Thomas Browne* (1931).

Kilburne, R., *Choice Presidents . . . Relating to the Office and duty of A Justice of the Peace* (1685).

King, G., *Natural and Political Observations . . . upon the State and Condition of England* (1696).

King, W. (ed.), *Memoirs of Sarah, Duchess of Marlborough* (1930).

The Ladies Law (1737).

Lambarde, W., *Eirenarcha, or of the Office of the Justices of Peace* (1614).

Lancashire and Cheshire Wills and Inventories, 1563–1807, ed. J. P. Rylands, Chetham Society, NS 37 (1897).

Laslett, P. (ed.), *The Earliest Classics* (1973).

Le Strange, N., *'Merry Passages and Jeasts': A Manuscript Jestbook*, ed. H. Lippincott (1974).

Leigh, D., *The Mothers Blessing* (1616, 1618).

Lemnius, L., *A Discourse touching Generation* (1667).

—— *The Secret Miracles of Nature in Four Books* (1658).

—— *The Touchstone of Complexions* (1576).

Lessius, L., *Hygiasticon: Or the Right Course of Preserving Life and Health unto Extream Old Age* (Cambridge, 1634).

Letter Book of Sir John Parkhurst, ed. R. Houlbrooke, Norfolk Record Society, 43 (1974).

Letters from Lady Margaret Kennedy to John, duke of Lauderdale, Bannatyne Club, 24 (Edinburgh, 1828).

Levett, J., *The Ordering of Bees* (1634).

Lewis, J., *Memoirs of Prince William Henry* (1789).

Ley, J., *A Patterne of Pietie or the Religious Life and Death of . . . Mrs Jane Ratcliffe, Widow and Citizen of Chester* (1640).

Liber Familicus of Sir James Whitelocke, ed. J. Bruce, Camden Society, 70 (1858).

Locke, J., *The Correspondence of John Locke and Edward Clarke*, ed. B. Rand (Cambridge, Mass., 1927).

—— *Two Treatises of Government*, ed. P. Laslett (Cambridge, 1960).

Loftis, J. (ed.), *The Memoirs of Anne, Lady Halkett and Ann, Lady Fanshawe* (Oxford, 1979).

Lord, G. de F. (ed.), *Poems on Affairs of State: Augustan Satirical Verse, 1660–1714*, 7 vols. (New Haven, 1963–75).

Lowe, R., *The Diary of Roger Lowe, 1663–74*, ed. W. Sachse (New Haven, 1938).

Luttrell, N., *A Brief Historical Relation of State Affairs, 1678–1714*, 6 vols. (Oxford, 1857).

[Makin, B.], *An Essay to Revive the Antient Education of Gentlewomen* (1673).

Mandeville, B., *The Fable of the Bees: Or, Private Vices, Publick Benefits*, ed. F. B. Kaye, 2 vols. (Oxford, 1924).

Markham, G., *Country Contentments* (1615).

Martindale, A., *The Life of Adam Martindale*, ed. R. Parkinson, Chetham Society, 4 (1845).

Mauquest de La Motte, G., *Treatise of Midwifery* (1746).

Memoirs of Queen Mary II (1689–1693), ed. R. Doebner (Leipzig, 1886).

Memoirs of Sarah, Duchess of Marlborough, ed. W. King (1930).

Memoirs of Sir Hugh Cholmley (1787).

Memorandum Book of Sir Walter Calverley, Yorkshire Diaries and Autobiographies, ii, Surtees Society, 77 (1883).

Meriton, G., *The Touchstone of Wills* (1668).

—— *A Guide for Constables, Churchwardens, Overseers of the Poor* (1669).

Minutes of the Norwich Court of Mayoralty, 1630–1631, ed. W. L. Sachse, Norfolk Record Society, 15 (1942).

Minutes of the Norwich Court of Mayoralty, 1632–1635, ed. W. L. Sachse, Norfolk Record Society, 36 (1967).

Minutes of Proceedings in Quarter Sessions held for the Parts of Kesteven in the County of Lincoln, 1674–95, 2 parts, ed. S. A. Peyton, Lincoln Record Society, 25–6 (1931).

Mordaunt, E., *The Private Diarie of Elizabeth, Viscountess Mordaunt* (Duncairn, 1856).

Morris, C. (ed.), *The Illustrated Journeys of Celia Fiennes, 1685–c.1712* (1982).

[Neville, H.] *The Ladies, A Second Time, assembled in Parliament* (1647).

—— *The Ladies Parliament* (1647).

Newnham, J., *Newnams Nighcrowe. A Bird that Breedeth Brauls in Many Families and Households* (1590).

Nicolson, M. H. (ed.), *Conway Letters: The Correspondence of Anne, Viscountess Conway, Henry More, and Their Friends, 1642–1684* (1930).

Norfolk Quarter Sessions Order Book, 1650–1657, ed. D. E. Howell James, Norfolk Record Society, 26 (1955).

North, R., *The Autobiography of the Hon Roger North*, ed. A. Jessopp (1887).

Norwich Census of the Poor, 1570, ed. J. F. Pound, Norfolk Record Society, 40 (1971).

Osborne, D., *Letters from Dorothy Osborne to Sir William Temple, 1652–54*, ed. G. Moore Smith (Oxford, 1928).

Oxford Dictionary of Proverbs, ed. W. Smith (Oxford, 2nd edn., 1952).

Paré, A., *The Workes of that famous Chirurgion* (1634).

Parsloe, G., *Wardens' Accounts of the Worshipful Company of Founders of the City of London, 1497–1681* (1964).

Pechey, J., *A Collection of Chronical Diseases* (1692).

—— *The Store-house of Physical Practice* (1695).

Peele, G., *The Old Wives Tale* [1595].

Penington, M., *Some Account of Circumstances in the Life of Mary Penington* (1821).

Pepys, S., *The Diary of Samuel Pepys*, ed. R. Latham and W. Matthews, 11 vols. (1970–83).

Petition of the Oppressed Market People [1699?].

Petyt, G., *Lex Parliamentaria* (1690).

Poverty in Early-Stuart Salisbury, ed. P. Slack, Wiltshire Record Society, 31 (1975).

Prévost, J., *Medicaments For the Poor*, trans. N. Culpeper (2nd edn., Edinburgh, 1664).

Purchas, S., *Purchas his Pilgrim: Microcosmus, or the Historie of Man* (1619).

Ray, J., *A Collection of English Proverbs* (1678).

Raymond, T., *Autobiography of Thomas Raymond*, ed. G. Davies, Camden Society, 3rd ser., 28 (1917).

Records of the Borough of Leicester, . . . 1603–1688, ed. H. Stocks (Cambridge, 1923).

Reports of the Historical Manuscripts Commission.

Riverius, L., *The Practice of Physick*, trans. N. Culpeper, A. Cole, and W. Roland (1655).

Rogers, J., *Ohel or Beth-Shemesh* (1653).

Ross, A., *Arcana Microcosmi* (1651).

Rowlands, S., *A Whole Crew of Kind Gossips, All Met to be Merry* (1609).

The Roxburghe Ballads, ed. W. Chappell and J. Ebsworth, 9 vols. in 8 (London and Hertford, 1866–99).

[Rueff, J.] *The Expert Midwife* (trans., 1637).

Rushworth, J., *Historical Collections*, 8 vols. (1659).

Russell, R., *Letters of Rachel Lady Russell* (1773); 2 vols. (1853).

Sad and True Relation of a Most Barbarous and Bloody Murder by one Thomas Watson (1686).

Second Humble Address from the Poor Weavers and Manufacturers to the Ladies [*c.*1690].

Sennert, D., *The Institutions or Fundamentals of the Whole Art . . . of Physick* (1656).

Sermon, W., *The Ladies Companion, or the English Midwife* (1671).

Sharp, J., *The Midwives Book* (1671).
Shaw, H., *A Plaine Relation of My Sufferings* (1653).
Shirley, J., *The Illustrious History of Women* (1686).
Simmonds, M., *A Lamentation for the Lost Sheep* (1655).
Singer, S. W. (ed.), *The Correspondence of Henry Hyde, Earl of Clarendon*, 2 vols. (1828).
Six North Country Diaries, Surtees Society, 118 (1910).
Some Account of the Life of Rachel Wriothesley Lady Russell (1819).
Stout, W., *The Autobiography of William Stout of Lancaster, 1665–1752*, ed. J. D. Marshall (Manchester, 1967).
Swinburne, H., *A Briefe Treatise of Testaments and Last Willes* (1590).
—— *A Treatise of Spousals* (1686).
[Tate, N.] *A Present for the Ladies* (1692).
Thirsk, J., and Cooper, J. P. (eds.), *Seventeenth-Century Economic Documents* (Oxford, 1972).
Thornton, A., *The Autobiography of Mrs. Alice Thornton*, ed. C. Jackson, Surtees Society, 62 (1875).
Tilley, M. P., *A Dictionary of the Proverbs in England in the Sixteenth and Seventeenth Centuries* (Ann Arbor, 1950).
Tixall Letters; Or the Correspondence of the Aston Family, 2 vols. (1815).
To the Honourable Knights . . . The Most Humble Petition of the Gentlewomen, Tradesmens Wives, and many others of the Female Sex (1642).
Transcription of the 'Poor Book' of the Tithings of Westbury-on-Trym, . . . 1656–1698, ed. H. J. Wilkins (Bristol, 1910).
True Relation of the Tryals . . . particularly of Elizabeth Wigenton (1681).
Trye, M., *Medicatrix, or the Woman-Physician* (1675).
Turner, G. L. (ed.), *Original Records of Early Nonconformity*, 3 vols. (1911–14).
Tusser, T., *Five Hundred Points of Good Husbandry* (Oxford, 1984).
Unto Every Individual Member of Parliament; the . . . Representation of . . . Women . . . on Behalf of Mr John Lilburn (1653).
Vaughan, W., *Naturall and Artificial Directions for Health* (1600).
Vestry Minute Books of the Parish of St Bartholomew Exchange in the City of London, 1567–1676, ed. E. Freshfield (1890).
Walker, A., *The Holy Life of Mrs Elizabeth Walker* (1690).
Warwick County Records. Quarter Session Records Easter, 1674, to Easter, 1682 (1946).
Warwick County Records. Quarter Sessions Order Book, Easter, 1625 to Trinity, 1637, ed. S. C. Ratcliff and H. C. Johnson (1935).
Wentworth, A., *A Vindication* (1677).
Wesley, J., *The Journal of John Wesley*, ed. N. Curnock (Epworth, 1912).
West Riding Sessions Records 1611–1642, ed. J. Lister, Yorks. Archaeological Society, 54 (1915).
Wheatcroft, L., 'The Autobiography of Leonard Wheatcroft', *Journal of Derbyshire Archaeological and Natural History Society*, 18 (1896) and 21 (1899).

—— *The Courtship Narrative of Leonard Wheatcroft*, ed. G. Parfitt and R. Houlbrooke (Reading, 1986).

Whitelocke, R. H., *Memoirs, Biographical and Historical, of Bulstrode Whitelocke* (1860).

Williams, J. B. (ed.), *The Lives of Philip and Matthew Henry* (1828; 1974).

Wills and Inventories from the Registry at Durham, ed. H. M. Wood, Surtees Society, 142 (1929).

Wolley, H., *A Supplement to the Queen-like Closet* (1674).

—— *The Gentlewomans Companion; Or, A Guide to the Female Sex* (1675; 3rd edn., 1682).

Wolveridge, J., *Speculum Matrices: Or, the Expert Midwives Handmaid* (1671).

Woodhouse, A. S. P. (ed.), *Puritanism and Liberty* (1974).

Wortley Montagu, M., *The Complete Letters of Lady Mary Wortley Montagu*, ed. R. Halsband, 3 vols. (1965).

Wright, L. B., *Advice to a Son: Precepts of Lord Burghley, Sir Walter Raleigh, and Francis Osborne* (Ithaca, NY, 1962).

York Civic Records, vii [1570–78], ed. A. Raine, Yorks. Archaeological Society, Record Series, 119 (1952).

York Civic Records, ix [1588–90], ed. D. Sutton, Yorks. Archaeological Society, Record Series, 138 (1978).

Yorkshire Diaries and Autobiographies in the Seventeenth and Eighteenth Centuries, ii, Surtees Society, 77 (1886).

SELECTED SECONDARY WORKS

Adair, R., *Courtship, Illegitimacy and Marriage in Early Modern England* (Manchester, 1996).

Allen, R., *Enclosure and the Yeoman* (Oxford, 1992).

Alsop, J., 'The Act for the Queen's Regal Power, 1554', *Parliamentary History*, 13 (1994), 261–76.

Amussen, S. D., 'Elizabeth I and Alice Balstone: Gender, Class, and the Exceptional Woman in Early Modern England', in B. S. Travitsky and A. F. Seeff (eds.), *Attending to Women in Early Modern England* (Newark, NJ, 1994).

—— 'The Gendering of Popular Culture in Early Modern England', in T. Harris (ed.), *Popular Culture in England, c.1500–1850* (1995).

—— *An Ordered Society: Gender and Class in Early Modern England* (Oxford, 1988).

—— 'Punishment, Discipline, and Power: The Social Meanings of Violence in Early Modern England', *Journal of British Studies*, 34 (1995), 1–34.

Andreadis, H., 'The Sapphic-Platonics of Katherine Philips, 1632–1664', *Signs*, 15 (1989), 34–60.

Anstruther, G., *Vaux of Harrowden: A Recusant Family* (Newport, 1953).

Arber, A., *Herbals: Their Origin and Evolution* (Cambridge, 3rd edn., 1986).

Archer, I., *The Pursuit of Stability: Social Relations in Elizabethan London* (Cambridge, 1991).

Aveling, J. H., *English Midwives: Their History and Prospects* (1872).

Aylmer, G. E., *The King's Servants: The Civil Service of Charles I, 1625–1642* (1961).

Baker, J. H., *An Introduction to English Legal History* (2nd edn., 1979).

—— 'Male and Married Spinsters', *The American Journal of Legal History*, 21 (1977), 255–9.

Barron, C., 'The "Golden Age" of Women in Medieval London', *Reading Medieval Studies*, 15 (1989), 35–58.

Barry, J. (ed.), *The Tudor and Stuart Town: A Reader in English Urban History* (1990).

Bashar, N., 'Rape in England between 1550 and 1700', in London Feminist History Group, *The Sexual Dynamics of History: Men's Power, Women's Resistance* (1983).

Beattie, J. M., *Crime and the Courts in England, 1660–1800* (Oxford, 1986).

Beier, L. M., 'The Good Death in Seventeenth-Century England', in R. Houlbrooke (ed.), *Death, Ritual, and Bereavement* (1989).

Ben-Amos, I. K., *Adolescence and Youth in Early Modern England* (New Haven, 1994).

—— 'Women Apprentices in the Trades and Crafts of Early Modern Bristol', *Continuity and Change*, 6 (1991), 227–63.

Bennett, J. M., '"History that Stands Still": Women's Work in the European Past', *Feminist Studies*, 14 (1988), 269–83.

—— 'Misogyny, Popular Culture, and Women's Work', *History Workshop*, 31 (1991), 166–88.

Berg, M., 'Women's Work, Mechanization and the Early Phases of Industrialization in England', in R. E. Pahl (ed.), *On Work: Historical, Comparative and Theoretical Approaches* (Oxford, 1988).

Berry, P., *Of Chastity and Power: Elizabethan Literature and the Unmarried Queen* (New York, 1989).

Bevan, B., *Charles II's French Mistress* (1972).

—— *Nell Gwynn* (1969).

Biographical Dictionary of British Radicals, ed. R. L. Greaves and R. Zaller, 3 vols. (Brighton, 1982).

Boswell, E., *The Restoration Court Stage (1660–1702)* (New York, 1932).

Boulton, J., *Neighbourhood and Society: A London Suburb in the Seventeenth Century* (Cambridge, 1987).

Brewer, J., and Styles, J. (eds.), *An Ungovernable People* (1980).

Brodsky, V., 'Single Women in the London Marriage Market: Age, Status and Mobility, 1598–1619', in R. B. Outhwaite (ed.), *Marriage and Society: Studies in the Social History of Marriage* (1981).

—— 'Widows in Late Elizabethan London: Remarriage, Economic Opportunity and Family Orientations', in L. Bonfield, R. M. Smith, and K. Wrightson (eds.), *The*

World We Have Gained: Histories of Population and Social Structure (Oxford, 1986).

Brown, I. Q., 'Domesticity, Feminism, and Friendship: Female Aristocratic Culture and Marriage in England, 1660–1760', *Journal of Family History*, 7 (1982), 406–24.

Brown, W. Newman, 'The Receipt of Poor Relief and Family Situation: Aldenham, Hertfordshire, 1630–90', in R. Smith (ed.), *Land, Kinship and Life-Cycle* (Cambridge, 1984).

Bucholz, R. O., *The Augustan Court: Queen Anne and the Decline of Court Culture* (Stanford, Calif., 1993).

Busby, D. (ed.), *The Bedfordshire Schoolchild: Elementary Education before 1902*, Bedfordshire Historical Record Society, 67 (1988).

Butler, J., and Scott, J. (eds.), *Feminists Theorize the Political* (1992).

Carlton, C., 'The Widow's Tale: Male Myths and Female Reality in 16th and 17th Century England', *Albion*, 10 (1978), 118–29.

Charles, L., and Duffin, L. (eds.), *Women and Work in Pre-Industrial England* (1985).

Cioni, M., 'The Elizabethan Chancery and Women's Rights', in D. J. Guth and J. W. McKenna (eds.), *Tudor Rule and Revolution: Essays for G. R. Elton from his American Friends* (Cambridge, 1982).

Clark, A., *Working Life of Women in the Seventeenth Century* (1919; 2nd edn., 1982; 3rd edn., 1992).

Clark, P. (ed.), *The Transformation of English Provincial Towns, 1600–1800* (1984).

—— and Slack, P. (eds.), *Crisis and Order in English Towns, 1500–1700* (1972).

Cockburn, J. S. (ed.), *Crime in England, 1550–1800* (1977).

Colley, L., *Britons: Forging the Nation, 1707–1837* (New Haven, 1992).

Collinson, P., *The Religion of Protestants: The Church in English Society, 1559–1625* (Oxford, 1982).

Cope, E. S., *Handmaid of the Holy Spirit: Dame Eleanor Davies, Never Soe Mad a Ladie* (Ann Arbor, 1992).

Copeland, A. J., 'Extracts from Bridewell Court Books', *Under the Dome*, 11 and 12 (1902, 1903).

Corfield, P., 'A Provincial Capital in the Late Seventeenth Century: The Case of Norwich', in P. Clark and P. Slack (eds.), *Crisis and Order in English Towns, 1500–1700* (1972).

Crawford, P., 'Attitudes to Menstruation in Seventeenth-Century England', *Past and Present*, 91 (1981), 47–73.

—— 'The Construction and Experience of Maternity', in V. Fildes (ed.), *Women as Mothers in Pre-Industrial England* (1990).

—— 'Katharine and Philip Henry and their Children: A Case Study in Family Ideology', *Transactions of the Historic Society of Lancashire and Cheshire*, 134 (1984), 39–73.

—— '"The Only Ornament in a Woman": Needlework in Early Modern England', in *All Her Labours, ii. Embroidering the Framework* (Sydney, 1984).

—— 'Printed Advertisements for Women Medical Practitioners in London, 1670–1710', *Society for the Social History of Medicine, Bulletin*, 35 (1984), 66–70.

—— 'Public Duty, Conscience, and Women in Early Modern England', in J. Morrill, P. Slack, and D. Woolf (eds.), *Public Duty and Private Conscience in Seventeenth-Century England* (Oxford, 1993).

—— 'The Savile Affair', *English Historical Review*, 110 (1975), 76–93.

—— 'Sexual Knowledge in England, 1500–1750', in R. Porter and M. Teich (eds.), *Sexual Knowledge, Sexual Science: The History of Attitudes to Sexuality* (Cambridge, 1994).

—— '"The Sucking Child": Adult Attitudes to Child Care in the First Year of Life in Seventeenth-Century England', *Continuity and Change*, 1 (1986), 23–51.

—— 'Women's Published Writings, 1600–1700', in M. Prior (ed.), *Women in English Society, 1500–1800* (1985).

—— *Women and Religion in England, 1500–1720* (1993).

—— and Mendelson, S., 'Sexual Identities in Early Modern England: The Marriage of Two Women in 1680', *Gender & History*, 7 (1995), 362–77.

Cressy, D., 'Purification, Thanksgiving and the Churching of Women in Post-Reformation England', *Past and Present*, 141 (1993), 106–46.

Daston, L., and Park, K., 'The Hermaphrodite and the Orders of Nature: Sexual Ambiguity in Early Modern France', *GLQ: A Journal of Gay & Lesbian Studies*, 1 (1995), 419–38.

Davis, N. Z., 'Women in the Crafts in Sixteenth-Century Lyon', *Feminist Studies*, 8 (1982) 47–80.

Dekker, R. M., and van de Pol, L. C., *The Tradition of Female Transvestism in Early Modern Europe* (1989).

Demos, J. and V., 'Adolescence in Historical Perspective', *Journal of Marriage and the Family*, 31 (1969), 632–8.

Diehl, H., *An Index of Icons in English Emblem Books, 1500–1700* (1986).

Dolan, F., *Dangerous Familiars: Representations of Domestic Crime in England, 1550–1700* (Ithaca, NY, 1994).

Donnison, J., *Midwives and Medical Men: A History of Inter-Professional Rivalries and Women's Rights* (1977).

Donoghue, E., *Passions Between Women: British Lesbian Culture, 1668–1801* (1993).

Doolittle, I. G., 'The Plague in Colchester, 1579–1666', *Transactions of the Essex Archaeological Society*, 3rd ser., 4 (1972).

Doran, S., *Monarchy and Matrimony: The Courtships of Elizabeth I* (1996).

—— 'Religion and Politics at the Court of Elizabeth I: The Habsburg Marriage Negotiations, 1559–1567', *English Historical Review* (1989), 908–26.

Dunster, S., 'An Independent Life? Nottingham Widows, 1594–1650', *Transactions of the Thoroton Society of Nottingham*, 5 (1991), 29–37.

Earle, P., 'The Female Labour Market in London in the Late Seventeenth and Early Eighteenth Centuries', *Economic History Review*, 2nd ser., 42 (1989), 328–53.

—— *The Making of the English Middle Class: Business, Society and Family Life in London, 1660–1730* (Berkeley, 1989).

Edwards, V. C., 'The Case of the Married Spinster: An Alternative Explanation', *The American Journal of Legal History*, 21 (1977), 260–5.

Emmison, F. G., *Elizabethan Life: Home, Work and Land* (Chelmsford, 1976).

Erickson, A. L., 'Common Law Versus Common Practice: The Use of Marriage Settlements in Early Modern England', *Economic History Review*, 2nd ser., 43 (1990), 21–39.

—— 'Maternal Management and the Cost of Raising Children in Early Modern England', in R. Wall and O. Saito (eds.), *Social and Economic Aspects of the Family Life Cycle* (Cambridge, forthcoming).

—— *Women and Property in Early Modern England* (1993).

Everitt, A., 'Farm Labourers', in J. Thirsk (ed.), *The Agrarian History of England and Wales*, iv. *1500–1640* (Cambridge, 1967).

Ezell, M. J., *The Patriarch's Wife: Literary Evidence and the History of the Family* (Chapel Hill, NC, 1987).

Faderman, L., *Surpassing the Love of Men: Romantic Friendship and Love between Women from the Renaissance to the Present* (New York, 1981).

Ferguson, M. (ed.), *First Feminists: British Women Writers, 1578–1799* (Bloomington, Ind., 1985).

Fieldhouse, R., 'Parliamentary Representation in the Borough of Richmond', *Yorks. Archaeological and Topographical Journal*, 44 (1972), 207–12.

Fildes, V. *Wet Nursing: A History from Antiquity to the Present* (Oxford, 1988).

—— (ed.), *Women as Mothers in Pre-Industrial England* (1990).

Finlay, R., *Population and Metropolis: The Demography of London, 1580–1650* (Cambridge, 1981).

Fletcher, A., *Gender, Sex and Subordination in England, 1500–1800* (New Haven, 1995).

—— 'Men's Dilemma: The Future of Patriarchy in England 1560–1660', *Transactions of the Royal Historical Society*, 6th ser., 4 (1994), 61–81.

Forbes, T. S., 'The Searchers', *Bulletin of the New York Academy of Medicine* (1974), 1031–8.

Fox, L., 'The Coventry Guilds and Trading Companies', in *Essays in Honour of Philip B. Chatwin*, Birmingham Archaeological Society (Oxford, 1962).

Fraser, A., *The Weaker Vessel: Woman's Lot in Seventeenth-Century England* (1984).

Freist, D., 'The King's Crown is the Whore of Babylon: Politics, Gender and Communication in Mid-Seventeenth-Century England', *Gender & History*, 7 (1995), 457–81.

Frith, V. (ed.), *Women and History: Voices of Early Modern England* (Toronto, 1995).

Gardiner, D., *English Girlhood at School: A Study of Women's Education through Twelve Centuries* (1929).

Gentles, I., 'London Levellers in the English Revolution: The Chidleys and their Circle', *Journal of Ecclesiastical History*, 29 (1978), 281–309.

—— *The New Model Army* (Oxford, 1992).

Gillis, J., *For Better, For Worse: British Marriages, 1600 to the Present* (Oxford, 1985).

Gilmour, M., *The Great Lady: A Biography of Barbara Villiers, Mistress of Charles II* (1944).

Gittings, C., *Death, Burial and the Individual in Early Modern England* (1984).

Gowing, L., *Domestic Dangers: Women, Words and Sex in Early Modern London* (1996).

—— 'Gender and the Language of Insult in Early Modern London', *History Workshop Journal*, 35 (1993), 1–21.

Graham, R. 'The Civic Position of Women at Common Law before 1800', in *English Ecclesiastical Studies* (1929).

Greaves, R. L., *Deliver Us From Evil* (Oxford, 1986).

—— *Enemies Under His Feet* (Stanford, Calif., 1990).

—— *Secrets of the Kingdom* (Stanford, Calif., 1992).

—— 'The Role of Women in Early English Nonconformity', *Church History*, 52 (1983), 299–311.

—— (ed.), *Triumph over Silence: Women in Protestant History* (Westport, Conn., 1985).

Green, D. B., *Queen Anne* (1970).

—— *Sarah, Duchess of Marlborough* (1967).

Greenberg, J., 'The Legal Status of the English Woman in Early Eighteenth-Century Common Law and Equity', *Studies in Eighteenth-Century Culture* (1975).

Gregg, E., *Queen Anne* (1980).

Griffiths, P., 'The Structure of Prostitution in Elizabethan London', *Continuity & Change*, 8 (1993), 39–63.

Hair, P. E. H., 'Bridal Pregnancy in Rural England in Earlier Centuries', *Population Studies*, 20 (1966), 233–43.

—— 'Bridal Pregnancy in Earlier Rural England Further Examined', *Population Studies*, 24 (1970), 59–70.

Hanawalt, B. A., *Women and Work in Preindustrial Europe* (Bloomington, Ind., 1986).

Hannay, M. P. (ed.), *Silent but for the Word: Tudor Women as Patrons, Translators and Writers of Religious Works* (Kent, Ohio, 1985).

Harley, D., 'Provincial Midwives in England: Lancashire and Cheshire, 1660–1760', in H. Marland (ed.), *The Art of Midwifery* (1993).

Harris, B. J., 'Women and Politics in Early Tudor England', *Historical Journal*, 33 (1990), 259–81.

Harris, F., '"The Honourable Sisterhood": Queen Anne's Maids of Honour', *The British Library Journal*, 19 (1993), 181–98.

—— *A Passion for Government: The Life of Sarah, Duchess of Marlborough* (Oxford, 1991).

Harris, T., *London Crowds in the Reign of Charles II: Propaganda and Politics from the Restoration until the Exclusion Crisis* (Cambridge, 1987).

—— (ed.), *Popular Culture in England, c.1500–1850* (1995).

Hartmann, C. H., *La Belle Stuart . . . Frances . . . Duchess of Richmond and Lennox* (1924).

Heal, F., *Hospitality in Early Modern England* (Oxford, 1990).

Heisch, A., 'Queen Elizabeth and the Persistence of Patriarchy', *Feminist Review*, 4 (1980), 45–56.

Herrup, C., *The Common Peace: Participation and the Criminal Law in Seventeenth-Century England* (Cambridge, 1987).

Hibbard, C., *Charles I and the Popish Plot* (Chapel Hill, NC, 1983).

—— 'The Role of a Queen Consort: The Household and Court of Henrietta Maria, 1625–1642', in R. Asch and A. Birke (eds.), *Princes, Patronage and the Nobility: The Court at the Beginning of the Modern Age, c.1450–1650* (1991).

Higgins, P., 'The Reactions of Women with Special Reference to Women Petitioners', in B. Manning (ed.), *Politics, Religion and the English Civil War* (1973).

Hill, B., 'The Marriage Age of Women and the Demographers', *History Workshop*, 28 (1989), 129–54.

—— 'A Refuge from Men: The Idea of a Protestant Nunnery', *Past and Present*, 117 (1987), 107–30.

—— *Women, Work and Sexual Politics in Eighteenth-Century England* (Oxford, 1989).

Hirst, D., *The Representative of the People?* (Cambridge, 1975).

Hobby, E., 'Katherine Philips: Seventeenth-Century Lesbian Poet', in E. Hobby and C. White (eds.), *What Lesbians Do In Books* (1991).

—— *Virtue of Necessity: English Women's Writing, 1649–1688* (1988).

Hoffer, P. C., and Hull, N. E. H., *Murdering Mothers: Infanticide in England and New England, 1558–1903* (New York, 1981).

Holderness, B. A., 'Credit in a Rural Community, 1600–1800: Some Neglected Aspects of Probate Inventories', *Midland History*, 3 (1975), 94–115.

—— 'Credit in English Rural Society before the Nineteenth Century, with Special Reference to the Period 1650–1720', *Agricultural History Review*, 24 (1976), 97–109.

—— 'Widows in Pre-Industrial Society: An Essay upon their Economic Functions', in R. M. Smith (ed.), *Land, Kinship and Life-cycle* (Cambridge, 1984).

Hole, C., *British Folk Customs* (1976).

Hollingsworth, T., 'The Demography of the British Peerage', suppl. to *Population Studies*, 18 (1964), 3–104.

Holmes, C., 'Women: Witnesses and Witches', *Past and Present*, 140 (1993), 45–78.

Houlbrooke, R. (ed.), *Death, Ritual, and Bereavement* (1989).

—— (ed.), *English Family Life, 1576–1716: An Anthology from Diaries* (Oxford, 1988).

—— *The English Family, 1450–1700* (1984).

—— 'Women's Social Life and Common Action in England from the Fifteenth Century to the Eve of the Civil War', *Continuity and Change*, 1 (1986), 339–52.

Howard, J. E., 'Crossdressing, the Theatre, and Gender Struggle in Early Modern England', *Shakespeare Quarterly*, 39 (1988), 418–40.

Howell, C., *Land, Family, and Inheritance in Transition: Kibworth Harcourt, 1280–1700* (Cambridge, 1983).

Hughes, A., 'Gender and Politics in Leveller Literature', in S. Amussen and M. Kishlansky (eds.), *Political Culture and Cultural Politics in England: Essays presented to David Underdown* (Manchester, 1995).

Hunt, M., 'Wife Beating, Domesticity and Women's Independence in Eighteenth-Century London', *Gender & History*, 4 (1992), 10–33.

Ingram, M., *Church Courts, Sex and Marriage in England, 1570–1640* (Cambridge, 1987).

—— 'Ridings, Rough Music and Mocking Rhymes in Early Modern England', in B. Reay (ed.), *Popular Culture in Seventeenth-Century England* (1985).

—— '"Scolding Women Cucked or Washed": A Crisis in Gender Relations in Early Modern England?', in J. Kermode and G. Walker (eds.), *Women, Crime and the Courts in Early Modern England* (Guildford, 1994).

Jamison, C., *The History of the Royal Hospital of St Katharine by the Tower of London* (Oxford, 1952).

Johansson, S. R., 'Welfare, Mortality, and Gender: Continuity and Change in Explanation for Male/Female Differences over Three Centuries', *Continuity and Change*, 6 (1991), 135–77.

Jones, M. G., *The Charity School Movement: A Study of Eighteenth-Century Puritanism* (Cambridge, 1938; 1964).

Jordan, C., *Renaissance Feminism: Literary Texts and Political Models* (Ithaca, NY, 1990).

—— 'Woman's Rule in British Political Thought', *Renaissance Quarterly*, 10 (1987), 421–51.

Karlsen, C. F., *The Devil in the Shape of a Woman: Witchcraft in Colonial New England* (New York, 1989).

Kent, J., *The English Village Constable, 1580–1642* (Oxford, 1986).

Kermode, J., and Walker, G. (eds.), *Women, Crime and the Courts in Early Modern England* (1994).

Kussmaul, A., *Servants in Husbandry in Early Modern England* (Cambridge, 1981).

Lake, P., 'Feminine Piety and Personal Potency: The "Emancipation" of Mrs Jane Ratcliffe', *The Seventeenth Century*, 2 (1987), 143–65.

Laqueur, T., *Making Sex: Body and Gender from the Greeks to Freud* (Cambridge, Mass., 1990).

Larminie, V., *Wealth, Kinship and Culture: The Seventeenth-Century Newdigates of Arbury and their World* (1995).

Larner, C., *Enemies of God: The Witch-hunt in Scotland* (Oxford, 1981).

Laslett, P., *Family Life and Illicit Love in Earlier Generations: Essays in Historical Sociology* (Cambridge, 1980).

—— 'Mean Household Size in England Since the Sixteenth Century', in P. Laslett and R. Wall (eds.), *Household and Family in Past Time* (Cambridge, 1972).

Laurence, A., 'Godly Grief: Individual Responses to Death in Seventeenth-Century Britain', in R. Houlbrooke (ed.), *Death, Ritual, and Bereavement* (1989).

—— 'A Priesthood of She-Believers: Women and Congregations in Mid-Seventeenth-Century England', *Studies in Church History*, 27 (1990), 345–63.

—— *Women in England, 1500–1760: A Social History* (1994).

Lemire, B., 'Consumerism in Preindustrial and Early Industial England: The Trade in Secondhand Clothes', *Journal of British Studies*, 27 (1988), 1–24.

—— *Dress, Culture and Commerce: The English Clothing Trade before the Factory* (1997).

—— 'The Theft of Clothes and Popular Consumerism in Early Modern England', *Journal of Social History*, 24 (1990), 255–76.

Leonard, E. M., *The Early History of English Poor Relief* (Cambridge, 1930).

Levin, C., *'The Heart and Stomach of a King': Elizabeth I and the Politics of Sex and Power* (Philadelphia, 1994).

Levine, M., 'The Place of Women in Tudor Government', in D. Guth and J. McKenna (eds.), *Tudor Rule and Revolution* (1982).

Lindley, K., *Fenland Riots and the English Revolution* (1982).

Lloyd, G., *The Man of Reason: 'Male' and 'Female' in Western Philosophy* (1984).

Ludlow, D., 'Shaking Patriarchy's Foundations: Sectarian Women in England, 1641–1700', in R. Greaves (ed.), *Triumph over Silence: Women in Protestant History* (Westport, Conn., 1985).

Macdonald, M., *Mystical Bedlam: Madness, Anxiety and Healing in Seventeenth-Century England* (Cambridge, 1981).

—— and Murphy, T., *Sleepless Souls: Suicide in Early Modern England* (Oxford, 1990).

Macfarlane, A., *The Family Life of Ralph Josselin, a Seventeenth-Century Clergyman: An Essay in Historical Anthropology* (Cambridge, 1970).

—— *Marriage and Love in England: Modes of Reproduction, 1300–1840* (Oxford, 1986).

—— *Witchcraft in Tudor and Stuart England: A Regional and Comparative Study* (1970).

McInnes, E. M., *St Thomas's Hospital* (1963).

McIntosh, M., *A Community Transformed: The Manor and Liberty of Havering, 1500–1620* (Cambridge, 1991).

Mack, P., *Visionary Women: Ecstatic Prophecy in Seventeenth-Century England* (Berkeley, 1992).

McLaren, A., *A History of Contraception from Antiquity to the Present Day* (Oxford, 1990).

—— *Reproductive Rituals: The Perception of Fertility in England from the Sixteenth Century to the Nineteenth Century* (1984).

Maclean, I., *The Renaissance Notion of Woman: A Study in the Fortunes of Scholasticism and Medical Science in European Intellectual Life* (Cambridge, 1980).

Maguire, N. K., 'The Duchess of Portsmouth: English Royal Consort and French Politician, 1670–85', in R. M. Smuts (ed.), *The Stuart Court and Europe* (Cambridge, 1996).

Malcolmson, R. W., 'Infanticide in the Eighteenth Century', in J. S. Cockburn (ed.), *Crime in England, 1550–1800* (1977).

Manchee, W. H., *The Westminster City Fathers (The Burgess Court of Westminster), 1585–1901* (1924).

Manning, B. (ed.), *Politics, Religion and the English Civil War* (1973).

Manning, R. B., *Village Revolts: Social Protest and Popular Disturbance in England, 1509–1640* (Oxford, 1988).

Marchant, R., *The Church under the Law: Justice, Administration and Discipline in the Diocese of York, 1560–1640* (Cambridge, 1969).

Marland, H. (ed.), *The Art of Midwifery: Early Modern Midwives in Europe* (1993).

Marshall, D., *The English Domestic Servant in History* (1949).

Mendelson, S. H., 'Debate: The Weightiest Business: Marriage in an Upper-Gentry Family in Seventeenth-Century England', *Past and Present,* 85 (1979), 126–35.

—— *The Mental World of Stuart Women: Three Studies* (Brighton, 1987).

—— 'Stuart Women's Diaries and Occasional Memoirs', in M. Prior (ed.), *Women in English Society, 1500–1800* (1985).

—— '"To Shift For a Cloak": Disorderly Women in the Church Courts', in V. Frith (ed.), *Women and History: Voices of Early Modern England* (Toronto, 1995).

Menefee, S. P., *Wives for Sale: An Ethnographic Study of British Popular Divorce* (Oxford, 1981).

Miller, J., *Charles II: Royal Politician* (1991).

Moore, N., *The History of St Bartholomew's Hospital,* 2 vols. (1918).

Myers, S. H., *The Bluestocking Circle: Women, Friendship, and the Life of the Mind in Eighteenth-Century England* (Oxford, 1990).

Nagy, D. E., *Popular Medicine in Seventeenth-Century England* (Bowling Green, Ohio, 1988).

Neeson, J. M., *Commoners: Common Right, Enclosure and Social Change in England, 1700–1820* (Cambridge, 1993).

Nenner, H., *By Colour of Law: Legal Culture and Constitutional Politics in England, 1660–1689* (Chicago, 1977).

Oldham, J., 'On Pleading the Belly: A History of the Jury of Matrons', *Criminal Justice History,* 6 (1985), 1–64.

Park, K., 'The Rediscovery of the Clitoris: French Medicine and the Tribade, 1570–1620', in C. Mazzio and D. Hillman (eds.), *The Body in Parts: Discourses and Anatomies in Early Modern Europe* (New York, 1995).

Pateman, C., *The Sexual Contract* (Stanford, Calif., 1988).

Pelling, M., 'Knowledge Common and Acquired: The Education of Unlicensed

Medical Practitioners in Early Modern London', in V. Nutton and R. Porter (eds.), *The History of Medical Education in Britain* (1995).
—— 'Occupational Diversity: Barbersurgeons and the Trades of Norwich, 1550–1640', *Bulletin of the History of Medicine*, 56 (1982), 484–511.
—— 'Old Age, Poverty, and Disability in Early Modern Norwich', in M. Pelling and R. M. Smith (eds.), *Life, Death and the Elderly* (1991).
—— and Smith, R. M. (eds.), *Life, Death, and the Elderly: Historical Perspectives* (1991).
Perry, R., *The Celebrated Mary Astell: An Early English Feminist* (Chicago, 1986).
Phillips, P., *The Scientific Lady: A Social History of Women's Scientific Interests, 1520–1918* (1990).
Phillips, R., *Putting Asunder: A History of Divorce in Western Society* (Cambridge, 1988).
Pinchbeck, I., and Hewitt, M., *Children in English Society* (1969).
Pollard, A. W., and Redgrave, G. R., *A Short-Title Catalogue of Books . . . 1475–1640*, 2nd edn., 2 vols. (1976–86).
Pollock, L., *Forgotten Children: Parent–Child Relations from 1500–1900* (Cambridge, 1983).
—— '"Teach Her to Live Under Obedience": The Making of Women in the Upper Ranks of Early Modern England', *Continuity and Change*, 4 (1989), 231–58.
Poovey, M., 'Feminism and Deconstruction', *Feminist Studies*, 14 (1988), 51–65.
Powell, C. L., *English Domestic Relations* (New York, 1917).
Prest, W. R., 'Law and Women's Rights in Early Modern England', *The Seventeenth Century*, 6 (1991), 169–87.
—— (ed.), *The Professions in Early Modern England* (1987).
Prior, M., 'Wives and Wills, 1558–1700', in J. Chartres and D. Hey (eds.), *English Rural Society, 1500–1800: Essays in Honour of Joan Thirsk* (Cambridge, 1990).
—— 'Women and the Urban Economy: Oxford, 1500–1800', in M. Prior (ed.), *Women in English Society* (1985).
—— (ed.), *Women in English Society, 1500–1800* (1985).
Putnam, B., *Early Treatises on the Practice of the Justices of the Peace in the Fifteenth and Sixteenth Centuries* (Oxford, 1924).
Radzinowicz, L., *A History of English Criminal Law and its Administration from 1750* (1948).
Raine, H., 'Christopher Fawsett Against the Inmates: An Aspect of Poor Law Administration in the Early Seventeenth Century', *Surrey Archaeological Collections*, 66 (1969), 79–85.
Reay, B. (ed.), *Popular Culture in Seventeenth-Century England* (1985).
Reynolds, M., *The Learned Lady in England, 1650–1760* (Cambridge, Mass., 1920).
Richards, J., 'Mary Tudor as "Sole Quene"? The Gendering of Tudor Monarchy', forthcoming, *Historical Journal*.
Rizzo, B., *Companions without Vows: Relationships Among Eighteenth-Century British Women* (Athens, Ga., 1994).

Roberts, M., '"Words They are Women, and Deeds They are Men": Images of Work and Gender in Early Modern England', in L. Charles and L. Duffin (eds.), *Women and Work in Pre-Industrial England* (1985).

Roper, L., *Oedipus and the Devil: Witchcraft, Sexuality and Religion in Early Modern Europe* (1994).

Rosaldo, M., 'Women, Culture and Society: A Theoretical Overview', in L. Lamphere and M. Z. Rosaldo (eds.), *Women, Culture and Society* (Stanford, Calif., 1974).

Schofield, R., 'Did the Mothers Really Die? Three Centuries of Maternal Mortality in "The World We Have Lost"', in L. Bonfield, R. M. Smith, and K. Wrightson (eds.), *The World We Have Gained: Histories of Population and Social Structure* (Oxford, 1986).

—— 'English Marriage Patterns Revisited', *Journal of Family History*, 10 (1985), 2–20.

Schwoerer, L. G., *The Declaration of Rights, 1689* (Baltimore, 1981).

—— 'Images of Queen Mary II, 1689–1695', *Renaissance Quarterly*, 42 (1989), 717–48.

—— 'The Queen as Regent and Patron', in *The Age of William III and Mary II: Power, Politics and Patronage, 1688–1702* (Washington, DC, 1989).

—— 'Women and the Glorious Revolution', *Albion*, 18 (1986), 195–218.

Scott, J., 'Gender: A Useful Category of Historical Analysis', in J. Scott, *Gender and the Politics of History* (New York, 1988).

Scott-Elliot, A. H., and Yeo, E., 'Calligraphic Manuscripts of Esther Inglis (1571–1624): A Catalogue', *The Papers of the Bibliographic Society of America*, 84 (1990), 11–63.

Shammas, C., *The Pre-Industrial Consumer in England and America* (Oxford, 1990).

Sharp, B., *In Contempt of All Authority: Rural Artisans and Riot in the West of England, 1586–1660* (Berkeley, 1980).

Sharpe, J., *Defamation and Sexual Slander in Early Modern England: The Church Courts at York*, Borthwick Papers, 58 (York, 1980).

—— 'Witchcraft and Women in Seventeenth-Century England: Some Northern Evidence', *Continuity and Change*, 6 (1991), 179–99.

Sharpe, K., *The Personal Rule of Charles I* (New Haven, 1992).

Sharpe, P., 'Literally Spinsters: A New Interpretation of Local Economy and Demography in Colyton in the Seventeenth and Eighteenth Centuries', *Economic History Review*, 44 (1991), 46–65.

—— 'Poor Children as Apprentices in Colyton, 1598–1830', *Continuity and Change*, 6 (1991), 1–18.

—— 'The Total Reconstitution Method: A Tool for Class-Specific Study?', *Local Population Studies*, 44 (1990), 41–51.

Shoemaker, R., 'The London "Mob"', *Journal of British Studies*, 26 (1987), 273–304.

—— *Prosecution and Punishment: Petty Crime and the Law in London and Rural Middlesex, c.1660–1725* (Cambridge, 1991).

Slack, P., *The Impact of Plague in Tudor and Stuart England* (1985).

—— *Poverty and Policy in Tudor and Stuart England* (1988).

Slater, M., 'The Weightiest Business: Marriage in an Upper-Gentry Family in Seventeenth-Century England', *Past and Present*, 72 (1976), 25–54.

Smith, A. H., 'Labourers in Late Sixteenth-Century England: A Case Study from North Norfolk', *Continuity and Change*, 4 (1989), 11–52, 367–94.

Smith, H., *Reason's Disciples: Seventeenth-Century English Feminists* (Urbana, Ill., 1982).

Smith, R. M. (ed.), *Land, Kinship and Life-Cycle* (Cambridge, 1984).

—— 'The Manorial Court and the Elderly Tenant in Late Medieval England', in M. Pelling and R. M. Smith (eds.), *Life, Death and the Elderly* (1991).

Smuts, R. M., *Court Culture and the Origins of a Royalist Tradition in Early Stuart England* (Philadelphia, 1987).

—— 'The Puritan Followers of Henrietta Maria in the 1630s', *English History Review*, 93 (1978), 26–45.

Snell, K. D. M., *Annals of the Labouring Poor* (Cambridge, 1985).

Sommerville, M. R., *Sex and Subjection: Attitudes to Women in Early-Modern Society* (1995).

Souden, D., 'Migrants and the Population Structure of Later Seventeenth-Century Provincial Cities and Market Towns', in P. Clark (ed.), *The Transformation of English Provincial Towns, 1600–1800* (1984).

Spring, E., *Law, Land, and Family: Aristocratic Inheritance in England, 1300 to 1800* (Chapel Hill, NC, 1993).

Spufford, M., *Contrasting Communities: English Villagers in the Sixteenth and Seventeenth Centuries* (Cambridge, 1974).

—— *Great Reclothing of Rural England: Petty Chapmen and their Wares in the Seventeenth Century* (1984).

Starkey, D. (ed.), *The English Court: From the Wars of the Roses to the Civil War* (1987).

Staves, S., *Married Women's Separate Property in England, 1660–1833* (Cambridge, Mass., 1990).

Stone, L., *The Crisis of the Aristocracy, 1558–1641* (Oxford, 1965).

—— *The Family, Sex and Marriage in England, 1500–1800* (1977).

—— *Road to Divorce: England, 1530–1987* (Oxford, 1990).

—— *Uncertain Unions: Marriage in England, 1660–1753* (Oxford, 1992).

—— and Stone, J. C. F., *An Open Elite? England, 1540–1880* (Oxford, 1984).

Stopes, C. C., *British Freewomen* (1894).

Taylor, E. (ed.), *The Suffolk Bartholomeans: A Memoir* (1840).

Thirsk, J. (ed.), *The Agrarian History of England and Wales*, iv. *1500–1640* (Cambridge, 1967).

—— *Economic Policy and Projects: The Development of a Consumer Society in Early Modern England* (Oxford, 1978).

Thomas, K., *Age and Authority in Early Modern England* (1976).

—— 'The Double Standard', *Journal of the History of Ideas*, 20 (1959), 195–216.

—— 'Numeracy in Early Modern England', *Transactions of the Royal Historical Society*, 5th ser., 37 (1987), 103–32.

—— *Religion and the Decline of Magic: Studies in Popular Beliefs in Sixteenth and Seventeenth Century England* (1971).

—— 'Women and the Civil War Sects', *Past and Present*, 13 (1958), 42–62.

Thompson, E. P., *Customs in Common* (Harmondsworth, 1993).

Todd, B. J., 'The Remarrying Widow: A Stereotype Reconsidered', in M. Prior (ed.), *Women in English Society* (1985).

Todd, J. (ed.), *A Dictionary of British and American Women Writers, 1660–1800* (1987).

—— *Women's Friendship in Literature* (New York, 1980).

Turnbull, G. H., *Hartlib, Dury and Comenius: Gleanings from Hartlib's Papers* (Liverpool, 1947).

Underdown, D. *Fire From Heaven: Life in an English Town in the Seventeenth Century* (1993).

—— *Revel, Riot and Rebellion: Popular Politics and Culture in England, 1603–1660* (Oxford, 1985).

—— 'The Taming of the Scold: The Enforcement of Patriarchal Authority in Early Modern England', in A. Fletcher and J. Stevenson (eds.), *Order and Disorder in Early Modern England* (Cambridge, 1985).

Verney, F. P. and M. M., *Memoirs of the Verney Family during the Seventeenth Century* (3rd edn., 2 vols., 1925).

Walby, S., *Theorizing Patriarchy* (Oxford, 1990).

Wales, T., 'Poverty, Poor Relief and the Life-Cycle: Some Evidence from Seventeenth-Century Norfolk', in R. M. Smith (ed.), *Land, Kinship and Life-Cycle* (Cambridge, 1984).

Walker, G., 'Women, Theft and the World of Stolen Goods', in J. Kermode and G. Walker (eds.), *Women, Crime and the Courts in Early Modern England* (1994).

Wall, A., 'Elizabethan Precept and Feminine Practice: The Thynne Family of Longleat', *History*, 75 (1990), 22–38.

Wall, R., 'The Age at Leaving Home', *Journal of Family History*, 3 (1978), 181–202.

—— 'Inferring Differential Neglect of Females from Mortality Data', *Annales de démographie historique* (1981), 119–40.

—— 'Leaving Home and the Process of Household Formation in Pre-Industrial England', *Continuity and Change*, 2 (1987), 77–101.

Walter, J., 'Grain Riots and Popular Attitudes to the Law: Maldon and the Crisis of 1629', in J. Brewer and J. Styles (eds.), *An Ungovernable People* (1980).

—— 'The Social Economy of Dearth in Early Modern England', in J. Walter and R.

Schofield (eds.), *Famine, Disease and the Social Order in Early Modern Society* (Cambridge, 1989).

—— and Wrightson, K., 'Dearth and the Social Order in Early Modern England', *Past and Present*, 71 (1976), 22–42.

Wardroper, J., *Jest Upon Jest* (1970).

Warnicke, R., 'Private and Public: The Boundaries of Women's Lives in Early Stuart England', in J. R. Brink (ed.), *Privileging Gender in Early Modern England* (Kirksville, Mo., 1993).

—— *Women of the English Renaissance and Reformation* (Westport, Conn., 1983).

Weatherill, L., 'A Possession of One's Own: Women and Consumer Behaviour in England, 1660–1740', *Journal of British Studies*, 25 (1986), 131–56.

Weil, R., '"If I Did Say So, I Lyed": Elizabeth Cellier and the Construction of Credibility in the Popish Plot Crisis', in S. D. Amussen and M. Kishlansky (eds.), *Political Culture and Cultural Politics in Early Modern England* (Manchester, 1995).

—— 'The Politics of Legitimacy: Women and the Warming-Pan Scandal', in L. G. Schwoerer (ed.), *The Revolution of 1688–1689: Changing Perspectives* (Cambridge, 1992).

Whiteman, A., 'The Protestation Returns of 1641–2', *Local Population Studies*, 55 (1995), 14–25.

Wiener, C. Z., 'Is a Spinster an Unmarried Woman?' *The American Journal of Legal History*, 20 (1976), 27–31.

—— 'Sex Roles and Crime in Late Elizabethan Hertfordshire', *Journal of Social History*, 8 (1975), 38–59.

Willan, T. S., *Elizabethan Manchester*, Chetham Society (1980).

Willen, D. '"Communion of the Saints": Spiritual Reciprocity and the Godly Community in Early Modern England', *Albion*, 27 (1995), 19–41.

—— 'Godly Women in Early Modern England: Puritanism and Gender', *Journal of Ecclesiastical History*, 43 (1992), 561–80.

—— 'Guildswomen in the City of York, 1560–1700', *The Historian*, 46 (1984), 204–18.

—— 'Women and Religion in Early Modern England', in S. Marshall (ed.), *Women in Reformation and Counter-Reformation Europe* (Bloomington, Ind., 1989).

—— 'Women in the Public Sphere', *Sixteenth Century Journal*, 19 (1988), 559–75.

Williams, J. B., *Memoirs of the Life and Character of Mrs Sarah Savage* (1818, 1821).

Wilson, A., *The Making of Man-Midwifery: Childbirth in England, 1660–1770* (1995).

Wilson, J. H., *Nell Gwynn* (1952).

Wing, D., *Short-Title Catalogue of Books printed in England . . . and of English Books . . . 1641–1700*, 2nd edn., 3 vols. (New York, 1972–88).

Woodbridge, L., *Women and the English Renaissance: Literature and the Nature of Womankind, 1540–1620* (Urbana, Ill., 1984).

Wordsworth, C., 'The Conversion of Mary Hurll, Lace-Maker's Apprentice at

Marlborough, 1675: With her Indentures, 21 June 1671', *Wiltshire Archaeological and Natural History Magazine*, 35 (1907–8), 103–13.

Wright, L. B. *Middle-Class Culture in Elizabethan England* (Chapel Hill, NC, 1935).

Wright, P., 'A Change in Direction: The Ramifications of a Female Household, 1558–1603', in D. Starkey (ed.), *The English Court from the Wars of the Roses to the Civil War* (1987).

Wright, S., '"Churmaids, Huswyfes and Hucksters": The Employment of Women in Tudor and Stuart Salisbury', in L. Charles and L. Duffin (eds.), *Women and Work in Pre-Industrial England* (1985).

Wrightson, K., *English Society, 1580–1680* (1982).

—— 'Infanticide in Earlier Seventeenth-century England', *Local Population Studies*, 15 (1975), 10–22.

—— and Levine, D., *The Making of an Industrial Society: Whickham, 1560–1765* (Oxford, 1991).

—— *Poverty and Piety in an English Village: Terling, 1525–1700* (New York, 1979).

Wrigley, E. A., and Schofield, R. S., *The Population History of England, 1541–1871: A Reconstruction* (Cambridge, 1981; 1989).

Wyman, A. L., 'The Surgeoness: The Female Practitioner of Surgery, 1400–1800', *Medical History*, 28 (1984), 22–41.

Zook, M., 'History's Mary: The Propagation of Queen Mary II, 1689–1694', in L. O. Fradenburg (ed.), *Women and Sovereignty* (Edinburgh, 1992).

THESES

Adair, R., 'Regional Variations in Illegitimacy and Courtship Patterns in England, 1538–1754', Ph.D. diss., University of Cambridge (1992).

Archer, I., 'Governors and Governed in Late Sixteenth-Century London, *c.*1560–1603: Studies in the Achievement of Stability', D.Phil. diss., University of Oxford (1988).

Campbell, L., 'The Women of Stiffkey', MA diss., University of East Anglia (1985).

Cioni, M., 'Women and Law in Elizabethan England with particular reference to the Court of Chancery', Ph.D. diss., University of Cambridge (1974).

Davies, J., 'The Growth and Implementation of Laudianism with Special Reference to the Southern Province', D.Phil. diss., University of Oxford (1987).

Davies, T. A., 'The Quakers in Essex, 1655–1725', D.Phil. diss., University of Oxford (1986).

Dillow, K., 'The Social and Ecclesiastical Significance of Church Seating Arrangements and Pew Disputes, 1500–1740', D.Phil. diss., University of Oxford (1990).

Evenden-Nagy, D., 'Seventeenth-Century London Midwives: Their Training, Licensing and Social Profile', Ph.D. diss., McMaster University (1991).

Glanz, L. M., 'The Legal Position of English Women under the early Stuart Kings and the Interregnum', Ph.D. diss., Loyola University of Chicago (1973).

Goldsmith, J., 'All the Queen's Women: The Changing Place and Perception of Aristocratic Women in Elizabethan England, 1558–1628', Ph.D diss., Northwestern University (1987).

Kirby, D., 'The Parish of St Stephen's Coleman Street, London', B.Litt. diss., University of Oxford (1971).

MacFarlane, S., 'Studies in Poverty and Poor Relief in London at the End of the Seventeenth Century', D.Phil. diss., University of Oxford (1983).

McIntosh, J. L., 'English Funeral Sermons, 1560–1640: The Relationship between Gender, Death, Dying, and the Afterlife', M.Litt. diss., University of Oxford (1990).

Merton, C., 'The Women who Served Queen Mary and Queen Elizabeth: Ladies, Gentlewomen and Maids of the Privy Chamber, 1553–1603', Ph.D. diss., University of Cambridge (1991).

Muldrew, C., 'Credit, Market Relations, and Debt Litigation in Late Seventeenth-Century England', Ph.D. diss., University of Cambridge (1990).

Roberts, M., 'Wages and Wage-earners in England, 1563–1725', D.Phil. diss., University of Oxford (1981).

Sawyer, R. C., 'Patients, Healers, and Disease in the South-East Midlands, 1597–1634', Ph.D. diss., University of Wisconsin-Madison (1986).

Sharpe, P., 'Gender-Specific Demographic Adjustment to Changing Economic Circumstances: Colyton, 1538–1837', Ph.D. diss., University of Cambridge (1988).

Stretton, T., 'Women and Litigation in the Court of Requests', Ph.D. diss., University of Cambridge (1993).

Walker, C., 'Contemplative Communities: English Catholic Convents in France and the Low Countries, 1598–1700', Ph.D. diss., University of Western Australia (1996).

Index